Photosynthesis and productivity in different environments

THE INTERNATIONAL BIOLOGICAL PROGRAMME

The International Biological Programme was established by the International Council of Scientific Unions in 1964 as a counterpart of the International Geophysical Year. The subject of the IBP was defined as 'The Biological Basis of Productivity and Human Welfare', and the reason for its establishment was recognition that the rapidly increasing human population called for a better understanding of the environment as a basis for the rational management of natural resources. This could be achieved only on the basis of scientific knowledge, which in many fields of biology and in many parts of the world was felt to be inadequate. At the same time it was recognised that human activities were creating rapid and comprehensive changes in the environment. Thus, in terms of human welfare, the reason for the IBP lay in its promotion of basic knowledge relevant to the needs of man.

The IBP provided the first occasion on which biologists throughout the world were challenged to work together for a common cause. It involved an integrated and concerted examination of a wide range of problems. The Programme was co-ordinated through a series of seven sections representing the major subject areas of research. Four of these sections were concerned with the study of biological productivity on land, in freshwater, and in the seas, together with the processes of photosynthesis and nitrogen fixation. Three sections were concerned with adaptability of human populations, conservation of ecosystems and the use of biological resources.

After a decade of work, the Programme terminated in June 1974 and this series of volumes brings together, in the form of syntheses, the results of national and international activities.

IBP Synthesis Meeting on the Functioning of Photo-synthetic Systems in Different Environments, Aberystwyth, 1973.

INTERNATIONAL BIOLOGICAL PROGRAMME 3

Photosynthesis and productivity in different environments

EDITED BY

J. P. Cooper

Director, Welsh Plant Breeding Station,
Aberystwyth, UK

CAMBRIDGE UNIVERSITY PRESS

CAMBRIDGE
LONDON · NEW YORK · MELBOURNE

Published by the Syndics of the Cambridge University Press
The Pitt Building, Trumpington Street, Cambridge CB2 1RP
Bentley House, 200 Euston Road, London NW1 2DB
32 East 57th Street, New York, NY 10022, USA
296 Beaconsfield Parade, Middle Park, Melbourne 3206, Australia

© Cambridge University Press 1975

First published 1975

Printed in Great Britian by Aberdeen University Press

Library of Congress Cataloguing in Publication Data

IBP Synthesis Meeting on the Functioning of Photosynthetic Systems in Different Environments,
Aberystwyth, 1973.
Photosynthesis and productivity in different
environments.

At head of title: International Biological Programme 3.
Includes indexes.
1. Photosynthesis—Congresses. 2. Primary
productivity (Biology)—Congresses. I. Cooper,
John Philip, 1923– . II. International Biological
Programme. III. Title.

QK882.I2 1973   581.1'3342   74–31808
ISBN 0 521 20573 5

Contents

v

Contents

Table des matières

A*

Table des matières

6e Partie. Influence des facteurs de stress et l'emploi des assimilats

7e Partie. Productivité réelle et potentielle dans les systèmes photosynthetiques

8e Partie. Conclusions

Содержание

Содержание

Содержание

Contenido

xiv

10 Producción primaria en micrófitos de agua dulce
J. F. Talling *página* 225
11 Producción primaria en micrófitos marinos
T. Platt & D. V. Subba Rao 249
12 Producción primaria en plantas acuáticas: conclusiones
J. F. Talling 281

Parte III. Distribución de la energía radiante y el CO_2 con relación a la estructura y estratificació ⊐ de la comunidad

13 Distribución de la energía radiante y el CO_2 en las comunidades terrestrestres
T. Saeki 297
14 Papel de la circulación de nutrientes y de energía radiante en comunidades acuáticas
D. W. Schindler & E. J. Fee 323
15 Radiación solar y di óxido de carbono en comunidades vegetales: conclusiones
Margaret C. Anderson 345

Parte IV. Actividad fotosintética en plantas y tejidos aislados

16 Mecanismos fotosintéticos en plantas superiores
J. H. Troughton 357
17 Fotosíntesis en musgos y líquenes
P. Kallio & L. Kärenlampi 393
18 Sistemas fotosintéticos: conclusiones
Ph. Chartier & J. Čatský 425

Parte V. Empleo de las sustancias asimiladas en el mantenimiento, crecimiento y desarrollo

19 Vías metabólicas en plantas unicelulares
G. E. Fogg 437
20 Empleo de sustancias asimiladas en plantas superiores
F. W. T. Penning de Vries 459
21 Relaciones producción–consumo, y distribución en la planta de sustancias asimiladas
P. F. Wareing & J. Patrick 481
22 Más allá de la fotosíntesis: el papel de la respiración, el transporte y el potencial de crecimiento en la determinación de la productividad
L. T. Evans 501

Contenido

Contributors

Alberda, Th.	IBS, Bornsesteeg 65–67, Wageningen, Netherlands
Anderson, Margaret C.	Division of Land Use Research, CSIRO, P.O. Box 1666, Canberra City, ACT 2601, Australia
Bamberg, S. A.	Laboratory of Nuclear Medicine and Radiation Biology, University of California, Los Angeles, California, USA
Bauer, H.	Institut für allgemeine Botanik, Universität Innsbruck, A. 6020 Innsbruck, Sternwartestrasse 15, Austria
Buschbom, U.	Botanisches Institut II, Universität Würzburg, 87 Würzburg, Mittlerer Dallenbergweg 64, Germany (BRD)
Caldwell, M. M.	Department of Range Science, Utah State University, Logan, Utah 84321, USA
Čatský, J.	Institute of Experimental Botany, ČSAV, 1600 Prague 6, Czechoslovakia
Chapman, A. R. O.	Department of Biology, Dalhousie University, Halifax, Nova Scotia, Canada
Chartier, Ph.	Station de Bioclimatologie, INRA, Route de St Cyr, 78000 Versailles, France
Cooper, J. P.	Welsh Plant Breeding Station, University College of Wales, Plas Gogerddan, Aberystwyth, Wales, UK
Eckardt, F. E.	Section d'Ecophysiologie du CEPE–Louis Emberger (CNRS), BP 5051, 34033 Montpellier, France
Evans, L. T.	Division of Plant Industry, CSIRO, P.O. Box 1600, Canberra City, ACT 2601, Australia

List of contributors

Evenari, M. Department of Botany, Hebrew
University of Jerusalem, Jerusalem,
Israel

Fee, E. J. Freshwater Institute, 510, University
Crescent, Winnipeg 19, Manitoba,
Canada

Fogg, G. E. Marine Science Laboratories, UCNW,
Menai Bridge, Anglesey, Wales, UK

Gerakis, P. A. Faculty of Agriculture and Forestry,
University of Thessaloniki,
Thessaloniki, Greece

Kallio, P. Department of Botany, University of
Turku, SF 20500 Turku 50, Finland

Kappen, L. Botanisches Institut II, Universität
Würzburg, 87 Würzburg, Mittlerer
Dallenbergwerg 64, Germany (BRD)

Kärenlampi, L. Department of Botany, University of
Turku, SF 20500 Turku 50, Finland

Kira, T. Department of Biology, Faculty of
Science, Osaka City University, Osaka,
Japan

Koller, D. Department of Agricultural Botany,
Hebrew University of Jerusalem,
P.O. Box 12, Rehovot, Israel

Lange, O. L. Botanisches Institut II, Universität
Würzburg, 87 Würzburg, Mittlerer
Dallenbergweg 64, Germany (BRD)

Larcher, W. Institut für allgemeine Botanik,
Universität Innsbruck, A. 6020
Innsbruck, Sternwartestrasse 15,
Austria

Loomis, R. S. Department of Agronomy and Range
Science, University of California,
Davis, California 95616, USA

Louwerse, W. IBS, Bornsesteeg 65–67, Wageningen,
Netherlands

Málek, I.	PP/IBP Secretariat, c/o Czechoslovak Academy of Sciences, Institute of Landscape Ecology, 25243 Průhonice u Prahy, Czechoslovakia
Mann, K. H.	Department of Biology, Dalhousie University, Halifax, Nova Scotia, Canada
Nátr, L.	Institute of Cereal Crops, Kroměříž, Havličkova 2787, Czechoslovakia
Patrick, J.	School of Biological Sciences, University of Newcastle, Newcastle, New South Wales, Australia
Penning de Vries, F. W. T.	Department of Theoretical Production Ecology, Landbouwhogeschool, De Dreijen 4, Wageningen, Netherlands
Platt, T. C.	Marine Ecology Laboratory, Bedford Institute of Oceanography, Dartmouth, Nova Scotia, Canada
Saeki, T.	Department of Botany, Faculty of Science, University of Tokyo, Hongo, Tokyo 113, Japan
Schindler, D. W.	Freshwater Institute, 501, University Crescent, Winnipeg 19, Manitoba, Canada
Schulze, E.-D.	Botanisches Institut II, Universität Würzburg, 87 Würzburg, Mittlerer Dallenbergweg 64, Germany
Sibma, L.	IBS, Bornsesteeg 65–67, Wageningen, Netherlands
Slavík, B.	Institute of Experimental Botany, ČSAV, 16000 Prague 6, Czechoslovakia
Soeder, C. J.	Gesellschaft für Strahlen- und Umweltsforschung MBH, 46 Dortmund, Bunsenkirchhoff Strasse 13, Germany (BRD)

List of contributors

Stengel, E. — Gesellschaft für Strahlen- und Umweltsforschung MBH, 46 Dortmund, Bunsenkirchhof Strasse 13, Germany (BRD)

Stern, W. R. — Department of Agronomy, University of Western Australia, Nedlands 6009, Western Australia, Australia

Subba Rao, D. V. — Marine Ecology Laboratory, Bedford Institute of Oceanography, Dartmouth, Nova Scotia, Canada

Talling, J. F. — Freshwater Biological Association, The Ferry House, Ambleside, Cumbria, UK

Troughton, J. H. — Physics and Engineering Laboratory, DSIR, Lower Hutt, New Zealand

van Keulen, H. — IBS, Bornsesteeg 65–67, Wageningen, Netherlands

Walker, R. B. — Department of Botany, University of Washington, Seattle, Washington, USA

Wareing, P. F. — Department of Botany and Microbiology, University College of Wales, Aberystwyth, Wales, UK

Wassink, E. C. — Laboratory for Plant Physiology, Landbouwhogeschool, General Foulkesweg 72, Wageningen, Netherlands

Westlake, D. F. — Freshwater Biological Association, River Laboratory, East Stoke, Wareham, Dorset, UK

Wielgolaski, F. E. — Botanical Laboratory, University of Oslo, Blindern, Oslo 3, Norway

Zalensky, O. V. — Komarov Botanical Institute, USSR Academy of Sciences, Leningrad, USSR

Foreword

In view of the need to find answers to urgent problems of environmental management, ecologists are nowadays exposed to a stress as well as a temptation to formulate and solve their problems rapidly and in rather broad terms. It is obvious that such an approach is based on rather broadly defined assumptions and can lead to conclusions which are of general and qualitative or only semi-quantitative character. Such conclusions may not stand the test of practical application. In spite of all good intentions, ecology may thus lose rather than gain the confidence of the lay public.

The IBP Production Process section, together with its Photosynthesis subsection, and later also the intersectional Photosynthesis Liaison Group, have been aware of this danger, and have been emphasising the value of the fundamental 'processes approach' to ecology. This approach stresses the importance of the study of physiological processes underlying the functioning and behaviour of ecological systems.

Primary production tends to be taken for granted by some ecologists, as if the plants acted as mere accumulators of energy and matter which they acquire from their environment. Ecological relationships, in this interpretation, become complex only during the further transfers and transformations of this matter and energy in the ecosystem. But things are by no means so simple; the primary producers operate differently in different ecosystems although, at the same time, the general principles of the process are common. The study of these common principles, as well as of the most important differences, should assist us in determining the minimum useful diversity which we must understand if we wish to analyse and predict the functioning of photosynthetic systems in different environments. The reactions and adaptation of the photosynthesising plants to the varied environmental factors can only be understood when we intensify our investigations from the ecosystem and community levels to most of the lower levels of biological organisation, and then extrapolate our results back to the higher and more complex levels.

The present concluding operations of the IBP consist largely of the synthesis of the great amount of unique data and ideas that have resulted from investigations of plant photosynthetic production pursued in a number of countries. How can ecology make use of these results? In order to understand the role played by photosynthesis and plant productivity in various ecosystems and biomes, the data on photosynthesis should be related to other ecosystem characteristics, such as the origin of the constituent taxa, the structure of the ecosystem and that of the populations present there, and the variation of these structures with time, habitat, and human influence. Also of importance is the relationship between photosynthesis and the genetic and morphological features of the taxa. When investigating these relationships we are analysing the variation in time of the photosynthetic function, particularly during successions taking place in ecosystems affected by man.

An analysis of the spatial variation of the photosynthetic function is also of great importance. It is meaningful to pursue comparative studies of the photosynthesis of taxa which occur both within one biome and in different biomes. Investigations of photosynthesis under controlled conditions represent an extremely useful tool for clarifying the dependence of photosynthesis on irradiation density, temperature, and water potential as well as on other important environmental factors. In such studies, we can also link the processes of gas exchange with the anatomical structure of the assimilatory organs, with the ultrastructure of the chloroplasts, and with the metabolism of the plant. Intensive work will undoubtedly be pursued along these lines in the post-IBP period also.

Finally, a few comments on the mathematical modelling of processes taking place in the leaf, plant, ecosystem, and biome. Apart from its usefulness as a method of clearly defining the objectives of our research, a fascinating aspect of mathematical modelling is the possibility of predicting changes in the processes, which will occur as a result of various kinds of environmental or other influences. Moreover, mathematical modelling has made it possible to investigate new characteristics, hitherto not studied, that are important for rightly understanding the photosynthetic function, e.g. the role which the spatial orientation of the leaves plays in the attenuation of photosynthetically active radiation. As a result of the recent rapid development of systems ecology, all of us seem to be at present under a 'stress' of mathematical modelling. With due respect to the outstanding advantages of mathematical modelling, its use should always be based on a critical and careful analysis of the data employed. The level of resolution of the model is determined both by the complexity of the system studied and by the actual level of our knowledge of that system. If the system is very complicated and our knowledge is comparatively little, the model inevitably contains many 'holes' each having a different significance for the quality of the model. Bearing in mind their 'hierarchy', the numbers of these 'holes' should be reduced by further carefully planned experiments and observations.

The present IBP volume concludes one period of international collaboration in investigations of plant production processes. This is an opportunity to thank all those whose enthusiasm and mutual understanding in carrying the burden of international collaboration – however rewarding it has been – have brought the Photosynthesis subsection as well as the intersectional Photosynthesis Liaison Group to our present situation. Among those few to be named, out of many others, Professor E. C. Wassink is to be thanked first of all. As Deputy Convener, he has always emphasised the fundamental and experimental approach to the study of plant photosynthetic production. Together with his work, that of all the members and corresponding members of the PP Photosynthesis subcommittee deserves high appreciation, the more so when we recall the hesitations and doubts about the subsection's programme in the early phases of the IBP. The idea of organising the Aberystwyth IBP technical meeting, on whose proceedings this volume is based, was first put forward by the Photosynthesis Liaison Group, and the Group has been most active in putting this idea into practice. Dr P. Gaastra deserves the credit for maintaining the activity of the Liaison Group for nearly four years, while Professors J. P. Cooper, and G. E. Blackman, FRS, and all the other British organisers are to be thanked for having enabled the meeting to take place in the United Kingdom, particularly in the hospitable environment of the University College of Wales at Aberystwyth. Last but not least, all the encouragement and assistance received from SCIBP, UNESCO and IUBS are gratefully acknowledged. The representatives of the MAB programme of UNESCO have also often expressed their interest in our activities; all of us would like to regard this as a guarantee that the results presented here will be fully used and further developed by the MAB programme. Dr F. E. Eckardt has been particularly active in promoting the contacts with UNESCO. We are also grateful for the assistance of the Royal Society towards this meeting, as well as for the various national supports given to the participants at Aberystwyth and the authors of this IBP volume.

It is with confidence, as always, that we look forward to future international collaboration in the study of photosynthesis and other plant processes essential for ecosystem functioning. We shall carry on with

Foreword

our effort aimed at breaking through both the national and inter-disciplinary barriers separating us one from another. The role IBP has played in this most desirable development has not been in vain. We believe that our plant will continue to grow, flourish and bear fruit even now, after the IBP has served its term and handed over to other more and more complex programmes, because ours is a vigorous living plant!

Prague and Leningrad   IVAN MÁLEK
June 1973   *IBP/PP Convener*

OLEG ZALENSKY
IBP/PP – Photosynthesis Deputy Convener

1. Introduction

J. P. COOPER

Photosynthesis forms the basis of primary production in all ecosystems, and studies on photosynthetic production serve as the starting point for all analyses of energy flow through these systems. The present volume therefore sets out to provide a comparative survey of the photosynthetic activity of different ecosystems, both terrestrial and aquatic, including an examination of the physiological basis of such activity and its possible modification by management and breeding.

This approach involves the following sequence:

(i) the comparison of photosynthetic production in different ecosystems, both terrestrial and aquatic;

(ii) the examination of the morphological and physiological basis of these differences in primary production, in terms of light and CO_2 distribution in the community, of variation in the photosynthetic process itself, and of the distribution and use of assimilates for growth and maintenance;

(iii) the study of the effects of stress factors, such as temperature or water stress or the shortage of soil nutrients, on photosynthetic activity and the strategy of use of assimilates, and

(iv) the control and management of photosynthetic production in different ecosystems, with a consideration of the potential production in different climatic regions.

The present volume does not attempt to synthesize in detail all IBP results on photosynthesis and photosynthetic production, but to present a comparative survey based on both IBP and non-IBP results. It is hoped that it will serve as a useful background to the extended accounts of specific projects on photosynthesis to be presented in the various national syntheses, and also as an introduction to the more detailed discussions of the photosynthetic basis of primary production in the forthcoming biome syntheses, which are planned to cover Woodlands, Grasslands, Tundra and Arid lands among the terrestrial biomes, and Freshwater and Marine ecosystems among the aquatic biomes.

The simulation and prediction of photosynthetic production, although discussed in a number of chapters, are not emphasized in the present volume as these aspects were dealt with extensively in the earlier IBP/PP Technical Meeting on Prediction and Measurement of Photosynthetic Productivity, held in Třeboň, Czechoslovakia in September 1969.

1

Introduction

The present synthesis volume is based on the papers and discussions at the IBP Synthesis Meeting on The Functioning of Photosynthetic Systems in Different Environments held in Aberystwyth, Wales, UK in April 1973. Each of the main papers presented at the meeting forms the basis of a chapter in this volume. In addition, a number of shorter contributions dealing with specific research projects were discussed at the meeting, and many of their results incorporated in the synthesis volume. These shorter contributions, many of which have been or will be published in full elsewhere, are listed by titles and authors at the end of the volume.

The discussions at the meeting emphasized the value of the complementary 'processes' and 'biome' approach in ecology. A large amount of comparative data on the plant processes governing primary production in both natural and managed ecosystems is being collated in the individual syntheses of the various IBP sections, as well as by national groups. The comparative and critical evaluation of these data is of great importance to post-IBP developments in environmental biology.

The Aberystwyth meeting was organized by the Photosynthesis Liaison Group of IBP (Secretary: Dr P. Gaastra, Wageningen) which contains members from all sections of IBP concerned with photosynthesis, in collaboration with the IBP–PP Photosynthesis sub-section and with the assistance of a local organizing committee consisting of Dr J. P. Cooper (Chairman), Professor G. E. Fogg, Dr J. F. Talling, Professor P. F. Wareing and Dr E. B. Worthington.

It was attended by some 150 scientists from the following 28 countries: Austria, Australia, Canada, Czechoslovakia, Denmark, Finland, France, Federal Republic of Germany, Hungary, India, Ireland, Israel, Italy, Japan, Morocco, Netherlands, New Zealand, Nigeria, Norway, Poland, Rhodesia, Sierra Leone, Sweden, Switzerland, Trinidad, Uganda, the UK and the USA.

The organizing committee would like to express their thanks to the IUBS for finance for overseas speakers, the Royal Society and the Commonwealth Foundation for welcome financial and other support, and to a number of IBP national committees and other agencies who provided funds for the attendance of individual participants. The University College of Wales provided an attractive venue for the meeting. We should also like to thank all those whose lively discussion contributed to this volume, and those at Aberystwyth who valiantly coped with the day-to-day organization of the meeting.

PART I

Primary production in terrestrial ecosystems

2. Primary production of forests[*]

T. KIRA

Pre-IBP researches on primary production of forests were extensively surveyed and reviewed by Ovington (1962), Satoo (1966), Kira & Shidei (1967), etc. to prepare a threshold on which IBP work was to be started. The appearance of the IBP handbook by Newbould (1967) considerably cleared any methodological, conceptual and terminological confusions concerned. The operational phase of the IBP (1967–72) thus opened the stage of exponential growth of the production ecology of forest. More than one hundred research projects have been launched within the framework of the IBP, working on various forest ecosystems of the world. Nearly half of them are concerned with primary production, while about one-third aim at the analysis of integrated ecosystem processes (SCIBP, 1969).

During the course of the operational phase, several workshop meetings were held to synthesise the results of these projects at Gatlingburg (1968), Brussels (1969), Kratte Masugn (1971), Oak Ridge (1972), etc. Some of their proceedings have already been published (Reichle, 1970; Duvigneaud, 1971; Rosswall, 1971).

As far as the primary production side is concerned, a considerable amount of net production data has been accumulated, enabling a fairly reasonable estimation of the range and mean value of net production in temperate forests, although the forests of the tropics and southern hemisphere, especially of Latin America, are very poorly represented in current literature. Only a limited number of publications are available concerning the photosynthetic activity of forest canopies as related to their structure and solar energy utilisation (e.g. Denmead, 1968; Hozumi, Yoda & Kira, 1969; Hozumi & Kirita, 1970; Hozumi, Kirita & Nishioka, 1972; Hozumi, Nishioka, Nagano & Kirita, 1973; Kira, Shinozaki & Hozumi, 1969; Lange & Schulze, 1971; Lemon, Allen & Muller, 1970; Baumgartner, 1969; Miller, 1972; Odum, 1970; Schulze & Koch, 1971).

The present chapter is, therefore, intended to present
(1) an outline of the net production estimation so far made in various types of forests;
(2) discussion on the efficiency of dry matter production and the net

* Contributions from J IBP–PT no. 170.

production–gross production ratio within the extent of the limited available data sources in comparison with other types of terrestrial plant communities;

(3) some preliminary data on the penetration and distribution of light within forest canopies;

(4) descriptions of the vertically anisotropic structure of the canopies in terms of the vertical trends of certain morphological and physiological properties of component leaves, and

(5) the way in which these properties can be incorporated into models for estimating total canopy functions on a land area basis.

I am indebted to the Japanese IBP/PT working group on forest primary production for the free use of original data, and to Drs K. Shinozaki, K. Hozumi, H. Ogawa and K. Yoda for useful discussion and co-operation.

Net production

The results of biomass and net production studies in Japanese forests were recently summarised by Satoo (1970*b*; 1971*b*) with special reference to the distribution of biomass and net production in different parts of the forest community and the efficiency of leaves in producing dry matter and stem wood. Therefore, mention is only made here of the range and mean value of their net productivity. Fig. 2.1 illustrates the frequency distribution of annual above-ground net production in 258 forest stands of Japan classified in five major types.

Apparently evergreen broad-leaf forests of the warm-temperate zone (central part of Honshu Island and southwestwards) are the most productive (mode of productivity around 20 t ha^{-1} yr^{-1}), forests of pines and temperate conifers (10–15 t ha^{-1} yr^{-1}) come next, followed by coniferous forests of the boreal zone (northeastern half of Hokkaido) and the subalpine zone of Honshu (around 10 t ha^{-1} yr^{-1}), while deciduous broad-leaf forests of the cool-temperate zone are the lowest in productivity (5–10 t ha^{-1} yr^{-1}).

As collated in Table 2.1, these estimates do not differ greatly from those obtained in Europe and North America, except that deciduous forests in these regions seem nearly as productive as coniferous forests. However, there is enough evidence to indicate that deciduous hardwoods are significantly less productive than evergreen conifers under the same environmental condition (e.g. Ovington, 1956; Satoo, 1970*b*, 1971*b*; Post, 1970; Reiners, 1972).

Table 2.1 also includes the global means of forest productivity adopted by a few authors for estimating the total primary production of the earth. If the figures in Fig. 2.1 and Table 2.1 are corrected for under-ground production by 20–25%, the resultant values of total net production become somewhat greater than these global means.

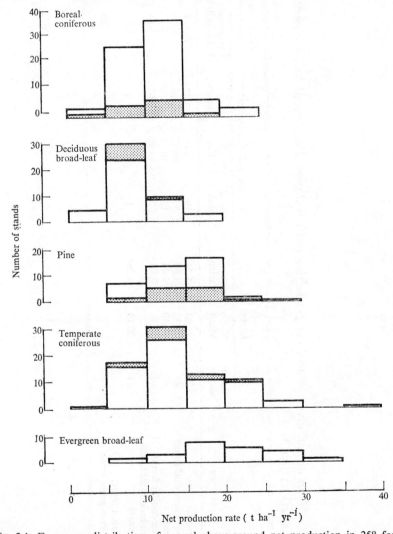

Fig. 2.1. Frequency distribution of annual above-ground net production in 258 forest stands of Japan. Boreal coniferous forests: Japanese larch (*Larix leptolepis*) in black, evergreen species in white. Deciduous broad-leaf forests: Japanese beech (*Fagus crenata*) in white, other species in black. Pine forests: Japanese red pine (*Pinus densiflora*) in black, other species in white. Temperate coniferous forests: Japanese cedar (*Cryptomeria japonica*) in white, other species in black.

7

Table 2.1. *Mean annual above-ground net production rates in Japan, Europe and North America* (Metric ton (dry matter) ha^{-1} yr^{-1})

Forest type	Japan			Europe and N. America*			Global mean productivity (incl. root production)	
	No. of stands	Mean	Variance	No. of stands	Mean	Variance	Whittaker & Woodwell, 1971	Lieth, 1972
Boreal conifer forest	74	11.23	3.74	19	9.01	3.47	8	5
Deciduous broad-leaf forest	48	8.32	3.68	57	10.17	2.26		10
Pine forest	42	14.40	4.44	15	10.41	5.72	} 13	} 10
Evergreen broad-leaf forest (temperate)	67	14.46	3.36	5	14.96	9.01		
Tropical rain forest	27	20.19	6.36	1	7.0	–	} 20	20
Tropical rain-green forest								15

As for tropical forests, very few estimates are available so far,

	t ha^{-1} yr^{-1}
Tropical rain forest, S. Thailand	28.6 (total net production)
(Kira, Ogawa, Yoda & Ogino, 1967)	28.2 (above-ground)
Dry evergreen forest, C. Thailand	17.6 (total)
(Ogino, Ratanawongs, Tsutsumi &	16.5 (above-ground)
Shidei, 1967)	
Tropical subhumid forest, Ivory Coast	13.4 (total)
(Müller & Nielsen, 1965)	

e.g. Wycherley (1969) reported a range of mean periodic increments of timber of 2.4–10.1 t ha^{-1} yr^{-1} (maximum rates 5.8–12.8 t ha^{-1} yr^{-1}) in various types of West Malaysian forests and tree plantations, which may approximately correspond to 10–25 t ha^{-1} yr^{-1} of total net production. These figures suggest that the productivity of tropical forest communities is not always greater than that of temperate evergreen forests.

On the other hand, fairly high net production rates are known in tropical tree crops, indicating the high potential productivity of the humid tropics. A maximum annual net production of 35.5 t ha^{-1} yr^{-1} in rubber plantations after four years from bud-grafting (Templeton, 1968) and 30.7–36.8 t ha^{-1} yr^{-1} in oil palm plantations at eight to fifteen years of age (Ng, Thamboo & de Souza, 1968) are examples.

Comparably high rates, however, have been reported also from the temperate zone; e.g. 43.7 t ha^{-1} yr^{-1} in a dense *Cryptomeria japonica* plantation (17 yr-old) (Research Group on Forest Productivity, 1966), 31.5–34.8 t ha^{-1} yr^{-1} in four- to seven-year-old plantations of *Acacia mollissima* (Tadaki, 1968*b*), both in Kyushu, Japan. *Pinus radiata* plantations in Australia and New Zealand are also known for their high productivity. Forrest & Ovington (1970) obtained net above-ground production rates of 19.4–25.9 t ha^{-1} yr^{-1} in plantations of this pine five to twelve years in age in New South Wales, while Miller (1971) estimated the rate in a twenty-six to twenty-nine year-old plantation of New Zealand at 38 t ha^{-1} yr^{-1}. Fujimori (1971) called attention to the very large biomass accumulation and high net productivity of temperate conifer forests in the Pacific Northwest of the United States, obtaining a net production rate of 36.2 t ha^{-1} yr^{-1} in a young stand of *Tsuga heterophylla*. Even the deciduous hardwood forests of the same region seem to be unusually productive as shown by the net production rate of 26 t ha^{-1} yr^{-1} in red alder forests (10–15 yr-old) (Zavitkovski & Stevens, 1972).

9

The differences in average net production rate among different forest types may be ascribed in the first place to climate, especially to the length of growing season when both thermal and moisture conditions are favourable. Compared with evergreen leaves, the deciduous habit of the leaves is a decisive drawback for dry matter production, because it can prevent trees from fully utilising climatically favourable periods. The low productivity of deciduous broad-leaf forests is probably caused partly by their short leafy period and partly by their small leaf area

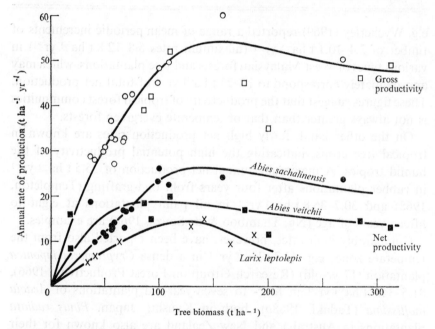

Fig. 2.2. Trends of productivity change in natural stands of two fir species and plantations of larch associated with the increase in stand biomass. Drawn from the data by Tadaki *et al.* (1970), Sato (1963) and Research Group on Forest Productivity (1964).

index (LAI) (Tadaki, 1966), while evergreen coniferous forests are favoured by a greater leaf surface and a longer duration of photosynthetic activity. The same may also be true for evergreen broad-leaf forests of lower latitudes where a greater amount of solar radiation and a greater tree height may increase LAI. An attempt to incorporate these two factors in a single leaf area duration index is given later in Fig. 2.3.

On the other hand, wide variability of net production rate within a forest type is also caused by inter-stand differences in community structure, especially in tree age distribution. Kira & Shidei (1967) pro-

10

posed a model to interpret the change of net productivity in growing even-aged stands of the same tree species. It is based on the fact that leaf biomass and gross production rate tend to reach a ceiling value within a relatively short period around the closure of forest canopy, whereas total tree biomass and community respiration continue to increase with age slowly but steadily. As a result, net production rate is expected to reach a maximum immediately after the complete closure of canopy. The same model may be applied to uneven-aged forests, if we take total forest biomass, instead of stand age, as a measure of time as well as of tree age distribution.

Three examples from Japanese conifer forests and plantations are given in Fig. 2.2. The net productivity reaches a maximum value at 80–140 t ha^{-1} of stand biomass and thereafter declines gradually as the biomass or the percentage of big trees increases.

It should be emphasised, according to Kira & Shidei (1967), that net productivity may amount to a level of 25–35 t ha^{-1} yr^{-1} in most forest types, provided a stand is young in age, sufficiently dense and fully closed. All of the very high productivity figures mentioned above were obtained under such conditions. Estimating the productivity of young regenerating forests in the humid tropics is of considerable interest in this connection in order to explore the highest possible level of net production rate.

Gross production and production efficiencies

Net production rate is controlled by two kinds of ecological efficiency, first by the efficiency of solar energy conversion in the process of gross production, and then by the ratio of net production to gross production. (The gross production is defined here as the sum of net production and dark respiration. Photorespiration is not taken into consideration for technical reasons.)

Available estimates of gross production rate are still limited both in number and in reliability because of the technical difficulties involved in the assessment of total community respiration. Particularly elaborate techniques are needed to estimate total respiration in woody organs such as stem, branch and root, in which respiration rate on a weight basis varies profoundly according to their size or diameter (Möller, Müller & Nielsen, 1954; Müller & Nielsen, 1965; Yoda et al., 1965; Kira, 1968; Yoda, 1967). Exact comparison of the gross production rates worked out by different authors is therefore not always justified.

11

Table 2.2. *Gross and net production rates in forest communities*

	Localities	Age (yr)	LAI (ha ha⁻¹)	Rate (t ha⁻¹ yr⁻¹) of		$\Delta P_n/\Delta P_g$ ratio	Authors
				Gross production (ΔP_g)	Net production (ΔP_n)		
Tropical rain forest	S. Thailand	–	11.4	123.2	28.6	0.23	Kira et al., 1967
Tropical subhumid forest	Cote d'Ivoire	–	3.2	52.5	13.4	0.26	Müller & Nielsen, 1965
Climax warm-temperate ever-green forest dominated by Distylium racemosum	S. Kyushu	–	8.8	73.0	20.6	0.28	Kimura, 1960
Secondary forest of Castanopsis cuspidata	S. Kyushu	11	8.0	45.3	18.7	0.41	Tadaki, 1965
	S. Kyushu	14	8.9	51.7	22.7	0.44	Tadaki, 1968a
Cryptomeria japonica plantation	S. Kyushu	5	8.6	84.1	29.1	0.35	Tadaki & Kawasaki, 1966
	S. Kyushu	24	7.4	73.3	15.1	0.21	Tadaki et al., 1965
	N. Kyushu	28	4.3	54.4	18.8	0.35	Tadaki et al., 1967
	W. Kyushu	31	6.8	64.1	16.7	0.26	Tadaki et al., 1965
	N. Kyushu	34	–	57.1	16.0	0.28	
Chamaecyparis obtusa plantation	S. Kyushu	45	5.1	40.9	15.4	0.38	Tadaki et al., 1966
Pinus densiflora plantation	C. Honshu	15	–	53.9	15.8	0.68	Satoo, 1968b

Fagus crenata secondary forest	C. Honshu	30–70	5.7	27.5	15.3	0.56	Maruyama et al., 1968
Fagus crenata plantation	C. Honshu	50	7.8	44.1	19.3	0.44	Tadaki et al., 1969
	Denmark	8	4.2	13.9	7.5	0.54	Möller et al., 1954
Fagus sylvatica plantation	Denmark	25		22.3	13.5	0.61	
	Denmark	46	5.4	23.5	13.5	0.57	
	Denmark	85		21.4	11.3	0.53	
Fraxinus excelsior plantation	Denmark	35–45		21.5	13.5	0.63	Möller, 1945
Oak-pine secondary forest	New York		3.8	26.4	13.5	0.45	Whittaker & Woodwell, 1969
Picea abies plantation	Denmark	40–50		26.5	18.0	0.68	Möller, 1945
Abies sachalinensis forest	Hokkaido	35–40		50.2	23.8	0.47	Sato, 1963
Subalpine *Abies* forest	C. Honshu	c. 15		19.9	7.4	0.37	Kimura et al., 1968
	C. Honshu			40	11.1	0.28	
Subalpine *Abies veitchii* forest	C. Honshu	4	5.5	16	8.4	0.53	Tadaki et al., 1970
	C. Honshu	25	9.7	45	16.8	0.37	
	C. Honshu	60	10.6	49	12.8	0.26	

Note. LAI in *Cryptomeria japonica* was calculated by dividing total surface area of needles by two.

Yet the data accumulated in Table 2.2 may allow some tentative analyses of the production efficiencies.

The highest known gross production rates, 123 t ha^{-1} yr^{-1} and 117 t ha^{-1} yr^{-1} (both in dry matter equivalent), were obtained in tropical rain forests of Southeast Asia. Evergreen forests, either broad-leaved or coniferous, of the warm-temperate zone have a gross productivity range of 40–85 t ha^{-1} yr^{-1}, while that of cool-temperate deciduous hardwood forests does not exceed 30 t ha^{-1} yr^{-1}. The corresponding rates in evergreen conifer forests of the boreal zone may reach 40–50 t ha^{-1} yr^{-1}. The effect of the long growing season in lower latitudes is thus more apparent on gross production than on net production, though the advantage of evergreen trees over deciduous species is recognised in both cases.

Kira, Ogawa, Yoda & Ogino (1967) suggested that climate might affect the gross production rate of forests mainly through the length of the growing season and the total leaf area which they supported, if water supply was not limiting. Since LAI of a forest is controlled by incident light intensity and tree height (Monsi & Saeki, 1953; Saeki, 1960; Kira Shinozaki & Hozumi, 1969), it tends to increase toward lower latitudes, its normal range being 5–6 ha ha^{-1} in deciduous broad-leaf forests (cool-temperate), 7–8 ha ha^{-1} in evergreen broad-leaf forests (warm-temperate) and 8–10 ha ha^{-1} in tropical rain forests (Tadaki, 1966; Kira & Shidei, 1967). On the other hand, the absolute level of temperature during growing season may not influence photosynthetic activity of trees so much, because the plants are usually well adapted to the prevailing thermal range in their habitat.

Fig. 2.3 illustrates a more or less proportional relationship between the rate of gross production and the leaf area duration in terrestrial plant communities, where the latter is approximated by the product of LAI and the length of growing season in months. The proportional coefficient is approximately 0.85 t ha^{-1} yr^{-1} LAI^{-1} month^{-1}. It is interesting to note that this coefficient is common to both broad-leaved and needle-leaved forests.

In Table 2.3 are tabulated existing estimates of the energy efficiency of gross and net production during the growing period of the year on a total short-wave radiation basis. The efficiency of gross production for closed forests mostly ranges between 2.0% and 3.5%. These figures would be doubled if the incident amount of photosynthetically active radiation (PAR) is taken as the basis. It is noteworthy that the efficiency of gross production during the growing season differs little among

14

forests of different thermal zones. Forest canopies seem to be able to utilise solar energy equally efficiently under different radiation climates. A survey of available data has led to the generalisation given in Table 2.4 concerning the comparison of primary production efficiencies in three main types of terrestrial plant community. The efficiency of gross production in perennial herbaceous communities ranges between 1% and 2% (Midorikawa, 1959; Hogetsu *et al.*, 1960; Iwaki, Monsi & Midorikawa, 1966), while it may generally be less than 1.5% in annual

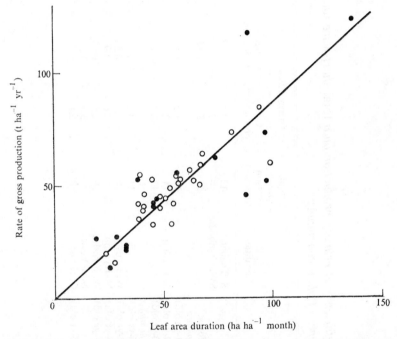

Fig. 2.3. Correlation between the rate of gross production and the leaf area duration (LAI × length of growing season in months) of forests. (●) Broad-leaved forests; (○) needle-leaved forests.

herb and crop communities. The efficiency is even lower in aquatic communities of phytoplankton, being about one-tenth of the values in closed forests, although rooted macrophyte and sessile algae communities in shallow waters may be as efficient in their gross productivity as terrestrial communities. High efficiency of gross production is obviously a characteristic feature of forest communities.

On the contrary, the net production–gross production ratio is expected to be smaller in forests than in herbaceous communities, because

Table 2.3. *Estimated energy efficiency of primary production on a total short-wave radiation basis during the growing season in various types of plant community*

	Localities	Length of growing season (months)	Energy efficiency (%)		Authors and data source
			Gross production	Net production	
Tropical rain forest	S. Thailand	12	3.4	0.85	Kira et al., 1967
Evergreen seasonal forest*	SW. Cambodia	–	2.8	–	Hozumi et al., 1969
Climax warm-temperate evergreen forest		11	2.7	0.86	Kimura, 1960
Secondary forest of *Castanopsis cuspidata*					
(11-yr old)	S. Kyushu	11	1.9	0.80	Tadaki, 1965
(14-yr old)		11	2.2	0.96	Tadaki, 1968a
(c. 50-yr old)		12	2.2	–	Hozumi et al., 1972
Dense sapling stand of *Cryptomeria japonica* (5-yr old)		11	3.1	1.4	Tadaki & Kawasaki, 1966
Cryptomeria japonica plantation (22-yr old)	W. Kyushu	10	2.2	0.58	Tadaki et al., 1965
(28-yr old)	N. Kyushu	9	2.6	0.9	Tadaki et al., 1967
(31-yr old)	W. Kyushu	9	2.6	0.69	Tadaki et al., 1965
Mixed oak–pine forest	New York	5	3.6	1.5	Whittaker & Woodwell, 1969
Chamaecyparis obtusa plantation (45-yr old)	C. Kyushu	8	2.1	0.8	Tadaki et al., 1966

Fagus crenata forest (600 m alt.)	C. Honshu	6	2.1	0.8	Maruyama, 1971
— (1500 m alt.)	C. Honshu	4	3.6	1.4	Maruyama, 1971
Subalpine *Abies veitchii* forest (4-yr old)	C. Honshu	5	1.0	0.5	⎫ Tadaki *et al.*, 1970
— (25-yr old)	C. Honshu	5	2.7	1.0	⎬
— (60-yr old)	C. Honshu	5	2.9	0.8	⎭
Abies sachalinensis forest	Hokkaido	6	3.2	1.6	Sato, 1963
Solidago altissima community	C. Honshu	7	1.6	0.71	Iwaki *et al.*, 1966
Miscanthus sinensis grassland	NE. Honshu	6	1.3	0.55	Shimada *et al.*, 1969
Paddy rice field (for average yield in Japan)	C. Honshu	6	1.2	0.67	
Rooted macrophyte (submerged) community[†]	Florida	12	2.6	–	Odum, 1957
Algal communities of a coral reef[†]	Micronesia	12	2.9	–	Odum & Odum, 1955
Phytoplankton community (Lake Mendota, eutrophic)	Wisconsin	12	0.40	0.27	Lindeman, 1942
— (Lake Suwa, eutrophic)	C. Honshu	12	0.22	0.15	Hogetsu & Ichimura, 1954
Mass culture of *Chlorella*[‡]	C. Honshu	12	–	3.5	Tamiya, 1957

[*] Observation of canopy photosynthesis was made only in two winter months.
[†] Efficiency calculation was based on the solar radiation reaching the community surface under water.
[‡] Pond water was enriched with mineral nutrients and air supply.

17

B[*]

the ratio of the amount of supporting organs (stem, branch and root) to that of foliage is much greater in forests, resulting in an increase of community respiration relative to total photosynthesis by the leaf canopy. The latter ratio is usually less than ten in communities of herbaceous dicotyledons, but may reach 30–100 or even more in broadleaf forests. Annual herbs have the greatest advantage in this respect (Müller, 1962). High efficiency of gross production in long-lived communities such as forest tends to be counterbalanced by a small net production–gross production ratio which results from the large accumulation of supporting tissues. Consequently, all of the three types of plant community seem to have a more or less similar efficiency of net production, mostly around 1%. It is perhaps surprising that even net production by moss-like mats of tiny alpine shrubs corresponds to an efficiency of solar energy conversion of about 1% (Bliss, 1966).

Table 2.4. *Normal ranges of production efficiencies in three types of terrestrial plant communities*

	Net production/gross production ratio (I)	Energy efficiency* of	
		Gross production (II)	Net production (I) × (II)
Forest communities	0.25–0.50	2.0–3.5%	0.5–1.5%
Perennial herbaceous communities	0.50–0.55	1.0–2.0	0.5–1.0
Annual herb and crop communities	0.55–0.70	~1.8	~1.0

* On the basis of *total* short wave radiation.

This normal level of net production efficiency is surpassed only by intensively managed crop fields; e.g. about 1.6% for the maximum recorded yield of paddy rice in Japan, a little over 2% for record yields of sugar-cane (Westlake, 1963), and more than 3% for a densely planted stand of *Gladiolus* (Blackman, 1968).

The net production–gross production ratio in forests is not only smaller than in other plant communities but also very variable, ranging from 0.25 to 0.55. The correlation between observed rates of net and gross production shown in Fig. 2.4 exhibits a ceiling trend of net production rate with increasing gross production. A smooth curve fitted to broad-leaved communities only is hyperbolic with an asymptote of net production rate at *c.* 40 t ha^{-1} yr^{-1}. This may represent the upper limit of net productivity for ordinary plant communities, probably with

18

the exception of C$_4$-plants. Sugar-cane, a representative of the C$_4$ 'tropical grasses' can produce up to 80–90 t ha^{-1} yr^{-1} (Westlake, 1963).

A high level of gross production efficiency is attained with the increase of leaf biomass (Fig. 2.3). On the other hand, however, greater LAI is usually associated with greater plant height and canopy depth, as stated later, and hence with an inevitable increase of stem, branch and root biomass. This leads to the relative increase of community respiration and smaller net production–gross production ratio. The high efficiency of gross production in well-developed forests is apparently realised at the expense of the yield ratio of net production.

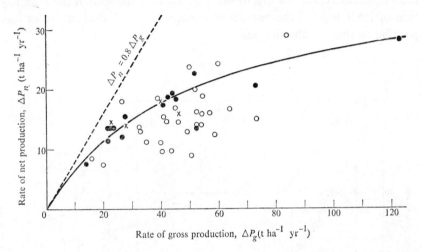

Fig. 2.4. Correlation between the rates of net and gross production in terrestrial plant communities. The smooth curve is fitted to the data of broad-leaved communities (both arboreal and herbaceous) only. The initial gradient of the curve shown by a broken line suggests that the net production–gross production ratio in an ideal leaf community might be about 0.8.

Light distribution within forest canopy

The physical process by which light penetrates through a forest canopy is no different from the case of a herbaceous canopy. In both types of leaf canopy, for instance, the mean flux density of light on a horizontal plane at a certain height level z within a canopy can well be approximated by

$$I(z) = I_0 e^{-KF(z)} \tag{1}$$

where I_0 is the value of I above the canopy surface and $F(z)$ is the cumulative leaf area density between z-plane and the canopy surface

(Monsi & Saeki, 1953; Kira, Shinozaki & Hozumi, 1969). The co-efficient of light extinction K represents the efficiency of the leaves in intercepting the light flux.

In some cases, the relative light intensity I/I_0 decreases exponentially with increasing depth from the canopy surface, indicating vertically even distribution of leaf area density (Fig. 2.5(a)). In ordinary forests, however, the gradient of log $(I/I_0) \sim z$ curve reflects the vertical change of leaf area density sensitively. The curve obtained in a West Malaysian rain forest (Fig. 2.5(b)) shows a sudden decline of relative illuminance at 30–25 m, 15–10 m and 5–10 m levels, respectively, corresponding to the four-storied structure of this forest. Fig. 2.5 also shows that the attenuation of PAR toward the bottom of canopy (Fig. 2.5(c)) is more or less parallel to that of illuminance.

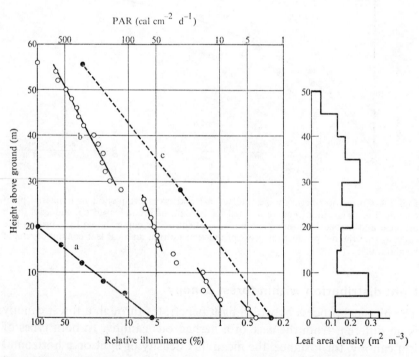

Fig. 2.5. Vertical distribution of relative illuminance and PAR in an evergreen oak forest (a; Minamata, Kyushu) and a tropical rain forest (b; relative illuminance; c; PAR. Pasoh Forest, West Malaysia). The profile diagram on the right side illustrates the vertical distribution of leaf area density in Pasoh Forest. Although the light measurements and the destructive sampling were made at different parts of the forest, the discontinuities in the illuminance $\sim$ height curve approximately correspond to the three maxima of leaf area density in the forest profile. Unpublished data by K. Yabuki (Minamata) and K. Yoda (Pasoh).

As pointed out by Kira, Shinozaki & Hozumi (1969) and in Tables 2.3 and 2,4, forest communities tend to have a greater LAI, larger canopy depth and higher level of gross productivity than herbaceous communities under the same latitude and climate. However, the amount of light that penetrates the canopy is not necessarily smaller in forests as recognised by the comparison of illuminance on the ground surface under the two types of community (e.g. Monsi & Saeki, 1953). The coefficient *K* of equation (1) thus becomes smaller in forests than in herbaceous communities, though the physical nature of the leaves, including their inclination, is similar in trees and herbs as far as dicotyledonous plants are concerned. Similar differences in *K* values are also observed between young sapling stands and tall mature stands of one and the same tree species as shown in Table 2.5. Apparently *K* tends to become smaller as forest stands grow older and taller.

Table 2.5. *Comparison of the coefficients of light extinction* (K) *in pure stands of different ages*

	Age (yr)	Approximate height of stand (m)	LAI (ha ha^{-1})	K (1/LAI)	Authors
Castanopsis cuspidata	c. 12	3–8	5.2–7.2	0.67–0.69	Kan et al., 1965
	14	—	8.9	0.38	Tadaki, 1968a
	c. 40	13	7.6–8.5	0.37	Kan et al., 1965
Quercus phillyraeoides	sapling	1.5	6.5	0.75	Yim et al., 1969
	c. 70	10	5.4–6.1	0.45	Kan et al., 1965
Abies veitchii	5	0.7	7.7	0.63	Tadaki et al.,
	25	5–15	8.1–10.9	0.34–0.42	1970
	60	12–19	7.8–10.6	0.43	

The value of *K* depends primarily on the average inclination of leaves, but it seems unreasonable to assume a significant change in leaf angle from young to older trees. Shinozaki explained this phenomenon by the change in leaf arrangement from an evenly dispersed state in low stands to an aggregated distribution in taller stands, in which the leaves tend to form clusters at the end of branches (Kira, Shinozaki & Hozumi, 1969). When a homogeneous water suspension of yeast cells is treated with a certain agent that enhances agglutination between cells, the optical density of the suspension decreases rapidly as cells begin to form clusters of various sizes (C. Shimoda, personal communication).

The same process is evidently taking place in deep forest canopies. Such a process would greatly facilitate light penetration through the canopy without a significant decrease in the amount of light available to each component of leaves, if inter-cluster distances are comparable to, or greater than, the average cluster diameter.

Shinozaki (personal communication) recently developed a new cluster model of a forest canopy. According to the model, let us assume that a single leaf cluster is composed of leaves with a light extinction coefficient K_1 and has a mean LAI of F_1, while the corresponding values for the whole forest stand are K and F. We may then define F_2 as

$$F_2 = F/F_1, \tag{2}$$

where F_2 is the sum of cluster area divided by land area, and may be called the cluster area index (CAI). If F_1 is sufficiently large ($F_1 > 3$) and the light transmission by leaf cluster is negligibly small, it is concluded that

$$K_2 \simeq F_1 K = (F/F_2)K. \tag{3}$$

Assuming that the canopy structure in young sapling stands is more or less similar to that of individual leaf clusters, we may put

$$K_1 = 0.7 \text{ LAI}^{-1}, F_1 = 5 \text{ ha ha}^{-1}, K = 0.4 \text{ LAI}^{-1} \text{ and } F = 8 \text{ ha ha}^{-1}$$

for mature *Castanopsis* forest according to Table 2.5. Then we get

$$F_2 = 1.6 \text{ ha ha}^{-1}$$
$$K_2 = 2 \text{ LAI}^{-1}.$$

The CAI value of 1.6 ha ha^{-1} suggests a certain degree of overlap between leaf clusters in this case. However, K_2 is considerably greater than one, indicating a more or less continuous arrangement of clusters on a horizontal plane. If the value of K_2 is close to one, the distribution of clusters in the canopy space would be approximately random.

A fully developed shoot system and sufficiently large depth of canopy are no doubt essential for a forest stand to have such a clustered canopy structure. Leaf clusters may develop in twofold or even threefold structures in the case of a very tall forest. Each tree crown, which is in itself an assemblage of small leaf clusters described above, may serve as a cluster of bigger size for the whole forest canopy, and big boughs may also behave in a similar way. Each of these superimposing cluster structures may increase the total LAI of the forest to a certain extent. Therefore, the increase of LAI toward lower latitudes mentioned earlier may be caused partly by a greater tree height as well as by the increase in solar radiation.

Great depth of forest canopy, sometimes as large as several tens of metres, naturally results in very low leaf area density. As noted by Kira (Kira, Shinozaki & Hozumi, 1969), mean leaf area density is generally ten times as large in herbaceous canopies as in forest canopies (Table 2.6). It is not yet certain whether low leaf area density really favours the penetration of the diffused fraction of light into forest canopies, but this may be advantageous for the photosynthesis of tree leaves in preventing the daytime depression of atmospheric CO_2 concentration, which is frequent in dense herbaceous canopies. In any case, the height factor seems to deserve more attention in the study of primary production by terrestrial plant communities.

Table 2.6. *Leaf area densities in forest and herbaceous communities. Calculated from the data of Kira, Shinozaki & Hozumi (1969)*

		Leaf area density (m^2/m^3)		
	LAI (m^2 m^{-2})	Average of whole canopy	Max. value in a layer of z cm thickness	z (cm)
Forest communities				
Castanopsis cuspidata (mature stand)	7.4	0.32	0.77	200
Castanopsis cuspidata (young stand)	8.1	0.88	3.65	100
Fagus crenata	6.1	0.26	0.42	200
Larix leptolepis	4.1	0.19	0.73	200
Herbaceous communities				
Solidago altissima	4.5	2.82	8.0	20
Fagopyrum esculentum (cultivated)	6.3	3.96	12.0	20
Zea mays, normal stand (cultivated)	3.2	1.77	5.2	20
Zea mays, dense stand (cultivated)	10.6	6.64	16.0	20
Gladiolus, dense stand (cultivated)	19.1	15.9	31.2	10

Another aspect of light distribution is the uneven distribution of light flux density on a horizontal plane within the forest canopy, as demonstrated by the occurrence of sun-flecks. Considering only the mean value of light intensity may lead to a fairly serious bias.

Making repeated simultaneous observations of illuminance inside and outside a beech forest, Ogawa (1967) found that the frequency distribution of relative illuminance inside the canopy is very close to a lognormal distribution at any height level. Similar observations in the West

Malaysian rain forest also resulted in approximately lognormal distribution curves of relative illuminance at various z-levels under the main canopy layer (30–35 m above the ground) (Fig. 2.6).

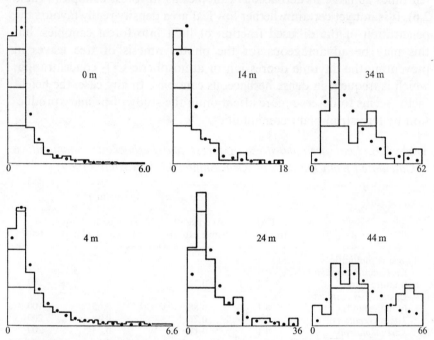

Fig. 2.6. Frequency distribution histograms of relative illuminance (%) at different height levels in Pasoh rain forest. Black dots indicate lognormal distributions fitted to the data (K. Yoda, unpublished data).

If light comes down vertically and the law of equation (1) holds, the relative light intensity at a point (i/I_0) is expected to be equal to $\exp(-K\phi)$, where ϕ is the amount of leaves existing right above the point in terms of LAI. Therefore $\phi = -\ln(i/I_0)/K$, so that the lognormal distribution of i/I_0 corresponds to a normal distribution of ϕ. In other words, if the whole stand space is divided into unit vertical columns having equal and sufficiently small cross-sectional area, the fraction of LAI contained in each cylinder is considered to be equivalent to ϕ, and the intensity of light at the bottom of each cylinder is solely determined by ϕ. Although ϕ is distributed normally, the resultant distribution of light intensity becomes extremely skew, especially near the ground under a dense forest stand.

Therefore, the mean light intensity on a z-plane is better represented by the geometric mean of a large enough number of observed values

581.13342 In8p
c. 1

Forests

than by their arithmetic mean. The latter is always greater than the former, if light intensity at a point is distributed lognormally, and does not correspond to the mean value of ϕ. If the arithmetic mean is used for calculating total canopy photosynthesis using some sort of mathematical model, an overestimation is always expected. It is further necessary to consider the skew distribution of light intensity in constructing such models as those presented in the following section.

Vertical gradient of leaf properties and canopy function models

In herbaceous communities, most leaves unfold at the top of shoots near the canopy surface under strong sunlight, but afterwards sink gradually towards the darker depths of the canopy as the plants grow and new leaves are added to the canopy surface. The oldest leaves may eventually be shed at the bottom of the canopy due to the lack of light. During such a life cycle, the physiological activities of leaves continue to deteriorate due either to senescence or to prompt adaptation to shading (McCree & Troughton, 1966), resulting in a vertical gradient of leaf functions.

A tree leaf in a forest canopy, on the other hand, tends to remain in nearly the same degree of shade throughout its life cycle, according to its situation in the profile of the canopy. Morphological and physiological differentiation of sun and shade leaves is therefore much more pronounced, as compared with the case of herb leaves. Our experience tells us that the transition from sun leaf to shade leaf is gradual and continuous, as shown by the example of *Castanopsis cuspidata*, a dominant oak species in the warm-temperate evergreen forests of Japan (Fig. 2.7).

For instance, the specific leaf area (SLA = leaf area–leaf dry weight ratio) of *Castanopsis* leaves increases 2.5-times from the top to the bottom of the forest canopy. Thus, the total LAI of the forest might be over- or underestimated more than two times, if leaf samples were not properly taken. The stratified clip technique (Monsi & Saeki, 1953; Newbould, 1967) and taking samples from all strata are indispensable in the destructive sampling of forest communities.

Fig. 2.7 shows that the gradient of leaf properties is closely correlated to that of light intensity. Tadaki (1970) found the following correlation between mean SLA(f) at z height and mean relative illuminance (I/I_0) on the same height level (Fig. 2.8).

$$f(z) = c(I(z)/I_0)^{-k}. \tag{4}$$

25

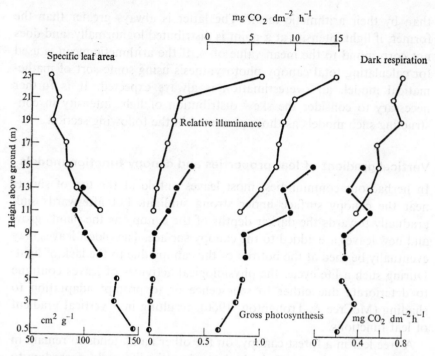

Fig. 2.7. Vertical gradient of relative illuminance in the evergreen oak forest at Minamata and a few leaf properties in the dominant species, *Castanopsis cuspidata*. Unpublished data by M. Nishioka & M. Nagano taken in October, 1972.

Hozumi & Kirita (1970) and Hozumi, Kirita & Nishioka (1972) elaborated the well known Monsi–Saeki canopy photosynthesis model by taking the vertical gradient of the photosynthetic capacity of leaves into consideration. The rate of gross photosynthesis in leaves at z height above the ground was found to follow the widely accepted formulation,

$$p_g = \frac{bI}{1+aI}, \tag{5}$$

where p_g stands for gross photosynthetic rate and I for the intensity of light at the leaf surface. On the other hand, mean light intensity on the z plane I' is given by equation (1),

$$I'(z) = I_0 e^{-KF(z)},$$

and mean light intensity at the surface of the leaves (I) by

$$I(z) = KI_0 e^{-KF(z)}/(1-m), \tag{6}$$

in which m is the mean light transmissibility of the leaf (Monsi & Saeki, 1953; Saeki, 1960; Monsi, 1968). In the original Monsi–Saeki model,

26

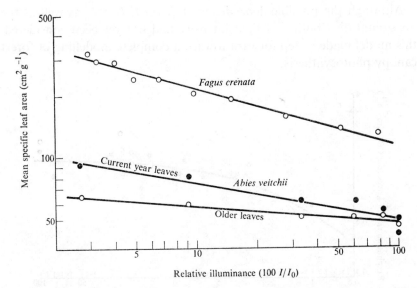

Fig. 2.8. Linear regressions between the logarithms of mean specific leaf area at various depths in forest canopy and of relative illuminance at corresponding heights. Equation (4) in the text. Redrawn from Tadaki (1970).

the coefficients a and b of equation (5) were assumed to be constant in all component leaves of the canopy. Hozumi and his collaborators, however, found that both a and b changed as the functions of light intensity. The proposed empirical formulation for the light-dependence of a and b was as follows.

$$a = \frac{A}{I'/I_0} + B \tag{7}$$

$$b = \frac{C}{I'/I_0} + D. \tag{8}$$

Combining equations (5), (6), (7) and (8) together, they arrived at;

rate of total canopy photosynthesis P_g

$$= \int_0^{F^*} p_g \mathrm{d}F$$

$$= \frac{KCF^*I_0}{(1-m)+KAI_0} + \left(\frac{D}{BK} - \frac{CI_0}{(1-m)+KAI_0}\right) \times$$

$$\ln\frac{(1-m)+KAI_0+KBI_0}{(1-m)+KAI_0+KBI_0\mathrm{e}^{-KF^*}}. \tag{9}$$

(F^*: total LAI of the canopy)

27

Although the possible dependency of K on I'/I_0 or z as well as the horizontal distribution of light intensity had not yet been considered, this model made a step forward toward a complete modelling of forest canopy photosynthesis.

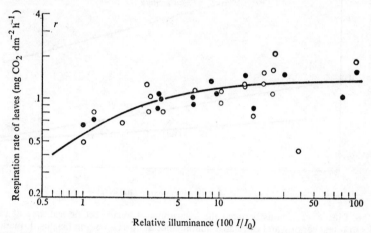

Fig. 2.9. Hyperbolic relationship between the rate of dark respiration in oak leaves and mean relative illuminance which they receive. Unpublished data by M. Nishioka and M. Nagano taken in August–September, 1972 at Minamata. (○) *Castanopsis cuspidata.* (●) *Quercus ilva.*

As for canopy respiration, the model proposed by Hozumi is much simpler (Kira, Shinozaki & Hozumi, 1969). The rate of dark respiration (r) in leaves of evergreen oaks was found to increase hyperbolically with increasing mean light intensity to which they were exposed in the canopy (Fig. 2.9), namely

$$\frac{1}{r(z)} = \frac{X}{I'(z)/I_0} + Y. \tag{10}$$

From equations (1) and (10), it follows that;

$$\text{rate of total canopy respiration } R = \int_0^{F^*} r\mathrm{d}F$$

$$= \frac{1}{YK} \ln\frac{1+(Y/X)}{1+(Y/X)\mathrm{e}^{-KF^*}}. \tag{11}$$

Just the same relation is also true for the chlorophyll content of oak leaves (leaf area basis) (Fig. 2.10). Thus Kirita & Hozumi (1973) derived the formulation as follows, where *CHL* denote the chlorophyll content of the leaf and *CHLF* the total amount of chlorophyll held by the whole canopy.

28

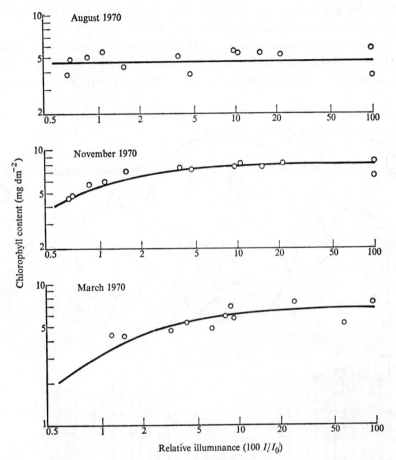

Fig. 2.10. Chlorophyll content of the leaves of *Castanopsis cuspidata* in relation to the mean relative illuminance to which they are exposed in the canopy. Differences in chlorophyll content become apparent after the leaves reach full maturity in August. Kirita & Hozumi (1973).

$$\frac{1}{CHL(z)} = \frac{A}{I'(z)/I_0} + B \tag{12}$$

$$CHLF = \int_0^{F^*} CHL \, dF$$

$$= \frac{1}{BK} \ln \frac{1+(B/A)}{1+(B/A)e^{-FK^*}}. \tag{13}$$

Equations (10)–(13) shows that a serious overestimation may result if R or $CHLF$ is calculated simply by multiplying the value of r or CHL of the canopy surface leaves by the total LAI. An overestimation by

86% was mentioned by Hozumi with respect to the total canopy respiration (Kira, Shinozaki & Hozumi, 1969).

Results of calculations based on these models as applied to a warm-temperate evergreen oak forest at Minamata special IBP research area, Kyushu, Japan, are summarised in Fig. 2.11. Gross production, canopy

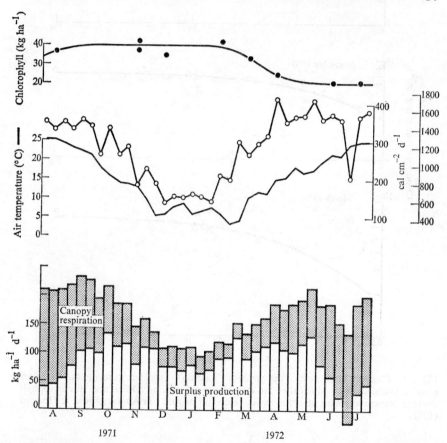

Fig. 2.11. Annual march of total incident radiation, air temperature, chlorophyll content of whole canopy, and the calculated rates of surplus production, canopy respiration and gross production in the evergreen oak forest at Minamata, Kyushu, Japan. Unpublished data by M. Nishioka & M. Nagano except those on chlorophyll content (1969–70; Kirita & Hozumi, 1973).

respiration and surplus production (gross production minus canopy respiration) are calculated for each ten-day period from average radiation records based on bi-monthly observations of photosynthesis and respiration. Dominant oak species of this forest shed almost all of their leaves in April–May, when new leaves unfold simultaneously. The total

30

chlorophyll content of the canopy gradually declines prior to leaf-fall, stays at a low level during late spring and early summer, and recovers again in late summer, but it is not directly correlated with gross productivity. Evidently the rate of gross production is closely correlated with the amount of radiation, whereas the respiration rate depends primarily on temperature. It is worth noting that surplus production remains at a fairly high level in spite of low temperatures throughout the winter season. On the contrary, high temperatures in mid-summer lower surplus production through accelerated respiratory consumption, especially when a spell of rainy weather occurs. Two peaks of surplus production in spring and fall seem to be the most remarkable feature in the production processes of this type of forest, which have been very little known to science so far.

Sources of net production data (used in Table 2.1 and Fig. 2.1)

(1) Akai, Ueda & Furuno, 1970; (2) Akai, Ueda & Furuno, 1971; (3) Akai, Furuno, Ueda & Sano, 1968; (4) Ando, 1965; (5) Ando, 1967; (6) Ando, Chiba, Tanimoto & Tagawa, 1972; (7) Ando, Takeuchi & Miyamoto, 1970; (8) Ando, Takeuchi, Saito & Watanabe, 1969; (9) Asada & Akai, 1963; (10) Asada & Akai, 1965; (11) Chiba & Nagano, 1967; (12) Chiba, Nagano & Tozawa, 1968; (13) Duvigneaud, 1971; (14) Fujimori, 1971; (15) Furuno, 1971; (16) Furuno & Kawanabe, 1967; (17) Harada *et al.*, 1972; (18) Hatiya, Doi & Kobayashi, 1965; (19) Hatiya, Tadaki, Karizumi & Harada, 1968; (20) Hatiya, Tochiaki & Fujimori, 1966; (21) Hughs, 1971; (22) Kabaya, Ikusima & Numata, 1964; (23) Kakubari & Maruyama, 1972; (24) Kan, Saito & Shidei, 1965; (25) Kimura, 1960; (26) Kimura, 1963; (27) Kimura, Mototani & Hogetsu, 1968; (28) Madgwick, 1968; (29) Maruyama, Yamada & Nakazawa, 1968; (30) Medwecka-Kornas, 1967; (31) Monk, Child & Nicholson, 1970; (32) Nihlgård, 1972; (33) Ogawa, 1967; (34) Ovington, 1957; (35) Post, 1970; (36) Reiners, 1972; (37) Research Group on Forest Productivity, 1960; (38) Research Group on Forest Productivity, 1964; (39) Research Group on Forest Productivity, 1966; (40) Saito, Kawahara, Shidei & Tsutsumi, 1970; (41) Saito, Tamai, Ogino & Shidei, 1968; (42) Saito, Yamada & Shidei, 1967; (43) Sato, 1963; (44) Satoo, 1968*a*; (45) Satoo, 1968*b*; (46) Satoo, 1970*a*; (47) Satoo, 1970*b*; (48) Satoo, 1971*a*; (49) Satoo, 1971*b*; (50) Satoo & Senda, 1966; (51) Tadaki, 1965; (52) Tadaki, 1968*a*; (53) Tadaki, 1968*b*; (54) Tadaki, Hatiya & Tochiaki, 1969; (55) Tadaki *et al.*, 1970; (56) Tadaki, Ogata & Nagatomo, 1965; (57) Tadaki, Ogata & Nagatomo, 1967; (58) Tadaki, Ogata, Nagatomo & Yoshida, 1966; (59) Tadaki, Shidei, Sakasegawa & Ogino, 1961; (60) Tadaki & Kawasaki, 1966; (61) Tamai & Shiedei, 1971; (62) Yamakura & Saito, 1970; (63) Yamakura, Saito & Shidei, 1972; (64) Zavitkovski & Stevens, 1972.

References

Akai, T., Ueda, S. & Furuno, T. (1970). Mechanisms related to matter production in a young slash pine forest. *Bulletin of the Kyoto University Forests*, **41**, 56–79.

Akai, T., Furuno, T., Ueda, S. & Sano, S. (1968). Mechanisms of matter production in young loblolly pine forests. *Bulletin of the Kyoto University Forests*, **40**, 26–49.

Akai, T., Ueda, S. & Furuno, T. (1971). Mechanisms related to matter production in a young white pine forest. *Bulletin of the Kyoto University Forest*, **42**, 143–62.

Ando, T. (1965). Estimation of dry-matter production and growth analysis of the young stand of Japanese black pine (*Pinus thunbergii*). *Advancing Frontiers of Plant Sciences, New Delhi*, **10**, 1–10.

Ando, T. (1967). Primary productivity of *Acacia* plantations. In: *Progress Report for 1966, JIBP/PT* (*Primary Productivity of Artificially Managed Forests*), ed. T. Satoo, pp. 27–9.

Ando, T., Chiba, S., Tanimoto, T. & Tagawa, R. (1972). Primary production of a *Tsuga* forest. *Progress Report for 1971, JIBP/PT* (*Comparative Study of Primary Productivity in Forest Ecosystems*), ed. T. Shidei, pp. 1–6.

Ando, T., Takeuchi, I. & Miyamoto, T. (1970). Seasonal variations of biomass and litterfall and nutrient cycling in a young *Cryptomeria japonica* plantation. *Progress Report for 1969, JIBP/PT* (*Comparative Study of Primary Productivity in Forest Ecosystems*), ed. T. Shidei, pp. 35–41.

Ando, T., Takeuchi, I., Saito, A. & Watanabe, H. (1969). Some observation of dry-matter production on the artificial two-storied forest. *Journal of the Japanese Forestry Society*, **51**, 102–7.

Asada, S. & Akai, T. (1963). On the management of subalpine forests, with special reference to the productivity and natural regeneration of *Abies veitchii* forest. *Nagano-Ringyo, Nagano*, **38**, 1–48.

Asada, S. & Akai, T. (1965). *On the productivity and regeneration of beech forest*, pp. 30. Nagano Regional Forest Office, Nagano.

Baumgartner, A. (1969). Meteorological approach to the exchange of CO_2 between the atmosphere and vegetation, particularly forest stands. *Photosynthetica*, **3**, 127–49.

Blackman, G. E. (1968). The application of the concepts of growth analysis to the assessment of productivity. In: *Functioning of Terrestrial Ecosystems at the Primary Production Level*, ed. F. E. Eckardt, pp. 243–59. Paris, UNESCO.

Bliss, L. C. (1966). Plant productivity in alpine microenvironments on Mt. Washington, New Hampshire. *Ecological Monographs*, **36**, 125–55.

Chiba, M. & Nagano, S. (1967). Primary productivity of larch plantations. *Progress Report for 1966, JIBP/PT* (*Primary Productivity of Artificially Managed Forests*), ed. T. Satoo, pp. 29–30.

Chiba, M., Nagano, S. & Tozawa, S. (1968). Productivity of larch plantations – primary production in mixed stands of larch and red pine. *Progress*

Report for 1967, JIBP/PT (*Primary Productivity of Artificially Managed Forests*), ed. T. Satoo, pp. 40–3.

Denmead, O. T. (1968). Comparative micrometeorology of a wheat field and a forest of *Pinus radiata*. *Agricultural Micrometeorology (Amsterdam)*, **6**, 357–71.

Duvigneaud, P. (ed.) (1971). *Productivity of Forest Ecosystems, Proceedings of the Brussels Symposium*, 707 pp. Paris, UNESCO.

Forrest, W. G. & Ovington, J. D. (1970). Organic matter changes in an age series of *Pinus radiata* plantations. *Journal of Applied Ecology*, **7**, 177–86.

Fujimori, T. (1971). *Primary productivity of a young* Tsuga heterophylla *stand and some speculations about biomass of forest communities on the Oregon coast*. USDA Forest Service, Research Pamphlet, PNW–123. 11 pp.

Furuno, T. (1971). Investigations on the productivity of Japanese fir (*Abies firma* Sieb. et Zucc.) and hemlock (*Tsuga sieboldii* Carr.) stands in Kyoto University forest in Wakayama (II). On the mixed stand of Japanese fir and hemlock. *Bulletin of the Kyoto University Forests*, **42**, 128–42.

Furuno, T. & Kawanabe, S. (1967). Investigations on the productivity of Japanese fir (*Abies firma* Sieb. et Zucc.) and hemlock (*Tsuga sieboldii* Carr.) stands in Kyoto University forest in Wakayama (I). On the growth of Japanese fir stands. *Bulletin of the Kyoto University Forests*, **39**, 9–26.

Harada, H., Satoo, I., Hotta, K., Hatiya, K. & Tadaki, Y. (1972). Study on the nutrient contents of mature *Cryptomeria* forest. *Bulletin of the Government Forest Experiment Station, Tokyo*, **249**, 17–74.

Hatiya, K., Doi, K. & Kobayashi, R. (1965). Analysis of the growth in Japanese red pine (*Pinus densiflora*) stands – a report on the matured plantation in Iwate Prefecture. *Bulletin of the Government Forest Experiment Station, Tokyo*, **176**, 75–88.

Hatiya, K., Tadaki, Y., Karizumi, N. & Harada, A. (1968). Primary productivity of Japanese red pine plantations – relation of productivity to stand age in dense stands. *Progress Report for 1967, JIBP/PT* (*Primary productivity of Artificially Managed Forests*), ed. T. Satoo, pp. 27–30.

Hatiya, K., Tochiaki, K. & Fujimori, T. (1966). Analysis of growth of a young larch (*Larix leptolopis*) plantation with excessively high stand density. *Journal of the Japanese Forestry Society, Tokyo*, **48**, 445–8.

Hogetsu, K. & Ichimura, S. (1954). Studies on the biological production of Lake Suwa. VI. The ecological studies on the production of phytoplankton. *Japanese Journal of Botany*, **14**, 280–303.

Hogetsu, K., Oshima, Y., Midorikawa, B., Tezuka, Y., Sakamoto, M., Mototani, I. & Kimura, M. (1960). Growth analytical studies on the artificial communities of *Helianthus tuberosus* with different densities. *Japanese Journal of Botany, Tokyo*, **17**, 278–305.

Hozumi, K. & Kirita, H. (1970). Estimation of total photosynthesis in forest canopies. *The Botanical Magazine, Tokyo*, **83**, 144–51.

Hozumi, K., Kirita, H. & Nishioka, M. (1972). Estimation of canopy photosynthesis and its seasonal change in a warm-temperate evergreen oak forest at Minamata (Japan). *Photosynthetica*, **6**, 158–68.

Hozumi, K., Nishioka, M., Nagano, M. & Kirita, H. (1973). Estimation of total photosynthesis by forest canopies. *Proceedings of the East Asian Regional Seminar for the IBP, Kyoto, 1973*, eds. S. Mori & T. Kira, pp. 45–56. Japanese National Committee for IBP, Kyoto.

Hozumi, K., Yoda, K. & Kira, T. (1969). Production ecology of tropical rain forests in southwestern Cambodia. II. Photosynthetic production in an evergreen seasonal forest. *Nature and Life in Southeast Asia, Tokyo*, ed. T. Kira & K. Iwata, **6**, 57–81.

Hughs, M. K. (1971). Tree biocontent, net production and litterfall in a deciduous woodland. *Oikos*, **22**, 62–73.

Iwaki, H., Monsi, M. & Midorikawa, B. (1966). *Dry matter production of some herb communities in Japan*. Pre-print, 11th Pacific Science Congress, Tokyo, 1966. 15pp.

Kabaya, H., Ikusima, I. & Numata, M. (1964). Growth and thinning of *Pinus thunbergii* stand – ecological studies of coastal pine forest, I. *Bulletin of the Marine Laboratory of Chiba University, Chiba*, **6**, 1–26.

Kakubari, Y. & Maruyama, K. (1972). On the permanent plots in natural beech forests at different altitudinal zones – (1) On biomass and productivity. *Progress Report for 1971, JIBP/PT (Comparative Study of Primary Productivity in Forest Ecosystems)*, ed. T. Shidei, pp. 7–13.

Kan, M., Saito, H. & Shidei, T. (1965). Studies of the productivity of evergreen broadleaved forests. *Bulletin of the Kyoto University Forests*, **37**, 55–75.

Kimura, M. (1960). Primary production of the warm-temperate laurel forest in the southern part of Osumi Peninsula, Kyushu, Japan. *Miscellaneous Report of the Research Institute for Natural Resources, Tokyo*, **52/53**, 36–47.

Kimura, M. (1963). Dynamics of vegetation in relation to soil development in northern Yatsugatake Mountains. *Japanese Journal of Botany, Tokyo*, **18**, 255–87.

Kimura, M., Mototani, I. & Hogetsu, K. (1968). Ecological and physiological studies on the vegetation of Mt. Shimagare. VI. Growth and dry matter production of young *Abies* stand. *The Botanical Magazine, Tokyo*, **81**, 287–94.

Kira, T. (1968). A rational method for estimating total respiration of trees and forest stands. In *Functioning of Terrestrial Ecosystems at the Primary Production Level*, ed. F. E. Eckardt, pp. 399–407. Paris, UNESCO.

Kira, T., Ogawa, H., Yoda, K. & Ogino, K. (1967). Comparative ecological studies on three main types of forest vegetation in Thailand. IV. Dry matter production, with special reference to the Khao Chong rain forest. *Nature and Life in Southeast Asia, Kyoto*, eds. T. Kira & K. Iwata, **6**, 149–74.

Kira, T. & Shidei, T. (1967). Primary production and turnover of organic matter in different forest ecosystems of the Western Pacific. *Japanese Journal of Ecology, Sendai*, **17**, 70–87.

Kira, T., Shinozaki, K. & Hozumi, K. (1969). Structure of forest canopies as related to their primary productivity. *Plant and Cell Physiology, Tokyo*, **10**, 129–42.

Kirita, H. & Hozumi, K. (1973). Estimation of total chlorophyll amount and its seasonal change in a warm-temperate evergreen oak forest at Minamata, Japan. *Japanese Journal of Ecology, Sendai*, **23**, 195–200.

Lange, O. L. & Schulze, E. D. (1971). Measurement of CO_2 gas-exchange and transpiration in the beech (*Fagus silvatica*). In *Integrated Experimental Ecology: Methods and Results of Ecosystem Research in the German Solling Project*, ed. H. Ellenberg, pp. 16–28. Berlin, Heidelberg & New York, Springer-Verlag.

Lemon, E., Allen Jr, L. H. & Muller, L. (1970). Carbon dioxide exchange of a tropical rain forest. Part II. *BioScience*, **20**, 1054–9.

Lieth, H. (1972). Modelling the primary productivity of the world. *Ciencia e Cultura, Julho*, **24**, 621–5.

Lindeman, R. L. (1942). The trophic-dynamic aspect of ecology. *Ecology*, **23**, 399–418.

McCree, K. J. & Troughton, J. H. (1966). Non-existence of an optimum leaf area index for the production rate of white clover grown under constant conditions. *Plant Physiology*, **41**, 1615–22.

Madgwick, H. A. I. (1968). Seasonal changes in biomass and annual production of an old-field *Pinus virginiana* stand. *Ecology*, **49**, 149–52.

Maruyama, K. (1971). Effect of altitude on dry matter production of primeval Japanese beech forest communities in Naeba Mountains. *Memoirs of the Faculty of Agriculture, Niigata University, Niigata*, **9**, 86–171.

Maruyama, K., Yamada, S. & Nakazawa, M. (1968). A tentative estimation of the gross photosynthetic production – Ecological studies of beech forest (17). *Proceedings of the 79th Annual Meeting of the Japanese Forestry Society*, pp. 286–8.

Medwecka-Kornas, A. (1967). Estimation of primary production as a basis for studies of secondary production. In *Secondary Productivity of Terrestrial Ecosystems*, ed. K. Petrusewicz, pp. 83–93. Kraków & Warsaw, Polish Acad. Sci.

Midorikawa, B. (1959). Growth-analytical study of altherbosa on Mt. Hakkoda, northeast Japan. *Ecological Review, Sendai*, **15**, 83–117.

Miller, P. C. (1972). Bioclimate, leaf temperature, and primary production in red mangrove canopies in South Florida. *Ecology*, **53**, 22–45.

Miller, R. B. (1971). Forest productivity in the temperate-humid zone of the southern hemisphere. In *Productivity of Forest Ecosystems, Proceedings of the Brussels Symposium*, ed. P. Duvigneaud, pp. 299–305. Paris, UNESCO.

Möller, C. M. (1945). Untersuchungen über Laubmenge, Stoffverlust und Stoffproduktion des Waldes. *Det forstlige Forsögsvaesen i Danmark*, **17**, 1–287.

Möller, C. M., Müller, D. & Nielsen, J. (1954). The dry matter production of European beech. *Det forstlige Forsögsvaesen i Danmark*, **21**, 253–335.

Monk, C. D., Child, G. I. & Nicholson, S. A. (1970). Biomass, litter and leaf surface area estimates of an oak–hickory forest. *Oikos*, **21**, 138–41.

Monsi, M. (1968). Mathematical models of plant communities. In *Functioning of Terrestrial Ecosystems at the Primary Production Level,* ed. E. F. Eckardt, pp. 131–49. Paris, UNESCO.

Monsi, M. & Saeki, T. (1953). Über den Lichtfaktor in den Pflanzengesellschaften und ihre Bedeutung für die Stoffproduktion. *Japanese Journal of Botany, Tokyo,* **14,** 22–52.

Müller, D. (1962). Wie gross ist der prozentuale Anteil der Nettoproduktion von der Bruttoproduktion? In *Die Stoffproduktion der Pflanzendecke,* ed. H. Lieth, pp. 26–8. Stuttgart, Gustav Fischer.

Müller, D. & Nielsen, J. (1965). Production brute, pertes par respiration et production nette dans la forêt ombrophile tropicale. *Det forstlige Forsögsvaesen i Danmark,* **29,** 69–110.

Newbould, P. J. (1967). *Methods for Estimating the Primary Production of Forests.* IBP handbook 2, 62pp. Oxford & Edinburgh, Blackwell.

Ng, S. K., Thamboo, S. & de Souza, P. (1968). Nutrient contents of oil palms in Malaya. II. Nutrients in vegetative tissues. *Malaysian Agricultural Journal, Kuala Lumpur,* **46,** 332.

Nihlgård, B. (1972). Plant biomass, primary production and distribution of chemical elements in a beech forest and a planted spruce forest in south Sweden. *Oikos,* **23,** 69–81.

Odum, H. T. (1957). Trophic structure and productivity of Silver Springs, Florida. *Ecological Monographs,* **27,** 55–112.

Odum, H. T. (1970). An emerging view of the ecological system at El Verde. In *A Tropical Rain Forest: A Study of Irradiation and Ecology at El Verde, Puerto Rico,* eds. H. T. Odum & R. F. Pigeon, pp. I–191–289. Oak Ridge, Information Services, US Atomic Energy Commission.

Odum, H. T. & Odum, E. P. (1955). Trophic structure and productivity of a windward coral reef community on Eniwetok Atoll. *Ecological Monographs,* **25,** 291–320.

Ogawa, H. & Kira, T. (1967). An estimation of the net production of Ashiu beech forest. *Progress Report for 1966, JIBP/PT (Studies on the Methods for Assessing Primary Production of Forests),* ed. T. Kira, pp. 21–5.

Ogawa, H. (1967). Three-dimensional structure of Ashiu beech forest in relation to light distribution. *Progress Report for 1966, JIBP/PT (Studies on the Methods for Assessing Primary Production of Forests),* ed. T. Kira, pp. 45–52.

Ogino, K., Ratanawongs, D., Tsutsumi, T. & Shidei, T. (1967). The primary production of tropical forests in Thailand. *The Southeast Asian Studies, Kyoto,* **5,** 121–54.

Ovington, J. D. (1956). The form, weight and productivity of tree species grown in close stands. *New Phytologist,* **55,** 289–304.

Ovington, J. D. (1957). Dry-matter production by *Pinus sylvestris* L. *Annals of Botany,* N.S., **21,** 287–314.

Ovington, J. D. (1962). Quantitative ecology and the woodland ecosystem concept. *Advances in Ecological Research,* ed. J. B. Cragg, **1,** 103–92.

Post, L. J. (1970). Dry-matter production of mountain maple and balsam fir in northwestern New Brunswick. *Ecology,* **51,** 548–50.

Reichle, D. E. (ed.) (1970). *Ecological Studies. Vol. I. Analysis of Temperate Forest Ecosystems.* Pp. xii + 304. London, Chapman & Hall; Berlin, Springer-Verlag.

Reiners, W. A. (1972). Structure and energetics of three Minnesota forests. *Ecological Monographs,* **42,** 71–94.

Research Group on Forest Productivity of the Four Universities (1960). *Studies on the Productivity of the Forest. Part I. Essential Needle-leaved Forests of Hokkaido,* 99pp. Tokyo, Kokusaku Pulp Industry Co.

Research Group on Forest Productivity of the Four Universities (1964). *Studies on the Productivity of the Forest. Part II. Larch Plantations in Shinshyu District,* 60pp. Tokyo, Nippon Ringyo-Gijutsu Kyokai.

Research Group on Forest Productivity of the Four Universities (1966). *Studies on the Productivity of the Forest. Part III. Matter Production in* Cryptomeria *Plantations,* 63pp. Tokyo, Nippon Ringyo-Gijutsu Kyokai.

Rosswall, T. (ed.) (1971). *Systems Analysis in Northern Coniferous Forests,* 194pp. Stockholm, Swedish Natural Science Council.

Saeki, T. (1960). Relationship between leaf amount, light distribution and total photosynthesis in a plant community. *The Botanical Magazine, Tokyo,* **73,** 55–63.

Saito, H., Kawahara, T., Shidei, T. & Tsutsumi, T. (1970). Productivity of young stands of *Metasequoia glyptostroboides. Bulletin of the Kyoto University Forests,* **41,** 80–95.

Saito, H., Tamai, S., Ogino, K. & Shidei, T. (1968). Studies on the effects of thinning from small diametered trees. III. Changes in stand conditions after the second growing season. *Bulletin of the Kyoto University Forests,* **40,** 81–92.

Saito, H., Yamada, I. & Shidei, T. (1967). Studies on the effects of thinning from small diametered trees. II. Changes in stand condition after single growing season. *Bulletin of the Kyoto University Forests,* **39,** 64–78.

Sato, H. (1963). *Dry Matter Production by Abies sachalinensis Forest in Hokkaido.* M.Sc. Thesis, Osaka City University, Osaka.

Satoo, T. (1966). Production and distribution of dry matter in forest ecosystem. *Miscellaneous Information, The Tokyo University Forests,* **16,** 3–15.

Satoo, T. (1968a). Primary production and distribution of produced dry matter in a plantation of *Cinnamomum camphora* – Materials for the studies of growth in stands, 7. *Bulletin of the Tokyo University Forests,* **64,** 241–75.

Satoo, T. (1968b). Primary production relations in woodlands of *Pinus densiflora.* In *Symposium on Primary Productivity and Mineral Cycling in Natural Ecosystems,* ed. H. E. Young, pp. 52–80. Orono, University of Maine Press.

Satoo, T. (1970a). Primary production in a plantation of Japanese larch, *Larix leptolepis:* a summarized report of JPTF–66 KOIWAI. *Journal of the Japanese Forestry Society, Tokyo,* **52,** 154–8.

Satoo, T. (1970b). A synthesis of studies by the harvest method: primary production relations in the temperate deciduous forests of Japan. In

Terrestrial ecosystems

Analysis of Temperate Forest Ecosystems, ed. D. E. Reichle, pp. 55–72. New York, Heidelberg & Berlin, Springer-Verlag.

Satoo, T. (1971a). Primary production relations of Norway spruce in Japan – Materials for the studies of growth in stands, 8. *Bulletin of the Tokyo University Forests*, **65**, 125–42.

Satoo, T. (1971b). Primary production relations of coniferous forests in Japan. In *Productivity of Forest Ecosystems: Proceedings of the Brussels Symposium*, ed. P. Duvigneaud, pp. 191–205. Paris, UNESCO.

Satoo, T. & Senda, S. (1966). Materials for the studies of growth in stands, 6. Biomass, dry matter production and efficiency of leaves in a young *Cryptomeria* plantation. *Bulletin of the Tokyo University Forests*, **62**, 117–46.

Schulze, E. D. & Koch, W. (1971). Measurement of primary production with cuvettes. In *Productivity of Forest Ecosystems: Proceedings of the Brussels Symposium*, ed. P. Duvigneaud, pp. 141–57. Paris, UNESCO.

Special Committee for the International Biological Programme (1969). *Index of National Projects. Part I. Section PT*. IBP News 12. London.

Shimada, Y., Iwaki, H., Midorikawa, B. & Oga, N. (1969). Biomass and annual net production of *Miscanthus sinensis* in the Special IBP Research Area at Kawatabi. *Progress Report for 1968, JIBP/PT–CT* (*Studies on the Productivity and Conservation of Grassland Ecosystems*), ed. M. Numata, pp. 5–18.

Tadaki, Y. (1965). Studies on the production structure of forest. VII. The primary production of a young stand of *Castanopsis cuspidata*. *Japanese Journal of Ecology, Sendai*, **15**, 142–7.

Tadaki, Y. (1966). Some discussions on the leaf biomass of forest stands and trees. *Bulletin of the Government Forest Experiment Station, Tokyo*, **184**, 135–61.

Tadaki, Y. (1968a). Studies on the production structure of forest. XIV. The third report on the primary production of a young stand of *Castanopsis cuspidata*. *Journal of the Japanese Forestry Society, Tokyo*, **50**, 60–5.

Tadaki, Y. (1968b). The primary productivity and the stand density control in *Acacia mollissima* stand. *Bulletin of the Government Forest Experiment Station, Tokyo*, **216**, 99–125.

Tadaki, Y. (1970). Studies on the production structure of forest. XVII. Vertical change of specific leaf area in forest canopy. *Journal of the Japanese Forestry Society, Tokyo*, **52**, 263–8.

Tadaki, Y., Hatiya, K. & Tochiaki, K. (1969). Studies on the production structure of forest. XV. Primary productivity of *Fagus crenata* in plantation. *Journal of the Japanese Forestry Society, Tokyo*, **51**, 331–9.

Tadaki, Y., Hatiya, K., Tochiaki, K., Miyauchi, H. & Matsuda, U. (1970). Studies on the production structure of forest. XVI. Primary productivity of *Abies veitchii* forests in the subalpine zone of Mt Fuji. *Bulletin of the Government Forest Experiment Station, Tokyo*, **229**, 1–22.

Tadaki, Y. & Kawasaki, Y. (1966). Studies on the production structure of forest. IX. Primary productivity of a young *Cryptomeria* plantation with excessively high stand density. *Journal of the Japanese Forestry Society, Tokyo*, **48**, 55–61.

Tadaki, Y., Ogata, N. & Nagatomo, Y. (1965). The dry matter productivity in several stands of *Cryptomeria japonica* in Kyushu. *Bulletin of the Government Forest Experiment Station, Tokyo*, **173**, 45–66.

Tadaki, Y., Ogata, N. & Nagatomo, Y. (1967). Studies on the production structure of forest. XI. Primary productivities of 28-year old plantations of *Cryptomeria* of cuttings and seedlings origin. *Bulletin of the Government Forest Experiment Station, Tokyo*, **199**, 47–65.

Tadaki, Y., Ogata, N., Nagatomo, Y. & Yoshida, T. (1966). Studies on the production structure of forest. X. Primary productivity of an unthinned 45-year old stand of *Chamaecyparis obtusa*. *Journal of the Japanese Forestry Society, Tokyo*, **48**, 387–93.

Tadaki, Y., Shidei, T., Sakasegawa, T. & Ogino, K. (1961). Studies on the production structure of forest. II. Estimation of standing crop and some analyses on productivity of young birch stand (*Betula platyphylla*). *Journal of the Japanese Forestry Society, Tokyo*, **43**, 19–26.

Tamai, S. & Shidei, T. (1971). Studies on the effects of thinning from small diametered trees. IV. Changes in stand conditions after the fourth growing season. *Bulletin of the Kyoto University Forests*, **42**, 163–73.

Tamiya, H. (1957). Mass culture of algae. *Annual Review of Plant Physiology*, **8**, 309–34.

Templeton, J. K. (1968). Growth studies in *Hevea brasilensis*. I. Growth analysis up to seven years after bud-grafting. *Journal of the Rubber Research Institute of Malaya, Kuala Lumpur*, **20**, 136.

Westlake, D. F. (1963). Comparison of plant productivity. *Biological Reviews*, **38**, 385–425.

Whittaker & Likens (1968). Cited by Whittaker & Woodwell (1971).

Whittaker, R. H. & Woodwell, G. M. (1969). Structure, production and diversity of the oak-pine forest at Brookhaven, New York. *Journal of Ecology*, **57**, 155–74.

Whittaker, R. H. & Woodwell, G. M. (1971). Measurement of primary production of forests. In *Productivity of Forest Ecosystems, Proceedings of the Brussels Symposium*, ed. P. Duvigneaud, pp. 159–75. Paris, UNESCO.

Wycherley, P. (1969). Forests and productivity. *Malayan Nature Journal, Kuala Lumpur*, **22**, 187–97.

Yamakura, T. & Saito, H. (1970). Growth of roots and branches in *Chamaecyparis obtusa* plantations. *Progress Report for 1969, JIBP/PT* (*Comparative Study of Primary Productivity in Forest Ecosystems*), ed. T. Shidei, 6pp.

Yamakura, T., Saito, H. & Shidei, T. (1972). Production and structure of underground part of Hinoki (*Chamaecyparis obtusa*) stand. 1. Estimation of root production by means of root analysis. *Journal of the Japanese Forestry Society, Tokyo*, **54**, 118–25.

Yim, Y. J., Ogawa, H. & Kira, T. (1969). Light interception by stems in plant communities. *Japanese Journal of Ecology, Sendai*, **19**, 233–8.

Terrestrial ecosystems

Yoda, K. (1967). Comparative ecological studies on three main types of forest vegetation in Thailand. III. Community respiration. *Nature and Life in Southeast Asia, Kyoto*, eds. T. Kira & K. Iwata, **5,** 83–148.

Yoda, K., Shinozaki, K., Ogawa, H., Hozumi, K. & Kira, T. (1965). Estimation of the total amount of respiration in woody organs of trees and forest communities. *Journal of Biology, Osaka City University, Osaka*, **16,** 15–26.

Zavitkovski, J. & Stevens, R. D. (1972). Primary productivity of red alder ecosystems. *Ecology*, **53,** 235–42.

Note added in proof

According to the recent investigation of a West Malaysian rain forest by K. Yoda (Malaysian IBP Synthesis Meeting, Kuala Lumpur, August 1974), the rate of community respiration in the rain forest of southern Thailand (Table 2.2; Yoda 1967) seems to have been considerably overestimated, owing to certain inadequate treatment of plant samples. He arrived at an estimate of *c.* 55 t (dry matter equivalent) $ha^{-1}yr^{-1}$ of annual community respiration in the former forest. This results in the increase of $\Delta P_n/\Delta P_g$ ratio in a climax rain forest up to *c.* 0.34 and the decrease in the energy efficiency of gross production (Table 2.3) to a level slightly less than 3%. Table 2.4 has to be somewhat modified, based on these findings.

3. Primary production of grazing lands

M. CALDWELL

A thorough coverage of grazing lands should rightfully include nearly all terrestrial ecosystems. Grazing usually implies herbivory by domestic livestock. However, consumption of forage by wildlife, whether by large ungulates or by smaller vertebrates such as the tundra lemming is also certainly grazing in the true sense of the word. Grazing lands then should logically include the world's prairies, steppes, savannahs, deserts, tundras and even the understory of most forested ecosystems. Insects, and soil invertebrates are also not to be underestimated as significant herbivores in most terrestrial ecosystems. This can be most apparent with plague populations of locusts and grasshoppers in grasslands (Blocker, 1969; Andrzejewska, 1967). Underground herbivory, such as by nematodes (Riffle, 1968; Paris, 1969), is also often overlooked as significant consumption of live plant material in many ecosystems. Grazers would only be unimportant in ecosystems where energy flows primarily through a detritus food chain. In view of the structure of this synthesis volume, however, grazing lands to be emphasized in this chapter are natural grassland prairies, grass and shrub steppes, and grassland savannahs to a lesser extent. In these systems, however, herbivory should be recognized as being carried out by invertebrates as well as vertebrates.

Because this volume has at its base a functional approach to photosynthetic systems, it is of interest here to compare the success as measured by productivity of plants possessing different pathways of carbon assimilation. Because grassland prairies and shrub steppes extend through a wide range of temperature and precipitation conditions on a world scale, plants possessing different photosynthetic strategies are well represented. For example, graminoids possessing the C_4-dicarboxylic acid pathway of photosynthesis and those possessing the normal C_3-pathway are well represented in varying proportions in grasslands extending through a range of latitudes. The productivity of species possessing these different photosynthetic pathways will be compared for plants growing in natural ecosystems.

In as much as possible, data from the International Biological Programme have been used in this synthesis. Often, however, much of this information is yet in a form not citable.

41

c

Primary production of grazing lands on a world scale

Rodin, Bazilevich and co-workers have undertaken a most comprehensive synthesis of the world distribution of plant biomass and productivity (Rodin & Bazilevich, 1965). In a relatively recent compilation, which includes results of the International Biological Programme, Bazilevich, Rodin & Rozov (1970) have summarized world primary productivity on a geographical basis. In Table 3.1 is a summary of net primary production data of steppes and savannahs abstracted from their compilations. These are broken down into four latitudinal belts used by Bazilevich *et al.*, and in turn into areas of varying precipitation. Net primary production, as used by these authors, is taken as the annual

Table 3.1. *Annual primary productivity for major plant formations of grazing ecosystems, abstracted from Bazilevich et al., 1971*

Latitudinal belts and plant formations		Annual productivity $(\text{g m}^{-2}\,\text{yr}^{-1})$
I. BOREAL BELT, HUMID AND SEMIHUMID REGIONS		
Mountain meadows on gray mountain forest soils		750
Mountain meadows on mountain meadow soils		1200
	Average	975
II. SUB-BOREAL BELT, HUMID REGIONS		
Herbaceous prairie on meadow chernozemlike soils (brunizems)		1500
	Average	1500
III. SUB-BOREAL BELT, SEMIARID REGIONS		
Steppe on typical and leached chernozems		1300
Steppe on ordinary and southern chernozems		800
Steppe on solonets chernozems		800
Steppified formations on solonets		500
Halophytic formations on solonchak		400
Psammophytic formations on sand		800
Dry steppe on dark chestnut soils		900
Desert steppe on light chestnut soils		500
Dry and desert steppe on chestnut and solonets complexes		500
Same, on solonets		500
Halophytic formations on solonchak		70
Psammophytic formations on sand		600
Mountain dry steppe on mountain chestnut soils		700
Mountain steppe on mountain chernozems		1000
Mountain meadow steppe on subalpine mountain meadow steppe soils		1100
	Average	639

Table 3.1 – *continued*

Latitudinal belts and plant formations		Annual productivity (g m^{-2} yr^{-1})
VI. SUB-BOREAL BELT, ARID REGIONS		
Steppified desert on brown semi-desert soils		400
	Average	400
SUB-BOREAL AND BOREAL BELTS AVERAGE		754
I. SUBTROPICAL BELT, HUMID REGIONS		
Herbaceous prairie on reddish black soils and rubrozems		1300
	Average	1300
II. SUBTROPICAL BELT, SEMIARID REGIONS		
Shrub-steppe formations on gray-brown soils		1000
Same, on gray-brown solonets soils with small solonets areas		600
Same, on subtropical chernozemlike and coalesced soils		800
Psammophytic formations on sandy soils and sand		500
Halophytic formations on solonchak soils and solonchak		50
Mountain shrub-steppe formations on gray-brown mountain soils		800
	Average	625
III. SUBTROPICAL BELT, ARID REGIONS		
Steppified desert on serozems and meadow-serozem soils		1000
	Average	1000
SUBTROPICAL AVERAGE		756
I. TROPICAL BELT, HUMID REGIONS		
Seasonally humid evergreen forest and secondary tall-grass savannah on red ferralitic soils		1600
Same, on black tropical soils		1500
	Average	1550
II. TROPICAL BELT, SEMIARID REGIONS		
Grass and shrub savannah on ferralitic red-brown soils		1200
Same, on tropical black soils		1100
Same, on tropical solonets soils		700
Mountain savannah on red-brown mountain soils		1200
	Average	1050
III. TROPICAL BELT, ARID REGIONS		
Desertlike savannah on reddish-brown soils		400
	Average	400
TROPICAL BELT AVERAGE		1100

production of living plant material, both above and below ground, as can be best measured by harvest techniques and calculations from source references. Since these data were drawn from several sources, considerable variation in methodological approach would be expected.

Not surprisingly average production data (see Table 3.1) do indicate the greatest productivity in lower latitudes and in more humid regions, as these authors found for total terrestrial world vegetation. It is clear, however, that considerable variation exists in average production values for these grazing ecosystem types.

Photosynthetic strategies in grazing ecosystems

Three basic strategies of carbon metabolism in plant photosynthesis are now widely recognized. The relatively recent discovery of the C_4-dicarboxylic pathway of carbon assimilation in species such as sugar cane and maize (Kortschak, Hartt & Burr, 1965; Hatch, Slack & Johnson, 1967) might help to explain the basis of the high productivity of these species in agronomic situations. Subsequent physiological studies on plants possessing the C_4-pathway have resulted in several generalizations concerning the leaf anatomy, carbon isotope discrimination ratios (Smith & Epstein, 1971), and biochemical pathways of C_4-plants which seem to be holding up rather well at present. Of prime interest to this discussion are the characteristics of C_4-plants which relate to their potential productivity in different environments. Many C_4-species possess remarkably high rates of photosynthesis (up to 70 mg dm^{-2} h^{-1}, Mooney, 1972) which has led some investigators to label these as 'efficient' plants (Black, 1971). In addition, they undergo light saturation of photosynthesis only at very high irradiation levels, have high temperature optima for photosynthesis (i.e., 35–40 °C), comparatively high photosynthesis–transpiration ratios and lack apparent photorespiration (Black, 1971). When compared to species possessing the normal C_3-pathway of photosynthesis, it is hardly surprising to find C_4-species widely distributed in tropical and subtropical latitudes particularly in arid and semiarid environments.

The crassulacean acid metabolism (CAM) pathway of succulent plant species has been known for many years. Because stomata of CAM plants are open during the night hours when CO_2 incorporation occurs, water loss is at a minimum, therefore these plants possess photosynthesis–transpiration ratios even superior to those of C_4-species (Neales, Patterson & Hartney, 1968). Since low night temperatures favor CO_2

assimilation in CAM-species, it is not surprising that they are primarily distributed in arid regions with widely divergent diurnal temperatures (Ting, 1971; Mooney, 1972). Carbon dioxide assimilation rates in CAM-species are, however, quite low (usually on the order of 5 to 10 mg CO_2 dm^{-2} h^{-1}) and they do not seem to be particularly competitive in densely vegetated communities (Patten, 1972; Mooney, 1972). The potential forage value of CAM-species, particularly in the genus *Opuntia* is, however, widely recognized in arid and semiarid regions (Goodin & McKell, 1971).

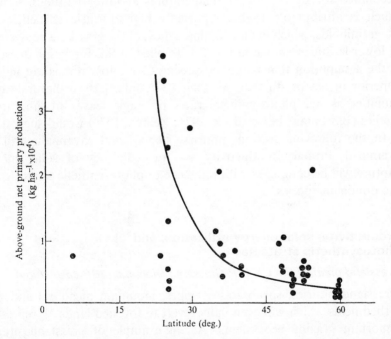

Fig. 3.1. Relationship between above-ground productivity and latitude for production values in grassland and tundra ecosystems. From the IBP Grassland/Tundra Workshop, Fort Collins, Colo., USA (Wielgolaski, personal communication).

Both the C_4- and CAM-pathways are widely scattered phylogenetically (Evans, 1971). It is not surprising, however, that graminoid genera possessing C_4-photosynthesis are primarily of tropical origin and distribution, while those genera possessing C_3-photosynthesis are more temperate in distribution. Succulents possessing CAM-metabolism are normally associated with warmer latitudes on a world scale.

A world pattern of primary production indicates the tropical latitudinal belt to be the most productive with decreasing productivities at higher latitudes (Bazilevich *et al.*, 1971). This has also evolved from the recent output of an International Grassland/Tundra Workshop held in Fort Collins, Colorado, 1972 (F. E. Wielgolaski, personal communication). In Fig. 3.1 is shown the regression relationship between above-ground primary productivity and latitude for thirty-one IBP sites in grassland and tundra areas of twelve participating countries. Although such a relationship between above-ground productivity and latitude in grazing ecosystems is certainly not surprising, the question might be posed as to how much of the increase in production can be accounted for by the higher temperatures at lower latitudes or how much is attributable to the reportedly high intrinsic efficiencies of C_4-graminoids, which in fact dominate most of the grassland ecosystems at lower latitudes, shown in Fig. 3.1. Implicit in this foregoing question is the assumption that plants possessing C_4-photosynthesis are indeed superior in net productivity to their C_3-counterparts in natural communities as net photosynthetic rates of single leaves in laboratory studies (Björkman, 1971; Black, 1971; Zelitch, 1971) would suggest.

In the following section, prairies, steppes and savannahs will be examined. Primary productivity and the efficiency of solar energy capture will be compared with reference to photosynthetic strategies of the dominant species.

Productivity, solar energy utilization, and photosynthetic strategies

Grassland prairies; the US IBP Grassland Biome, an IBP case study

Grassland prairies, shrub-grass steppes, mountain meadows and disturbed fields which will eventually revert to forested lands all represent important grazing ecosystems. As an example of grassland prairie productivity, synthesized data from the US IBP Grassland Biome will be presented here. This example has been chosen primarily because there exists a network of research sites covering a wide latitudinal range where similar methodologies have been employed.

The distribution of these sites is shown in Fig. 3.2. The Canadian IBP Matador site and the Curlew Valley site of the US IBP Desert Biome are also indicated on this map. The basic biome formations which are shown in Fig. 3.1 are the short-grass prairie dominated by xeric grasses of short stature, the most important of which are *Bouteloua gracilis* and *Buchloë dactyloides*; the mixed- and tall-grass prairies where tall grasses such as *Stipa spartea*, *Andropogon furcatus*, and *Sorghastrum nutans*,

46

and grasses of medium height such as *Andropogon scoparius* and *Bouteloua curtipendula* become more prevalent. The taller grasses become increasingly important to the east and more mesic end of the grassland formation. The Great Basin formation is also indicated in Fig. 3.2. It is essentially a shrub steppe with two major communities, one dominated by *Artemisia tridentata* and the other, at somewhat lower elevations, dominated by *Atriplex confertifolia*.

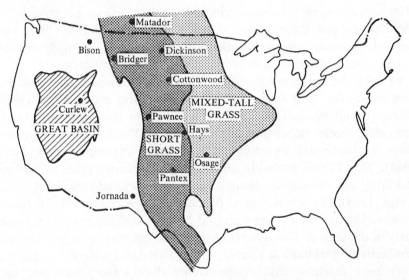

Fig. 3.2. Location of research sites of the US IBP Grassland Biome, the IBP Canadian Matador site and the Curlew Valley site of the US IBP Desert Biome (adapted from Van Dyne, 1971, and Rasmussen, 1971).

The distribution of dominant species according to photosynthetic pathways does tend to follow an expected latitudinal gradient. For example, in the US Grassland Biome sites, the 'warm season' grasses of tropical affinities clearly dominate in those sites below 45° N. latitude, i.e. Pawnee and Cottonwood south to the Jornada site. On the other hand the 'cool season' grasses of temperate affinities clearly predominate in the Bison, Bridger, and Dickinson sites above 45° N. latitude (Sims & Singh, 1971). Based upon anatomical and physiological characteristics from other studies (Black, 1971; Brownell & Crossland, 1972; Brown & Gracen, 1972; Brown, 1958; Downton, Berry & Tregunna, 1969; Krenzer & Moss, 1969; Downton & Tregunna, 1968; Tieszen, 1970; Williams, 1971) at least 90% of these 'warm season' grasses are C$_4$ in photosynthetic pathway and all of the 'cool season'

47

grasses are C_3 in pathway. This latitudinal distribution is not as abrupt as this description might sound. For example, some prominent C_4-grasses such as *Bouteloua gracilis* have an extensive range from Mexico into Canada. Similarly in the Great Basin formation, a C_4-plant, *Atriplex confertifolia*, extends throughout nearly the entire latitudinal range of this formation. The distribution of C_4- and C_3-grasses in the grasslands is also dependent on microsite variations, i.e., south- versus north-facing slopes (Tieszen, 1970) and elevational gradients (A. Harrison, personal communication). Succulent species occur only in the Pawnee and Pantex sites of this Grassland Biomenet work. In general, however, the distribution of succulents is definitely biased toward southern latitudes in the North American continent.

In Table 3.2 are shown the above- and below-ground annual production values for 1970 from the various Grassland Biome sites. These above-ground production data are based upon peak live weights of individual species rather than on simply the peak weight of the standing crop for the entire community (Ovington, Heitkamp & Lawrence, 1963). This is still probably an underestimate since rates of foliage mortality and subsequent disappearance were not included (Wiegert & Evans, 1964). The below-ground productivity is based on the difference between the maximum below-ground biomass and the minimum value early in the season. This difference then is an estimate of below-ground productivity (Dahlman & Kucera, 1965). This again is an underestimate since root mortality and disappearance during the season are not included in the production value.

This tabulation of productivities includes sites normally grazed, except during the season of production assay, and sites protected from grazing by large herbivores. The grazed Pawnee site was grazed with moderate intensity during the 1970 season when production was measured.

A calculation of the efficiency of solar energy capture is represented for total productivity values at each of these sites. This is based upon conversion of plant dry weight to caloric values by factors of 4 kcal g^{-1} (16.7 kJ g^{-1}) for above-ground material and 4.7 kcal g^{-1} (19.7 kJ g^{-1}) for below-ground material (Sims & Singh, 1971). The original values of Sims & Singh have been adjusted using a value of 47% of the total solar radiation as available for plant photosynthesis on a ground area basis (Yocum, Allen & Lemon, 1964). The average production and efficiency of energy capture values for the grassland sites dominated by C_3- and C_4-grasses clearly do not indicate that the C_4-grasses might be superior

Table 3.2. *Primary production of the US IBP Grassland Biome sites for 1970. Solar energy utilization efficiencies are based on 47% of total solar irradiation during the growing season. Adapted from Sims & Singh, 1971*

Sites	Ungrazed sites				Grazed sites			
	Above-ground ($g\,m^{-2}\,yr^{-1}$)	Below-ground ($g\,m^{-2}\,yr^{-1}$)	Total ($g\,m^{-2}\,yr^{-1}$)	Eff. (%)	Above-ground ($g\,m^{-2}\,yr^{-1}$)	Below-ground ($g\,m^{-2}\,yr^{-1}$)	Total ($g\,m^{-2}\,yr^{-1}$)	Eff. (%)
Dickinson	328	391	719	0.78	280	606	886	0.98
Bison	228	382	610	0.64	156	521	677	0.69
Bridger	179	372	551	1.03	156	510	666	1.28
Average for Northern sites	245	382	627	0.82	197	546	743	0.96
Pawnee	142	458	600	0.61	119	699	818	0.85
Cottonwood	197	269	466	0.50	111	385	496	0.54
Hays	273	288	561	0.49	357	412	769	0.67
Pantex	107	177	284	0.20	368	411	779	0.56
Osage	337	174	511	0.47	512	362	874	0.82
Jornada	172	104	276	0.17	114	133	247	0.14
Average for Southern sites	205	245	450	0.41	264	400	664	0.60
Average for all sites	218	291	509	0.54	241	449	690	0.72

Table 3.3. *Abiotic factors for US IBP Grassland Biome sites in 1970. Adapted from Sims & Singh, 1971*

| Site | Growing season | | Photosynthetically active solar radiation | | | | Mean annual temp. (°C) | Precipitation | | Evapotranspiration | | Available water storage (cm) |
	Beginning date 1970	Length (days)	1970 Growing season (kJ m⁻²)	(kcal m⁻²)	Daily (kJ m⁻² d⁻¹)	(kcal m⁻² d⁻¹)		Mean annual (cm)	1970 Growing season (cm)	Potential (mm)	Actual (mm)	
Dickinson	5/1	161	1704842	407467	10586	2530	4.8	41	36	646	422	15
Bison	4/28	164	1760686	420814	10736	2566	7.2	33	31	495	353	12
Bridger	6/10	92	997202	238337	10841	2591	7.7	61	*	*	*	12
Pawnee	4/22	170	1856357	443680	10916	2609	8.3	30	18	608	205	16
Cottonwood	4/22	171	1720080	411109	10058	2404	8.3	38	23	676	366	27
Hays	4/4	214	2088402	499140	9757	2332	12.2	58	40	723	463	8
Pantex	4/2	266	2542659	607710	9556	2284	13.9	53	20	831	257	3
Osage	3/30	218	1913778	457404	8778	2098	15.2	94	62	881	669	27
Jornada	2/22	267	2935365	701569	10991	2627	24.5	23	14	842	155	4

* Data unavailable.

in terms of production on a unit ground area basis or even solar energy utilization. Values of both production and efficiency in these grassland systems were quite low.

Table 3.3 contains a comparative summation of abiotic parameters during 1970 for the various grassland sites. The effective growing season is based on the occurrence of five consecutive days when the minimum temperature averaged at least 4.4 °C (Sims & Singh, 1971) and usable solar radiation is calculated as 47% of the total incoming shortwave radiation for the entire growing season.

When comparing the efficiencies of solar energy utilization for the various sites (see Table 3.2), it should be recognized that the assumption that the same temperature parameters can be used to arbitrarily define the growing season for all 'cool season' and 'warm season' grasses is unsound. After all, these classes of grasses were defined according to whether they develop primarily during the cooler or warmer portions of the spring–summer period (Sims & Singh, 1971). It must also be recognized that photosynthesis in green overwintering leaf tissues might account for a significant carbon gain to the plant before leaf expansion and active growth. This single arbitrary definition of the growing season upon which both daily productivity and available solar radiation are based might certainly bias solar energy utilization efficiencies in favor of the 'cool season' (C_3) grasses.

It would be expected too that available moisture would limit solar energy capture to a significant extent in many of these grassland sites. For example, at the Pawnee site, gas exchange measurements taken during the 1971 season for intact soil–plant systems indicate an abrupt decrease in photosynthetic rates from mid-June to mid-July which were judged largely to be a function of decreasing available moisture (Dye, 1972). Maximum net rates of photosynthesis on a leaf area basis for a community dominated by *Bouteloua gracilis* (C_4) were as high as 44 mg dm^{-2} h^{-1} following a substantial rainfall. (These rates were corrected for CO_2 evolution from the soil–plant system under dark conditions at the same temperatures.) Such rates of net photosynthesis on a leaf area basis, though not as high as for some C_4-species measured in the field (Björkman, Pearcy, Harrison & Mooney, 1972), are much higher than field CO_2 assimilation rates of other C_4-species (Jones, Hodgkinson & Rixon, 1969; Caldwell, 1972). Later in the season, following rains, similarly high values of photosynthesis were also measured by Dye (1972). Productivity at the Pawnee site as well as at most of the Grassland Biome sites seems to be clearly water-limited.

51

If the energy utilization efficiency is calculated for single days when water is apparently not limiting, such as on a single August day in 1971 from the work of Dye (1972), a net photosynthetic rate of 40.5 $gm^{-2} d^{-1}$ and a total radiation receipt of 705 $cal cm^{-2} d^{-1}$ (2950 $J cm^{-2} d^{-1}$) would result in an efficiency of 3.3% on the plant leaf area basis (assuming 2.7 $kcal g^{-1} CO_2$ (11.3 $kJ g^{-1} CO_2$) and 47% of the solar radiation as usable in photosynthesis). However, this would be only 1.1% on a ground area basis when calculated from values of leaf area index provided by Dye.

Although such an optimal daily energy utilization percentage is higher than the seasonal figures produced from harvest information in Table 3.2, these values still fall far short of some maximum energy utilization efficiencies reported for C_4-crop species growing under optimal agronomic conditions. For example, a maize field growing in New York State has been reported to exhibit a daily efficiency of 6.8%, assuming 47% of the incoming shortwave radiation is utilizable in plant photosynthesis (Yocum *et al.*, 1964). This was for CO_2 assimilation measurements of a whole stand by the aerodynamic method. High energy efficiencies have also been reported for both C_3- and C_4-crops based on harvests of above-ground plant material. A crop of *Pennisetum typhoides* growing at tropical latitudes had an efficiency of 9.5% based on solar energy receipt of the visible portion of the spectrum (Begg, 1965). Physiological characteristics of other species of this genus (Black, 1971; Downton & Tregunna, 1968) suggest this species does possess the C_4-pathway. *Zea mays* (C_4) and *Helianthus annuus* (C_3) cultured in Cairo were reportedly functioning at efficiencies of 10.2% and 10.9%, respectively when corrected for photosynthetically active irradiation (Mattei, Gibbon & Abd El-Rahman, 1972). These crops were, however, grown under ideal agronomic cultural conditions. It might be argued that if *Bouteloua gracilis* were cultured in a regime of continual optimal moisture instead of the sporadic moisture available to this species resulting from summer thunderstorms, a much greater leaf area index would result and the energy efficiency might approach that of agronomic species grown under cultural conditions.

A daily solar energy utilization efficiency for May 1960 based upon gas exchange data of Golley (1965) for an abandoned field progressing through the normal stages of old field succession was only 0.37%. This field in South Carolina would probably not be considered as water-limited, especially during the spring of the year, and the community consisted of a reasonably dense (leaf area index = 1.6) community of

Andropogon virginicus and *A. ternarius*. *Andropogon virginicus* is known to be C_4 in photosynthetic pathway (Brown & Gracen, 1972) and *A. ternarius* probably also possesses this pathway. Unfortunately, very few data exist in the literature to serve as a comparison of energy utilization efficiency from gas exchange measurements on a ground area basis in natural ecosystems.

In such considerations of efficiencies of solar energy utilization in natural systems whether dominated by C_3- or C_4-species, many other limitations other than moisture supply should also be taken into account. Nutrient limitations in natural systems have been discussed and yet little studied. Studies of the West German IBP Solling project in northern Germany have revealed, for example, that fertilization of grassland meadows with nitrogen, phosphorus, and potassium supplements does significantly increase total net production, especially above ground (Speidel & Weiss, 1972). This was also reflected in seasonal photosynthetic measurements (Ruetz, 1972). Other edaphic hardships such as soil salinity would also be expected to decrease this overall efficiency value.

Productivity and energy utilization in grazing ecosystems: comparative studies

A comparison of annual productivity rates for both above and below ground when available, and calculations of solar energy efficiency rates for a wide variety of the world's grazing systems is represented in Table 3.4. A few values from highly productive agronomic situations are also included for comparison. Production rates are on an annual basis unless otherwise stated. The probable photosynthetic pathway of the dominant species is indicated for each community. This evaluation is based upon physiological and anatomical characteristics of the dominant species or closely related taxa (Black, 1971; Brownell & Crossland, 1972; Brown & Gracen, 1972; Brown, 1958; Downton *et al.*, 1969; Krenzer & Moss, 1969; Downton & Tregunna, 1968; Williams, 1971; Welkie & Caldwell, 1970; Gould, 1968; Pearcy, Berry and Bartholomew, 1972). It has, however, been kept in mind that even species within the same genus do not necessarily possess the same photosynthetic pathway (Downton *et al.*, 1969; Welkie & Caldwell, 1970). The efficiency of solar radiation utilization has been calculated wherever sufficient information exists. This has been based simply on the caloric value of the annual net production divided by the photosynthetically

53

Table 3.4. *Net production and solar energy utilization efficiencies of grazing ecosystems*

Vegetation type	Probable photosynthetic pathway of dominant species	Above-ground production (g m⁻² yr⁻¹)	Below-ground production (g m⁻² yr⁻¹)	Total net production (g m⁻² yr⁻¹)	Efficiency (%)	Growing season (days)	Methods	References
Theoretical maximum crop yield					12			Loomis & Williams, 1963
Pennisetum typhoides crop, northern Australia (132° E. 14.3° S.)	C_4	54 (g m⁻² d⁻¹)			9.5	(Based on 14 d)	Two-week increment standing crop harvests	Begg, 1965
Maize, *Zea mays*, Cairo, Egypt	C_4	8161			10.2	110	Maximum standing crop	Mattei, Gibbon & Abd El-Rahman, 1972
Helianthus annuus, Cairo, Egypt	C_3	7936			10.9	110	Maximum standing crop	
Zea mays crop, Minnesota, USA	C_4	946	121	1067	2.1	92	Incremental standing crop	Ovington, Heitkamp & Lawrence, 1963; and Ovington & Lawrence, 1967
Tall-grass prairie Minnesota, USA	C_3, C_4	93			0.13	116	Incremental standing crop by species	Lawrence, 1967
Shrub–tree–grass savannah Minnesota, USA	C_3	526			0.74	116	Incremented standing crop by species	Ovington, & Heitkamp & Lawrence, 1963; and Ovington & Lawrence, 1967
Tall-grass prairie Missouri, USA	C_4	482	547	1029	1.2	180	Maximum standing crop plus root biomass increment	Kucera, Dahlman & Koelling, 1967

Site							Method	Reference
Tall-grass prairie Colorado, USA	C$_4$			1120	1.2	140	Seasonal shoot biomass increment and assuming root biomass = 0.7 total biomass	Moir, 1969a,b
Short-grass prairie Colorado, USA				900	1.3	100	Seasonal shoot biomass increment and assuming root biomass = 0.9 total biomass	Klipple & Costello, 1960 in Moir, 1969b
Dense *Festuca thurberi* USA	C$_3$			855	1.2	95	Seasonal shoot biomass increment and assuming root biomass = 0.7 total biomass	Turner & Dortignac, 1954 in Moir, 1969b
Shortgrass prairie Sidney, Montana, USA (unfertilized)	C$_4$, C$_3$	134			0.13	92	Maximum standing crop	Wight & Black, 1972
Same (fertilized)	C$_4$, C$_3$	443			0.42	92	Maximum standing crop	Wight & Black, 1972
Grassland (*Agropyron–Koeleria*) Matador site (see Fig. 3.2), Saskatchewan, Canada (1970)	C$_3$	252	410	662			Incremental biomass harvests	Coupland, 1973
Average for US Grassland Biome northern sites (ungrazed)	C$_3$	245	382	627	0.82	139	Incremental biomass harvests	See Table 3.2

Table 3.4 – *continued*

Vegetation type	Probable photosynthetic pathway of dominant species	Above-ground production (g m⁻² yr⁻¹)	Below-ground production (g m⁻² yr⁻¹)	Total net production (g m⁻² yr⁻¹)	Efficiency (%)	Growing season (days)	Methods	References
Average for US Grassland Biome southern sites (ungrazed)	C_4	205	245	450	0.41	218	Incremental biomass harvests	See Table 3.2
Festuca rubra montane meadow, Solling, northern Germany (unfertilized)	C_3				1.2†	153	Gas exchange of shoots with conversion factor of 1g CO_2 = 2.55 kcal	Ruetz, 1972
Festuca rubra montane meadow, Solling, northern Germany (fertilized)	C_3				1.6†	153	Gas exchange of shoots with conversion factor of 1g CO_2 = 2.55 kcal	Ruetz, 1972
Same (unfertilized)	C_3	316	371	687			Maximum shoot standing crop plus litter; maximum underground sand- and ash-free biomass increment	Speidel & Weiss, 1972
Same (fertilized)	C_3	808	381	1189				
Poa compressa Michigan, USA	C_3	385	1023	1408	1.1	180	Maximum standing crop increment for season	Golley, 1960
Old field abandoned for 1 year New Jersey, USA	C_3	396	1944	2340	3.8	120	Peak standing crop based on 2-week incremental harvests	Botkin & Malone, 1968

Site							Method	Reference
Old field abandoned for 8-years, South Carolina, USA	C_4	493	157	650	0.4*		Harvest according to Odum, 1960 and gas exchange of shoots	Golley, 1965
Field abandoned for 30 years, southeastern Michigan, USA (upland)	C_3, C_4	312	143	455			Incremental biomass harvests plus rates of mortality and disappearance	Wiegert & Evans, 1964
Same, (swales)	C_3, C_4	1004	358	1362				
Grassland meadow, Krakow, Poland	C_3	874					Modified Wiegert & Evans, 1964	Jankowska, 1971
Montane grassland, Montana, USA	C_3	140					Maximum standing crop (air dry)	Mueggler, 1972
Grassland pasture (*Phalaris, Trifolium*) (lightly grazed 10 sheep per ha) near Armidale, NSW, Australia	C_3			2014			Gas exchange of shoots plus estimated root respiration. $\lg CO_2 = 0.67$ g dry wt	Vickery, 1972
Grassland pasture (*Phalaris, Trifolium*) (lightly grazed 20 sheep per ha) near Armidale, NSW, Australia	C_3			2819			Gas exchange of shoots plus estimated root respiration. $\lg CO_2 = 0.67$ g dry wt	Vickery, 1972
Natural stands emergent Macrophytes: (Třeboň, Czechoslovakia)							Maximum standing crop of shoots plus estimates of litter in small trail plots; root production estimated from hydroponic studies	Dykyjová, 1971
Phragmites communis	C_3			3250	5.9	130		
Typha angustifolia	C_3			4038	9.2	103		
Scirpus lacustris				2959	4.2	137		

Table 3.4 – *continued*

Vegetation type	Probable photosynthetic pathway of dominant species	Above-ground production (g m^{-2} yr^{-1})	Below-ground production (g m^{-2} yr^{-1})	Total net production (g m^{-2} yr^{-1})	Efficiency (%)	Growing season (days)	Methods	References
Heathland, Southern Australia	C$_3$	308	5828	6136	5.3	283	Incremental biomass harvests plus estimated shoot and root litter	Jones, 1968
Zygophyllum gontscharovii arid steppe, southern Tajikistan, USSR	C$_3$	28	25	54	0.13	153		Shamsiev, 1972
'Dry' *Festuca sulcata* meadow mown twice in growing season	C$_3$	234	807	1041			Calculated from incremental biomass harvests	Petrík, 1972
'Moist' *Alopecurus pratensis* meadow mown twice in growing season	C$_3$	446	876	1322				
'Damp' *Phalaris arundinacea* meadow mown twice in growing season	C$_3$	683	772	1455				
'Wet' *Glyceria maxima* meadow	C$_3$	832	745	1577				

Community							Notes	Reference
Haloxylon persicum arid steppe, southern Tajikistan, USSR		54	104	158	0.10	153		Shamsiev, 1972
Aristida plumosa arid steppe, southern Tajikistan, USSR	C₄	4	51	55	0.06	153		Shamsiev, 1972
Short-grass semi-savannahs, southern Tajikistan, USSR	C₃	85	465	550	1.5	153		Shamsiev, 1972
Artemisia tridentata shrub steppe, Idaho, USA (ungrazed)	C₃	123	42	165	0.05*		Maximum standing crop; correlations of shrub biomass and age; assumed root age = shoot age	Pearson, 1965
Same, (grazed)	C₃	98	164	262	0.07*			
Bromus tectorum steppe, western Washington, USA	C₃	129					Maximum standing crop	Daubenmire, 1970
Aristida pennata community, southern Balkhash area, USSR	C₄			45				Kurochkina, Osmanova & Borovskaya, 1972
Ephedra lomatolepis–Calligonum alatiforme arid-shrub steppe				152				

Table 3.4 – *continued*

Vegetation type	Probable photosynthetic pathway of dominant species	Above-ground production (g m⁻² yr⁻¹)	Below-ground production (g m⁻² yr⁻¹)	Total net production (g m⁻² yr⁻¹)	Efficiency (%)	Growing season (days)	Methods	References
Perovskia–Agropyron steppe, Gissar Range, Tajikistan, USSR	C_3	1585	315	1900				Stanyukovich, Shukurov & Stanyukovich, 1972
Artemisia porrecta steppe, southern Tajikistan, USSR	C_3	30	21	51				
Montane shrub meadow (*Crataegus*) southern Tajikistan, USSR	C_3	811	629	1440				
Calamagrostis–Equisetum Syrdarya River Valley, southern Tajikistan, USSR	C_3	625	1150	1775				
Artemisia herba-alba steppe, Algeria	C_3	115	62	177				Rodin, Bazilevich, & Miroshnitchenko, 1972
Poa sinaica–Artemisia steppe, Syria		130	108	238				

				Method	Reference
Atriplex halimus, *Suaeda fruticosa,* Chellala region, Algeria	C_4	372			⎫ Miroshnitchenko, 1970 in Le Houerou, 1972
Salsola tetrandra, Chellala region, Algeria	C_4	277			⎬
Tropical grassland (*Dichanthium*) Varanasi, India (heavily disturbed)	C_4, C_3	510		Incremental harvests (Odum, 1960)	Singh & Misra, 1969
Ground vegetation of *Acacia* savannah, central Australia	C_4	245		Maximum standing crop	Perry, 1970
Heteropogon grassland, Jhansi, India (unfertilized)	C_4	334			⎫ Dabadghao & Shankarnarayan, 1970
Same (fertilized)	C_4	556			⎬
Grass-savannah (*Andropogon*) Ivory Coast, Africa	C_4	1000	1200 2200	Estimated from maximum shoot and root biomass increment plus shoot litter	Cesar, in Lamotte, 1972
Grass-savannah (*Hyparrhenia*) Costa Rica	C_4	1387		Incremental biomass harvests	Daubenmire, 1972

* Based on photosynthetically active radiation for total year. † On a leaf area basis.

active irradiation falling on a horizontal plane during the course of the growing season. Unless specifically stated or measured in the original work, photosynthetically active irradiation was taken as 47% of the total shortwave radiation (Yocum *et al.*, 1964). This efficiency was calculated on a unit ground area basis except in one case (Ruetz, 1972) where it was upon a leaf area basis. In two instances, sufficient information was not available to calculate the efficiency on the growing season basis so it was done on an annual energy receipt basis (Pearson, 1965; Golley, 1965). Unless caloric values were measured in a particular study they were assumed to be 4 kcal g^{-1} (16.7 kJ g^{-1}) dry weight. Production values are assumed in all cases to be oven dry weight unless otherwise indicated. The length of the growing season has been variously determined by different authors, e.g., based on temperature regimes for a given year, actual plant growth parameters, etc. Despite these obvious discrepancies in definitions of growing seasons, no attempt was made to adjust the original values as stated by the source references. Efficiency values taken from Moir (1969*b*) were usually based on climatological summaries. If total net production values were not available, the efficiency percentage was based upon above-ground production values. Methodologies employed by various authors are briefly stated when sufficient information was available. Whether or not these areas were grazed was seldom indicated in the original references. Unless indicated otherwise, these communities are considered as ungrazed, at least during the season of production measurements.

As an upper scale comparison, several highly productive crop species were placed at the beginning of Table 3.4. It is not surprising under optimal agronomic conditions, that C_4-species such as *Pennisetum* and *Zea* would have extremely high yields and solar utilization efficiencies. The equally impressive yields for *Helianthus* (C_3) species should warrant some caution in making generalizations concerning the superior yields of C_4-species under ideal cultural conditions (Black, 1971; Zelitch, 1971).

In natural non-irrigated systems, water and nutrient limitations would seem to be the most obvious limitations for yield and solar energy utilization efficiencies. The productivity values compiled in Table 3.4 certainly do not support a hypothesis that C_4-species in natural grazing ecosystems should be more productive. If anything the evidence is in the opposite direction. Notably high productivities and energy utilization efficiencies are apparent for some C_3-species growing in situations unlimited by water (e.g., *Typha* and the Australian heath).

In this compilation, only in tropical grassland savannahs were production values of communities dominated by C_4-species particularly impressive.

An inferential comparison of productivity of communities dominated by C_3- and C_4-species as is done in Table 3.4 is, however, biased against the C_4-species. As was stated earlier in this review, C_4-species do seem to be consistently associated with arid, water-limited ecosystems where total vegetal cover is also necessarily quite low. Caution must also be exercised in drawing conclusions from such a table since the successional status of these various grazing ecosystems cannot always be inferred. In early stages of succession, such as the abandoned agricultural fields where pioneer species are mainly annual in life cycle (see Table 3.4, Botkin & Malone, 1968) net community productivity would be expected to be much higher than in later stages of the successional process when perennials dominate (Odum, 1960; Golley, 1965).

The calculations of solar energy utilization efficiency must also be viewed with reservation. As was discussed earlier, the definition of the growing season upon which these efficiencies were calculated, varies with different studies. In agricultural systems growing seasons can be reasonably arbitrary, e.g. the number of frost-free days between seedling emergence and the date of harvest. However, in natural systems dominated by perennial species, periods of photosynthetic activity and growth do not always coincide. For example, many of the perennial cool season grasses and certainly many of the semiarid shrubs do carry on photosynthesis in the early spring periods and can also carry on photosynthesis following the termination of active shoot growth (Caldwell, 1972). The temperature limits for photosynthesis and growth also certainly vary substantially between species. However, despite the problems associated with defining the growing season in natural systems, the concept of energy utilization efficiency is still a useful basis for comparing primary productivity. In semiarid and arid systems, however, an efficiency based on water consumption might be even more appropriate. In such a case C_4-species should stand out as clearly more efficient (Shantz & Piemeisel, 1927; Dwyer & Wolde-Yohannis, 1972; Slatyer, 1970; Caldwell, 1972).

Recent syntheses from the US IBP Grassland Biome (J. K. Marshall, personal communication) have involved comparisons of primary production on several grassland sites in relation to available soil moisture during the growing season. In this case primary production has been calculated as described earlier in this review and available soil moisture was calculated from precipitation, soil characteristics and actual evapotranspiration. As might be expected when various sites of the Biome network are compared, productivity increases with available moisture storage with production values from various sites falling along a reasonably well-defined line. It is interesting in this context that sites dominated primarily by C_4-grasses and those sites dominated by C_3-grasses all fell along this line with no obvious deviation. Therefore, although gas exchange studies have been consistent in demonstrating that C_4-species do possess more favorable photosynthesis–transpiration ratios, a gross community comparison such as that of Marshall does not immediately reveal that grassland sites dominated by C_4-species are particularly more efficient in productivity with a given available soil moisture supply. Naturally, a refinement of such comparisons may show different results in the future.

Finally, it should be mentioned that even though this paper does not concern itself with methodologies *per se*, comparing production values, such as in Table 3.4, from many research efforts is indeed difficult. In terms of above-ground production, failure to consider species individually in terms of when they attain maximum biomass during the season (Ovington *et al.*, 1963), or the transfer of living biomass to standing dead and litter components and the subsequent disappearance of this dead material during the course of the growing season can also provide serious underestimates of above-ground productivity (Wiegert & Evans, 1964). Truly satisfactory estimates of underground productivity for perennial plants in natural systems are still not possible because of technological limitations. The use of the increment between minimum and maximum underground biomass during the course of the year is often employed. However, this certainly is an underestimate since root death and carbon loss, i.e. root turnover, are extremely difficult to estimate. These errors become particularly large in semiarid and arid systems where 80 to 90 % total plant biomass is underground.

The potential of natural forage species possessing different photosynthetic strategies

Species of forage potential which possess the C_4- or CAM-photosynthetic pathways have been cultured in trial programs. For example, Goodin & McKell (1971) report annual dry weight above-ground yields of three C_4 *Atriplex* species to be in the range of 760 to 1017 g m^{-2} when cultured in non-irrigated agronomic conditions in southern California. Even species of *Opuntia*, a CAM-species, have been cultured in Mexico with reported yields of 500 g m^{-2} according to Goodin & McKell.

Working with *Atriplex nummularia* (C_4), an important Australian rangeland shrub, Jones *et al.* (1969) reported that although photosynthetic rates on a unit leaf area basis from single-leaf studies indicated this species to be inferior to maize and other highly productive C_4 agronomic species, on a whole plant basis in the field this *Atriplex* species was superior in CO_2 uptake to maize. Apparently *A. nummularia* could carry on photosynthesis at approximately 67 % of the maximum rate for individual leaves, whereas the *Zea mays* was functioning in the field at only approximately 35 % of maximum leaf rates. In a 500-day growth analysis study, they grew *A. nummularia* under optimal soil moisture and nutrient conditions. Growth rates when computed over this period of time were in the same range of magnitude as highly productive C_4-crop species such as sugar-cane and maize (Jones *et al.*, 1969). These growth analyses included under-ground plant productivity.

Such growth analysis studies are necessary to evaluate the field performance of forage species. Simply extrapolating from single-leaf photosynthetic rates to whole-plant productivity is not always sound. Slatyer (1970) convincingly demonstrated this in a brief 23-day growth analysis study of *Atriplex spongiosa* (C_4) and *A. hastata* (C_3). Although net photosynthetic rates per unit leaf area of *A. spongiosa* were indeed usually higher and never less than those of *A. hastata*, the growth performance of the C_4-species was not always superior to that of the C_3-species. At the beginning of this experiment, total leaf area was initially greater in *A. spongiosa*, but later in the growth analysis period *A. hastata* was investing more energy into new leaf area development. Therefore, the daily growth rate of *A. spongiosa* on a plant basis actually fell below that of *A. hastata* in the latter part of the experiment. Certainly Slatyer's experiments must be extrapolated with great care since these were carried out with young potted greenhouse-grown plants. However, the importance of growth analysis in evaluating productivity is apparent.

A growth study using reciprocal transplants of annual C_3- and C_4- *Atriplex* species in California (Nobs, Pearcy, Berry & Nicholson, 1972) indicated that only in certain circumstances were the C_4-species truly superior in dry weight yield. Often, the C_3-species yielded as much as twice that of the C_4-species. The superiority of the C_4-species in terms of water requirements for growth were, however, quite clear in their results. Earlier photosynthetic studies of these species had, however, shown that on a leaf area basis the C_4-species was always superior (Björkman, 1971).

Because C_4-species are not always found in exactly comparable situations with C_3-species or CAM-species in natural environments, it is still quite difficult to draw meaningful conclusions concerning productivity of species possessing these different photosynthetic pathways on a natural community basis. However, it is possible, occasionally, to find situations where meaningful conclusions might be drawn. For example, near the Curlew Valley site of the US IBP Desert Biome (see Fig. 3.1) adjacent pure stands of *Atriplex confertifolia* (C_4) and *Eurotia lanata* (C_3) can be found, each in nearly monospecific communities in reasonably comparable microclimatic and edaphic situations. These two species also grow together in mixed communities. Photosynthetic rates on a leaf area basis for the C_4 *Atriplex* were not superior to those of the C_3 *Eurotia* species when measured under field conditions. The C_4-species was, however, able to extend its period of active CO_2 uptake longer into the drier portion of the late summer and fall periods of the year than the C_3-species (Caldwell, 1972). In adjacent pure stands of these two species, above-ground productivity per unit ground area was approximately 20% greater for the C_4-species (Bjerregaard, 1971); however, the total plant biomass (above-ground and below-ground) in the two communities was very nearly the same. No estimates were possible for root turnover, and therefore, root productivity values are not available. Nevertheless, it appears that the C_4-species is not necessarily more productive than the C_3-species in this water-limited ecosystem.

At the Pantex site of the IBP Grassland Biome there is a community dominated by *Bouteloua gracilis* (C_4) and *Opuntia polyacantha* (CAM) in distinct strata. Thus, adjacent and nearly pure stands of *Bouteloua* and *Opuntia* can be found. On a unit ground area basis, standing crop and litter samples from the *Bouteloua* and *Opuntia* stands were taken in 1971 (Fagan & Pettit, unpublished data).

Calculations of relative productivity rates per unit ground area (Květ, Ondok, Nečas & Jarvis, 1971) based upon seasonal standing crop data of Fagan & Pettit (unpublished data) for the 1971 growing season indicate that the relative growth rate of the above-ground biomass during the season for *Bouteloua* was only about 20% greater than for *Opuntia*. For shorter time periods, relative growth rates of *Opuntia* actually exceeded by a factor of two the relative growth rates of *Bouteloua*. The seasonal progression of crown and under-ground biomass of *Opuntia* and *Bouteloua* were almost identical both in trends and in absolute magnitude. Litter in the *Opuntia* community was much greater than in the *Bouteloua* stands. Although these data are preliminary, the conclusion seems clear that the C_4-species was certainly not greatly superior, if at all, to the CAM-species. This may seem contrary to the fact that net assimilation rates on a unit leaf basis for C_4 are known to be quite high and for CAM-species to be extremely low as was discussed in the early part of this review. Here again, however, a need for field growth analyses and productivity determinations for a complete evaluation of plant performance in natural communities becomes apparent.

Conclusions

Because of the great geographical extent of world grazing lands, annual primary productivity of these lands also covers a wide range of values. Productivity values for grazing ecosystems which include much of the recent IBP information (Table 3.4) coincide well with world summaries by Bazilevich *et al.* (1971) (Table 3.1). In the arid and semiarid grazing lands annual productivity can be expected to range between 50 and 1000 g m^{-2} yr^{-1} with average values around 400. According to summaries of Bazilevich *et al.* (1971) arid and semiarid areas would constitute 70% of what could be classified as world grazing lands in Table 3.1. In more humid situations a range of productivity values between 600 and 3000 g m^{-2} yr^{-1} should be expected with average values around 1500. These averages are of course only based on summaries of existing productivity studies, i.e., from Tables 3.1 and 3.4; however, they should give some indication of the magnitude of primary production in world grazing systems. As would be expected, productivity values do appear to increase with increasing precipitation and decreasing latitude.

Solar energy use efficiency in most grazing systems is quite low. If calculated for solar energy receipt in photosynthetically active wavelengths (usually taken as 47% of total solar radiation) during the growing season, values of 1% or less are usually to be expected. The only exceptions seem to be in cases where water is not limiting and very dense communities with high leaf area indices have been able to develop. In most grazing communities irradiation *per se* is probably seldom a limiting factor although very few data are available concerning radiation extinction within grazing communities. In addition to water limitations of primary productivity, there is some evidence (see Table 3.4) of nutrient limitation as well. However, it would seem that in a large proportion of the world's grazing systems water is the primary limiting factor.

Laboratory studies of net assimilation rates of individual leaves suggest that species possessing C_4-photosynthesis should be more productive than species possessing the normal C_3-photosynthesis and both should be highly superior to plants possessing CAM-metabolism. Although many agronomic species possessing C_4-metabolism are known for high yields (Zelitch, 1971), inferential data (Tables 3.2 and 3.4) for productivity and efficiency of solar energy utilization do not support this hypothesis for natural grazing systems. Even when C_4- and C_3-species are cultured together or are found growing in similar micro-environments, the C_4-species is not necessarily more productive. There is limited evidence that in certain environments, CAM-plants may be much more productive than their low rates of photosynthesis might indicate. Since C_4- and CAM-photosynthesis are considered evolutionary elaborations of normal C_3-photosynthesis (Evans, 1971), the benefits may be perhaps more related to water use efficiency rather than productivity *per se*.

References

Andrzejewska, L. (1967). Estimation of the effect of feeding of the sucking insect *Cicadella viridis* L. (Homoptera-Aucherorrhyncha) on plants. In *Secondary Productivity of Terrestrial Ecosystems*, ed. K. Petrusewicz, pp. 791–805. Warsaw, Inst. Ecol., Polish Acad. Sci.

Bazilevich, N. I., Rodin, L. E. & Gorina, A. I. (1972). Productivity and biogeochemistry of succulent communities on solonchaks. In *Eco-Physiological Foundations of Ecosystems Productivity in Arid Zone*, ed. L. E. Rodin, pp. 203–6. Int. Symp., Leningrad.

Bazilevich, N. I., Rodin, L. E. & Rozov, N. W. (1970). Geographical aspects of biological productivity, pp. 293–317. *Proc. Vth Congr. Geogr. Soc.*, Leningrad.

Begg, J. E. (1965). High photosynthetic efficiency in a low-latitude environment. *Nature*, **205**, 1025–6.

Bjerregaard, R. S. (1971). The nitrogen budget of two salt desert shrub plant communities of western Utah. Ph.D. Thesis. Utah State University, Logan.

Björkman, O. (1971). Comparative photosynthetic CO_2 exchange in higher plants. In *Photosynthesis and Photorespiration*, eds. M. D. Hatch, C. B. Osmond & R. O. Slatyer, pp. 18–31. New York, John Wiley & Sons.

Björkman, O., Pearcy, R. W., Harrison, A. T. & Mooney, H. (1972). Photosynthetic adaption to high temperatures: a field study in Death Valley, California. *Science*, **175**, 786–9.

Black, C. C. (1971). Ecological implications of dividing plants into groups with distinct photosynthetic production capacities. *Adv. Ecol. Res.* **7,** 87–109.

Blocker, H. D. (1969). The impact of insects as herbivores in grassland ecosystems. In *The Grassland Ecosystem: A Preliminary Synthesis.* Range Sci. Dep. Ser. no. 2, pp. 290–9. Fort Collins, USA, Colorado State University.

Botkin, D. B. & Malone, C. R. (1968). Efficiency of net primary production based on light intercepted during the growing season. *Ecology,* **49,** 438–44.

Brown, R. H. & Gracen, V. E. (1972). Distribution of the post-illumination CO_2 burst among grasses. *Crop. Sci.* **12,** 30–3.

Brown, W. V. (1958). Leaf anatomy in grass systematics. *Bot. Gaz.* **119,** 170–8.

Brownell, P. F. & Crossland, C. J. (1972). The requirement for sodium as a micronutrient by species having the C_4-dicarboxylic photosynthetic pathway. *Plant Physiol.* **49,** 794–7.

Caldwell, M. M. (1972). Adaptability and productivity of species possessing C_3 and C_4 photosynthesis in a cool desert environment. In *Eco-Physiological Foundation of Ecosystems Productivity in Arid Zone,* ed. L. E. Rodin, pp. 27–9. Int. Symp., Leningrad.

Coupland, R. T. (1973). Productivity of the Matador grassland site. In *Proc. Canadian IBP/PP Synthesis Meeting, Guelph,* Dec. 1972, in press.

Dabadghao, P. M. & Shankarnarayan, K. A. (1970). Studies of *Iseileman, Sehima,* and *Heteropogon* communities of the *Sehima-Dichanthium* zone. In *Proc. XI Int. Grassland Congr.,* ed. M. J. T. Norman, pp. 36–8. Brisbane, Watson Ferguson & Co.

Dahlman, R. C. & Kucera, C. L. (1965). Root productivity and turnover in native prairie. *Ecology,* **46,** 84–9.

Daubenmire, R. (1970). Steppe vegetation of Washington. *Wash. Agr. Exp. Sta. Tech. Bull.* 62.

Daubenmire, R. (1972). Standing crops and primary production in savanna derived from semideciduous forest in Costa Rica. *Bot. Gaz.* **133,** 395–401.

Downton, J., Berry, J. & Tregunna, E. B. (1969). Photosynthesis: Temperate and tropical characteristics within a single grass genus. *Science,* **163,** 78–9.

Downton, W. J. S. & Tregunna, E. B. (1968). Carbon dioxide compensation, its relations to photosynthesis, carboxylation reactions, systematics of the Gramineae, and leaf anatomy. *Can. J. Bot.* **46,** 207–15.

Dwyer, D. D. & Wolde-Yohannis, K. (1972). Germination, emergence, water use, and production of Russian Thistle. (*Salsola kali,* L.) *Agron. J.* **64,** 52–5.

Dye, A. J. (1972). Carbon dioxide exchange of blue grama swards in the field. Ph.D. Thesis, Colorado State University, Fort Collins, USA.

Dykyjová, D. (1971). Productivity and solar energy conversion in reedswamp stands in comparison with outdoor mass cultures of algae in the temperate climate of central Europe. *Photosynthetica,* **5,** 329–40.

Evans, T. L. (1971). Evolutionary, adaptive, and environmental aspects of the photosynthetic pathway: Assessment. In *Photosynthesis and Photorespiration*, eds. M. D. Hatch, C. B. Osmond & R. O. Slatyer, pp. 130–6. New York, John Wiley.

Golley, F. B. (1960). Energy dynamics of a food chain of an old-field community. *Ecol. Monogr.* **30,** 187–206.

Golley, F. B. (1965). Structure and function of an old-field broomsedge community. *Ecol. Monogr.* **35,** 113–37.

Goodin, J. R. & McKell, C. M. (1971). Shrub productivity: A reappraisal of arid lands. In *Food, Fiber and the Arid Lands*, ed. W. G. McGinnies, B. J. Goldman & P. Paylord, pp. 235–46. Tucson, University of Arizona Press.

Gould, F. W. (1968). *Grass Systematics*, p. 382. New York, McGraw-Hill.

Hatch, M. D., Slack, C. R. & Johnson, H. S. (1967). Further studies on a new pathway of photosynthetic carbon dioxide fixation in sugarcane and its occurrence in other plant species. *Biochem. J.* **102,** 417–22.

Jankowska, K. (1971). New primary production during a three-year succession on an unmowed meadow of the Arrhenatheretum elatoris plant association. *Bull. Acad. Polonaise des Sci.* **19,** 789–94.

Jones, R. (1968). Estimating productivity and apparent photosynthesis from differences in consecutive measurements of total living plant parts of an Australian heathland. *Austr. J. Bot.* **16,** 590–602.

Jones, R., Hodgkinson, K. C. & Rixon, A. J. (1969). Growth and productivity in rangeland species of *Atriplex*. In *The Biology of Atriplex*, ed. R. Jones, Canberra, Commonwealth Sci. Ind. Res. Org.

Kortschak, H. P., Hartt, C. E. & Burr, G. O. (1965). Carbon dioxide fixation in sugarcane leaves. *Plant Physiol.* **40,** 209–13.

Krenzer, E. G. & Moss, D. N. (1969). Carbon dioxide compensation in grasses. *Crop. Sci.* **9,** 619–21.

Kucera, C. L., Dahlman, R. C. & Koelling, M. R. (1967). Total new productivity and turnover on an energy basis for tall grass prairie. *Ecology*, **48,** 536–41.

Kurochkina, L. Ya., Osmanova, L. T. & Borovskaya, T. A. (1972). Bioecological characteristics and productivity of psammophilous communities in the southern Balkhash area. In *Eco-Physiological Foundation of Ecosystems Productivity in Arid Zone*, ed. L. E. Rodin, pp. 132–3. Int. Symp., Leningrad.

Květ, J., Ondok, J. P., Nečas, J. & Jarvis, P. G. (1971). Methods of growth analysis. In *Plant Photosynthetic Production: Manual of Methods*, eds. Z. Šesták, J. Čatský & P. G. Jarvis, pp. 343–91. The Hague, Junk.

Lamotte, M. le Pr. M. (1972). Productivité des communautés terrestres en zones tropicales. In *Compte-Rendu d'Activité des la Participation Francaise*, ed. Th. Monod, pp. 45–65. Paris, Progr. Biol. Int.

Le Houerou, H.-N. (1972). An assessment of the primary and secondary production of the arid grazing lands ecosystems of North Africa. In *Eco-Physiological Foundation of Ecosystems Production in Arid Zone*, ed. L. E. Rodin, pp. 168–72. Int. Symp., Leningrad.

Loomis, R. S. & Williams, W. A. (1963). Maximum crop productivity: an estimate. *Crop Sci.* **3**, 67–72.

Mattei, F., Gibbon, D. & Abd El-Rahman, A. A. (1972). Crop potential productivity and energy conversion efficiency in semi-arid climates. In *Eco-Physiological Foundation of Ecosystems Productivity in Arid Zone*, ed. L. E. Rodin, pp. 207–10. Int. Symp., Leningrad.

Moir, W. H. (1969a). Steppe communities in the foothills of the Colorado front range and their relative productivities. *Amer. Midl. Natural.* **81**, 331–40.

Moir, W. H. (1969b). Energy fixation and the role of primary producers in energy flux of grassland ecosystems. In *The Grassland Ecosystem: A Preliminary Synthesis*, Range Sci. Dept. Sci. Ser. no. 2, pp. 125–47. Fort Collins, USA, Colorado State University.

Mooney, H. A. (1972). The carbon balance of plants. *Ann. Rev. Ecol.* **3**, 315–46.

Mueggler, W. F. (1972). Plant development and yield on mountain grasslands in southwestern Montana. *USDA For. Ser. Res. Paper*, INT124.

Neales, T. F., Patterson, A. A. & Hartney, V. J. (1968). Physiological adaptation to drought in the carbon assimilation and water loss of xerophytes. *Nature*, **219**, 469–72.

Nobs, M. A., Pearcy, R. W., Berry, J. A. & Nicholson, F. (1972). Reciprocal transplant responses of C_3 and C_4 *Atriplexes*. *Carnegie Inst. Wash. Yr Bk*, **71**, 164–9.

Odum, E. P. (1960). Organic production and turnover in old field succession. *Ecology*, **41**, 34–49.

Ovington, J. D., Heitkamp, D. & Lawrence, D. B. (1963). Plant biomass and productivity of prairie, savanna, oakwood, and maize field ecosystems in central Minnesota. *Ecology*, **44**, 52–63.

Ovington, J. D. & Lawrence, D. B. (1967). Comparative chlorophyll and energy studies of prairie, savanna, oakwood and maize field ecosystems. *Ecology*, **48**, 515–24.

Paris, O. H. (1969). The function of soil fauna in grassland ecosystems. In *The Grassland Ecosystems: A Preliminary Synthesis*, Range Sci. Dept. Ser. no. 2, pp. 331–60. Fort Collins, USA, Colorado State University.

Patten, D. T. (1972). Growth and productivity of cacti in relation to environments in the Sonoran desert, North America. In *Eco-Physiological Foundation of Ecosystems Productivity in Arid Zone*, ed. L. E. Rodin, pp. 39–41. Int. Symp., Leningrad.

Pearcy, R. W., Berry, J. A. & Bartholomew, B. (1972). Field measurements of the gas exchange capacities of *Phragmites communis* under summer conditions in Death Valley. *Carnegie Inst. Wash. Yr Bk*, **71**, 161–4.

Pearson, L. C. (1965). Primary production in grazed and ungrazed desert communities in eastern Idaho. *Ecology*, **46**, 278–85.

Perry, R. A. (1970). The effects on grass and browse production of various treatments on a mulga community in central Australia. In *Proc. XI Grassland Congr.*, ed. M. J. T. Norman, pp. 63–6. Brisbane, Watson Ferguson.

71

Petřik, B. (1972). Season changes in plant biomass in four inundated meadow communities. In *Ecosystem Study on Grassland Biome in Czechoslovakia*, ed. M. Rychnovská, pp. 17–23. Czechosl. IBP–PT–PP Report no. 2. Brno.

Rasmussen, J. L. (1971). Abiotic factors in grassland ecosystem analysis and function. In *Preliminary Analysis of Structure and Function in Grasslands*, ed. N. R. French, Range Sci. Dept. Sci. Ser. no. 10, pp. 11–34. Fort Collins, USA, Colorado State University.

Riffle, J. W. (1968). Plant-parasitic nematodes in marginal *Pinus ponderosa* stands in central New Mexico. *Plant Dis. Reporter*, **52**, 52–5.

Rodin, L. E. & Bazilevich, N. E. (1965). *Production and Mineral Cycling in Terrestrial Vegetation*, 288pp. London, Oliver & Boyd.

Rodin, L. E., Bazilevich, N. E. & Miroshnicthenko, Yu. M. (1972). Productivity and biogeochemistry of Artemisieta in the Mediterranean area. In *Eco-Physiological Foundation of Ecosystems Productivity in Arid Zone*, ed. L. E. Rodin, pp. 193–7. Int. Symp., Leningrad.

Ruetz, W. F. (1972). Seasonal changes in the CO_2 gas exchange of red fescue (*Festuca rubra*) in a montane meadow community in northern Germany. Ph.D. Thesis. Oregon State University, Corvallis, USA.

Shantz, H. L. & Piemeisel, L. N. (1927). The water requirements of plants at Akron, Colorado. *J. Agr. Res.* **34**, 1093–190.

Shamsiev, A. (1972). Radiation conditions and biological productivity of plants in Southern Tajikistan. In *Eco-Physiological Foundation of Ecosystems Productivity in Arid Zone*, ed. L. E. Rodin, pp. 112–13. Int. Symp., Leningrad.

Sims, P. L. & Singh, J. S. (1971). Herbage dynamics and net primary production in certain ungrazed and grazed grasslands in North America. In *Preliminary Analysis of Structure and Function in Grasslands*. Range Sci. Dept. Sci. Ser. no. 10, pp. 59–113. Fort Collins, USA, Colorado State University.

Singh, J. S. & Misra, R. (1969). Diversity, dominance, stability and net production in the grasslands at Varanasi, India. *Can. J. Bot.* **47**, 425–7.

Slatyer, R. O. (1970). Comparative photosynthesis, growth and transpiration of two species of *Atriplex*. *Planta*, **93**. 175–89.

Smith, B. N. & Epstein, S. (1971). Two categories of ^{13}C/^{12}C ratios for higher plants. *Plant Physiol.* **47**, 380–4.

Speidel, B. & Weiss, A. (1972). Zur ober- und unterirdischen Stoffproduktion einer Goldhaferwiese bei verschiedener Düngung. *Angew. Bot.* **46**, 75–93.

Stanyukovich, K. V., Shukorov, A. Sh. & Stanyukovich, M. B. (1972). Biological productivity of various types of Tajikistan vegetation as related to humidity and altitude. In *Eco-Physiological Foundation of Ecosystems Productivity in Arid Zone*, ed. L. E. Rodin, pp. 142–3. Int. Symp., Leningrad.

Tieszen, L. L. (1970). Photosynthetic properties of some grasses in eastern South Dakota. *Proc. South Dakota Acad. Sci.* **49**, 78–89, South Dakota, USA.

Ting, I. P. (1971). Non-autotrophic CO_2 fixation and crassulacean acid metabolism. In *Photosynthesis and Photorespiration*, eds. M. D. Hatch, C. B. Osmond & R. O. Slatyer, pp. 169–85. New York, John Wiley.

Van Dyne, G. M. (1971). The US IBP Grassland Biome study – an overview. In *Preliminary Analysis of Structure and Function in Grasslands*, ed. N. R. French, Range Sci Dept. Sci. Ser. no. 10, pp. 1–10. Fort Collins, USA, Colorado State University.

Vickery, P. J. (1972). Grazing and net primary production of a temperate grassland. *J. Appl. Ecol.* **9,** 307–14.

Welkie, G. W. & Caldwell, M. (1970). Leaf anatomy of species in some dicotyledon families as related to the C_3- and C_4-pathways of carbon fixation. *Can. J. Bot.* **48,** 2135–46.

Wiegert, R. G. & Evans, F. C. (1964). Primary production and the disappearance of dead vegetation on an old field in southeastern Michigan. *Ecology*, **45,** 49–63.

Wight, J. & Black, A. L. (1972). Energy fixation and precipitation – use efficiency in a fertilized rangeland ecosystem of the northern Great Plains. *J. Range Manage.* **25,** 376–80.

Williams, G. J. (1971). Producer function on the intensive and comprehensive sites. In *Preliminary Analysis of Structure and Function in Grasslands*, Range Sci. Dept. Sci. Ser. no. 10, pp. 125–31. Fort Collins, USA, Colorado State University.

Yocum, C. S., Allen, L. H. & Lemon, E. R. (1964). Photosynthesis under field conditions. VI. Solar radiation balance and photosynthetic activity. *Agron. J.* **56,** 249–53.

Zelitch, I. (1971). *Photosynthesis, Photorespiration, and Plant Productivity*, 347pp. New York, Academic Press.

D

4. Primary production of tundra

F. E. WIELGOLASKI

Tundra may be defined in different ways, but usually as those areas with permafrost in the soil or with yearly average air temperatures below 0 °C. Sometimes, as in the work within the International Biological Programme, a wider definition is used, allowing oceanic moorland also to be included in tundra (Wielgolaski, 1972b). Within IBP, studies have been carried out in the Tundra Biome both in arctic and subarctic ecosystems in Canada, Finland, Greenland, USA and USSR, in antarctic ecosystems at South Georgia and Macquarie Island, and in the mountain areas with or without permafrost in Austria, Norway, Sweden and USA, as well as in tundra-like blanket bogs in Great Britain and Ireland.

Characteristics of tundra ecosystems

Rodin & Bazilevich (1966) state that quantitative studies of biological productivity of tundra ecosystems, including below-ground portions of vegetation have been carried out mostly after 1957. The difficulties in determining the below-ground biomass of plants in tundra are stressed by Alexandrova (1970), who was one of the first to collect this interesting information. The primary production of tundra regions is most comprehensively described in Soviet literature by Alexandrova (1958, 1960), Andreev (1966); Rodin & Bazilevich (1966); Pavlova (1969); Khodachek (1969); Tikhomirov (1971), as well as in many papers in the Proceedings from the Conference on Productivity of Biogeocoenosis in the subarctic (Firsova, Shijatov & Dobriskij, 1969). Bliss (1962) refers to work carried out in western tundra regions, especially in North America. He also gives important information on primary production in arctic regions in more recent papers (Bliss, 1966,1970), as do also Dennis & Johnson (1970). Primary production in tundra has been described in detail in dissertations given in North America by Pieper (1963) and Dennis (1968) and in Austria by Brzoska (1969). A survey of primary production in the subarctic is given by Pearsall & Newbould (1957). In antarctic and subantarctic tundra similar problems are reported by Ahmadjian (1970); Jenkin & Ashton (1970); Lewis & Greene (1970) and others.

The knowledge of primary productivity of tundra ecosystems has been greatly increased by the internationally co-ordinated work within the

Tundra Biome of IBP. Even if many results from these studies are not yet published, preliminary data are often available through good personal communication between workers in the various countries involved (see acknowledgement). Preliminary results are also found in proceedings from international tundra meetings, e.g., in Finland (Heal, 1971), USSR (Wielgolaski & Rosswall, 1972) and Ireland (Bliss & Wielgolaski, 1973), and from other international IBP meetings, e.g., Symposia in connection with IBP V General Assembly (Wielgolaski, 1975a), as well as from more locally arranged Symposia, e.g., by the US Tundra Biome of Lake Wilderness Center in spring 1972, and in project reports, e.g., on the Canadian IBP tundra studies (Bliss, 1972a).

Tundra is generally characterized by low plants (normally less than 0.5 m height), often with vegetative regeneration only, reduced plant cover, low biological diversity, low annual production (although at times rapid daily growth) and often high fragility and thus oscillations in the system (Bliss, 1962, 1970). This may, in part, be caused by the cyclicity of small mammals (Pitelka, 1972). The decomposition rate is usually slow in tundra, and accumulation of organic matter often occurs (Rodin & Bazilevich, 1966; Wielgolaski, 1975a). The small number of annual plants in tundra is stressed by Alexandrova (1970). Tundra plants also normally have a low top–root ratio (Alexandrova, 1958, 1970; Bliss, 1970; Wielgolaski, 1972b). This is similar to plants in desert communities (Rodin & Bazilevich, 1966) and many of the other characteristics of tundra plants may also be found in desert as well as in saline lake ecosystems (Bliss, 1970). Thus the typical tundra ecosystems may show many similarities in their vegetation to other stressed ecosystems, although climatic conditions, for example temperature and precipitation, may be different.

Some tundra vegetation types are, however, closely related to grassland ecosystems. The problems of grazing are especially important in these types in studies on primary production (Wielgolaski, 1975b), even if grazing, e.g. by reindeer, is also important in other tundra vegetation types (Makhaeva, 1959). In its typical form, tundra is treeless, but transition zones to the taiga–boreal forest zones are often included in tundra studies (Rodin & Bazilevich, 1966; Beschel, 1970).

Many attempts have been made to divide tundra into different types. Mostly climates combined with vegetation studies have been used as criteria for tundra classification in the USSR, see review by Alexandrova (1970). Similar methods have been used for example by Beschel (1970) in Canada. The soil nutrient status may also be used for grouping into more or less eutrophic and oligotrophic tundra types. A rough classification of the tundra sites within IBP is based on vegetation and plant biomass studies (Wielgolaski, 1972*b*). A more advanced technique for classification, using the cluster–dendrogram technique by the average linkage method of Sokal & Sneath (1963), has been tried for the IBP sites internationally (Wielgolaski & Webber, 1974). Ordination of tundra plant communities has been carried out in Canada by Beschel (1970) and Webber (1971), for IBP sites with principal component analysis by J. J. Moore (personal communication) and a more detailed analysis is now in progress using various techniques (Wielgolaski & Webber, 1974).

The rough zonal division of tundra in arctic and subarctic regions in the USSR used by Alexandrova (1970) and partly by Rodin & Bazilevich (1966), into polar desert, tundra zone and forest tundra zone gave a good starting point for classification of primary productivity. In the polar desert, the mean temperature of the vegetation period is by definition close to 0 °C (in the USSR the southern limit of this zone is found close to the 2 °C July isotherm), and the plant cover is sparse. This causes a very low primary productivity of the area. The tundra zone is defined by relatively closed plant cover, but with more bare spots of soil in the arctic tundra subzone (especially in the northern variant or arctic semidesert) than in the subarctic tundra subzone (the northern part of this subzone is sometimes called typical tundra or lichen–moss tundra and the southern part called shrub tundra). In the arctic tundra subzone, most of the woody vegetation consists of creeping dwarf shrubs, while the woody plants in the subarctic subzone often are dominated by, on an average, 50 cm high willow and even shrubby birch thickets. The limit between these two subzones, in the USSR, according to Alexandrova (1970) is roughly found at the 6 °C July isotherm. Similarly the limit between the subarctic tundra subzone and the forest tundra zone is found to be roughly at the 10 °C July isotherm. The forest tundra is defined by wide spacing of trees and unique life forms of the tree species with krumholz mats, half- and fully depressed growth and 'flagging'. Generally the relative amount of lichens is highest in the polar deserts, and of bryophytes in the southern tundra types.

The vegetation in alpine tundra has also been divided into vertical zones by several Russian workers, e.g. by Gorchakovsky (1966), as well as in western countries, e.g. oro-zones by Ahti, Hämet-Ahti & Jalas (1968) and altitudinal zones by Dahl (1956). The high-alpine belt, according to Dahl, has only patchy vegetation of solifluction communities and a relatively high content of cryptogams, especially lichens. The mid-alpine belt is dominated by heaths with gramineous plants and cryptogams. The low alpine belt has a high percentage of shrubs, especially dwarf shrubs, but also lichen heaths and, in some areas, bryophyte-dominated plant communities. The subalpine zone is a transition zone to forest vegetation, often with krumholz or other somewhat shrubby tree vegetation.

Special methodological problems

Estimates of primary productivity in tundra are mostly based upon changes in the dry weight of standing crops using the harvest or yield method (Rodin & Bazilevich, 1966). Often the estimates have been based only on above-ground biomass (Bliss, 1962). This will usually give an underestimate, especially in perennial plants with high below-ground biomass, as is common in tundra. Translocation between various organs, consumption and decomposition usually will also cause underestimates of primary productivity based on harvesting values. Dead material will be decomposing simultaneously with death of the live material. Thus, the measured production will not only include an increase in live and dead material (which is not caused by a decrease in other compartments), but the decomposition rate of dead material and a consumption rate, which must also be taken into account.

The harvesting method is the only *direct* method for estimation of primary productivity (Lieth, 1962). In the last decade, and especially within IBP studies, however, some indirect methods have also been used for estimation of primary productivity in tundra. Some of these methods may be expected to give more correct values than the yield method.

One promising method in tundra primary productivity studies involves morphology–age studies of the main species at a site (Flower-Ellis, 1973; Callaghan, 1973). This method might also be seen as a refinement of the harvesting method. The age of woody stems and rhizomes of woody or herbaceous perennials is determined, and so is the dry weight and number of shoots or plants per area specified for different age classes. The measurements for the various species may be used as a basis for a model for dry matter production on a unit area basis. For shrubs in typical shrub tundra the productivity may also be found by a method modified from the regression method of Whittaker (1968), for example, see Kjelvik (1973).

A rough estimate of primary productivity might be found from the plant cover when the regression is known between this and standing crop. In the IBP tundra studies this method is used to find the production for larger areas when detailed values are known for intensively studied sites. The plant cover of various communities is usually found from remote studies, e.g. by infra-red photography from an airplane or a similar technique (P. J. Webber, personal communication). A variant of the cover technique for primary productivity determination is the use of leaf area indices and their correlation with harvesting values (J. C. Emerich, D. C. Ebert & P. J. Webber, personal communication). The amount of chlorophyll per square metre has also been used for estimation of primary productivity in tundra areas, after initial calibration against harvesting values in different plant communities (Bliss, 1970).

The use of CO_2 exchange of plants as a measurement of primary productivity is well known in various vegetation types (Sestak, Čatsky & Jarvis, 1971). Both photosynthesis and respiration have been measured in alpine and arctic regions for some years (Billings, Clebsch & Mooney, 1960, and review in Shvetsova & Voznesenskii, 1970), but, through the IBP tundra studies, more detailed gas exchange studies are being carried out in different tundra plant communities and used for productivity estimates. From the values found by CO_2 measurements, estimates of primary production may be found if it is accepted that the plant incorporation of CO_2 measured may be converted to plant dry matter using a conversion factor; according to Sestak *et al.* (1971, p. 27) a factor of 0.648 may be used. This naturally provides a relatively rough estimate of dry matter production. On the other hand, these estimates are not influenced by decomposition and consumption. Theoretically, higher primary production values should therefore be expected from CO_2 exchange measurements than from harvesting. If the CO_2 incorporation by plants is measured by the ^{14}C method in short time exposures (e.g., 30 s) this does not allow sufficient time for the incorporated $^{14}CO_2$ to be lost by the photorespiratory processes. The values found for incorporation by this method will possibly represent therefore something between 'net' and 'gross' photosynthesis (L. L. Tieszen & D. A. Johnson, personal communication). Values found by infra-red gas analysis and similar methods will, on the other hand, mostly give estimates for net assimilation (in tundra by Mayo, Despain & van Zinderen Bakker, 1972).

79

Plant biomass

The standing crop of arctic and alpine tundra regions varies strongly with latitude and altitude as well as with the plant communities within an area (see Table 4.1). Warren Wilson (1957) and Alexandrova (1970) have measured only a few grams of live above-ground biomass of vascular plants in polar deserts and Svoboda (1972) states that vascular plants in that region are only found in small pockets sheltered by rocks. In these pockets, however, the total vascular plant biomass may be as high as 70 g m^{-2}. Cryptogams are more common in the polygons of the polar desert than vascular plants, and Alexandrova (1970) reports a lichen (dominant), bryophyte and algal biomass of about 125 g m^{-2} in this type at Franz Josef Land which, however, is higher than the expected average for the zone. This relatively high cryptogamic biomass causes the total live standing crop of some polar deserts to be higher than in many arctic semideserts. Andreev (1966) measured an above-ground vascular biomass in the semideserts of about 40 g m^{-2}. At sites with greater amounts of dwarf shrubs this value may be three times higher, as found (Svoboda, 1973) at the crest of the high arctic IBP study area Devon Island in North Canada (75 °N), if this site is characterized as an arctic semidesert. According to the average July temperature (about −5.5 °C), this site could also be classified within the southern variant of arctic tundra (Alexandrova, 1970).

Generally, however, the southern variant of arctic tundra is more dominated by graminoid plant species than by woody plants. The biomass of cryptogams, dominated by mosses, is normally higher and there are fewer bare spots in the southern variant of arctic tundra than found in the arctic semidesert. This results in the total biomass (above and below ground) of the southern variant of arctic tundra being two to ten times as high as that of the more northern variant and it may reach 1000 g m^{-2} (see Table 4.1). The depth of the active soil layer in early fall at Barrow is 30–45 cm (Brown, Rickard & Przybyla, 1970), while it is normally 20–30 cm at the intensive meadow site at Devon Island (Muc, 1973). This difference may be one reason for the slightly higher vascular above-ground biomass found at some of the Barrow plots than at Devon Island. The bryophyte biomass is, however, high at Devon Island; more than 250 g (dry weight) of live material per m^2 may be estimated at wet sites from values given by Pakarinen & Vitt (1973).

This is nearly as much as the lowest values found in the USSR in the next zone, the typical tundra within the subarctic tundra subzone, which is dominated by bryophytes and dwarf shrubs (Alexandrova, 1970; Shamurin, Polozova & Khodachek, 1972; Pospelova, 1972). The live biomass of cryptogams, especially due to bryophytes, in the zone is three to four times as high as the above-ground live vascular biomass. This is a higher relative value for cryptogams (Table 4.1) than in any of the other arctic zones except the polar desert, where it is usually due mostly to lichens. The lowest biomass of vascular plants, less than 100 g m^{-2} above ground, according to Shamurin *et al.* (1972), is found in spotted tundra in the zone. Normally the vascular plants, however, have a higher biomass both above ground and below ground in the typical tundra than in the southern variant of arctic tundra, and the total live biomass may as a maximum be above 2000 g m^{-2}.

This is still usually lower than the standing crop in shrub tundra (Alexandrova, 1970; Gorchakovsky & Andreyashkina, 1972; Pospelova, 1972). Because of the high amount of woody plants, the above-ground parts of vascular plants in particular have a higher live biomass in the shrub tundra than in the previous zones (Table 4.1). The tendency towards higher ratios of biomass of aerial parts of higher plants, in relation to cryptogams and below-ground parts, is for the same reason still more pronounced in the forest tundra (Andreev, 1966; Ignatenko, Knorre, Lovelius & Norin, 1972). The biomass, about 235 g m^{-2}, of the live above-ground vascular understory in a subarctic Finnish birch forest (Kallio & Kärenlampi, 1971) is of the same order as found in the Russian forest tundra.

The plant biomass in high alpine vegetation, as in polar deserts, is often dominated by lichens (see Chepurko, 1966 for the lower part of the belt), but patches of solifluction communities with some vascular plants may occur (Dahl, 1956), for example in the Alps *Ranunculus glacialis* and other forbs contributed strongly to the vascular plant biomass in this belt (Moser, 1971; Brzoska, 1973). The total biomass in the high alpine belt is comparable to the values in the polar desert, although in the lower parts it is more like the arctic semidesert.

In the mid-alpine belt the plant biomass, according to a few observations (Chepurko, 1966; Wielgolaski & Kjelvik, 1975) is of the same order as in the southern variant of the arctic tundra (Table 4.1), although there seems to be a still higher relative dominance of cryptogams. Some of the sites grouped in the mid-alpine belt are placed in this group because of extreme environmental conditions causing low productivity, e.g. in Norway, extreme snow beds and wind swept,

D*

Table 4.1. *Tundra plant biomass. Arctic vegetation grouped according to Russian zonation system (Alexandrova, 1970). Alpine vegetation grouped in belts according to Dahl (1956)*

	Live biomass (g m^{-2})				References
	Vascular plants		Cryptogams	Total	
	Above ground	Total	Total		
ARCTIC ZONES					
Polar desert (patchy vegetation)	4–20	25–60	100–125	125–185	Warren Wilson, 1957; Alexandrova, 1970; Svoboda, 1972
Arctic tundra semidesert (North. var.)	40–120	90–240	10–60	100–300	Andreev, 1966; Svoboda, 1973; Richardson & Finegan, 1973
arctic tundra (South. var.)	70–100	550–750	50–250	600–1000	Andreev, 1966; Alexandrova, 1970; Dennis & Tieszen, 1972; Muc, 1973; Pakarinen & Vitt, 1973
Subarctic tundra moss-lichen-dwarf shrub zone (typical tundra)	100–200	800–1550	300–800	1100–2350	Alexandrova, 1970; Shamurin et al., 1972; Pospelova, 1972
shrub tundra	200–800	1150–4500	250–1350	1400–5850	Alexandrova, 1970; Gorchakovsky et al., 1972; Pospelova, 1972
Forest tundra (scattered trees)	450–1300	2350–4200	200–1500	2550–5700	Andreev, 1966; Ignatenko et al., 1972

ALPINE BELTS					
High alpine (patchy vegetation)	35	110		25–110	Chepurko, 1966; Brzoska, 1973
Mid alpine (cryptog. gramineous heath)	40–75	250–850	150–400	400–1250	Chepurko, 1966; Wielgolaski & Kjelvik,1975
Low alpine dwarf shrub-cryptog. meadow belt	100–250	500–3000	50–300	550–3300	Pearsall & Newbould, 1957; Chepurko, 1972; Webber, 1972; Flower-Ellis, 1973; Kjelvik & Kärenlampi,1975; Wielgolaski, 1975
shrub–moss–tall forbs perennial community	250–1350	1300–7200	250–trace	1550–7200	Chepurko, 1972; Webber, 1972; Larcher *et al.*, 1973; Kjelvik, 1973; Kjelvik & Kärenlampi, 1975
Subalpine forest*	2500	4550	50	4600	Kjelvik, 1973; Kjelvik & Kärenlampi, 1975
* Understory and roots <0.5 cm diam.	200–235	825			

coarse, sandy eskers with lichen and dwarf shrub vegetation in the upper part of the low alpine belt.

Most of the primary productivity studies in alpine regions are from the low alpine belt (Pearsall & Newbould, 1957; Chepurko, 1972; Webber, 1972; Flower-Ellis, 1973; Wielgolaski & Kjelvik, 1973; Kjelvik & Kärenlampi, 1975; Wielgolaski, 1975*d*). It may be subdivided into two zones as the subarctic tundra, a dwarf shrub–cryptogam–meadow sub-belt and a shrub–moss–tall perennial forb sub-belt. The lowest biomass values in the first sub-belt (Table 4.1) are from sites on the border of the mid-alpine belt in Norway and from an alpine subarctic bog in northern Sweden. These low values and the high root biomass at some moist alpine meadows in Colorado, USA, cause a wider variation in the total biomass than in the similar zone (typical tundra) in the arctic. As expected, the biomass is generally high in the shrub sub-belt, which is often dominated by willow thickets with a rich understory of herbs and is often found along streams. The moss cover may be more or less missing.

The biomass values from the Norwegian IBP subalpine birch forest study (Kjelvik, 1973) are of same order as reported for subarctic forest tundra. The biomass of above-ground vascular plant understory and roots less than 0.5 cm diameter is similar to the values for a birch forest in northern Finland (Kallio & Kärenlampi, 1971; Kjelvik & Kärenlampi, 1975).

The ratio between tops and roots of vascular plants may be extremely low in tundra conditions, often as small as 1:10 to 1:20 or lower in some cases (Alexandrova, 1958,1970; Dennis & Johnson, 1970; Wielgolaski, 1972*b*,1975*a*; Webber, 1972; Muc, 1973). The calculated values are, of course, very much dependent on the criterion of separation between above- and below-ground parts. However, even when variation in the harvesting procedure is corrected for, it seems true that arctic environments are relatively more severe for above-ground than for below-ground plant production as stated by Bliss (1970), and also found for alpine conditions (Wielgolaski, 1972*b*). The lowest values are found in wet meadows in all cases, but various climatic and soil factors also seem to influence the top–root ratio directly. All factors causing a slow decomposition rate of organic material in the soil, e.g., low temperatures, extreme wet and dry soil, as well as oligotrophic, poor soil, will generally result in low top–root ratios (Wielgolaski, 1975*a*). With increasing biomass of woody plants the ratio increases. However, it is normally less than one in all tundra communities without trees. In the subalpine Norwegian birch forest the top–root ratio is about 1 : 4 for the understory, but about 1 : 0.6 when the biomass of the birch trees is included as well. Still higher values are found in forests and meadows in temperate regions (Bray, 1963; Wielgolaski, 1972*b*,1975*a*).

Although decomposition of the plant biomass is generally slow in the tundra ecosystem, this is the major pathway for the plant material produced. The decay rates vary strongly between plant species, up to 100% in one year being found in some cases in subantarctic vegetation (J. F. Jenkin, personal communication). At the other extreme, moss at Signy Island in the Antarctic loses only 2% per year (J. H. Baker, personal communication). Most of the tundra sites record rates of 10–30% loss in the first part of the year after plant death, with the highest values in subarctic and subalpine regions and tundra eutrophic conditions with medium soil moisture.

Dennis (1968) noted a change in the plant species in the years within a small mammal cycling period, both because of selective consumption by the small mammals, and of differences between plant species in reproduction possibilities in dense stands with high amounts of litter and more open vegetation with less litter caused by animal grazing. After relatively low small mammal grazing pressure (about 10% of above-ground biomass), an increased amount of plant shoots was found the following summer in the USSR (Smirnov & Tokmakova, 1972). However, after a lemming high year in Alaska, Schultz (1964) reports a strong reduction in vigour and yield of plants. This is also found for the vegetation types preferred by small mammals in Norwegian alpine tundra (F. E. Wielgolaski, unpublished observations), although the consumption is found to be not much more than $10 \text{ g m}^{-2} \text{ yr}^{-1}$ in a small mammal high year, or about 10% of the above-ground biomass. The year after the small mammal peak the consumption may be only 3–4% of the maximum values (E. Østbye, personal communication). Snow beds with *Salix herbacea* mats and hummocky moist meadow tundra seem to be amongst the most preferred vegetation types in Norwegian alpine tundra for small mammals.

The effect of sheep grazing on plants has also been studied in the Norwegian alpine tundra (Wielgolaski, 1975*b,c*). It is found that the regrowth of shoots was increased by relatively heavy grazing (30–60% of above-ground biomass) over a period of three years, while the root biomass was strongly reduced. The relative amount of monocotyledons increased after the sheep grazing while shrubs were strongly reduced and dicotyledonous herbs also to some degree. 'Broad-leaved' grasses

85

(*Anthoxanthum alpinum, Poa alpina* and *Phleum commutatum*) were preferred species by the sheep.

Large native mammals may be of importance for the plant biomass in some areas. In arctic Canada, the summer removal by musk-ox is estimated at 1.5% of above-ground biomass (Bliss, 1972*b*). Studies on native reindeer in the alpine tundra of Hardangervidda, Norway, show that most of their winter consumption is from the wind-blown plant community Loiseleurio–Arctostaphylion, and partly also from Phyllodoco–Myrtillion, especially the lichens *Cladonia mitis* and *Cetraria nivalis* and the shrub *Betula nana* (Gaare & Skogland, 1971). One animal is found to remove 1750 g dry plant material per day on an average during the winter months in the area, and above 100 g more per day during summer. Makhaeva (1959) found that each domestic reindeer in the Murmansk area grazed an area of 65 m^2 per day in the lichen tundra. If this estimate is used for the Norwegian alpine tundra the daily consumption per reindeer would be about 22 g m^{-2} on the lichen vegetation during winter. The area of this vegetation type limits the size of the reindeer population in the district.

The influence of invertebrates on plant biomass is difficult to estimate, but the consumption may sometimes totally kill the plants as has been the case for *Betula* in northern Finland subarctic tundra by *Oporinia* (Kallio & Kärenlampi, 1971). In the USSR, some estimates have been found for insect consumption on willows (Danilov, 1972; Bogatschova, 1972) and show values ranging from 1.3% to 3.3% of the green biomass in typical tundra and from 5% to 9% in shrub tundra on river banks.

Production

The vegetation period is short in the tundra, sometimes less than fifty days in snowbeds (M. C. Lewis, personal communication) and in polar deserts (L. C. Bliss, personal communication), but is most often between two and four months, when defined as the period when photosynthesis takes place in phanerogams and/or cryptogams. This may start even before snow melting in spring, as net assimilation for some plant species is found to occur beneath at least 5 cm snow cover (Billings & Bliss, 1959). For many cryptogams, net assimilation may take place at very low temperatures, as is found also for some phanerogams, e.g. positive assimilation of *Dryas* in northern Canada at 1 °C (Mayo *et al.*, 1972). In spite of this, the main reasons for low annual production in polar and alpine regions are the low temperatures and the short growing seasons. This is also a reason for the generally low above-ground biomass already reported in these regions. More locally, however, moisture and nutrients may strongly limit the primary production in tundra.

Primary production varies strongly between tundra sites. Bliss (1970), states, however, that usually the annual above-ground tundra primary production (based on harvestings) will vary within the range 50–200 g m^{-2}. There are also considerable differences in the values between years, because of such factors as the cyclicity of the small mammal population and climatic variations. Dennis & Johnson (1970) found variations in seasonal above-ground dry matter accretion in mesic arctic meadows from 60 to 97 g m^{-2} in a minimum small mammal year and from 3 to 48 g m^{-2} in a lemming high year. The lowest value (3 g m^{-2}) is of the same order as Warren Wilson (1957) found from harvesting in a *Salix* barren polar desert. Generally, as expected, the

Table 4.2. *Seasonal changes in tundra plant biomass* (*in g m^{-2} yr^{-1}*)

| | Vascular plants | | |
	Above ground	Total	Cryptogams
Polar desert	3		
Polar semidesert and high mid-alpine regions	10–30		25–75
Southern arctic tundra, subarctic typical tundra and low-alpine dwarf shrub meadow belt	40–250	100–600	50–270
Polar and alpine shrub tundra and moorlands	225–450	500–1000	50–400

annual primary production increases from polar to temperate regions and from high alpine to lowland areas, but the variation between plant communities in each zone is greater than for the biomass values. The annual production of lichens is small, 2.5–5 mm per thallus of *Cladonia* species according to Scotter (1963); Pegau (1968); Kärenlampi (1970), and/or approximately 5–10 mg per thallus. The growth of bryophytes is also usually slower than for vascular plants. Woody plants with a high living biomass have lower production per unit of biomass than the herbaceous plants. Often only above-ground biomass changes of vascular plants are studied. This, as already mentioned, will give too low values for estimated primary production.

Crude values of seasonal biomass changes in arctic and alpine tundra are given in Table 4.2. Low annual above-ground vascular plant production, i.e. in the range 10–30 g m^{-2}, is found in polar semideserts in the USSR (Andreev, 1966) and Canada (Svoboda, 1973), in the high alpine belt (Brzoska, 1973) and at mid-alpine sites as well as in snow beds and lichen heaths on the border between mid- and low-alpine belts in Norway (Wielgolaski, 1972*a* and unpublished data). Similar values are found in spotted tundras, even in the low-alpine dwarf shrub belt (Chepurko, 1972). Of course still lower values may be found in the patchy vegetation in high alpine belts and in polar deserts. Including cryptogams, however, the annual production of even polar semideserts and mid-alpine belts may be of the order 50–100 g m^{-2}, or even higher as found for example at the Norwegian alpine IBP lichen heath, in spite of the slow growth of lichens, if dieback and decomposition are taken into account (Kjelvik & Kärenlampi, 1975).

Many tundra sites have an annual above-ground vascular plant production of 40–100 g m^{-2} (measured as biomass changes). This has been found for many southern arctic tundras in Canada, USA and the USSR (Andreev, 1966; Dennis & Johnson, 1970; Dennis & Tieszen, 1972; Muc, 1973), as well as sites in subarctic typical tundra (Shamurin *et al.*, 1972). Similar values are found in the low-alpine dwarf shrub meadow belt (Chepurko, 1972; Wielgolaski, 1972*a*). For those sites where below-ground plant material has also been investigated, a total annual vascular plant accretion of 100–200 g m^{-2} is generally found. In addition, cryptogams contribute significantly to primary production at many of the sites, as in the bryophytes (about 50–200 g m^{-2}) at the Norwegian IBP mid-alpine meadow and low-alpine willow thicket sites (Wielgolaski, 1975*d*; Kjelvik & Kärenlampi, 1975) and 30–60 g m^{-2} at hummocky and wet meadow sites in the southern arctic tundra at Devon Island in Canada (Pakarinen & Vitt, 1973).

Still higher production of bryophytes was found in extremely wet conditions in the last mentioned area (up to above 200 g m^{-2} per year according to Pakarinen & Vitt, 1973). Similar values are found for *Sphagnum* production in moorland communities in the United Kingdom (Clymo, 1970). An annual bryophyte production, from about 250 g m^{-2} up to about 1000 g m^{-2}, is reported from the subantarctic (Clarke, Greene & Greene, 1971) and the maritime antarctic (Collins, 1973). Possibly a bryophyte production of some 100 g m^{-2} yr^{-1} would also be found in some of the USSR subarctic shrub tundras where the bryophyte biomass is as high as 1350 g m^{-2} (Alexandrova, 1970).

Both the arctic and the alpine shrub tundra zones may generally be highly productive, especially in meadow areas within the zones. The annual above-ground vascular plant accretion is found to be of the order 225–450 g m^{-2} (Rodin & Bazilevich, 1966, and Table 4.2) approximately doubled if below-ground production is included as well. The lowest values reported from the zones are found in the low alpine shrub communities at Hardangervidda, Norway, and Kola, USSR (Chepurko, 1972; Kjelvik & Kärenlampi, 1974) and in low alpine grassland communities at Abisko, northern Sweden (Pearsall & Newbould, 1957), the highest in swampy meadows in forest tundra (Gorchakovsky & Andreyashkina, 1972), in eutrophic meadows in sub-arctic shrub tundra in Greenland (Lewis, Callaghan & Jones, 1972) and in low latitude (40 °N) low-alpine shrub tundra (Webber, 1972). Similar annual production is also found in most of the other low-latitude plant community studies included in the IBP tundra network e.g. in the Austrian alps in the shrub communities Loiseleurietum and Vaccinietum (Larcher, Cernusca & Schmidt, 1973), in moorland communities in the United Kingdom (Forrest, 1971) and parts of Ireland (J. J. Moore, personal communication), in grassland and herb-field communities on the Australian Macquarie Island (Jenkin & Ashton, 1970) and in some types of moist alpine tundra (Scott & Billings, 1964).

However, in a few low-latitude (about 40 °N) tundra studies a some-what lower annual vascular plant production is found (of the order 100–200 g m^{-2} for above-ground only, twice as much if below-ground production is included). This is the case for some poorer alpine meadows in the USA (Bliss, 1962; Webber, 1972) and also for an open bog in Ireland (J. J. Moore, personal communication). This production is relatively low for these regions. On the other hand, similar values may be found under extremely good conditions even in southern arctic tundra at about 70 °N. (Shanks for sites at Barrow, Alaska according to Bliss, 1962).

In forest tundra, relative low annual production is mostly found for the understory. Based on traditional biomass changes, the annual above-ground vascular understory plant accretion is reported to be 40–70 g m^{-2} for both subarctic and subalpine forests (Andreev, 1966; Kallio & Kärenlampi, 1971; Wielgolaski, 1972a). According to pre-liminary results from Norwegian subalpine birch forest studies (Kjelvik, 1973) the production of green biomass may be of the order of 100 g m^{-2} for trees and the production of non-green woody above-ground material for trees nearly the same. This means that the annual production of an oligotrophic subalpine forest may be of the same order as of a eutrophic subarctic or subalpine shrub community.

The continuous illumination of polar days in summer may cause positive net assimilation twenty-four hours a day, as stated already in the nineteenth century (see e.g. Müller, 1928). The duration of the period for which assimilation is continuous is determined both by the light intensity at midnight and by the temperature; lower temperature is well known to result in greater net assimilation at low light intensity, as also in arctic plants (Müller, 1928; Stålfelt, 1937,1938; Russell, 1940; Pisek, 1960; Mooney & Billings, 1961; Ungerson & Scherdin, 1964; Billings & Mooney, 1968; Shvetsova & Voznesenskii, 1970). The light compensation point at a specific temperature is also known to vary with the plant species (Müller, 1928), which means that the net assimilation during the night hours of a polar summer might well be different for various species (Shvetsova & Voznesenskii, 1970). Mayo *et al.* (1972) have stressed that the compensation point must be very low at low temperatures for *Dryas integrifolia* and *Carex stans* as both species have 24-h net assimilation even at very low light intensities. On the other hand, Tieszen (1973) stresses that light saturation for photosynthesis of arctic grasses is found to be as high as 0.4 cal cm^{-1} min^{-1} (400–700 nm) which only occurred on relatively clear days around solar noon at Barrow. These results are in accordance with similar results found by Shvetsova & Voznesenskii (1970).

Cloudiness seems to be a very important factor determining the ability of many species to achieve 24-h net assimilation in polar tundra. Ungerson & Scherdin (1964) found negative CO_2 exchange of *Betula nana* in late June in northern Norway at 71 °N. during night time except on clear cold nights, which also seems to be the case in the results of Shvetsova & Voznesenskii (1970) for this and other species with relatively high respiration even at low temperatures. Tieszen (1972*b*, 1973) also states that for the same species CO_2 exchange may become negative during summer. Most of the arctic species studied (*Carex aquatilis*, *Eriophorum angustifolium* and *Salix pulchra*), however, have a very low compensation point and therefore normally show 24-h net assimilation during the period of the midnight sun (until August 2nd at Barrow, USA at about 71 °N.). Mayo *et al.* (1972) found that when cloud cover is present, positive net assimilation may occur mostly during daytime, while when clear skies prevail, night-time positive fixation may be more important for *Dryas integrifolia*. On clear days a reduced net assimilation in this species in the afternoon may have been caused by high leaf temperatures and thus increased respiration rate, as also found by Shvetsova & Voznesenskii (1970) for *Dryas punctata* and other species.

90

The incoming radiation increases with the height above sea level (Sauberer & Härtel, 1959). As in polar regions, the light conditions in alpine regions are generally favourable to assimilation and compensate to some degree for the short growth periods. This explains why the *daily* primary production in tundra is often higher than could be expected from the relatively small *annual* values. On the other hand a higher light intensity has been found necessary for saturation of assimilation in low-latitude alpine areas than in arctic lowland areas (D. A. Johnson, personal communication).

In areas where nutrients or lack of water (or water surplus) are not strongly limiting growth a mean daily increment of above-ground biomass is found to be from 2 to above 3 g m^{-2}, both in arctic systems (Bliss, 1962) and in alpine systems in the period from spring to peak above-ground biomass (Bliss, 1962; Webber, 1972; F. E. Wielgolaski, unpublished observations). These values are of the same order as the daily primary production often reported, by use of the harvesting method, in natural systems in temperate regions both in prairies (e.g., tall-grass prairie in USA; Odum, 1971) and in deciduous forests. Temperature and light are, however, usually very important limiting factors in the arctic and alpine plant communities with near optimum water and nutrient conditions. Then small variations in the energy supply cause great differences in the net assimilation as found by the author in Norwegian alpine tundra (Kjelvik, Wielgolaski & Jahren, 1975) and also seen in the examples mentioned earlier.

The often favourable conditions for plant growth in tundra regions during the summer season are reflected by the relatively high efficiency estimates found for net production. Bliss (1962) found for a low-alpine sedge meadow at Mt Washington in the USA (44 °N.) an efficiency estimate of about 0.97% for above-ground and below-ground production, as an average for the growing season. This was based on 50% of the total solar radiation, but if 45% of the total radiation is regarded as within the wavelengths 400–700 nm useful to photosynthesis (Anderson, 1967), the efficiency increases to 1.1%. This is nearly the same percentage as reported by Golley (1960) for herbaceous vegetation during the growing season in southern Michigan. Similar calculations are carried out for vegetation at the Norwegian IBP alpine tundra sites. The efficiency estimates for total net production (above and below ground, vascular and cryptogams) in the growth period are then found to be about 0.7% for the lichen heath (see Table 4.3), 1.4% for the dry meadow, 1.7% for the subalpine birch forest including the trees (1.1%

for understory) and 2.3% for the wet meadow. Webber (1972) reports efficiency estimates for net shoot photosynthesis in alpine communities at 40 °N. from 0.62% in a dry fell-field to 1.9% in a moist shrub tundra. Larcher *et al.* (1973) found the efficiency to be about 0.6% in shrub heaths in the Alps in Austria for the growing season. Even in high-alpine patchy vegetation (less than 20% cover) an efficiency of 0.1–0.4% is found for the growth period based on above-ground parts only (Brzoska, 1973).

Table 4.3. *Efficiency, as percentage of solar radiation used by plants for production (based on 45% of incoming global radiation). Calculated per day of growing season, and including both cryptogams and vascular plants, and also both above- and below-ground production, except where otherwise stated*

		%
Patchy vegetation with < 20% cover (above-ground only)	Austria	0.1–0.4
Shrub heath (alpine)	Austria	0.6
Fellfield (alpine)	Colorado, USA	0.6
Lichen heath (alpine)	Norway	0.7
Meadows (alpine)	Mt Washington, New Hampshire, USA	1.1
Herbs	Southern Michigan, USA	1.2
Dry alpine meadow	Norway	1.4
Subalpine birch forest	Norway	1.7
Moist shrub tundra (alpine)	Colorado, USA	1.9
Wet meadow (alpine)	Norway	2.3

As in other vegetation types of the world, water may be the main limiting factor, in some cases, for primary production in tundra, but is often, as in coarse sand, difficult to distinguish from low production caused by lack of nutrients. Bliss (1962) reports daily above-ground production rates of about 1 g m⁻² in rush–dwarf shrub heath in alpine tundra as well as in some *Carex* communities in Alaska. Lower values based on a similar harvesting technique are found at a sandy lichen heath in Norway, above-ground about 0.8 g m⁻² (Kjelvik & Kärenlampi, 1975), and at Devon Island in northern Canada, where Svoboda (1973) has calculated a daily above-ground primary production of about 0.35 g m⁻² at a sandy beach ridge. From the high alpine belt of the Alps, Brzoska (1973) reports a daily above-ground production of 0.66 g m⁻² from a 10% ground cover. Dennis & Tieszen (1972) found a nearly linear growth rate of 1.5 to 1.8 g m⁻² d⁻¹ for above-ground plant material in a medium wet meadow at Barrow, Alaska. This is of the same order as found by Forrest (1971) in poor moorlands in England. Muc (1973) at Devon Island has found about 0.70 g m^{-2} d^{-1} produced above ground in a mesic sedge meadow, when corrected for seasonal dieback.

Corrections for dieback are very important in primary production estimates, as stressed earlier (Wielgolaski, 1972a,1975d). If primary production at an alpine dry meadow in southern Norway is calculated only on the basis of differences in above-ground biomass (including cryptogams) at the peak and beginning of the vegetation period, a value of about 1–1.5 g m^{-2} is found per day as an average for the whole growing season. By taking the dieback and decomposition of dead material into consideration as well as the differences in growth seasons of tops and roots of vascular plants, an average value of about 4.5 g m^{-2} d^{-1} is found (Wielgolaski & Kjelvik, 1973), about half of which occurs in above-ground parts.

The below-ground vascular plant production is often found to be higher than the above-ground. This is reported by Dennis & Johnson (1970) for plots at Barrow, Alaska, and also from alpine tundra (Scott & Billings, 1964; Bliss, 1966). At sites with a relatively high amount of soil water it seems that root production is often higher compared to the production of above-ground parts than at drier sites. This has been found for the wet alpine tundra meadow and willow-thicket IBP sites in Norway, as well as in marshy tundra in Western Taimyr (Pospelova, 1972). At the last-mentioned site, the total daily primary production was found to be 5–6 g m^{-2}, while above-ground production accounted for only about 1 g m^{-2} per day (see Table 4.4). Lower daily production is found at other sites in the same area, down to a total of about 2 g m^{-2} in a spotted *Dryas*–moss tundra with only 0.25 g m^{-2} per day in above-ground production. In alpine shrub heaths in Austria it is found, by harvesting, that the daily vascular plant above-ground production in the community Loiseleurietum is about 2.1 g m^{-2} and the total daily growth is 3.6 g m^{-2}, while in the community Vaccinietum the above-ground biomass is found to increase to 2.7 g m^{-2} d^{-1} and the total biomass to 6.8 g m^{-2} d^{-1}, according to preliminary results by Larcher *et al.* (1973).

Thus it is obvious that measurements of primary production based on seasonal changes in above-ground biomass only will give strong underestimates. Tieszen (1972a) suggests that net carbon dioxide uptake may exceed that incorporated in above-ground material by a factor of three to five. This seems to hold also in Norwegian alpine studies. The net assimilation of vascular plants at the IBP tundra dry meadow site measured by simple field technique (Kjelvik, Wielgolaski & Jahren, 1975) is found to be on average above 3 g CO_2 incorporated per m^{-2} per day (probably underestimates), or using the conversion factor 0.648 about 2 g dry matter $m^{-2} d^{-1}$. This is about twice as much as is found by just comparing seasonal biomass changes in above-ground vascular plants, but as seen above is very close to the values calculated for vascular plants at the same site by harvesting, when dieback and translocations are taken into account. This indicates that both methods may give close estimates of the true net primary production.

Table 4.4. *Net primary production of tundra vascular plants (in $g\ m^{-2}\ d^{-1}$ of growing season)*

		Above ground	Total
Spotted Dryas–moss tundra	USSR	0.25	2.0
Lichen heath	Norway	0.8	1.7
Wet meadow	USA	–	4.0
Dry meadow	Norway	2.3	4.6
Marshy tundra	USSR	1.0	5.0–6.0
Alpine shrub heath	Austria	2.1–2.7	3.6–6.8
Willow thicket (understory)	Norway	2.0	4.2
(incl. shrubs)		4.5	6.7

Tieszen (1972*b*) in a recent preliminary paper, has found the accumulative CO_2 uptake of vascular plants to be of the order 800 g m^{-2} at a mesic meadow at Barrow, Alaska, during an eighty-day period from mid-June to early September. Even if reduced by 40% because of shading, this means an average daily production of vascular plants of 4 g dry weight m^{-2}. During the fifty-day period from mid-June to early August the uptake is about 550 g CO_2 m^{-2} or 4.5 g dry weight m^{-2}. This is about three times higher than the daily accretion of above-ground vascular plant biomass (1.5–1.8 g $m^{-2} d^{-1}$) found in the same plant community at Barrow (Dennis & Tieszen, 1972). Still higher values were obtained in the same studies when production of cryptogams were included (about 6 g $m^{-2} d^{-1}$), as also found by Coyne & Kelley (1972) by aerodynamic CO_2 studies. Calculations based on data from arctic Canada (Devon Island) for a beach ridge seem to indicate still higher differences (5–6 times) between production estimated from CO_2 gas-exchange studies (Mayo *et al.*, 1972) and from above-ground harvestings (Svoboda, 1973), respectively.

The net assimilation per unit ground area increased from spring to early August in the meadow at Barrow, Alaska (Tieszen, 1972*b*). During the same period, the above-ground dry weight was increasing approximately linearly (Dennis & Tieszen, 1972), but the increase in dry weight continued for some more days in the fall than did the increase of live leaf area index. Mayo *et al.* (1972) found that *Dryas* is photosynthetically active within a few days of snow-melt, which is in accordance with results on net assimilation at Barrow (Tieszen, 1972*c*) and earlier results.

The highest daily growth rates in tundra plants on a plant weight basis mostly occur soon after the release of the plants from the snow cover. This was found by Billings & Bliss (1959) by harvesting techniques in alpine snow beds, and seems to be confirmed both by harvesting and gas-exchange studies in the Norwegian alpine IBP studies (F. E. Wielgolaski, unpublished observations). Recently, a substantial shift in photosynthetic rates on a leaf area basis was found during the season for some plant species in alpine tundra studies in the USA (Moore *et al.*, 1973; M. Caldwell, personal communication). Moser (1973) also reports lower net assimilation in *Ranunculus glacialis* in fall than in summer in high alpine regions in Austria. One reason may be the shift in assimilation rates with leaf age (L. L. Tieszen & D. A. Johnson, personal communication). A seasonal shift in optimum temperature for net assimilation seems also to have occurred for some of the species in the alpine tundra study in the USA, with the lowest optimum temperature during the most rapid vegetative period. If these findings are confirmed, they will be of importance for the studies of primary production in relation to climatic factors.

The maximum net assimilation rate is found to vary strongly between tundra plant species. Shvetsova & Voznesenskii (1971) found maximum values of 28 mg CO_2 g^{-1} h^{-1} for *Oxyria digyna*, while the values were 9.5 mg CO_2 g^{-1} h^{-1} for *Dryas punctata* in typical tundra vegetation in western Taimyr, USSR. Mayo *et al.* (1973) report somewhat lower maximum net photosynthesis values for *Dryas integrifolia* in studies at Devon Island in arctic Canada and Skre (1975) intermediate values for *Dryas octopetala* in Norway (see Table 4.5). At Devon Island a maximum rate of 12–13 mg CO_2 g^{-1} h^{-1} was found for net assimilation of *Carex stans* which is of the same order as the maximum values found for *Eriophorum angustifolium* in western Taimyr and *Carex nigra* in Norway, but somewhat higher than the maximum rate found in USSR for *Carex ensifolia*. Tieszen (1972*b*) found that the maximum net photosynthesis of *Salix pulchra* at Barrow, Alaska, was nearly twice as high as for most monocotyledons. However, the values vary strongly between grasses as well. Shvetsova & Voznesenskii (1971) found highest rates for *Alopecurus alpinus* and *Arctophila fulva*. The same two species were amongst the grasses having the highest maximum rates in a detailed study on photosynthesis as a function of light intensity and temperature at Barrow, Alaska (Tieszen, 1973), while *Poa arctica, P. malacantha* and *Hierochloë alpina* showed the lowest maximum values in that study.

Table 4.5. *Examples of maximum net assimilation of arctic and alpine tundra plants in mg CO_2 g^{-1} h^{-1}*

Alopecurus alpinus, Western Taimyr, USSR	33
Arctophila fulva, Western Taimyr, USSR	28
Oxyria digyna, Western Taimyr, USSR	28
Polygonum bistortioides, alpine Colorado, USA	24
Ranunculus nivalis, USA	20
Deschampsia caespitosa, alpine Colorado, USA	20
Salix lapponum, Hardangervidda, Norway	18
Festuca rubra, Hardangervidda, Norway	16
Carex nigra, Hardangervidda, Norway	16
Eriophorum angustifolium, Western Taimyr, USSR	15
Ranunculus acris, Hardangervidda, Norway	14
Carex stans, Devon Island, Canada	13
Vaccinium myrtillus (leaves), Hardangervidda, Norway	11
Ranunculus glacialis, the Alps, Austria	10
Dryas punctata, Western Taimyr, USSR	10
Carex ensifolia, Western Taimyr, USSR	9
Dryas octopetala, Hardangervidda, Norway	8
Dryas integrifolia, Devon Island, Canada	7.4

In alpine regions at about 40 °N. in the USA, high maximum net assimilation rates are found for both some forbs and grasses. The author has calculated the value for *Polygonum bistortioides* to be about 24 mg CO_2 g^{-1} h^{-1} and somewhat lower for *Deschampsia caespitosa* (based on data kindly submitted by Dr Caldwell and collaborators). The maximum net assimilation rate for *Ranunculus glacialis* measured at high alpine sites in the Alps is found to be about 10 mg g^{-1} h^{-1} in late July (Moser, 1973), while the maximum value for *Ranunculus nivalis* in the USA may be about twice as high (D. Johnson, personal communication) and intermediate values are recorded for *R. acris* in Norway (Skre, 1975).

The maximum net assimilation rates for cryptogams in tundra areas are generally lower than for vascular plants. Mayo *et al.* (1972) report a maximum rate of $5 \, mg \, CO_2 \, g^{-1} \, h^{-1}$ for the moss *Polytrichum juniperinum* at Devon Island in arctic Canada, which is somewhat higher than that found by Bazzaz, Paolillo & Jagels (1970) for the same species in lower-latitude alpine regions and by Kärenlampi & Kallio (Chapter 17) in southern Finland. For various species of bryophytes these authors mostly report maximum values of the order of 1.5–3.0 mg $CO_2 \, g^{-1} \, h^{-1}$, but for some species much lower maximum values seem to be usual. Still lower values are found for lichens, mostly of the order of 0.3–0.5 mg $CO_2 \, g^{-1} \, h^{-1}$ (Kärenlampi & Kallio, Chapter 17). The CO_2 uptake in lichens is found to be strongly dependent on the moisture content, both in northern Finland (Kärenlampi, 1971) and in alpine regions of southern Norway (Kjelvik, Wielgolaski & Jahren, 1975).

The variation between plant groups and species in maximum net assimilation rate will also influence the average growth rates during the season. To get the best estimates of primary production in tundra, it is obviously preferable therefore to study the values for each species as a function of at least temperature (in the air or better in the leaf), light intensity, a humidity factor, and the time of the growing season, either in the laboratory or in the field, although such complete studies will never be possible under natural conditions. Even somewhat less sophisticated assimilation studies seem to lead to more correct primary production values, than do elaborate harvesting techniques.

Conclusions

The biomass and production of tundra plants as well as the top–root ratio of vascular plants generally decrease with latitude and altitude i.e. with decreasing temperature, modified by moisture and nutrient conditions. On a relative basis, the amount of lichens increases in the same direction, while bryophytes and vascular plants usually decrease. Woody plants decrease in height with latitude and altitude, and are absent under extreme conditions. The daily total production in tundra areas may be from nearly zero to about 8 g m^{-2} and the annual values from less than 10 g m^{-2} to about 1000 g m^{-2}. Methods for estimation of primary production are discussed. Similar results are obtained from assimilation studies and from detailed harvesting techniques, while values based on seasonal changes in above-ground biomass usually give strong underestimates or production. The efficiency of the use of incoming radiation (400–700 nm) for total plant production on a ground area basis per day of growing season is found to vary from less than 0.5% to about 2%, mostly around 1%. The assimilation rates vary strongly between species. Maximum values above 30 mg CO_2 g^{-1} h^{-1} incorporated are found for some vascular species, while maxima less than 10 mg g^{-1} h^{-1} for others. Positive net assimilation usually occurs for twenty-four hours a day in polar regions during mid summer, but on cloudy nights, however, CO_2 exchange may be negative for some species.

This paper would not have been possible without the very good co-operation of my colleagues in the IBP Tundra Biome internationally. I wish to thank all the scientists for allowing me to use their often unpublished data in this paper. In the USA I address my thanks to Drs M. Caldwell, L. Tieszen, and P. J. Webber, although many of their co-workers have contributed considerably as well, in Canada to Dr L. C. Bliss and his co-workers, in Ireland to Dr J. J. Moore and his co-workers, in the United Kingdom to Dr O. W. Heal and his co-workers, in the Bipolar project to Drs M. C. Lewis and T. Callaghan and their co-workers, in Sweden to Dr M. Sonesson and his co-workers, in Finland to Drs P. Kallio and L. Kärenlampi, in Austria to Drs W. Larcher and W. Moser and their co-workers, in the USSR to Drs B. A. Tikhomirov and S. S. Schwarz and their several co-workers, and at home in Norway to Drs S. Kjelvik, O. Skre, A. Berg, and A. K. Veum, and A. Skartveit and the technical assistants headed by Miss A. Polder.

I also thank my colleagues of the editorial board in the IBP Tundra Biome Steering Committee for their careful review of the manuscript and valuable suggestions. Finally I thank Mrs M. Espeland for correcting the language in the paper and for typing the manuscript.

References

Ahmadjian, V. (1970). Adaptations of Antarctic terrestrial plants. In *Antarctic Ecology*, ed. M. W. Holdgate, vol. 2, pp. 801–11. London, Academic Press.

Ahti, T., Hämet-Ahti, L. & Jalas, J. (1968). Vegetation zones in northwestern Europe. *Ann. Bot. Fennica*, **5**, 169–211.

Alexandrova, V. D. (1958). An attempt to determine the above-ground productivity of plant communities in the arctic tundra. (In Russian). *Bot. Zh.* **43**, 1748–61.

Alexandrova, V. D. (1960). Some regularities in the distribution of the vegetation in the arctic tundra. *Arctic*, **13**, 147–62.

Alexandrova, V. D. (1970). The vegetation of the tundra zones in the USSR and data about its productivity. In *Proceedings of the Conference on productivity and conservation in northern circumpolar lands, Edmonton 1969*, eds. W. A. Fuller & P. G. Kevan. IUCN publication new series no. 16, pp. 93–114. Morges, Switzerland.

Anderson, M. C. (1967). Photon flux, chlorophyll content and photosynthesis under natural conditions. *Ecology*, **48**, 1050–3.

Andreev, V. N. (1966). Peculiarities of zonal distribution of the arial and underground phytomass on the East European Far North. (In Russian). *Bot. Zh.* **51**, 1401–11.

Bazzaz, F. A., Paolillo Jr, D. J. & Jagels, R. H. (1970). Photosynthesis and respiration of forest and alpine populations of *Polytrichum juniperinum*. *The Bryologist*, **73**, 579–85.

Beschel, R. E. (1970). The diversity of tundra vegetation. In *Proceedings of the Conference on productivity and conservation in northern circumpolar lands, Edmonton 1969*, eds. W. A. Fuller & P. G. Kevan. IUCN publication new series no. 16, pp. 85–92. Morges, Switzerland.

Billings, W. D. & Bliss, L. C. (1959). An alpine snow-bank environment and its effect on vegetation, plant development and productivity. *Ecology*, **40**, 388–97.

Billings, W. D., Clebsch, E. E. C. & Mooney, H. A. (1960). Photosynthesis and respiration measurements on alpine plants under field conditions (abst.). *Bull. Ecol. Soc. Amer.* **41**, 77.

Billings, W. D. & Mooney, H. A. (1968). The ecology of arctic and alpine plants. *Biol. Rev.* **43**, 481–529.

Bliss, L. C. (1962). Net primary production of tundra ecosystems. In *Die Stoffproduktion der Pflanzendecke*, ed. H. Lieth, pp. 35–46. Stuttgart, Fischer-Verlag.

Bliss, L. C. (1966). Plant productivity in alpine microenvironments on Mt Washington, New Hampshire. *Ecol. Monogr.* **36**, 125–55.

Bliss, L. C. (1970). Primary production within arctic tundra ecosystems. In *Proceedings of the Conference on productivity and conservation in northern circumpolar lands, Edmonton 1969*, eds. W. A. Fuller & P. G. Kevan. IUCN publication new series no. 16, pp. 75–85. Morges, Switzerland.

Bliss, L. C. (ed.) (1972a). Devon Island IBP project high arctic ecosystem. *Project report 1970 and 1971*, 413pp. Edmonton: Department of Botany, the University of Alberta.

Bliss, L. C. (1972b). Devon Island research 1971. In *Proceedings IV International meeting on the biological productivity of tundra, Leningrad, October 1971*, eds. F. E. Wielgolaski & T. Rosswall, pp. 269–75. Oslo & Stockholm, IBP Tundra Biome Steering Committee.

Bliss, L. C. & Wielgolaski, F. E. (eds.) (1973). *Primary production and production processes, Tundra Biome*, 256pp. Edmonton & Oslo, IBP Tundra Biome Steering Committee.

Bogatschova, I. A. (1972). Leaf-eating insects on willows in tundra biocenoses of the Southern Jamal. In *Proceedings IV International meeting on the biological productivity of tundra, Leningrad, October 1971*, eds. F. E. Wielgolaski & T. Rosswall, pp. 131–2. Oslo & Stockholm, IBP Tundra Biome Steering Committee.

Bray, J. R. (1963). Root production and the estimation of net productivity. *Can. J. Bot.* **41**, 65–72.

Brown, J., Rickard, W. & Przybyla, J. E. (1970). USA CRREL study area Barrow, Alaska. Soils data, 1962–66. *Internal Report 67*, 117pp. Hanover, New Hampshire, Cold Regions Research and Engineering Laboratory, Corps of Engineers, US Army.

Brzoska, W. (1969). Stoffproduktion und Energiehaushalt der Vegetation auf hochalpinem Standort unter besonderer Berücksichtigung von *Ranunculus glacialis* L. Dissertation, Universität Innsbruck.

Brzoska, W. (1973). Stoffproduktion und Energiehaushalt von Nivalpflanzen. In *Ökosystemforschung*, ed. H. Ellenberg, pp. 225–33. Berlin, Heidelberg & New York, Springer-Verlag.

Callaghan, T. V. (1973). Studies on the factors affecting the primary production of bi-polar *Phleum alpinum* L. In *Primary Production in production processes, Tundra Biome*, eds. L. C. Bliss & F. E. Wielgolaski, pp. 177–83. Edmonton & Oslo, IBP Tundra Biome Steering Committee.

Chepurko, N. L. (1966). Biological productivity and cycling of mineral elements in forest and tundra ecosystems of Khibini mountains. (In Russian). *Vestnik*, Moscow University, ser. 5, Geogr. 1.

Chepurko, N. L. (1972). The biological productivity and the cycle of nitrogen and ash elements in the dwarf shrub tundra ecosystem of the Khibini mountains (Kola Peninsula). In *Proceedings IV International meeting on the biological productivity of tundra, Leningrad, October 1971*, eds. F. E. Wielgolaski & T. Rosswall, pp. 236–47. Oslo & Stockholm, IBP Tundra Biome Steering Committee.

Clarke, G. C. S., Greene, S. W. & Greene, D. M. (1971). Productivity of bryophytes in polar regions. *Ann. Bot.* **35**, 99–108.

Clymo, R. S. (1970). The growth of *Sphagnum*: methods of measurement. *J. Ecol.* **58**, 13–49.

Collins, N. J. (1973). The productivity of selected bryophyte communities in the maritime Antarctic. In *Primary production and production processes, Tundra Biome*, eds. L. C. Bliss & F. E. Wielgolaski, pp. 177–83. Edmonton & Oslo, IBP Tundra Biome Steering Committee.

Coyne, P. I. & Kelley, J. J. (1972). CO_2 exchange in the Alaskan arctic tundra: Meteorological assessment by the aerodynamic method. In *Proceedings 1972 Tundra Biome Symposium*, ed. S. Bowen, pp. 36–9. US Tundra Biome.

Dahl, E. (1956). Rondane mountain vegetation in South Norway and its relation to the environment. *Skrifter utgitt av Det Norske Videnskaps-Akademi i Oslo, I. Mat.-Naturv. Klasse*, no. 3, 374pp. Oslo, Aschehoug.

Danilov, N. N. (1972). Birds and arthropods in the tundra biogeocenosis. In *Proceedings IV International meeting on the biological productivity of tundra, Leningrad, October 1971*, eds. F. E. Wielgolaski & T. Rosswall, pp. 117–21. Oslo & Stockholm, IBP Tundra Biome Steering Committee.

Dennis, J. G. (1968). Growth of tundra vegetation in relation to arctic microenvironments at Barrow, Alaska. Ph.D. Thesis, Duke University.

Dennis, J. G. & Johnson, P. L. (1970). Shoot and rhizome–root standing crops of tundra vegetation at Barrow, Alaska. *Arctic and Alpine Res.* **2**, 253–66.

Dennis, J. G. & Tieszen, L. L. (1972). Seasonal course of dry matter and chlorophyll by species at Barrow, Alaska. In *Proceedings 1972 Tundra Biome Symposium*, ed. S. Bowen, pp. 16–21. US Tundra Biome.

Firsova, V. P., Shijatov, S. G. & Dobriskij, L. N. (eds.) (1969). Productivity of biogeocenoses in the subarctic. *Proceedings of all Union Conference*, pp. 1–246. USSR, Sverdlovsk.

Flower-Ellis, J. G. K. (1973). Growth and morphology in the evergreen dwarf shrubs *Empetrum hermaphroditum* and *Andromeda polifolia* at Stordalen. In *Primary production and production processes, Tundra Biome*, eds. L. C. Bliss & F. E. Wielgolaski, pp. 123–35. Edmonton & Oslo, IBP Tundra Biome Steering Committee.

Forrest, G. I. (1971). Structure and production of north Pennine blanket bog vegetation. *J. Ecol.* 59, 453–80.

Golley, F. (1960). Energy dynamics of a food chain of an old-field community. *Ecol. Monogr.* 30, 187–206.

Gorchakovsky, P. L. (1966). *Flora and vegetation of the Ural high mountains.* (In Russian). USSR, Sverdlovsk.

Gorchakovsky, P. L. & Andreyashkina, N. I. (1972). Productivity of some shrub, dwarf shrub and herbaceous communities of forest-tundra. In *Proceedings IV International meeting on the biological productivity of tundra, Leningrad, October 1971*, eds. F. E. Wielgolaski & T. Rosswall, pp. 113–16. Oslo & Stockholm, IBP Tundra Biome Steering Committee.

Gaare, E. & Skogland, T. (1971). Villreinens næringsvaner. *Report from the grazing project of the Norwegian IBP Committee*, pp. 1–25+tables. Trondheim.

Heal, O. W. (ed.) (1971). *Working meeting on analyses of ecosystems, Kevo, Finland, September 1970*, 297pp. London, IBP Tundra Biome Steering Committee.

Ignatenko, I. V., Knorre, A. V., Lovelius, N. V. & Norin, B. N. (1972). Standing crop in plant communities at the station Ary-Mas. In *Proceedings IV International meeting on the biological productivity of tundra, Leningrad, October 1971*, ed. F. E. Wielgolaski & T. Rosswall, pp. 140–9. Oslo & Stockholm, IBP Tundra Biome Steering Committee.

Jenkin, J. F. & Ashton, D. H. (1970). Productivity studies on Macquarie Island vegetation. In *Antarctic Ecology*, ed. M. W. Holdgate, vol. 2, pp. 851–63. London, Academic Press.

Kallio, P. & Kärenlampi, L. (1971). A review of the stage reached in the Kevo IBP in 1970. In *Working meeting on Analyses of Ecosystems, Kevo, Finland, September 1970*, ed. O. W. Heal, pp. 79–91. London, IBP Tundra Biome Steering Committee.

Khodachek, E. A. (1969). The plant matter of tundra phytocenoses in Western Taimyr. *Bot. Zh.* 54, 1059–73. (Translated by P. Kuchar.)

Kjelvik, S. (1973). Biomass and production in a willow thicket and a sub-alpine birch forest, Hardangervidda, Norway. In *Primary production and production processes, Tundra Biome*, eds. L. C. Bliss & F. E. Wielgolaski, pp. 115–22. Edmonton & Oslo, IBP Tundra Biome Steering Committee.

Kjelvik, S. & Kärenlampi, L. (1975). Plant biomass and primary production of Fennoscandian subarctic and subalpine forests and of alpine willow and heath ecosystems. In *Fennoscandian Tundra Ecosystems*, part. I. *Plants and micro-organisms*, ed. F. E. Wielgolaski. Berlin, Heidelberg & New York, Springer-Verlag. In press.

Kjelvik, S., Wielgolaski, F. E. & Jahren, A. (1975). Photosynthesis and respiration of plants studied by field technique at Hardangervidda, Norway. In *Fennoscandian Tundra Ecosystems*, part I, *Plants and micro-organisms*, ed. F. E. Wielgolaski. Berlin, Heidelberg & New York, Springer-Verlag. In press.

Kärenlampi, L. (1970). Morphological analysis of the growth and productivity of the lichen *Cladonia alpestris*. *Report Kevo Subarctic Research Station*, **7**, 9–15.

Kärenlampi, L. (1971). Studies on the relative growth rate of some fruticose lichens. *Report Kevo Subarctic Research Station*, **7**, 33–9.

Larcher, W., Cernusca, A. & Schmidt, L. (1973). Stoffproduktion und Energiebilanz in Zwergstrauchbeständen auf dem Patscherkofel bei Innsbruck. In *Ökosystemforschung*, ed. H. Ellenberg, pp. 175–94. Berlin, Heidelberg & New York, Springer-Verlag.

Lewis, M. C. & Greene, S. W. (1970). A comparison of plant growth at an Arctic and Antarctic station. In *Antarctic Ecology*, ed. M. W. Holdgate, vol. 2, pp. 838–50. London, Academic Press.

Lewis, M. C., Callaghan, T. V. & Jones, G. E. (1972). Bipolar botanical project. Arctic research programme phase II. *IBP Tundra Biome report*, pp. 1–34. York, Department of Biology, University of York.

Lieth, H. (ed.) (1962). *Die Stoffproduktion der Pflanzendecke*, pp. 1–156. Stuttgart, Fischer-Verlag.

Makhaeva, L. V. (1959). Winter pasture management in reindeer farming in Murmansk oblast. *Probl. Sev.* **3**, 66–77. (Translated from Russian).

Mayo, J. M., Despain, D. G. & van Zinderen Bakker Jr, E. M. (1972). CO_2 assimilation studies. In *Devon Island BIP project high arctic ecosystems. Project report 1970 and 1971*, ed. L. C. Bliss, pp. 217–42. Edmonton, Department of Botany, University of Alberta.

Mayo, J. M., Thompson, R. G., Despain, D. G. & van Zinderen Bakker Jr, E. M. (1973). CO_2 assimilation by *Dryas integrifolia* on Devon Island, Northwest Territories. *Can. J. Bot.* **51**, 581–8.

Mooney, H. A. & Billings, W. O. (1961). Comparative physiological ecology of arctic and alpine populations of *Oxyria digyna*. *Ecol. Monogr.* **31**, 1–29.

Moore, R. T., Ehleringer, J., Miller, P. C., Caldwell, M. M. & Tieszen, L. L. (1973). Gas exchange studies of four alpine tundra species at Niwot Ridge Colorado. In *Primary production and production processes, Tundra Biome*, eds. L. C. Bliss & F. E. Wielgolaski, pp. 211–17. Edmonton & Oslo, IBP Tundra Biome Steering Committee.

Moser, W. (1971). Microclimate and photosynthesis in the nival-zone of the Alps. In *Working meeting on Analyses of Ecosystems, Kevo, Finland, September 1970*, ed. O. W. Heal, pp. 22–33. London, IBP Tundra Biome Steering Committee.

Moser, W. (1973). Licht, Temperatur und Photosynthese an der Station 'Hoher Nebelkogel' (3184 m). In *Ökosystemforschung*, ed. H. Ellenberg, pp. 203–23. Berlin, Heidelberg & New York, Springer-Verlag.

Muc, M. (1973). Primary production of plant communities of the Truelove Lowland, Devon Island, Canada. Sedge meadows. In *Primary production and production processes, Tundra Biome*, eds. L. C. Bliss & F. E. Wielgolaski, pp. 3–14. Edmonton & Oslo, IBP Tundra Biome Steering Committee.

Müller, D. (1928). Die Kohlensäureassimilation bei arktischen Pflanzen und die Abhängigkeit der Assimilation von der Temperature. *Planta*, **6**, 22–39.

Odum, P. E. (1971). *Fundamentals of ecology*, pp. 1–574. Philadelphia & London, W. B. Saunders & Co.

Pakarinen, P. & Vitt, D. H. (1973). Primary production of plant communities of the Truelove Lowland, Devon Island, Canada. Moss Communities. In *Primary production and production processes, Tundra Biome*, eds. L. C. Bliss & F. E. Wielgolaski, pp. 37–46. Edmonton & Oslo, IBP Tundra Biome Steering Committee.

Pavlova, E. B. (1969). Vegetal mass of the Tundras of Western Taimyr. *J. Moscow Univ.* **5**, 62–7. (Int. Tundra Biome translation, 3, 1971, ed. S. L. Bowen.)

Pearsall, W. H. & Newbould, P. J. (1957). Production ecology. IV. Standing crops of natural vegetation in the subarctic. *J. Ecol.* **45**, 593–9.

Pegau, R. E. (1968). Growth rates of important reindeer forage lichens on the Seward Peninsula, Alaska. *Arctic*, **21**, 255–9.

Pieper, R. D. (1963). Production and chemical composition of arctic tundra vegetation and their relation to the lemming cycle. Ph.D. Thesis. Berkeley: University of California.

Pisek, A. (1960). Pflanzen der Arktis und des Hochgebirges. In *Handbuch der Pflanzenphysiologie*, ed. W. Ruhland, vol. 5, pp. 376–414. Berlin, Springer-Verlag.

Pitelka, F. A. (1972). Cycle pattern in lemming populations near Barrow, Alaska. In *Proceedings 1972 Tundra Biome Symposium*, ed. S. Bowen, pp. 132–5. US Tundra Biome.

Pospelova, E. B. (1972). Vegetation of the Agapa station and productivity of the main plant communities. In *Proceedings IV International meeting on the biological productivity of tundra, Leningrad, October 1971*, eds. F. E. Wielgolaski & T. Rosswall, pp. 204–8. Oslo & Stockholm, IBP Tundra Biome Steering Committee.

Richardson, D. H. S. & Finegan, E. J. (1973). Primary production of plant communities of the Truelove Lowland, Devon Island, Canada. Lichen communities. In *Primary production and production processes, Tundra Biome*, eds. L. C. Bliss & F. E. Wielgolaski, pp. 47–55. Edmonton & Oslo, IBP Tundra Biome Steering Committee.

Rodin, L. E. & Bazilevich, N. I. (1966). *Production and mineral cycling in terrestrial vegetation* (English translation, ed. G. E. Fogg) 253pp. London, Scripta Technica Ltd, Oliver & Boyd.

Russell, R. S. (1940). Physiological and ecological studies on an arctic vegetation. III. Observations on carbon assimilation, carbohydrate storage and stomatal movement in relation to the growth of plants on Jan Mayen Island. *J. Ecol.* **28**, 289–309.

Sauberer, F. & Härtel, O. (1959). *Pflanze und Strahlung*, 268pp. Leipzig, Akademische Verlagsgesellschaft Geest & Portig K.-G.

Schultz, A. M. (1964). The nutrient recovery hypothesis for arctic microtine cycles. II. Ecosystem variables in relation to arctic microtine cycles. In *Grazing in terrestrial and marine environments*, ed. D. J. Crisp, pp. 37–68. Oxford, Blackwell.

Scott, D. & Billings, W. D. (1964). Effects of environmental factors on standing crop and productivity of an alpine tundra. *Ecol. Monogr.* **34**, 243–70.

Scotter, G. W. (1963). Growth rates of *Cladonia alpestris*, *C. mitis* and *C. rangiferina* in the Talston River region, N.W.T. *Can. J. Bot.* **41**, 1199–202.

Sestak, Z., Čatsky, J. & Jarvis, P. G. (1971). *Plant photosynthetic production*, 818pp. The Hague, Junk.

Shamurin, V. F., Polozova, T. G. & Khodachek, E. A. (1972). Plant biomass of main plant communities at the Tareya station (Taimyr). In *Proceedings IV International meeting on the biological productivity of tundra, Leningrad, October 1971*, eds. F. E. Wielgolaski & T. Rosswall, pp. 163–82. Oslo & Stockholm, IBP Tundra Biome Steering Committee.

Shvetsova, V. M. & Voznesenskii, V. L. (1970). Diurnal and seasonal variations in the rate of photosynthesis in some plants of Western Taimyr. *Bot. Zh.* **55**, 66–76. (Int. Tundra Biome translation 2, 1971, ed. S. L. Bowen).

Skre, O. (1975). CO_2 exchange in norwegian tundra plants studied by infrared gas analyzer technique. In *Fennoscandian Tundra Ecosystems*, part I, *Plants and microorganisms*, ed. F. E. Wielgolaski. Berlin, Heidelberg & New York, Springer-Verlag. In press.

Smirnov, V, S. & Tokmakova, S. G. (1972). Influence of consumers on natural phytocenosis production variation. In *Proceedings IV International meeting on the biological productivity of tundra, Leningrad, October 1971*, eds. F. E. Wielgolaski & T. Rosswall, pp. 122–8. Oslo & Stockholm, IBP Tundra Biome Steering Committee.

Sokal, R. R. & Sneath, P. H. A. (1963). *Principles of numerical taxonomy*, 148 pp. San Francisco, W. H. Freeman & Co.

Stålfelt, M. G. (1937). Der Gasaustausch der Moose. *Planta*, **27**, 30–60.

Stålfelt, M. G. (1938). Der Gasaustausch der Flechten. *Planta*, **29**, 11–31.

Svoboda, J. (1972). Vascular plant productivity studies of raised beach ridges (semi-polar desert) in the Truelove Lowland. In *Devon Island IBP project high arctic ecosystem. Project report 1970 and 1971*, ed. L. C. Bliss, pp. 146–84. Edmonton, Department of Biology, the University of Alberta.

Svoboda, J. (1973). Primary production of plant communities of the Truelove Lowland, Devon Island, Canada. Beach ridges. In *Primary production and production processes, Tundra Biome*, eds. L. C. Bliss & F. E.

Wielgolaski, pp. 15–26. Edmonton & Oslo, IBP Tundra Biome Steering Committee.

Tieszen, L. L. (1972a). Photosynthesis in relation to primary production. In *Proceedings IV International meeting on the biological productivity of tundra, Leningrad, October 1971*, eds. F. E. Wielgolaski & T. Rosswall, pp. 52–62. Oslo & Stockholm, IBP Tundra Biome Steering Committee.

Tieszen, L. L. (1972b). CO_2 exchange in the Alaskan arctic tundra: Measured course of photosynthesis. In *Proceedings 1972 Tundra Biome Symposium*, ed. S. Bowen, pp. 29–35. US Tundra Biome.

Tieszen, L. L. (1972c). The seasonal course of above-ground production and chlorophyll distribution in a wet arctic tundra at Barrow, Alaska. *Arctic and Alpine Res.* **4**, 307–24.

Tieszen, L. L. (1973). Photosynthesis and respiration in arctic tundra grasses: Field light intensity and temperature responses. *Arctic and Alpine Res.* **5**, 239–51.

Tikhomirov, B. A. (ed.) (1971). *Biogeocenoses of Taimyr tundra and their productivity*, 237pp. Leningrad, Nauka.

Ungerson, J. & Scherdin, G. (1964). Untersuchungen über den Tagesverlauf der Photosynthese und der Atmung bei *Betula nana* L. in Fennoskandia. *Ann. Bot. Soc. Vanamo*, **35**, 1–35.

Warren Wilson, J. (1957). Arctic plant growth. *Adv. Sc.* **13**, 383–8.

Webber, P. J. (1971). Gradient analysis of the vegetation around the Lewis Valley North-Central Baffin Island, NWT, Canada. Ph.D. dissertation, Queens University, Kingston, Canada.

Webber, P. J. (1972). Comparative ordination and productivity of tundra vegetation. In *Proceedings 1972 Tundra Biome Symposium*, ed. S. Bowen, pp. 55–60. US Tundra Biome.

Whittaker, R. H. (1968). Dimensions and production relations of trees and shrubs in the Brookhaven forests, New York. *J. Ecol.* **56**, 1–25.

Wielgolaski, F. E. (1972a). Vegetation types and primary production in tundra. In *Proceedings IV International meeting on the biological productivity of tundra, Leningrad, October 1971*, eds. F. E. Wielgolaski & T. Rosswall, pp. 9–35. Oslo & Stockholm, IBP Tundra Biome Steering Committee.

Wielgolaski, F. E. (1972b). Vegetation types and plant biomass in tundra. *Arctic and Alpine Res.* **4**, 291–305.

Wielgolaski, F. E. (1975a). Productivity of tundra ecosystems. In *Productivity of world ecosystems*, eds. D. E. Reichle, J. F. Franklin & D. W. Goodall (in press). Washington, DC, US National Academy of Science.

Wielgolaski, F. E. (1975b). The effects of herbage intake by sheep on primary production, ratios top–root and dead–live above-ground parts. In *The human influence on energy-flows and cycling in grassland ecosystems*, ed. A. Breymeyer. Warsaw, Institute of Ecology, PAS. In press.

Wielgolaski, F. E. (1975c). Comparison of plant structure on grazed and ungrazed tundra meadows. In *Fennoscandian Tundra Ecosystems*, part I, *Plants and microorganisms*, ed. F. E. Wielgolaski. Berlin, Heidelberg & New York, Springer-Verlag. In press.

E

Wielgolaski, F. E. (1975*d*). Primary productivity of alpine meadow communities. In *Fennoscandian Tundra Ecosystems*, part I, *Plants and microorganisms*, ed. F. E. Wielgolaski. Berlin, Heidelberg & New York, Springer-Verlag. In press.

Wielgolaski, F. E. & Kjelvik, S. (1973). Production of plants (vascular plants and cryptogams) in alpine tundra, Hardangervidda. In *Primary production and production processes, Tundra Biome*, eds. L. C. Bliss & F. E. Wielgolaski, pp. 75–86. Edmonton & Oslo, IBP Tundra Biome Steering Committee.

Wielgolaski, F. E. & Kjelvik, S. (1975). Plant biomass at the Norwegian IBP sites at Hardangervidda 1969–1972. In *IBP in Norway. Methods and results. Sections PT-UM Grazing Project, Hardangervidda. Botanical Investigations* ed. R. Vik, pp. 1–88. App. I. Ann. Rep. 1974. Oslo, Norwegian Nat. IBP Comm.

Wielgolaski, F. E. & Rosswall, T. (eds.) (1972). *Proceedings IV International meeting on the biological productivity of tundra, Leningrad, October 1971*, 320 pp. Oslo & Stockholm, IBP Tundra Biome Steering Committee.

Wielgolaski, F. E. & Webber, P. J. (1974). A comparison of circumpolar arctic and alpine tundra vegetation. I. Classification. II. Ordination. In manuscripts, about 40pp.

5. Primary production of deserts[*]

E.-D. SCHULZE & L. KAPPEN

About one third of the terrestrial surface of the earth consists of arid regions, where the potential evapotranspiration exceeds the precipitation (Walter, 1960). These areas are covered by steppe formations, savannahs, semideserts, and deserts. Among these different arid types of vegetation the desert is characterized by eleven to twelve arid months per year (Troll, 1956) and by a great variability in annual rainfall (Shanan, Evenari & Tadmor, 1967; Hershfield, 1962). At this absolute border of plant existence small deviations from the mean of available water determine not only great changes in production but also the chance of survival and death. Therefore, under these conditions comparisons of primary production and its prediction can only be made on the basis of the structural and functional abilities of the species involved.

5.1. Physiological basis of primary production of perennial higher plants[†] in the Negev desert

E.-D. SCHULZE, O. L. LANGE, L. KAPPEN, M. EVENARI & U. BUSCHBOM

The drier the climate is, the greater are the demands for the functional adaptations of the growing organisms, in order to maintain an adequate hydration level of the protoplast necessary for any active metabolism. These demands are fulfilled only by a relatively small number of morphologically and physiologically highly adapted plant species (Stocker, 1970,1971,1972; Walter, 1960; Goodman & Caldwell, 1971). A number of these species were investigated together with cultivated plants in the Negev desert (mean annual rainfall 80 mm) (Lange, Koch & Schulze, 1969; Schulze, Lange & Koch, 1972*b*; Schulze *et al.*, 1973)

---

[*] Dedicated to Professor Dr Otto Stocker on the occasion of his 85th birthday.
[†] The physiology and production of the drought-evading grassland vegetation is discussed in Chapter 3 of this volume by M. M. Caldwell. The physiological adaptations of the drought-enduring succulents are explained in Chapter 16 by J. H. Troughton.

and some of the mechanisms of carbon dioxide and water vapour control in these plants will be reported here.

Net photosynthesis, when measured under favorable temperature and moisture conditions and when based on dry weight (Fig. 5.1), shows high values for plants of *Citrullus colocynthis* and *Datura metel* that

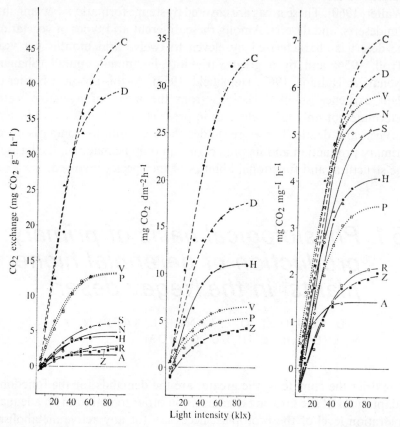

Fig. 5.1. The light dependency of net photosynthesis as related to dry weight (g) (left), surface area (dm²) (middle) and chlorophyll content (mg) (right) of the photosynthesizing organs. *Artemisia herba-alba* (A), *Citrullus colocynthis* (C), *Datura metel* (D), *Hammada scoparia* (H), *Noaea mucronata* (N), *Prunus armeniaca* (P), *Reaumuria negevensis* (R), *Salsola inermis* (S), *Vitis vinifera* (V), *Zygophyllum dumosum* (Z). (After Schulze *et al.*, 1972b.)

were continuously irrigated. Their photosynthetic rates are ten times as high as those of non-irrigated natural growing wild desert plants. But when net photosynthesis is based on the chlorophyll content of the photosynthesizing organs some native desert plants (*Salsola inermis*, *Noaea mucronata*) are now in the order of magnitude of *C. colocynthis* and *D. metel. Hammada scoparia* shows higher values than a cultivated apricot. Only *Reaumuria negevensis, Zygophyllum dumosum* and *Artemisia herba-alba* remain at the lower level. Obviously the desert plants can keep up a high efficiency of photosynthesis far into the dry season only because their photosynthetic apparatus is protected against damaging water loss by the high dry weight of xeromorphic structures and a relatively small surface area.

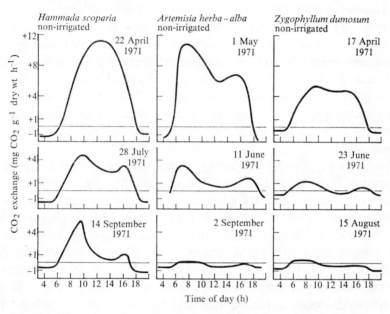

Fig. 5.2. The daily course of net photosynthesis of natural growing *Hammada scoparia*, *Artemisia herba-alba*, and *Zygophyllum dumosum* in the different seasons. From Lange *et al.* (1975). Copyright © Springer-Verlag New York Inc.

High rates of net photosynthesis, as achieved under optimum light, temperature and humidity conditions, occur only rarely during the course of a desert day. The water deficit and the climatic conditions soon cause a decline in CO_2 uptake (Stocker, 1960; Hellmuth, 1971; Schulze *et al.* 1972*c*; Oechel, Strain & Odening, 1972). The specific reactions of some desert plants during the year are shown in Fig. 5.2. In April, *H. scoparia* has a single-peaked daily course of photosynthesis with highest rates at noon, whereas for *A. herba-alba* and *Z. dumosum* there is a slight depression of CO_2 uptake in the afternoon. In June *A. herba-alba* and *Z. dumosum* have a pronounced two-peaked daily curve with a deep depression down to the compensation point around midday. For *H. scoparia* this large midday depression occurs first in

109

September. At that season *A. herba-alba* and *Z. dumosum* have only a low rate of net photosynthesis in the morning hours and a respiratory loss during the rest of the day.

The intensity and the extent of the midday depression considerably determines the primary production in the desert. The hydroactive closure of the stomata which follows from a water deficit in the leaves after a high water loss in the morning hours is the classic explanation of the two-peaked curves. This interpretation cannot fully explain why the stomata stay closed for many hours during midday, and open again in the afternoon when the water potential in the xylem measured by the Scholander method is still low. It seems therefore, that in addition to the hydroactive mechanism which controls stomatal resistance via the water potential of the entire leaf (see Slavík, Chapter 23), there are also other controlling mechanisms at the same time. Temperature and air humidity have to be considered as factors involved in this control system.

As far as the direct influence of temperature on the photosynthetic apparatus is concerned, it seems that generally the photosynthetic system of plants is quite well adapted to the temperature regime of their habitat (Pisek, Larcher, Moser & Pack, 1969). This is also true for desert plants which show a high photosynthetic capacity even at high leaf temperatures (Adams & Strain, 1968; Hellmuth, 1969; Schulze *et al.*, 1972*b*; Björkman, Pearcy, Harrison & Mooney, 1972). Concerning the influence of temperature on stomatal movement (Fig. 5.3), all investigated species exhibited stomatal opening with increasing temperature when the water stress was low (Schulze *et al.*, 1973). With increasing water stress, at a certain point, different for each species, the opening response was reversed to a closing reaction. This change of stomatal reaction is an adaptation important for desert plants in their environment: at low water stress the increasing transpiration due to stomatal opening leads to increasing cooling which results in a more favourable temperature range in the leaf tissue (Lange, 1959; Lange & Lange, 1963). Under water stress, which also induces an increased heat resistance of the cytoplasm in the leaves (Hammouda & Lange, 1962; Kappen, 1966) the restriction of water loss brought about by stomatal closure is of significant importance for the survival of the plants.

As far as air humidity as a controlling factor is concerned, there is the principal question whether stomatal closing reactions are possible without a decrease in the water potential of the leaf tissue. An experiment with isolated epidermis (Lange, Lösch, Schulze & Kappen, 1971) has

110

shown that dry air at the outer side of the epidermis leads to stomatal closure also when the inner side is water-saturated. Schulze *et al.* (1972*a*) carried out an experiment in which the diffusion resistance for water vapour of *Prunus armeniaca* increased simultaneously with an increased water vapour concentration difference. Since the water content increased at the same time, it is unlikely that the stomatal closure was caused by water stress in the entire leaf. With subsequent raising of the

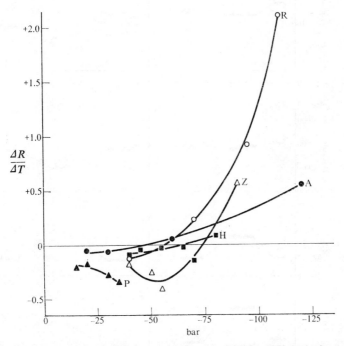

Fig. 5.3. The change in total diffusion resistance per 1 °C increase in leaf temperature ($\Delta R/\Delta T$) as related to the minimal pressure potential in the xylem of the experimental plants during the day (bar). Positive values of $\Delta R/\Delta T$ designate stomatal closure, and negative values indicate stomatal opening with increasing temperature. *Artemisia herba-alba* (A), *Hammada scoparia* (H), *Prunus armeniaca* (P), *Reaumuria negevensis* (R), and *Zygophyllum dumosum* (Z). (After Schulze *et al.*, 1973.)

air humidity the stomata were reopened in spite of an increased water stress in the leaf. For xeromorphic and succulent native desert plants Fig. 5.4 shows in principle the same result. Since this stomatal response controlled by air humidity prevents excess water loss from the whole plant apparently before the water stress develops in the photosynthesizing organs, it has special ecological significance for plants in an arid habitat.

111

Apparently a complicated steering mechanism – a combination of climatic factors and water stress – controls to a great extent the daily balance of CO_2 exchange, the water relations, and the primary production on a desert site (Moore, White & Caldwell, 1973). How far the climatic factors are involved can be shown when diffusion resistances

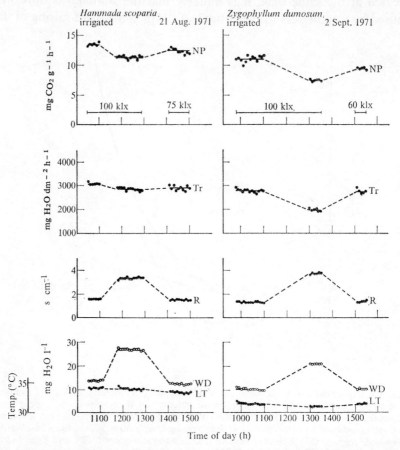

Fig. 5.4. The changes in net photosynthesis (NP), transpiration (Tr) and total diffusion resistance (R) as a response to a change in water vapour concentration difference (WD) between the leaf and the air in the irrigated *Hammada scoparia* and the irrigated *Zygophyllum dumosum*. The leaf temperature is kept constant. (After Schulze *et al.*, 1972*a*.)

are calculated from the meteorological data and from the temperature and humidity experiments. This curve can be compared with the actual observations of gas exchange under natural conditions in the field. Fig. 5.5*a* shows the change in stomatal aperture of apricot leaves caused by a pronounced change in water vapour concentration difference ($\Delta r_{(WD)}$)

112

during a dry desert day. At this plant–water status the leaf temperature causes stomatal opening, reducing the humidity-induced stomatal closure ($\Delta r_{(LT)}$, hatched area). The predicted change in diffusion resistance (r_p, half-hour intervals) is almost identical with the observed one (r_o) at least for the first part of the day. It is obvious that the large noon depression of CO_2 uptake and the following second peak are primarily caused by the climate-controlled stomatal reaction. The water status of the leaf is stabilized during the day. The significance of the climate-controlled stomatal response become seven more evident when comparing a dry day (Fig. 5.5a) with a moist day (Fig. 5.5b). For that day the humidity-controlled stomatal closure is almost compensated by temperature-induced stomatal opening. The predicted and observed resistance values are low, making a high rate of photosynthesis possible throughout the day. The transpiration loss leads to a permanent increasing water stress. Starting from the same morning value as in Fig. 5.5a, the pressure potential in the xylem reaches as low values as on the dry day.

Under the same plant–water stress, two distinctly different daily courses of net photosynthesis are possible. These results demonstrate the great influence of the external climatic conditions on the daily course of CO_2 uptake for the dry and hot desert habitat, although Bamberg & Kleinkopf (p. 689) have shown that there are differences among species, some not showing a two-peaked curve. Internal factors probably have the greatest effect on the range within which the diffusion resistance is variable by external control. They also determine the maximum rates of CO_2 uptake in the morning, which decreases throughout the season (Fig. 5.2; Oechel *et al.*, 1972; Hellmuth, 1968; Slatyer, 1957). But even under extreme water stress, Moore *et al.* (1972) found a controlled transpiration rate at -115 bar, and Kappen *et al.* (1972) showed that *A. herba-alba* still is photosynthetically active at -123 bar.

The daily gain of net photosynthesis per gram dry weight, together with the minimal daily pressure potential in the xylem, are shown in Fig. 5.6 for *H. scoparia* and *Z. dumosum* for the vegetation period. *H. scoparia* has high rates of CO_2 uptake almost throughout the year. The minimum water potential is the same in June, at a high daily rate of CO_2 uptake, as in September at a low one. This depression is caused not by water stress, but by the climatic conditions and by the increasing dry weight of the xeromorphic structures in the photosynthesizing organs during the year. There are days of low and high CO_2 gain

113

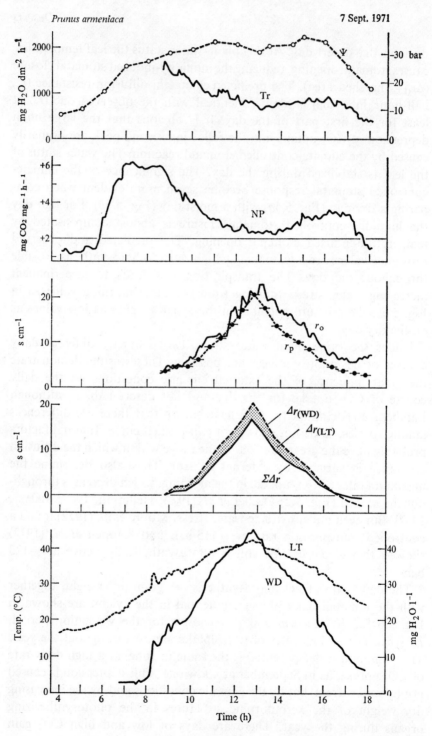

Fig. 5.5. (a)

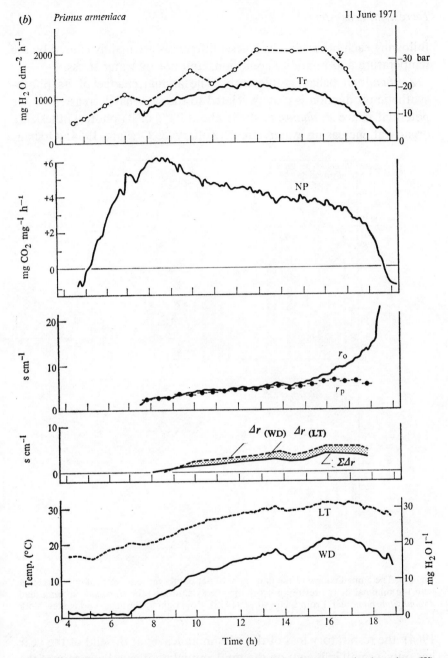

Fig. 5.5. (a),(b) The daily course of the negative hydrostatic pressure in the xylem (Ψ), transpiration (Tr), net photosynthesis (NP), observed values of total diffusion resistance (r_o), predicted values of total diffusion resistance (r_p), change in diffusion resistance caused by changes in the water vapour concentration difference between the leaf and the surrounding air ($\Delta r_{(WD)}$), change in diffusion resistance caused by changes in leaf temperature ($\Delta r_{(LT)}$), total change in diffusion resistance caused by changes in leaf temperature and water vapour concentration difference ($\Sigma\Delta r$), leaf temperature (LT), and water vapour concentration difference between the leaf and the surrounding air (WD). From Lange *et al.* (1975). Copyright © Springer-Verlag New York Inc.

following each other closely. These differences are mainly caused by the temperature and humidity conditions and not by water stress.

Z. *dumosum* behaves differently. The annual change of its photosynthetic production is closely related to the seasonal decrease in water potential. Since Z. *dumosum* sheds about 90 % of its photosynthesizing organs at increasing water stress (Zohary & Orshan, 1954; Orshan,

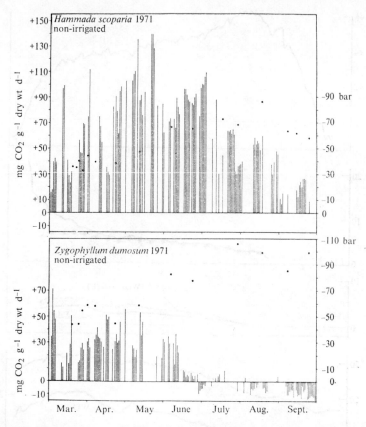

Fig. 5.6. The annual course of the daily gain of net photosynthesis (vertical lines) together with the minimal daily pressure potential in the xylem (dots) for *Hammada scoparia* and *Zygophyllum dumosum*. From Lange *et al.* (1975). Copyright © Springer-Verlag New York Inc.

1964), the respiratory loss of the remaining leaves at the end of the year has only a small influence on the total annual photosynthetic gain of the plant. The main proportion of the total annual CO_2 gain is photosynthesized in the time before leaf-shedding, during the time of a high photosynthetic activity until June. However, during this time of high metabolic activity the large effect of the temperature and humidity-controlled stomatal reactions is also obvious from the change in CO_2 gain from one day to the next. The reduction of the daily CO_2 gain through climate-controlled stomatal reactions is certainly limiting primary production, but it is absolutely necessary for keeping the water economy of the plants in balance (Evenari & Richter, 1937–8; Evenari, Shanan & Tadmor, 1971; Orshan, 1973). Under the stress conditions of the desert this mechanism stabilizes the plant's water relations over a long dry period. Without this, even a limited primary production would be impossible.

References

Adams, M. S. & Strain, B. R. (1968). Photosynthesis in stems and leaves of *Cercidium floridum*: spring and summer diurnal field response and relation to temperature. *Oecologia Plantarum*, **3**, 285–97.

Björkman, O., Pearcy, R. W., Harrison, A. T. & Mooney, H. A. (1972). Photosynthetic adaptation to high temperatures: A field study in Death Valley, California. *Science*, **175**, 786–9.

Evenari, M. & Richter, R. (1937–8). Physiological–ecological investigations in the wilderness of Judaea. *J. Linnean Soc. London*, **51**, 333–51.

Evenari, M., Shanan, L. & Tadmor, N. (1971). *The Negev. The Challenge of a Desert.* Cambridge, Mass., Harvard University Press.

Goodman, P. J. & Caldwell, M. M. (1971). Shrub ecotypes in a salt desert. *Nature*, **232**, 571–2.

Hammouda, M. & Lange, O. L. (1962). Zur Hitzeresistenz der Blätter höherer Pflanzen in Abhängigkeit von ihrem Wassergehalt. *Naturwissenschaften*, **21**, 500–1.

Hellmuth, E. O. (1968). Eco-physiological studies on plants in arid and semi-arid regions in Western Australia. I. Autecology of *Rhagodia baccata* (Labill.) Moq. *J. Ecol.* **56**, 319–44.

Hellmuth, E. O. (1969). Eco-physiological studies in plants in arid and semi-arid regions in Western Australia. II. Field physiology of *Acacia craspedo-carpa* F. Muell. *J. Ecol.* **57**, 613–34.

Hellmuth, E. O. (1971). Eco-physiological studies on plants in arid and semi-arid regions in Western Australia. III. Comparative studies on photosynthesis, respiration and water relations of ten arid zone and two semi-arid zone plants under winter and late summer climatic conditions. *J. Ecol.* **59**, 225–59.

Hershfield, D. M. (1962). A note on the variability of annual precipitation. *J. Appl. Meteorol.* **1**, 575–8.

Kappen, L. (1966). Der Einfluß des Wassergehaltes auf die Widerstandsfähigkeit von Pflanzen gegenüber hohen und tiefen Temperaturen, untersucht an Blättern einiger Farne und von *Ramonda myconi*. *Flora* (*Jena*), Abt. B, **156**, 427–45.

117

Kappen, L., Lange, O. L. Schulze, E.-D., Evenari, M. & Buschbom, U. (1972). Extreme water stress and photosynthetic activity of the desert plant *Artemisia herba-alba* Asso. *Oecologia (Berl.)*, **10**, 177–82.

Lange, O. L. (1959). Untersuchungen über Wärmehaushalt und Hitzeresistenz mauretanischer Wüsten- und Savannenpflanzen. *Flora (Jena)*, **147**, 596–651.

Lange, O. L., Koch, W. & Schulze, E.-D. (1969). CO₂-Gaswechsel und Wasserhaushalt von Pflanzen in der Negev-Wüste am Ende der Trockenzeit. *Ber. dtsch. bot. Ges.* **82**, 39–61.

Lange, O. L. & Lange, R. (1963). Untersuchungen über Blattemperaturen, Transpiration und Hitzeresistenz an Pflanzen mediterraner Standorte (Costa Brava, Spanien). *Flora (Jena)*, **153**, 387–425.

Lange, O. L., Lösch, R., Schulze, E.-D. & Kappen, L. (1971). Responses of stomata to changes in humidity. *Planta*, **100**, 76–86.

Lange, O. L., Schulze, E.-D., Kappen, L., Buschbom, U. & Evenari, M. (1975). Photosynthesis of desert plants as influenced by internal and external factors. In *Ecological Studies*, vol. 12, *Perspectives of biophysical ecology* (eds. D. M. Gates, R. B. Schmerl). Berlin, Heidelberg & New York, Springer-Verlag.

Moore, R. T., White, R. S. & Caldwell, M. M. (1973). Transpiration of *Atriplex confertifolia* and *Eurotia lanata* in relation to soil, plant, and atmospheric moisture stress. *Canadian J. Bot.* **50**, 2411–18.

Oechel, W. C., Strain, B. R. & Odening, W. R. (1972). Photosynthetic rates of a desert shrub *Larrea divaricata* Cav. under field conditions. *Photosynthetica*, **6**, 183–8.

Orshan, G. (1964). Seasonal dimorphism of desert and Mediterranean chamaephytes and their significance as a factor in their water economy. In *The water relations of plants*, eds. A. J. Rutter & F. H. Whitehead, pp. 206–22. Oxford, Blackwell.

Orshan, G. (1973). Morphological and physiological plasticity in relation to drought. In *Wildland Shrubs – Their Biology and Utilization*, USDA Forest Service General Technical Report INT–I, pp. 245–54, Ogden, Utah, Intermountain Forest and Range Experiment Station.

Pisek, A., Larcher, W., Moser, W. & Pack, I. (1969). Kardinale Temperaturbereiche und Grenztemperaturen des Lebens der Blätter verschiedener Spermatophyten. III. Temperaturabhängigkeit und optimaler Temperaturbereich der Netto-Photosynthese. *Flora (Jena)*, Abt. B, **158**, 608–30.

Schulze, E.-D., Lange, O. L., Buschbom, U., Kappen, L. & Evenari, M. (1972a). Stomatal responses to changes in humidity in plants growing in the desert. *Planta*, **108**, 259–70.

Schulze, E.-D., Lange, O. L. & Koch, W. (1972b). Ökophysiologische Untersuchungen an Wild- und Kulturpflanzen der Negev-Wüste. II. Die Wirkung der Außenfaktoren auf CO₂-Gaswechsel und Transpiration am Ende der Trockenzeit. *Oecologia (Berl.)*, **8**, 334–55.

Schulze, E.-D., Lange, O. L. & Koch, W. (1972c). Ökophysiologische Untersuchungen an Wild- und Kulturpflanzen der Negev-Wüste. III.

Tagesläufe von Nettophotosynthese und Transpiration am Ende der Trockenzeit. *Oecologia (Bler)*,. **9**, 317–40.

Schulze, E.-D., Lange, O. L., Kappen, L., Buschbom, U. & Evenari, M. (1973). Stomatal responses to changes in temperature at increasing water stress. *Planta*, **110**, 29–42.

Shanan, L., Evenari, M. & Tadmor, N. (1967). Rainfall patterns in the Central Negev Desert. *Israel Exploration Journal*, **17**, 163–84.

Slatyer, R. O. (1957). The influence of progressive increases in total soil moisture stress on transpiration, growth, and internal water relationships of plants. *Australian Journal of Biological Sciences*, **10**, 320–36.

Stocker, O. (1960). Die photosynthetischen Leistungen der Steppen- und Wüstenpflanzen. In *Handbuch der Pflanzenphysiologie*, ed. W. Ruhland, Vol. 5, pp. 460–91, Berlin, Göttingen & Heidelberg, Springer-Verlag.

Stocker, O. (1970). Der Wasser- und Photosynthesehaushalt von Wüstenpflanzen der mauretanischen Sahara. I. Regengrüne und immergrüne Bäume. *Flora (Jena)*, **159**, 539–72.

Stocker, O. (1971). Der Wasser- und Photosynthese-Haushalt von Wüstenpflanzen der mauretanischen Sahara. II. Wechselgrüne, Rutenzweig- und stammsukkulente Bäume. *Flora (Jena)*, **160**, 445–94.

Stocker, O. (1972). Der Wasser- und Photosynthesehaushalt von Wüstenpflanzen der mauretanischen Sahara. III. Kleinsträucher, Stauden und Gräser. *Flora (Jena)*, **161**, 46–110.

Troll, C. (1956). Das Wasser als pflanzengeographischer Faktor. In *Handbuch der Pflanzenphysiologie*, ed. W. Ruhland, vol. 3, pp. 750–85. Berlin, Göttingen & Heidelberg, Springer-Verlag.

Walter, H. (1960). *Einführung in die Phytologie. III. Grundlagen der Pflanzenverbreitung*. I. Teil, Standortslehre. Stuttgart, Eugen Ulmer Verlag.

Zohary, M. & Orshan, G. (1954). Ecological studies in the vegetation of the near eastern deserts. V. The Zygophylletum dumosi and its hydroecology in the Negev of Israel. *Vegetatio*, **5–6**, 340–50.

5.2. The biomass production of some higher plants in Near-Eastern and American deserts

M. EVENARI, S. BAMBERG, E.-D. SCHULZE, L. KAPPEN, O. L. LANGE & U. BUSCHBOM

One of the most outstanding adaptations of arido-active* desert plants is the continuous reduction of their metabolically active shoot surface during the dry season (Evenari, Shanan & Tadmor, 1971). This reduction is brought about in various ways (Evenari & Richter, 1937; Orshan, 1953; Evenari et al., 1971), and its magnitude varies from year to year according to the special climatic and humidity conditions of each year (Orshan & Zand, 1962). The survival value of this phenomenon is considerable during water stress since through it the water loss of the whole plant is drastically reduced, enabling the plant to use the scarce available water to maintain photosynthesis and all other metabolic functions of the reduced surfaces (Evenari & Richter, 1937; Evenari, 1953; Orshan, 1954; Zohary, 1961; Orshan, 1964; Adams & Strain, 1968; Cunningham & Strain, 1969; Lange, Koch & Schulze, 1969). But because of the reduction of the metabolically active surface, the overall dry matter production of the plant is affected, limiting growth and phytomass production even though the reduced surfaces may keep up a high rate of photosynthesis.

Table 5.1 gives an example of the biomass production in terms of standing phytomass at the time of its annual maximum (peak phytomass) of three dominant plant communities in the Negev desert (Hammadetum scopariae, Artemisietum herbae-albae, Zygophylletum dumosi) studied at the Advat Desert Station of the Hebrew University.†

The dominant arido-active dwarf shrubs and two arido-passive geophytes (Carex pachystylis and Poa sinaica) form the bulk of the phytomass. The geophyte C. pachystylis shows the highest phytomass figure. In contrast to the dwarf shrubs more than 80 % of the phytomass of the two geophytes C. pachystylis and P. sinaica is in the biomass of their below-ground or near-ground storage organs (rhizomes and bulbs) which in bad years remain completely dormant without forming any

---

* Arido-active plants: plants which are metabolically active during the dry season.
Arido-passive plants: plants dormant during the dry season.
† Our thanks are due to Professor Dr Otto Stocker, Darmstadt, for his valuable help. Additional detailed information will be published later.

Table 5.1. *Peak phytomass (dry weight in g m⁻²) of the plant communities of Avdat (Negev Highlands)*

Artemisietum I is a mixed Artemisietum–Zygophylletum, Artemisietum II a nearly pure stand of *Artemisia herba-alba*. (ap = annual growth, pp = perennial parts of the shoots)

Species	Shoot			Root	Total plant
	ap	pp	Total		
ZYGOPHYLLETUM					
Zygophyllum dumosum	9.0	54.0	63.0	54.0	117.0
Hammada scoparia	2.1	3.9	6.0	7.0	13.0
Artemisia herba-alba	0.7	0.7	1.4	1.3	2.7
Reaumuria negevensis	–	–	5.0	5.5	11.0
Gymnocarpos fruticosum	–	–	0.9	0.6	1.5
Total	–	–	76.3	68.0	145.0
ARTEMISIETUM I					
Artemisia herba-alba	17.0	18.0	35.0	32.0	67.0
Zygophyllum dumosum	7.0	35.0	42.0	38.0	80.0
Gymnocarpos fruticosum	–	–	5.0	3.0	8.0
Reaumuria negevensis	–	–	0.5	0.6	1.0
Poa sinaica	0.2	–	0.2	4.4*	5.0
Total	–	–	83.0	78.0	161.0
ARTEMISIETUM II					
Artemisia herba-alba	21.0	23.0	44.0	40.0	84.0
Reaumuria negevensis	–	–	0.3	0.3	0.6
Helianthemum kahiricum	–	–	0.2	0.2	0.4
Carex pachystylis	0.9	–	0.9	3.9†	4.8
Total	–	–	45.0	44.0	90.0
HAMMADETUM					
Hammada scoparia	12.0	23.0	35.0	37.0	72.0
Peganum harmala	–	–	15.0	1.8	17.0
Carex pachystylis	44.0	–	44.0	190.0†	234.0
Total	–	–	94.0	229.0	323.0

* Includes bulblets.   † Includes rhizomes.

green shoots or leaves. At least for the year of measurement (1971) the annuals were so few that they could be neglected.

The Hammadetum has by far the highest phytomass because as far as available water is concerned its habitat (flood plain with deep loess soil receiving a large amount of runoff from the slopes) is more favourable than the stony slopes on which the Artemisietum and Zygophylletum thrive. The nearly pure stand of *Artemisia herba-alba* (Artemisietum II) has a lower phytomass than the mixed stand (Artemisietum I) because the small *A. herba-alba* plants, even when comparatively densely spaced, have a considerably smaller total phytomass than the mixed stand of *A. herba-alba/Zygophyllum dumosum*. The dry weight of one *Z. dumosum* is about 20–40 times higher than that of one *A. herba-alba*.

The phytomass values found by Rodin, Bazilevich & Miroshnichenko (1972) for two Artemisieta with 611 and 419 g m⁻² in Syria and Algeria are considerably higher than our values. Artemisieta are basically steppical associations which reach their limit of existence in the Negev (70–80 mm annual rainfall) and are therefore least productive there.

A comparison of the above ground biomass of the Negev plants with that of other areas (Table 5.2) shows that the Negev values for the individual species are, with the exception of *P. sinaica* in the Syrian Artemisietum, and *Eurotia lanata* and *Atriplex confertifolia* in the Western Utah salt desert, more or less of the same order of magnitude as those of plants of other deserts. The difference lies in the lower *total* values of the Zygophylletum and Artemisietum of the Negev. In contrast to other regions within the Negev these two plant communities are formed only by two or three main phytomass producers, showing that the slope habitats in the Negev are very extreme ones. Slope habitats in some other desert regions in North America have similarly reduced phytomass production.

Since above-ground biomass values of 30–200 g m⁻² are thought to be typical for arid regions and 100–600 g m⁻² for semiarid areas (Bazilevich & Rodin, 1971; Noy-Meir, 1973) the figures of Table 5.2 characterize all these habitats as arid to semiarid with the two slope habitats measured in the Negev at the extreme arid end of the scale.

The total root biomass (Table 5.3) of the Negev and also of the Mojave desert vegetation types show the same relationship to each other as the above-ground biomass. The values of the Artemisieta from Algeria and Syria are relatively higher, but the total root biomass of the two communities of the Western Utah salt desert are 4.6 and 3.8 times higher respectively than the highest value found in the other deserts. Perhaps the high salinity of the Utah habitat is responsible for this fact. (*Poa sinaica* and *Carex pachystylis* were excluded from the calculation of root biomass and root–shoot ratio since comparison of geophytes with below ground storage organs with other life-forms would give a wrong picture. See also Noy-Meir (1973).)

The root–shoot ratio (Table 5.4) of the Negev plants, which according to Noy-Meir (1973) lies for desert shrubs between one and three, falls quite well into this category, as do the corresponding values found in

123

Table 5.2. *Peak above-ground biomass* ($g \; m^{-2}$) *of plants of the dominant vegetation types of the Negev desert, the North American Mojave and Utah salt desert* (*Bjerregaard, 1971*) *and two Artemisieta* (*Algeria and Syria: Rodin et al., 1972*)

NEGEV DESERT	
(80 mm annual rainfall)	
Zygophylletum	
Zygophyllum dumosum	63.0
Hammada scoparia	6.0
Artemisia herba-alba	1.4
Reaumuria negevensis	5.0
Gymnocarpos fruticosum	0.9
Total	76.3
Artemisietum I	
Artemisia herba-alba	35.0
Zygophyllum dumosum	42.0
Gymnocarpos fruticosum	5.0
Reaumuria negevensis	0.5
Poa sinaica	0.2
Total	82.7
Artemisietum II	
Artemisia herba-alba	44.0
Reaumuria negevensis	0.3
Helianthemum kahiricum	0.2
Carex pachystylis	0.9
Total	45.4
Hammadetum	
Hammada scoparia	35.0
Peganum harmala	15.0
Carex pachystylis	44.0
Total	94.0
ALGERIA	
(301 mm annual rainfall)	
Artemisietum	
Artemisia herba-alba	102.7
Anabasis oropediorum	0.8
Stipa parviflora	5.0
Stipa retorta	3.6
Forbs (perennial)	10.3
Legumes (perennial)	0.2
Grasses (perennial)	0.3
Grasses (ephemerals)	0.7
Forbs (ephemerals)	13.1
Total	136.7

SYRIA	
(120–190 mm annual rainfall)	
Artemisietum	
Artemisia sieberi	10.9
Salsola rigida	19.3
Noea mucronata	2.0
Pyrethrum sp.	0.1
Poa sinaica	230.0
Ephemerals	1.2
Total	263.5
MOJAVE DESERT	
(115 mm annual rainfall)	
Terrace vegetation	
Ephedra nevadensis	16.3
Ambrosia dumosa	40.1
Krameria parvifolia	26.7
Larrea tridentata	46.6
Lycium andersonii	35.5
Lycium pallidum	8.9
Rest	4.8
Total	178.9
Annuals	0.6
SLOPE VEGETATION	
Ephedra nevadensis	9.3
Ambrosia dumosa	20.1
Krameria parvifolia	26.3
Larrea tridentata	51.1
Lycium andersonii	43.9
Lycium pallidum	2.4
Rest	3.4
Total	156.5
Annuals	0.5
WESTERN UTAH SALT DESERT	
(200–250 mm annual rainfall)	
Eurotia lanata community	241.0
Atriplex confertifolia community	417.0

Table 5.3. *Total root biomass of various vegetation types*

Vegetation type	Location	Root biomass $(g\,m^{-2})$
Zygophylletum	Negev	68
Artemisietum I	Negev	74
Artemisietum II	Negev	41
Hammadetum	Negev	55
Artemisietum	{Algeria	282
	{Syria	348
Terrace vegetation	Mojave	187
Slope vegetation	Mojave	158
Eurotia lanata community	Western Utah salt desert	1607
Artiplex confertifolia community	Western Utah salt desert	1313

Algeria and the Mojave desert. The values given for the Syrian desert plants are abnormally high and even higher than the values for the Western Utah salt desert.

In order to understand the productivity of a vegetation type, in addition to the peak phytomass, the annual dry matter production has to be measured. We give here as an example the annual above-ground production of *Z. dumosum* of the Negev (Table 5.5). The annual biomass production of the other plants is very similar.

At the beginning of the growing season the woody shoot biomass amounted to 54 g m^{-2} (see Table 5.1). Shortly after the start of the growing season the plants had produced 1.5 g m^{-2} of green shoot

Table 5.4. *Root–shoot ratio (dry weight) of some desert plants at peak phytomass development*

NEGEV DESERT		SYRIA	
Hammada scoparia	1.14	(Rodin *et al.*, 1972)	
Artemisia herba-alba	0.92	*Artemisia sieberi*	7.61
Zygophyllum dumosum	0.87	*Salsola rigida*	7.20
Reaumuria negevensis	1.10	*Noea mucronata*	6.75
		Pyrethrum sp.	8.00
WESTERN UTAH SALT DESERT			
(Bjerregaard, 1971)		MOJAVE DESERT	
Eurotia lanata	6.67	*Ephedra nevadensis*	0.84
Atriplex confertifolia	3.15	*Ambrosia dumosa*	1.16
		Krameria parvifolia	0.79
ALGERIA		*Larrea tridentata*	1.24
(Rodin *et al.*, 1972)		*Lycium andersonii*	0.84
Artemisia herba-alba	1.80	*Lycium pallidum*	1.65
Anabasis oropediorum	1.25		

biomass (*a* in Table 5.5). A few days later lignification of the newly formed biomass sets in (*b* in Table 5.5). In May the green shoot biomass reaches its peak with 4.9 g m^{-2}. This figure is nearly identical with that given by Orshan & Diskin (1967) for *Zygophyllum* of another Zygophylletum stand. A month later lignification is up to 4.8 g m^{-2}. Since 0.9 g m^{-2} of the 4.9 g m^{-2} of green shoot biomass are green stems which later lignify, this means therefore that 8.8 g m^{-2} of the above-ground biomass has been produced at the peak of development. This figure rounded up to 9 g m^{-2} appears in Table 5.1 (annual growth: ap) for *Z. dumosum* in the Zygophylletum. Towards the end of the dry season the metabolically active surface of the shoot has been reduced to 1.28 g m^{-2}. Later in the year of 1971 this reduction proceeds further and the remaining green shoot biomass approaches zero at the beginning of

Table 5.5. *Annual dry weight above-ground production* (*g m^{-2}*) *of Zygophyllum dumosum in 1971.* (a) *green photosynthesizing parts;* (b) *lignified parts*

Dates	(a)	(b)
12.III	1.54	0
25.III	2.55	0.20
7.IV	3.56	0.67
18.V	4.90	1.39
22.VI	2.95	4.80
20.VII	1.41	4.80
13.IX	1.28	4.80

the new growing season (1972). The 4.8 g m^{-2} of lignified shoot biomass formed in 1971 does not remain either. But, since the litter fall of these lignified parts is much more irregular thanth at of the green biomass, it is very difficult to provide a meaningful measure, and the question remains how much permanent shoot biomass was added in 1971 to the 54 g m^{-2} of permanent shoot biomass (pp of Table 5.1). Most possibly the real figure is much smaller than 4.8 g m^{-2}. The price of survival for desert plants and plant communities is the utter restriction of growth and production (see also Stocker, 1969).

References

Adams, M. S. & Strain, B. R. (1968). Photosynthesis in stems and leaves of *Cercidium floridum*: Spring and summer diurnal field response and relation to temperature. *Oecol. Plant*, **3**, 285–97.

Bazilevich, N. I. & Rodin, L. Ye. (1971). Geographical regularities in productivity and the circulation of chemical elements in the earth's main vegetation types. *Soviet Geography*, Review and Translation by American Geographical Society, pp. 24–53.

Bjerregaard, R. S. (1971). The nitrogen budget of two salt desert shrub communities of Western Utah. Ph.D. Thesis, Utah State University, Logan, Utah.

Cunningham, G. L. & Strain, B. R. (1969). Ecological significance of seasonal leaf variability in a desert shrub. *Ecology*, **50**, 400–8.

Evenari, M. (1953). The water balance of plants in desert conditions. *Desert Res. Proceed. Symp. Jerusalem*, 266–74.

Evenari, M. & Richter, R. (1937). Physiological–ecological investigations in the wilderness of Judaea. *J. Linnean Soc. London*, **51**, 333–51.

Evenari, M., Shanan, L. & Tadmor, N. (1971). *The Negev. The Challenge of a Desert*. Cambridge, Mass., Harvard University Press.

Lange, O. L., Koch, W. & Schulze, E.-D. (1969). CO_2-Gaswechsel und Wasserhaushalt von Pflanzen in der Negev-Wüste am Ende der Trockenzeit. *Berichte der Deutschen Botanischen Gesellschaft*, **82**, 39–61.

Noy-Meir, I. (1973). Desert ecosystems. *Ann. Rev. Ecol. Syst.* **4**, 25–52.

Orshan, G. (1953). Note on the application of Raunkiaer's system on life forms in arid regions. *Palestine Journal of Botany*, **6**, 120–2.

Orshan, G. (1954). Surface reduction and its significance as a hydroecological factor. *J. Ecol.* **42**, 442–4.

Orshan, G. (1964). Seasonal dimorphism of desert and Mediterranean chamaephytes and their significance as a factor in their water economy. In *The water relations of plants*, eds. A. J. Rutter & F. H. Whitehead, pp. 206–22, Oxford, Blackwell Scientific Publications.

Orshan, G. & Diskin, S. (1967). Seasonal changes in productivity under desert conditions. *Proc. UNESCO Symp. Ecosystems Copenhagen*, pp. 191–201.

Orshan, G. & Zand, G. (1962). Seasonal body reduction of certain desert halfshrubs. *Bull. Res. Counc. Israel*, **11D**, 35–42.

Rodin, L. E., Bazilevich, N. Z. & Miroshnichenko, T. M. (1972). Productivity and biogeochemistry of Artemisieta in the Mediterranean area. *Symp. Eco-Physiol. Found. Ecosyst. Product. Nauka, Leningrad*, pp. 193–8.

Stocker, O. (1969). Die 'Stoffproduktion' in Urwäldern und anderen Pflanzengesellschaften im Gleichgewicht. *Mitteilungen der Floristisch-soziologischen Arbeitsgemeinschaft* NF, **14**, 422–34.

Zohary, D. (1961). On hydro-ecological relations of the near east desert vegetation. In *Plant water relationship in arid and semi arid conditions*. Proceedings of the Madrid Symposium. *Arid Zone Research*, **16**, 199–212, Paris, UNESCO.

5.3. Potential photosynthesis of Central Asian desert plants

O. V. ZALENSKY

A distinctive feature of the desert biome is the often highly hetero-geneous origin of its flora. This is especially true for the Central Asian deserts,* the species of which originated in the surrounding high mountain areas and on the littorals of the ancient Tetis. Its long evolutionary history under gradually increasing xeric conditions and its large gene pool may explain the high percentage of endemics and a considerable diversity with respect to adaptive characters, both morpho-logical and physiological.

Two groups of plants can be distinguished with respect to photo-synthetic behaviour in the Karakum desert (Table 5.6). Ephemers and ephemeroids which complete their life cycle before May are char-acterized by high potential photosynthesis attaining values of 40–190 mg CO_2 g^{-1} dry matter h^{-1}. In drought-enduring shrubs and trees (*Haloxylon, Calligonum, Salsola* and *Ephedra*) the corresponding values are generally considerably lower, ranging from 10 to 40 mg CO_2 g^{-1} dry weight h^{-1}. Maximum rates of photosynthesis are attained, on the other hand, at different times of the year for the different life forms: for the ephemers and ephemeroids they coincide with the onset of fructi-fication (end-March to mid-April, in *Ferula, Carex* and *Horaninovia*), for plants completing their vegetative period at the beginning of the summer, they precede summer dormancy and partial leaf shedding (e.g. *Smirnovia, Astragalus* and *Convolvulus*), and for drought-enduring shrubs and trees they occur during the hottest and driest period of the year in the middle of June.

In the Karakum desert, the water content of the drought-enduring species is low and remains almost constant during the day, with water saturation deficits not exceeding 6–15% even on a midsummer day (sublethal saturation deficits are in the range 46–53%).

Photorespiration was only found in few species in the Karakum (*Haloxylon, Aristida, Calligonum*), as appears from the low L/D ratio

---

* Eco-physiological investigations on desert plants are carried out within the Soviet Union in (1) the sandy desert at Repetek in the South Eastern Karakum with psammo-phytic vegetation, (2) the Kyzylkum clay desert in Uzbekistan with *Artemisia* and *Salsola*, (3) the southern Tadzhikistan loess desert and (4) the cold high mountain desert of the Pamirs with *Eurotia ceratoides, Stipa glareosa* and *Acantholimon dina-persoides*.

Table 5.6. *Maximum values of photosynthesis in desert plants (south-eastern Karakum)*

Plant species	Net photosynthesis (mg CO_2 h⁻¹)			Potential photosynthesis (mg CO_2 h⁻¹)		
	g⁻¹ dry matter	dm⁻²	mg⁻¹ chlorophyll	g⁻¹ dry matter	dm⁻²	mg⁻¹ chlorophyll
Ammodendron conollyi	20	19	7.1	71	66	25
Haloxylon aphyllum	10	13	5.3	40	52	21
Haloxylon persicum	10	15	7.7	30	45	23
Salsola richteri	18	23	11	35	46	20
Calligonum caput medusae	12	18	7.5	23	35	14
Ephedra strobilacea	4	13	4.0	30	96	30
Smirnovia turkestana	40	33	19	135	110	64
Astragalus paucijugus	22	13	7.6	90	54	27
Convolvulus korolkovii	25	17	8.6	70	49	24
Heliotropium arguzioides	24	34	10	78	109	32
Jurinea derderoides	22	16	6.9	105	79	33
Aristida karelini	52	52	22	110	110	46
Ferula litwinowiana	40	40	12	115	115	35
Rheum turkestanicum	16	12		110	79	
Carex physodes	28	15		65	34	
Eminium lehmannii	18	11		110	66	
Senecio subdentatus	60	19	7.5	190	61	24
Horaninovia ulicina	25		12	40		19
Populus pruinosa	22	17	6.5	62	48	18
Tamarix ramosissima	15		4.4	40		12
Alhagi camelorum	7		1.4	35		10

Table 5.7. *Photosynthesis of desert plants in relation to temperature and irradiance (south-eastern Karakum)*

| Plant species | Temperature (°C) | | | | | | Irradiance for light saturation | |
| | Net photosynthesis | | | Potential photosynthesis | | | (cal cm⁻² min⁻¹) | (J cm⁻² min⁻¹) |
	Minimum	Optimum	Maximum	Minimum	Optimum	Maximum		
Ammodendron conollyi		22–35	33–47	0	27–45	50–55	0.8–0.9	3.35–3.77
Haloxylon aphyllum	−5	10–30	40–50	−5	20–45	48–54	0.7–0.8	2.93–3.35
Haloxylon persicum	+7	10–30	30–50	0	20–40	55	0.7–0.8	2.93–3.35
Salsola richteri		20–30	47	−2.5	25–35	50–55	0.8–0.9	3.35–3.77
Calligonum caput medusae	−2	25	42	−5	22–45	54	0.7–0.9	2.93–3.77
Ephedra strobilacea	−2.5	5–20	35	0	30	50		
Smirnovia turkestana	+2.5	20–30	37–48	−3	20–42	50–55	1.2	5.02
Astragalus paucijugus	−3	15–23	40–44	0	27–32	55	1.1	4.60
Convolvulus korolkovii	<−5	25–30	37–44	−5	25–35	55	1.3	5.44
Heliotropium arguzioides	−2.5	15–30	40–45	0	20–45	55	1.4	5.86
Aristida karelini	+4	30–40	46	<−3	25–35	55	1.4	5.86
Ferula litwinowiana	<−5	20	43–45	<−5	15–25	50		
Rheum turkestanicum	<−5	15–30	38–44	−3	20–35	55		
Carex physodes	−1.5	17–30	42	<−2.5	15–30	45–55	0.6–0.7	2.51–2.93
Senecio subdentatus	+4	12–25	35–45		25–37	50–55		
Horaninovia ulicina					25–32	55	1.1	4.60
Populus pruinosa	+5	20–28	27–45	0	30–40	55		

(ratio between $^{14}CO_2$ produced by photosynthesizing organs in the light and in the dark following photosynthetic assimilation of $^{14}CO_2$). In some species (*Atriplex dimorphostegia*), lack of photorespiration does not coincide with the presence of bundle sheath chloroplasts. Similarly, the rate of photosynthesis and the rate of photorespiration may not always be correlated. In *Aristida karelini* and *Haloxylon aphyllum*, the L/D ratios are almost the same (0.1 and 0.2) whereas the rates of photosynthesis are very different (52 and 12 mg CO_2 g^{-1} dry weight h^{-1}).

In most plants, light saturation is attained only at high irradiances (50–70% of full sun light), in others not even in full sunlight (Table 5.7). Similar behaviour has been observed in plants from the Kyzylkum and the high mountain deserts of the Pamir with respect to potential photosynthesis. The high temperature compensation point is attained in most species at between 46 °C and 54 °C, increasing about 5 °C during the dry period. In some psammophytes, in particular (*Ammodendron, Aristida, Horaninovia, Convolvulus, Haloxylon*), potential photosynthesis becomes nil at 55–56 °C. The high temperature compensation point for net photosynthesis, on the other hand, is reached at temperatures (40–51 °C) rarely attained in the natural environment.

Maximum values of net and potential photosynthesis are in most cases observed at 28–30 °C, although the range of optimal temperatures may be large in many species (10–30 °C in *Haloxylon aphyllum*). These values, however, may vary quite significantly with time during the vegetative period.

Thermostability of photosynthesis seems to be a characteristic feature of desert plants. In spite of large differences with respect to genetic origin and physiology, whether characterized by high or low rates of photosynthesis, they are all equally adapted to the particular temperature regime of their habitat. This high thermostability together with a capacity to maintain a sufficient CO_2 exchange balance, constitutes an essential basis for survival under desert conditions.

5.4.Primary production of lower plants (lichens) in the desert and its physiological basis

L. KAPPEN, O. L. LANGE, E.-D. SCHULZE, M. EVENARI & U. BUSCHBOM

Non-vascular cryptogams are small and therefore generally not very apparent in the vegetation. Their importance in the cycles between the aerial and the edaphic sphere, as well as for the fertility of the soils, especially for the desert, has been repeatedly remarked (Cameron, 1961). Terrestrial algae are widely distributed in most of the deserts, living on soil (Cameron, 1964), below translucent rock particles (Vogel, 1955), or in rock fissures, and even within the peripheral layers inside the rocks (Friedman, Lipkin & Ocampo-Paus, 1967). The fungal population can also be well developed in a desert (Cameron, 1972). Loess soils, rich in organic material, show a wide diversity of species (Borut, 1960). Apart from several soil microbiological investigations (Cameron, 1972) the biomass production of lower plants in deserts has been rarely determined. One of the few investigations was done by Novichkova-Ivanova (1972), who found that soil algae in Central Asian deserts were present in high amounts.

In contrast to free-living algae and fungi, the lichens can be very apparent in the desert. Locally their abundant growth seems to show that in this habitat the symbiosis between alga and fungus is especially favourable for their productivity. In the cold desert continent of Antarctica, lichens are the most obvious representatives of the vegetation (Rudolph, 1967). In the Namib desert, lichens locally dominate the vegetation (Walter, 1936; Logan, 1960). In the Lomas of the Chilenian desert the lichens even serve as food for the Guanacos (Follmann, 1964).

In an area of 50–80 mm annual rainfall, as, for example, the Central Negev and parts of the Northern Sinai, where higher plants are very scattered, a considerable lichen vegetation is developed. It is represented by a high frequency of endolithic species and by epilithic crustaceous lichens consisting primarily of the genera *Aspicilia, Buellia, Caloplaca, Diploschistes* and others (Galun & Reichert, 1960; Galun, 1970). Even fruticose forms such as *Teloschistes lacunosus* (Rup.) Sav. and *Ramalina maciformis* (Del.) Nyl. are present. Investigations were carried out with representative species of this lichen vegetation.

Physiological bases of photosynthetic production

One basic requirement for survival in the desert is a high resistance to extreme environmental conditions. In this respect lichens are remarkably well adapted to a desert habitat. Lange (1969) found that the photosynthetic activity of *R. maciformis* recovered fully within a short time after severe artificial desiccation for almost one year. The thalli were better able to survive a strong desiccation (1 % water content based on

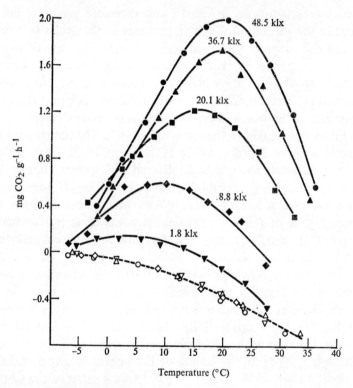

Fig. 5.7. Net photosynthesis (black symbols) of *R. maciformis* at different light intensities and temperatures (abscissa) and dark respiration (white symbols) at different temperatures. Rates of CO_2-exchange in mg CO_2 g^{-1} h^{-1} are given on the ordinate. The water relations were always kept optimal. (After Lange, 1969.)

dry weight) than exposure to a higher humidity (15 % water content). In the desiccated state *R. maciformis* tolerates heating up to 65 °C (Lange, 1969). Thus, this lichen is able to survive almost any naturally occurring hot and dry period.

However, when the thalli are hydrated and active they become heavily damaged by an exposure of one hour at 38 °C (Lange, 1965). Fig. 5.7

shows the relationship between net CO_2 exchange and temperature under various light intensities. It appears that *R. maciformis* is adapted more to cooler than to hot conditions. Higher temperatures thus lead to a decrease of photosynthetic gain and finally to injury of the metabolically active lichen.

The lichens do not take up water from the ground. The water content of the thalli always tends to get into equilibrium with the water vapour

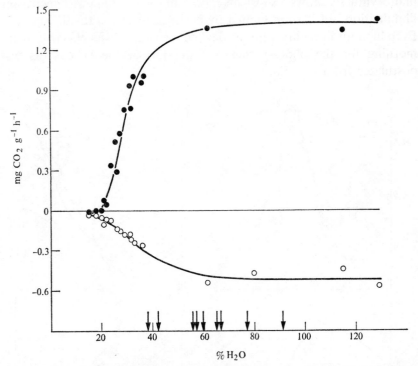

Fig. 5.8. Net photosynthesis (●) and dark respiration (○) in relation to water content (per cent of dry weight) of *R. maciformis* under experimental conditions: 10 klx, 10 °C. Arrows indicate water contents determined from thalli in their natural environment after dew fall. (After Lange, 1969.)

conditions of the surrounding air. Photosynthetic activity already begins at a very low water content. Fig. 5.8 shows that at 10 °C and 10 klx there is a moisture compensation point for CO_2 exchange at approximately 20% relative water content based on dry matter. This water content already could be induced by a relative air humidity of 80%, which corresponded to a water potential of about −285 bar. At 60% water content photosynthesis reaches a saturation level. This water content can easily be provided solely by dewfall (see Fig. 5.8: arrows).

135

Moistening of the lichens by rainfall is too sporadic in the desert and can hardly provide for growth of the lichens. Increases in air humidity and dew fall occur regularly in deserts, such as in the Negev, especially in spring, fall and winter. The possibility that lichen growth depends predominantly on the frequency of dewfall, fog and high air humidity was demonstrated in their natural habitats by Lange, Schulze & Koch (1970*a*). By means of natural dew imbibition the general course of photosynthesis shows a short steep peak in the morning with increasing illumination but is soon limited by desiccation of the thalli (Fig. 5.9). Even high air humidity without dew condensation was effective in the morning for the photosynthetic production of the lichens; as was postulated from Fig. 5.8.

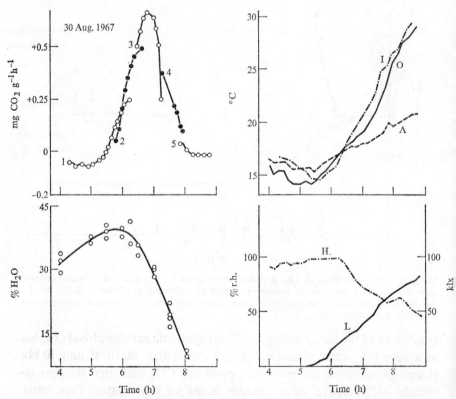

Fig. 5.9. Apparent CO_2-exchange rates of *R. maciformis* due to dew imbibition in the morning in the natural environment. The numbers near the curves indicate the parts of different samples sequentially measured. Water content is shown below. Also shown are: temperatures of thalli inside (I) and of thalli outside (O) the Siemens plant chamber, air temperature (A), relative humidity (H), and light intensity (L). (After Lange, Schulze & Koch, 1970.)

If later, during the hot desert day, humid conditions or rain-fall were simulated by spraying with water, the lichens had no photosynthetic gain, as also would be expected from Fig. 5.7. Only an intensively raised respiration was measured until the thalli became dry again. Thus, inactivation of gas exchange due to the period of desiccation, as on a normal desert day, is most favourable for the CO_2 balance of the lichens. Photosynthesis was measured on several lichen species and all showed similar results (Lange, Schulze & Koch, 1970*b*).

The dependence of photosynthetic production on the exposure of the habitat

Since dew fall seems to be an essential parameter for productivity of the lichens, measurements of dew imbibition were made by means of a recording Hiltner dew balance (Fa. Thies, Göttingen) at four exposures around the top of a typical desert mesa in the Central Negev.

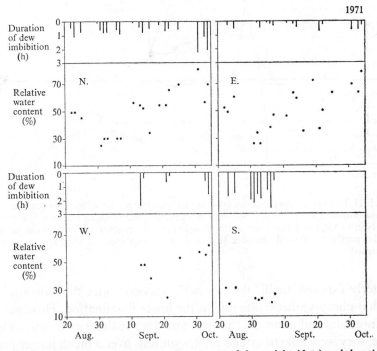

Fig. 5.10. Amount of dew water content in per cent of dry weight (dots) and duration in hours (small columns) of dew imbibition in the thalli of *R. maciformis* according to recordings by a Hiltner dew balance in the fall of 1971. The four main expositions around the top of a mesa about 7 km SSW. of Advat, Negev, where the balances were installed, are indicated by the symbols N., E., W., S. No measurements were made in W. exposure from 20 Aug. to 10 Sept. and in S. exposure from 11 Sept. to 2 Oct.

137

F

Thalli exposed to the east showed a slightly higher maximum increase of fresh weight in the morning than those exposed to the other directions (Fig. 5.10). Consequently, one would expect the lichen growth to be most abundant on the slopes of eastern exposure.

Photosynthesis measurements, using two Siemens plant chambers, one exposed to the north and the other to the east, show that lichens, equally moistened with dew, have quite different patterns of CO_2 exchange according to the exposure (Fig. 5.11). In contrast to the

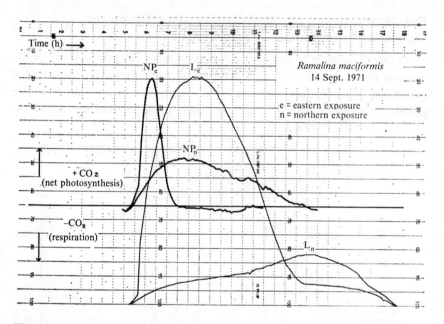

Fig. 5.11. Recording chart showing apparent CO_2-exchange rates of almost equal samples of *R. maciformis* equally dew-imbibed in plant chambers, one of which was exactly exposed to the North (NP_n) and the other to the East (NP_e). The courses of illumination intensities in the northerly exposed chamber (L_n) and in the east exposed chamber (L_e) are also presented.

easterly exposed thalli, the northerly exposed ones did not attain as high a photosynthetic rate due to the lower illumination. However, the diffuse solar radiation did not heat and dry the thalli as rapidly. Therefore, they were able to extend photosynthesis over a much longer period of time. An analysis of twelve dew events in September 1971 indicates that the mean photosynthetic gain of northerly exposed *R. maciformis* was 250% of that obtained from those with easterly exposition. Here, the thalli had a higher but less extended rate of photosynthesis. Fig. 5.10

shows that the smaller amount of dew in the lichens of western exposure remains in the thalli for longer periods than on the northern exposure. This was surprisingly similar to the southerly exposed site, where the dew fall is smallest but long-lasting on a low level.

Fig. 5.12 shows the pattern of the lichen vegetation on a desert mesa in terms of species composition and frequency. The abundance of species and the amount of biomass was greatest for a northerly exposure, which can be interpreted as a result of the long-lasting effects of dew imbibition. On the eastern exposure the striking decrease of lichen

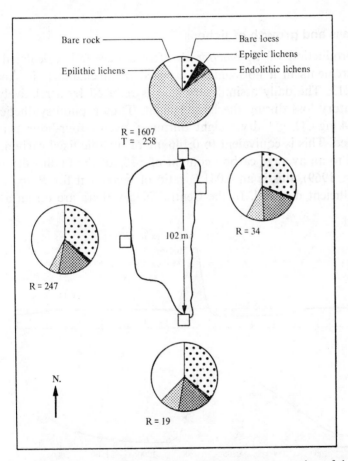

Fig. 5.12. Cover of lichen vegetation around the four main compass points of the top of the mesa 7 km SSW. of Avdat, Negev. In the circles the sectors indicate the relation between rock and loess (heavy lines) and the relative covering by different growth forms of lichens on the rock surfaces and on the loess ground in areas of 60 m². The numbers of specimens of fruticose lichens as *R. maciformis* (R) and *Teloschistes lacunosus* (T) are shown below the circles.

production and the high amount of bare rock is due to the short periods of dew availability. It is possible that the endolithic species dominating here benefit more from the dew which has trickled into the rock. On the westerly sites the conditions will cause similar production and vegetation patterns as for the easterly exposed sites. The higher number of specimens of *R. maciformis* show an overlapping influence of the north. In the southern exposure the production of fruticose lichens appears to be near the borderline. However, the pattern of endolithic and epilithic species can be interpreted by a low but sufficiently long-lasting dew gain.

Biomass and growth of lichens

The production of *R. maciformis* after a dew fall, calculated from measurements in a horizontally exposed plant chamber, is shown in Fig. 5.13. The daily assimilatory gain is reduced by a relatively high respiratory loss during the humid night. Thus a photosynthetic yield of 0.54 mg CO_2 g^{-1} dry weight during a twenty-four-hour period is obtained. This is equivalent to 0.146 mg of organic fixed carbon. With regard to an average carbon content of 34% of the thallus dry matter (Lange, 1969), this is an 0.041% ratio of increment for *R. maciformis* per sufficient dew fall. In the Central Negev there are on an average

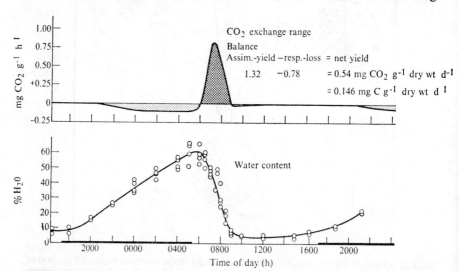

Fig. 5.13. Apparent CO_2-exchange rate during 24 h in September 1967 and calculation of the daily balance and carbon gain of *R. maciformis*. The curve of CO_2-exchange rate is a result of several fragmentary curves (cf. Fig. 5.11). Water content of the thalli in per cent of dry weight is shown below. (After Lange, Schulze & Koch, 1970.)

198 dew events per annum. If one assumes such mean dew fall conditions as shown above, a yearly increment of the thallus of 8.4% would be possible. Consequently on a dew fall basis only, a small thallus might grow ten-fold within a period of about thirty years. On an average of several places with abundant lichen growth, there is an estimated biomass of 73 g dry matter of *R. maciformis* per m² of the tested area (i.e. 28.5 g of organic bound carbon).

Crustose lichens from the Negev desert show similar productivity after dew imbibition as *R. maciformis*. This follows from the maximum photosynthetic rates of six species ranging between 0.6 and 2.21 mg CO_2 dm^{-2} h^{-1}. The primary production was evaluated from direct growth measurements over several years. The average yearly radial increment of *Caloplaca aurantia* (Pers.) Hellb. in the Negev was approximately 0.6 mm (Lange & Evenari, 1971). The average yearly production per unit of the actively growing area of the crustose thalli of 5–10% corresponds well to the production of the differently shaped *R. maciformis*. This annual growth is even more than that of lichens from alpine habitats and is comparable to that of species in temperate environments.

The biomass of crustose lichens was measured on several northerly exposed rocks of a desert mesa in the Negev. *Diploschistes calcareus* Stein., which is common here, covers around 24% of the rock surface with a compact mass of hyphae and algae. On an average 311.8 g of thallus dry matter can be found per m². However, because the crustose thalli are interspersed with a high amount of inorganic material, the amount of crude ash of 54.9% of the dry matter must be subtracted and thus a biomass of 140.6 g m^{-2} is obtained. Besides *D. calcareus*, other crustose species mostly with a less compact biomass cover 62% of the northerly exposed rock surface. Their total biomass per m² may be approximately two or three times of that calculated for *D. calcareus*.

Conclusions

These preliminary biomass measurements provide only a first estimation. They need to be extended in order to obtain a more precise concept of biomass production of lichens in a desert. In extreme environments, where there is generally a low productivity of higher plant biomass, the production of slowly growing plants such as the lichens, appears to be considerable. The ability of the poikilohydric lichens to fall into an anabiotic state for either short- or long-term periods, when conditions are unfavourable, makes respiratory loss minimal. Their capability of being rapidly activated when air humidity rises above a certain level or dew condensation moistens the thalli is a very advantageous adaptation to the desert conditions. Precipitation is of little importance to lichen existence in such an environment. Above all factors, the frequency, intensity and persistence of dew in the early morning and, in some deserts also, fog are decisive for lichen growth. In this environment the standing biomass per unit area is locally as high as that of higher plants (cf. 5.2 of this chapter). But because lichens depend on special microclimatic conditions, their productivity changes markedly with the exposure of the habitat.

References

Borut, S. (1960). An ecological and physiological study on soil fungi of the northern Negev (Israel). *Research Council of Israel Bulletin*, **8D**, 65–80.

Cameron, R. E. (1961). Algae of the Sonoran Desert in Arizona. Ph.D. Dissertation. University of Arizona.

Cameron, R. E. (1964). Terrestrial algae of southern Arizona. *Transactions of the American Microbiological Society*, **83**, 212–18.

Cameron, R. E. (1972). A comparison of soil microbial ecosystems in hot, cold and polar desert regions. In *Eco-physiological Foundation of Ecosystems Productivity in Arid Zone*, ed. L. E. Rodin, pp. 185–92. Leningrad, USSR Academy of Sciences.

Follmann, G. (1964). Nebelflechten als Futterpflanzen der Küstenguanacos. *Die Naturwissenschaften*, **51**, 19–20.

Friedmann, I., Lipkin, T. & Roseli Ocampo-Paus (1967). Desert algae of the Negev (Israel). *Phycologia*, **6**, 185–95.

Galun, M. (1970). *The lichens of Israel*. Jerusalem, The Israel Academy of Sciences and Humanities.

Galun, M. & Reichert, I. (1960). A study of lichens of the Negev. *The Bulletin of the Research Council of Israel*, **9D**, 127–48.

Lange, O. L. (1965). Der CO_2-Gaswechsel von Flechten nach Erwärmung im feuchten Zustand. *Berichte der deutschen botanischen Gesellschaft*, **78**, 441–54.

Lange, O. L. (1969). Experimentell-ökologische Untersuchungen an Flechten der Negev-Wüste. I. CO_2-Gaswechsel von *Ramalina maciformis* (Del.) Bory unter kontrollierten Bedingungen im Laboratorium. *Flora (Jena)*, **158**, 324–59.

Lange, O. L. & Evenari, M. (1971). Experimentell-ökologische Untersuchungen an Flechten der Negev-Wüste. IV. Wachstumsmessungen an *Caloplaca aurantia* (Pers.) Hellb. *Flora (Jena)*, **160**, 100–4.

Lange, O. L., Schulze, E.-D. & Koch, W. (1970a). Experimentell-ökologische Untersuchungen an Flechten der Negev-Wüste. II. CO_2-Gaswechsel und

Wasserhaushalt von *Ramalina maciformis* am natürlichen Standort während der sommerlichen Trockenperiode. *Flora (Jena)*, **159**, 38–62.

Lange, O. L., Schulze, E.-D. & Koch, W. (1970*b*). Experimentell-ökologische Untersuchungen an Flechten der Negev-Wüste. III. CO_2-Gaswechsel und Wasserhaushalt von Krusten- und Blattflechten am natürlichen Standort während der sommerlichen Trockenperiode. *Flora (Jena)*, **159**, 525–8.

Logan, R. F. (1960). The central Namib Desert, South West Africa. *National Academy of Sciences/National Research Council, Publication 758 (ONR Foreign Field Research Program Report, 9)* 162pp.

Novichkova-Ivanova, L. N. (1972). Soil algae of Middle Asia Deserts. In *Eco-Physiological Foundation of Ecosystems Productivity in Arid Zone*, ed. L. E. Rodin, pp. 180–1. Leningrad, USSR Academy of Sciences.

Rudolph, E. D. (1967). Lichen distribution. In *Terrestrial life of Antarctica*, ed. V. L. Bushnell. *Antarctic Map Folio* Ser. 5, pp. 9–11. New York, American Geophysical Society.

Vogel, S. (1955). Niedere 'Fensterpflanzen' in der südafrikanischen Wüste. Eine ökologische Schilderung. *Beitr. Biol. Pflanzen*, **31**, 45–135.

Walter, H. (1936). Die ökologischen Verhältnisse in der Namib-Nebelwüste (Südwestafrika). *Jahrbuch für Wissenschaftliche Botanik*, **84**, 58–222.

6. Productivity of agricultural ecosystems

R. S. LOOMIS & P. A. GERAKIS

Agricultural ecosystems differ from more natural systems in a number of ways which strongly influence our approach to measuring and interpreting primary production. Our objectives in evaluating primary production data lie in two general areas. In this brief review, we will focus on one of these, the assessment of genotype–environment interactions, to see if certain broad generalizations can be reached regarding domesticated species. The second area involves the detailed understanding of production processes and is beyond our resources of time and space.

An examination of agricultural productivities on a global basis reveals several levels for syntheses. However, agricultural yields are highly variable and commercial production in a particular region seldom provides a clear measure of either genotypic or environmental potentials. Such data are confounded by a series of cultural and economic constraints for the utilization of particular crop systems and for minimizing the influence of limiting factors. Even within uniform social, soil and climatic environments there are large differences in the skill of individual growers in achieving production potentials. It would be well to look at some examples of these characteristics before proceeding further.

Characteristics of agricultural systems

Profitable cropping systems are usually extended geographically to their environmental limits before being replaced by better adapted systems. At the limits, production will be considerably less than the potential and may be distorted by adjustments which are made to avoid environmental stress. The history of research in agricultural physiology and ecology and in breeding is an elegant record of the emphasis on resistance or tolerance to frost, drought, salinity, heat and chilling. While the pressure on environmental limits is very evident, farmers operate rather conservatively with inputs and decisions (on locations, varieties and dates) designed as much to give a high probability of success as to maximize production from the resources at hand.

F*

Primary production data are also influenced by the fact that agricultural systems are exploited through the periodic removal of portions of the primary production. The export of economic yield represents material drains, particularly of inorganic nutrients, and the degree and manner of replacement differ for every system. A grazing system offers rather tight nutrient recycling with minimum export whereas the 'refuging' (Hamilton & Watt, 1970) system of the giant, centralized feedlots of North America become massive nutrient sinks with little recycling economically feasible. A California lot with 60000 beef animals fed out each year may occupy only 120 ha. But more than 1600 t (tonnes) of nitrogen drawn from over 20000 ha of widely dispersed crop lands may be excreted in the lot each year.

Intensification of crop production can be achieved by reducing limitations imposed by nutrient and water resources. The tactics employed vary widely for different cultures: additional external fossil energy inputs (chemical fertilizers and pesticides, tractor power, pumped water) may be used where the cost of labor is high relative to the cost of energy; while additional labor (recycling of animal dung, hand weeding, and transplanting) might be used where labor is inexpensive relative to energy. The agricultural systems of Europe and North America have exploded in their use of fossil energies during the past forty years. In mechanized American corn production, 2.5–4J of food energy are returned for each J of fuel energy input (P. R. Stout, personal communication; Pimental *et al.* 1973). Since all agricultural systems seem to fall within a single technological continuum, we can expect advances and retreats in productivity of each system as energy and labor supplies change.

The intensification of agricultural systems is also heavily influenced by man–land ratios and the associated relative values of agricultural products. As a single example, human diets in North America derive two-thirds of the daily protein intake from animal products because of a highly favorable man–land ratio (1.5 cultivated ha cap^{-1}). The proportion of diet energy drawn from animals is much greater than in Western Europe yet because of the extensive pasturage available very few pastures are managed as intensively as in Europe, and yields even in favorable climates are typically lower than in Britain and the Netherlands.

What we have said is that, in crop distributions and in the use of labor and capital, agricultural systems are operated so as to optimize economic returns rather than biological productivity. This is also true in other

146

aspects such as the choice of plant spacings. Usually only a portion of the plant (e.g. fruit, roots or tubers) has economic value and plant spacings are chosen so as to provide high yields of this portion, and the density is generally much lower than the optimum for primary productivity. Maize (*Zea mays* L.) provides a good example: forage yields and primary productivity are generally maximized at densities of 200000 plants ha^{-1} or more. At this density, intraplant competition is so severe that the plants may be barren of grain; maximum grain yield is obtained with only 40000 to 70000 plants ha^{-1}. This situation is especially common with horticultural crops where, because of their relatively high value, greater emphasis is given to product quality. Only a few such as potato (*Solanum tuberosum* L.) are cultivated so as to approach their production potential.

Finally, it might seem that crop management activities would effectively conceal major aspects of the genotype–environment interactions since practices such as fertilization, irrigation, and pest and weed control are designed for this purpose. There are real advantages from minimizing genotype–environment interactions so that similar high yields can be achieved year after year. However, this is seldom done in a genetic sense except for incorporation of resistance to environmental extremes and pests. Even in the sugar industry where markets and processing capacities are relatively fixed, the varieties employed are designed to exploit through higher yields the occasionally more favorable environments. This is particularly evident with cereal grains where there is a strong trend for the newer cultivars to be more opportunistic in behavior, i.e. as good yielding in poor environments as older strains and much better yielding under the best circumstances.

An ecological survey of agricultural productivity

We have outlined what are perhaps the main issues to be considered in ecological assessments of agricultural productivity. If one wants to determine a global carbon budget for such systems, the only feasible way is to utilize crop reporting information on area and total economic production and apply corrections for noneconomic production. Further subdivision of such data to show the degree to which nutrition, water, cultivar or climate is limiting has been attempted only for specific crops and regions. However, by limiting our attention to maximum crop yields, certain differences in biological capabilities are revealed.

We have attempted such a survey. The hypotheses to be tested were

147

that C_4- and C_3-species, and indeterminate and determinate growth habits, would perform differently in different climates. No really suitable climate index is available. On the basis that solar altitude is related to maximum levels of radiant flux and hence to a possible relative advantage of the C_4-species, we used latitude as our index. An implicit assumption of considering only maximum yields for a given latitude is that only the optimum combinations of growing season, altitude, nutrition, moisture and other factors are recorded. An analysis of factor gradients within latitudes was not attempted.

As Westlake (1963) found, careful studies of primary production in agricultural fields are rare and seldom represent maximum production situations. The Japanese IBP work (Togari, Murata & Saeki, 1969, 1970,1971,1972) is by far the most extensive. Measurements of standing crop (above ground parts, except where tubers or storage roots are considered) are more common but most observations of high performance involve only economic yield. For example, the greatest verified yield of potatoes from a commercial field is 83.8 t ha⁻¹ of fresh tubers (Delta area, California; O. A. Lorenz, personal communication, U. C. Davis; Anon, 1969) whereas the most detailed ecological data come from a production study which produced 38 t ha⁻¹ of fresh tubers (Lorenz, 1944). The 38 t crop produced 10.0 t ha⁻¹ of dry matter including 0.1 t ha⁻¹ of roots and 1.0 t ha⁻¹ of ash. Partition factors are reasonably constant for potato so by applying Lorenz's factors to the record 83 t crop, we can conclude that total dry matter production was near 22 t ha⁻¹ and that its mean growth rate was about 17 g m⁻² d⁻¹.

Partition factors are also needed to estimate total standing crop for the record commercial crop of maize, 16.3 t ha⁻¹ of dry grain (La Salle, Michigan). This is somewhat more than the 14.5 t ha⁻¹ (assuming grain/ear = 0.8) achieved in the Japanese maximum production trials at a similar latitude (Togari, Murata & Saeki, 1969). Maize grain is commonly about 0.5 of the above ground dry matter so the 16 t record corresponds to about 32 t ha⁻¹ of total dry matter with a mean growth rate near 27 g m⁻² d⁻¹.

Such partition factors are reasonably well documented and conservative values may be used. Fewer data are available on root production. Fortunately, fibrous root production by intensely managed annual crops usually amounts to only 5–10% of the total primary production (e.g. Togari, Murata & Saeki, 1972). By ignoring fibrous roots (and discarded parts) we greatly facilitate a broad survey without introducing appreciable error. This would not be true for crops grown under moisture or nutrient limitations where fibrous roots may represent a much larger fraction of the total biomass. Similarly we have considered only dry matter production. Mineral nutrients commonly constitute 5–10% of dry matter. While not organic and thus of photosynthetic origin, they do represent an essential physiological component of living plants and detailed analyses are rare. A somewhat similar problem arises in relation to energy content but since the heats of combustion of dry matter from annual crop plants vary little from 17 kJ g^{-1} except

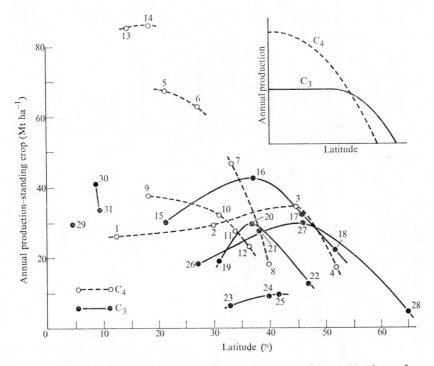

Fig. 6.1. Annual standing crop production by various cultivated crops. Numbers refer to entries in Table 6.1. The inset is a summary hypothesis of the relationships shown.

for oil seeds (Lieth, 1968) there is little to be gained from independent conversions to an energy basis. Also, some of the major energy costs of plant growth such as nitrate reduction may take place photosynthetically without an intermediate carbon assimilation step. Thus, none of the alternative bases for expressing production (dry matter, organic matter, carbon, and energy) is uniquely the best index of net photosynthesis.

The results of our annual productivity survey are presented in Fig. 6.1. The sources and principal features of the data are listed in

149

Table 6.1. *Documentation for the data points in Fig. 6.1*

Species	No.	Lat.	Location	Annual production (standing crop)* (t ha⁻¹)	Notes†‡	Reference
C₄ Corn (*Zea mays* L.)	1	12° N.	V. Chillon, Peru	(25.8)	10.3 t ha⁻¹ dry grain taken as 0.4 total crop; S, R, I.	CIMMYT, 1971
	2	30° N.	Egypt	(29.1)	11.6 t ha⁻¹ dry grain taken as 0.4 total crop; S, R, I.	CIMMYT, 1971
		39° N.	Fruita, Colorado, USA	26.6	117 d; 26 t ha⁻¹ also observed in Japan, Togari *et al.*, 1969, and California, see text, at similar latitudes; S, R, I.	Cuany, Shafer & Swink, 1972
		42° N.	Rome, Italy	(26)	140 d; 30 t ha⁻¹ primary production; 0.85 taken as standing crop; S, R, I.	Gibbon, Holliday, Mattei & Luppi, 1970
	3	45° N.	Turin, Italy	(34)	140 d; 40 t ha⁻¹ primary production; 0.85 taken as standing crop; S, R, I.	Gibbon *et al.*, 1970
	4	52° N.	Cawood, England	(17)	140 d; 20 t ha⁻¹ primary production; 0.85 taken as standing crop; S, R.	Gibbon *et al.*, 1970
		38° N.		(26)	Record grain crop at Stockton, Cal. USA; see text	
C₄ Sugar-cane (*Saccharinum* sp.)	5	21° N.	Hawaii, USA	(67.3)	365 d; 64.1 t ha⁻¹ organic; 1.05 taken as standing crop; C.	Burr *et al.*, 1957
	6	27° S.	Swaziland	(63)	365 d; 23.7 t ha⁻¹ sucrose; taken as 0.38 total crop; C.	Humbert, 1972
C₄ Sorghum–Sudangrass (*Sorghum* sp.)	7	33° N.	El Centro, Cal., USA	46.6	210 d; forage trials (*Sorghum biocolor* Moench); S, R, I.	Worker & Marble, 1968.
	8	40° N.	Urbana, Illinois, USA	17.9	140 d; forage trials sorghum × sudangrass Hybrid (*S. bicolor* Moench × *S. sudanesis* Staff)	Burger & Hittle, 1967

Crop	No.	Latitude	Location	Yield	Notes	Reference
C$_4$ Bermuda and Stargrass (*Cynodon* sp.)	9	18° N.	Puerto Rico	37.3	365 d; *Cynodon plectostachyus* (K. Schum.) Pilger, Stargrass; SB, R.	Caro-Costas, Abruña & Figarella, 1972
	10	31° N.	College Station, Tex., USA	31.8	365 d; *Cynodon dactylon* (L.) Pers., Coastal Bermuda; S, R.	Fisher & Caldwell, 1959
	11	34° N.	Tifton, Georgia, USA	27.0	365 d; *Cynodon dactylon* (L.) Pers., Coastal Bermuda, S, R.	Burton, Jackson & Knox, 1959
	12	35.5° N.	Springfield, Tenn., USA	23.1	365 d; *Cynodon dactylon* (L.) Pers., Midland Bermuda; S, R.	Fribourg, Edwards & Barth, 1971
C$_4$ Napiergrass (*Pennisetum purpureum* Shum.)	13	14° N.	El Salvador	85.3	365 d; SB, R.	Watkins & Lewy-van Severen, 1951
	14	18° N.	Puerto Rico	85.9	365 d; SB, R.	Vincente-Chandler et al., 1959
C$_3$ Sugar-beet (*Beta vulgaris* L.)	15	21° N.	Maui, Hawaii, USA	(30.7)	Reported as 13.8 t sucrose ha^{-1} for two crops per year (365 d). Sucrose assumed to be 0.45 total crop (annual production) on the basis that a single crop would have produced at least as well as two crops; S, R, I.	Young & Butchart, 1963
	16	33° N. / 36° N.	El Centro, Cal., USA / Salinas, Cal., USA	33.8 / (42.4)	240 d; winter crop; S, R, I. Two fields both with sucrose yields of 19.1 t ha^{-1}; taken at 0.45 total crop. One crop 240 d, 8.9 ha, C, I. The second 290 d, 8.7 ha, C, I.	Loomis & Worker, 1963 / W. R. Duckworth, Spreckels Sugar Co. (personal communication)
	17	46° N.	Prosser, Wash., USA	(32.0)	230 d; sucrose yield 14.4 t ha^{-1}; taken at 0.45 total crop; C, I.	J. Law, Utah–Idaho Sugar Co. (personal communication)
	18	52° N.	The Netherlands	22	160 d; R.	Sibma, 1968

Table 6.1 – *continued*

Species	No.	Lat.	Location	Annual production (standing crop)* (t ha⁻¹)	Notes†‡	Reference
C₃ Alfalfa (*Medicago* sp)	19	31° N.	Rohovat, Israel	(18.6)	Interpolated from growth rate data; S, R, I.	Stanhill, 1962
	20	37° N.	Fresno, Cal., USA	29.7	Maximum annual commercial production with 8–10 cuttings; C, I.	E. H. Stanford (personal communications)
	21	38° N.	Davis, Cal., USA	27.6	Maximum annual commercial production with 6–8 cuttings; C, I.	
	22	47° N.	Brookings, ND, USA	12.5	Yield trials; S, R.	
C₃ Soybean (*Glycine max* (L.) Merrill)	23	33° N.	Kumamoto, Japan	6.3	120 d, IBP test; S, R.	Togari *et al.*, 1969, 1970, 1971, 1972
	24	40° N.	Morioka, Japan	8.9	130 d IBP test; S, R.	Weber, Shibles & Byth, 1966
	25	42° N.	Ames, Iowa, USA	10.4	S, R.	
C₃ Wheat (*Triticum vulgare* L.)	26	27° N.	Obregon, Sonora, Mexico	(18.3)	7.3 t ha⁻¹ dry grain; taken at 0.4 total crop; S, R, I.	R. A. Fischer, CIMMYT (personal communication)
	27	46° N.	Pullman, Wash., USA	(29.8)	209 bu. grain; taken at 0.85 dry matter and 0.4 total crop; C, I.	Reitz, 1967
	28	65° N.	Fairbanks, Alaska, USA	(4.5)	1.9 t ha⁻¹ grain; taken at 0.85 dry matter and 0.4 total crop; S, R.	Guitard *et al.*, 1965
C₃ Oil palm (*Elaeis quineensis* Jacq.)	29	4° N.	Malaysia	29.4	365 d; 1.3% roots subtracted; 5.0 t ha⁻¹ oil; R.	Corley, Gray & Kee, 1971

C₃ Manioc (*Manihot esculenta* Crantz)	30	8.5° S.	Java	(41)	365 d; see text	De Vries *et al.*, 1967
	31	9° N.	Sierra Leone	(33.3)	230 d; see text	Enyi, 1972*a,b,c*
C₃ Potato (*Solanum tuberosum* L.)	32	38° N.	Stockton, Cal., USA	(22)	See text	M. L. Peterson, U. C. Davis (personal communication)
C₃ Rice (*Oryza sativa* L.)	33	38° N.	Davis, Cal., USA	(22.4)	11.2 t ha⁻¹ dry grain; taken as 0.5 total crop; 0.4 ha, R, I.	Alberda, 1968
C₃ Ryegrass (*Lolium* sp.)	34	52° N.	The Netherlands	(22)		

* Figures in parentheses estimated generally from economic yield; all others observed directly.
† Correction factors, developed from various sources, are conservative values; e.g., grain-straw ratios for dwarf wheats are commonly near 0.5 whereas 0.67 is used here.
‡ S = small plots, generally greater than 4 m²; SB = small plots with possible border effect; 8.9 ha = the size of a commercial (C) field; R = research; and I = irrigated.

Table 6.1. Additional data and background on annual and daily production rates can be found in the recent papers by Cooper (1970) and Loomis, Williams & Hall (1971). Several important patterns are immediately evident:

(1) Graminaceous C_4-species of tropical and subtropical origin excel at the lower latitudes. Records for sugar cane (*Saccharinum* sp.) are seldom found in the open literature (the industry conducts most of its own research) and the recorded values may underestimate its potential. Lacking access to the original publication, we have not included Westlake's value for cane production in Java (94 t ha^{-1}). Westlake based this on a reported air-dry yield of 2300 Pikol Bouw^{-1}. He gives the value of the Pikol as 16.1 g and the Bouw as 0.7 ha for a yield of 53 kg ha^{-1}. Taking the Pikol to be the picul (61.76 kg) of the old Dutch East Indies, the yield is 142 t ha^{-1} and would seem to contain a large amount of water or have been subject to a large border effect. Napiergrass (*Pennisetum purpureum* Shumach.) produced the greatest standing crop of any species but there may have been some border effect influencing both the Puerto Rico and El Salvador reports. As we shall see later, a relatively small portion of such crops in useful economically and less productive species may have more value agriculturally.

(2) As one proceeds to higher latitudes, forage sorghums (*Sorghum bicolor* (L.) Moench), sudangrass (*S. sudanensis* (Piper) Staph.) and their hybrids replace *Saccharinum* and *Pennisetum*. Bermuda grass (*Cynodon dactylon* (L.) Pers.) performs well up to 30° latitude. This species has a very extensive root and rhizome system, sometimes reaching 14 t ha^{-1}, but Holt & Lancaster (1968) found that the under-ground biomass reached a maximum during the first year or two after establishment and then declined whereas the annual increase in above-ground biomass was greatest in older stands. In Fig. 6.1, we have used only above-ground data from well established old swards of *Cynodon* with the reasonable assumption that there were no net annual changes in under-ground biomass.

An especially significant feature of Fig. 6.1 is that maize is the only C_4-species which performs well at latitudes higher than 40°. *Sorghum* sp. are grown to 50° but the yields which we found were not exceptional.

(3) Considering the C_3-species, manioc (*Manihot esculenta* Crantz) probably gives the highest yields at low latitudes. Enyi (1972*a*,*b*,*c*) conducted several detailed growth studied with this species. We have interpreted from his Fig. 1 (1972*c*) that 33.3 t ha^{-1} of dry plants were produced in 230 days and from his Fig. 1 (1972*b*) that 18.6 t ha^{-1} of

154

this was in storage roots (at 7400 plants h⁻¹). At final harvest, he reported that storage roots and stems constituted about 95% of plant weight (Enyi, 1972*a*) and the data above seem to involve only these parts. Comparison with his yields of fresh roots indicates that the dry matter content was near 65%. De Vries, Ferwerda & Flach (1967) cite a manioc yield from Java at 71.1 t ha⁻¹ of fresh roots in a single year. Using their caloric value per ha d⁻¹ and 17 J g⁻¹ dry matter, the dry storage root yield was 23 t ha⁻¹ (32% dry matter). Using Enyi's stem–root ratio of 0.8, total production was 41 t ha⁻¹. While the frailty of such calculations is apparent, they are sufficient to show that C_3-plants can produce well at low latitudes.

Another root crop, the sugar beet (*Beta vulgaris* L.), excels in production at intermediate latitudes. Above 50°, the indeterminate forages such as ryegrass (*Lolium* sp.) and the determinate grains such as wheat (*Triticum* sp.) are superior to other crops. Legumes are inferior at all latitudes. Soybean (*Glycine max* (L.) Merrill) seems to be rather typical whereas alfalfa (*Medicago sativa* L.) gives quite high production. This may be explained in part from alfalfa's adaptation to arid regions with high radiation.

Considering only the peak daily crop growth rates and maximum observed efficiencies in solar energy conversion, a somewhat different picture emerges (Table 6.2). Here again we encountered difficulties in evaluating the quality of published data. As an example, Robinson (1969) reported a yield of carrots (*Daucus carota* L.; tops and storage roots) of 54.5 t ha⁻¹ dry matter after 160 days with 22305 plants m⁻². The data in his Table 2 indicate growth rates up to 146 g m⁻² d⁻¹, the highest ever observed for any plant. After smoothing the data for each harvest date by fitting a regression of ln plant dry weight against ln density, the peak growth was reduced to 81 g m⁻² d⁻¹ with other values as high as 56 and 60. The difficulty seems to lie with having harvested a set number of plants rather than a precise area; mortality was certainly high and was not considered. The maximum growth rate of carrots at densities which yielded roots of commercial size was only 20 to 30 g m⁻² d⁻¹. On the occasion of the IBP Synthesis meeting in Aberystwyth, several speakers cited very high growth rates for another C_3-species, sunflower (*Helianthus annuus* L.). We are inclined to discount the original reports (79 g m⁻² d⁻¹ by Hiroi & Monsi, 1966; 104 g m⁻² d⁻¹ by Repka & Kostrej, 1970). In both cases plots were small with possibly large border effects. Growth rates as great as 110 g m⁻² d⁻¹ can be calculated from the unreplicated data in Table 2 of Hiroi & Monsi. The estimate is improved by taking the mean rate of their full-sun treatments over the final three weeks of the 1968 season. But even this value, 63.8 g, is equivalent to an improbable efficiency in total solar energy conversion of 7.5% (1.450 kJ cm^{-2} d^{-1} radiation, their Table 1; 17 kJ g^{-1} as the heat of combustion). There is a similar anomality in Repka & Kostrej's data. They reported (Repka & Kostrej, 1970) 1.22 kJ cm^{-2} d^{-1} as mean daily radiation at their site for July 1968. Even if radiation during the period July 12 to 22 averaged twice this amount or 2.42 kJ cm^{-2}, the calculated efficiency of 7.2% is well beyond theoretical predictions of 5 to 6% (Loomis & Williams, 1963). The highest sunflower rate observed (1966–70) in their IBP tests at the same site was 31 g m^{-2} d^{-1} (Repka & Kostrej, 1970).

Table 6.2. *Maximum crop growth rates (total dry weight of communities, above and below ground parts)*

	Maximum C observed (gm^{-2} d^{-1})	Reference	Maximum efficiency observed (% DTR*)	Reference
C$_4$-species				
Bulrush Millet (*Pennisetum typhoides*)	54	Begg, 1965	4.2	Begg, 1965
Corn	52	Togari et al., 1969	4.6	Togari et al., 1971
Corn	51	Williams et al., 1965a	–	
Sudangrass	51	Loomis & Williams, 1963	–	
C$_3$-species				
Rice	36	Togari et al., 1969	3.2	Togari et al., 1972
Sugar-beet	31	Blackman & Black, 1959	4.5	Togari et al., 1969
Soybean	27	Togari et al., 1971	4.4	Togari et al., 1971
Potato	37	Lorenz, 1944	–	
Sunflower	See text			
Carrot	See text			

*DTR = Daily total short-wave radiation.

If we ignore the reports of unusual performance by sunflower and carrot, the selected data in Table 6.2 reveal a consistent pattern in that C$_4$-plants have higher daily maximum growth rates, and that both C$_3$- and C$_4$-plants, under appropriate irradiance conditions, approach the limit of one CO$_2$ molecule fixed for each ten quanta of photosynthetically active radiation (PAR) absorbed (5–6% efficiency after correction for albedo and respiration loss).

Agricultural ecosystems

Canopy relations

Studies of crop growth rates show that the annually cultivated crops are particularly limited by the time required to achieve a full foliage canopy. A great deal of attention has been given to tolerance of cultivars to early planting and to space and resource relationships which might minimize this time. It appears to be general for both C_3- and C_4-species that production rates during early season are a simple linear function of PAR interception (Fig. 6.2a).

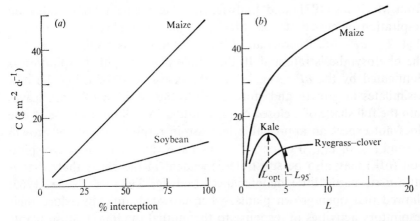

Fig. 6.2. (a) Crop growth rates (C) for maize (Williams, Loomis & Lepley, 1965a) and soybean (Shibles & Weber, 1966) communities as a function of light interception. An illuminance meter was used with maize; Ozalid paper stacks with soybean. (b) Crop growth rates (C) for maize (Williams, Loomis & Lepley, 1965b), ryegrass–clover (Brougham, 1956) and kale (Watson, 1958) communities as a function of leaf-area index (L). Plateau and optimum responses are illustrated.

The picture becomes more complex as foliage density is increased beyond the value required for full interception. Observations of crop growth rates at various foliage densities have revealed two types of response functions (Fig. 6.2b): one a parabolic response indicating an optimum L (Watson, 1958); the other a plateau, or asymptotic, relationship (Brougham, 1956; Williams, Loomis & Lepley, 1965a). However, it is increasingly evident that many crops show a plateau response (McCree & Troughton, 1966; Ludwig, Saeki & Evans, 1965; Buttery, 1970; Pearce, Brown & Blaser, 1967). Brougham (1956) employed the term 'critical' leaf area index for this situation to denote the L value which resulted in the interception of 95% of the incident PAR at local solar noon. L_{95} also corresponds to the breaking point in the plateau

157

curves, i.e. it is the minimum or threshold L for near maximal growth rate. The L_{opt} concept has been applied to plateau curves where there is no optimum; we suggest using L_{opt} for parabolas, L_{crit} for plateau threshold, and L_{95} for 95 % interception. It is also important to realize that most crop situations involve plant densities which optimize economic production and that the associated L values are usually below L_{opt} or L_{crit}.

The optimum relationship is generally explained by the assumption that the additional heavily shaded leaves represent a severe respiratory drain. An explanation for the plateau response can be seen most clearly from McCree's (1971) and Ludwig, Saeki & Evans' (1965) studies on respiration of closed stands. McCree found with clover communities that $R = aP + bW$ where a and b are constants, R is respiration rate, P the photosynthesis rate and W the whole plant weight. Respiration is dominated by the aP term, i.e. by the energy cost of using the new assimilates in growth and storage. Since the addition of more leaves into the full shade of a closed canopy ordinarily will not increase P, one does not expect an appreciable increase in respiration cost of growth beyond L_{opt} or L_{crit}. Further, it seems likely that maintenance respiration (bW) may also be substrate-dependent in the sense that what is little used needs little maintenance. Ludwig, Saeki & Evans (1965) showed that open-grown plants, when crowded, quickly reduce their respiratory activities in response to the mutual shading. Cotton plants which gave an optimal response at the onset of crowding, within a few days yielded a plateau response. Respiration is also attenuated in other ways: for example, the proportion of the biomass in stem and roots is sharply reduced in dense stands; and many plants quickly dispense with heavily shaded leaves, flowers and other parts through senescence.

Community photosynthesis models show a remarkable sensitivity to leaf respiration rates in simulations of C versus L relationships (Loomis, Williams & Duncan, 1967). It appears that Zelitch's (1971) simulations, all of which show optimum L relationships, failed to take this vital point into account.

Tooming (1971) and Tooming & Kallis (1972) have come to a similar conclusion regarding shade adaptation but from a de-novo logic that adaptation of leaf and whole plant processes occurs so as to maximize community production. The adaption response he employs in his models has analogies to McCree's equation and involves changes in leaf dark respiration and in P_{max} of apparent photosynthesis as a function of light intensity. This changes the shape of the light response curves so

158

that with shading the light intensity corresponding to the intercept with the curve of a tangent line drawn through the origin (this corresponds to the irradiance for maximum efficiency, i.e. P/I is maximum) is shifted to lower irradiance. In an ideal foliage canopy, this 'irradiation density of adaptation' (IDA) shifts to lower values for the shaded leaves in the same manner as real plants. One can perhaps draw a parallel with C_3- and C_4-plants as starting, before adaptation, with low and high IDA values.

Using this approach, Tooming & Kallis (1972) predict from simulations with a community photosynthesis model that optimum L will occur only when the leaves fail to adapt to shading and that plateau responses occur when adaptation occurs. In a point which relates well with Fig. 6.1 and Table 6.2, they find species with high IDA (C_4?) should have higher growth rates and be most productive at low latitudes while low IDA species (C_3?) should have lower growth rates and be less sensitive to latitude.

A second feature of the C versus L relationship involves modifications in productivity which occur with changes in canopy architecture (Loomis & Williams, 1969). Early qualitative predictions that assemblages of clumped, random or regularly dispersed leaf elements of varying leaf inclinations should be quite different in their production relations were provided quantitative substance by the light distribution models of Monsi & Saeki (1953), de Wit (1965), Monteith (1965) and Duncan, Loomis, Williams & Hanau (1967). Three main points were evident in the hypotheses drawn with the Duncan model (Duncan, Loomis, Williams & Hanau, 1967; Loomis & Williams, 1969; Duncan, 1971): (1) at less than L_{opt} or L_{crit}, horizontally displayed leaves would maximize interception and productivity; (2) in the range of leaf area indices normally achieved by crop plant communities at full leaf development, leaf angle would have little influence on production rate; and (3) in communities which could be allowed to go to very high leaf area index ($L = 6$ to 10), there would be a strong production advantage to erect leaves (the erect-leaf hypothesis), at least below 50–60° N. or S.

These predictions have led to a number of efforts to confirm the leaf angle point experimentally with maize and to exploit it for improvements in agricultural production. However, most of these efforts have ignored the main features of the hypotheses. For example, Russell (1972) and Hicks & Stucker (1972) conducted their experiments at a low leaf area index (4 or less) and with inadequate differences in leaf angle. Primary production and crop growth rates were not determined

159

and the advantages observed in grain yield may simply have resulted from alterations in source–sink patterns as suggested by Pendleton, Smith, Winter & Johnson (1968) rather than from greater photosynthesis. The experiments performed by Winter & Ohlrogge (1973) with maize and Angus, Jones & Wilson (1972) with barley were far superior in conception and execution. Winter & Ohlrogge found that erect leaves increased grain yields with $L > 3$ to 4, and reduced it below $L = 3$ to 4; production rates were not determined. Angus, Jones & Wilson (1972) conducted their detailed measurements of leaf display and light interception (which revealed marked differences between erect and lax leaf cultivars) at a location where the crop was limited by moisture supply, rather than at their second site where moisture supply was not so limiting and the variety with erect leaves gave superior crop growth rates and grain yields. However, with small grains such as barley much of the erectly displayed area consists of sheaths enclosing the culm with only one surface fully exposed for gas exchange. Thus, an increasing density of tillers (to obtain high L) leads to a greater percentage of the light interception being accomplished by organs having a lower photosynthetic capability. The experiments of Angus, Jones & Wilson (1972) offer encouragement for the demonstration of the erect-leaf hypothesis, but the principle may be defeated if one has to substitute sheaths for leaves in order to obtain a high L.

Adaptation

The production rates observed for agricultural ecosystems exceed the values observed for most natural ecosystems. One reason is that agriculture is practiced in the most favorable soil–climate situations. In addition, domesticated species have been selected for rapid growth. This is related in turn to nitrogen nutrition and photosynthetic ability.

We shall consider nitrogen nutrition first by returning to the origins of crop plants and examining the special relationships which may have developed in domestication. These relationships are clearer for the New World species, and have been reviewed by Sauer (1969). The principal New World crop species of *Zea, Manihot, Solanum, Lycopersicum, Cucurbita, Ipomoea, Dioscorea, Amaranthus, Nicotiana, Gossypium,* and *Phaseolus* all seem to have had their center of origin in northern and western South America (Peru, Ecuador, Columbia and Venezuela) or in Meso America (Mexico, Guatamala, Honduras, Nicaragua, and Costa Rica). The southern and Caribbean extensions from these origins initially emphasized vegetative propagation of the root and tuber crops followed by sown cultures of *Amaranthus* and *Phaseolus*. The northern extensions rested on seed crops, principally *Zea*, *Phaseolus* and *Cucurbita*. It is interesting that manioc cultivation once extended to high latitudes in South America but to only about 25 °N. Present cultivars are clonally propagated and are seldom grown beyond 15° from the equator. Part of the reason is that they require short days for root thickening, a factor which may have limited the northward spread of clonal lines by early man. *Zea mays* has developed only recently and has displaced *Amaranthus* and, to some extent, the root and tuber crops as starch sources in South American agriculture.

Several distinctive features of the domestication process in the New World seemed evident to Sauer. There was an initial emphasis on carbohydrate crops, particularly root and tuber species, perhaps because the gathering of roots and tubers leads to rapid regeneration of a second crop with even less competition from other species, i.e. a natural conversion towards monoculture. The species involved were found in hill and mountain lands on forest margins free of intense competition with either grasses or trees. Man presumably found the grasslands untenable due to fire and his inability to cultivate the soil, and the forests relatively devoid of productive food plants. It is significant that domesticated plants are all tolerant or requiring of high irradiance and grow rapidly with an abundance of water and nitrogen. While drought tolerance is a characteristic of these early crop plants and is essential to good performance in tropical dry seasons, the use of nitrogen is perhaps more important.

Very tight nutrient recycling patterns characterize mature natural vegetations. While large amounts of organic nitrogen may accumulate in soils (up to 10 t ha^{-1} in the central grasslands and Pacific rainforests of North America), the concentration of available inorganic nitrogen is low unless the soils are disturbed to increase aeration. The ability of crop plants to respond to nitrogen availability with rapid growth fits with a presumed original adaptation as weedy species to disturbed soils in the forest boundary. Root and tuber harvest and seed sowing both involve soil disturbance, aeration and nitrification. It is logical that weedy growth characteristics would be selected among the progeny in both instances. A high-nitrogen environment would also characterize the midden heaps where some consider that the rapid growth of volunteer plants would lead early man to discover the possibilities of cultivation.

161

It is our view that this relatively greater availability of nitrogen and other nutrients in the soil has been generally true for agricultural environments and distinguishes agricultural fields from all but occasional events in natural vegetation.

Originally this would result from aeration of soils and nitrification upon tillage and, more recently, from inclusion of legumes in rotations and applications of chemical fertilizer. Nitrogen cycling may be much greater in agricultural systems than in natural vegetation. The sugar-beet crops shown at 42 t ha^{-1} in Fig. 6.1 are estimated to have assimilated nearly 700 kg of N ha^{-1} annually. Average beet crops cycle about one-half this amount. The outstanding performance by the C$_4$-grasses likewise occurs only with high nitrogen. This is seen clearly in Table 6.3 where the responses shown for *Cynodon* are rather typical of

Table 6.3. *Forage yield components relative to ruminant nutrition for a tropical grass* (Cynodon plectostachyus (*K. Schum.*) *Pilger.* (*Caro-Costas* et al., *1972*)

Cutting interval (d)	N applied (kg ha^{-1} yr^{-1})	N uptake (kg ha^{-1} yr^{-1})	Above ground dry matter yield (t ha^{-1} yr^{-1})	Apparent in vitro digestible yield (t ha^{-1} yr^{-1})	Crude protein yield (t ha^{-1} yr^{-1})
30	0	210	12.2	–	1.6
	670	580	20.6	12.4	3.5
90	0	230	23.4	–	1.6
	670	490	36.0	16.6	2.9

Yields are averages for 2 years; the maximum yield, 37.3 mt ha, was achieved with 90-d interval and 800 kg N ha^{-1} yr (Table 6.1).

observations with other C$_4$-grasses. Nitrogen enrichments of 1000 to 2000 kg ha^{-1} yr^{-1} as used to achieve 85 t ha^{-1} production with Napier-grass (Vicente-Chandler, Silva & Figarella, 1959) are seldom feasible economically and the full potential of these species is not exploited even in intensive agriculture. Also, while the highest yields of C$_4$-grasses are obtained with long cutting cycles, the older tissues are less digestible by ruminant animals, due principally to lignification (Table 6.3). Thus, the most profitable agriculture would involve frequent cutting at less than luxury levels of nitrogen, or the use of more digestible species. Since luxury nutrition is rare even with chemical fertilizers, the evolutionary success of the nitrogen utilization ability would lie more with the short-time advantage from exploitation of small increments of nitrogen from animal dung, aerated soil or alluvial deposits.

Our comments regarding the nitrogen responsiveness of domesticated species seems to be generally true for all except the leguminous crops. A noteworthy feature of Fig. 6.1 was the failure of legumes except alfalfa to accomplish significant annual production. Even with indeterminate growth no other forage or seed legumes came within range of the best C_3-species. The food value of seed legumes, such as *Arachis*, *Phaseolus* and *Glycine*, lies in their storage of protein and oil. They presumably would come to domestication on nitrogen-poor lands, or in places with a low supply of animal protein. The forage legumes are natural invaders of nitrogen-poor grasslands but are not successful against grasses when nitrogen is not limiting (Stern & Donald, 1962). Alfalfa was used by the Romans as forage for horses but many of the forage legumes have been domesticated only recently as population pressures caused crop-fallow swidden systems to be replaced by legume rotations as a means for maintaining soil nitrogen supply.

As a starting point in accounting for the differences among species in their behavior to nitrogen, let us consider the analysis presented by de Wit, Dijkshoorn & Noggle (1963). Starting with Ulrich's (1941) observation that cation uptake by excised barley root systems is balanced electrochemically by organic acid anions, Dijkshoorn (1962) found that similar balances were maintained by whole plants. Briefly, the total cation $(K^+ + Na^+ + Ca^{2+} + Mg^{2+})$ content minus total inorganic anion $(NO_3^- + H_2PO_4^- + SO_4^{2-} + Cl^-)$ content $(C-A)$ is remarkably constant for a species and appears to be regulated as a condition for rapid growth rather than a result for growth. C_3-grasses maintain $C-A$ near 1000 meq kg^{-1} dry matter; unnodulated legumes near 2000 meq and sugar-beet near 4000 meq.

The $C-A$ balance seems tied directly to a circulatory pattern between roots and shoots of higher plants. In the upward xylem flux, NO_3^- is balanced by K^+. In leaves, NO_3^- is reduced to a neutral amino group and is replaced by an organic anion which accumulates or moves downward in the phloem (balanced by K^+) to the roots. Ben-Zioni, Vaadia & Lips (1971) showed that such organic anions may be decarboxylated in the root and the HCO_3^- produced exchanged stoichiometrically for additional NO_3^- from the external solution, while the K^+ recycles to the leaves.

There are many possible variants of this scheme depending upon the plant, its rate of growth and the ion supply in the external medium: H^+ exchange to balance NH_4^+ or other cation uptake; cation uptake paired with anion uptake; and HCO_3^- or OH^- exchange to balance Cl^-,

163

SO_4^{2-} or HPO_4^{2-} uptake. What has been found for rapid growth on NO_3^-, though, is that organic anions accumulate as charge replacement in the plant in an amount equal electronegatively to the amount of NO_3^- reduced to organic N with neutral charge; and that $C-A =$ organic anions. The apparent cost of nitrate metabolism is thus quite high. If we start with CH_2O units (glucose equivalent from photosynthesis) and ignore the carbon skeleton of the amino acids, we need:

1 CH_2O for HCO_3^- exchange in absorption

2 CH_2O for $4NADPH_2$ for NO_3^- reduction

4 CH_2O for a C_4-organic anion for electronegative balance

---

7 CH_2O per NO_3^- amino NH_2.

Since the energy for NO_3^- reduction may come from photosynthesis without concomitant CO_2 assimilation (Beevers & Hageman, 1969), the carbon requirement may be as low as 5 CH_2O/NO_3^-, in which case the equivalent assimilation of 2 CO_2 is probably lost. In either case, a sugar-beet with 1.4 mol (2%) organic N kg^{-1} dry matter would accumulate 1.4 mol of organic anions, in this case principally oxalate, or about 13% of the dry weight (Joy, 1964; Houba, van Egmond & Wittich, 1971).

One point seems clear. Plants carry with them massive amounts of their own 'sewage' and a high protein content necessarily means more problems per unit dry weight (production) in cation and organic anion accumulation. High growth rates and hence high photosynthesis rates can occur in both C_3- and C_4-species when the need for reduced nitrogen per unit dry weight is kept to a minimum and the plant has an efficient disposal system.

Plants which accumulate significant amounts of carbohydrates as sugar or starch can continue to accumulate dry matter against a limited amount of protein. It probably is significant that two of the most productive species in Fig. 6.1, sugar-cane and sugar-beet, are sucrose accumulators with indeterminate habits of growth and storage. Peak storage rates for both species were found to be near 10 g sucrose $m^{-2} d^{-1}$ (the rates for sugar-beet were greater, perhaps because of the longer days in the temperate summer). These rates are less than have been observed with potato tubers (26 g $m^{-2} d^{-1}$; Lorenz, 1944) and maize ears (24 g $m^{-2} d^{-1}$; Togari, Murata & Saeki, 1969) but potato and maize are to some degree determinate in growth habit and the storage rates in each case reflect considerable redistribution of assimilates previously accumulated in other plant parts. The generally high photosynthetic capability of crop plants is also a logical consequence of domestication processes which emphasized selection for rapid growth. At low latitudes, the principal advantage of C_4-species probably lies with their greater photosynthesis in the intense radiation which occurs with high solar elevations. It is also possible that C_4-metabolism, by producing the necessary organic anions directly as a principal product of CO_2 assimilation in mesophyll cells, is more effective in nitrate assimilation. Higher temperature optima in photosynthesis and greater water-use efficiency (g net production to g H_2O transpired) have also been advanced (Downton, 1971a; Björkman, 1971). But many C_3-plants such as *Helianthus* and *Gossypium* also have high temperature optima (El-Sharkawy & Hesketh, 1964, 1965). Also, C_4-plants retain their advantage at low latitudes even with irrigation. While C_4-plants are probably more tolerant of the mid-day plant water deficits which develop even when soil moisture is not limiting, their greater water-use efficiency comes more from higher peak photosynthesis than from lower transpiration rates.

The limited success of C_4-species at high latitudes deserves attention. While most authors have emphasized the high temperature optima for growth and photosynthesis of C_4-species, the situation at high latitudes is better stated as resulting from a poor ability to grow in cool temperatures, which is an entirely different problem. Maximum solar elevations and hence peak radiation levels are lower than in the tropics and the superior photosynthetic capability of C_4-species in intense radiation thus finds less opportunity for expression. The models of both Tooming & Kallis (1972) and de Wit (1965) predict that the C_4-species would have an advantage in community photosynthesis rate at 66° latitude but the relative advantage is not nearly as great as it is at 23°. It would be useful to explore the point in more detail with the Duncan simulation model.

Among the cultivated C_4-species, only maize is significant above 40–50° latitude. Its origins seem to have been in the cool tropics where it does extremely well at high altitudes. The record for maize grain yield given earlier was attained in a region in California with cool nights from a strong marine influence. Thus maize is best characterized as a warm climate rather than a hot climate species. But like most other C_4-species it is subject to chilling injury (Taylor & Rowley, 1971; Lyons, 1973). At high latitudes, maize performance is closely geared to its determinate growth habit and only late-sown, early maturing cultivars are successful through avoidance of chilling temperatures.

There has been considerable effort spent in seeking C_4-photosynthesis variants within the C_3-crop species. These efforts are encouraged by the wide distribution of the C_4-system among higher plants (Evans, 1971; Downton, 1971*b*) and because *Atriplex, Kochia, Amaranthus* and several other genera contain both types. Thus far, no C_4-variants have been found in genetic collections of soybean, wheat and *Beta* sp. (Cannell, Brun & Moss, 1969; Menz, Moss, Cannell & Brun, 1969; Moss, Krenzer & Brun, 1969; Hall, 1972). Further, the experience of Björkman *et al.* (1971) with intraspecific hybrids of C_3- and C_4-*Atriplex* indicate that genetic transfer of the C_4-system would be difficult even if variants are found. But the reverse logic of finding C_4-types which possess chilling tolerance and grow well in cool climates is a rather promising approach and is being pursued by New Zealand workers (Taylor & Rowley, 1971).

The distribution noted in Fig. 6.1 for C_4-crop plants parallels the distribution of wild C_4-species (Downton, 1971*a,b*). B. Crampton of our group has surveyed Canadian and the northern US flora for occurrence of the C_4-wild species in Downton's (1971*b*) checklist. The majority of those found at high latitudes (e.g. *Setaria* sp.) are short-season plants of a weedy character and exist principally on disturbed sites. But a few, including *Andropogon scoparius, Axonopus compressus, Panicum virgatum,* and *Sorghastrum nutans* are native to northern grasslands and, like high-altitude tropical plants, may represent successful adaptations to cool climates. However, these species do not occur as dominants in northern communities so any photosynthetic advantage over C_3-species which they possess is probably not very great.

Conclusions

Our survey of productivity rates in agricultural systems revealed a strong latitudinal dependence. C_4-species excel at low latitudes but are inferior to C_3-species above 40° to 50°. This crossover, i.e. genotype–environment interaction, is correlated with peak radiation levels and the occurrence of chilling temperatures.

Cultivated species are generally highly responsive to luxury environments, a trait apparently selected for and nurtured during domestication. Legume species appear to represent an exception. The capability for rapid growth by crop plants is reciprocally linked with rapid photo-

166

synthesis and effective mechanisms for nitrogen assimilation. Indeterminate plants are the most productive and are matched by determinate plants only where the growth duration of the determinate types is similar to the length of the growing season.

References

Alberda, Th. (1968). Dry matter production and light interception of crop surfaces. IV. Maximum herbage production as compared with predicted values. *Neth. J. Agr. Sci.* **16**, 142–53.

Angus, J. F., Jones, R. & Wilson, J. H. (1972). A comparison of barley cultivars with different leaf inclinations. *Aust. J. Agr. Res.* **23**, 945–57.

Anonymous. (1969). Can we break the 50-ton barrier? *Am. Veg. Growers*, **17**, 11–14.

Beevers, L. & Hageman, R. H. (1969). Nitrate reduction in higher plants. *Ann. Rev. Plant Physiol.* **20**, 495–522.

Begg, J. E. (1965). High photosynthetic efficiency in a low-latitude environment. *Nature*, **205**, 1025–6.

Ben-Zioni, A., Vaadia, Y. & Lips, S. H. (1971). Nitrate uptake by roots as regulated by nitrate reduction products of the shoot. *Physiol. Plant.* **24**, 288–90.

Björkman, O. (1971). Comparative photosynthetic CO_2 exchange in higher plants. In *Photosynthesis and Photorespiration*, eds. M. D. Hatch, C. B. Osmond & R. O. Slayter, pp. 3–17. New York, Wiley-Interscience.

Björkman, O., Nobs, M., Pearcy, R., Boynton, J. & Berry, J. (1971). Characteristics of hybrids between C_3 and C_4 species of *Atriplex*. In *Photosynthesis and Photorespiration*, eds. M. D. Hatch, C. B. Osmond & R. O. Slayter, pp. 105–19. New York, Wiley-Interscience.

Blackman, G. E. & Black, J. N. (1959). Physiological and ecological studies in the analysis of plant environment. 12. The role of light factors in limiting growth. *Ann. Bot.* NS, **22**, 131–45.

Brougham, R. W. (1956). Effect of intensity of defoliation on regrowth of pasture. *Aust. J. Agr. Sci.* **7**, 377–87.

Burger, A. W. & Hittle, C. N. (1967). Yield, protein, nitrate, and prussic acid content of sudangrass, sudangrass hybrids, and pearl millets harvested at two cutting frequencies and two stubble heights. *Agron. J.* **59**, 259–62.

Burr, G. O., Hartt, C. E., Brodie, H. W., Tanimoto, T., Kortschak, H. P., Takashahi, D., Ashton, F. M. & Coleman, R. E. (1957). The sugarcane plant. *Ann. Rev. Plant Physiol.* **8**, 275–308.

Burton, G. W., Jackson, J. E. & Knox, F. E. (1959). The influence of light reduction upon the production, persistence and chemical composition of Coastal bermudagrass, *Cynodon dactylon. Agron. J.* **51**, 537–42.

Buttery, B. R. (1970). Effects of variation in leaf area index on growth of maize and soybeans. *Crop Sci.* **10**, 9–13.

Cannell, R. Q., Brun, W. A. & Moss, D. N. (1969). A search for high net photosynthetic rate among soybean genotypes. *Crop Sci.* **9**, 840–1.

Caro-Costas, R., Abruna, J. & Figarella, J. (1972). Effect of nitrogen rates, harvest interval and cutting heights on yield and composition of star grass in Puerto Rico. *J. Agr. Univ. Puerto Rico*, **56**, 267–79.

CIMMYT (1971). *Annual report, 1970–1*. Mexico, Int. Maize Wheat Improve. Center. 115pp.

Cooper, J. P. (1970). Potential production and energy conversion in temperate and tropical grasses. *Herb. Abs.* **40**, 1–15.

Corley, R. H. V., Gray, B. S. & Kee, N. S. (1971). Productivity of the oil palm (*Elaeis quineensis* Jacq.) in Malaysia. *Expl. Agr.* **7**, 129–36.

Cuany, R. L., Shafer, S. L. & Swink, J. F. (1972). Performance tests of corn hybrids grown in various regions of Colorado in 1971. *Gen. Ser.* **921**, 43pp. Fort Collins, Colorado State Univ. Expt. Sta.

De Vries, C. A., Ferwerda, J. D. & Flach, M. (1967). Choice of food crops in relation to actual and potential production in the tropics. *Neth. J. Agr. Sci.* **15**, 241–8.

Dijkshoorn, W. (1962). Metabolic regulation of the alkaline effect of nitrate utilization in plants. *Nature (London)*, **194**, 165–7.

Downton, W. J. S. (1971a). Adaptive and evolutionary aspects of C_4-photosynthesis. In *Photosynthesis and Photorespiration*, eds. M. D. Hatch, C. B. Osmond & R. O. Slayter, pp. 3–17. New York, Wiley-Interscience.

Downton, W. J. S. (1971b). Check list of C_4-species. In *Photosynthesis and Photorespiration*, eds. M. D. Hatch, C. B. Osmond & R. O. Slayter, pp. 554–58. New York, Wiley-Interscience.

Duncan, W. G. (1971). Leaf angles, leaf area, and canopy photosynthesis. *Crop. Sci.* **11**, 482–5.

Duncan, W. G., Loomis, R. S., Williams, W. A. & Hanau, R. (1967). A model for simulating photosynthesis in plant communities. *Hilgardia*, **38**, 181–205.

El-Sharkawy, M. A. & Hesketh, J. D. (1964). Effects of temperature and water deficit on leaf photosynthetic rates of different species. *Crop Sci.* **4**, 514–18.

El-Sharkawy, M. & Hesketh, J. (1965). Photosynthesis among species in relation to characteristics of leaf anatomy and CO_2 diffusion resistance. *Crop Sci.* **5**, 517–21.

Enyi, B. A. C. (1972a). Effect of shoot number and time of planting on growth, development and yield of cassava (*Manihot esculenta* Crantz). *J. Hort. Sci.* **47**, 457–66.

Enyi, B. A. C. (1972b). The effects of spacing on growth, development and yield of single and multi-shoot plants of cassava (*Manihot esculenta* Crantz). I. Root tuber yield and atributes. *East Afr. Agr. For. J.* **38**, 23–6.

Enyi, B. A. C. (1972c). II. Physiological factors. *East Afr. Agr. For. J.* **38**, 27–34.

Evans, L. T. (1971). Evolutionary, adaptive and environmental aspects of the photosynthetic pathway: assessment. In *Photosynthesis and Photorespiration*, eds. M. D. Hatch, C. B. Osmond & R. O. Slayter, pp. 130–6. New York, Wiley-Interscience.

Fisher, F. L. & Caldwell, A. G. (1959). The effects of continued use of heavy rates of fertilizers on forage production and quality of Coastal bermuda-grass. *Agron. J.* **51,** 99–102.

Fribourg, H. A., Edwards, N. C., Jr & Barth, K. M. (1971). *In vitro* dry-matter digestibility at several levels of N fertilization. *Agron. J.* **63,** 786–8.

Gibbon, D., Holliday, R., Mattei, F. & Luppi, G. (1970). Crop production potential and energy conversion efficiency in different environments. *Expl. Agr.* **6,** 197–204.

Guitard, A. A., Taylor, R. L., Brinsmade, J. C., Gilbey, J. A., Newman, J. A. & Tsukamoto, J. Y. (1965). Growth of spring cereals in North-western Canada and Alaska. *Canad. Dept. Agr. Publ.* **1220,** 11 pp.

Hall, A, E. (1972). Photosynthesis in the genus *Beta. Crop Sci.* **12,** 701–2.

Hamilton, W. J., III & Watt, K. E. F. (1970). Refuging. *Ann. Rev. Ecol. Systematics,* **1,** 263–86.

Hicks, D. R. & Stucker, R. E. (1972). Plant density effect on grain yield of corn hybrids diverse in leaf orientation. *Agron. J.* **64,** 484–7.

Hiroi, T. & Monsi, M. (1966). Dry-matter economy of *Helianthus annuus* communities grown at varying densities and light intensities. *J. Fac. Sci., Univ. Tokyo,* III, **9(8),** 241–85.

Holt, E. C. & Lancaster, J. A. (1968). Yield and stand survival of 'Coastal' bermudagrass as influenced by management practices. *Agron. J.* **60,** 7–11.

Houba, V. J. G., van Egmond, F. & Wittich, E. M. (1971). Changes in production of organic nitrogen and carboxylates $(C-A)$ in young beets with nitrogen nutrition. *Neth. J. Agr. Sci.* **19,** 39–47.

Humbert, R. P. (1972). Mechanization of sugarcane harvesting. *Outlook Agr.* **7,** 10–13.

Joy, K. W. (1964). Accumulation of oxalate in tissues of sugar-beet, and the effect of nitrogen supply. *Ann. Bot.* NS, **28,** 689–701.

Lieth, H. (1968). The measurement of calorific value of biological material and the determination of ecological efficiency. In *Functioning of Terrestrial Ecosystems at the Primary Production Level,* ed. F. E. Eckardt, pp. 233–42, Paris, UNESCO.

Loomis, R. S. & Williams, W. A. (1963). Maximum crop productivity: an estimate. *Crop Sci.* **3,** 67–72.

Loomis, R. S. & Worker, G. F. Jr (1963). Responses of the sugar beet to low soil moisture at two levels of nitrogen nutrition. *Agron. J.* **55,** 509–15.

Loomis, R. S., Williams, W. A. & Duncan, W. G. (1967). Community architecture and the productivity of terrestrial plant communities. In *Harvesting the Sun,* eds. A. San Pietro, F. A. Greer & T. J. Army, pp. 291–308. New York, Academic Press.

Loomis, R. S. & Williams, W. A. (1969). Productivity and the morphology of crop stands: patterns with leaves. In *Physiological Aspects of Crop Yield,* eds. J. D. Eastin, F. A. Haskins, C. Y. Sullivan & C. H. M. van Bavel, pp. 27–47. Madison, Wisconsin, Amer. Soc. Agron.

Loomis, R. S., Williams, W. A. & Hall, A. E. (1971). Agricultural pro-ductivity. *Ann. Rev. Plant Physiol.* **22,** 431–68.

G

Lorenz, O. A. (1944). Studies on potato nutrition. II. Nutrient uptake at various stages of growth by Kern County potatoes. *Am. Soc. Hort. Sci. Proc.* **44**, 389–94.

Ludwig, L. J., Saeki, T. & Evans, L. T. (1965). Photosynthesis in artificial communities of cotton plants in relation to leaf area. I. Experiments with progressive defoliation of mature plants. *Aust. J. Biol. Sci.* **18**, 1103–18.

Lyons, J. L. (1973). Chilling injury in plants. *Ann. Rev. Plant Physiol.* **24**, 445–66.

McCree, K. J. & Troughton, J. H. (1966). Nonexistence of an optimum leaf area index for the production rate of white clover grown under constant conditions. *Plant Physiol.* **41**, 1615–22.

McCree, K. J. (1971). An equation for the rate of respiration of white clover plants grown under controlled conditions. In *Prediction and Measurement of Photosynthetic Productivity*, ed. I. Šetlik, pp. 221–9. Wageningen, PUDOC.

Menz, K. M., Moss, D. N., Cannell, R. Q. & Brun, W. A. (1969). Screening for photosynthetic efficiency. *Crop Sci.* **9**, 692–4.

Monsi, M. & Saeki, T. (1953). Über den Lichtfaktor in den Pflanzengesellshaften und seine Bedeutung für die Stoffproduktion. *Jap. J. Bot.* **14**, 22–52.

Monteith, J. L. (1965). Light distribution and photosynthesis in field crops. *Ann. Bot.* NS, **29**, 17–37.

Moss, D. N., Krenzer, E. G. & Brun, W. A. (1969). Carbon dioxide compensation points in related plant species. *Science*, **164**, 187–8.

Pearce, R. B., Brown, R. H. & Blaser, R. E. (1967). Photosynthesis in plant communities as influenced by leaf angle. *Crop Sci.* **7**, 321–4.

Pendleton, J. W., Smith, G. E., Winter, S. R. & Johnson, R. J. (1968). Field investigations of the relationships of leaf angle in corn (*Zea mays* L.) to grain yield and apparent photosynthesis. *Agron. J.* **60**, 422–5.

Pimental, D., Hurd, L. E., Belloti, A. C., Forster, M. J., Oka, I. N., Sholes, O. D. & Whitman, R. J. (1973). Food production and the energy crisis. *Science*, **182**, 443–8.

Reitz, L. P. (1967). Wheat distribution and importance of wheat. In *Wheat and Wheat Improvement*, eds. K. S. Quisenberry & L. P. Reitz, pp. 1–18. Madison, Wisconsin, Amer. Soc. Agron.

Repka, J. & Kostrej, A. (1970). An analysis of the production process of cultivated plants in the conditions of Southern Slovakia. II. Manuring and various leaf surface rate(s) in relation to the production of dry matter. *Polnohospodarstvo*, **16**, 830–41.

Repka, J. & Kostrej, A. (1972). Seasonal changes of net photosynthetic production in plants under the climatic conditions of South Slovakia. *Biol. Prace*, **XVIII/8**, 79 pp.

Robinson, F. E. (1969). Carrot population density and yield in an arid environment. *Agron. J.* **61**, 499–500.

Russell, W. A. (1972). Effect of leaf angle on hybrid performance in maize (*Zea mays* L.). *Crop Sci.* **12**, 90–2.

Sauer, C. (1969). *Seeds, Spades, Hearths and Herds: The domestication of animals and foodstuffs.* 175 pp. Cambridge, Mass., MIT Press.

Shibles, R. M. & Weber, C. R. (1966). Interception of solar radiation and dry matter production by various soybean planting patterns. *Crop Sci.* **6,** 55–9.

Sibma, L. (1968). Growth of closed green crop surfaces in the Netherlands. *Neth. J. Agr. Sci.* **16,** 211–6.

Stanhill, G. (1962). The effect of environmental factors on the growth of alfalfa in the field. *Neth. J. Agr. Sci.* **10,** 247–53.

Stern, W. R. & Donald, C. M. (1962). Light relations in grass-clover swards. *Aust. J. Agr. Res.* **13,** 599–614.

Taylor, A. O. & Rowley, J. A. (1971). Plants under climatic stress. I. Low-temperature, high-light effects on photosynthesis. *Plant Physiol.* **47,** 713–18.

Togari, Y., Murata, Y. & Saeki, T. (1969). PP: Photosynthesis and utilization of solar energy. Level I experiments. *Report II (1967 data).* J IBP/PP-Photosynthesis, Local Productivity Group. Tokyo. 83 pp. (1970). *Report III (1968 data).* 100 pp. (1971). *Report IV (1969 data).* 79 pp. (1972). *Report V (1970 data).* 72 pp.

Tooming, H. 1971. Mathematical description of net photosynthesis and adaptation processes in the photosynthetic apparatus of plant communities. In *Prediction and Measurement of Photosynthetic Productivity,* ed. I. Šetlik, pp. 103–13. Wageningen, PUDOC.

Tooming, H. & Kallis, A. (1972). Productivity and growth calculations of plant stands. In *Solar Radiation and Productivity of Plant Stand,* pp. 1–121. Tartu, Estonian Acad. Sci., Inst. Physics Astron. (Russian, English summary).

Ulrich, A. (1941). Metabolism of non-volatile organic acids in excised barley roots as related to cation-anion balance during salt accumulation. *Am. J. Bot.* **28,** 526–37.

Vicente-Chandler, J., Silva, S. & Figarella, J. (1959). The effect of nitrogen fertilization and frequency of cutting on the yield and composition of three tropical grasses. *Agron. J.* **51,** 202–6.

Watkins, J. M. & Lewy-van Severen, M. (1951). Effect of frequency and height of cutting on the yield, stand, and protein content of some forages in El Salvador. *Agron. J.* **43,** 291–6.

Watson, D. J. (1958). The dependence of net assimilation rate on leaf area index. *Ann. Bot.* NS, **22,** 37–55.

Weber, C. R., Shibles, R. M. & Byth, D. E. (1966). Effect of plant population and row spacing on soybean development and production. *Agron. J.* **58,** 99–102.

Westlake, D. F. (1963). Comparisons of plant productivity. *Biol. Rev.* **38,** 385–425.

Williams, W. A., Loomis, R. S. & Lepley, C. R. (1965a). Vegetative growth of corn as affected by population density. I. Components of growth net assimilation rate and leaf-area index. *Crop Sci.* **5,** 215–19.

Williams, W. A., Loomis, R .S. & Lepley, C. R. (1956b). II. Productivity in relation to interception of solar radiation. *Crop Sci.* **5,** 211–15.

Winter, S. R. & Ohlrogge, A. J. (1973). Leaf angle, leaf area, and corn (*Zea mays* L.) yield. *Agron. J.* **65**, 395–7.

Wit, C. T. de (1965). Photosynthesis of leaf canopies. *Versl. Landbouwk. Onderz.* **66**, 81 pp.

Wit, C. T. de, Dijkshoorn, W. & Noggle, J, C. (1963). Ionic balance and growth of plants. *Versl. Landbouwk. Onderz.* **69**, 68 pp.

Worker, G. F., Jr & Marble, V. L. (1968). Comparison of sorghum forage types as to yield and chemical composition. *Agron. J.* **60**, 669–72.

Younge, O. R. & Butchart, D. H. (1963). Irrigated sugar beet production in Hawaii. *Haw. Agr. Exp. Sta. Bul.* **52**, 36 pp.

Zelitch, I. (1971). *Photosynthesis, Photorespiration, and Plant Productivity.* 347 pp. New York, Academic Press.

7. Functioning of the biosphere at the primary production level—objectives and achievements

F. E. ECKARDT

Research at high levels of organizational order has often been considered unproductive on the ground that important discoveries in recent years have been made, not at the biosphere level, but at much lower organizational levels, in particular at the macromolecular level. As one of the main objectives of the International Biological Programme has been to study the biomes of the planet on a worldwide scale, a general appreciation of the value of efforts made up to the present would be in order. In the following a short account will be given of the basic principles in the organizational pattern of biological systems and their bearing on the interpretation of results of scientific inquiry in this area. This will lead to a more general discussion of the state of progress in biosphere research with a view to defining areas of particular interest for future studies.

Characteristics of biological systems

Without bringing up the moot question of the self-sufficiency of the reductionist approach, one can accept with Nagel (1961) that biological inquiry has greatly profited by the adoption of systems of explanation which employ concepts and assert relations neither defined in nor derived from the physical sciences. Few biologists would deny today that the biosphere can be considered as an organic whole which has evolved as a whole. It is accepted that the behaviour of its components cannot be fully understood if just considered as so many independent but additive entities. This would seem too obvious to be mentioned. The full scope of its implications, however, may not yet have been realized.

One of the conceptual tools appropriate to the study of such systems is that of *hierarchical organization*. Biologists are faced with the fact that each of the hierarchically superimposed levels of integration: organelle, cell, organ, organism, population, etc. possesses properties specifically ascribable to their particular organization. In consequence, it is often

173

extremely difficult to predict behaviour at a given level from that of its various components at the underlying level.

The second, and by far the most important concept, is that of *adaptedness*. The study of adaptation is the inquiry into how and to what extent components of biological systems are or can be fitted together into higher groups of organizational order. It is thus implicit in all research on the structure and functioning of the biosphere. It is also, however, a most difficult concept as it implies in each case the clear specification of the time and space perspectives considered. What increases, for example, the chances of survival of the species at present may later contribute to its extinction, and what seems useful for a population if considered in isolation, such as a high rate of reproduction, may in fact prove unfavourable, in particular if leading to the depletion of essential food resources. Malthusianism is a form of adaptation, and probably a greatly underestimated form.

Of more immediate usefulness in recent years has been the concept of *strategy*. Central in the idea of strategy is the recognition that evolution has been based on a series of choices between different alternatives, exploiting already acquired genetic information to a maximum degree. It has been particularly useful as a tool for linking together many already well known facts and in particular for establishing the most likely evolutionary history of the biosphere.

Acceptance of the merits of these concepts carries with it the acceptance of the necessity of research at high levels of organizational order. Protein structures at the molecular level may well determine which strategic choices are possible, but it is from studies at higher levels of organizational order, where the phenomenological aspects of evolution obtain, i.e. where selection pressure acts to favour specific evolutionary trends, that it is possible to discover which strategies succeeded and why. It also implies, as often stressed by Dobzhansky (1970), that the most spectacular findings are to be expected at lower levels of organizational order, but that it is studies at higher levels of organizational order that make possible the establishment of judiciously conceived research programmes that can lead to such findings. The analytical and the holistic approach should go hand in hand.

Evolutionary history of the biosphere

To be acceptable, a theory of the origin of life must keep to a minimum the number of unlikely events. Following this principle, it is highly

174

likely that the origin of life occurred in the absence of oxygen. As Wald (1964) so convincingly points out, it would be extremely difficult to rationalize the ingenuity displayed by present-day organisms in conducting so many of their metabolic transformations in oxygen-independent manners. One would expect with Hochachka & Somero (1973) that biochemical evolution started with fermentative sequences, the first essential invention being structures capable of trapping energy, released in oxidation–reduction processes, in bonds of organo-phosphate compounds. The activity of these first organisms would be accompanied by an enrichment of CO_2 in the atmosphere.

The next major achievement might have been the invention of the pentose phosphate cycle enabling the production, independently from that of high energy compounds, of biosynthetic power, thus gaining for the organism increased independence from the external environment. It would have been followed by the evolution of pigmented compounds capable of absorbing solar energy and transducing it into a metabolically usable form. The integration of this first pattern of photophosphorylation with the pentose phosphate cycle, now to be used essentially in the reverse direction, thus paved the way for photosynthesis. Solar energy could be used for reducing CO_2 of the air to the oxidation level of carbohydrate. An important change in the environment would take place due to the release in the atmosphere by green plants of molecular oxygen.

The newly created environment, in its turn, could provide the necessary conditions for the evolution of a variant pattern of metabolism, respiration, to a large extent a reversal of photosynthesis. The high efficiency of this process would make possible the existence of the present day highly organized biosphere with its complex interactions between living organisms. This evolution was possible because of the parallel development of special hierarchically organized metabolic control mechanisms enabling plants to cope with different types of environmental variation. An almost instantaneous regulation could be achieved, for example, through the mechanism of allosteric modulation at the enzyme level, medium range control through gene activation, whereas long term adaptation would require a recombination of DNA base sequences in the process of sexual reproduction. Adaptation at higher levels of organizational order constituted a sort of coarse regulation which would dispense from excessive demands on lower level regulation mechanisms.

Accepting with Stebbins (1972) that the processes of evolution

175

operated in the past essentially as they do now, it is likely that initial stages of phylum differentiation resulted from interactions between populations and various environmental features, both biotic and abiotic. Selection for tolerance to specific stresses such as drought, salinity, extreme temperatures, etc. played a major role, but so did selection for structures enabling the plants to escape from or protect themselves against grazing animals. Of particular importance might have been the advent during Paleocene of herbivorous ungulates. Plants, to survive, adopted various tactics so as to protect essential organs. Phanerophytes placed their leaves high above the ground, hemicryptophytes gave shelter to their growing points close to the surface of the soil. Other plants specialized in the rapid colonization of disturbed surfaces such as the 'fugitive' (Harper, 1967) annual species. Others again developed special devices for surviving in the face of special stresses. Geophytes let above-ground organs wither away during the unfavourable seasons after having accumulated sufficient reserves in bulbs and corms to ensure a rapid re-formation of photosynthetic tissues at the onset of more propitious conditions. These life-forms, combined in different ways, make up the various biomes, forests, grasslands, etc. which characterize the landscapes of the planet as we know them today.

Organization of the biosphere

Granting that this general outline of the evolutionary history of the biosphere, based essentially on works by Broda (1970) and Hochachka & Somero (1973), is valid, to what extent can it be related to quantitative data on the structure and functioning of the biosphere which have been obtained within the framework of the IBP? First it is important to define what the two concepts life-form and biome, cover.

Raunkiaer (1905) used as a basis for his definition of life-forms the ways and means by which plants protect their leaf buds during the unfavourable season. In choosing this criterion he was able to describe life-forms which still today can be considered as excellent examples of major successful evolutionary strategies. In point of fact, several more recent and more detailed classifications of life-forms are still based on his basic plant types (Ellenberg & Mueller-Dombois, 1966). At present, more stress might be put on other criteria, such as protection against grazing animals, for example, but the basic idea of strategic choice remains the same. Some relationships exist between the world-wide distribution of life-forms and climate, but, as clearly stated by

Raunkiaer, they are of statistical character. The major life forms can be encountered together in a great variety of conditions.

The concept of biome is much more difficult to define. Gray (1967) defines it as a large community of living organisms having a peculiar form of dominant vegetation and associated characteristic animals. The biome is thus largely characterized by the life-form of the dominant plant species whether single or not and as most life-forms can be found under a great variety of conditions, so biomes can be encountered over considerable climatic gradients. On the other hand, biomes are to a large extent dependent on the stability of the environment. In stabler conditions, in later phases of succession, perennials, in particular woody species, will prevail, i.e. species devoting a large part of available energy resources to persistent vegetative organs. Forests, and to a lesser degree, grasslands, with respectively phanerophytes and hemicryptophytes as dominant life forms, are examples of such biomes. Under unstable conditions, in earlier stages of succession, colonizing species will dominate. Biomes also depend on the predominance of specific environmental constraints such as found in areas occupied by deserts, tundras, etc. Crops, for the most part, can maintain themselves only if Man intervenes so as to reduce natural stresses, e.g. competition and lack of soil nutrients.

In a sense, in the same way as for life-forms, biomes can be defined as special types of strategies which have succeeded in a given environment. One difficulty, however, persists. In some areas of the world, in particular in the arctic–alpine regions, the plant cover is composed of a great variety of smaller, physiognomically very different vegetation units (Wielgolaski, Chapter 4), each of which can be considered as representing a special form of survival strategy. To this can be added that most of the world biomes have been so much altered in the last decades that they do not represent any more the outcome of a long evolutionary history in which only forces other than Man's have been at play. Many biomes today in fact can be considered as unretrievable, the time needed for the restoration of soils, for example, exceeding that of several human generations. For want of something better, it seems quite reasonable, however, for the time being, to use the concept of biome as a basic although crude unit of organization of the biosphere. It has proven to be useful for the study of the performance of the biosphere to a large extent because of the links between life-forms and biomes.

Performance of the biosphere

Bearing in mind the large number of higher plant species, which may amount to more than a quarter of a million, it quite obviously is impossible to study in each biome more than an almost infinitesimally small part of its total flora. This implies that emphasis must be laid on a few dominant species, which will often mean a few typical life-forms. To what extent generalizations from the behaviour of these few species to that of the whole biosphere are permissible, remains an open question. There are signs, however, that they may lead to useful working hypotheses on which to base future research on the biosphere considered as a whole.

The survival of green plants is based on their ability to maintain a positive balance between gain of energy through photosynthesis and loss due to respiration, death of tissues and grazing. This has been achieved through a combination of many different structural and functional features such as those well exemplified by the life-forms mentioned. Some plants have increased their energy input by investing a considerable part of products of photosynthesis in chlorophyll-containing tissues. Others have reduced losses by developing special organs enabling them to defend themselves against grazing, etc.

As many of these life-forms, as already mentioned, can perfectly well exist under similar macroclimatic conditions, it is interesting to compare their performances as regards interception, transformation and use of solar energy. Kira (Chapter 2) in his penetrating study of the forest biome proposes two basic principles. The first is that most plants under optimal soil conditions will develop leaf canopies capable of absorbing almost all the photosynthetically usable radiation. The second is that the efficiency of the process of fixing this energy in dry matter is on the whole similar whatever the amount of radiant energy received, i.e. it is independent of geographical latitude. Kira evaluates the efficiency to about one percent (based on *total* short-wave radiation) which is considerably less than that generally given for potential production.

This discrepancy between actual and potential production is at first sight surprising if one takes into account the strong selection pressures prevailing in Nature (Levins, 1968). Several reasons, however, can be invoked. One is that plants must pay a price for defending themselves. With each strategy can be associated a cost (Harper, 1967) and Kira gives good examples of the respiratory costs linked with the maintaining of tree trunks. Eckardt (1973) in the Mediterranean region finds that

178

net primary production actually becomes negative in some perennial species during the warm summer, and if it were not for the strongly reduced stem respiration in winter it might be difficult for the evergreen climactic forest there to survive. From an evolutionary point of view it seems quite permissible to pay a very high price for a given structure, if this structure enables the species to become the dominant plant of a mature ecosystem. It was also found that a perennial shrub species had a light-response curve of photosynthesis quite similar to that of a closely related annual species occupying adjacent sites. The costs associated with the maintenance of large quantities of ligneous tissues appeared to be almost as high as those associated with the behaviour of the short-lived colonizing species.

There is another reason also, which perhaps is too often neglected; it is that plants to survive, except perhaps in the equatorial region, do need to maintain a certain capacity to adapt to rapidly changing conditions. This may imply a large enzyme turnover rate (Penning de Vries, 1974) and in this respect it is significant to note that the large amounts of ribulose diphosphate carboxylase present in the cells of C_3-plants have been considered favourable under changing light conditions (Björkman, 1970). It should also be remembered that evolution is a slow process. Plants, so to say, are doing the right thing at the wrong moment. It implies that the variables, both structural and functional, on which production depends, never attain optimum values for this production at the same time. In the above-mentioned work in the Mediterranean region it was found that in spite of large variations from one life-form to the other with respect to canopy architecture, length of the photosynthetic season, the efficiency of photosynthesis on a leaf area basis, total respiration, etc., the annual dry matter production of the different vegetation types studied was surprisingly similar. Survival is obtained by a combination of many potentialities, only a few of which are exploited to the full.

To these reasons can be added that there is a price to be paid for genetic variability. If variability is lost, as is the case in some self-fertilizing species, the future of the phylum may be sacrified in exchange for some short-term advantage (Stebbins, 1966). Although activities of living beings seem to be directed towards the attainment of goals that lie in the future, their behaviour just reflects the fact that they have evolved under changing conditions which favoured great variability. It can also be added that selection pressure may not always have favoured production as such. Just as Man, in selecting directly for a given desirable quality in a crop (Loomis & Gerakis, Chapter 6) has often failed to select first for increased productivity, so the action of numerous grazing animals in the past may have diverted plant evolution from its way towards increased production capacity.

Under more unfavourable soil conditions, due to lack of water, lack of nutrients, extreme temperatures or high salt content, primary production is in most cases considerably reduced, stress resistance, whether based on the principle of tolerance or endurance, taking precedence over capacity to harvest the sun's energy (Levitt, 1972). Survival may hinge on specific behavioural patterns: shedding of leaves linked with drought, stomatal control linked with complex combinations of climatic factors and water stress (Schulze & Kappen, Chapter 5), rapid CO_2 absorption when stomata are open ensured by high CO_2-affinity systems as found in C_4-plants, etc.

Present difficulties in biosphere research

In spite of the considerable amount of research made in recent years, we are still far from having acquired a synthetic view of the biosphere (Margalef, 1963). One reason is that very little is known as yet about the adaptative significance of structural and functional traits in plants. An important stumbling bloc is that such traits or characteristics are, quoting from Dobzhansky, only semantic devices employed by biologists to facilitate the description of the organism. The importance of a trait depends on the whole developmental nexus in which it is part.

As stated above, one cannot affirm that a trait is of adaptive value, without at the same time specifying the time and space perspectives taken into consideration. Plants are adapted to live in a community of organisms so that a given behavioural pattern may be interpreted quite differently according to whether a single leaf, a rosette or a whole canopy is considered (Lewis, 1972), or a crop or an ecosystem. Comparisons of the adaptive role of the C_4-pathway with that of the C_3-pathway for example may give different results if made in cultures or under natural environmental conditions (Caldwell, Chapter 3). This already in itself represents a considerable difficulty because quite evidently it is impossible to take into account all possible relations between the organism and the rest of the biosphere. But what makes things even more difficult is that plants are adapted to maintain themselves in a community over long intervals of time. The value of self-fertilization for the survival of the phylum is entirely different if considered over short- instead of

180

long-term intervals. Yet, it would be quite aberrant to take into account the entire evolutionary history of the entire biosphere considered at that level. As aptly observed by Ayala (cited in Dobzhansky, 1970), the primordial organisms from which all the rest have descended would be the fittest.

Adding to this difficulty is the fact that selection pressure may give rise to adaptive responses at all levels of organizational order of the plant except perhaps at the lowest, i.e. the macromolecular level (Crow, 1972), and that in many cases these responses are correlated. As a result of this, for example, selection for high productivity can perfectly well give rise to plants with erect photosynthetic organs but lower rate of photosynthesis per unit leaf area (Cooper, Chapter 21). A frequent cause of correlated responses is pleiotropism, i.e. manifold effects of gene activity. Another is canalizing selection which tends to stabilize the developmental pattern.

One consequence arising from the existence of such correlated responses is that it is almost impossible to assert if, or to what degree, a given trait contributes to the survival of a species without supporting experimental evidence. Intuitively, one would infer adaptive significance of characteristic traits found in desert, alpine, prairie, tundra, tropical forest and many other types of vegetation, from the fact that they are often linked with a specific habitat. In many cases the inference may be correct, in many cases it may not. Only in rare cases are biologists faced with such apparently clear-cut examples of adaptation as found in *Ranunculus aquatilis* where the shapes of leaves during ontogenesis change according to habitat so as, seemingly, to maintain an optimum balance between the two factors most needed in photosynthesis, light and water. In most instances, the problem is most difficult to disentangle and the physiognomical convergence of systematically different species in areas of the world with Mediterranean type of climate is a case in point (Specht, 1969; Mooney & Dunn, 1969). Does sclerophylly increase chances of survival under such conditions or is it just accompaning increased tolerance to water deficits? Close links between morphology and drought tolerance may have existed in early forms of plant life.

Another consequence is that the extent to which ecological systems operate as integrated wholes may have been considerably underestimated. For the individual plant, Mousseau (p. 692) has shown how the rate of photosynthesis during ontogenesis is kept roughly constant under changing light conditions through simultaneous and co-ordinated adjustments at the levels of the chloroplast, the leaf, the shoot and the entire plant, and at a much higher level of organizational order, MacArthur (1973) has convincingly demonstrated how regeneration of, for example, an artificially destroyed island ecosystem proceeds according to fixed rules. New species enter and established ones become extinct all the time, but the overall number remains almost the same.

With respect to the heritability of structural and functional characteristics, the situation is similar. Very little information is available on how readily the various traits are selected and how far selection can go before the store of genetic variation is depleted. In theories relating to the origin of the world's biomes, little evidence is available to indicate the actual role of environmental factors. One might well suspect, as mentioned earlier, that many groups of animals, ungulates in particular, played an essential role in the past in differentiating plants into life forms of various kinds. This would have implied an adjustment of the rate of photosynthesis, *a postiori*, so as to permit the development of canopy structure which neither underexploited available light resources, nor left too many leaves under unfavourable conditions. Clearly some knowledge of relevant heritabilities could provide a lead. Similarly, it has been suggested that differences between ligneous and herbaceous plants can be considered as depending not just on phylogenetic age, but actually resulting from an environmentally induced change in cambial activity and that during evolution one form has been able to change into the other, and vice versa, when exposed to strong selection pressure favouring such changes (Scharfetter, 1953). Little experimental evidence is available as yet, however, to substantiate such hypotheses.

It is generally acknowledged that mathematical modelling may prove useful in many areas of ecological inquiry. Models can be constructed so as to permit the study of large-scale flows of energy and matter within the ecosystem. Simulation experiments on the computer can contribute to the solving of problems of ordination, and the establishment of the hierarchical role in productivity of various structural and functional features of the plant is a case in point. It is apparent, however, that as soon as one leaves the safe ground of geometry as related to canopy structure or transport phenomena obeying Fick's law, and enters the realm of biochemistry, modelling may become a less worthwhile proposition. Very little is known, for example, about the process of translocation and the role of hormones and sink potentialities, i.e. what governs allocation of energy and matter during growth. Very little is known too of the transport of CO_2 from intercellular space to the carboxylation centres and the role of concentrations of carbonic anhydrase at the external membrane level and of ribulose diphosphate carboxylase at the operating level of the Calvin cycle.

Finally, it should be mentioned that the plant's environment is often very difficult to describe, let alone to quantify. What matters for the plant are the mass and energy exchanges across the surface-to-air and surface-to-soil interfaces, and these may bear only little relationship to macroclimate and soil type. Microclimate within the plant cover will change during growth and Leafe, Stiles & Dickinson (p. 689) have aptly demonstrated how a decline in productivity in grasslands during the growing season can be ascribed to progressively deteriorating light conditions at the sites where young leaves are developed. In general, microclimatic changes within the canopy during growth are so important that one may expect a considerably higher net production, notably at low latitudes, if leaves are capable of adapting their metabolism *pari passu* with increasing shade (Loomis & Gerakis, Chapter 6).

Conclusions

Considering PT activities of the International Biological Programme in retrospect, what has been achieved? To what extent has it been possible to put the initial general objectives into a concrete form? How much insight has been gained into the more detailed aspects of the structure and functioning of the biosphere?

An important achievement of the programme has been the acquisition of many new quantitative data on productivity parameters of the world's biomes. An even greater achievement, however, may have been to focus attention to the apparent low efficiency of energy conversion in the biosphere and to demonstrate how this low efficiency is related to essential characteristics of the living world. The study of low efficiency *per se* may, in fact, lead to a better understanding of basic principles governing the evolution of biological systems. Several circumstances can be invoked to explain this low efficiency:

(1) Strategic choices in the past, related to metabolism, reproduction, life-form, etc., have channelled evolution so as to restrict adaptability except in certain privileged directions.

(2) Adjustments to environmental change have taken place with time lags varying from one structural and functional trait to the other.

(3) Isolation and the invention of new mechanisms enabling the

183

exploitation of unoccupied territories and niches, have resulted in high productivity becoming less important for survival.

(4) Efficient resource exploitation implied highly complex structures, the maintenance costs of which were, and still are, high, notably under changing environmental conditions.

To these circumstances can be added the possible existence of un-coupled biochemical reactions, in relation, for example, to respiration and photorespiration, although this postulate may be somewhat academic. On the one hand, it is difficult to assert that no intermediate products in the reactions are useful. On the other, we know that evolution has always exploited with a fair amount of success bits and pieces of already existing metabolic pathways.

The present flora of the planet clearly bears the stamp of a tumultuous past combined with an evolution, based on chance and deterministic laws, which gave premium to variability. This variability must be considered as an essential feature which cannot be substituted by some generalized plant behaviour, however desirable this may be in an effort of synthesis. It is within this variability only that we can seek indications of general principles relative to the distribution of plants on the earth. It is apparent that a huge field of promising research awaits the ecologist as almost nothing is known as yet about the survival value of individual structural and functional traits, of their heritability, of the costs associated with different survival strategies and the costs of maintaining high gene redundancy.

Research at high levels of organizational order, as stated in the introduction, may not have led to important discoveries at that level. Clearly, however, it has helped to systematize the formulation of existing problems and thus to establish a sound strategy for future research on the structure and functioning of the biosphere at the primary production level.

References

Björkman, O. (1970). Characteristics of the photosynthetic apparatus as revealed by laboratory measurements. In *Prediction and Measurement of Photosynthetic Productivity*, pp. 267–81. Wageningen, PUDOC.

Broda, E. (1970). The evolution of bioenergetic processes. *Progress in Biophysics and Molecular Biology, London*, **21**, 143–208.

Crow, J. F. (1972). The dilemma of nearly neutral mutations. *Journal of Heredity*, **6**, 306–16.

Dobzhansky, Th. (1970). *Genetics of the evolutionary process*, 505 pp. New York, Columbia University Press.

Eckardt, F. E. (1973). Plant strategy, CO_2-exchange and primary production. *Oecologia Plantarum*, **8**, 309–12.

Ellenberg, H. & Mueller-Dombois, D. (1966). A key to Raunkiaer plant life forms with revised subdivisions. *Berichte der geobotanisches Institutes der Eidgenössichen technischen Hochschule, Stiftung Rübel*, **37**, 56–73.

Gray, P. (1967). *The dictionary of the biological sciences*, 602 pp. New York, Reinhold.

Harper, J. L. (1967). A Darwinian approach to plant ecology. *Journal of Ecology*, **55**, 247–70.

Hochachka, P. W. and Somero, G. N. (1973). *Strategies of biochemical adaptation*, 385 pp. Philadelphia, W. B. Saunders.

Levins, R. (1968). *Evolution in changing environments*, 120 pp. Princeton, N.J., Princeton University Press.

Levitt, J. (1972). *Responses of plants to environmental stresses*, 697 pp. New York, Academic Press.

Lewis, M. C. (1972). The physiological significance of variation in leaf structure. *Science Progress*, **60**, 25–51.

Margalef, R. (1963). On certain unifying principles in ecology. *American Naturalist*, **97**, 357–74.

MacArthur, R. H. (1973). *Patterns in the distribution of species*. New York, Harper & Row.

Mooney, H. A. & Dunn, E. L. (1969). Convergent evolution of mediterranean-climate evergreen sclerophyll shrubs. *Evolution*, **24**, 292–303.

Nagel, E. (1961). *The structure of science. Problems in the logic of scientific explanation*, 618 pp. London, Routledge & Kegan Paul Ltd.

Penning de Vries, F. W. T. (1974). The cost of maintenance processes in plant cells. *Annals of Botany* (in press).

Raunkiaer, C. (1905). Types biologiques pour la géographie botanique. *Bulletin de l'Académie royale des Sciences*, Copenhagen.

Scharfetter, R. (1953). *Biographien von Pflanzensippen*, 546 pp. Vienna, Springer-Verlag.

Specht, R. L. (1969). A comparison of the sclerophyllous vegetation characteristic of Mediterranean type climates in France, California, and Southern Australia. *Australian Journal of Botany*, **17**, 277–92.

Stebbins, G. L. (1966). *Processes of organic evolution*, 191 pp. New York, Prentice-Hall.

Stebbins, G. L. (1972). Ecological distribution of centers of major adaptive radiation in Angiosperms. In *Taxinomy, Phytogeography and Evolution*, ed. D. H. Valentine, pp. 6–34. London, Academic Press.

Wald, G. (1964). The origins of life. *Proceedings of the National Academy of Sciences, USA*, **52**, 595 pp.

PART II

Primary production in aquatic ecosystems

8. Primary production of freshwater macrophytes

D. F. WESTLAKE

This chapter is based on a general knowledge of research both within and outside IBP and the proceedings of four preliminary PF and Wetlands meetings.

The magnitude of production and the relations between the production processes and the environment differ greatly between submerged and emergent macrophytes. Hence each will be treated separately throughout. Emergent plants have aerial leaves and a gaseous source of carbon dioxide, which makes them resemble terrestrial plants, but they are normally free from restrictions imposed by water supply. Submerged plants resemble phytoplankton in having to compete with water for light and in having aqueous carbon dioxide and mineral nutrient sources, but can maintain a fixed position in the water column, have very different relations to water movement and are severely restricted in distribution by depth.

In the classical limnologists' lake, which is deep and fairly steep sided, the marginal areas, where submerged and emergent macrophytes can grow on the bottom, are small compared with the total area of the lake, where phytoplankton can grow, and their contribution to the total primary production of lakes is small. However, on a global basis it is probable that the majority of lakes are shallow and macrophyte production is correspondingly more important (cf. Rich, Wetzel & Van Thuy, 1971). In rivers much depends on depth, length and turbidity, but in general macrophytes are more important in short, shallow, clear streams and phytoplankton in long, deep, turbid rivers. Emergent plants are often only found in a narrow margin along rivers, but extensive marginal and deltaic areas occur, particularly where man has not interfered with the natural drainage.

Periphytic algae have more resemblances with macrophytes than phytoplankton, but can only occur in thin layers and are unable to make active responses to changes in depth (macrophytes can grow towards the surface). Macrophytes with floating leaves occupy an intermediate position in the series – terrestrial plants, emergent plants, submerged plants – being dependent on water for support, yet having some access to gaseous as well as aqueous carbon dioxide sources.

Marine and freshwater macrophytes appear to have very similar relations between the environment and their productive processes. Appearances may be deceptive, however, since the great difference in productivity between these communities, emphasised during the Aberystwyth symposium (see Chapman & Mann, Chapter 9), suggests that production processes are somehow favoured in the marine littoral.

The determination and interpretation of biomass changes remains the main basis for estimations of the annual productivity of freshwater macrophytes, but difficulties have arisen with stands with stable or irregularly changing biomass (e.g. Rich, Wetzel & Van Thuy, 1971; Thompson, p. 691). The importance of translocation and accumulation in underground organs is now more generally recognised and some special studies have been made (e.g. Imhof & Burian, 1972; Fiala, 1973a; Thompson, p. 691). More attention has also been paid to problems arising from losses of biomass by grazing, damage or mortality (e.g. Mathews & Westlake, 1969; Pieczyńska, 1972; Kajak, Hillbricht-Ilkowska & Pieczyńska, 1972; Dawson, 1973).

There has been increasing use of metabolic methods, experimental techniques and population studies to improve the interpretation of biomass changes, as well as for their value in gaining a fuller understanding of the behaviour of the plants (e.g. Ikusima, 1970; Květ, 1971; Burian, 1971,1973; Gaudet, 1973; Rejmánková, 1973a). In a few cases, not during the IBP, entire unenclosed stands have been studied by metabolic methods (e.g. Odum, 1957; Edwards & Owens, 1962; Hannan & Dorris, 1970).

The importance for plant growth of the balance between light energy fixed (true gross photosynthesis) and heat energy lost (total respiration) is becoming more widely recognised but, apart from determinations of respiratory rates, little detailed work has been done on aquatic macrophytes. Photorespiration has been indicated, or shown to occur, in many aquatic macrophytes (e.g. Goldsworthy & Day, 1970; McNaughton & Fullem, 1970; Spence, 1972; Stanley & Naylor, 1972; Hough, 1974). However, plant morphology, the problems of aqueous diffusion of gases, the large internal air spaces and the variety of carbon sources make the photorespiratory behaviour of submerged macrophytes differ from terrestrial plants, and some emergent macrophytes may have special features. Photorespiration may be less important for aquatic macrophytes than for terrestrial plants and phytoplankton. Submerged macrophytes, like algae, also lose energy by excretion of organic materials (e.g. Wetzel & Manny, 1972).

Table 8.1. Cover and productivity of freshwater macrophytes, on fertile sites, during optimum growth period (references in text)

	Net photosynthetic capacity of photosynthetic organs			Crop growth rate change in dry wt per unit stand area (g m⁻² d⁻¹)	Seasonal maximum cover		Rate of net production		Climate
	Rate of carbon uptake		Rate of CO_2 uptake per unit leaf area (unit leaf rate) (mg dm⁻² h⁻¹)		Biomass as organic wt (kg m⁻²)	Total chlorophyll (g m⁻²)	Annual as organic wt (kg m⁻² yr⁻¹)	Mean for growing season (g C m⁻² d⁻¹)	
	Per unit dry wt (mg g⁻¹ h⁻¹)	Per unit total chlorophyll (mg mg⁻¹ h⁻¹)							
Emergent probable C₄: C. papyrus	–	–	~26	~41 (mean)	3–5	3–9*	9–15	12–19†	Tropical
Emergent C₃: e.g. P. communis Typha spp.	3–9	1–2.5	15–34	12–48	4–10	3–6‡	4–6	10–13§	Temperate
Submerged: e.g. Chara spp. M. spicatum	2–10(−20)	0.2–0.9	1–5(−11)	2–10(−25)	0.6 / 0.4–0.7	~6 / 2–6	~2 / 0.5–0.8	~3 / 1–3¶	Tropical / Temperate

* Assuming 1–3 mg chl. (g org. wt)⁻¹ in shoots.
‡ See text; 2–4 kg aerial shoots m⁻² and 1.5 mg chl. (g org. wt)⁻¹; and some direct results.
§ Assuming 470 mg C (g org. wt)⁻¹ and 180–200 d.

† Assuming 480 mg C g⁻¹ and 365 d.
¶ Assuming 470 mg C (g org. wt) and 120–200 d.

Aquatic ecosystems

Comparisons of biomass, photosynthesis and production are sum-marised in Table 8.1. Preparation of this table has involved some selection of data, and assumed conversion factors have often been necessary to obtain probable ranges. Throughout the table more weight should be given to general differences between plant types than to the absolute values of the upper and lower limits of the ranges. Oxygen–carbon interconversions have been based on $0.37(O_2) = C$.

Photosynthetic capacity

The rate at which the photosynthetic organs can fix carbon and energy under optimum conditions sets an upper limit to the potential pro-ductivity of a plant community. Data on photosynthetic capacity are summarised in the first three columns of Table 8.1 using the three most common criteria.

Emergent macrophytes

The few investigations on the net photosynthetic capacity of emergent macrophytes give values in the range 3–9 mg C (g dry leaf wt)$^{-1}$ h^{-1} at or near light saturation for *Phragmites communis* and *Typha latifolia* (Walker & Waygood, 1968; McNaughton & Fullem, 1970; Burian, 1973). Walker & Waygood's results are rather low, but if allowance is made for seasonal differences and technical problems (cf. Burian, 1973) and some confusion in units, they indicate an optimum value well within this range.

After a similar correction Walker & Waygood's results (1968) give ~ 0.8 mg C fixed (mg total chlorophyll)$^{-1}$ h^{-1}. Assuming typical chloro-phyll contents for the leaves of these plants (Bray, 1960; Walker & Waygood, 1968; Rejmánková, 1973*b*) of 2.0–5.5 mg chlorophyll (g dry wt of leaf)$^{-1}$ the other capacities are 1.0–2.5 mg C(mg chl.)$^{-1}$ h^{-1}.

Metabolic measurements of the unit leaf rate of net photosynthesis made with leaf cuvettes and infra-red gas analysis (from Ikusima, 1970; Gloser, 1972; Burian, 1973) on *Nuphar japonicum*, *Nymphoides indica*, *Potamogeton distinctus*, *Glyceria maxima*, *Phalaris arundinacea* and *Phragmites communis* have found net rates of 15–30 mg CO_2 dm^{-2} h^{-1} at optimum temperatures and light intensities. Lower values, about 5–11 mg CO_2 dm^{-2} h^{-1}, were found by Walker & Waygood (1968) but if the points discussed above are correct these rates would become comparable with the others.

McNaughton & Fullem (1970) measured the net photosynthesis of isolated leaves of *Typha latifolia* by infra-red gas analysis, finding very high unit leaf rates of photosynthesis of 44–69 mg CO_2 dm^{-2} h^{-1}. The paper does not indicate how the leaf areas were measured and, as Dykyjová & Ondok (1973) point out, it may be better to use both surfaces of such thick erect leaves. If only one surface was measured, these rates would become 22–34 mg CO_2 dm^{-2} h^{-1} in terms of both surfaces, which are similar to those for *Phragmites* and *Phalaris*. This explanation is supported by the fact that the photosynthetic capacity (per unit dry weight) of this species is also similar to those species.

McNaughton & Fullem thought the high unit leaf rate indicated that *T. latifolia* might be a C_4-plant, but other biochemical and morphological evidence was found to show that it was a C_3-plant. Jones & Milburn (personal communication) have made similar experiments using rays from the umbel of *Cyperus papyrus* and found net rates of up to 26 mg CO_2 dm^{-2} h^{-1} with light saturation reached at about 350 J m^{-2} s^{-1} (quartz–iodine radiation filtered through water). Their findings that the CO_2 compensation point is zero, that the temperature optimum is around 32 °C and that bundle sheath cells are present strongly support the view that this is a C_4-plant, yet the unit leaf rate and light saturation level suggest a C_3-metabolism. However, some morphological peculiarities of the rays may affect these responses and it would be interesting to know photosynthetic rates expressed on chlorophyll or dry weight. No other aquatic plants are known to have a C_4-metabolism at present.

Submerged macrophytes

Photosynthetic capacity has often been measured, usually by means of the oxygen output, but also using radiocarbon. Both are assumed to give net photosynthesis. Optimum rates for a great variety of species usually lie between 2 and 10 mg C(g dry wt)$^{-1}$ h^{-1} and a value of about 4 may be regarded as typical (5–10–25 mg O_2 g^{-1} h^{-1}; e.g. Whitwer, 1955; Wetzel, 1964; Ikusima, 1965,1970; Westlake, 1967; McGahee & Davis, 1971; Adams, 1972; Kumano, 1972; Stanley & Naylor, 1972). Carr (1969) gives rates of photosynthesis for *Ceratophyllum demersum* of between '35 and 65 O_2 (ml/(200 min 0.1 g dry wt))' which imply net carbon fixation rates of the order of 75 mg C g^{-1} h^{-1}, but elsewhere in her paper she states that 'productivity was found to be 6 mg C/(g h)' in a context that clearly intends the biomass to still be in dry weight.

Aquatic ecosystems

The highest rates reported, free from anomalies, are ~ 13–18 mg C $g^{-1} h^{-1}$ (38–51 mg gross O_2 $g^{-1} h^{-1}$; Ikusima, 1965, see also p. 690).

There are fewer data for capacity expressed in terms of chlorophyll. Values reported are mostly between 0.2 and 0.9 mg C (mg chl.)$^{-1} h^{-1}$ (Hammann, 1957; Ikusima, 1966), which correspond well to a value of 0.5 estimated from the typical capacity of 4 mg C(g dry wt)$^{-1} h^{-1}$ and an assumed mean chlorophyll content of 8 mg g^{-1} (see p. 200).

There are few unit leaf rates of net photosynthesis available, largely because measurements of leaf area are extremely difficult and not obviously relevant for the many species with finely divided leaves and green stems. Most are between 1 and 5 mg CO_2 $dm^{-2} h^{-1}$ (Hammann, 1957; Ikusima, 1965,1966; Spence & Campbell, 1971). The highest reported is ~ 11 mg CO_2 $dm^{-2} h^{-1}$ (Spence & Chrystal, 1970) for *Potamogeton pectinatus*.

Crop growth rates

Daily rates of change in biomass ultimately depend on photosynthetic capacity, but many other factors such as biomass, self-shading, variations in irradiance and proportions of non-photosynthetic tissue are involved. Generally these rates are found directly from changes in biomass over a period of days but sometimes integrations of hourly determinations of carbon exchange are attempted. This approach is usually essential in communities, such as phytoplankton, subject to heavy losses. The rates given in Table 8.1 are generally those found during the period of optimum growth.

Emergent plants

High growth rates, mostly derived from changes in aerial standing crop, are in the range 25–48 g dry wt $m^{-2} d^{-1}$, but several of these include material translocated from rhizomes or rootstocks (*Typha latifolia*, Penfound, 1956;* *Justicia americana*, Boyd, 1969; *Typha angustifolia*, *Phragmites communis*, Dykyjová, Ondok & Přibáň, 1970; Květ, 1971; Dykyjová, 1971; Monteith, 1972; Burian, 1973). However, Boyd's value was based on a plant which has only a small rootstock and Burian's value was based on metabolic measurements with an infra-red gas analyser. He found rates within this range throughout the summer

* A value of 52.6 g $m^{-2} d^{-1}$, often quoted from Penfound, is derived from an arithmetical error in his paper which gives 14 days between 4.5 and 28.5 instead of 24 days.

194

while the standing crop growth rate was much lower or even negative. Also Dykyjová (1971) gives values towards the upper end of the range based on increments of both under and above ground parts. Květ (1971) gives rates of 16 g m^{-2} d^{-1} for *P. communis* in July, when translocation in either direction was low, and 7.3 g m^{-2} d^{-1} for *T. latifolia* after correction for translocation. *Stratiotes aloides*, which is emergent when growing most rapidly, achieves at least 30–46 g m^{-2} d^{-1} (Geus-Kruyt & Segal, 1973). This plant has rather rapid leaf-shedding and addition of this loss would increase the net production; on the other hand, the ash content is probably high. Dykyjová (1971) and Dykyjová & Ondok (1973) give values of 12–36 g m^{-2} d^{-1} for aerial shoots of *P. communis*, *Schoenoplectus lacustris*, *Sparganium erectum* and *T. angustifolia* averaged over long periods.

The only available data for *Cyperus papyrus* in natural stands derives from the estimates of annual production discussed later (p. 198). It is not affected by translocation and in an equable climate an annual mean is unlikely to be far below the optimum. Thompson (p. 691) reported that in hydroponic cultures five 'plant units', arranged so that the photosynthetic organs were contained within one square metre and enclosed round the sides in black polyethylene to reduce edge effects, could sustain 125 g m^{-2} d^{-1} (50 g C m^{-2} d^{-1}). Similarly in a temperate climate Dykyjová, Véber & Přibáň (1971*a,b*) found rates of 30–60 g total dry wt m^{-2} d^{-1} for many established hydroponic cultures of *P. communis*, *Typha* spp., *S. lacustris* and *Bulboschoenus maritimus* (but they had minimal guarding). These total rates involve some assumptions about the annual increments of rhizomes which are only given in detail in the 1971*a* paper. For aerial shoots alone many values lie between 10 and 55 g m^{-2} d^{-1}. All these very high values require further investigation.

Submerged macrophytes

The majority of crop growth rates found for natural stands at fertile temperate sites over the period of their most rapid growth are in the range 2–10 g dry wt m^{-2} d^{-1} (e.g. Edwards & Owens, 1960,1962; Forsberg, 1960; Owens & Edwards, 1962; Wetzel, 1964; Ikusima, 1966; Westlake *et al.*, 1972). Since few submerged aquatic species have large perennating organs, translocation errors are unlikely to arise. Most of these rates are derived from biomass changes over periods of a month or more. Two estimates of the maximum crop growth rate attained over

195

a single day, based on radiocarbon methods, are very much higher. Adams & McCracken (1974) calculated stand production from measurements of the net photosynthetic capacity of *Myriophyllum spicatum*, making allowance for stand density and the vertical profiles of biomass and capacity and underwater irradiance. This gave a value of 10.8 g C m^{-2} d^{-1}, greater than 25 g dry wt m^{-2} d^{-1}. The photosynthetic capacity of the plant apices was a normal 5.7 mg C(g dry wt)$^{-1}$ h^{-1}. They appear to have made no allowance for night-time respiration, which probably reduces this rate to > 20 g dry wt m^{-2} d^{-1}. Wetzel (1964) enclosed a stand of *Chara* sp. for four to six hours and converted this result to a daily rate of 15.9 g C m^{-2} d^{-1}, 75 g dry wt m^{-2} d^{-1}. This is a very high rate even allowing for the possibility of under-correcting for night respiration and for exaggeration of the crop growth rate in terms of dry weight by the high ash content assumed (55%, typical for this genus).

Biomass, cover and annual production

The optimum crop growth rates are not sustained throughout a year and in many climates growth is confined to part of the year. There is some evidence in Table 8.1, that the optimum and mean crop growth rates for the growing season are not very different between comparable temperate and tropical stands, but when growth occurs all the year in a tropical or subtropical climate the annual production can greatly exceed that of similar temperate communities. Higher respiratory losses towards the end of the growth cycle of individual shoots may make the final net production available to the secondary consumers less than the previous cumulative net production.

Table 8.1 summarises the available data on biomass and production on fertile sites. Clearly on less fertile or otherwise unfavourable sites much lower values will be found.

Emergent macrophytes

Many authors (e.g. Seidel, 1959; Bray, Lawrence & Pearson, 1959; Rudescu, Niculescu & Chivu, 1965; Stake, 1967; Boyd, 1969; Dykyjová, 1971; Květ, 1971; Korelyakova, 1971; Imhof & Burian, 1972; Szajnowski, 1973) have reported biomasses of aerial shoots of emergent plants in the temperate zone equivalent to from 1.5–3.5 kg m^{-2} of dry organic (ash-free) matter. The species involved include *Butomus umbellatus, Phragmites communis, Schoenoplectus*

196

lacustris, Sparganium erectum and *Typha angustifolia.* All these have extensive rhizome systems which were not always sampled, but there is enough data in the literature to show that the underground parts are often two to five times the weight of the aerial parts (some of the above papers; Westlake, 1965; Fiala, 1973*b*).

There are many fewer data on tropical and subtropical emergent plants and it is not always clear if the sampling pattern has overcome the problems of clumped distributions and edge effects. Several workers have given data equivalent to aerial shoot biomasses often exceeding 2.0 kg m⁻² dry organic weight (Zohary, Orshansky, Muhsam & Lewin, 1955; Pearsall, 1959; Ogawa, Yoda & Kira, 1961; Sinha, 1970; Ambasht, 1971; Howard-Williams, 1973; Thompson, p. 691). A wide variety of species is involved, but *Cyperus papyrus* occurs frequently.

Thompson (p. 691) reported areas of 5 m² containing 100 kg dry organic weight of this species (20 kg total biomass m⁻²) but 3–5 kg m⁻² seemed more likely over large areas. The aerial shoots formed 60–70 % of the biomass, which explains why the total biomass is lower than the biomass of temperate emergent plants. *Typha domingensis* reaches a total biomass of 4.4 kg m⁻², with 52 % underground (Howard-Williams, 1973). There may well be other species in tropical regions with a greater proportion of long-lived rhizome and hence higher biomass. Ogawa, Yoda & Kira (1961) found 10 kg m⁻² of aerial shoots in an *Arundo donax* stand. Kaul (1971) found aerial shoot biomasses of *Typha angustata* and *Phragmites communis* of 3.5–4.7 kg m⁻² dry weight in Kashmir. If the underground parts are in the same proportions as in Europe this implies total biomasses of at least 5–14 kg m⁻².

There are not many data on the chlorophyll content of emergent plants and there is probably a wide range of 1–20 mg chlorophyll per gram organic weight of aerial shoots, depending on whether the plant consists largely of young green leaves or has a high proportion of stem or older tissues. To some extent these are complementary, so that plants with much stem or older tissue have a higher biomass than those with mostly young green leaves. The data in the table (based on: Bray, 1960; Aruga & Monsi, 1963; Walker & Waygood, 1968; Boyd, 1970*a,b*; Gaudet, 1973; Rejmánková, 1973*b*; Szajnowski, 1973; Szczepański, 1973; and my own preliminary determinations) show this reduced range.

The estimations of annual production from the biomass have involved making assumptions about the transfer of material from the aerial shoots to the rhizomes, the age of the rhizomes and losses from all parts of the plant before the seasonal maximum. Observations on the age of

197

rhizomes (Westlake, 1968), the proportions of aerial and underground parts (Westlake, 1965; Szczepański, 1969; Dykyjová, 1971), the annual increments of rhizomes to cultured plants (Hejný, 1960; Fiala, Dykyjová, Květ & Svoboda, 1968; Dykyjová, Véber & Přibáň, 1971*a*; Fiala, 1973*b*), growth analysis (Květ, 1971), and interpretation of biomass changes, biochemical changes and net photosynthetic rates (Imhof & Burian, 1972; Burian, 1973; Fiala, 1973*a*; Sieghardt, 1973*a,b*) suggest that those species with a large underground biomass have more persistent rhizomes of a higher average age, and that in general the annual underground increment approaches the maximum biomass of aerial shoots. Hence the annual net production of such species is estimated in Table 8.1 as twice the maximum aerial shoot biomass (without further correction for any losses), although this factor is certainly very variable with species, clone and site.

Reserves are mobilised in the spring and replenished in the summer, though the exact timing depends on the species. During the transfer to aerial shoots these shoots grow rapidly while the leaf area index is very low, giving abnormally high unit leaf rates ('net assimilation rates', determined from aerial crop growth rates). These may reach 35–90 g aerial dry wt (m leaf)$^{-2}$ d^{-1} (Dykyjová, Ondok & Přibáň, 1970; Květ, 1971) as compared with 2–14 g m^{-2} d^{-1} for emergent macrophytes or 4–13 g m^{-2} d^{-1} for C_3 terrestrial plants (Evans, 1972) during growth dependent on photosynthesis. When transfer to rhizomes is occurring carbon dioxide uptake remains high, but unit leaf rates and crop growth rates based on aerial shoots may become very low or negative (Burian, 1973).

Communities with a constant biomass necessitate studies of the population dynamics and the life cycle of individual shoots (Thompson, p. 691). He estimated that the annual production of *Cyperus papyrus* on a favourable site was 12.5 kg organic wt m^{-2} yr^{-1}; 2.5 times the biomass. This is probably an underestimate, and interpretation of his data on the turnover of aerial shoots and rhizomes and the weight of mature shoots suggests that the annual production may be nearly three times the biomass. This factor has been applied to obtain the crop growth rate and annual production estimates used in Table 8.1 to represent productive tropical emergent communities, without any further correction for losses. *Typha domingensis*, however, has an annual turnover of aerial shoots of only 0.56 and its annual production is less than the maximum biomass (Howard-Williams, 1973).

In general the annual production estimates in Table 8.1 have not been specifically corrected for losses since so little evidence is available, though some authors have taken some account of them. It is likely that sites achieving high seasonal maximum biomasses, on which the Table 8.1 entries are based, are not subject to heavy losses before the maximum is reached. The extent of leaf mortality before this time is very variable with species and site, varying from 2 to 20% of the seasonal maximum biomass in various reedswamp species (Harper, 1918; Borutskiĭ, 1949; Westlake, 1966; Dykyjová, Ondok & Přibáň, 1970; Květ, 1971; Dykyjová, 1973, Burian, 1973; Lack, 1973). The total losses can be much higher with plants like *Glyceria maxima* or *Rorippa nasturtium-aquaticum* which are subject to both leaf and shoot mortalities throughout much of their growing season and have an indistinct maximum. The annual production may be 1.5 to 2 times the maximum biomass (Mathews & Westlake, 1969; Castellano, personal communication). *C. papyrus* can be regarded as an extreme example of this trend.

Invertebrate grazing losses may be much less than 8% (Smirnov, 1961; Westlake, 1965; Imhof, 1973; Lack, 1973; Thompson, p. 691) but heavy grazing by vertebrates can occur at some sites, often exceeding 10% of the maximum biomass (e.g. Květ & Hudec, 1971; Pelikán, Svoboda & Květ, 1971).

Submerged plants

There are numerous studies for the temperate zone describing biomasses of around 0.5 kg m^{-2} of dry organic weight at fertile sites (e.g. Forsberg, 1960; Edwards & Owens, 1960; Wetzel, 1964; Boyd, 1967; Ikusima, 1970; Rejmánková, 1973c). Various species are present, but *Chara* is often mentioned. This frequently has a very high biomass as dry weight since calcareous deposits give it a very high ash 'content'. Few of these species have very large underground components and these are often sampled, at least partially.

There is very little information on the biomass of tropical submerged plants apart from Odum (1957); Sinha (1970) and Kumano (1972). Most of the work on tropical waters has been carried out in large deep lakes with a negligible submerged littoral area or in ponds. Most of these latter seem to be dominated by algal blooms or floating emergent plants such as *Salvinia, Azolla, Trapa, Eichhornia* and duckweeds (Ambasht, 1971; Kaul, 1971; Ganapati, 1971; Gopal, 1973). They are unlikely to be representative of all tropical waters.

199

Chlorophyll contents range from 2 to 20 mg chlorophyll per gram dry weight of shoot, but most are in the range 5–15 mg g^{-1} (Hammann, 1957; Odum, 1957; Wetzel, 1964; Boyd, 1970a; Ikusima, 1966,1970; Dokulil, 1972; Maier, 1973). There is evidence of correlation with age and physiological condition. The estimates in Table 8.1 are based on an assumption of 15% ash and a range of 4–8 mg g^{-1} of chlorophyll, and direct determinations by Odum (1957) and Ikusima (1965,1966).

Losses and turnover in submerged aquatic plants. Although devastating grazing is probably not as common in submerged communities as in emergent communities, there must be occasions when it occurs. Wild-fowl such as ducks and swans, mammals such as the manatee, and fish such as the grass carp and possibly the common carp, are known to eat quantities of submerged aquatic plants, but there are few or no data on their grazing pressure in natural systems. Grazing by invertebrates also occurs, though the extent again is very dependent on the species present and their abundance. At many sites there is little direct consumption of the living plant, while at other sites it can be up to 90% of the maximum biomass by the autumn (Westlake, 1965; Pieczyńska, 1972; Kajak, Hillbright-Ilkowska & Pieczyńska, 1972; McNabb & Tierney, 1972).

Losses by damage or leaf-shedding are probably more often important and frequently exceed 10% (Pieczyśńka, 1972; Adams, 1972; Dawson, 1973).

Annual production estimates in Table 8.1 have been made by adding 20–25% to the seasonal maximum biomass for the temperate region, and are based on Odum's sub-tropical metabolic data (1957) for the tropical regions.

References

* IBP/PF Data Reports will be kept in the Library of the Freshwater Biological Association, Ambleside, England.

Adams, M. S. (1972). Lake Wingra, USA – Primary productivity of submergent aquatic macrophytes and periphyton. *IBP/PF Data Report** no. 12a,b and c, 1–150.

Adams, M. S. & McCracken, M. D. (1974). Seasonal production of the *Myriophyllum* component of the littoral of Lake Wingra, Wisconsin. *J. Ecol.* **62**, 457–67.

Ambasht, R. S. (1971). Ecosystem study of a tropical pond in relation to primary production of different vegetational zones. *Hidrobiologia*, **12**, 57–61.

Aruga, Y. & Monsi, M. (1963). Chlorophyll amount as an indicator of matter productivity in bio-communities. *Pl. Cell Physiol. Tokyo*, **4**, 29–39.

Borutskiĭ, E. V. (1949). Changes in the growth of the macrophytes in Lake Beloie at Kossino from 1888 to 1939. (In Russian). *Trudȳ vses. gidrobiol. Obshch.* **1**, 44–56.

Boyd, C. E. (1967). Some aspects of aquatic plant ecology. *Reservoir Fisheries Resources Symposium*, April 5–7, Athens, Georgia, pp. 114–29. Am. Fish. Soc. Washington, DC.

Boyd, C. E. (1969). Production, mineral nutrient absorption, and biochemical assimilation by *Justicia americana* and *Alternanthera philoxeroides*. *Arch. Hydrobiol.* **66**, 139–60.

Boyd, C. E. (1970a). Chemical analyses of some vascular aquatic plants. *Arch. Hydrobiol.* **67**, 78–85.

Boyd, C. E. (1970b). Production, mineral accumulation and pigment concentrations in *Typha latifolia* and *Scirpus americanus*. *Ecology*, **51**, 285–90.

Bray, J. R. (1960). The chlorophyll content of some native and managed plant communities in central Minnesota. *Can. J. Bot.* **38**, 313–33.

Bray, J. R., Lawrence, D. B. & Pearson, L. C. (1959). Primary production in some Minnesota terrestrial communities for 1957. *Oikos*, **10**, 38–49.

Burian, K. (1971). Primary production, carbon dioxide exchange and transpiration in *Phragmites communis* Trin. on the lake Neusiedler See, Austria. *Hidrobiologia*, **12**, 203–18.

Burian, K. (1973). Das Schilfgürtel – Ökosystem eines Steppensees. A. *Phragmites communis* Trin. im Röhricht des Neusiedler Sees. Wachstum, Produktion und Wasserverbrauch. In *Ökosystemforschung*, ed. H. Ellenberg, pp. 61–78. Berlin, Springer-Verlag.

Carr, J. L. (1969). The primary productivity and physiology of *Ceratophyllum demersum*. II. Micro primary productivity, pH, and the P/R ratio. *Aust. J. mar. Freshwat. Res.* **20**, 127–42.

Dawson, F. H. (1973). The production ecology of *Ranunculus penicillatus* var. *calcareus* in relation to the organic input into a chalk stream. Ph.D. Thesis, Birmingham, University of Aston. 356 pp.

Dokulil, M. (1972). Neusiedlersee, Austria – Primary production level. *IBP/PF Data Report** no. 50, 1–8.

Dykyjová, D. (1971). Productivity and solar energy conversion in reedswamp stands in comparison with outdoor mass cultures of algae in the temperate climate of central Europe. *Photosynthetica*, **5**, 329–40.

Dykyjová, D. (1973). Specific differences in vertical structures and radiation profiles in the helophyte stands (a survey of comparative measurements). In *Ecosystem Study on Wetland Biome in Czechoslovakia*, ed. S. Hejný, *Czech. IBP/PT-PP Rep.* no. 3, pp. 121–31, Třeboň, Czech. Acad. Sci.

Dykyjová, D. & Ondok, J. P. (1973). Biometry and the productive stand structure of coenoses of *Sparganium erectum* L. *Preslia*, **45**, 19–30.

Dykyjová, D., Ondok, J. P. & Přibáň, K. (1970). Seasonal changes in productivity and vertical structure of reed-stands (*Phragmites communis* Trin.) *Photosynthetica*, **4**, 280–7.

201

H

Dykyjová, D., Véber, K. & Přibáň, K. (1971a). Production and root/shoot ratio of dominant reedswamp species growing in outdoor summer hydroponic cultures. In *Productivity of Terrestrial Ecosystems. Production Processes, Czech. IBP/PT–PP Rep.* no. 1, pp. 101–4. Prague, Czech. Acad. Sci.

Dykyjová, D., Véber, K. & Přibáň, K. (1971b). Productivity and root/shoot ratio of reedswamp species growing in outdoor hydroponic cultures. *Folia Geobot. Phytotax. Praha*, **6**, 233–54.

Edwards, R. W. & Owens, M. (1960). The effects of plants on river conditions. I. Summer crops and estimates of net productivity of macrophytes in a chalk stream. *J. Ecol.* **48**, 151–60.

Edwards, R. W. & Owens, M. (1962). The effects of plants on river conditions. IV. The oxygen balance of a chalk stream. *J. Ecol.* **50**, 207–20.

Evans, G. C. (1972). *The Quantitative Analysis of Plant Growth, Studies in Ecology*, vol. 1, 734 pp. Oxford, Blackwell Sci. Publ.

Fiala, K. (1973a). Seasonal changes in the growth and total carbohydrate content in the underground organs of *Phragmites communis* Trin. In *Ecosystem Study on Wetland Biome in Czechoslovakia*, ed. S. Hejný, *Czech. IBP/PT–PP Rep.* no. 3, pp. 107–10. Třeboň, Czech. Acad. Sci.

Fiala, K. (1973b). Growth and production of underground organs of *Typha angustifolia* L., *Typha latifolia* L. and *Phragmites communis* Trin. *Pol. Arch. Hydrobiol.* **20**, 59–65.

Fiala, K., Dykyjová, D., Květ, J. & Svoboda, J. (1968). Methods of assessing rhizome and root production in reed-bed stands. In *Methods of Productivity Studies in Root Systems and Rhizosphere Organisms*, eds. M. S. Ghilarov, V. A. Kovda, L. N. Novichkova-Ivanova, L. E. Rodin & V. M. Sveshnikova. Int. Symp. USSR, pp. 36–47. Leningrad, USSR Acad. Sci.

Forsberg, C. (1960). Subaquatic macrovegetation in Ösbysjön, Djursholm. *Oikos*, **11**, 183–99.

Ganapati, S. V. (1971). Organic production in seven types of aquatic ecosystems in India. *Int. Symp. on Tropical Ecology Emphasising Organic Production*, INTECOL, ISTE, INSA, New Delhi, January 1971, pp. 312–50.

Gaudet, J. J. (1973). Growth of a floating aquatic weed, *Salvinia*, under standard conditions. *Hydrobiologia*, **41**, 77–106.

Geus-Kruyt De M. & Segal, S. (1973). Notes on the productivity of *Stratiotes aloides* in two lakes in the Netherlands. *Pol. Arch. Hydrobiol.* **20**, 195–205.

Gloser, J. (1972). Temperature-dependence of apparent photosynthesis and dark respiration in grasses dominant in alluvial meadows. In *Ecosystem Study on Grassland Biome in Czechoslovakia*, ed. M. Rychnovská, *Czech. IBP/PT–PP Rep.* no. 2, pp. 47–9. Brno, Czech. Acad. Sci.

Goldsworthy, A. & Day, P. R. (1970). Further evidence for reduced role of photorespiration in low compensation point species. *Nature*, **228**, 687–8.

Gopal, B. (1973). A survey of the Indian studies on ecology and production of wetland and shallow water communities. *Pol. Arch. Hydrobiol.* **20**, 21–9.

Hammann, A. (1957). Assimilationszahlen submerser Phanerogamen und ihre Beziehung zur Kohlensäureversorgung. *Schweiz. Z. Hydrol.* **19**, 579–612.

Hannan, H. K. & Dorris, T. C. (1970). Succession of a macrophyte community in a constant temperature river. *Limnol. and Oceanogr.* **15**, 442–53.

Harper, R. M. (1918). Some dynamic studies of Long Island vegetation. *Pl. Wld.* **21**, 38–46.

Hejný, S. (1960). *Ökologische Charakteristik der Wasser-und Sumpfpflanzen in den Slowakischen Tiefebenen.* (Donau- und Theissgebiet), 487 pp. Bratislava, Czech. Acad. Sci.

Howard-Williams, C. (1973). Vegetation and environment in the marginal areas of a tropical African lake (L. Chilwa, Malawi). Ph.D. Thesis. University of London.

Hough, R. A. (1974). Photorespiration and productivity in submersed aquatic vascular plants. *Limnol. and Oceanogr.* In press.

Ikusima, I. (1965). Ecological studies on the productivity of aquatic plant communities. I. Measurement of photosynthetic activity. *Bot. Mag. Tokyo,* **78**, 202–11.

Ikusima, I. (1966). Ecological studies on the productivity of aquatic plant communities. II. Seasonal changes in standing crop and productivity of a natural submerged community of *Vallisneria denserrulata. Bot. Mag. Tokyo,* **79**, 7–19.

Ikusima, I. (1970). Ecological studies on the productivity of aquatic plant communities. IV. Light condition and community photosynthetic production. *Bot. Mag. Tokyo,* **83**, 330–41.

Imhof, G. (1973). Aspects of energy flow by different food chains in a reed-bed. A review. *Pol. Arch. Hydrobiol.* **20**, 165–8.

Imhof, G. & Burian, K. (1972). Energy-flow studies in a wetland ecosystem. (Reed belt of the Lake Neusiedler See). *Spec. publ. Austrian Acad. Sci. IBP,* 1–15. Vienna, Springer-Verlag.

Kajak, Z., Hillbricht-Ilkowska, A. & Pieczyńska, E. (1972). The production processes in several Polish lakes. In *Productivity Problems of Freshwaters,* eds. Z. Kajak & A. Hillbricht-Ilkowska, pp. 129–47. Warsaw & Kraków, Polish Sci. Publ.

Kaul, V. (1971). Production and ecology of some macrophytes of Kashmir lakes. *Hidrobiologia,* **12**, 63–9.

Korelyakova, I. L. (1971). Distribution and productivity of communities of *Phragmites communis* Trin. in Dnieper Reservoirs. *Hidrobiologia.* **12**, 149–54.

Kumano, S. (1972). Tasek-Bera, Malaysia – standing crop and relationship between photosynthesis and light intensity. *IBP/PF Data Report** no. 76, pp. 83–90 and 116–19.

Květ, J. (1971). Growth analysis approach to the production ecology of reedswamp plant communities. *Hidrobiologia,* **12**, 15–40.

Květ, J. & Hudec, K. (1971). Effects of grazing by grey-lag geese on reedswamp plant communities. *Hidrobiologia,* **12**, 351–9.

Lack, T. J. (1973). Studies on the macrophytes and phytoplankton of the rivers Thames and Kennet at Reading. Ph.D. Thesis, University of Reading, pp. 96.

McGahee, C. F. & Davis, G. J. (1971). Photosynthesis and respiration in *Myriophyllum spicatum* L. as related to salinity. *Limnol. and Oceangr.* **16**, 826–9.

McNabb, C. D. & Tierney, D. P. (1972). Growth and mineral accumulation of submersed vascular hydrophytes in pleioeutrophic environs. *Inst. Wat. Res. Mich. St. Univ. Tech. Rep.* no. 26, 33 pp.

McNaughton, S. J. & Fullem, L. W. (1970). Photosynthesis and photorespiration in *Typha latifolia*. *Plant Physiol.* **45**, 703–7.

Maier, R. (1973). Produktions- und Pigmentanalysen an *Utricularia vulgaris* L. In *Ökosystemforschung*, ed. H. Ellenberg, pp. 87–101. Berlin, Springer-Verlag.

Mathews, C. P. & Westlake, D. F. (1969). Estimation of production by populations of higher plants subject to high mortality. *Oikos*, **20**, 156–60.

Monteith, J. L. (1972). Solar radiation and productivity in tropical ecosystems. *J. appl. Ecol.* **9**, 747–66.

Odum, H. T. (1957). Trophic structure and productivity of Silver Springs, Florida. *Ecol. Monogr.* **27**, 55–112.

Ogawa, H., Yoda, K. & Kira, T. (1961). A preliminary survey on the vegetation of Thailand. *Nature & Life in SE. Asia*, **1**, 21–157.

Owens, M. & Edwards, R. W. (1962). The effects of plants on river conditions. III. Crop studies and estimates of net productivity of macrophytes in four streams in southern England. *J. Ecol.* **50**, 157–62.

Pearsall, W. H. (1959). Production ecology. *Sci. Progr.* **47**, 106–11.

Pelikán, J., Svoboda, J. & Květ, J. (1971). Relationship between the population of muskrats (*Ondatra zibethica*) and the primary production of Cattail (*Typha latifolia*). *Hidrobiologia*, **12**, 177–80.

Penfound, W. T. (1956). Primary production of vascular aquatic plants. *Limnol. Oceangr.* **2**, 92–101.

Pieczyńska, E. (1972). Ecology of the littoral zone of lakes. *Ecol. Pol.* **20**, 637–732.

Rejmánková, E. (1973a). Biomass, production and growth rate of duckweeds (*Lemna gibba* and *L. minor*). In *Ecosystem Study on Wetland Biome in Czechoslovakia*, ed. S. Hejný, *Czech. IBP/PT–PP Rep.* no. 3, pp. 101–6. Třeboň, Czech. Acad. Sci.

Rejmánková, E. (1973b). Chlorophyll content in leaves of *Phragmites communis* Trin. In *Ecosystem Study on Wetland Biome in Czechoslovakia*, ed. S. Hejný, *Czech. IBP/PT–PP Rep.* no. 3, pp. 143–5. Třeboň, Czech. Acad. Sci.

Rejmánková, E. (1973c). Biomass of submerged macrophytes growing in the Nesyt Fishpond. In *Littoral of the Nesyt Fishpond*, ed. J. Květ, pp. 107–10. Prague, Czech. Acad. Sci.

Rich, P. H., Wetzel, R. G. & Van Thuy, N. (1971). Distribution, production and role of aquatic macrophytes in a southern Michigan marl lake. *Freshwat. Biol.* **1**, 3–21.

Rudescu, L., Niculescu, C. & Chivu, I. P. (1965). *Monografia Stufului din Delta Dunării*. 542 pp. Bucharest, Editura Academiei Republicii Socialiste.

Seidel, K. (1959). *Scirpus*-Kulturen. *Arch. Hydrobiol. (Plankt.)*, **56**, 58–92.

Seighardt, H. (1973a). Strahlungsnutzung von *Phragmites communis*. In *Ökosystemforschung*, ed. H. Ellenberg, pp. 79–86. Berlin, Springer-Verlag.

Seighardt, H. (1973b). Utilization of solar energy and energy content of different organs of *Phragmites communis* Trin. *Pol. Arch. Hydrobiol.* **20**, 151–6.

Sinha, A. B. (1970). Studies on the bioecology and production of Ramgarh Lake, Gorakhpur. Ph.D. Thesis, University of Gorakhpur.

Smirnov, N. N. (1961). Consumption of emergent plants by insects. *Verh. int. Verin. theor. angew. Limnol.* **14**, 232–6.

Spence, D. H. N. (1972). Light on freshwater macrophytes. *Trans. Proc. Bot. Soc. Edinb.* **41**, 491–505.

Spence, D. H. N. & Campbell, R. M. (1971). *In situ* measurement of carbon fixation rates by submerged freshwater macrophytes. *Proc. Eur. Weed Res. Coun. 3rd Int. Symp. Aquatic Weeds*, pp. 43–51.

Spence, D. H. N. & Chrystal, J. (1970a). Photosynthesis and zonation of freshwater macrophytes. I. Depth distribution and shade tolerance. *New Phytol.* **69**, 205–15.

Stake, E. (1967). Higher vegetation and nitrogen in a rivulet in central Sweden. *Schweiz. Z. Hydrol.* **29**, 107–24.

Stanley, R. A. & Naylor, A. W. (1972). Photosynthesis in Eurasian water-milfoil (*Myriophyllum spicatum* L.) *Pl. Physiol.* **50**, 149–51.

Szajnowski, F. (1973). The relation between the leaf area and production of the above-ground parts of common reed (*Phragmites communis* Trin.). *Pol. Arch. Hydrobiol.* **20**, 157–8.

Szczepański, A. (1969). Biomass of underground parts of the reed *Phragmites communis* Trin. *Bull. Acad. Pol. Sci.* **17**, 245–6.

Szczepański, A. (1973). Chlorophyll in the assimilation parts of helophytes. *Pol. Arch. Hydrobiol.* **20**, 67–71.

Walker, J. M. & Waygood, E. R. (1968). Ecology of *Phragmites communis*. I. Photosynthesis of a single shoot *in situ*. *Can. J. Bot.* **46**, 549–55.

Westlake, D. F. (1965). Some basic data for investigations of the productivity of aquatic macrophytes. *Mem. Ist. Ital. Idrobiol.* **18** Suppl. 229–48.

Westlake, D. F. (1966). The biomass and productivity of *Glyceria maxima*. I. Seasonal changes in biomass. *J. Ecol.* **54**, 745–53.

Westlake, D. F. (1967). Some effects of low-velocity currents on the metabolism of aquatic macrophytes. *J. exp. Bot.* **18**, 187–205.

Westlake, D. F. (1968). Methods used to determine the annual production of reedswamp plants with extensive rhizomes. In *Methods of Productivity Studies in Root Systems and Rhizosphere Organisms*, eds. M. S. Ghilarov, V. A. Kovda, L. N. Novichkova-Ivanova, L. E. Rodin, V. M. Sveshnikova, Int. Symp. USSR, Aug.–Sept. 1968, pp. 226–34. Leningrad, USSR Acad. Sci.

Westlake, D. F., Casey, H., Dawson, H., Ladle, M., Mann, R. H. K. &

Marker, A. F. H. (1972). The chalk-stream ecosystem. In *Productivity Problems of Freshwaters*, eds. Z. Zajak & A. Hillbricht-Ilkowska, pp. 615–35. Warsaw & Kraków, Pol. Sci. Publ. Revised Oct. 1972, *Coll. Reprint Freshwat. Biol. Assoc.* no. 934.

Wetzel, R. G. (1964). A comparative study of the primary productivity of higher aquatic plants, periphyton and phytoplankton, in a large, shallow lake. *Int. Revue ges. Hydrobiol. Hydrogr.* **49**, 1–61.

Wetzel, R. G. & Manny, B. A. (1972). Secretion of dissolved organic carbon and nitrogen by aquatic macrophytes. *Verh. int. Verein. theor. angew. Limnol.* **18**, 162–70.

Whitwer, E. E. (1955). Efficiency of finely-divided *vs* tape-like aquatic plant leaves. *Ecology*, **36**, 511–12.

Zohary, M., Orshansky, G., Muhsam, H. & Lewin, M. (1955). Weight estimate of the papyrus culms growing in the Hula Marshes. *Bull. Res. Coun. Israel.* **5c** (1).

9. Primary production of marine macrophytes

K. H. MANN & A. R. O. CHAPMAN

Within a comparatively narrow zone at the edge of the sea are found areas of extremely high primary productivity. In some instances the rate of carbon fixation is as high as anywhere on earth; comparable, for instance, with that of luxurious tropical rain forest. The plant forms living in this zone are very varied, and include seaweeds, sea grasses, marsh grasses, and mangroves. The most spectacular rates of primary production are found in the kelps and giant kelps, i.e. brown algae of the genera *Laminaria* and *Macrocystis*. These plants live subtidally on rocky shores of temperate and subarctic waters, and achieve annual net production in the range 1000–2000 g C m^{-2}. Intertidally in the same general areas are found rockweeds such as *Fucus* and *Ascophyllum* which commonly produce 500–1000 g C m^{-2}. On sedimented shores in temperate climates sea grasses such as *Zostera* live subtidally or intertidally and may fix annually up to 1500 g C m^{-2}. Marsh grasses such as *Spartina* act as natural traps for silt, producing distinct salt marsh communities at or near high water level. These marshes may extend almost unbroken for hundreds of hectares and have a net annual productivity of 200–1000 g C m^{-2}.

In tropical waters various marine grasses are important sublittoral producers. For instance, Turtle grass, *Thalassia*, may have an annual productivity of 500–1500 g C m^{-2}. At the edge of the tropical seas, mangrove swamps cover large areas. Their productivity has not been well documented, but appears to be of the order of 350–400 g C m^{-2} yr^{-1}. The evidence for the foregoing statements was reviewed in the IBP Symposium 'Detritus and its ecological role in aquatic ecosystems' (Mann, 1972c). The data are summarized in Fig. 9.1. During an IBP study of the productivity of the seaweed zone in a marine bay on the Atlantic coast of Canada (Mann, 1972a,b) it was discovered that *Laminaria longicruris*, *L. digitata* and *Agarum cribrosum* had particularly high rates of production, and that most of their growth in length occurred during winter and early spring. This has led to an interest in the mechanisms by which the high productivity is achieved in large marine algae, and to a consideration of the strategic value of seasonal variations in photosynthesis and respiration in various algal types.

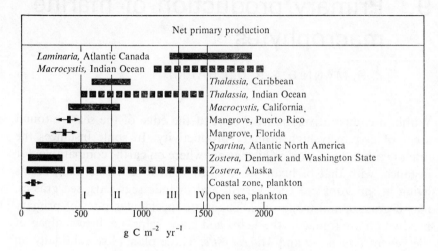

I = Medium aged oak—pine forest, New York
II = Young pine plantation (England)
III = Mature rain forest, Puerto Rico
IV = Alfalfa field, USA, an intensively managed system
Quoted in Odum (1971) Calculated as k cal x 0.1

Fig. 9.1. Estimates of net primary production by various marine macrophytes. Solid bars show the range of published values, broken lines are the result of applying reasonable production: biomass ratios to published biomass data. Vertical lines are comparative values from terrestrial situations. From Mann (1973).

The seasonal pattern of growth in *Laminaria longicruris*

In St Margaret's Bay, Nova Scotia, individual plants of *Laminaria longicruris* (as well as other species) were identified by numbered tags, and holes were punched at 10 cm intervals along the blades (Fig. 9.2). It was shown that as time progressed the holes moved towards the tip of the blade, showing that growth in length was confined to the meristem near the junction of stipe and the blade. At the same time that this growth was occurring, erosion was occurring at the tips of the blades, so that the blades could be regarded as 'moving belts' of tissue, producing new growth at the bases and shedding particulate and dissolved organic matter to the environment from the tips.

The movement of holes along the blades was followed, by SCUBA divers, for two years. As a result, it was possible to plot the seasonal pattern of growth shown in Fig. 9.3. From a minimal rate of length increase between July and October, the growth rate increased to reach a maximum between January and April. Specimens growing in deeper water lagged behind those in shallow water by about two months. When length increments were summed for a year, it was found that individual plants grew by amounts equivalent to one to five times their initial length. As they grew longer they also grew wider and thicker, so that their biomass increased approximately in proportion to the square of the length increase, and the community produced annually four to twenty times its initial biomass. The weighted mean net primary productivity was calculated as 1750 g C m^{-2}, or 648 000 g C per m of shore line.

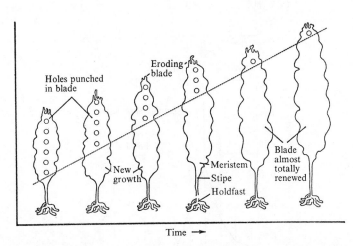

Fig. 9.2. Diagram illustrating the movement of punched holes along the blade of a laminarian as a result of growth. The size of the holes is exaggerated.

The surprising feature was the great increase in length during periods of short day length, low light intensity and low water temperature. This period of rapid growth coincided with a period of minimum dry weight per g of live tissue. Dry weight was 14.7% of fresh weight in December, 16.2% in March, 20.8% in June and 21.7% in August (Mann, 1972a). Hence, it appeared that in winter the plants might be using some of the dry matter stored during summer as an energy and material source for part of their winter growth. Since winter is a time of high dissolved nitrogen and phosphorus in the sea water, it seemed possible that the plants were making some of their new tissue by using a stored carbon source and taking up other nutrients from the sea water. This could place them in an advantageous position for making maximum use of sunlight for photosynthesis in early spring.

Although the geometry of the blades is different in *Laminaria longicruris* and *Agarum cribrosum*, the seasonal pattern of growth was found to be similar (Mann, 1972b).

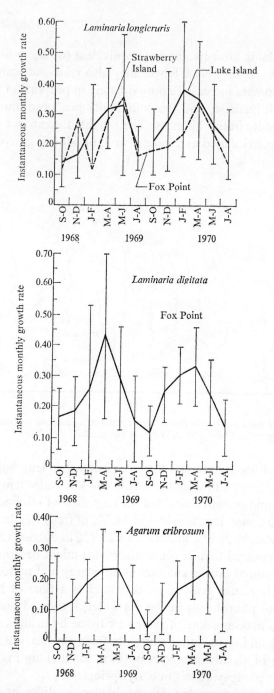

Fig. 9.3. Seasonal growth patterns of *Laminaria* and *Agarum*. Heavy lines and broken lines join points which are instantaneous monthly growth rates averaged over 2-month periods. Vertical lines are standard deviations. *Laminaria longicruris* was studied at three named sites; *L. digitata* at one site but three different depths (results combined); *Agarum cribrosum* also at Fox Point, depth 12 m. From Mann (1972b).

The seasonal pattern of growth in other seaweeds

Sublittoral forms

In some sublittoral kelps the sporophyte is annual, and there is a seasonal alternation of microscopic and macroscopic phases. Examples are *Chorda filum* (South & Burrows, 1967) and *Saccorhiza polyschides* (Norton & Burrows, 1969). The young sporophyte appears during the spring, grows during the summer and disintegrates after fruiting in the autumn. The spores form microscopic stages which survive the winter and produce a new population of macrophytic sporophytes in the following spring. Experiments show that during the winter the gametophytes are inhibited in their development by low levels of irradiance. When available light energy increases in the spring, growth is resumed.

This life history is well adapted to the particular environmental conditions. These two species often colonize unstable substrata such as sand and small pebbles. During calm summer conditions a population of large sporophytes grows up, having very little anchorage. The autumn gales dislodge them and may cast them ashore, but the microscopic forms remain on the sea bed and start a new colony in the spring.

Many sublittoral seaweeds with a perennial macroscopic phase resemble the kelps in having a period of rapid growth during winter. Thus, *Desmarestia aculeata* in Britain begins regeneration in November after a quiescent period extending from mid-summer (Chapman, 1971). *Cystoseira granulata* and *Hijikia fusiforme* (fucoids which are predominantly sublittoral) also grow throughout the winter (A. R. O. Chapman, unpublished data; Suto, 1951). On the other hand, the microscopic gametophytes of *Desmarestia aculeata* remain dormant during the winter. Spores are produced from November (Chapman, 1971), and they settle and produce gametophytes, but young sporophytes do not become visible until the following spring. Their period of growth starts several months later than that of the large sporophytes.

Kain (1971*a*) found that in her study area on the Isle of Man, the average light intensity at 10 m in December was 5.4 μg cal cm^{-2} s^{-1} (22.6 μJ cm^{-2} s^{-1}). In culture levels of 5 μg cal cm^{-2} s^{-1} (20.9 μJ cm^{-2} s^{-1}) gametophytes of *D. aculeata* were near the compensation point and maturation took 88 days from the establishment of cultures. On the other hand, large sporophytes grew rapidly, doubling their length in ten days, at light intensities of only 3.3 μg cal cm^{-2} s^{-1} (13.8 μJ cm^{-2} s^{-1}) (Chapman, 1970). This difference between macroscopic and microscopic forms suggests that winter growth is made possible by the use of carbon reserves stored in the large sporophytes.

Littoral forms

In the fucoids there is no alternation of gametophyte and sporophyte. The diploid plant produces gametes meiotically. Gametic fusion produces an embryo which reconstitutes the diploid phase. The macroscopic fucoid plants which are so typical of the littoral region of temperate waters are usually perennial, and some species may live as long as fifteen years, e.g. *Ascophyllum nodosum* (Baardseth, 1968). Although irradiance levels are high during the summer, these plants are usually less productive than the kelps (Westlake, 1963). In relatively harsh winter conditions, such as those found on the east coast of Canada, it is obvious that the intertidal species, which may be encased in ice or subjected to freezing temperatures during exposure to the air, are in much less favourable conditions for growth than the sublittoral forms.

Seasonal patterns of photosynthesis and respiration in seaweeds

A seasonal cycle of rapid growth in summer and quiescence in winter is familiar enough, but the cycle observed in many sublittoral seaweeds with perennial sporophytes, in which the most rapid growth occurs in winter, is sufficiently unusual to be worth further investigation. One hypothesis advanced to explain the phenomenon is that in certain species where under winter conditions the light intensity is insufficient to provide a photosynthetic surplus, the plants grow by utilizing stored materials. It is possible that carbon is obtained from stored products while nitrate, phosphate, etc. are obtained from the seawater.

The early work of Kniep (1914) and Harder (1915), on the effects of temperature on photosynthetic and respiratory rates of marine plants led to misconceptions widely held during the early part of this century. Both authors found that with decreasing temperature the respiratory rate fell more rapidly than the photosynthetic rate. This implies that for a given light intensity a greater surplus remains for synthesis of organic substances at low temperatures than at high temperatures. This theory has two important faults. First, photosynthesis is temperature-independent at very low light intensities, but at the high light intensities required to build up an assimilatory surplus, photosynthetic rate, like respiration rate, is strongly influenced by temperature.

Secondly, it is clear from more recent studies that seaweeds are capable of seasonal adaptation of photosynthetic and respiratory rates. Thus, Black (1950*b*) found that in May at 8 °C the respiration rate of

212

Laminaria hyperborea was 6.9 ml O_2 (g crude protein)$^{-1}$ h^{-1} while in August at 16 °C it was only 2.8. Clearly the plant had reduced its respiratory rate in spite of higher temperatures in August. Kanwisher's (1966) results for *Laminaria* in Labrador show the reverse seasonal adaptation. He measured respiration at various temperatures between 0 °C and 20 °C on plants collected during the winter and during the summer. The rate for winter plants at 20 °C was somewhat lower than

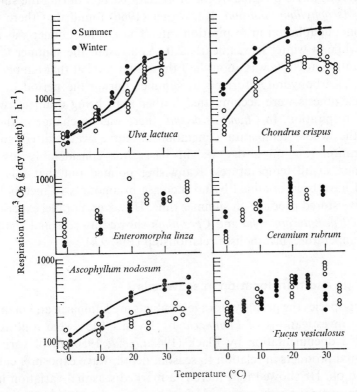

Fig. 9.4. Respiration of named seaweeds, in summer and winter, plotted against temperature. Adapted from Kanwisher (1966).

for summer plants. He interpreted the winter decrease as an adaptation to survival through the long winter period of low light intensity, when the plants might otherwise metabolize the whole of their reserves.

It is now clear from the extensive work of Lüning (1971) that *Laminaria hyperborea* (at least in temperate waters) is capable of seasonal adaptations of rates of photosynthesis and respiration, with the result that an assimilatory surplus may be built up in the summer. With rising temperatures, between May and August, the rate of respiration per unit dry weight decreased, while light-saturated rates of gross photosynthesis increased. An investigation of conditions at a depth of 2.5 m off Heligoland showed that saturation levels of irradiance were reached for most of the day between June and August, but that irradiance was below the compensation level most of the time from October until March. It seems inevitable that the rapid growth which took place in winter was made possible by the storage of carbon during the summer.

In *Ascophyllum nodosum*, Kanwisher (1966) found that there was a seasonal adaptation in respiration rate. The Q_{10} in summer was about 1.5, while in winter it was nearly 2.0. As a result, the summer level of respiration at 20 °C was about half the winter level at that temperature. Hence, carbohydrates formed in summer during the period of rapid photosynthesis were accumulated, rather than being drained away in rapid respiration. In *Chondrus crispus* there was no change in the Q_{10}, but the whole temperature–metabolism curve was shifted so that respiration rate on a dry weight basis was considerably lower in summer, at all temperatures. Kanwisher pointed out that this effect could have been obtained by an increase in amounts of metabolically inactive stored products in summer time. However, parallel experiments with *Ulva, Enteromorpha* and *Ceramium* showed no seasonal change in the temperature–metabolism relationship (Fig. 9.4).

Storage and translocation in seaweeds

In kelp species the primary storage products are laminarin and mannitol. Initial investigations of *Laminaria* by Kylin (1915) were followed by detailed documentation by Black (1948a,b,c,d; 1950a,b) of variations in stored products in relation to season, depth, wave exposure, current, and so on. He showed that there is a marked seasonal variation in dry matter content, with mannitol reaching a peak in mid-summer and laminarin reaching a maximum in late autumn. In *L. hyperborea* the blade may contain as much as 36% of the dry weight as laminarin. Black (1950a) found that the dry matter content was higher in more sheltered water. By the end of winter the stores of laminarin are usually severely depleted. The ranges of concentrations of storage products in various kelp species, as given by Boney (1965), are shown in Table 9.1.

Black (1954) found no laminarin in the stipe of *L. digitata*. If this is also true of other species, it might explain why growth of the stipe is delayed until the summer (A. R. O. Chapman, unpublished data).

Table 9.1. *Maximum and minimum levels of storage products in kelp species expressed as percentage dry weight (after Boney, 1965)*

| | Minimum | | Maximum | |
	Laminarin	Mannitol	Laminarin	Mannitol
L. saccharina	0	4.5	23	22
L. digitata	0	6	21	26
L. hyperborea	0	5	18	18
Alaria esculenta	0	4	34	12.5

In fucoids the seasonal fluctuation in storage products is much less marked than in kelps. In *Ascophyllum nodosum* laminarin reaches a maximum of 5% of dry weight in November, and a minimum of 1% in May. Mannitol varies from about 10% in September to about 7% in February (Jensen, 1960). Since, as we have seen, there is little winter growth in fucoids, the ability to store carbohydrates and mobilize them for subsequent growth is much less important. Material for growth is

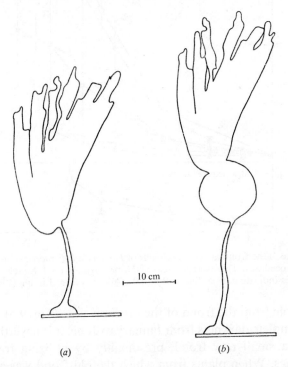

(a) (b)

Fig. 9.5. *Laminaria hyperborea* (a) before, and (b) after exposure to 5.5 months darkness, beginning in December. Note the constriction between old and new frond. From Lüning (1969).

215

provided directly by the high photosynthetic output during summer. Storage products are needed mainly for respiration during the winter, when light levels are below those needed for photosynthetic production.

The best evidence for translocation of storage products is that given by Lüning (1969,1971) and by Schmitz, Lüning & Willenbrink (1972). *Laminaria hyperborea* develops new frond tissue which is clearly

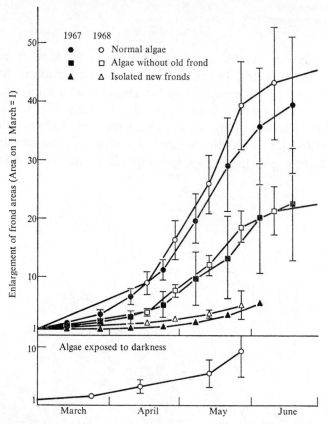

Fig. 9.6. Increase in the frond area of specimens of *Laminaria hyperborea* subject to various experimental procedures. The average area of the new fronds on 1 March was set at 1. The vertical lines indicate fiducial limits, $P = 0.05$. Adapted from Lüning (1969).

distinguishable from the frond of the previous year (Fig. 9.5). If a plant is kept in complete darkness from January to June, it is nevertheless able to produce a small new frond, presumably by utilizing translocated stored reserves. When plants from which the old frond was amputated were grown in the sea along with normal intact plants, the growth of new frond was reduced by 50% in the amputated plants (Fig. 9.6). Young

216

new fronds isolated from both stipe and old frond, grew only about one-tenth as much as the new fronds of intact plants.

When an old frond was allowed to assimilate radiocarbon from NaH^{14}CO$_3$ for fourteen hours at 10 °C, significant radioactivity was found in the new frond, but none in the stipe. An autoradiogram of a frond of *L. hyperborea* twenty-four hours after localized application of H^{14}CO$_3^-$ showed clear evidence of translocation from the old frond to the new (Fig. 9.7). The radioactive material was conducted in well-defined groups of cells within the medulla of the fronds. The material translocated was identified as 53% mannitol, 45% amino acids and 2% malate.

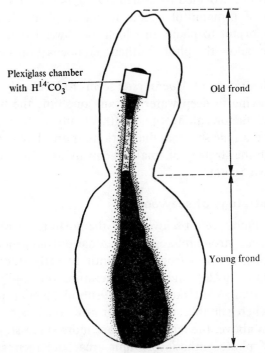

Fig. 9.7. Autoradiogram of a specimen of *Laminaria hyperborea* 24 h after localized application of H^{14}CO$_3$. From Schmitz, Lüning & Willenbrink (1972).

Growth in *Macrocystis pyrifera* in southern California

A detailed study of the biology of giant kelp beds in southern California has been carried out since 1956 under the direction of W. J. North.

Measurement of growth in *Macrocystis* is difficult because of the complex construction of the plant. However, whichever method measurement is used, there is very little seasonal fluctuation in rate. Many of the factors which are important in kelp growth vary individually with season and North (1971) thus concludes that the fluctuations tend to compensate for one another. In mid-summer when surface irradiance is highest, attenuation through the water column is greatest, while in winter the converse applies. The maintenance of a high growth rate through the year in *Macrocystis* is closely related to seasonal adaptation of photosynthesis to temperature (Clendenning, 1971). The photosynthetic capacity of healthy blades was found to be essentially constant through the year.

Detailed information on seasonal fluctuation of storage products in *Macrocystis* is not provided by North (1971), but it is known that rapid translocation of D-mannitol occurs in intact plants. This activity is extremely important to plants in which the lower fronds in very deep water may be below the photosynthetic compensation point for much of the year.

The growth strategy of *Macrocystis* seems to be closely related to the problems of living in deep water. At any one time the fluctuations in environmental factors along the length of any mature plant will be much greater than the seasonal fluctuations at one depth. This contrasts markedly with the strategy of smaller kelps living in the cold temperate waters of Nova Scotia.

The overall strategy of seaweeds

Although the literature on seaweeds of the north temperate waters has tended to reflect a strong interest in the zonation and general biology of intertidal forms, it is clear from the quantitative IBP studies in Eastern Canada (Mann, 1972a) and other literature on exploitable stocks (MacFarlane, 1952; Westlake, 1963) that subtidal laminarians dominate the biomass where suitable substrates for firm attachment are available. As was shown above, the laminarians are more successful in achieving high levels of photosynthesis per unit area, and their success is apparently related to their habit of storing carbon reserves during summer and early autumn. In the case of *Laminaria hyperborea*, winter growth is limited to the production of a new area of frond with the old frond still attached, and Lüning's work has clearly shown that translocation from the old to the new takes place. However, in the case of *Laminaria longicruris* and *L. digitata* in Canada, the blade is completely renewed at least once in the course of the winter, by growth at the base and erosion at the tip. It is therefore difficult to see how this amount of growth can be supported by stored material from any part of the plant. Presumably, then, these species are able to photosynthesize and produce an assimilatory surplus during the winter. This is an hypothesis which must be tested.

Whatever the basis for winter growth, it is obvious that the plants which develop a large blade area are placing themselves in the best position for making the maximum use of increased light intensity in early spring. Fig. 9.8 shows that, in Nova Scotian waters, winter and early spring is a period of high nutrient levels. There is also good light transmission in the water column. In so far as phytoplankton and seaweeds may be competing for limited nutrients, it is possible that by translocating and metabolizing stored carbon during winter or by performing winter photosynthesis the seaweeds are able to use the nutrients for growth at a time when the phytoplankton cells are prevented from growing and dividing, for lack of an energy source.

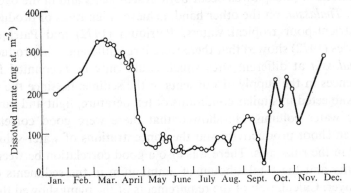

Fig. 9.8. Seasonal variation in the integrated value of dissolved nitrate in the water column at a station in St Margaret's Bay, Nova Scotia, in 1967. From Platt & Irwin (1968).

It is tempting to speculate that in the strongly seasonal light regime of high latitudes this strategy may give the seaweeds a particularly strong competitive advantage. Kain (1971*b*) has shown that at Tromsø in Norway (about 70 °N.) the longer day length in summer compensates for the lower light intensity, so that total daily incident radiation is similar to that of the Isle of Man (54 °N.). Moreover, fresh weight production by *Laminaria hyperborea* is similar at the two sites. Hence, the ability of the seaweeds to carry out intensive photosynthesis in the arctic summer, store carbon reserves and mobilize them during periods of low light intensity may enable them to greatly extend their growing season.

Production strategies of some other marine macrophytes

Since seaweeds have no root system it is reasonable to suppose that they take their nutrients from the water, and that the sublittoral region, which is subjected to strong wind-induced and tidal water movements is a good location for plants which may need to extract large amounts of nutrients from low concentrations. In fact, Ryther (1963) took the view that marine benthic plants are provided with a virtually inexhaustible supply of nutrients in the water moving past them.

However, marine angiosperms such as *Thalassia* and *Zostera* do have roots, although the xylem system tends to be somewhat reduced (Sculthorpe, 1967). McRoy & Barsdate (1970) demonstrated uptake of ^{32}P by the roots of *Zostera*, and Reimold (1972) showed that *Spartina* takes up ^{32}P from depths of 100 cm in the sediments. However, both *Zostera* and *Spartina* grow in situations where moderately high concentrations of phosphorus occur both in sediments and in the overlying water. *Thalassia*, on the other hand, achieves high rates of productivity in nutrient-poor tropical waters. Patriquin (1972) and Patriquin & Knowles (1972) showed that there were large differences in productivity of *Thalassia* at different sites which could only be accounted for by differences in the supply of nutrients in the sediments, since the plants were subjected to similar conditions of temperature, light and nutrients in the water column. He showed that there were good correlations between shoot productivity and the concentrations of water-soluble N and P in the rhizomes. There was also a good correlation between productivity and the total amount of ammonium in the sediments of the root layer. Calculation of the requirements of the plant showed that the sediments contained 300–1000 days' supply of P, but only 5–15 days' supply of N. Patriquin & Knowles (1972) subsequently showed that there was a high rate of acetylene reduction in the rhizosphere of *Thalassia*, and estimated that nitrogen fixation was occurring at a rate of 100 to 500 kg N ha^{-1} yr^{-1} in *Thalassia* beds. The fixation appeared to be mediated by very high concentrations of nitrogen-fixing anaerobic bacteria in the sediments.

Patriquin also suggested that most of the forty or so species of marine angiosperms occurring in nutrient-poor tropical waters probably obtain most of their nitrogen from N$_2$ fixation. Experiments with *Zostera marina*, a typical temperate water species, showed that strong acetylene reduction also occurred, but the highest rate was obtained in aerobic incubation.

220

Hence marine macrophytes form a very productive fringe to the ocean. This fringe makes a major contribution to the input of primary production to bays and estuaries. In St Margaret's Bay, Nova Scotia, with a total area of about 130 km², the annual productivity of the seaweed is estimated as three times the annual productivity of the phytoplankton. This area of high productivity provides a nursery area for many commercially important species of fish. It appears that the kelps owe their high efficiency to their strategy of winter growth, using stored carbon reserves, while the angiosperms are able to grow in nutrient-poor water as a result of the large scale nitrogen-fixation which takes place in the sediments in which they are rooted.

References

Baardseth, E. (1968). Synopsis of biological data on *Ascophyllum nodosum* (Linn.). *Le Jolis. FAO Fisheries Synopsis*, no. **38**.

Black, W. A. P. (1948*a*). Seasonal variation in the chemical constitution of some British Laminariales. *Nature (London)*, **161**, 174.

Black, W. A. P. (1948*b*). Seasonal variation in chemical constitution of some of the sublittoral seaweeds common to Scotland. I. *Laminaria cloustoni. J. Soc. Chem. Ind. (London)*, **67**, 165–8.

Black, W. A. P. (1948*c*). Seasonal variation in chemical constitution of some of the sublittoral seaweeds common to Scotland. II. *Laminaria digitata. J. Soc. Chem. Ind. (London)*, **67**, 169–72.

Black, W. A. P. (1948*d*). Seasonal variation in chemical constitution of some of the sublittoral seaweeds common to Scotland. III. *Laminaria saccharina* and *Saccorhiza bulbosa. J. Soc. Chem. Ind. (London)*, **67**, 172–6.

Black, W. A. P. (1950*a*). Seasonal variation in weight and chemical composition of the common British Laminariaceae. *J. Mar. Biol. Assoc. UK*, **29**, 45–72.

Black, W. A. P. (1950*b*). Effect of the depth of immersion on the chemical constitution of some of the sublittoral seaweeds common to Scotland. *J. Soc. Chem. Ind. (London)*, **69**, 161–5.

Black, W. A. P. (1954). Concentration gradients and their significance in *Laminaria saccharina. J. Mar. Biol. Assoc. UK*, **33**, 49–60.

Boney, A. D. (1965). Aspects of the biology of the seaweeds of economic importance. *Adv. Mar. Biol.* **3**, 105–253.

Chapman, A. R. O. (1970). Experimental investigations into the controlling effects of light conditions on the development and growth of *Desmarestia aculeata. Phycologia*, **9**, 103–8.

Chapman, A. R. O. (1971). Field and culture studies of *Desmarestia aculeata. Phycologia*, **10**, 63–76.

Clendenning, K. A. (1971). Photosynthesis and general development in *Macrocystis*. In *The Biology of giant kelp beds (Macrocystis) in California*, ed. W. J. North. *Beih. Nova Hedwigia*, **32**, 169–90.

Harder, R. (1915). Beitrage zur Kenntnis des Gaswechsels der Meeresalgen. *Jb. Wiss. Bot.* **56**, 254–98.

Jensen, A. (1960). Produksjon au tangmel. *Rep. Norw. Inst. Seaweed Res.* no. **24**, 23 pp.

Kain, J. M. (1971*a*). Continuous recording of underwater light in relation to *Laminaria* distribution. *Fourth European Marine Biology Symposium*, ed. D. J. Crisp, pp. 335–45. London, Cambridge University Press.

Kain, J. M. (1971*b*). The biology of *Laminaria hyperborea*. 6. Some Norwegian populations. *J. Mar. Biol. Assoc. UK*, **51**, 387–408.

Kanwisher, J. W. (1966). Photosynthesis and respiration in some seaweeds. In *Some contemporary Studies in Marine Science*, ed. H. Barnes, pp. 407–20. London, George Allen & Unwin Ltd.

Kniep, H. (1914). Über die Assimilation und Atmung der Meeresalgen. *Int. Revue ges. Hydrobiol. Hydrogr.* **7**, 1–18.

Kylin, H. (1915). Untersuchungen über die Biochemie der Meeresalgen. *Hoppe-Seyler's Z. physiol. Chem.* **101**, 236–47.

Lüning, K. (1969). Growth of amputated and dark-exposed individuals of the brown alga *Laminaria hyperborea*. *Mar. Biol.* **2**, 218–23.

Lüning, K. (1971). Seasonal growth of *Laminaria hyperborea* under recorded underwater light conditions near Heligoland. In *Fourth European Marine Biology Symposium*, ed. D. J. Crisp, pp. 347–61. London, Cambridge University Press.

Mann, K. H. (1972*a*). Ecological energetics of the seaweed zone in a marine bay on the Atlantic coast of Canada. I. Zonation and biomass of seaweeds. *Mar. Biol.* **12**, 1–10.

Mann, K. H. (1972*b*). Ecological energetics of the seaweed zone in a marine bay on the Atlantic coast of Canada. II. Productivity of the seaweeds. *Mar. Biol.* **14**, 199–209.

Mann, K. H. (1972*c*). Macrophyte production and detritus food chains in coastal water. *Mem. Ist. Ital. Idrobiol.* **29**, Suppl. 353–83.

MacFarlane, C. (1952). A survey of certain seaweeds of commercial importance in southwest Nova Scotia. *Can. J. Bot.* **30**, 78–97.

McRoy, P. & Barsdate, R. J. (1970). Phosphate absorption in eelgrass. *Limnol. Oceanogr.* **15**, 6–13.

North, W. J. (1971). Growth of individual fronds of the mature giant kelp *Macrocystis*. In *The biology of giant kelp beds (Macrocystis) in California*, ed. W. J. North. *Beih. Nova Hedwigia*, **32**, 123–68.

Norton, T. A. & Burrows, E. M. (1969). Studies on the marine algae of the British Isles. 7. *Saccorhiza polyschides*. *Br. Phycol. J.* **4**, 19–53.

Patriquin, D. G. (1972). The origin of nitrogen and phosphorus for growth of the marine angiosperm *Thalassia testudinum*. *Mar. Biol.* **15**, 35–46.

Patriquin, D. G. & Knowles, R. (1972). Nitrogen fixation in the rhizosphere of marine angiosperms. *Mar. Biol.* **16**, 49–58.

Platt, T. & Irwin, B. (1968). Primary productivity measurements in St Margaret's Bay, 1967. *Fish. Res. Bd. Canada Tech. Rep.* 77.

Reimold, R. J. (1972). The movement of phosphorus through the salt marsh cord grass, *Spartina alterniflora* Loisel. *Limnol. Oceanogr.* **17**, 606–11.

Ryther, J. H. (1963). Geographic variations in productivity. In *The Sea*, ed. M. N. Hill, vol. 2, pp. 347–80. New York, Wiley-Interscience.

Schmitz, K., Lüning, K. & Willenbrink, J. (1972). CO$_2$-Fixierung und Stofftransport in benthischen marinen Algen. II. Zum Ferntransport ^{14}C-markierter Assimilate bei *Laminaria hyperborea* und *Laminaria saccharina*. *Z. Pflanzenphysiol.* **67,** 418–29.

Sculthorpe, C. D. (1967). *The Biology of Aquatic Plants*, 610 pp. London, Edward Arnold.

South, G. R. & Burrows, E. M. (1967). Studies on the marine algae of the British Isles. 5. *Chorda filum* (L.) Stackh. *Br. Phycol. Bull.* **3,** 379–402.

Suto, S. (1951). On the growth of 'buds' in *Hijikia fusiforme Bull. Jap. Soc. Sci. Fish.* **17,** 13–14.

Westlake, D. F. (1963). Comparisons of plant productivity. *Biol. Rev.* **38,** 385–425.

10. Primary production of freshwater microphytes

J. F. TALLING

Although communities of freshwater microphytes do not attain the extensive geographical development of their marine counterparts, their production is an important part of the natural economy of inland waters, and their functioning as photosynthetic systems is of great theoretical and practical interest. They are based, predominantly, on a great diversity of algae of simple construction, at least above the cellular level, which inhabit waters with compositions ranging from near-distilled water to saturated soda lakes. Their resources of nutrients (including CO_2) are correspondingly varied, and their energy income is subject to the attenuation of solar radiation in an aqueous medium. The accessibility of most inland waters has led to an historically extensive study of their population dynamics. However, because of the difficulties of assessing 'turnover' and losses from diffuse populations, such a crop-census approach can rarely give reliable estimates of organic production. For this end more direct measurements of photosynthesis have been used extensively during the last forty years, stimulated (as in marine work) by the development of methods applicable to dilute cell suspensions and low rates of gas exchange. Nevertheless, the high or intense localised rates of photosynthesis associated with dense communities may also raise important problems of methodology and photosynthetic performance. The present contribution aims to illustrate the photosynthetic activities of freshwater microphytes and controlling variables in a geographically diverse array of environments, paying particular attention to sites prominent in the International Biological Programme. Results from these sites will be considered in greater detail in the IBP PF synthesis volume edited by Le Cren.

Attached and bottom-living microphytes (phytomicrobenthos, periphyton)

The attractions of dealing with natural cell suspensions, as exemplified by *phytoplankton*, are obvious and have been discussed at an earlier IBP meeting (Talling, 1970). Although the present contribution deals chiefly with this dispersed type of microphytic vegetation, the existence

225

of microphyte communities associated with some substratum of mud, stone, or submerged vegetation should not be neglected. They are often important as an aggregated source of food for aquatic animals, but their uneven horizontal distribution increases the difficulties of assessing biomass and (cf. Schindler, Frost & Schmidt, 1973) photosynthetic production. Variability in development across and along the littoral of a Polish lake is illustrated by Pieczyńska (1971), where both the biomass and photosynthetic production per unit area of littoral may be governed by the area of suitable substratum available for colonization (Pieczyńska, 1968), as well as by other seasonal factors including ice-cover (Pieczyńska & Szczepańska, 1966).

These benthic communities will not extend to the central areas of deep lakes, and their photosynthetic performance *in situ* may suffer as a result of shading from host macrophytes, such as *Phragmites* (Pieczyńska & Straškraba, 1969). In some shallow lakes, rendered 'optically deep' by turbid water, their development can be controlled to a considerable extent by the varying penetration of photosynthetically active radiation. In turn, this may be controlled by the overlying phytoplankton; Hickman & Round (1970) discuss a probable example affecting the microbenthos in an English pond. In the Neusiedlersee, Austria, the increased penetration associated with calm conditions under clear ice cover is significant (M. V. Prosser, personal communication).

A fairly considerable development of phytomicrobenthos is not uncommon in oligotrophic lakes unproductive in phytoplankton, a feature perhaps not unrelated to mutual competition for nutrients and light penetration. Bottom-attached mats of blue-green algae are a conspicuous feature of some shallow Antarctic lakes (Fogg & Horne, 1970; Heywood, 1972) where their photosynthetic activity has been studied by Goldman, Mason & Wood (1963, 1972). An extensive benthic development of mosses may also exist in lakes at high latitudes, as in Lapland (Bodin & Nauwerck, 1968) and in the Antarctic islands of Signy and South Georgia (Light & Heywood, 1973). In the contrasting environment of hot springs, the growth and photosynthetic activity of blue-green mats can be intense and periodic (Brock & Brock, 1969; Stockner 1968; Wiegert & Fraleigh, 1972). The estimates of cover density compiled by Moss (1968), for benthic microphyte communities, show that densities exceeding 1 g chlorophyll a m^{-2} can be reached.

Phytoplankton: volume-based concentrations and photosynthetic activity

In the planktonic world of cell suspensions, the most obvious and most used measures of population have been related to unit volume of water. Unfortunately, the one-sided supply of radiant energy implies that no natural photosynthetic cover can be assessed without substituting area- for volume-based estimates of crop cover and activity. Some of the difficulties and complications involved in this transition are explored below, but first some volume-based relationships may be considered.

It is evident that there are no absolute lower or (allowing excess water!) upper limits to crop concentrations, but that the concentrations encountered are likely to be regulated by the nutrient resources per unit volume. The enormous range of crop concentrations in freshwaters is illustrated by records from two IBP sites, involving the most widely used index – chlorophyll *a* content – of crop quantity. Three orders of magnitude separate the concentrations found (Kalff, Welch & Holmgren, 1972) in the high latitude (75° N.) Char Lake and those in the equatorial Lake George (Ganf, 1972, 1974*b*; Ganf & Viner, 1973). Yet, when successive years are compared, both lakes are relatively stable systems with regard to the time-variation of phytoplankton density. In Char Lake, Kalff, Welch & Holmgren (1972) consider that the recovery from lowest density involves a response to ice-penetrating fluxes of solar radiation as low as 0.1 cal cm^{-2} d^{-1} (4 kJ m^{-2} d^{-1}).

For middle latitudes there are numerous descriptions of seasonal variation in phytoplankton concentration, but fewer in which the associated photosynthetic activity was also assessed. Fig. 10.1 shows an example from the River Thames, England (Kowalczewski & Lack, 1971). Here the periodic development of high algal concentrations is reflected in maxima of photosynthetic production per unit area; the latter were assessed from samples exposed *in situ* at different depths, yielding rates per unit volume that were integrated with respect to depth. It is noticeable, however, that the increases in area-based rates are less than proportional to the increases in volume-based algal concentrations.

In a wider survey, both between or within individual water-bodies, this last feature could be expected to be even more marked. Several distinct reasons exist, involving the limited resources of radiation and nutrient income in relation to the potentially unlimited scale of algal concentration. First, nutrient-rich waters (like the River Thames) are likely to have a high 'background' (i.e., non-algal) attenuation which will compete with the photosynthetic pigments for energy capture, and so restrict the photosynthesis per unit area of potentially dense algal populations. Second, the populations themselves introduce an element of 'self-shading', which increases with population density, but will be proportionately greater in situations (unlike the River Thames) of low background attenuation. This self-shading effect constitutes the ultimate limitation on the increase with population density of area-based rates

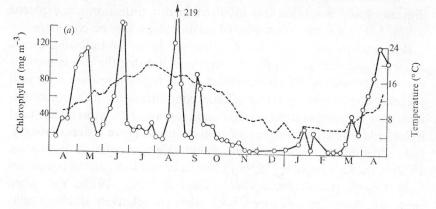

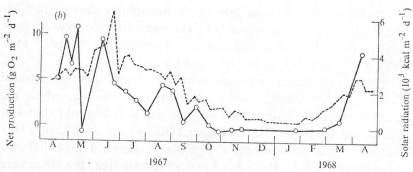

Fig. 10.1. Seasonal variation in the River Thames near Reading, England, of (*a*) chlorophyll *a* concentration — and temperature - - -; (*b*) daily net oxygen production per unit area — and solar radiation income - - - (from Kowalczewski & Lack, 1971).

of photosynthetic production, and of area-based contents of population, within the well-illuminated depth zone (euphotic, photosynthetic, or trophogenic layers). Examples, supported by measurements of the underwater attenuation of light, are described by Sakamoto (1966) for Japanese lakes, Talling (1965), Ganf (1972, 1974*b*), and Ganf & Viner (1973) for equatorial African lakes, Talling, Wood, Prosser & Baxter (1973) for Ethiopian lakes, Pyrina, Rutkovskaya & Il'inskii (1972) for a

Russian reservoir, Bindloss, Holden, Bailey-Watts & Smith (1972) and Bindloss (1974) for Loch Leven, Scotland, and Steel (1972) for water reservoirs in England.

The consequences of increasing population density for rates of photosynthetic productivity per unit area have been described for many individual lakes. Some wider comparisons (e.g. Talling, 1965) have brought out the marked non-linearity of the relationship at higher population densities, to be expected on the two optical grounds discussed above. However, there is strong evidence, especially from variations encountered within a lake, for a third source – a trend of declining photosynthetic capacity (per unit population) with increasing population density (Mikheeva, 1970). In some cases this trend might result, at least in part, from secondary issues, such as possible underestimation of rates in long exposures or of lower densities of population, or from correlations between cell size, abundance and photosynthetic capacity. In others, including Loch Leven (Bindloss, Holden, Bailey-Watts & Smith, 1972; Bindloss, 1974) such explanations are very improbable, and nutrient limitation may be suspected as a more meaningful correlate of depressed photosynthetic capacity. Less regularity in an inverse density/specific activity relationship can be expected from comparisons between lakes; Findenegg (1965) describes examples. Using chlorophyll *a* content as an index of crop, several Japanese workers (e.g., Ichimura & Aruga, 1964) have emphasised a trend towards reduced photosynthetic capacity in oligotrophic lakes, but Talling (1965) and Talling, Wood, Prosser & Baxter (1973) found little variation of capacity with population density in a wide range of tropical African lakes. If photosynthetic capacity is assessed on the basis of chlorophyll *a* content the values normally encountered with freshwater (also marine) microphytes lie in the range 1–10 mg C (mg chlorophyll $a)^{-1}$ h^{-1}.

Especially in recent years, human activities have led to increased nutrient inputs and higher densities of phytoplankton in many lakes – so-called 'eutrophication'. Increases in photosynthetic activity may result, both per unit area, and per unit volume under conditions of light-saturation, as at the 'optimum depth'. A relatively mild example, Lago Maggiore in Italy, is described by Gerletti (1972) on the basis of measurements of photosynthesis extending from 1957 to 1967. Some of the most extreme examples are recorded among some polluted lakes in Denmark (Fig. 10.2), for which Mathiesen (1970, 1971) has demonstrated the development of very high rates of photosynthesis per unit volume (e.g. 10–25 mg C l^{-1} d^{-1}) with decline in transparency (Secchi disc) to under 0.5 m. Other examples of very intense but vertically localised activity of phytoplankton has also been followed in sewage oxidation ponds (Winberg, Ostapenya, Sivko & Levina, 1966; Uhlmann, 1966) and fertilised fishponds (Hepher, 1962; Fott, 1972), in the unmodified natural environment of soda lakes (Talling *et al.*, 1973), and in other shallow tropical waters (Ganf, 1972, 1974*b*; Ganapati & Kulkani, p. 690, Sreenivasan, p. 690). It raises rather severe problems in the estimation of photosynthetic rates by the usual field methods, owing to the rapid modifications induced in the medium, especially when

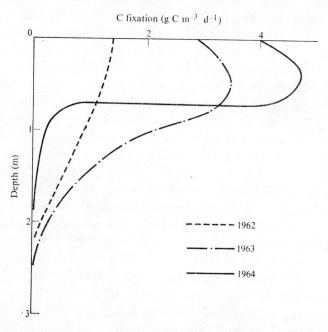

Fig. 10.2. Vertical profiles of daily photosynthetic activity (^{14}C method) by phytoplankton measured at station F1 in a Danish lake, Furesø, at the times of summer maxima in the years indicated (from Mathiesen, 1970, 1971).

enclosed in small vessels. Diurnal changes *in situ* are also accentuated, and in the less seasonal tropical environments play a greater role (Ganf, 1974*a*; Ganf & Viner, 1973; Ganf & Horne, 1975).

These problems of technique are one obstacle, but not necessarily the most important one, in assessing the upper limits of production by phytoplankton. Other difficulties (discussed by Talling, Wood, Prosser & Baxter, 1973) concern the distinction between estimates of gross and net photosynthesis in relation to the methods used, and the lack of sufficient information to check the derivation of most of the highest published estimates. A considerable number of better documented studies on productive lakes or ponds have yielded estimates of 4–7 g C $m^{-2} d^{-1}$, which, in my view, may approximate gross rather than net daily photosynthesis. Examples can be cited from Denmark (Mathiesen, 1970), Scotland (Bindloss, 1974), Sweden (Ahlgren, 1970), East Africa (Talling, 1965; Ganf, 1972), Israel (Hepher, 1962), and USA (Wetzel, 1966). Reasonably well-established estimates of 10 g C $m^{-2} d^{-1}$, or higher, appear to be extremely rare for natural lakes (possible examples are discussed by Talling, Wood, Prosser & Baxter, 1973), but apparently not for mass cultures of planktonic algae under natural irradiation (cf. Vendlová, 1969, and Soeder & Stengel, Chapter 29). In the latter, net organic production can be more safely assessed from the yield of dry matter. The relatively indirect (gas exchange) methods applied to natural communities involve more uncertainties, including the calculation of daily rates from the short exposure periods permitted by high rates per unit volume. The absolute calibration of rates deduced from ^{14}C uptake has also been challenged on several grounds, and large correction factors applicable to much previous data have been discussed by Steemann Nielsen (1965); Arthur & Rigler (1967); Goldman (1968); Wood (1971); Schindler & Holmgren (1971); and Williams, Berman & Holm–Hansen (1973).

From the earlier discussion, it will be seen that highest rates of gross photosynthesis per unit area should be realized when (i) algal absorption of photosynthetically active radiation predominates over the background absorption, and (ii) the population density is not so high as to generate a greatly reduced specific activity or photosynthetic capacity. In terms of population density, these are often conflicting requirements. The conflict may, perhaps, be reduced in two ways. In the uncommon situation of low 'background' light absorption, yet favourable nutrient supply, condition (i) may be realized at relatively low population densities that also satisfy condition (ii). Possible examples may exist in the large lakes of Africa (cf. Talling, 1965). Alternatively, condition (i) may be achieved by high population densities in a medium of considerable background absorption, where nutrient supply is sufficiently high to enable high population density and high photosynthetic capacity to coexist. Examples are provided by certain Ethiopian crater lakes (Talling *et al.*, 1973) and, in lesser degree, by Lake George, Uganda (Ganf, 1972).

The relationship between population density and net photosynthetic production per unit area is more uncertain. High densities are rarely

231

encountered throughout deep water columns, but this situation would imply large cover densities and large respiration losses per unit area which would lead to low net yields. Even in shallow lakes, where high densities per unit volume are most typically found, the water column is often optically deep as a result of light attenuation by algae and by sediments resuspended from wind-induced turbulence. Examples include Lake Balaton (Entz & Fillinger, 1961), Neusiedlersee (Sauberer, 1952; Dokulil, 1973), and Tjeukemeer (Beattie *et al.*, 1972) in Europe, and Lake George (Ganf, 1972,1974*b*) and Lake Chad (Lemoalle, 1969,1973) in Africa. As a result, the average planktonic cell spends a large fraction of its time in darkness, and again net yields of photosynthesis are likely to be much lower than the gross yields. From these considerations, the interconversion of gross to net yields using some widely applied factor (e.g. 0.7) could often be misleading.

Regular and irregular depth-profiles of photosynthesis

Estimates of rates of photosynthesis per unit volume, plotted against depth, provide the basic information from which the great majority of production estimates for phytoplankton are derived. Any wide ranging survey will show that such depth profiles exhibit a variation of three or four orders of magnitude in the absolute scales of the two axes, with the depth axis contracting as the rate axis expands. Four examples are shown in Fig. 10.3, using double logarithmic scales. These bring out (as do the optical depth scales used by Talling, 1965 and Rodhe, 1965) the intrinsic shape of the profiles, governed primarily by the photosynthetic rate–irradiance characteristic and the near-exponential decline of irradiance with depth. They also enable the derived rates of integral photosynthesis per unit area (ΣA) to be represented by diagonal lines, which pass through points (▲) defined by the maximum rate per unit volume (A_{max}) and the 'average profile depth' as indicated by the quotient between the integral photosynthesis per unit area and A_{max}. This representation is particularly useful when an approach to some suspected upper limit of areal production is being examined.

The widespread occurrence of a 'regular' intrinsic shape in depth profiles is a striking feature of the literature on primary production by phytoplankton, and has stimulated theoretical models based on irradiance–rate–depth relationships. It is particularly well shown in studies on shallow lakes without wind-shelter, where effective vertical mixing by turbulence over a restricted euphotic zone is commonplace.

However, more irregular profiles are far from uncommon. There can be little doubt that the most important single factor in generating irregularity is uneven vertical distribution of population density, as described in detail by Findenegg (1964,1965,1971) for European alpine lakes. Pronounced examples (e.g. subsurface maxima) are usually associated

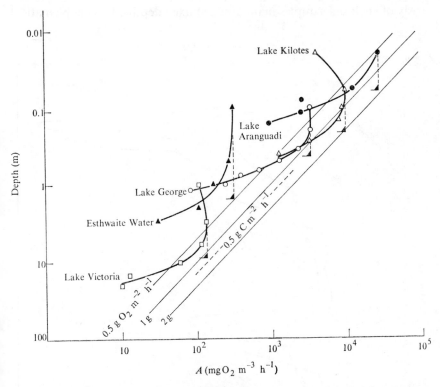

Fig. 10.3. Vertical profiles of photosynthetic activity per unit volume, A (gross oxygen production) measured during short (0.5 to 3 h) exposures in four productive lakes, plotted on a double-logarithmic diagram. The mean vertical depth of each profile ($=\Sigma A/A_{max}$: see text) is indicated by ▲, linked to the corresponding value of A_{max} by an interrupted line, and shown in relation to diagonal lines representing values of estimated gross production per unit area (ΣA). Sources of data: Lakes Kilotes and Aranguadi, Ethiopia (Talling, Wood, Prosser & Baxter, 1973); Lakes George and Victoria, East Africa (Talling, 1965); Esthwaite Water, England (Talling, unpublished observations).

with thermal (density) stratification, but even for passive and non-buoyant cells this is not always essential. Gross distortions of the 'regular' form of photosynthesis-depth profile can arise from surface aggregations of buoyant blue-green algae, and from active vertical migrations of phytoflagellates (e.g. Happey & Moss, 1967; Pechlaner,

233

I

1971; Tilzer, 1972,1973). Production in both these situations may be difficult to study with the methods usually employed. This is well shown (Fig. 10.4) by detailed measurements *in situ* of daily migrations of the dominant dinoflagellate, *Peridinium westii*, in Lake Kinneret, Israel (Berman & Rodhe, 1971). In such a mobile type of vegetation, it is more difficult to estimate daily photosynthetic production from a vertical array of enclosed samples maintained at fixed depths. It is problematical

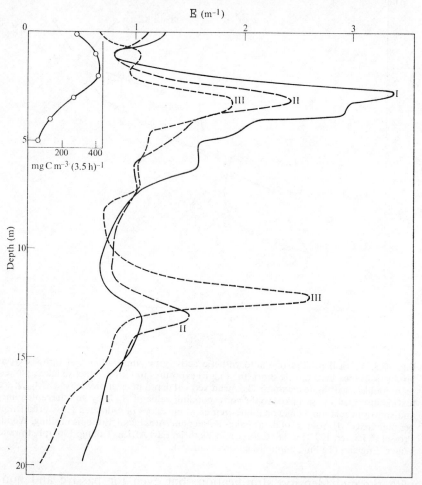

Fig. 10.4. Changes in localised depth-maxima of a dinoflagellate, *Peridinium westii*, over a single day (16 May 1969) in Lake Kinneret, Israel, as indicated by the extinction coefficient (E) of a horizontal light beam. The three extinction profiles were recorded at 09 45 h (I), 11 00 h (II), and 13 50 h (III). The upper inset shows a depth-profile of carbon assimilation (^{14}C method), based upon material collected from 2.5 m depth at 09 45 h and exposed for 3.5 h (from Berman & Rodhe, 1971).

234

whether or not such daily migrations tend to increase the daily photosynthetic production, bearing in mind such features as negative phototaxis and possibly intrinsic diurnal rhythms in tactic response.

An equally difficult problem is the corresponding consequence, for the daily integral photosynthesis, of differentiation between 'sun' and 'shade' characteristics in cells at different depths. Examples in freshwaters are discussed by Ohle (1964); Talling (1966), and Ichimura, Nagasawa & Tanaka (1968). Such differentiation will normally take place in a stratified water column, within which population density – and probably composition and photosynthetic capacity – will be strongly stratified, and it is difficult to distinguish the relative contributions involved. In my view the generalized scheme of Odum, McConnell & Abbott (1958), which depicts a direct enhancement of production per unit area, is likely to be a gross simplification. Sorokin (1959) has introduced a weighting factor or K_r coefficient to assess the consequences of stratification on population density and photosynthetic capacity, based on rates of photosynthesis measured in surface exposures. However, this would not fully represent the consequences for photosynthetic production of a pronounced sun–shade differentiation in the phytoplankton.

The significance of respiration losses

Compared with the abundance of recent estimates of photosynthesis (usually labelled 'production'), remarkably few detailed studies have been made of respiration rates of freshwater (or marine) microphytes in relation to ecological problems. The reason lies chiefly in the limitations of current methodology (cf. Vollenweider, 1973), especially as used in 'routine' estimations of production by the ^{14}C method or by measurements of oxygen changes in light and dark bottles. The latter yield estimates of oxygen uptake that have often been interpreted as algal respiration, but which usually include a contribution of unknown magnitude from associated bacteria, small invertebrates, and possibly (e.g. Abeliovich & Shilo, 1972; Serruya & Serruya, 1972) other non-respiratory oxidations. Further, the rates per unit volume are often too low for accurate measurement; they are usually not assessed for depths below the photosynthetic zone, to which cells may circulate; and the classic assumption of equality in light and darkness is increasingly challenged (e.g., Golterman, 1971; Lex, Silvester & Stewart, 1972). The ^{14}C method is even less useful in this respect: although estimations of respiration have been made (Steemann Nielsen & Hansen, 1959) the analysis of the kinetics involved is controversial and the method has not been widely applied in work on primary production. It is often supposed that the usual estimates of ^{14}C fixation are equivalent to production of particulate carbon, as in some small-scale growth experiments (e.g. Eppley & Sloan, 1965), and that the need for taking respiration losses into account is thereby circumvented. This neglects the extent of respiration in water layers and diurnal periods not encompassed by experimental measurements. It is also doubtful whether the basic postulate is well established for cell systems in which the depth–time dark sector is predominant, as mentioned earlier for shallow, turbid lakes. Development of additional experimental approaches, as by Golterman (1971), is therefore to be welcomed.

It is not difficult to show that net photosynthetic production per unit area must often be influenced by very considerable respiration losses, as is also suggested by estimates for terrestrial vegetation (e.g. McCree, 1970; Kira, Chapter 2). Thus quantitative models of organic production by phytoplankton (e.g. Talling, 1957b,1971; Steel, 1972; Ganf & Viner, 1973) usually show a marked sensitivity to values of the ratio between specific rates of respiration and photosynthetic capacity. A simple calculation will show that a normal order of magnitude for specific respiration rate, 1 mg O_2 (mg chlorophyll a)$^{-1}$ h^{-1}, in a not exceptionally high cover density of 500 mg chlorophyll a m^{-2}, will lead to a rate of 12 g O_2 m^{-2} d^{-1}, comparable with estimates of gross photosynthesis in productive waters. Some examples from field experience are described by Fott (1972) for fishponds in Czechoslovakia, by Bindloss (1974) for a Scottish loch, and by Ganf (1972,1974b); Ganf & Viner (1973), and Talling, Wood, Prosser & Baxter (1973) for productive lakes in Africa. In my opinion reliable estimates of net photosynthetic production, trustworthy to within $\pm 50\%$, are probably non-existent. I believe that more recognition should be made of this 'Achilles heel' in present-day production biology, and the unqualified description of rate estimates (based upon gas exchange) as 'production' avoided, in view of the overtones of meaning introduced by this word.

Photosynthetic productivity, nutrient consumption, and population growth

Historically, the increasing use (since around 1955) of gas exchange measurements to assess organic production of freshwater microphytes followed a period with quantitative study centred upon the population dynamics of individual species or species-groups. The two approaches have rarely been combined effectively, to the detriment of wider issues of quantitative ecology if not of production numerology. One deduction, from general experience in the two fields, is that photosynthetic capacity (per unit of population) tends to be maintained to a remarkable extent at times of population constancy or even decline (e.g. Tilzer, 1972). This would not be surprising if the population decline was effected by external rates of depletion (e.g. cell sedimentation) superimposed upon an actively growing population. In many instances of nutrient depletion, however, this is not true since cell division itself is limited; an example for the primary limitation of spring diatom growth by silicon depletion is given by Talling (1957*a*,1966). Other alternative explanations involve periods of intracellular storage of photosynthate or accelerated losses by respiration or extracellular products. It should not be forgotten that much of the classic work on kinetics of algal photosynthesis was performed with carbonate media incapable of maintaining cellular growth. This approach did involve some severe penalties, as shown above, all by Myers and his co-workers (Myers, 1970). Nevertheless, measurements of photosynthesis by natural populations may give even less trustworthy information on the capacity for further population growth than on momentary rates of net organic production. This is a gloomy outlook for modellers attempting to predict population dynamics, but in mitigation one may cite some correlations between observed increments of population and experimental 'production' estimations (Goldman *et al.* 1968; de Amezaga, Goldman & Stull, 1974).

An almost universal difficulty in the interrelation of population dynamics and photosynthetic production lies in the usual neglect of species difference in studies on the latter compared with its obvious importance in the former. Comparisons of differing specific photosynthetic activity, recorded for different algal species in natural communities, are given by Findenegg (1971) and Mikheeva (1970). Any calculation of specific activity depends upon the selected index of biomass; a common index, chlorophyll *a* content, may vary considerably between species in relation to dry weight (Pyrina & Elizarova, 1971). The consequences of neglect are well illustrated in the few autoradiographic studies of ^{14}C uptake by individual planktonic algae yet carried out (Watt, 1971; Gutel'makher, 1973; Stull, de Amezaga & Goldman, 1974). As another example, one may consider the mathematically untenable course of averaging the differing specific growth rates of several coexisting species in order to predict future population growth

237

in a mixed culture. Averages of differing specific rates of photosynthesis may be equally useless for prediction.

Returning to early history, the derivation of rates of net organic production by microphytes was attempted using the product of population density with an estimate of either the specific (relative) growth rate or the reciprocal of the 'turnover time' (Boysen Jensen, 1914; Juday, 1940). More recently calculations of the 'turnover time' have often been made (e.g. Rodhe, 1958; Javornický, 1966; Ahlgren, 1970) from a combination of experimental estimates of 'production' (as C uptake, from CO_2 or O_2 exchange) with estimates of population density (as carbon equivalent) per volume or unit area. Estimates of a few days duration are frequently obtained. For several reasons, these may be very different from the mean generation time of cells in the populations involved, which in simple cell division is proportional (as $\ln 2/k$) to the reciprocal of the specific growth rate k. Two reasons, already discussed, are the possible under-representation of respiration losses in the experimental measurements and the consequences of a heterogeneous composition of the populations. Further, the quantities are distinct in their derivation, as the specific growth rate and mean generation time involve logarithmic measures of population size whereas the turnover time (as usually derived) does not. The concept of turnover time for cellular material is not readily applicable to prolonged periods of exponential population increase, often observed during spring diatom growth (e.g. Lund, 1949; Pechlaner, 1970). In my view, the dynamics involved are best characterised by exponential rate constants such as specific growth rate. For most microphytes, excluding certain thermophilic strains, these are unlikely to appreciably exceed 1.5 to 2 (ln units) d^{-1} (Hoogenhout & Amesz, 1965), which may be regarded as upper limits to relative production rate that are rarely approached for entire natural populations. However, specific rates of photosynthesis per unit population (expressed as carbon) may attain such values in the optimum or light-saturation region of a depth profile. I do not know of a systematic comparison of such rate constants for growth and photosynthesis of species important in freshwater communities comparable to the marine work of McAllister, Shah & Strickland (1964) or the studies on *Chlorella* by Myers and his co-workers (Myers, 1970). Some laboratory and field comparisons are available for the common planktonic diatom *Asterionella formosa* (Talling, 1955), and Pechlaner (1970) shows a compatibility between rate constants deduced from measurements of photosynthesis and the spring increase of phytoplankton in Lake Erken, Sweden.

Greater differences may appear in populations subject to opposed depletion rates, as described by Uhlmann (1971) and Steel, Duncan & Andrew (1972).

It has often been found, especially in densely populated lakes, that the measured rates of carbon fixation would imply a rapid exhaustion of another dissolved nutrient(s) if nutrient uptake followed the proportions to carbon represented in the average composition of organic material. Examples can be cited from Lake George, Uganda (Viner, 1973; Ganf & Viner, 1974), Tjeukemeer, Netherlands (Golterman, 1971), and Lough Neagh, N. Ireland (Gibson, Wood, Dickson & Jewson, 1971). Despite such calculations, considerable photosynthetic activity and dense crops are often maintained for long periods. Explanations can be sought in (i) the recycling of nutrients by bacteria, animals, and algal products; (ii) other chemical equilibria involving nutrient flux between the water and solid phases (compartments) of the aquatic environment; (iii) the possible overestimation of net organic production by the usual short-term measurement of gas exchange, mentioned above but often neglected. Recycling mechanisms are considered to be of great importance in the equatorial Lake George (evidence in Golterman, 1971; Ganf & Viner, 1973; Ganf & Blažka, 1974), and the subject is discussed elsewhere in this volume (Schindler & Fee, Chapter 14). Possibility (iii) has some implications for the assessment of the photosynthetic quotient $(+O_2/-CO_2)$ applicable to experimental field data, as values higher than 1 (e.g. 1.3) are often adopted (though rarely tested directly) from considerations of average crop composition.

Among the possible rate-limiting nutrients carbon dioxide has a special place in view of its immediate involvement in photosynthesis, and of the large net uptake of carbon required relative to such elements as N and P. Although in most freshwaters the reserves of dissolved inorganic carbon are large, and supported by variable exchange rates with the atmospheric reservoir (Schindler *et al.*, 1972; Schindler & Fee, 1973, and Chapter 14), the chemical species involved in cellular uptake may be reduced to rate-limiting concentrations during the depletions of total CO_2 often observed in productive lakes. Examples of rate limitation described for lakes in Canada (Schindler & Fee, 1973, and Chapter 14) and Scotland (Bindloss, 1974) may be interpreted in this way, although other consequences of the alkaline conditions associated with CO_2 depletion may also be relevant. In Loch Leven, Scotland, Bindloss (1974) has shown that a CO_2-linked pH limitation of photosynthetic rate is one of the causes (not necessarily the most important) of the inverse

239

relationship observed between photosynthetic capacity and population density.

Stimulated by the increased availability of estimates of microphyte production rates, based primarily upon photosynthesis, the supremacy of the dynamic treatment of freshwater systems has been advocated in comparison with the more 'static' products of crop census and chemical analysis prevalent in the past. In my view, a bigger challenge is posed by the desired interrelation of the two aspects. Many of the 'production', especially net production, rates at present in circulation rest on precarious foundations of methodology. Other dangers implicit in the uncritical integration of rates of photosynthetic production with time have been well stated by Ryther (1960):

In modern, dynamic ecology, it has become unfashionable to speak of the 'standing crop' of organisms. The important question is not 'how much is there?' but 'how fast is it being produced?' There is no doubt that this concept has opened up new and extremely interesting avenues of ecological research. But the population ecologist or fisheries biologist should beware of these values. The sociologist who compares the productive capacity of the land and sea may be sadly deluding himself. For animals eat food, not photosynthesis. What is the significance of organic matter which is produced, consumed, decomposed and remineralized almost simultaneously? Why add up a daily production which is daily expended into a non-existent annual total. Is this comparable to a barn full of corn?

References

Abeliovich, A. & Shilo, M. (1972). Photo-oxidative death in blue-green algae. *Journal of Bacteriology*, **111**, 682–9.

Ahlgren, G. (1970). Limnological studies of Lake Norrviken, a eutrophicated Swedish lake. II. Phytoplankton and its production. *Schweizerische Zeitschrift für Hydrologie*, **32**, 353–96.

Arthur, C. R. & Rigler, F. H. (1967). A possible source of error in the ^{14}C method of measuring primary productivity. *Limnology and Oceanography*, **12**, 121–4.

Beattie, M., Bromley, H. J., Chambers, M., Goldspink, C., Vijverberg, J., van Zalingen, N. P. & Golterman, H. L. (1972). Limnological studies on Tjeukemeer – a typical Dutch 'polder reservoir'. In *Productivity Problems of Freshwaters*, eds. Z. Kajak & A. Hillbricht-Ilkowska, pp. 421–46. Warsaw & Kraków, Polish Scientific Publishers.

Berman, T. & Rodhe, W. (1971). Distribution and migration of *Peridinium* in Lake Kinneret (Lake Tiberias). *Mitteilungen der Internationale Vereinigung für theoretische und angewandte Limnologie*, **19**, 266–75.

Bindloss, M. E. (1974). Primary productivity of phytoplankton in Loch Leven, Kinross. *Proceedings of the Royal Society of Edinburgh*, **74**, 157–81.

Bindloss, M. E., Holden, A. V., Bailey-Watts, A. E. & Smith, I. R. (1972). Phytoplankton production, chemical and physical conditions in Loch Leven. In *Productivity Problems of Freshwaters*, eds. Z. Kajak & A. Hillbricht-Ilkowska, pp. 639–59. Warsaw & Kraków, Polish Scientific Publishers.

Bodin, K. & Nauwerck, A. (1968). Produktionsbiologische Studien über die Moosvegetation eines klaren Gebirgssees. *Schweizerische Zeitschrift für Hydrologie*, **30**, 318–52.

Boysen Jensen, P. (1914). Studies concerning the organic matter of the sea bottom. *Reports of the Danish Biological Station*, **22**, 1–39.

Brock, T. D. & Brock, M. L. (1969). Effect of light intensity on photosynthesis by thermal algae adapted to natural and reduced sunlight. *Limnology and Oceanography*, **14**, 334–41.

de Amezaga, E., Goldman, C. R. & Stull, E. A. (1974). Primary productivity and rate of change of biomass of various species of phytoplankton in Castle Lake, California. *Verhandlungen der Internationale Vereinigung für theoretische und angewandte Limnologie*, **18**, 1768–75.

Dokulil, M. (1973). Zur Steuerung der planktischen Primärproduktion durch die Schwebstoffe. In *Ökosystemforschung*, ed. H. Ellenberg, pp. 109–10. Berlin, Springer-Verlag.

Entz, B. & Fillinger, E. M. (1961). Angaben zur Kenntnis des Lichtklimas des Balaton. *Annales Biologicae Tihany*, **28**, 49–89.

Eppley, R. W. & Sloan, P. R. (1965). Carbon balance experiments with marine phytoplankton. *Journal of the Fisheries Research Board of Canada*, **22**, 1083–97.

Findenegg, I. (1964). Produktionsbiologische Planktonuntersuchungen an Ostalpenseen. *Internationale Revue der gesamten Hydrobiologie und Hydrographie*, **49**, 381–416.

Findenegg, I. (1965). Factors controlling primary productivity, especially with regard to water replenishment, stratification, and mixing. *Memorie dell'Istituto Italiano di Idrobiologia*, **18** Suppl. 105–19. Reprinted in *Primary Productivity in Aquatic Environments*, ed. C. R. Goldman, pp. 105–19. Berkeley, University of California Press.

Findenegg, I. (1971). Die Produktionsleistungen einiger planktischer Algenarten in ihrem natürlichen Milieu. *Archiv für Hydrobiologie*, **69**, 273–93.

Fogg, G. E. & Horne, A. J. (1970). The physiology of Antarctic freshwater algae. In *Antarctic Ecology*, ed. M. W. Holdgate, vol. 2, pp. 632–8. London, Academic Press.

Fott, J. (1972). Observations on primary production of phytoplankton in two fish ponds. In *Productivity Problems of Freshwaters*, eds. Z. Kajak & A. Hillbricht-Ilkowska, pp. 673–83. Warsaw & Kraków, Polish Scientific Publishers.

Ganf, G. G. (1972). The regulation of net primary production in Lake George, Uganda, East Africa. In *Productivity Problems of Freshwaters*, eds. Z. Kajak & A. Hillbricht-Ilkowska, pp. 693–708. Warsaw & Kraków, Polish Scientific Publishers.

1*

Ganf, G. G. (1974a). Diurnal mixing and the vertical distribution of phytoplankton in a shallow equatorial lake (Lake George, Uganda). *Journal of Ecology*, **62**, 611–30.

Ganf, G. G. (1974b). Incident solar irradiance and underwater light penetration as factors controlling the chlorophyll *a* content of a shallow equatorial lake (Lake George, Uganda). *Journal of Ecology*, **62**, 593–610.

Ganf, G. G. & Blažka, P. (1974). Oxygen uptake, ammonia and phosphate excretion by zooplankton of a shallow equatorial lake (Lake George, Uganda). *Limnology and Oceanography*, **19**, 313–25.

Ganf, G. G. & Horne, A. J. (1975). Diurnal stratification, primary production and nitrogen fixation in a shallow equatorial lake (Lake George, Uganda). *Freshwater Biology*, **5**, in press.

Ganf, G. G. & Viner, A. B. (1973). Ecological stability in a shallow equatorial lake (Lake George, Uganda). *Proceedings of the Royal Society* B, **184**, 321–46.

Gerletti, M. (1972). Comparative trends of primary productivity and some chemical parameters in Lake Maggiore. In *Productivity Problems of Freshwaters*, eds. Z. Kajak & A. Hillbricht-Ilkowska, pp. 709–13. Warsaw & Kraków, Polish Scientific Publishers.

Gibson, C. E., Wood, R. B., Dickson, E. L. & Jewson, D. H. (1971). The succession of phytoplankton in Lough Neagh 1968–70. *Mitteilungen der Internationale Vereinigung für theoretische und angewandte Limnologie*, **19**, 146–60.

Goldman, C. R. (1968). The use of absolute activity for eliminating serious errors in the measurement of primary productivity with C^{14}. *Journal du Conseil, Conseil permanent international pour l'exploration de la Mer*, **32**, 172–9.

Goldman, C. R., Gerletti, M., Javornický, P., Melchiorri-Santolini, V. & de Amezaga, E. (1968). Primary productivity, bacteria, phyto- and zooplankton in Lake Maggiore: correlations and relationships with ecological factors. *Memorie dell'Istituto Italiano di Idrobiologia*, **23**, 49–127.

Goldman, C. R., Mason, D. T. & Wood, B. J. B. (1963). Light injury and inhibition in Antarctic freshwater phytoplankton. *Limnology and Oceanography*, **8**, 313–22.

Goldman, C. R., Mason, D. T. & Wood, B. J. B. (1972). Comparative study of the limnology of two small lakes on Ross Island, Antarctica. In *Antarctic terrestrial biology*, ed. G. A. Llano, pp. 1–50. Washington, DC, Antarctic Research Series, American Geophysical Union.

Golterman, H. L. (1971). The determination of mineralization losses in correlation with the estimation of net primary production with the oxygen method and chemical inhibitors. *Freshwater Biology*, **1**, 249–56.

Gutel'makher, B. L. (1973). Radioautographic method of determination of comparative significance of individual species of algae in primary production of plankton. *Gidrobiologicheskii Zhurnal, Kiev*, **9** (1), 103–7.

Happey, C. & Moss, B. (1967). Some aspects of the biology of *Chrysococcus diaphanus* in Abbots Pond, Somerset. *British Phycological Bulletin*, **3**, 269–79.

Hepher, B. (1962). Primary production in fishponds and its application to fertilization experiments. *Limnology and Oceanography*, **7**, 131–6.

Heywood, R. B. (1972). Antarctic limnology: a review. *British Antarctic Survey Bulletin*, **29**, 35–65.

Hickman, M. & Round, F. E. (1970). Primary production and standing crops of epipsammic and epipelic algae. *British Phycological Journal*, **5**, 247–55.

Hoogenhout, H. & Amesz, J. (1965). Growth rates of photosynthetic microorganisms in laboratory cultures. *Archiv für Mikrobiologie*, **50**, 10–24.

Ichimura, S. & Aruga, Y. (1964). Photosynthetic natures of natural algal communities in Japanese waters. In *Recent Advances in the Fields of Hydrosphere, Atmosphere and Nuclear Geochemistry*, eds. Y. Miyake & T. Koyama, pp. 13–37. Tokyo, Maruzen Co.

Ichimura, S., Nagasawa, S. & Tanaka, T. (1968). On the oxygen and chlorophyll maxima found in the metalimnion of a mesotrophic lake. *Botanical Magazine, Tokyo*, **81**, 1–10.

Javornický, P. (1966). Measurements of production and turnover of phytoplankton in four localities of Poland. *Ekologia Polska, Ser. A*. **14**, 203–14.

Juday, C. (1940). The annual energy budget of an inland lake. *Ecology*, **21**, 438–50.

Kalff, J., Welch, H. E. & Holmgren, S. K. (1972). Pigment cycles in two high-arctic Canadian lakes. *Verhandlungen der Internationale Vereinigung für theoretische und angewandte Limnologie*, **18**, 250–6.

Kowalczewski, A. & Lack, T. J. (1971). Primary production and respiration of the phytoplankton of the Rivers Thames and Kennet at Reading. *Freshwater Biology*, **1**, 197–212.

Lemoalle, J. (1969). Premieres données sur la production primaire dans la region de Bol (avril–octobre, 1968) (lac Tchad). *Cahiers ORSTOM, séries Hydrobiologie*, **3**, 107–19.

Lemoalle, J. (1973). L'energie lumineuse et l'activé photosynthétique du phytoplancton dans le lac Tchad. *Cahiers ORSTOM, séries Hydrobiologie*, **7**, 85–116.

Lex, M., Silvester, W. & Stewart, W. D. P. (1972). Photorespiration and nitrogenase in the blue-green alga *Anabaena cylindrica*. *Proceedings of the Royal Society of London* B, **180**, 87–102.

Light, J. J. & Heywood, R. B. (1973). Deep-water mosses in Antarctic lakes. *Nature, London*, **242**, 535–6.

Lund, J. W. G. (1949). Studies on *Asterionella*. I. The origin and nature of the cells producing seasonal maxima. *Journal of Ecology*, **37**, 389–419.

Mathiesen, H. (1970). Miljøaendringer og biologisk effekt i søer. *Vatten*, **2**, 149–73.

Mathiesen, H. (1971). Summer maxima of algae and eutrophication. *Mitteilungen der Internationale Vereinigung für theoretische und angewandte Limnologie*, **19**, 161–81.

McAllister, C. D., Shah, N. & Strickland, J. D. H. (1964). Marine phytoplankton photosynthesis as a function of light intensity: a comparison of methods. *Journal of the Fishery Research Board of Canada*, **21**, 159–81.

McCree, K. J. (1970). An equation for the rate of respiration of white clover plants grown under controlled conditions. In *Prediction and Measurement of Photosynthetic Productivity*, Proceedings IBP/PP Technical Meeting, Třeboň, September 1969, pp. 221–9. Wageningen, PUDOC.

Mikheeva, T. M. (1970). Evaluation of potential production of a unit of phytoplankton biomass. (In Russian). In *Biological Productivity of an Eutrophic Lake*, ed. G. G. Winberg, pp. 50–70. Moscow, Nauka.

Moss, B. (1968). The chlorophyll *a* content of some benthic algal communities. *Archiv für Hydrobiologie*, **65**, 51–62.

Myers, J. (1970). Genetic and adaptive physiological characteristics observed in the chlorellas. In *Prediction and Measurement of Photosynthetic Productivity*, Proceedings IBP/PP Technical Meeting, Třeboň, September 1969, pp. 447–54. Wageningen, PUDOC.

Odum, H. T., McConnell, W. & Abbott, W. (1958). The chlorophyll *a* of communities. *Publications of the Institute of Marine Science, University of Texas*, **5**, 65–96.

Ohle, W. (1964). Interstitiallösungen der Sedimente, Nährstoffgehalt des Wassers und Primärproduktion des Phytoplanktons in Seen. *Helgoländer Wissenschaftliche Meeresuntersuchungen*, **10**, 411–29.

Pechlaner, R. (1970). The phytoplankton spring outburst and its conditions in Lake Erken (Sweden). *Limnology and Oceanography*, **15**, 113–30.

Pechlaner, R. (1971). Factors that control the production rate and biomass of phytoplankton in high-mountain lakes. *Mitteilungen der Internationale Vereinigung für theoretische und angewandte Limnologie*, **19**, 125–43.

Pieczyńska, E. (1968). Dependence of the primary production of periphyton upon the substrate area suitable for colonization. *Bulletin de l'Académie Polonaise des Sciences*, **16** (3), 165–9.

Pieczyńska, E. (1971). Mass appearance of algae in the littoral of several Mazurian lakes. *Mitteilungen der Internationale Vereinigung für theoretische und angewandte Limnologie*, **19**, 59–69.

Pieczyńska, E. & Straškraba, M. (1969). Field experiments on the effect of light conditions in Phragmites stands on the production of littoral algae. *Bulletin de l'Académie Polonaise des Sciences*, **17**, 43–6.

Pieczyńska, E. & Szczepańska, W. (1966). Primary production in the littoral of several Mazurian lakes. *Verhandlungen der Internationale Vereinigung für theoretische und angewandte Limnologie*, **16**, 373–9.

Pyrina, I. L. & Elizarova, V. A. (1971). Spectrophotometric measurements of chlorophyll in cultures of some algae. (In Russian). *Trudi Instituta Biologii Vnytnennikh Vodokhranilishch*, **21**, 56–65.

Pyrina, I. L., Rutkovskaya, V. A. & Il'inskii, A. L. (1972). Influence of phytoplankton on penetrating solar radiation into water of the Volga reservoirs. (In Russian). *Trudi Instituta Biologii Vnutrennikh Vodokhranilishch*, **23** (26), 97–106.

Rodhe, W. (1958). Primärproduktion und Seetypen. *Verhandlungen der Internationale Vereinigung für theoretische und angewandte Limnologie*, **13**, 121–41.

Rodhe, W. (1965). Standard correlations between pelagic photosynthesis and light. *Memorie dell'Istituto Italiano di Idrobiologia*, **18** Suppl. 365–81.

Ryther, J. H. (1960). Organic production by plankton algae, and its environmental control. In *The ecology of algae*, eds. C. A. Tryon & R. T. Hartman, pp. 72–83. Special Publication no. 2. University of Pittsburgh, Pymatuning Laboratory of Field Biology.

Sakamoto, M. (1966). The chlorophyll amount in the euphotic zone in some Japanese lakes and its significance in the photosynthetic production of phytoplankton community. *Botanical Magazine, Tokyo*, **79**, 77–88.

Sauberer, F. (1952). Der Wind-Einfluss auf die Trübung des Neusiedlersees. *Wetter und Leben*, **5**, 200–3.

Schindler, D. W., Brunskill, G. J., Emerson, S., Broeckner, W. S. & Peng, T.-H. (1972). Atmospheric carbon dioxide: its role in maintaining phytoplankton standing crops. *Science*, **177**, 1192–4.

Schindler, D. W. & Fee, E. J. (1973). Diurnal variation of dissolved inorganic carbon and its use in estimating primary production and CO_2 invasion in Lake 227. *Journal of the Fisheries Research Board of Canada*, **30**, 1501–10.

Schindler, D. W., Frost, V. E. & Schmidt, R. V. (1973). Production of epilithiphyton in two lakes of the Experimental Lakes Area, Northwestern Ontario. *Journal of the Fisheries Research Board of Canada*, **30**, 1511–24.

Schindler, D. W. & Holmgren, S. K. (1971). Primary production and phytoplankton in the Experimental Lakes Area, northwestern Ontario, and other low carbonate waters, and a liquid scintillation method for determining ^{14}C activity in photosynthesis. *Journal of the Fisheries Research Board of Canada*, **28**, 189–201.

Serruya, C. & Serruya, S. (1972). Oxygen content in Lake Kinneret: physical and biological influences. *Verhandlungen der Internationale Vereinigung für theoretische und angewandte Limnologie*, **18**, 580–7.

Sorokin, Y. I. (1959). Determination of the productivity of photosynthesis of phytoplankton in water by carbon-14. *Fiziologiya Rastenii*, **6**, 118–25.

Steel, J. A. (1972). The application of fundamental limnological research in water supply system design and management. *Symposium of the Zoological Society of London*, no. 29, 41–67.

Steel, J. A. P., Duncan, A. & Andrew, T. E. (1972). The daily carbon gains and losses in the seston of Queen Mary Reservoir, England, during early and mid 1968. In *Productivity problems of freshwaters*, ed. Z. Kajak & A. Hillbricht-Ilkowska, pp. 515–27. Warsaw & Kraków, Polish Scientific Publishers.

Steemann Nielsen, E. (1965). On the determination of the activity in C-14 ampoules for measuring primary production. *Limnology and Oceanography*, **10**, Suppl. R247–R252.

Steemann Nielsen, E. & Hansen, V. K. (1959). Measurements with the C-14 technique of the respiration rates in natural populations of phytoplankton. *Deep-Sea Research*, **5**, 222–32.

Stockner, J. G. (1968). Algal growth and primary productivity in a thermal stream. *Journal of the Fishery Research Board of Canada,* **25,** 2037–58.

Stull, E. A., de Amezaga, E. & Goldman, C. R. (1974). The contribution of individual species of algae to primary productivity in Castle Lake. *Verhandlungen der Internationale Vereinigung für theoretische und angewandte Limnologie,* **18,** 1776–83.

Talling, J. F. (1955). The relative growth rates of three plankton diatoms in relation to underwater radiation and temperature. *Annals of Botany, London,* **19,** 329–41.

Talling, J. F. (1957a). Photosynthetic characteristics of some freshwater plankton diatoms in relation to underwater radiation. *New Phytologist,* **56,** 29–50.

Talling, J. F. (1957b). The phytoplankton population as a compound photosynthetic system. *New Phytologist,* **56,** 133–49.

Talling, J. F. (1965). The photosynthetic activity of phytoplankton in East African lakes. *Internationale Revue der gesamten Hydrobiologie und Hydrographie,* **50,** 1–32.

Talling, J. F. (1966). Photosynthetic behaviour in stratified and unstratified lake populations of a planktonic diatom. *Journal of Ecology,* **54,** 99–127.

Talling, J. F. (1970). Generalized and specialized features of phytoplankton as a form of photosynthetic cover. In *Prediction and Measurement of photosynthetic productivity,* Proceedings IBP–PP Technical Meeting, Třeboň, September 1969. Wageningen, PUDOC.

Talling, J. F. (1971). The underwater light climate as a controlling factor in the production ecology of freshwater phytoplankton. *Mitteilungen der Internationale Vereinigung für theoretische und angewandte Limnologie,* **19,** 214–43.

Talling, J. F., Wood, R. B., Prosser, M. V. & Baxter, R. M. (1973). The upper limit of photosynthetic productivity by phytoplankton: evidence from Ethiopian soda lakes. *Freshwater Biology,* **3,** 53–76.

Tilzer, M. (1972). Dynamik und Produktivität von Phytoplankton und pelagischen Bakterien in einem Hochgebirgssee (Vorderer Finstertaler See, Österreich). *Archiv für Hydrobiologie,* **40,** Suppl. 201–73.

Tilzer, M. (1973). Diurnal periodicity in the phytoplankton assemblage of a high mountain lake. *Limnology and Oceanography,* **18,** 15–30.

Uhlmann, D. (1966). Produktion und Atmung im hypertrophen Teich. *Verhandlungen der Internationale Vereinigung für theoretische und angewandte Limnologie,* **16,** 934–41.

Uhlmann, D. (1971). Influence of dilution, sinking and grazing rate on phytoplankton populations of hyperfertilized ponds and micro-ecosystems. *Mitteilungen der Internationale Vereinigung für theoretische und angewandte Limnologie,* **19,** 100–24.

Vendlová, J. (1969). The problems of technology of the cultivation of algae on a large scale in outdoor units. *Annali di Microbiologia,* **19,** 1–12.

Viner, A. B. (1972). Responses of a mixed phytoplankton population to nutrient enrichments of ammonia and phosphate, and some associated ecological implications. *Proceedings of the Royal Society* B, **183,** 351–70.

Vollenweider, R. A. (1973). *A manual on methods for measuring primary production in aquatic environments.* IBP Handbook no. 12. Oxford, Blackwell.

Watt, W. D. (1971). Measuring the primary production rates of individual phytoplankton species in natural mixed populations. *Deep-Sea Research,* **18,** 329–39.

Wetzel, R. G. (1966). Variations in productivity of Goose and hypereutrophic Sylvan lakes, Indiana. *Investigations of Indiana Lakes of Streams,* **7,** 147–84.

Weigert, R. G. & Fraleigh, P. C. (1972). Ecology of Yellowstone thermal effluent systems: net primary production and species diversity of a successional blue-green algal mat. *Limnology and Oceanography,* **17,** 215–28.

Williams, P. J. Le B., Berman, T. & Holm-Hansen, O. (1973). Potential sources of error in the measurement of low rates of planktonic photosynthesis and excretion. *Nature, London,* **236,** 91–2.

Winberg, G. G., Ostapenya, P. V., Sivko, T. N. & Levina, R. I. (1966). *Biological Oxidation Ponds.* (In Russian). Minsk, Izd. Belarus.

Wood, K. G. (1971). Self-absorption corrections for the ^{14}C method with $BaCO_3$ for measurement of primary productivity. *Ecology,* **52,** 491–8.

11. Primary production of marine microphytes

T. PLATT & D. V. SUBBA RAO

Two important points emerge from a survey of the world literature on marine primary production. First, that although an immense amount of effort has been expended in the acquisition of field data, many of the results are of little value for comparative purposes; there is considerable variation between (and sometimes even within) authors in experimental and analytical methodology; some of the results have been obtained by methods which are now considered unreliable; the data are often incomplete in that they lack one or more critical collateral measurements which would permit the calculation of indices of comparison; there has been little attempt to control variance in the measurements by sound experimental design. It is therefore difficult at best to make valid comparisons between the productivities of different regions, and interpretations are often ambiguous.

Second, and more encouraging, is that recent work in marine primary production has been characterised by renewed synthesis of the ideas of plant physiologists and marine ecologists. This marriage of minds has provided the stimulus for several new insights and concepts in biological oceanography and laid the foundation for what will probably be an accelerated progress in the near future. There is considerable scope and opportunity for further expansion of this collaboration: only in this way will a satisfactory synthesis be made of the results of laboratory experiments with those of measurements on natural populations.

The present review is not claimed to be exhaustive, either in the sense of covering all aspects of marine primary production, or in that of treating all of the available literature on those aspects which are covered. We have chosen, in the space allowed, to deal with a limited number of topics of current interest or controversy in primary production research, selected from among those which have been the subject of intensive study during the International Biological Programme, and according to the particular interests of the authors. A number of important topics have been treated superficially, or excluded from our review, since they will be given a detailed discussion in other chapters in this volume. In particular we regret that we have not been able to give the Soviet literature the full attention it deserves. Within these limitations, our coverage should be quite up to date, as far as late 1972.

Effect of light and the energy efficiency of primary production

We note first that in the sea, light intensity decreases exponentially with depth, the attenuation coefficient being as high as 0.2 or more in coastal waters. The availability of light, then, for photosynthesis depends strongly on depth, and it is customary to define a photic zone within which there is sufficient light for daily photosynthesis to exceed respiration. The thickness of this zone depends on the turbidity of the water.

Many studies have shown that the effect of light intensity on photosynthetic rate in phytoplankton can be described by a curve which is generally hyperbolic in shape (Vollenweider, 1965), but there has not been the same agreement among investigators on the equation which should be used to quantify the relationship as there has been for the effect of nutrients on photosynthetic rate. The reason is that in phytoplankton ecology, at least, we are still lacking a conceptual model of the way in which plankton cells assimilate light: the equations which have been used to date have had merely descriptive convenience, with no particular biological significance attached to their parameters. But there seems no reason, for the want of something better, why one should not apply the Michaelis–Menton equation here also, interpreting the parameter V_m as proportional to the availability of uptake sites for light, i.e. the concentration of photosynthetic pigments (Caperon & Meyer, 1972).

A major problem in primary productivity studies in marine ecosystems has been to establish suitable diagnostic indices by which the productivity of different waters could be compared without the benefit of a prohibitively long data series. Absolute levels are themselves of little value, except in the long-term average, since the results of the individual measurements are subject to the influence of many factors which are outside the control of the observer, such as incident radiation, temperature, salinity, inorganic nutrients, the abundance and species composition of the phytoplankton.

Most workers have utilised the assimilation number θ to normalise their data. This is defined as $\theta = P(z)/B(z)$ with units of mg C fixed $m^{-3} h^{-1}$/mg chl. a m^{-3}, the rate of primary production per unit chlorophyll a *at light saturation*. The optimal light intensity for photosynthesis must be chosen, given all the other existing environmental conditions: for in-situ studies, optimal light intensity should be considered as that prevailing at the depth for which the assimilation number is largest; for incubator measurements, a light intensity is selected which is not so low as to limit the rate of photosynthesis, nor so high that photosynthesis is inhibited.

The strength of the concept of assimilation number lies in the fact that it recognises the importance of chlorophyll *a* as the unit of response to light in photosynthesis. Its weakness is that it contains no information on relative response at sub-optimal intensities. In particular it is important to avoid confusing the assimilation number with values of $P(z)/B(z)$ calculated from in-situ studies, but not selected according to light intensity.

Many measurements have been made of the assimilation numbers of natural phytoplankton populations in the world oceans. All of the data known to us are summarised by ocean in Table 11.1. Most of the results fall within the range from 1 to 10 mg C mg chl. a^{-1} h^{-1}. The table shows that the methodology employed is far from standardised and it is not always possible to make a valid comparison among the results of different workers. Within workers, however, interesting comparisons can be made; by way of example we may quote the work of Thomas (1970) who found, in the Pacific, assimilation numbers in nitrogen-rich water roughly double those in nitrogen-poor water, and that of Caperon, Cattell & Krasnick (1971) who showed an increase of roughly 100% in assimilation numbers of a coastal inlet over a ten-year period as a result of progressive eutrophication.

Another way in which different ecosystems may be compared with respect to their primary productivities is by calculating their efficiency in the utilisation of solar energy. A major problem arises with respect to primary production in aquatic ecosystems (but not terrestrial) because the productivity $P(z)$, is expressed in terms of unit volume whereas the light energy $I(z)$ is measured in terms of unit area. Thus the simple ratio $P(z)/I(z)$ has the dimensions of (L^{-1}) and cannot be considered a true efficiency (which should be dimensionless). The only true efficiency is $\int P(z) \, dz / I_0$, the ratio of the total production in the water column to the surface radiation. There are few measurements of this efficiency which are detailed enough to compute a yearly mean. However, there does not seem to be a very wide spread in the values which are available. Thus Qasim, Bhattathiri & Abidi (1968) found 0.4% for a polluted tropical estuary; Platt (1971) found 0.52% (using the revised calorific values of Platt & Irwin, 1973) for an unpolluted coastal inlet in temperate waters, while Patten (1961) measured 0.88% averaged over the summer months for a polluted temperate estuary. The average of Platt's (1971) data for the same summer period was 0.66%.

Table 11.1. *Summary of published values of assimilation number, mg C fixed h⁻¹ (mg chl. a)⁻¹, measured for natural marine phytoplankton populations. Arranged by ocean.*

Region	Lat.	Date	Depth(m)	Method	Incub.	Light	Temp.(°C)	mg C (mg chl. a)⁻¹ h⁻¹ Max.	Min.	Avg.	Remarks	References
ATLANTIC												
Woods Hole	Coastal	Mar.–Jul. 56		ΔO₂	*In vitro*	2000 fc		5.2	3.4	5.7		Ryther & Yentsch, 1957
New York		Sep./56– Jul./57		¹⁴C	*In vitro* 12 h	1500 fc		4.0	1.0	3.7		Ryther & Yentsch, 1958
Sargasso	~32° N.	27–28 Apr.	0	¹⁴C	*In situ* 24 h		21.30	4.83	2.98		Fixed stn 15 m off Bermuda. Measurements made 1330, 2100, 0030, 0800 h Impoverished No₂, No₃, Po₄	Ryther et al., 1961
			15				20.36	3.08	2.83			
			25				20.28	2.33	1.04			
			50				19.58	0.31	0.28			
			100				18.82	0.14	0.03			
Sargasso	~28° N.	Winter/60		¹⁴C	*In vitro* 24 h		~2	~2	0		Samples collected at 100, 50, 25, 10, 1% of the incident radiation which varied from 70 to 380 g cal/cm² per day	Ryther & Menzel, 1961
Fladen Ground		Mar./59 Jan./60	0– 50	¹⁴C	*In vitro* 6 h			19.9	0		Production values mg c/m³ per day were divided by 12	Steele & Baird, 1961
Gulf of Panama	8° 45' N.	May/57	10	¹⁴C				5.70	0.18			Smayda, 1965
Tropical Atlantic	1° 22' N.– 15° 39' S.	Sept.– Oct./63		¹⁴C	*In vitro* 5–6 h	60–70% surface light		17.0	2.15	4.04	Creitz & Richards chl equations used. Authors suggest a +30% re-vision of values	Suschenya & Finenko, 1965
Woods Hole	Coastal			¹⁴C	*In vitro*	7000 lx		25.0	1.7		Over 10-day dark period. During 12–22 days following 10 days dark period. Water with low phaeophytin was used. Water from 200 m with high phaeophytin was used over 194 h. Values in ( ) refer to samples from 500 m.	Yentsch, 1965a
								36.9	2.8			
								18.8	0.6			
								(2.45)	(0.4)			

Location	Latitude	Date	Depth	Method	Incubation	Light	Temp.			Notes	Reference
Beaufort Channel		14 Oct.–Dec.		ΔO_2	In situ 24 h			3.26	12.66	mg c/m³ per day were divided by 12	Williams & Murdoch, 1966
	10° N. 10° N. 7° N. 7° N.	Jun. 7–Oct.	10 75 10 75	14C 14C 14C 14C 14C		8000 lx 4500 lx 8000 lx 4700 lx 5 1000 lx	20° 20° 20° 20° 25°	4.0 1.0 3.0 1.2		Light is for P_{max}, $IK \equiv \dfrac{P_{max}}{P/I}$	Yentsch & Lee, 1966
Puerto Rico Bay	7° N.	Feb. 18–Apr. 19/63, Jul. 10–19 1964	75	14C	4 h			13.0	1.0		Burkholder et al., 1967
New York	40° 30′ N.	1966	3 depths	14C	In situ noon to sunset			3.5 3.1 3.4		Estuarine Nearshore Offshore	Mandelli et al., 1970
St Margaret's Bay	44° 35′ N.	Mar. 27–Apr. 28/69	10	14C	In situ 4 h		2.6°	12.3	1.0	Top 10 m	Platt & Subba Rao, 1970a
Chesapeake Bay	39° 30′ N.	29 Aug./66–12 Sept./67, Apr./65–Mar./66		ΔO_2	In vitro 12–24 h	675–1400 fc		11.9 10.3	0 1.3	Up-bay stns. Down-bay stns. The lower values below the sensitivity of the method used.	Flemer, 1970
Bedford Basin	44° 40′ N.	Jun. 1–2 1970	1 5 10 15 2	14C	In situ 24 h			4.74 0.66 0.24 0.104 10.8 (7.3)	2.14 0.26 0.04 0.003 2.3 (0.8)	Based on 6 stns. mg c/ m³ per day were divided by 15	Platt & Conover, 1971
Caribbean				14C		0.06 ly/ min		6.35 (3.88)		Values for <22 μ fractions. Values in ( ) for >22 μ fractions	Malone, 1971b
Chesapeake Bay	39° 30′ N.	Jun.–Oct./ 67		ΔO_2	In situ			57	23	Incubation from sunrise to sunset	Flemer & Olmon, 1971
Murman Coast		Apr.–Oct. 1966		14C	In situ 24 h			4	0		Sokolova & Solov'yeva, 1971
Chesapeake Bay	39° 30′ N.	Aug./71	0.7	14C	1 h	Surf.	Surf.	10.0	4.7	Incubated in surf. water	Loftus et al., 1972
PACIFIC Eniwetok Lagoon		Jun.–Aug./58		ΔO_2				5.505 2.41			Sargent & Austin, 1949
Tokyo Bay		Jun./59 May/58		14C				16.95 9.1	9.09 1.24	*Skeletonema* bloom	Hogetsu et al., 1959; Ichimura & Saijo, 1959

Table 11.1 – continued

Region	Lat.	Date	Depth(m)	Method	Incub.	Light	Temp.(°C)	mg C (mg chl. a)$^{-1}$ h^{-1} Max.	Min.	Avg.	Remarks	References
Stn P1	38° 46' N.	15 Jul./59	Offshore	^{14}C	*In vitro* 6 h	0.08 ly/min				1.34		McAllister et al., 1960
2		22 Jul.								1.31		
3		29 Jul.								1.50		
4		6 Aug.								1.83		
5	13 Aug.									1.07		
6										0.63		
Kanaohe Bay		19 Aug.		^{14}C						5.83		Doty & Capurro, 1961
			15	^{14}C	*In vitro* 24 h	0.11 ly/min		1.75	0.95		19 days plastic sphere expts	McAllister et al., 1961
			20									
			15	^{14}C	*In vitro* 24 h	80 × 10^3 ly/min		2.55	0.5		23 days plastic sphere expts.	Antia et al., 1963
			20									
Stn P	50° N.	Jul./61	0	^{14}C	*In vitro* 4 h	0.07 ly/min		3.5	1.5			McAllister, 1963
	61° N. 42° N.	Jun./Aug./60	0		*In vitro* 5 h	8000 lx		7.1	0.8			Motoda & Kawamura, 1963
Tasman and Coral Seas	0–45° S.	Jan.–Mar.	0–150	^{14}C	*In vitro*	1100 fc		4.5	0.2	3.7		Jitts, 1965
Oregon	44° 40' N.			^{14}C	*In situ* 2 h	I_0 300–375		25% I_0 8.9	10% I_0 4.5		Mean values at 25% and 10% of incident solar radiation which is measured as gc/cm^2 per day	Curl & Small, 1965
						215		4.0	2.9			
						150		3.7	2.1			
		15 Nov./64				115				8.6	Extinction coefficient $K = 0.11$	
		12 Apr./65				435				4.3	Extinction coefficient $K = 0.10$	
		15 Apr./65				96				5.7	Extinction coefficient $K = 0.13$	
Cromwell Current	2° N.–2° S.	Apr./66						10.0	5.34		Values based on integrating measurements at 5 depths within the euphotic zone and assumed 12 h daylight	Barber & Ryther, 1969

Location	Lat.	Date	No.	Isotope	Incubation	Light				Notes	Reference
La Jolla		Apr.–Sep./67		¹⁴C	*In situ* 24 h	0.09 ly/min	10.4	6.5		Nitrate undetectable (shallow sample) nutrients added prior to incub. nitrate present (deeper samples)	Eppley *et al.*, 1970
							13.5	6.8			
Stn Calcofi 3	14°49′ S. 19°39′ N.	Feb.–Apr./68	10		*In vitro* 3 h		2.9	2.4	3.15	N₂-poor water	Thomas, 1970
Offshore				¹⁴C			5.18	1.15	4.95	N₂-rich water Values for <22 μ fractions in ( )	Malone, 1971a
Inshore							6.19	3.53	7.42 (4.21) 8.18 (3.68)		
Neritic			2	¹⁴C		0.06	14.0 (11.6)	2.1 (1.8)	7.02 (5.84)	Values for <22 μ fractions in ( )	Malone, 1971b
Peru Cur.							24.1 (7.1)	5.9 (1.6)	11.50 (5.31)		
Tr. Surf. Wt							4.6 (4.3)	0.8 (0)	2.29 (1.50)		Malone, 1971b
Calif. Curr. I									9.4 (4.7)		
Calif. Curr. O									8.3 (4.1)		
A	50° N.–10° S.		2	¹⁴C	*In vitro* 2–3 h	0.06 ly/min	<22 μ 6.7–6.4	>22 μ 3.8–3.4		Samples collected at 3 h before and 3 h after local noon A = Cal. curr. sys. B = oligotrophic tr. C = eutrophic tr.	Malone, 1971c
B							2.1–1.1	2.6–0.8			
C							18.3– 12.1–	11.1– 6.3			
Peru	10°–12° S.	Jun./69		¹⁴C			3.35	2.17		Assuming 12 h daylight gc/m² per day values were divided by 10. 7 stns data only at phytopl. patches	Beers *et al.*, 1971
PISCO	~15° S.	17 Apr./69		¹⁴C		Natural		5.16		Stn 49 Assuming 12 h day	Barber *et al.*, 1971
		19 Apr./69				light		11.26		Stn 53 light, values were calculated	
Hawaii	~21° N.		1	¹⁴C	*In vitro* 3 h		11.50 (7.94) 11.49 (6.50) 13.04 (6.15)	7.15– 14.54		Values for 1970 after eutrophication. Values in ( ) from Doty 1959–60 prior to eutrophication	Caperon *et al.*, 1971

Table 11.1 – *continued*

Region	Lat.	Date	Depth(m)	Method	Incub.	Light	Temp.(°C)	mg C (mg chl. *a*)⁻¹ h⁻¹ Max.	Min.	Avg.	Remarks	References
Fanning Lagoon		9 Jan./70	0.5 2.5 4.5 7.0	¹⁴C	*In situ* 3 h					16.7 20.6 17.1 13.4		Gordon *et al.,* 1971
		17 Jul./65– 22 Jun./66	10 15	¹⁴C	*In situ* 12–24 h			4.6 11.1 18.7 14.3	0.1 0.2 0.2 0.2		Control N-NaNo₂ P-NaH₂Po₄H₂O Fe-Fe-EDTA enrichment	Glooschenko & Curl, 1971
ANTARCTIC												
	10531			¹⁴C		300 fc		0.8			Dana Stn 10531	Steemann Nielsen & Hansen, 1959
McMurdo Sound		Dec./61 Jan./62	0	¹⁴C	*In vitro* 4 h	1100 fc	−1.5° −0 °C	0.07			Under sea ice	Bunt, 1964
Drake Passage	55° 06– 62° 31 S.	Mar./63	0	¹⁴C	4 h	1200 fc	2–3 °C	10.47	2.81	4.52		El-Sayed *et al.,* 1964
South Pole	50°–64° S.	Dec./63 Jan./64	0 10 12 13 14 15 16 20 22	¹⁴C	*In vitro*	10 000 lx	Surf.	2.04 1.56 1.00 0.75 1.05 1.64 1.89 0.48 1.20	0.81		Temp. of water ranged from 1.5 to 4.0. Max. solar radiation. 65 per g cal/cm² per h	Saijo & Kawashima, 1964
Palmer Penin. Gerlache Str. Bellingshausen Sea Martha Str. Martha Str. Marguerite Bay		Feb./65		¹⁴C	*In vitro*	18 000 lx				2.6 0.63 2.58 2.22 2.65 2.61	Values for brown sea ice water samples Ice samples	Burkholder & Mandelli, 1965
Bansfield Gerlache Str. Bansfield Bellingshausen Sea Foster Hbr.	64°–62° S.	Summer Feb. Mar./65	0 to 50	¹⁴C	*In vitro*			3.50 2.5 5.2	0.4		Samples were incubated at simulated *in situ* light intensity	Mandelli & Burkholder, 1966

Region	Position	Date	Depth (m)	Isotope	In vitro / In situ	Light	Values	Notes	Reference
Drake Passage	50°–62° S.	Sep./63		^{14}C	In vitro	0.16 ly/min.	~2.6		Mandelli, 1967
	35°–40°	Nov./63 Mar./63		^{14}C	In vitro 4 h		59.21 / 3.0 / 14.87	Values based on 9 cruises conducted during Mar. 12/62 to Mar. 6/65. Samples were incubated in simulated *in situ*, light intensity	El-Sayed, 1968
	40°–45°						22.47 / 2.5 / 6.45		
	45°–50°						72.48 / 2.05 / 10.75		
	50°–55°						98.82 / 1.59 / 8.51		
	55°–60°						8.08 / 2.28 / 3.0		
	60°–65°						13.00 / 1.25 / 5.23		
	65°–70°						2.89 / 2.0 / 1.90		
	70°–75°						12.14 / 1.73 / 9.45		
	75°–80°						15.05 / 2.69 / 8.10		
Signey Island	60° 43′ S.	Summer 1966–7	0 / 3 / 6	^{14}C	In situ		0.88 / 0.48 / 0.93 — 1.65 / 0.41 / 1.07		Horne et al., 1969
	40°–43° S.		15 / 0	^{14}C	In situ or In vitro		0.14 / 12.8 / 0.18 / 3.2	Subtropical Convergence Subantarctic	Taniguchi & Nishizawa, 1971
	43°–46° S.		0				5.6 / 0.01		
	46°–48° S.		0				1.2 / 1.2		
INDIAN									
	10° N. 30° S.		0 (Surf.)	^{14}C	In vitro	15 000 lx	7.4 (2.4) / 5.53 (0.81) / 2.3 (0.2)	Values for <90 μm fractions. Values in ( ) for >90 μm fractions	Saijo & Takesue, 1965
			25				8.5 (2.2) / 7.16 (1.41) / 4.1 (0.3)		
			75				6.3 (2.4) / 2.97 (1.30) / 0.6 (0.7)		
Ernakulam	9° 58′ N.		2	^{14}C	In situ		13 / 10.7 (8.2) — 3 / 1.2 (1.1)	Values refer to respiration corrected gross prod. Those in ( ) to uncorrected values	Sournia, 1968; Qasim et al., 1969
Inshore	8° 10′ N.	Aug.–Oct. 1967		^{14}C			4.63 / 2.66	At 13 stns based on 12 h day light calculation	Radhakrishna, 1969
Waltair	17° 43′ N.	Apr./67	0	ΔO_2	22	16 000 lx	6.04 / 4.57	*Asterionella japonica* red water bloom	Subba Rao, 1969
ARCTIC									
Davis Str. Dana Stn 10531	64° N.	Jul.	0 / 27 / 50	^{14}C	In vitro		~3.3 / ~2.5 / ~1.0	I_K = 9500 lx / 7300 lx / 3200 lx	Steemann Nielsen & Hansen, 1959
Faroes and Iceland Dana Stn 10460		Jul.	0+16 / 35				~3.5 / ~3.0	I_K = 9800 lx / 8500 lx	

Considerations of dimensionality led Platt (1969) to define an index k_b^z in (m^{-1}) which represents that contribution to the absorption co-efficient of light energy at any depth which is due to photosynthesis. This should be equal to the absorption of light in photosynthetic pigments multiplied by a factor measuring the efficiency with which light is utilised in the photosynthetic process. It was shown that this index k_b^z was very nearly equal to the ratio $P(z)/I(z)$, when both are measured in joules or calories. Calculating $P(z)$ in joules or calories permits the inclusion of information on the quality, as well as the quantity, of what is produced.

Two major problems are involved in the measurement of such an index in natural populations. One is the extreme difficulty of making good measurements of light energy under water. Some progress was made here with the development of an instrument which measures, in absolute units and independent of wavelength, the light available at depth in an in-situ productivity incubation (Platt *et al.*, 1970). The other is the conversion of productivity, which is measured in carbon units, into energy units. It has been argued recently, however (Platt & Irwin, 1973), on both theoretical and empirical grounds, that calorific value of phytoplankton can be predicted quite well from the percentage of carbon, which is relatively simple to measure. These two developments should facilitate a more widespread study of the utility of indices like k_b^z.

It was found that in natural populations at least, k_b^z depends linearly on the concentration of chlorophyll *a* (Platt, 1969; Platt & Subba Rao, 1970*b*). This can be interpreted as a unit response of the photosynthetic pigments to light. If this concept has any validity for organisms (as opposed to isolated chloroplasts), then we should see it in the plankton, where we are dealing with responses at the cellular level of organisation. The slope of the regression increased (slightly) with depth; those populations living at depth having either a slightly higher efficiency of chlorophyll *a* response than those living at the surface, or using a slightly different suite of photosynthetic pigments. It was suggested that the slope of the regression of k_b^z on the chlorophyll concentration $B(z)$ could be used as an index of comparison in primary productivity studies, but as yet insufficient comparative data have been accumulated. In any event it seems that productivity, available light and pigment concentration form the minimum set of data which will allow the calculation of indices of comparison in marine primary production.

Physiological structure and age of phytoplankton populations

Steemann Nielsen (1955) distinguished four marine ecosystem types in tropical and subtropical areas based on production characteristics: (1) regions with considerable admixture of new water from mid-depth to photic zone, with daily production 0.5–3.0 g C m^{-2}; example, Benguela Current. (2) Regions with steady admixture of new water to photic zone, with daily production 0.2–0.5 g C m^{-2}; example, Equatorial counter-current divergence regions. (3) Regions with pronounced admixture of nutrient rich water, with daily production 0.1–0.2 g C m^{-2}; typical of much of the tropical and subtropical ocean. (4) Regions where the water in the photic zone is old or renewed very seldom, with daily production ~ 0.05 g C m^{-2}; example, Sargasso Sea.

The distinction between *new* and *old* surface water is a useful one which can help in the interpretation of differences in phytoplankton production in terms of the physiological age of the populations.

Under optimal growth conditions, phytoplankton pass through four distinct growth phases: the lag, log, stationary and senescent phases. The last three of these correspond to the 'activity structure' scheme of classification of the phytoplankton community given by Soeder (1965) and based on metabolic activity: active organisms, strongly anabolic (log phase); neutral organisms, slightly anabolic (stationary phase); inactive organisms, catabolic (senescent phase).

Several investigations have shown that high assimilation numbers are characteristic of healthy log phase populations and low assimilation numbers typical of senescent or old populations (Yentsch & Lee, 1966; Subba Rao, 1969 and unpublished data). Jeffrey & Allen (1964) showed a decrease in the photosynthetic carbon assimilation of cultures of *Coccolithus huxleyi* and *Hymenomonas* sp. over a thirty-day period. In cultures of *Dunaliella tertiolecta* the rates of both photosynthesis and nitrate assimilation per mg chlorophyll decreased rapidly with age (Grant, 1968). Besides carbon assimilation, the photosynthesis–respiration ratio also decreased with the age of the culture in the diatom *Cylindrotheca closterium* (Humphrey & Subba Rao, 1967) and in cultures of five neritic phytoplankters (D. V. Subba Rao, unpublished data). Ryther (1954) with *Chlamydomonas*, Zgurovskaya & Kustenko (1968) with *Skeletonema costatum* showed a similar age effect when the cultures were grown in nitrogen-deficient medium. In the culture experiments of Humphrey (1963), Madgwick (1966) and D. V. Subba Rao (unpublished data) the ratio of chlorophyll *c* to *a* followed a consistent parabolic pattern with age. On the basis of laboratory experiments therefore, we can recognise the *c–a* ratio, the assimilation number and *P–R* ratio as indicators of the physiological age of the culture.

Turning to the natural populations, phytoplankton bloom communities have been shown to be satisfactory analogues of monospecific culture populations although they are polyspecific, growing under fluctuating environmental conditions and in dilute nutrient concentrations (Platt & Subba Rao, 1970*a*). There are several published instances of high assimilation numbers associated with natural bloom populations (Table 11.1). When inorganic nutrients are added to nutrient-poor waters characterized by low assimilation numbers, a definite increase in the assimilation number occurs (Thomas, 1970; Eppley, Strickland & Solorzano, 1970; Glooschenko & Curl, 1971). Caperon *et al.* (1971) showed, in a Hawaiian coastal inlet, a doubling of assimilation number following ten years of progressive eutrophication. The photosynthesis–respiration ratio has been shown to decline with age in natural bloom populations (Eppley & Sloan, 1965; Subba Rao, 1969; Platt & Subba Rao, 1970*a*; Subba Rao, 1973). Another physiological index which has been shown to decline with the age of blooms is the calorific value of the cells (Platt & Subba Rao, 1970*a*).

The perfect indicator of physiological age in natural phytoplankton populations has not been found, and more study should be devoted to it. It would have important theoretical implications in the refining of predictive equations for primary production and practical utility in the stimulation of natural productivity by artificial enrichment, since maximum productivity can be achieved by maintaining the populations in a sustained log-phase condition. The work of Dunstan & Menzel (1971), who succeeded in developing a polyspecific steady-state phytoplankton population by enrichment with treated sewage effluent in the New York Bight, provides an example.

Global productivity of marine microphytes

The first systematic data series covering different marine ecosystem-types which permitted an estimate of the primary productivity of the world oceans was collected during the Galathea Expedition (Steemann Nielsen & Jensen, 1957). On that cruise, 194 stations were occupied representing on the average 2×10^6 km^2 each. Since then, both temporal and spatial coverage of primary productivity measurements have improved considerably: the most serious gaps in our knowledge are for the tropical inshore waters and the polar waters in general.

Estimates of global plankton production have varied widely, as shown in Table 11.2.

Our survey of the literature has persuaded us that a recalculation of global productivity is justified. The raw data we have used are summarised by ocean in Table 11.3. There is some confusion in detail on the estimates of the surface areas of the principal seas. We have included the results of Cushing's (1971) detailed analysis of primary production in the upwelling areas and those of an extensive series of measurements of annual primary production in various Atlantic coastal waters: neither of these were available at the time Ryther (1969) prepared his estimate of global primary production in the sea.

Table 11.2. *Estimates of global plankton production*

Year	10^9 t C yr^{-1}	References
1942	50–130	Sverdrup, Johnson & Fleming
1946	126	Riley
1950	45	Skopintsev
1957	20–25	Steemann Nielsen & Jensen
1960	35–70	Vinberg
1968	25–30	Koblents-Mishke, Volkovinshii & Kabanova
1969	20	Ryther
1971	33	Bruyevich & Ivanenkov
1973	31	Present study

We have divided the oceans into shelf (<200 m) and offshore (> 200 m) regions, their areal extent being recalculated from the FAO data presented in Moiseev (1971); the principal difference between our figures for area and those of Moiseev is that we have separated out the polar oceans (Table 11.4). We have included the data for primary production of the upwelling regions (Cushing, 1971) under shelf area in calculating total production for each ocean.

A major difficulty is the estimation of the production of the Antarctic Ocean. The surface area of the productive region is in doubt. Taking an annual production of 130 g C m^{-2} yr^{-1} (Horne, Fogg & Eagle, 1969) and an area of 23.8×10^6 km^2, Antarctic production would be 3.1×10^9 t C yr^{-1}, which compares well with the estimate of 3.3×10^9 t C yr^{-1} made by El-Sayed (1968). If a productive area of 11.8×10^6 km^2 is used,

261

Table 11.3. *World summary of published values on marine primary productivity providing raw data for recalculation of global production of marine microphytes. Arranged by ocean*

Region	Area (km² · 10⁶)	Season	$g\ C\ m^{-2}\ d^{-1}$			Annual prod. ($t\ C\ km^{-2}\ yr^{-1}$ or $g\ C\ m^{-2}\ yr^{-1}$)	Reference
			Max.	Min.	Avg.		
ATLANTIC							
Fladen Ground		3 yr study				54–82	Steele, 1956
Inshore						104–127	Steele, 1956
Eng. Channel						55–91	Riley, 1956
Long Is. Sound	0.002	Annual				380	Riley, 1956
Caribbean Sea	1.920	May–Jun.	0.19	0.10			Steeman Nielsen & Jensen, 1957
Antilles Cur.			0.056				
Cap Blanc			0.67	0.56			
Walvis Bay			3.4				
New York Shelf	0.566	Sept.–July				100–160	Ryther & Yentsch, 1958
North Sea						45–110	Steele, 1958
Off Portugal						Open sea / Coastal sea	Currie, 1958
Danish inshore waters		Annual				74	Steemann Nielsen, 1958
Ville Franche	2.931	Annual	0.5	0.1		64–83	Bouardel & Rink, 1963
Monaco		Annual	1.1	0.5		60	Bouardel & Rink, 1963
Sargasso 30°–15°		March	0.04	0.03		160	Ryther & Menzel, 1960
Subtrop. Sargasso			0.1			55–127	Menzel & Menzel, 1960
Sargasso		3 yr study	2.0 / 0.20	0.13 / 0.10	0.44	90.7	Menzel & Ryther, 1961
Sargasso 30°–15°	0.075	Feb.	0.05	0.05			Ryther & Menzel, 1961
English Channel			3.5	0.7			Sorokin & Klyashtorin, 1961
English Channel			1.4				Sorokin & Klyashtorin, 1961
Gulf of Panama	0.290	Annual	1.93	0.05	0.33	180 (net)	Forsbergh, 1963
New York Shelf		Spring	0.08	0.02		120	Ryther, 1963
Gulf of Guinea		Fall	0.90	0.60			Chmyr, 1965

Location		Period					Reference
West African waters							
Canaries Cur.		Apr.–Oct.	0.04†	0.43‡	0.162§		Bessonov & Fedosov, 1965
Cap Blanc area			0.06†	1.90‡	–	300–600	
Dakar area			0.20†	3.40‡	2.78§		
Conakry area			0.60†	0.61‡	1.08§		
Guinea Cur.			0.14†	0.03‡	1.990§		
Takoradi area			0.28†	–	1.552§	150–300	
Equatorial area			0.28†	0.04‡	1.990§		
Walvis Bay			2.13†	3.50‡	–		
S. trade Cur.				1.15‡	0.735§		
W. African Coast		Sept.–Oct.	1.7	0.3		200	Sushchenya & Finenko, 1965
S. Eq. Cur.			0.38	0.13		70	
W. Eq. area			0.67	0.16		100	
Gulf of Panama	0.290					255–280 (gross)	Smayda, 1966
Black Sea offshore	0.431	Annual				40–45	Finenko, 1966
coastal						100–150	
Sevastopol Bay		Annual				200–280	
Pamlico Sound	0.0004	Annual	1.62	0.15	0.464	99.6	Williams, 1966
Puerto Rico			8.3	0.8			Burkholder et al., 1967
Mediterranean		2-yr study				75	Margalef & Ballester, 1967
Costa Catalana		2-yr study				85	Margalef & Castelli, 1967
Jamaican waters		3-yr study	0.52	0.08	0.18	66	Beers et al., 1968
Barbados		Annual	0.62	0.19	0.38	139	Beers et al., 1968
Aegean Sea		2-yr study	334	70		64	Becacos-Kontos, 1968
Haifa		4-yr study				31–65 Avg. 34.2	Becacos-Kontos, 1968
Gulf of Mexico	1.792	Oct.	0.379	0.062		175¶	Franceschini & El-Sayed, 1968
Beaufort Channel		Annual	0.72	0.12		113–225	Williams & Murdoch, 1966
Off Guinea and Sierra Leone		Feb.–Mar.	1.61				Corcoran & Mahken, 1969
Off Congo		July–Sept.	1.678				
Kattegat		Annual					Bertelsen & Hansen, 1969
Long Is. Sound		Feb.–Dec.	1.35 (inshore)			85	Mandelli et al., 1970
Long Is. Sound			0.94 (offshore)				Mandelli et al., 1970

Table 11.3 – *continued*

Region	Area (km² · 10⁶)	Season	g C m⁻² d⁻¹ Max.	g C m⁻² d⁻¹ Min.	g C m⁻² d⁻¹ Avg.	Annual prod. (t C km⁻² yr⁻¹, or g C m⁻² yr⁻¹)	Reference
Chesapeake Bay	0.162	2-yr study	1.0	0.2		73 upper bay	Flemer, 1970
			0.31	0.12		365 lower bay	Flemer, 1970
			1.07	0.75			
St Margaret's Bay		Annual	1.92	0.13	0.520	190	Platt, 1971
Bedford Basin		Annual	2.431	0.086	0.602	220	Platt & Irwin, 1971
Near Barbados		22-month study			0.288	105	Steven, 1971
Cape Blanc		May–Jun.	3.35	1.12			Lloyd, 1971
NW. Baltic Sweden		Annual				40.93–46.66	Fonselius, 1971
Baltic and Gulf of Finland	2.624	Annual				35–40	Sen Gupta, 1972
Scillian Channel		August	1.613	0.040			Magazzu & Andreoli, 1972
Canary 1	0.040				0.400	3.48	Cushing, 1971*
2	0.105				0.390	12.19	
3	0.306				2.087	114.95	
4	0.150				–	–	
5	0.090				0.600	8.10	
Guinea Dome	–				0.500	–	
Guinea	0.100				0.600	7.20	
Benguela 1	0.035				0.280	3.46	
2	0.240				1.130	94.38	
3	0.360				0.530	98.60	
4	0.240				1.560	78.15	
ANTARCTIC							
Palmer Pen.	2.6	Dec.–Feb.	0.15	0.01	0.19	0.5 × 10⁶/area	Saijo & Kawashima, 1964
Bellingshausen Sea		Summer			0.09		Burkholder & Mandelli, 1965a

Location		Date					Reference
Gerlache Str.		Summer			0.66		Burkholder & Mandelli, 1965b
Bellingshausen Sea					0.040		
Bansfield Str.					0.273		
Gerlache Str.					0.646		
Oceanic area		Feb.–Mar.	0.93	0.12	0.37		Mandelli & Burkholder, 1966
Bansfield Str.			1.59	0.21	0.70		
Gerlache Str.			1.20	0.58	0.86		
Deception Is.			3.62	–	3.62		
McMurdo Sound	2.6	1962–5					El-Sayed, 1968
Weddell Sea	23.8	Summer 64, 65			0.68		
Drake Passage	11.8	Spr. Sum. Fall, 63–65			0.77		
Bellingshausen Sea		Summer 65			0.24		
Marguerite Bay		Summer 65			0.46		
Gerlache Str.		Summer 65			1.31		
Bansfield Str.		Spr. Sum. Fall, 63–65			2.76		
Antarctic Inshore					1.23		
Antarctic Offshore					0.42		
Sub-antarctic							
Inshore					0.77		
Offshore					0.10		
Antarctic	23.8	March			21.24	0.45×10^{10} t C/area per yr	Horne et al., 1969
	11.8	Sept.			10.53	0.22×10^{10} t C/area per yr	
					($\times 10^6$/area)	Average = 0.33×10^{10} t C/area per yr	
South Orkney		Feb.	0.25/h			130	Taniguchi & Nishizawa, 1971
		Mid Dec./66– May/67				150 (tentative)	
		May–Jul.			0.35		
		Winter			0.23		

Table 11.3 – *continued*

Region	Area (km²·10⁶)	Season	g C m⁻² d⁻¹ Max.	g C m⁻² d⁻¹ Min.	g C m⁻² d⁻¹ Avg.	Annual prod. (t C km⁻² yr⁻¹, or g C m⁻² yr⁻¹)	Reference
ARCTIC							
Faroes–Arctic		Summer	0.75	0.5			Steemann Nielsen & Jensen, 1957
			1.60	0.8 (coastal waters)			
N. polar waters	13.10	Jun./Aug.	0.024	0.005		1	English, 1959
Spitsbergen		June	2.4				Sokolova & Solov'yeva, 1971
Murman Coast		Apr.–Oct.	0.262	0.007	0.094		
Okhatsk Sea	1.5		5.1	0.0065		25.90¶	
PACIFIC							
Kuroshio (warm)			0.10	0.05			Saijo & Ichimura, 1959
Oyashio (cold)			0.15	0.07			
Oregon Coast		Nov.–Apr.	0.42	0.16		43–78	Anderson, 1964
Oregon Coast							Curl & Small, 1965
Pac. Total	165.467				0.632	8 × 10⁹ tons C/zone per yr	Koblents-Mishke, 1965
Oceanic Trop.	90.105				0.076	6.8	
Transition Zone	33.357				0.135	4.5 10⁶ tons C/	
Oceanic	31.319				0.250	7.8 km²/day/	
Coastal	10.422				0.288	3.0 zone	
Neritic	0.243				0.650	0.16	
Tasman and Coral Seas		Summer	66 mg/hr per m²				Jitts, 1965
		Jan.–Mar.		6 mg/hr per 2			
Pac. Inshore						105	Koblents-Mishke, 1966
Pac. Eutrophic						237	
Departure Bay		Annual				200	Stephens et al., 1967
Str. Georgia		Annual				150	Stephens et al., 1969
49° 18′ N.		Feb.–May				50 g C/m² per 4 mth	Parsons et al., 1969
Stn 'P'		Annual				50–70	McAllister et al., 1960

Location		Month					Reference
~55° N.		Mar.–May	0.5	0.1	0.318–		Parsons & Anderson, 1970
E. Trop. Pac.		Annual	0.612	0.044	0.127	75	Owen & Zeitschel, 1970
Cen. Pac. 20° N.–30° S.			5.6	0.058			Sorokin, 1970
S. Trade Cur.			0.15	0.05			Sorokin, 1970
33°–43° N.		Feb.–Jul.	2.30	0.8			Starodubtsev, 1970
Peru 15°S.		Mar.–Apr.	3.5	1.075			Barber et al., 1971
Peru		Mar.–Apr.	11.74	3.14			Ryther et al., 1971
Peru 1°–20° S.		Apr.			10	290	Guillen, 1971; Cushing, 1971*
California 1	0.169				0.8	11.03	
2	0.106				0.250	4.45	
3	0.230				0.161	15.01	
Costa Rica Dome	0.148				0.250	16.73	
E. Trop.					0.260	1245.55	
Peru 1	0.288				0.325	36.64	
2	0.191				1.020	76.27	
Chile 1	0.375				0.242	35.53	
2	0.150				0.205	8.03	
Marquesas	8.760				0.135	514.46	
New Guinea	0.460				0.205	41.04	
INDIAN							
West Arabian			0.24	0.10			Steemann Nielsen & Jensen, 1957
Indo-Malayan			1.08	0.24			
Gulf of Thailand	2.291		1.36	0.35	0.61		Kabanova, 1961
10°–8°			0.12	0.05	0.87		Kabanova, 1964
Somali			0.27	0.088			Kabanova, 1964
Open Indian Ocean	23		0.02	0.01		143	Ryther & Menzel, 1965
Arabian		May–Nov.	6.7	0.35	1.8		Ryther & Menzel, 1965
W. Arabian			6.7		1.5		Saijo, 1965
94° E.		Dec.	0.2	0.1			Saijo, 1965
110° E.		Jan.	0.7	0.3			Subba Rao, 1965
Gulf of Thailand		May	0.84	0.44	0.59		Prasad, 1966
Coastal					2		

Table 11.3 – continued

Region	Area (km² · 10⁶)	Season	g C m⁻² d⁻¹ Max.	Min.	Avg.	Annual prod. (t C km⁻² yr⁻¹, or g C m⁻² yr⁻¹)	Reference
Open Ocean							Prasad, 1966
Agulhas Cur.					0.2–0.5		Mitchell-Innes, 1967
Durban	0.013	Winter	1.08	0.03			Burchall, 1968
Arabian		6 yr	2.191	0.032	0.618	225.5¶	Kuzmenko, 1968
Indian Ocean	40 × 10⁶	Summer	3.0	0.1		115–120	Kabanova, 1968
			1.0	0.1	0.3	120	
			0.5	0.1	0.1		
Cen. Arabian Sea }							
S. Bay of Bengal }							
Gulf of Aden							
EC. Africa			1.0	0.5			
SW. Madagascar	2.2						
N. Bay of Bengal							
NW. Australian			2.5	0.75			
Indo Malayan							
110° E.		May			0.18	135¶	Jitts, 1969
		Aug.			0.13–0.27		
		Oct.–May.			0.08		

Location	ΔO$_2$ (§)	Period	Radhakrishna, 1969	Qasim et al., 1969	Cushing, 1971*	Annual production 10^6 tons C/area
10°–8°	0.005	Aug.–Oct.	1.108	0.377	0.807	294.4¶
10°–8°	0.095	Jan.–Dec.	1.523	0.349		281
Somali	0.131				0.690	17.10
S. Arabia	0.112				1.000	34.19
Malabar	1.014				1.000	16.80
Madagascar Wedge	0.072				0.750	8.66
NE. Madagascar	0.096				1.100	9.50
Orissa (SW. Monsoon)	0.096				0.415	8.67
Orissa (NE. Monsoon)	0.100				0.620	12.92
Andaman	0.010				0.225	3.42
W. Ceylon					0.410	1.14
Indonesia; etc						
Java	0.300				0.415	27.09
NW. Australia	0.300				0.284	18.53
E. Arufura	0.250				0.390	16.97
Flores	0.100				0.505	8.79
Banda	0.100				0.650	11.31
Gulf of Thailand	0.075				1.298	20.75
Vietnam	0.200				1.270	44.20

* Extracted from Cushing 1971 Table IV. † Steemann Nielsen's ^{14}C data Nov. 1950. ‡ Sorokin and Klyashtorin's ^{14}C data Apr., Dec.
§ Bessonov's ΔO$_2$ data Apr.–Oct. ¶ Our calculation. Annual production 10^6 tons C/area.

Table 11.4. *Summary table of recalculated values for annual plankton productivity of the five oceans, divided into inshore and offshore zones*

	Area (10^6 km^2§)			(g C m^{-2} d^{-1})		Primary production (10^6 t C yr^{-1} per zone)		Total production (10^6 t C yr^{-1} per ocean)
Ocean	Total	Shelf	Offshore	Shelf	Offshore	Shelf	Offshore	
Indian*	73.82	2.80	71.02	0.71	0.23	725	5875	6 600
Atlantic	92.57	8.65	83.92	0.41	0.28	1295	8461	9 760
Pacific	177.56	10.67	166.89	0.52	0.15	2037	9360	11 400
Antarctic	23.8†–11.8†	4.80		0.89				3 300
Arctic	13.10	6.11‡	6.99					13¶
Total		33.03				4057	23 696	31 100

* Includes Indo Malayan waters.
† MacKintosh & Brown's estimate cited in El-Sayed, 1968.
‡ Including 800 000 km^2 in Barents, White and Norwegian Seas.
§ Calculated from the data in Tables 19 and 20 given by Moiseev, 1971. Shelf = < 200 m; offshore = > 200 m.
¶ Assuming 1 g C m^{-2} yr^{-1} see English, 1961.

then annual production for the region would be 1.5×10^9 t C, and our estimate of global production would be decreased by 3%.

Our estimate of average annual production for shelf regions is 183 g C m^{-2} compared with 175 g C m^{-2} given by Cushing (1971). The main reason for the discrepancy is that Cushing's calculation does not include that contribution to annual production which is made on non-upwelling days.

Table 11.5. *Some relationships among primary production, nutrient content and water exchange of the major oceans*

Ocean	Area (10^6 km^2)	Primary production (10^6 t C yr^{-1})	Total SiO$_2$* (10^9 t)	Total PO$_4$* (10^9 t)	Ann. exch.* (10^6 km^3)	Ann. exch. ÷ vol. of ocean	Ann. prim. prod. (10^6 t C yr^{-1}) ÷ area of ocean (10^6 km^2)
Indian	73.82	6 600	4.5	0.31	6.98	0.24	89.4
Atlantic	92.57	9 760	5.0	0.35	6.58	0.19	105
Pacific	177.56	11 400	5.9	0.40	6.00	0.008	64.2

* From Bruyevich & Ivanenko (1971).

Our estimate of 31×10^9 C yr^{-1} (Table 11.4) for the global production of marine microphytes is consistent with the estimate of 33×10^9 t C yr^{-1} calculated by Bruyevich & Ivanenko (1971) from a consideration of the oxygen budget of the world oceans. The annual productivity per unit area of the major oceans is related to their relative annual water exchange (Table 11.5). On this basis the Pacific Ocean is much less productive than the Atlantic and Indian Oceans, and has considerable less annual exchange compared to its total volume.

We are grateful to Dr K. Denman for constructive discussion and to Miss D. Rutherford and Mrs D. Chalmers for assistance in the compilation of the bibliography.

References

Anderson, G. C. (1964). The seasonal and geographic distribution of primary productivity off the Washington and Oregon coasts. *Limnology and Oceanography*, **9**, 284–302.

Antia, N. J., McAllister, C. D., Parsons, T. R., Stephens, K. & Strickland, J. D. H. (1963). Further measurements of primary production using a large volume plastic sphere. *Limnology and Oceanography*, **8**, 166–83.

Barber, R. T., Dugdale, R. C., MacIsaac, J. J. & Smith, R. L. (1971). Variation in phytoplankton growth associated with source and conditioning of upwelling water. *Investigación pesquera*, **35**, 171–94.

Barber, R. T. & Ryther, J. H. (1969). Organic chelators: factors affecting primary production to the Cromwell Current upwelling. *Journal of Experimental Marine Biology and Ecology*, **3**, 191–9.

Becacos-Kontos, T. (1968). The annual cycle of primary production in the Sarconicos Gulf (Aegean Sea) for the period November 1963–October 1964. *Limnology and Oceanography*, **13**, 485–9.

Beers, J. R., Steven, D. M. & Lewis, J. B. (1968). Primary productivity in the Caribbean Sea off Jamaica and the tropical North Atlantic off Barbados. *Bulletin Marine Science, Miami*, **18**, 86–104.

Beers, J. R., Stevenson, M. R., Eppley, R. W. & Brooks, E. R. (1971). Plankton production and upwelling off the coast of Peru, June 1969. *Fishery Bulletin*, **69**, 859–76.

Bertelsen, E. & Hansen, P. M. (1969). Fiskeriundersogelser i 1969 Danmark, Färöarne og Grönlang. H. plankton. *Skrifter Danmarks Fiskeri og Havundersogelser*, **30**, 1–101.

Bessonov, N. M. & Fedosov, M. V. (1965). Primary productivity in the shelf waters off the West African coast. *Okeanologiia, Moskva*, **5**, 88–93.

Bouardel, J. & Rink, E. (1963). Mesure de la production organique un Mediterranee dans les parages de Monaco, a l'aide du C^{14}. *Annales de l'Institut océanographique*, **40**, 109–64.

271

Aquatic ecosystems

Bruyevich, S. & Ivanenkov, V. N. (1971). Chemical balance of the world oceans. *Okeanologiia, Moskva*, **11**, 694–99.
Bunt, J. S. (1964). Primary production under sea ice in Antarctic waters. I. Concentrations and photosynthetic activities of microalgae in the waters of McMurdo Sound, Antarctica. In *Biology of the Antarctic Seas*, ed. Milton O. Lee, American Geophysical Union of the National Academy of Sciences – National Research Council Publication 1190.
Burchall, J. (1968). An evaluation of primary productivity studies in the continental shelf region of the Agulhas current near Durban. *Investigational Reports of Oceanographic Research, Institute of South Africa, Durban*, **21**, 44 pp.
Burkholder, P. R., Burkholder, L. M. & Almodovar, L. R. (1967). Carbon assimilation of marine flagellate blooms in neritic waters of southern Puerto Rico. *Bulletin of Marine Science, Miami*, **17**, 1–15.
Burkholder, P. R. & Mandelli, E. F. (1965*a*). Carbon assimilation of marine phytoplankton in Antarctica. *Proceedings of the National Academy of Sciences, United States*, **54**, 437–44.
Burkholder, P. R. & Mandelli, E. F. (1965*b*). Productivity of microalgae in Antarctic ice. *Science*, **149**, 872–4.
Caperon, J., Cattell, S. A. & Krasnick, G. (1971). Phytoplankton kinetics in a subtropical estuary: Eutrophication. *Limnology and Oceanography*, **16**, 599–607.
Caperon, J. & Meyer, J. (1972). Nitrogen-limited growth of marine phytoplankton. II. Uptake kinetics and their role in nutrient limited growth of phytoplankton. *Deep-Sea Research*, **19**, 619–32.
Chmyr, V. D. (1965). Some data on the determination of primary production of plankton in the equatorial Atlantic. *First Conference of the All-Union Hydrobiological Society, Abstracts*, Moscow.
Corcoran, E. F. & Mahnken, C. V. (1969). Productivity of the tropical Atlantic Ocean. *Proceedings of the Symposium on the Oceanography and Fisheries Resources of the Tropical Atlantic*, pp. 57–67. Paris, UNESCO.
Curl, H. Jr & Small, L. F. (1965). Variations in photosynthetic assimilation ratios in natural, marine, phytoplankton communities. *Limnology and Oceanography*, **10**, 67–73.
Currie, R. I. (1958). Some observations on organic production in the northeast Atlantic. *Rapport et procès-verbaux des réunions. Commission internationale pour l'exploration scientifique de la Mer Méditerranée. Paris*, **144**, 96–102.
Cushing, D. H. (1971). A comparison of production in temperate seas and the upwelling areas. *Transactions of the Royal Society of South Africa*, **40**, 17–33.
Doty, M. S. & Capurro, L. R. A. (1961). Productivity measurements in the world oceans. Part I. *IGY Oceanography Report*, **4**, 298 pp.
Dunstan, W. M. & Menzel, D. W. (1971). Continuous cultures of natural populations of phytoplankton in dilute, treated sewage effluent. *Limnology and Oceanography*, **16**, 623–32.
El-Sayed, S. Z. (1968). On the productivity of the southwest Atlantic Ocean

272

and the waters west of the Antarctic Peninsula. *Antarctic Research Series, Biology of the Antarctic Seas III, American Geophysical Union of the National Academy of Sciences, National Research Council Publication*, 11, 15–47.

El-Sayed, S. Z., Mandelli, E. F. & Sugimura, Y. (1964). Primary organic production in the Drake Passage and Bransfield Strait. *Antarctic Research Series, Biology of the Antarctic Seas I, American Geophysical Union of the National Academy of Sciences, National Research Council*, 1, 1–11.

English, T. S. (1959). Primary production in the central North Polar Sea Drifting station Alpha 1957–8. *Paper presented at First International Oceanographic Conference, New York, 1959.*

English, T. S. (1961). Some biological oceanographic observations in the central North Polar Sea, Drift Station Alpha, 1957–8. *Research Papers, Arctic Institute of North America*, 13, (viii)+80 pp.

Eppley, R. W. & Sloan, P. R. (1965). Carbon balance experiments with marine phytoplankton. *Journal of the Fisheries Research Board of Canada*, 22, 1083–97.

Eppley, R. W., Strickland, J. D. H. & Solorzano, L. (1970). General introduction, hydrography and chemistry. (The ecology of plankton off La Jolla, California, in the period April through September, 1967). *Report of the Scripps Institution of Oceanography*, 14, 1–22.

Finenko, Z. Z. (1966). Primary production in Southern Seas and some aspects of its utilisation. *Second International oceanographic congress, Moscow*, 116–17.

Flemer, D. A. (1970). Primary productivity in the Chesapeake Bay. *Chesapeake Science*, 11, 117–29.

Flemer, D. A. & Olmon, J. (1971). Daylight incubator estimates of primary production in the mouth of the Patuxent River, Maryland. *Chesapeake Science*, 12, 105–10.

Fonselius, S. H. (1971). Hydrography of the Baltic deep basins. *Report of the Fishery Board for Sweden. Series Hydrography*, 13, 1–41.

Forsbergh, F. J. (1963). Phytoplankton production in the south-eastern Pacific. *Nature*, 200, 87–8.

Franceschini, G. A. & El-Sayed, S. Z. (1968). Effect of hurricane Inez (1966) on the hydrography and productivity of the western Gulf of Mexico. *Deutsche hydrographische Zeitschrift*, 21, 193–202.

Glooschenko, W. A. & Curl, H. (1971). Influence of nutrient enrichment on photosynthesis and assimilation ratios in natural North Pacific phytoplankton communities. *Journal of the Fisheries Research Board of Canada*, 28, 790–3.

Gordon, L. I., Kilho Park, P., Hager, S. W. & Parsons, T. R. (1971). Carbon dioxide partial pressures in North Pacific surface waters – time variations. *Journal of the Oceanographical Society of Japan*, 27, 81–90.

Grant, B. R. (1968). Effect of carbon dioxide concentration and buffer system on nitrate and nitrite assimilation in *Dunaliella tertiolecta*. *Journal of General Microbiology*, 54, 444–55.

Guillen, O. (1971). The *El Nino* phenomenon in 1965 and its relations with the productivity in coastal Peruvian waters. In *Fertility of the Sea*, ed. John D. Costlow, vol. 1, pp. 187–96. Gordon Breach.

Hogetsu, K., Sakamoto, M. & Sumekawa, H. (1959). On the high photosynthetic activity of *Skeletonema costatum* under the strong light intensity. *Botanical Magazine, Tokyo*, **72**, 421–2.

Horne, A. J., Fogg, G. E. & Eagle, D. J. (1969). Studies *in situ* of the primary production of an area of inshore Antarctic Sea. *Journal of the Marine Biological Association of the United Kingdom*, **49**, 393–405.

Humphrey, G. F. (1963). Chlorophyll *a* and *c* in cultures of marine algae. *Australian Journal of Marine and Freshwater Research*, **14**, 148–54.

Humphrey, G. F. & Subba Rao, D. V. (1967). Photosynthetic rate of the marine diatom *Cylindrotheca closterium. Australian Journal of Marine and Freshwater Research*, **18**, 123–7.

Ichimura, S. & Saijo, Y. (1959). Chlorophyll content and primary production of the Kuroshio off the southern midcoast of Japan. *Botanical Magazine, Tokyo*, **75**, 212–20.

Jeffrey, S. W. & Allen, M. B. (1964). Pigments, growth and photosynthesis in cultures of two chrysomonads, *Coccolithus huxleyi* and a *Hymenomonas sp. Journal of General Microbiology*, **36**, 277–88.

Jitts, H. R. (1965). The summer characteristics of primary production in the Tasman and Coral Seas. *Australian Journal of Marine and Freshwater Research*, **16**, 151–62.

Jitts, H. R. (1969). Seasonal variation in the Indian Ocean along 110°E. IV. Primary production. *Australian Journal of Marine and Freshwater Research*, **20**, 65–75.

Kabanova, Yu. G. (1961). Primary production and nutrients in the Indian Ocean. *Okeanologicheskiye issledovaniiya, Mezhdunarodnovo Komitet. Provednie Mezhdunarodnovo Geofizicheskovo Goda, Prezidiume, Akademiya Nauk, SSSR*, **4**, 72–5.

Kabanova, Yu G. (1964). Primary production and nutrient salts content in the Indian Ocean waters in October–April 1960–61. *Trudy Instituta okeanologii, Akademiya nauk, SSSR*, **64**, 85–93.

Kabanova, Yu. G. (1968). Primary production in the northern Indian Ocean. *Okeanologiia (Moskva)*, **8**, 214–25.

Koblents-Mishke, O. I. (1965). The magnitude of primary productivity in the Pacific Ocean. *Fisheries Research Board of Canada Translation Series* no. 828.

Koblents-Mishke, O. I. (1966). Primary production of the Pacific Ocean. *Second International Oceanographic Congress, Moscow*, pp. 198–9.

Koblents-Mishke, O. I., Volkovinshii, V. V. & Kabanova, Yu G. (1968). Distribution and magnitude of the primary production of the Oceans. *Sbornik Nauchno-Tekhnicheskoi Informatsii Vniro*, no. 5.

Kuz'menko, L. V. (1968). Primary production in the Arabian Sea during the summer monsoon. *Okeanologiia (Moskva)*, **8**, 367–71.

Lloyd, I. J. (1971). Primary production off the coast of North-west Africa. *Journal du Conseil permanent international pour l'exploration de la mer*, **33**, 312–23.

Loftus, M. E., Subba Rao, D. V. & Seliger, H. H. (1972). Growth and dissipation of phytoplankton in Chesapeake Bay I. Response to a large pulse of rainfall. *Chesapeake Science*, **13**, 282–99.

McAllister, C. D. (1963). Measurements of diurnal variation in productivity at Ocean Station 'P'. *Limnology and Oceanography*, **8**, 289–92.

McAllister, C. D. (1969). Aspects of estimating zooplankton productivity from phytoplankton production. *Journal of the Fisheries Research Board of Canada*, **26**, 199–220.

McAllister, C. D., Parsons, T. R., Stephens, K. & Strickland, J. D. H. (1961). Measurements of primary production in coastal sea water using a large volume plastic sphere. *Limnology and Oceanography*, **6**, 237–58.

McAllister, C. D., Parsons, T. R. & Strickland, J. D. H. (1960). Primary productivity and fertility at station 'P' in the Northeast Pacific Ocean. *Journal du Conseil permanent international pour l'exploration de la mer*, **25**, 240–59.

Madgwick, J. C. (1966). Chromatographic determination of chlorophyll in algal cultures and phytoplankton. *Deep-Sea Research*, **13**, 459–66.

Magazzu, G. & Andreoli, C. (1972). Contributions to the knowledge of phytoplankton and of primary production on the Sicilian coasts. (Sicilian Channel and West Tyrrhenian Sea.) *Memorie di biologia marina e di oceanografia*, **2**, 30 pp.

Malone, T. C. (1971a). The relative importance of nannoplankton and netplankton as primary producers in the California Current System. *Fisheries Bulletin, United States NOAA*, **69**, 799–820.

Malone, T. C. (1971b). The relative importance of nannoplankton and netplankton as primary producers in tropical oceanic and neritic phytoplankton communities. *Limnology and Oceanography*, **16**, 633–9.

Malone, T. C. (1971c). Diurnal rhythms in netplankton and nannoplankton assimilation ratios. *Marine Biology*, **10**, 285–9.

Mandelli, E. F. (1967). Enhanced photosynthetic assimilation ratios in Antarctic polar front (convergence) diatoms. *Limnology and Oceanography*, **12**, 484–91.

Mandelli, E. F. & Burkholder, P. R. (1966). Primary productivity in the Gerlache and Bransfield Straits of Antarctica. *Journal of Marine Research*, **24**, 15–27.

Mandelli, E. F., Burkholder, P. R., Doheny, T. E. & Brody, R. (1970). Studies of primary productivity in coastal waters of Southern Long Island, New York. *Marine Biology*, **7**, 153–60.

Margalef, R. & Ballester, A. (1967). Fitoplancton y produccion primaria de la costa Catalana, de Junio de 1965 a Junio de 1966. *Investigación pesquera*, **31**, 165–82.

Margalef, R. & Castelli, J. (1967). Fitoplancton y produccion primaria de la costa catalana, de julio de 1966 a julio de 1967. *Investigación pesquera*, **31**, 491–502.

Menzel, D. W. & Ryther, J. H. (1960). The annual cycle of primary production in the Sargasso Sea off Bermuda. *Deep-Sea Research*, **6**, 351–67.

Menzel, D. W. & Ryther, J. H. (1961). Annual variations in primary

275

production of the Sargasso Sea off Bermuda. *Deep-Sea Research*, **7,** 282–8.

Mitchell-Innes, B. A. (1967). Primary production studies on the southwest Indian Ocean, 1961–3. *Investigational Report. Oceanographic Research Institute, Durban*, **14,** 1–20.

Moiseev, P. A. (1971). *The Living Resources of the World Oceans* (Translated from the Russian). Published for National Marine Fish Service, National Oceanic and Atmospheric Administration, US Dept. of Commerce and the National Science Foundation, Washington, DC by Israel Program for Scientific Translations, Jerusalem.

Motoda, S. & Kawamura, T. (1963). Light assimilation curves of surface phytoplankton in the North Pacific. In *Marine Microbiology*, ed. C. Oppenheimer, pp. 251–9. Springfield, Ill., C. Thomas.

Owen, R. W. & Zeitschel, B. (1970). Phytoplankton production: seasonal change in the oceanic eastern tropical Pacific. *Marine Biology*, **10,** 32–6.

Parsons, T. R. & Anderson, G. C. (1970). Large-scale studies of primary production in the North Pacific Ocean. *Deep-Sea Research*, **17,** 765–76.

Parsons, T. R., Lebrasseur, R. J., Fulton, J. D. & Kennedy, O. D. (1969). Production studies in the Strait of Georgia. II. Secondary production under the Fraser River plume, February to May 1967. *Journal of Experimental Marine Biology and Ecology*, **3,** 39–50.

Patten, B. (1961). Plankton energetics of Raritan Bay. *Limnology and Oceanography*, **6,** 369–87.

Platt, T. (1969). The concept of energy efficiency in primary production. *Limnology and Oceanography*, **14,** 653–9.

Platt, T. (1971). The annual production by phytoplankton in St Margaret's Bay, Nova Scotia. *Journal du Conseil international pour l'exploration de la mer*, **33,** 324–34.

Platt, T. & Conover, R. J. (1971). Variability and its effect on the 24-hour chlorophyll budget of a small marine basin. *Marine Biology*, **10,** 52–65.

Platt, T., Conover, R. J., Loucks, R., Mann, K. H., Peer, D. L., Prakash, A. & Sameoto, D. D. (1970). Study of a eutrophicated marine basin. *FAO Technical Conference on Marine Pollution and its effects on Living Resources and Fishing, Rome*.

Platt, T. & Irwin, B. (1971). Phytoplankton production and nutrients in Bedford Basin, 1969–70. *Fisheries Research Board of Canada, Technical Report*, **247,** 172 pp.

Platt, T. & Irwin, B. (1973). Caloric content of phytoplankton. *Limnology and Oceanography*, **18,** 306–10.

Platt, T. & Subba Rao, D. V. (1970a). Primary production measurements on a natural plankton bloom. *Journal of the Fisheries Research Board of Canada*, **27,** 887–99.

Platt, T. & Subba Rao, D. V. (1970b). Energy flow and species diversity in a marine phytoplankton bloom. *Nature*, **227,** 1059–60.

Prasad, R. R. (1966). Recent advances in the study of production in the Indian Ocean. *Second International Congress, Moscow*, pp. 239–48. Paris, UNESCO.

Qasim, S. Z., Bhattathiri, P. M. A. & Abidi, S. A. H. (1968). Solar radiation and its penetration in a tropical estuary. *Journal of Experimental Marine Biology and Ecology*, **2**, 87–103.

Qasim, S. Z., Wellershaus, S., Bhattathiri, P. M. A. & Abidi, S. A. H. (1969). Organic production in a tropical estuary. *Proceedings of the Indian Academy of Sciences. Series B*, **69**, 51–94.

Radhakrishna, K. (1969). Primary production studies in the shelf waters off Alleppey, southwest India, during the post monsoon. *Marine Biology*, **4**, 174–81.

Riley, G. A. (1956). Factors controlling phytoplankton populations on George's Bank. *Journal of Marine Research*, **6**, 54–73.

Riley, G. A. (1956). Oceanography of Long Island Sound, 1952–1954. IX. Production and utilization of organic matter. *Bulletin of the Bingham Oceanographic Collection, Yale University*, **15**, 324–34.

Ryther, J. H. (1954). The ratio of photosynthesis to respiration in marine plankton algae and its effect upon the measurement of productivity. *Deep-Sea Research*, **2**, 134–9.

Ryther, J. H. (1963). Geographic variations in productivity. *The Sea: Ideas and observations in the study of the seas*, ed. M. N. Hill, pp. 347–80. New York, Interscience.

Ryther, J. H. (1969). Photosynthesis and food production in the sea. *Science*, **166**, 72–6.

Ryther, J. H., Hall, J. R., Pease, A. K., Bakun, A. & Jones, M. M. (1966). Primary organic production in relation to the chemistry and hydrography of the western Indian Ocean. *Limnology and Oceanography*, **11**, 371–80.

Ryther, J. H. & Menzel, D. W. (1960). The seasonal and geographical range of primary production in the western Sargasso Sea. *Deep-Sea Research*, **6**, 235–8.

Ryther, J. H. & Menzel, D. W. (1961). Primary production in the southwest Sargasso Sea, January–February 1960. *Bulletin of Marine Science of the Gulf and Caribbean*, **11**, 381–8.

Ryther, J. H. & Menzel, D. W. (1965). On the production, composition and distribution of organic matter in the Western Arabian Sea. *Deep-Sea Research*, **12**, 199–209.

Ryther, J. H., Menzel, D. W., Hulburt, E. M., Lorenzen, C. J. & Corwin, N. (1971). Production and utilization of organic matter in Peru coastal current. *Investigación pesquera*, **35**, 43–59.

Ryther, J. H., Menzel, D. W. & Vaccara, R. F. (1961). Diurnal variations in some chemical and biological properties of the Sargasso Sea. *Limnology and Oceanography*, **6**, 149–53.

Ryther, J. H. & Yentsch, C. S. (1957). The examination of phytoplankton production in the ocean from chlorophyll and light data. *Limnology and Oceanography*, **2**, 281–6.

Ryther, J. H. & Yentsch, C. S. (1958). Primary production of continental shelf waters off New York. *Limnology and Oceanography*, **3**, 327–35.

Saijo, Y. (1965). Summary report on photosynthesis and chlorophyll on the

Eastern Indian Ocean observed by Japanese ships during 110°E. *Information Bulletin on Planktology in Japan*, **12**, 72–8.

Saijo, Y. & Ichimura, S. (1959). *Primary production in the Northwestern Pacific Ocean.* Paper presented at the First Oceanographic Congress, New York.

Saijo, Y. & Kawashima, T. (1964). Primary production in the Antarctic Ocean. *Journal of the Oceanographical Society of Japan*, **19**, 190–6.

Saijo, Y. & Takesue, K. (1965). Further studies on the size distribution of photosynthesizing phytoplankton in the Indian Ocean. *Journal of the Oceanographical Society of Japan*, **20**, 10–17.

Sargent, M. C. & Austin, T. S. (1949). Organic productivity of an atoll. *Transactions of the American Geophysical Union*, **30**, 245–9.

Sen Gupta, R. (1972). Photosynthetic production and its regulating factors in the Baltic Sea. *Marine Biology*, **17**, 82–92.

Skopintsev, B. A. (1950). Organic matter in natural waters (water humus). *Trudy Gosudarstvennogo okeanograficheskogo instituta*, no. **17**(29).

Smayda, T. J. (1965). A quantitative analysis of the phytoplankton of the Gulf of Panama. II. On the relationship between C^{14} assimilation and the diatom standing stock. *Inter-American Tropical Tuna Commission Bulletin*, **9**, 467–531.

Smayda, T. J. (1966). A quantitative analysis of the phytoplankton of the Gulf of Panama. III. General ecological conditions and the phytoplankton dynamics at 8° 45′ N., 79° 23′ W. from November 1954 to May 1957. *Inter-American Tropical Tuna Commission Bulletin*, **11**, 355–612.

Soeder, C. J. (1965). Some aspects of phytoplankton growth and activity. In *Primary productivity in Aquatic Environments*, ed. C. R. Goldman, *Memorie dell'instituto italiano di idrobiologia*, **18** Supplement, pp. 48–59. Berkeley, University of California Press.

Sokolova, S. A. & Solov'yeva, A. A. (1971). Primary production in the Dal'nezelenetskaya Bay (Murman Coast) in 1967. *Okeanologiia* (*Moskva*), **11**, 460–70.

Sorokin, Yu. I. (1970). Some data on primary production in the central Pacific. *Okeanologiia* (*Moskva*), **10**, 691–4.

Sorokin, Yu. I. & Klyashtorin, L. B. (1961). Primary production in the Atlantic Ocean. *Trudy Vsesoiuznogo gidrobiologicheskogo obshchestva*, **11**.

Sournia, A. (1968). Variations saisonnières et nycthémerales phytoplancton maria et de la production primarire dans une baie tropicale, a Nosy-Bé (Madagascar). *Internationale Revue der gesamten Hydrobiologie und Hydrographie*, **53**, 1–76.

Starodubtsev, E. G. (1970). Primary production in the Kuroshio Current area. *Okeanologiia* (*Moskva*), **10**, 686–90.

Steele, J. H. (1956). Plant production on the Fladen ground. *Journal of the Marine Biological Association of the United Kingdom*, **35**, 1–33.

Steele, J. H. (1958). Plant production in the northern North Sea. *Marine Research. Department of Agriculture and Fisheries for Scotland*. Series **7**, 3–36.

Steele, J. H. & Baird, I. E. (1961). Relations between primary production,

Chlorophyll and particulate carbon. *Limnology and Oceanography*, **6**, 68–78.

Steemann Nielsen, E. (1955). Production of organic matter in the oceans. *Journal of Marine Research*, **14**, 374–86.

Steemann Nielsen, E. (1958). Experimental methods for measuring organic production in the sea. *Rapport et procès-verbaux des réunions.(Conseil permanent international pour l'exploration de la mer*, **144**, 38–46.

Steemann Nielsen, E. & Hansen, V. (1959). Measurements with the C^{14} technique of the respiration rates in natural populations of phytoplankton. *Deep-Sea Research*, **5**, 222–33.

Steemann Nielsen, E. & Jensen, A. (1957). Primary oceanic production, the autotrophic production of organic matter in oceans. *Galathea Report I*, 47–135.

Stephens, K., Fulton, J. D. & Kennedy, O. D. (1969). Summary of biological investigations in the Strait of Georgia, 1965–8. *Fisheries Research Board of Canada Technical Report*, no. **110**.

Stephens, K., Sheldon, R. W. & Parsons, T. R. (1967). Seasonal variations in the availability of food for benthos in a coastal environment. *Ecology*, **48**, 852–5.

Steven, D. M. (1971). Primary productivity of the tropical western Atlantic Ocean near Barbados. *Marine Biology*, **10**, 261–4.

Subba Rao, D. V. (1965). The measurement of total carbon dioxide in dilute tropical waters. *Australian Journal of Marine and Freshwater Research*, **16**, 273–80.

Subba Rao, D. V. (1969). *Asterionella Japonica* bloom and discoloration off Waltair, Bay of Bengal. *Limnology and Oceanography*, **14**, 632–4.

Subba Rao, D. V. (1973). Effects of environmental perturbations on short-term phytoplankton production off Lawson's Bay, a tropical coastal embayment. *Hydrobiologia*, **43**, 77–91.

Sushchenya, L. M. & Finenko, Z. Z. (1965). Primary productivity in the tropical part of the Atlantic. *Okeanologiia (Moskva)*, **5**, 60–70.

Sverdrup, H. U., Johnson, M. W. & Fleming, R. H. (1942). *The Oceans*, 1087 pp. New York, Prentice Hall.

Taniguchi, A. & Nishizawa, S. (1971). Primary production in the sea area east of New Zealand in winter 1968. *Kaiyo Report*, **3**, 17–25.

Thomas, W. H. (1970). A nitrogen deficiency in tropical Pacific Oceanic phytoplankton: Photosynthetic parameters in poor and rich water. *Limnology and Oceanography*, **15**, 380–5.

Vinberg, G. G. (1960). *Pervichnaya produktsiya vodoemov. (Primary production of water bodies.)* Minsk, Izdatel'stov Akademii Nauk, BSSR.

Vollenweider, R. A. (1965). Calculation models of photosynthesis depth curves. In *Primary Productivity in Aquatic Environments*, ed. C. R. Goldman, *Memorie dell'instituto italiano di idrobiologia*, **18** Supplement, pp. 426–57. Berkeley, University of California Press.

Williams, R. B. (1966). Annual phytoplanktonic production in a system of shallow temperate estuaries. In *Some Contemporary Studies in Marine Science*, ed. H. Barnes, pp. 699–716. London.

Williams, R. B. & Murdoch, M. B. (1966). Phytoplankton production and chlorophyll concentration in the Beaufort Channel, N.C. *Limnology and Oceanography*, **11**, 73–82.

Yentsch, C. S. (1965*a*). Distribution of chlorophyll and phaeophytin in the open ocean. *Deep-Sea Research*, **12**, 653–66.

Yentsch, C. S. (1965*b*). The relationship between chlorophyll and photosynthetic carbon production with reference to the measurement of decomposition products of chloroplastic pigments. In *Primary Productivity in Aquatic Environments*, ed. C. R. Goldman, *Memorie dell' instituto italiano di idrobiologia*, **18** Supplement, pp. 323–46. Berkeley, University of California Press.

Yentsch, C. S. & Lee, R. W. (1966). A study of photosynthetic light reactions, and a new interpretation of sun and shade phytoplankton. *Sears Foundation Journal of Marine Research*, **24**, 319–37.

Zgurovskaya, L. N. & Kustenko, N. G. (1968). Effects of different concentrations of nitrite nitrogen of photosynthesis pigment accumulation and cell division in *Sceletonema costatum* (Grev.) CL. *Okeanologiia* (*Moskva*), **8**, 830–4.

12. Primary production of aquatic plants – conclusions

J. F. TALLING

For the greater part of geological time, the survival of plant communities on the earth depended upon the effective functioning of photosynthetic systems with a watery environment. The carbon fixed by these systems was the support for a succession of faunas and, in fossil fuels, for modern industrial economy. The oxygen evolved first established the terrestrial environmental characteristics favourable for organisms sensitive to short-wave ultraviolet radiation and dependent upon aerobic oxidative metabolism. The present-day success of aquatic photosynthetic systems is attested by their large share in the estimated total annual photosynthetic production, as reviewed by Platt & Subba Rao (Chapter 11). Yet this large share depends chiefly upon the extensive areas of the oceans: by terrestrial standards, low standing crops and low rates of primary production per unit area are the rule rather than the exception.

We have chosen to divide our discussion of photosynthetic production according to whether the aquatic plants are microscopic in size (microphytes) or relatively large (macrophytes), and whether they inhabit fresh or sea water. Though convenient, these divisions are of unequal significance. In fundamentals, the problems of primary production by microphytes are similar in fresh and salt water; those of the emergent, largely subaerial, freshwater macrophyte have more in common with terrestrial vegetation. Many of the distinctions between work on microphytes originate in enforced differences of methodology. Few investigators are familiar with both freshwater and marine aquatics, and extremely few work with marine macrophytes; the resulting specializations and traditions need not reflect essential biological or environmental differences.

The distinctive characteristics of photosynthetic production underwater arise partly from the physical properties of the medium, and partly from the prevalence of vegetation types of delicate or diffuse construction, with algae predominant in the larger water-masses. The mechanical support offered by water provides opportunities for maintaining photosynthetic cover with a minimum of mechanical and nonphotosynthetic tissues. Below the water surface the physiological problems of very low temperatures, and frost damage, disappear, but

281

the potential extension of the growing season in cold climates is often offset by the interception of radiant energy by ice plus snow cover. In dry climates, especially of the tropics and subtropics, the benefits of superabundant water in extending the growing season – amidst withered terrestrial vegetation – are often striking. Winds are replaced by water currents, which may have a more significant role in the supply of CO_2 to bulky organs, and often decide the vertical and horizontal location of the many unattached aquatics and the structure of the canopy of attached aquatics. Disadvantages of being surrounded by water can particularly concern the twin inputs of CO_2 and radiant energy; these penalties have been discussed in other chapters of this volume by Talling, Westlake, Schindler & Fee. Among such constraints and opportunities, effective primary production has, as on land, three main requirements: that a light-intercepting cover is established, that photosynthetic activity is maintained by the available environmental resources, and that a positive net production of organic matter is achieved, available for further growth in excess of sources of depletion.

Comparative magnitudes of crop cover and activity

From previous discussions of various forms of aquatic production, two important conclusions may be drawn about the order of magnitudes of crop cover and photosynthetic activity per unit area. First, an effective light-intercepting cover can be established by a remarkably small cover-density of biomass. This is illustrated by the estimates, for phytoplankton, of the maximum content of chlorophyll a which can be accommodated within unit area of the euphotic zone, a situation that implies the near-complete absorption of PAR by algal pigments. If the figure of 300 mg chl. a m^{-2} is accepted as an order-of-magnitude estimate, the corresponding cover density in terms of dry organic matter will be ~ 15 g m^{-2} or 150 kg ha^{-1}. Under most hydrographic conditions, these estimates will be increased by a part of the population present below the euphotic zone, but this addition is not a necessary part of an effective photosynthetic cover, and usually does not affect the order of magnitude involved. It may be contrasted with the crop densities for dense stands cited by Westlake (Chapter 8) of ~ 400–700 g dry organic weight m^{-2} for submersed freshwater macrophytes, of 3000–6000 g m^{-2} for seaweeds, and 3000–10000 g m^{-2} for emergent freshwater macrophytes.

The scale of these cover densities, along the series phytoplankton –

freshwater submersed macrophytes, seaweeds, emergent freshwater macrophytes, involves increases totalling three orders of magnitude. A large part is connected with the increasing ratio of supporting tissues to photosynthetic tissues, and would be extended if terrestrial forest canopies (~ 50000 g m^{-2}: Kira (Chapter 2)) were also included. If the content of chlorophyll was to be taken as the index of cover (e.g. Gessner, 1949; Odum, McConnell & Abbott, 1958; Bray, 1960,1962), the range of variation would probably not exceed one order of magnitude.

These inter-comparisons are unrepresentative of the usual situation in nature, in that they concern maximum or near-maximum cover densities. These are approached much more frequently in stands of macrophytes than in the extensive oceanic areas occupied by phytoplankton. The low cover densities in the latter are well demonstrated in the survey by Platt & Subba Rao (Chapter 11), and Williams & Robinson (p. 691) provide a detailed seasonal illustration for the North Atlantic. Consequently, although the biomass requirement for an effective light-intercepting cover of phytoplankton is small, it is apparently much larger than that permitted by the very restricted nutrient supply of most offshore oceanic areas. Even in freshwaters, where population densities of phytoplankton per unit volume are typically higher, Talling (Chapter 10) has pointed out that the expected increase in euphotic cover density per unit area is often offset by an increased background absorption of residual pigments in the water column.

The second general conclusion concerns rates of photosynthetic production per unit area in the microphytic and macrophytic aquatic communities. Disregarding for the present the difficulties of deriving net production estimates for microphytes, and the 'net'–'gross' ambiguities in much published work noted by Talling, Stengel & Soeder, and Westlake (this volume), it seems clear that the areal rate of carbon fixation rarely exceeds 5 g C m^{-2} d^{-1} in microphyte communities but frequently does so in emergent freshwater macrophytes, including *Cyperus papyrus* (Thompson, see p. 691). The overall position for other submerged aquatic macrophytes is less clear; the relatively low areal rates of net biomass production for freshwater aquatics noted by Westlake (Chapter 8) contrast with some remarkably high rates per annum (1–2 kg C m^{-2} yr^{-1}) summarized by Mann & Chapman (p. 208) for certain seaweeds. Most estimates for productivity by seaweeds are based upon repeated census of the standing crop, and some thallus-marking methods have to contend with problems due to translocation.

283

However, high areal estimates (> 10 g C m^{-2} d^{-1}) based upon short-term measurements of gas exchange have previously and independently impressed some workers, notably Blinks (1955) and Kanwisher (1966), although the detailed derivation of these estimates is often not given. Blinks commented 'Perhaps, like all specialists, its productivity is greater the narrower it becomes'. Though this has particular reference to the narrow horizontal zone of seaweed abundance, it might also epitomize the high production rates often associated with vertically compressed profiles of photosynthetic activity, discussed by Talling (Chapter 10 and 12) for planktonic microphytes, and further illustrated by Sreenivasan (p. 690) and by Ganapati & Kulkani (p. 690) for shallow tropical ponds.

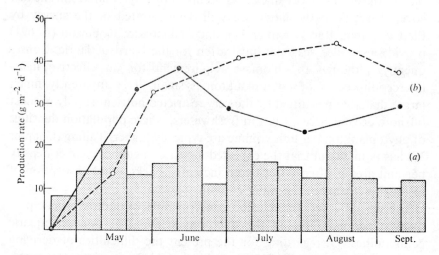

Fig. 12.1. A comparison of seasonal changes in rates of dry matter production by (*a*) outdoor mass cultures of a unicellular green alga (*Scenedesmus*) – shaded histograms, and (*b*) natural stands of two reedswamp plants, *Typha angustifolia* (○) and *Phragmites communis* (●), in Southern Bohemia, Czechoslovakia (from Dykyjová, 1971*b*).

There are greater difficulties, theoretical and practical, in attempts to compare the maximum rates of production by different types of aquatic vegetation. For natural populations of phytoplankton, I believe that technically satisfactory estimations that exceed 10 g C m^{-2} d^{-1} are extremely rare, even in such densely populated habitats as the freshwaters in India described by Ganapati & Kulkarni (p. 690) and by Sreenivasan (p. 690). There is no doubt that net production rates (based on crop census) of emergent freshwater macrophytes can considerably exceed this level. The particularly high estimates (~ 15 g C m^{-2} d^{-1}) for tropical papyrus swamps, reported by Thompson (p. 691), are particularly interesting in this connexion, but, as Westlake (Chapter 8) shows, there are also some well-documented estimates for temperate reedswamp vegetation in excess of 10 g C m^{-2} d^{-1}. The examples described for *Typha* and *Phragmites* by Dykyjová (1971*b*) are particularly interesting, as they are directly compared with measurements of net production in outdoor mass cultures of a planktonic alga (Fig. 12.1). Further work on seaweeds, to substantiate the relatively few but similarly high estimates (already mentioned), would be most desirable.

Production determinants: specific activity, cover display, depletion-rates

Estimates of rates of organic production per unit area can, and have, been obtained, and incorporated into a comparative numerology, without reference to the characteristics of the producing biomass or to opposing rates of depletion. This is particularly prevalent in the field of phytoplankton production, where the organisms exist in mixed microscopic assemblages and are often subject to heavy depletions that are difficult to measure. However, many authors have used chlorophyll *a* content, as an index of crop quantity, to calculate the specific activity at (or near) light-saturation as a measure of photosynthetic capacity. Values for phytoplankton, in both seas (Platt & Subba Rao, Chapter 11) and fresh waters (Talling, Chapters 10 and 12), usually lie in the range 1–10 mg C (mg chl. *a*)$^{-1}$ h^{-1}; values for submerged macrophytes are typically much lower (e.g. Hammann, 1957; Westlake, Chapter 8). Most estimates of the photosynthetic capacity of aquatic macrophytes are based upon dry weight as index. The typical value of about 4 mg C g^{-1} h^{-1} for freshwater species, indicated by Westlake (Chapter 8), and even the higher values (to ~20 mg C g^{-1} h^{-1}) given by Ikusima (p. 690), are low when compared with similarly based estimates for phytoplankton. Among a range of seaweeds, Kanwisher (1966) recorded the highest value (equivalent to ~20 mg C g^{-1} h^{-1}) for the membranaceous *Ulva* sp., but even in the bulkier fronds of *Laminaria* and *Macrocystis* the values corresponded to short doubling times of a few days. He commented: 'Such an impressive autotrophic performance must indicate a real minimum of cellular structural material. They are more purely photosynthetic machines'.

Systematic trends in the magnitude of photosynthetic capacity, in relation to environmental or community factors, have often been

285

described. Few are free from controversy. Thus a strong positive relationship with temperature is usually shown (within limits) by homogeneous plant material, but is often obscured when wider comparisons, e.g. between seasons or climatic zones, are attempted. Examples are discussed by Eppley (1972) for marine phytoplankton, and by Kanwisher (1966), Healey (1972), and Mann & Chapman (Chapter 9) for seaweeds; the role and basis of compensatory temperature 'adaptation' has been especially controversial. The widespread tendency, among freshwater phytoplankton, towards an inverse relationship between photosynthetic capacity and algal concentration was referred to by Talling (Chapters 10 and 12) and discussed in more detail by Javornický (p. 690). For marine phytoplankton, relationships between capacity and inorganic

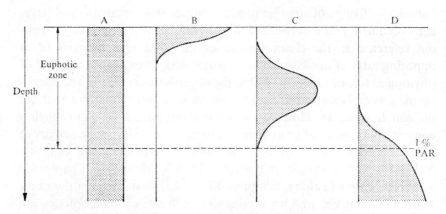

Fig. 12.2. Diagrammatic representation of some common vertical profiles of biomass concentration in relation to the euphotic zone.

nitrogen concentrations in some low-latitude areas were mentioned by Platt & Subba Rao (Chapter 11). These may be viewed against a background of other evidence for nitrogen as a limiting nutrient in the oceans, including that presented by Taylor (p. 691) from culture experiments in New Zealand. A tendency for lower capacities to be exhibited by freshwater plankton in more oligotrophic lakes in Japan was noted by Sakamoto (p. 690), although in a European region such a relationship, now based upon cell volume rather than chlorophyll as the crop index, was not found by Elster (1965).

The realization of photosynthetic capacity in a natural plant cover, and its relationship to photosynthetic production per unit area, will be strongly influenced by the mode of display of photosynthetic biomass within the vertical light gradient. A diagrammatic representation of four common types of display, as depth profiles of photosynthetic biomass, is given in Fig. 12.2. In most shallow waters there are two, three, or four superimposed components or tiers of plant cover with dissimilar organizations, recruited from emergent macrophytes, buoyant surface associations, dispersed phytoplankton, and bottom-living microphytes and macrophytes. Thus, at Aberystwyth, comparisons of biomass and/or production rates were made for a marine phytoplankton/bottom microphyte system (Steele, Munro & Reddy, p. 690), and Kvĕt gave evidence (cf. Rejmánková, 1973*a*) of interactions between emergent macrophytes and surface duckweeds in feshwater ponds. In such interactions competition for light is usually important, as illustrated by Pieczyńska & Straškraba (1969) for reedswamp/periphyton. Light interception within reedswamp biomass profiles is described, for example, by Dykyová (1971*a*).

The limiting and simplest case (A), of a uniform distribution of homogeneous biomass, is not uncommonly shown by the phytoplankton of isothermal and turbulently mixed water-bodies. It has been used as the basis for a number of model solutions of the photosynthesis-depth integral (e.g. Vollenweider, 1965,1970) including the effect of variation in photosynthetic capacity (e.g. Talling, Wood, Prosser & Baxter, 1973) and of generalised depth-profiles of photosynthesis (e.g. Rodhe, 1965). The non-uniform distributions B, C, and D can also be illustrated by phytoplankton, under the influences of motility (flagellates), buoyancy (e.g. gas-vacuolate blue-green algae), sinking, and locally restricted multiplication. Thus, Bohr (p. 690) describes an example of type C from Lake Jasne in Poland, and shows how a corresponding weighting was introduced into the depth-profiles of photosynthetic activity. Soeder (in discussion) pointed out that this might well vary diurnally as active flagellates were involved, and in amplification Schindler mentioned examples from his experience with Chrysomonads in Canadian lakes. Findenegg (1964,1965) has illustrated, for central European lakes, the influence of a wide variety of non-uniform depth-distributions of planktonic biomass. Fee (1973) and Schindler & Fee (Chapter 14) have shown how non-analytical solutions of the photosynthesis-depth integral can be developed to deal with such non-uniform distributions. For freshwater macrophytes, with further complexities, both analytical (Ikusima, 1967,1970) and non-analytical (Westlake, 1966) solutions have been attempted.

Situations with optically deep, and so poorly displayed, maxima of

287

biomass (type D) are likely to be associated with low ratios of photo-synthesis per unit area to photosynthetic capacity. Illustrations can be found, seasonally, among the phytoplankton of high-altitude, ice-covered lakes (Rodhe, Hobbie & Wright, 1966; Pechlaner, 1971; Tilzer, 1972,1973), where the mobility of flagellates is all-important. Other examples are shown by deep mats or swards of freshwater and marine macrophytes (see, e.g. Gessner, 1955), including young stages (cf. Kain, 1966, for some seaweeds). The mid-water biomass maximum (type C) is also commonplace in stands of submerged macrophytes, as noted by Westlake, who drew attention to the optical penalties often suffered by communities of freshwater macrophytes.

Heavy concentrations of biomass near the air–water interface (cf. type B) are not uncommon: examples include blooms of blue-green algae, floating-leaved macrophytes, and such free floating freshwater macrophytes as lemnids and *Salvinia*, and the more emergent plants of *Pistia* and *Eichhornia*. In these dense covers the vertical light gradient is determined more by self-absorption than by attenuation from other components in the water column. The same is true of the benthic mats of microphytes and macrophytes often well-developed in clear shallow waters. The luxuriant and strongly stratified mats of blue-green algae in hot springs afford one extreme and recently much studied example (e.g. Brock & Brock, 1969); the communities of stream periphyton (e.g. Tominaga & Ichimura, 1966) another.

Cover-display has also an important time-dependence, as illustrated by the concept of leaf area duration applied to terrestrial crops. Inter-ruptions during winter at higher latitudes and during dry seasons at lower latitudes have been mentioned. Mann & Chapman (Chapter 9) have emphasised the probable importance of winter translocation and use of assimilates as part of an adaptive 'strategy' in some seaweeds, enabling an effective cover to be presented early in the year. More familiar is the translocation and use of rhizome-stored assimilates for shoot development in spring, discussed by Westlake (Chapter 8) in connexion with temperate freshwater reedswamps (e.g. *Phragmites*). Delays in cover development are often responsible for inefficient utiliza-tion of the vernal increase in solar radiation. One neglected yet striking instance of this among microphytes is the very widespread spring increase of diatoms in deep temperate water-bodies, marine and fresh-water. The population increases from over-wintering 'inocula' are often as great as 10^3 or 10^4:1, and take many weeks to complete. Their inception or development may be greatly advanced by a reduction in depth of the upper mixed zone due to thermal stratification, as described by Robinson (1970) and Williams & Robinson (p. 691) for North Atlantic waters. Conversely, they may be delayed by the persistence of a winter ice cover, as described by Steven (p. 691) for the Gulf of St Lawrence. At another extreme, the significance for annual production of year-long dense cover needs no comment. An equatorial locality in Uganda, Lake George, has yielded illustrative results for both a swamp macrophyte (papyrus: Thompson, p. 691) and phytoplankton (Burgis *et al.*, 1973; Ganf & Viner, 1973).

The rates of depletion to which aquatic plant covers are subjected vary greatly. For phytoplankton, the uncertainties introduced by relatively large respiration losses are emphasized by Talling (Chapter 10), and Schindler & Fee (Chapter 14) refer to the importance of cell sedimentation losses in short-term nutrient dynamics. For some emergent freshwater macrophytes, however, Westlake notes that the further depletion of net photosynthetic production by various sources of mortality or grazing may be inconsiderable during the main growing season. Although any removal of photosynthetic biomass will be directly opposed to gains by photosynthetic production, the input rates of photosynthetic production may not be greatly impaired – especially in dense stands with marked self-shading. This insensitivity has received little attention in connexion with the production dynamics of dense phytoplankton communities subjected to heavy grazing or sedimentation losses. In some situations with self-shading, heavy respiratory losses and strong inverse relationships between photosynthetic capacity and population density, reductions of biomass could theoretically enhance the net yield per unit area. Applications to fish ponds have been discussed by Hepher (1962) and Prowse (1964).

Change and adaptation of components within the cover

Some differentiations with the cover, affecting the vertical profile of biomass, and photosynthetic production, have been discussed and compared. In practice, profiles of biomass concentration and photosynthetic capacity are often superimposed. The mechanisms of internal, biological control of these gradients are less developed in the systems of planktonic microphytes, but examples have been cited by several speakers. They include the migration responses of flagellates and the vertical differentiation between 'sun' and 'shade' cells. The 'adaptive' significance of the latter has been the subject of recent controversy (e.g. Yentsch & Lee,

1966; Steemann Nielsen & Jørgensen, 1968*a,b*). Westlake also refers to the long-established knowledge of sun–shade differentiation in the shoot systems of submerged freshwater macrophytes, which may affect gross morphology.

Internal changes which affect the photosynthetic performance or growth of aquatic plants will often occur in time. Platt & Subba Rao (1973) emphasized their probable importance for marine phytoplankton on two time scales of the diurnal and of the population cycle. Their data and discussion show that unequivocal examples from natural populations are difficult to establish, in view of the problems of 'normalizing' photosynthetic rates in relation to algal biomass of variable concentration and composition. For freshwater phytoplankton, Talling (Chapter 10) points out that there is often an unexpected persistence of considerable photosynthetic capacity into the final declining phase of a population cycle. For seaweeds, the internal regulation of effective cover via seasonal translocation of assimilates is described by Mann & Chapman (Chapter 9). The exploitation of this capability in many freshwater emergent macrophytes is further documented by Westlake (Chapter 8). Although such extensive seasonal translocations are precluded in the simpler floating duckweeds, such as *Lemna, Wolffia,* and *Spirodela,* Květ referred to both laboratory field evidence of internally controlled rhythms affecting relative (specific) growth rate.

Intercomparability of methods and factor-groupings

Any comparative review of primary production estimates for aquatic plants is hampered, at times frustrated, by the usual dependence upon gas exchange measurements for microphytes and crop census for macrophytes. For phytoplankton, I have argued that the differences of interpretation are much greater than is often assumed, and affect the foundations of mathematical models of production based upon the kinetics of photosynthesis. An obvious remedy, the careful study of suitable populations by both approaches, is rarely attempted: no examples were reported in the symposium on which the present volume is based.

The relative or specific growth rate is unique among parameters of production rate in simplicity of dimensions (time^{-1}) and scope of application. A formal derivation from data on gas exchange is possible if both net assimilation and biomass are expressed in the same terms (e.g. carbon), and such derivations appear in literature on phytoplankton (e.g. Eppley, 1972). However, Myers (1970) has pointed out several grounds for caution; as several differently controlled processes and forms of biomass are involved, the derived rates are really 'mixed' parameters. A similar reservation is applicable to a common alternative use of the same type of data, to calculate 'turnover times' for phytoplankton – essentially as reciprocals of the P/B coefficient based upon carbon.

For unicellular algae and for duckweeds, there is much experimental work on true relative growth rates; Květ points out how useful the characteristic could be in field studies on duckweeds, as in the work of Rejmánková (1973b).

Another, more controversial link between photosynthetic characteristics and growth is represented by the methods of 'growth analysis', with such 'mixed' parameters as net assimilation rate (unit leaf rate). Applications to aquatic plants (excepting duckweeds and reedswamp; cf. Květ, 1971) have not been numerous, and the factor-groupings that have been used for planktonic algae (e.g. Lemoalle, 1973) would at first appear quite unrelated. My own view (not shared by all contributors) is that there are considerable analogies, as between leaf area index and euphotic chlorophyll content, and that both systems reflect operationally effective (if 'mixed') groupings of factors. Although they are blunt or even inappropriate instruments for much finer analysis, they may provide more information about the production characteristics of plant cover than such traditional summarizing parameters as percentage utilization of incident solar energy.

References

Blinks, L. R. (1955). Photosynthesis and productivity of littoral marine algae. *Journal of Marine Research*, **14,** 363–73.

Bray, J. R. (1960). The chlorophyll content of some native and managed plant communities in central Minnesota. *Canadian Journal of Botany*, **38,** 313–33.

Bray, J. R. (1962). The primary productivity of vegetation in central Minnesota, USA and its relationship to chlorophyll content and albedo. In *Die Stoffproduktion der Pflanzendecke*, ed. H. Leith, pp. 102–16. Stuttgart, G. Fischer.

Brock, T. D. & Brock, M. L. (1969). Effect of light intensity on photosynthesis by thermal algae adapted to natural and reduced sunlight. *Limnology and Oceanography*, **14,** 334–41.

Burgis, M. R., Darlington, J. P. E. C., Dunn, I. G., Ganf, G. G., Gwahaba, J. J. & McGowan, L. M. (1973). The biomass and distribution of organisms in Lake George, Uganda. *Proceedings of the Royal Society*, B **184,** 271–98.

Aquatic ecosystems

Dykyjová, D. (1971*a*). Production, vertical structure and light profiles in littoral stands of reed-bed species. *Hidrobiologia*, **12**, 361–76.

Dykyjová, D. (1971*b*). Productivity and solar energy conversion in reed-swamp stands in comparison with outdoor mass cultures of algae in the temperate climate of Central Europe. *Photosynthetica*, **5**, 329–40.

Elster, H. J. (1965). Absolute and relative assimilation rates in relation to phytoplankton populations. *Memorie dell'Istituto Italiano di Idrobiologia*, **18** Suppl. 77–103. Reprinted in *Primary productivity in aquatic environments*, ed. C. R. Goldman, pp. 77–103. Berkeley, University of California Press.

Eppley, R. W. (1972). Temperature and phytoplankton growth in the sea. *Fisheries Bulletin* (US), **70**, 1063–86.

Fee, E. J. (1973). Modelling primary production in water bodies: a numerical approach that allows vertical inhomogeneities. *Journal of the Fishery Research Board of Canada*, **30**, 1469–73.

Findenegg, I. (1964). Produktionsbiologische Planktonuntersuchungen an Ostalpenseen. *Internationale Revue der gesamten Hydrobiologie und Hydrographie*, **49**, 381–416.

Findenegg, I. (1965). Factors controlling primary productivity, especially with regard to water replenishment, stratification, and mixing. *Memorie dell'Istituto Italiano di Idrobiologia*, **18** Suppl. 105–19. Reprinted in *Primary productivity in aquatic environments*, ed. C. R. Goldman, pp. 105–19. Berkeley, University of California Press.

Ganf, G. G. & Viner, A. B. (1973). Ecological stability in a shallow equatorial lake (Lake George, Uganda). *Proceedings of the Royal Society*, B **184**, 321–46.

Gessner, F. (1949). Der Chlorophyllgehalt im See und seine photosynthetische Valenz als geophysikalische Problem. *Schweizerische Zeitschrift für Hydrologie*, **11**, 378–410.

Gessner, F. (1955). *Hydrobotanik. I. Energiehaushalt*. Berlin, VEB Deutscher Verlag der Wissenschaften, 517 pp.

Hamman, A. (1957). Assimilationszahlen submerser Phanerogamen und ihre Bezeichung zur Kohlensäureversorgung. *Schweizerische Zeitschrift für Hydrologie*, **19**, 579–612.

Healey, F. P. (1972). Photosynthesis and respiration of some Arctic seaweeds. *Phycologia*, **11**, 267–71.

Hepher, B. (1962). Primary production in fishponds and its application to fertilization experiments. *Limnology and Oceanography*, **7**, 131–6.

Ikusima, I. (1967). Ecological studies on the productivity of aquatic plant communities. III. Effect of depth on daily photosynthesis in submerged macrophytes. *Botanical Magazine, Tokyo*, **80**, 57–67.

Ikusima, I. (1970). Ecological studies on the productivity of aquatic plant communities. IV. Light condition and community photosynthetic production. *Botanical Magazine, Tokyo*, **83**, 330–41.

Kain, J. M. (1966). The role of light in the ecology of *Laminaria hyperborea*. In *Light as an ecological factor*, eds. R. Bainbridge, G. C. Evans & O. Rackham, pp. 319–33. Oxford, Blackwell.

Kanwisher, J. (1966). Photosynthesis and respiration in some seaweeds. In *Some contemporary studies in marine science*, ed. H. Barnes, pp. 407–20. London, Allen & Unwin.

Květ, J. (1971). Growth analysis approach to the production ecology of reed-swamp plant communities. *Hidrobiologia*, **12**, 15–40.

Lemoalle, J. (1973). L'energie lumineuse et l'activé photosynthétique du phytoplancton dans le lac Tchad. *Cahiers ORSTOM, sér. Hydrobiologie*, **7**, 85–116.

Myers, J. (1970). Genetic and adaptive physiological characteristics observed in the chlorellas. In *Prediction and measurement of photosynthetic productivity*, Proceedings IBP/PP Technical Meeting, Třeboň, September 1969, pp. 447–54. Wageningen, PUDOC.

Odum, H. T., McConnell, W. & Abbott, W. (1958). The chlorophyll *a* of communities. *Publications of the Institute of Marine Science, University of Texas*, **5**, 65–96.

Pechlaner, R. (1971). Factors that control the production rate and biomass of phytoplankton in high-mountain lakes. *Mitteilungen der internationale Vereinigung für theoretische und angewandte Limnologie*, **19**, 125–43.

Pieczyńska, E. & Straškraba, M. (1969). Field experiments on the effect of light conditions in *Phragmites* stands on the production of littoral algae. *Bulletin de l'Académie Polonaise des Sciences*, **17**, 43–6.

Platt, T. & Subba Rao, D. V. (1973). Some current problems in marine phytoplankton productivity. *Technical Report, Fisheries Research Board of Canada*, no. 370, 90 pp.

Prowse, G. A. (1964). Some limnological problems in tropical fish ponds. *Verhandlungen der internationale Vereinigung für theoretische und angewandte Limnologie*, **15**, 480–4.

Rejmánková, E. (1973*a*). Biomass, production and growth rate of duckweeds (*Lemna gibba* and *L. minor*). In *Ecosystem study on Wetland Biome in Czechoslovakia*. Czechosl. IBP/PT–PP Report no. 3, pp. 101–6, Třeboň.

Rejmánková, E. (1973*b*). Seasonal changes in the growth rate of duckweed community (*Lemnetum gibbae*). *Folia Geobotanica et Phytotaxonomia, Praha*, **8**, 1–13.

Robinson, G. A. (1970). Continuous plankton records: variation in the seasonal cycle of phytoplankton in the North Atlantic. *Bulletin of Marine Ecology*, **6**, 333–45.

Rodhe, W. (1965). Standard correlations between pelagic photosynthesis and light. *Memorie dell'Istituto Italiano di Idrobiologia*, **18** Suppl. 365–81.

Rodhe, W., Hobbie, J. E. & Wright, R. T. (1966). Phototrophy and hetero-trophy in high mountain lakes. *Verhandlungen der internationale Vereinigung für theoretische und angewandte Limnologie*, **16**, 302–13.

Steemann Nielsen, E. & Jørgensen, E. G. (1968*a*). The adaptation of plankton algae I. General part. *Physiologia Plantarum*, **21**, 401–13.

Steemann Nielsen, E. & Jørgensen, E. G. (1968*b*). The adaptation of plankton algae III. With special consideration of the importance in nature. *Physiologia Plantarum*, **21**, 647–54.

Talling, J. F., Wood, R. B., Prosser, M. V. & Baxter, R. M. (1973). The upper limit of photosynthetic productivity by phytoplankton: evidence from Ethiopian soda lakes. *Freshwater Biology*, **3**, 53–76.

Tilzer, M. (1972). Dynamik und Produktivität von Phytoplankton und pelagischen Bakterien in einem Hochgebirgssee (Vorderer Finstertaler See, Österreich). *Archiv für Hydrobiologie*, Suppl. **40**, 201–73.

Tilzer, M. (1973). Diurnal periodicity in the phytoplankton assemblage of a high mountain lake. *Limnology and Oceanography*, **18**, 15–30.

Tominaga, H. & Ichimura, S. (1966). Ecological studies on the organic matter production in a mountain river ecosystem. *Botanical Magazine, Tokyo*, **79**, 815–29.

Vollenweider, R. A. (1965). Calculation models of photosynthesis-depth curves and some implications regarding day rate estimates in primary production measurements. *Memorie dell'Istituto Italiano di Idrobiologia*, **18** Suppl. 425–57.

Vollenweider, R. A. (1970). Models for calculating integral photosynthesis and some implications regarding structural properties of the community metabolism of aquatic systems. In *Prediction and measurement of photosynthetic productivity*. Proceedings IBP/PP Technical Meeting, Třeboň, September 1969, pp. 455–72. Wageningen, PUDOC.

Westlake, D. F. (1966). A model for quantitative studies of photosynthesis by higher plants in streams. *International Journal of Air and Water Pollution*, **10**, 883–96.

Yentsch, C. S. & Lee, R. W. (1966). A study of photosynthetic light reactions, and a new interpretation of sun and shade phytoplankton. *Journal of Marine Research*, **24**, 319–37.

PART III

Distribution of radiant energy and CO_2 in relation to community structure and stratification

13. Distribution of radiant energy and CO_2 in terrestrial communities

T. SAEKI

The light flux density observed under a plant canopy is often very low, as is typically shown on the floor of a climax forest. This reduction of light flux density is a result of light interception by plant organs within the canopy. It also means that light attenuation proceeds along the vertical axis. Although the flux of light is very variable in time and space, the mean horizontal flux densities indicate the gradient of 'light intensity' down through the canopy.

The particular pattern of light reduction along the vertical axis was correlated with the downward cumulative LAI, and mathematical models were developed for a model canopy composed only of very thin flat leaves with idealized properties of reflection and transmission.

Further investigations were made, in connection with the activities of IBP, of the horizontal variation of light flux density. On sunny days distinct sunflecks make an apparent sharp contrast with the shaded portions of foliage. It is evident in principle that averaging the light flux densities over a stratum overestimates the rate of total photosynthesis, since the photosynthetic rate of single leaves is a curvilinear function of the light flux density.

Models had also been simplified in terms of leaf inclination. Assuming a mean angle of leaves or uniform angle distribution simplifies theoretical analyses considerably. The actual foliage involves, however, a wide range of leaf angles even in the same stratum. In recent years, therefore, great efforts were directed to the assessment of canopy architecture or leaf display, including leaf orientation towards various points of the compass. The results were summarized by Loomis & Williams (1969).

These distribution functions were used to estimate light extinction within the canopy with the basic assumption that the horizontal leaf distribution is random. Although non-randomness of leaf distribution might exert greater influence on the light distribution within the canopy than does leaf inclination, the theoretical analyses of non-random distribution have so far only had limited success. Point quadrat methods applied to computer models might stimulate a further development,

L

because such a quasi-experimental procedure does not require any pre-supposition about foliage models or actual leaf distribution and does not require random leaf arrangement (Oikawa & Saeki, 1972).

The considerable work of the Institute of Physics and Astronomy, Academy of Sciences of the Estonian SSR on the theories and measurements of light penetration in plant stands was summarized by Niilisk, Nilson & Ross (1970), who give much information on the multiple scattering and selective absorption of light by leaves theoretically and experimentally. Miller & Norman (1971*a,b*) and Norman, Miller & Tanner (1971) advanced for the first time a unique theoretical analysis of penumbral fuzziness in relation to gap distribution in the canopy.

At the Třeboň Technical Meeting in 1969 Loomis indicated three gaps remaining in the models of radiation regime in a plant canopy, and two more were added by Anderson (Landsberg, 1970) analytical descriptions for non-random dispersion; penumbral effects; relationships of complex communities; size of plant parts in relation to frequency distribution of flux density both in time and space within a stand; and significance of very short period fluctuations. Substantial steps appear to have been taken in some of these aspects.

Aerodynamic and heat balance approaches were developed as a non-destructive method for estimating total CO_2 uptake and water vapour evolution in a plant community. Further sophistication of this method has enabled us to work within the foliage and evaluate the sink and source intensity of CO_2 and other physical parameters. Compared with the studies of light regime in stands, the studies of CO_2 stratification in stands have been limited to a small number of sites, probably because these involve the installation and complete operation of a full set of costly instruments. The need for a very long fetch has also restricted the application of such technique.

Although the stratification of CO_2 concentration along the vertical axis of stands shows very similar patterns, the connection with the plant structure is still indefinite. Many technical difficulties obstruct the establishment of empirical laws. Also, it is very difficult to provide a theoretical analysis of the contribution of eddies to the vertical transport of CO_2.

Although in this chapter light refers to visible radiation or photosynthetically active radiation (PAR), mention will also be made of radiation of longer wavelengths.

Horizontal variation of light

On cloudy days, light distribution on a horizontal surface within a canopy is unimodal. When expressed by the coefficient of variation, light variability generally increases with increasing depth in the canopy (Acock, Thornley & Warren Wilson, 1970). But, if we attempt to relate light variability to the photosynthesis of leaves, the standard error will be a more appropriate expression (Isobe, 1969). In this expression, light distribution in the lower strata of the canopy is mostly in the lower range of light intensity.

On sunny days, very intense direct sunlight penetrates to various depths of the canopy and light variability is increased, although the coefficient of variation does not show any clear difference between strata. According to measurements with small photocells, Acock, Thornley & Warren Wilson (1970) demonstrated that near the top of the canopy the horizontal distribution of light is clearly bimodal, and on descending into the canopy the fraction of diffuse light is more and more increased, and the pattern becomes unimodal. Laisk (1968) found a clearly bimodal flux density distribution at two wavelengths (663 and 772 nm) in a corn canopy at three solar altitudes. In the near-infrared wavelength, flux densities of more than the value above the canopy were recorded in the lower strata (LAI 2.04).

The frequency distribution of light flux density naturally changes with the ratio of incident direct sunlight to diffuse skylight. Kumura (1968) made his measurements on each leaf surface of a soybean crop. This brings in another complexity due to leaf angle and orientation, but the measurements can be related directly to the light–photosynthesis curves. The pattern of distribution was similar to that shown by Acock, Thornley & Warren Wilson (1970) and Isobe (1969).

As is clear from all the theories of light penetration, increasing the percentage of diffuse skylight in the total sunlight may contribute to the horizontal uniformity of light distribution within the canopy and to the increase of total canopy photosynthesis. Such an effect was confirmed by actual measurements of crop photosynthesis (Kumura, 1968; Ito, 1971; Tanaka, 1972).

The distribution of light flux density on different leaf planes in the same stratum depends upon solar altitude and the leaf distribution function actually measured (Nichiporovich, 1961; Laisk, 1965; de Wit, 1965; Shiman, 1967; Květ, Svoboda & Fiala, 1967; Uchijima, Udagawa, Horie & Kobayashi, 1968; Udagawa & Uchijima, 1969). With an assumption of non-overlap of leaves in a unit layer of a canopy it can be calculated theoretically (Ross & Nilson, 1965; Uchijima, Udagawa, Horie & Kobayashi, 1968). In a corn crop such a calculated distribution of radiation flux density on the leaves showed that the peak of distribution frequency was transferred from lower short-wave radiation flux density at lower sun altitudes to the higher radiation flux density at higher sun altitudes. Owing probably to the erectophile leaves in rice and barley, radiation flux density on the sunlit leaf surface at higher solar altitudes had a peak frequency in the lower part of the whole range of radiation flux (Ito, 1969; Udagawa & Uchijima, 1969).

Ogawa (1969) suggested that radiation flux densities measured on a horizontal plane within a plant canopy often show log-normal distributions. He revealed that such light distribution corresponds to the extinction coefficient calculated from the geometrical mean of luminous flux densities but not from the arithmetical mean, although the extinction coefficients actually calculated from the horizontal light variability in a beech forest were not much different (0.67 and 0.65, respectively). Such log-normal curves, however, would not fit Laisk's (1968) bimodal distributions.

Penetration of sky radiation

Skylight penetrates plant canopies directly through gaps between leaves in the canopy, which are usually most frequent near the zenith, because the path length of radiation through the canopy increases with the distance from the zenith.

Measurements of the percentage direct penetration of skylight under the canopy (diffuse site factor) as well as the direct site factor are conveniently obtained by fish-eye photographs and diffuse spider's web estimates (Anderson, 1964, 1971). Anderson (1966) assumed a standard overcast sky (SOC) and horizontally random distribution of leaves, when calculating the theoretical values of light penetration under different combinations of leaf angle and LAI. The corresponding values under uniform overcast sky (UOC) are a little lower, up to a maximum of 10% in the case of a constant leaf angle of 90° from the horizontal. Brightness of sky on a clear day is not uniform but is related to the position of the sun. So far no theory has examined this effect on light penetration.

The fraction of diffuse sky radiation transmitted by a forest or a crop each day is not much affected by weather, shows little spatial variation for a uniform crop, and is usually higher than that of direct solar radiation, since transmission of the canopy increases towards the zenith (Anderson, 1970*a*).

Penetration of direct sunlight

The sun has usually been regarded as a point source at infinite distance. In reality the sun has the finite angular diameter of 0.5° and causes fuzziness of sunflecks. The penumbral area at the edge of a sunfleck increases with the distance between the gap and the measuring height.

Miller & Norman (1971*a,b*) presented a theory which enables us to obtain the horizontal variability due to penetration of direct sunlight. This theory, together with the exponential decrease of skylight penetration and a new scattering theory, favourably predicted light distribution under the canopies with horizontal sumac and sunflower leaves and artificial opaque discs (Norman, Miller & Tanner, 1971). However, its extension to more general cases, e.g. application to canopies with inclined leaves, would require a more complex theory.

If it is assumed that the direct sunlight is composed of parallel light beams, its penetration into a canopy can be examined by the point quadrat of Warren Wilson (1960) or with a fish-eye photograph (Anderson, 1964). With a lucerne stand, Warren Wilson (1965) recorded the proportions of quadrats making first contacts within successive 10 cm layers for six quadrat inclinations. Their profiles were not much different for inclinations larger than the mean foliage angle 50° of this stand, corresponding to the theory in random distribution foliage, although the stand showed clumping for larger inclinations of the quadrat from the horizontal. With lower altitudes of the sun the sunlit foliage area is largely confined to the upper layers of canopy and less than one unit of LAI. Under-dispersed leaf arrangement enhances the sunlit leaf area and overdispersed arrangement reduces it. The sunlit foliage area index gives a simple and clear image of total sunlit area in relation to leaf angle and solar altitude. Nevertheless, it is not a proper measure of the light regime for predicting canopy photosynthesis, as it neglects the distribution of flux density on the leaf surfaces and of photosynthetic characteristics of foliage at different depths.

With a small sensor, radiation flux under a plant canopy is found to vary rapidly on clear days. Recording with a large sensor averages out these fluctuations (Anderson, 1970*a*). According to Ino (1969, 1970) records of luminous flux density under a *Betula* canopy showed four to five peaks per ten seconds when the wind speed was 1–3 m s^{-1}. When the wind speed increased to 4–6 m s^{-1}, numerous fine peaks appeared but the frequency of large peaks was three to six per ten seconds. He showed that a fluctuation between high and low luminous flux densities brought about more than double the photosynthetic rate than is expected under steady-state illumination. Similar photosynthetic enhancement was found in grapevines by Kriedemann, Törökfalny & Smart (1973).

Light penetration, receipt and absorption

There have been many computations of flux densities on a horizontal plane or on the leaves on that plane in the canopy. These are mostly based on the conventional model canopy with flat, infinitely thin, black leaves or leaves having specific scattering properties. The leaves may have a constant angle, uniform distribution of angle, or make heliotrophic movements; light sources may be parallel beams of specific inclination and orientation, or diffuse skylight of UOC or SOC; and sometimes various combinations of parallel light beams and skylight are assumed (Kuroiwa & Monsi, 1963*a,b*; de Wit, 1965; Anderson, 1966; Kuroiwa, 1968*b*, 1970; Ross & Nilson, 1967, 1968*a,b*; Duncan, Loomis, Williams & Hanau, 1967; Niilisk, Nilson & Ross, 1970; Isobe, 1969). Leaf-geometrical characters actually measured were sometimes used instead of the simplified foliage models (Niilisk, 1964; de Wit, 1965; Uchijima, Udagawa, Horie & Kobayashi, 1968; Horie & Udagawa, 1971). These computations are summarized in tables and figures in each paper, and can conveniently be utilized for general understanding of the effects of leaf angle, leaf orientation, different light sources, solar angle and latitude and can be applied to individual specific situations. Characteristic points are indicated in each paper and not mentioned here. It should be noted, however, that leaf dispersion is assumed to be at random, and miscalculation is found in some papers.

We have also made many field measurements of light penetration in plant canopies. These measurements use sensors of various properties, in different types of natural or artificial stands, and the results are expressed in different forms. A majority of measurements was made in crops and these have been individually extracted by Monteith (1969). He concluded that the extinction coefficient in relation to cumulative LAI does not vary much at least over the central eight hours of the day, although theoretically this result is valid only when there is a preponderance of leaf angles less than 30°.

Acock, Thornley & Warren Wilson (1970) noted that the mean light flux density (without scattering) on the horizontal leaves dispersed in a regular arrangement on a plane is higher than the mean light flux density on that plane. When leaf arrangement is clumped the situation is reversed. This is part of the general rule that governs the relation between penetration and interception. The larger the penetration, the lower the absorption (or the receipt without scattering).

Light absorption is the first prerequisite of photosynthesis. When light falls perpendicularly on a leaf, reflection is minimum and transmission is maximum. With increasing obliquity of light beams, reflection increases and transmission decreases. As a result of this, absorption is held relatively constant in a wide range of incident angle (Tagayava & Brandt, 1960).

Leaves in a canopy receive light from diverse directions. Even if the flux density of very oblique light beams could be correctly measured on a leaf surface with a photometer with ideal cosine response, these measurements could not be applied without error to the light–response curve of photosynthesis of single leaves, because the photosynthetic rate is usually measured under vertical light beams and the proportion of light absorbed will differ for oblique beams. Photosynthetic rate is, therefore, most suitably related to the *absorbed* light flux, as stressed by the Russian scientists and de Wit (1965).

The light flux density absorbed by leaves is easily calculated by measuring upward and downward light flux densities with a normally positioned and an inverted photometer. Niilisk (1964) gave an integral form for the absorption of light. When $I\downarrow$ and $I\uparrow$ are the downward and upward flux densities at F (downward cumulative LAI), respectively, the absorbed light flux density at F is obtained in differential form as follows: $-\partial(I\downarrow - I\uparrow)/\partial F$ (see Saeki, 1960). Horizontal variation in both received and absorbed light presents a similar problem.

Scattering by leaves

Within a canopy there is direct penetration of sunlight and diffuse skylight through gaps of the canopy. A third component of radiation originates from the scattering of radiation by leaves, because a leaf is an excellent diffuser of radiation over the whole range of visible and near-infrared regions (e.g., Woolley, 1971). The amount of this component within a canopy is small in the waveband of PAR, but large in the range 0.7–3 μm, because the latter involves the waveband of very low absorbancy.

This third scattering component of radiation was theoretically evaluated by assuming that incident radiation on leaves is ideally scattered, i.e. scattered according to the cosine law and scattered in the same flux density to both upward and downward directions. Any scattering reiterated more than twice was ignored (de Wit, 1965; Kuroiwa, 1968*a*; Duncan, Loomis, Williams & Hanau, 1967; Cowan, 1968; Isobe, 1969; Horie & Udagawa, 1971). Ross & Nilson (1967,1968*a*) and Nilson (1968) developed a detailed multiple scattering theory and applied it also to near-infrared radiation of low absorbancy wavebands. Norman, Miller & Tanner (1971) also proposed a scattering theory only applicable to horizontal leaves.

An alternative approach, using the Duntley equations for propagation of light through a diffusing medium, and working from spectrophotometrically measured leaf properties, has been adopted by a group in Texas, e.g. Allen & Richardson (1968); Allen, Gayle & Richardson (1970). Recently, Suits (1972*a*,*b*) and Suits & Safir (1972) have extended the approach to examine azimuthal variations in crop properties, and suggest that there is a hot spot opposite the sun.

The scattered radiation flux as a complementary radiation field is split into two components, downward and upward. The downward flux is zero at the top of the canopy, increases with canopy depth to attain the maximum at a certain depth (cumulative LAI 1–2) and then decreases monotonically. Although this pattern of profile is clear, it cannot be proved by actual measurement, because the (leaf) scattered radiation cannot be separated from the direct diffuse-sky radiation by the ordinary methods.

On the other hand, the same theory predicts that the upward flux diminishes monotonically with the depth of the canopy. The theoretical values agreed well with the experimental values in various spectral intervals (Niilisk, Nilson & Ross, 1970) and in the short-wave radiation (Horie & Udagawa, 1971), though in the latter only the first scattering was considered. Anderson (1969) measured hourly percentage transmissions of PAR and NIR (0.7–2.5 μm) under two experimental crops. By taking PAR/NIR ratio she was able to confirm the adequacy of the scattering theory proposed by Russian scientists, which predicted the ratio to decrease with LAI.

The reflectance of the leaf in general increases with the angle of incidence. When radiation impinges on leaves at higher incident angles, it is mostly reflected as in a mirror and this specular reflection is independent of wavelength (Woolley, 1971). With erect leaves and a high solar altitude this specular reflected radiation might be very high, and could supply a considerable amount of radiation to deeper layers of canopy.

Ordinary measurements of PAR sum up total energy within this waveband. This means that the efficiency in blue light is nearly twice that in red light in a low flux density (McCree, 1972).

Within a single leaf, light is mostly absorbed through a long pathway by means of multiple reflection and refraction, but part of the light passes through the intercellular spaces between the mesophyll cells by the 'sieve effect' of Rabinowich (1951). Light penetration in a stand is in a similar situation. Light of different colours is selectively absorbed due to different absorptances, and the transmitted and reflected fractions constitute the scattered light regime within the canopy. The flux density of this leaf-scattered light loses the original sharp contrast of leaf absorptance owing to multiple scattering. The resultant components of scattered radiation are well indicated by graphs given theoretically by Niilisk, Nilson & Ross (1970). Even green light, which has the least absorptance among the PAR wavebands, occupied, at the peak in the LAI depth of 1–2, only 10% of the original flux density on the canopy surface. The spectral distribution in PAR measured under the canopy, therefore, shows no sharp peak at green light (Yocum, Allen & Lemon, 1964; Federer & Tanner, 1966; Kriedemann & Smart, 1971). This may allow us, as a first approximation, to assume non-selective absorption of PAR or to neglect the complementary radiation field in the PAR waveband (Ross & Nilson, 1968b). At lower solar angles the bias toward red light of direct sunlight is compensated by the increase of skylight/direct light ratio (Shulgin, 1967).

In constructing models, e.g. for canopy photosynthesis, the number of parameters and the complexity of the model are being continuously increased. An apparent agreement between simulation and measurement can easily be obtained by different modifications of many of the parameters. The importance of simplification in the substeps of a model cannot be underestimated.

Radiation of longer wavelengths

The measurement of PAR requires a sharp cut-off at the wavelengths of 0.4 (or 0.38) and 0.7 (or 0.71) μm, a difficult task with available

305

L*

filters. Some PAR meters retain sensitivity to radiation of higher wavelengths which include the band of very low leaf absorbancy (0.75–1.3 μm). Since the scattered light within this band is rich within and beneath plant canopies, such photometers will give erroneous PAR values (Anderson, 1971). Similarly, original short-wave radiation above a canopy is transformed in the canopy to produce much near-infrared radiation (Anderson, 1969).

Long-wave radiation refers to the radiation of wavelengths exceeding 3–4 μm which cannot penetrate into the glass dome of pyranometers. Net radiation measures the difference of downward and upward flux densities of radiation over the full range of wavelengths. Since it contains long-wave radiation, net radiation depends on leaf temperature, and is intimately connected with the heat budget of canopy. On the other hand, the absorption of net radiation provides an important basis of the heat budget method. Net radiation in sunflecks within a plant canopy can exceed net radiation above the plant canopy, while net radiation in shade can be negative (Allen & Lemon, 1972).

Since net radiation decreases with the depth of canopy in the daytime like short-wave radiation, it is often plotted against height or downward cumulative LAI (e.g. Brown & Covery, 1966), and rough estimates of extinction coefficient are calculated, as in the case of light flux density. There is however no foundation to warrant either of these plottings, except that net (effective) long-wave radiation may occupy only a minor part of the total net radiation.

Non-random leaf arrangement

The leaf arrangement is rarely at random, often clumped and sometimes regular, and the degree of randomness depends upon inclination of rays (Warren Wilson, 1959,1961,1965). In swards of clover and ryegrass, leaf arrangement was individually at random, but collectively regular (Warren Wilson, 1959). A regular arrangement toward the direction of the incident rays implies that leaves are located at less covered positions, while a clumped arrangement implies that leaves are located at more covered positions, except at the top of the canopy where light distribution is more or less uniform.

Positive and negative binomials can describe the horizontal variability of radiation flux density more adequately than a Poisson distribution (Mototani, 1968; Acock, Thornley & Warren Wilson, 1970). These distribution patterns and a Markov model (Nilson, 1971) are examples of non-random distribution. No other mathematical models have been adopted. Analytical theories on light penetration in non-random distribution foliage are scarce, and only binomial distributions of leaves have been combined to the level of light extinction (Monteith, 1965; Ross, 1972).

Forest canopies are often characterized by very high LAI values and low light-extinction coefficients. Kira, Shinozaki & Hozumi (1969) interpreted this phenomenon by the 'leaf cluster model': tree leaves are not evenly distributed, but clustered around twigs. These units form clusters (branches), single tree crowns, and finally the stratified structure of the whole canopy. Horn (1971) has discussed the advantages of such forest structure for evening out the distribution of light on the lower leaf strata. Young smaller leaves located around the upper stem of *Solidago altissima* show a clear cluster (Monsi, 1968).

The assumption of non-overlap within a finite thickness of stratum in a canopy contradicts the assumption of random distribution; it implies underdispersion or regular arrangement (Warren Wilson, 1967). Anderson (1970b) could partly explain an apparent clumping effect on increasing light penetration, simply by taking the variation of foliage angle into account on the random-distribution model. The calculated light penetration approached that of the fish-eye observation and was much better than that predicted from a mean foliage angle.

Ross (1972) proposed a new theory which takes into account non-randomness of plant and leaf distributions. In reality only binomial regular arrangements were considered. Light penetrates into an assemblage of plants distributed at random or regularly. Each plant is confined within a cylindrical form in which the leaves are distributed at random or regularly. Only vertical or nearly vertical light is allowed to penetrate according to the given equations. Analytical solution of light penetration in non-random distribution foliage is thus a very difficult problem.

The point quadrat method of Warren Wilson produced a great deal of useful information on the distribution patterns of foliage and leaf angle distribution in the field, but it involves laborious quadrat counts and has not been much used by other researchers. When it was used to estimate the mean angle distribution in each of the stratified layers of tree crowns, the values did not show good agreement with the values obtained by de Wit's protractor method (Ford & Newbould, 1971). This might be due to an insufficient number of quadrats relative to the degree of heterogeneity of the foliage structure. In order to clarify the light regime of non-random foliage, Tanaka (1969,1970) and Oikawa &

Radiant energy, CO_2 *and community structure*

Saeki (1972) applied a Monte Carlo method using a high quality computer. In principle this method is the same as the point quadrat method. Foliage structure either of actual plants or of idealized foliage model is put into the memories of the computer, light beams of the desired constitution are emitted, and penetration and interception are *experimentally* examined.

This method was applied to the study of light penetration in the isolated segment of a population where border effects are important, and also to the study of the light regime in square-planted populations in relation to planting density, leaf angle, leaf area density, leaf size etc. (Oikawa & Saeki, 1972). It revealed many characteristics in the light regime that had not been predicted from the assumption of random distribution of the foliage. Although here UOC and black leaves were assumed, extension to other conditions may be an easy matter.

A square-planted population consists of plants that have a regular horizontal distribution. The leaves are confined within the cylindrical form of the plant, just like the model of Ross (1972). With larger leaf areas, however, the total leaf dispersion was clumped, which was clearly indicated by the relative-variance criterion. The Monte Carlo simulation method showed that one of the square-planted populations, which was clumped when examined in the vertical direction, intercepted light more than in random distribution foliage. It might mean that the leaf dispersion was regular for UOC.

Lang (1973) has recently described a modification of the point quadrat technique using an on-line computer. This measures both angular elevation and azimuth of leaves as well as LAI. His studies bring out clearly the large changes in leaf position and azimuth during the day in a cotton plant, and must shed doubts on the reliability of a single set of measurements of leaf distribution for explaining light distribution in canopies over a period of time.

Light interception by plant organs other than leaves

Radiation is intercepted not only by leaves but also by stems, sheaths, inflorescences and fruits. These organs sometimes afford a substantial contribution to the total CO_2 uptake, as is well demonstrated in the sheaths and awns of some gramineous crops. So light interception by such organs not only affects the light diminution within a stand but also contributes to additional CO_2 uptake, or reduces the CO_2 loss in chlorophyll-containing tissues. Although in some herbaceous plants and trees, more than half of the green area is occupied by sheaths and stems, the bulk of those areas exists in the lower strata, and their effect on the canopy photosynthesis is not as serious as suspected (Loomis & Williams, 1969).

Warren Wilson (1967) proposed the term foliage area index for use instead of leaf area index when the photosynthetic surface includes organs other than leaves, while Ross & Nilson (1965) have defined the stem surface density function and the stem distribution function. Low light flux densities at the bottom of the forest floor in leafless seasons may give rough estimates of the light interception by twigs, branches and boles. Owing to the interception by trunks and branches, forest-floor plants can only expect to receive light from small solid angles near the zenith, and the tree crown itself is subject to the shading effect of the twigs and branches on which leaves are sustained in position.

Yim, Ogawa & Kira (1969) measured vertical light extinction in four herbaceous stands and in an artificially planted dense stand of two-year old oak before and after leaves were removed by hand. Stems alone intercepted 28–69% of the total incident luminous flux (I_o) at the bottom of these stands. With regard to light extinction, leaf distribution was regarded as independent of stem distribution, so that the total extinction was the product of both these independent extinctions. Luminous flux density at height z of a leafy stand $I(z)$ divided by luminous flux density after the leaves are removed $I_c(z)$ gives the degree of interception by leaves alone. The value I/I_c, when plotted on a log scale, was linearly related to the cumulative leaf area index (F) from the foliage top, that is $\log_e I/I_c = -K_F F$. In the small oak stands, $\log_e (I_c(z)/I_o)$ proved to be most closely correlated with the summed area of the stem cross-sections at height z, $A(z)$, giving the equation, $I_c(z)/I_o = \exp(-K_c A(z))$. Using the pipe model hypothesis proposed by Shinozaki, Yoda, Hozumi & Kira (1964a,b), Yim, Ogawa & Kira (1969) finally came to the conclusion that $K = K_F + aK_c$, where K is the apparent extinction coefficient and a is a constant.

Federer (1971) described a leafless hardwood forest in terms of a uniformly light-absorbing crown space plus a stem space of randomly arranged vertical cylinders.

Vertical distribution of CO2 concentration

CO_2 profiles and fluxes above or within plant stands have been extensively studied in rice (Inoue, Tani, Imai & Isobe, 1958b), in wheat

(Inoue, Tani, Imai & Isobe, 1958*a*; Denmead, 1969), in sugar beet (Monteith & Szeicz, 1960), in corn (Lemon, 1960; Wright & Lemon, 1966*a,b*; Uchijima, Kobayashi & Ito, 1966; Uchijima, Udagawa, Horie & Kobayashi, 1967; Inoue *et al.*, 1968; Gillespie, 1971), in spruce forest (Baumgartner, 1969), in pine forest (Denmead, 1969) and in tropical forest (Lemon, Allen & Müller, 1970). Although short time fluctuations of CO_2 concentration are found inside a canopy (Lemon, Wright & Drake, 1969), ten- and twenty-minute averages of CO_2 concentration have usually been observed.

The shapes of the CO_2 profile are very similar. During daylight hours the profiles are characterized by a minimum concentration of CO_2 near the top or in the middle layer of the canopy. At the soil surface the CO_2 concentration is high owing to soil respiration and low diffusivity and a large concentration gradient is formed above the soil surface. The characteristic shape of the CO_2 profile indicates that the downward flux from the atmospheric CO_2 penetrates into the upper canopy down to this minimum point, and another flux originating from soil respiration and stem respiration is directed upwards. At the level of the minimum concentration, the CO_2 flux is zero, indicating no net upward or downward CO_2 transport. On a clear windless day the depression of CO_2 concentration in the middle layer of canopy is conspicuous, while on windy days and cloudy days it is not so clear. A pronounced minimum of CO_2 concentration in the profile shows that potentially high activity of photosynthesis is restricted by insufficient CO_2 supply due to low turbulence.

The height of the minimum concentration in the profile shows a clear diurnal change, which can be attributed to the change of flux density of incident solar radiation and is well simulated by a mathematical model, with the main assumption that eddy diffusivity decreases linearly with depth (Uchijima, Udagawa, Horie & Kobayashi, 1967; Uchijima & Inoue, 1970). The observations obtained at about fortnightly intervals during the growing season of the corn crop revealed that typical profiles became established with the increasing growth of the leaf area.

During the night CO_2 profiles are quite different. A rich accumulation of respiratory CO_2 establishes a continuously decreasing gradient of CO_2 concentration toward the atmosphere above the canopy, indicating that only an upward flux prevails during the night. A striking feature of night CO_2 profiles reported by Gillespie (1971) was associated with the special turbulent diffusivity profile in the canopy (Gillespie & King, 1971). Many field observations indicate that the rich accumulation of

CO_2 within the canopy during the night is associated with low wind speed (e.g., Lemon, Allen & Müller, 1970). This accumulation of CO_2 is rapidly removed with the beginning of photosynthesis in the early morning or sometimes even earlier with the increase of wind speed (Allen, Lemon & Müller, 1972).

A different CO_2 profile was observed in a tall tropical forest (Lemon, Allen & Müller, 1970), in which the stand showed an increase of CO_2 concentration in the middle layer, where there were relatively few leaves. Lemon, Allen & Müller ascribed the occurrence of this bulge to an advective effect due to a short upwind fetch. There was a corresponding increase of wind speed in the wind profiles.

Since drag is always directed against air flow, wind speed should continuously decline with depth, so far as horizontal homogeneity is warranted. If it is assumed that the three dimensional mixing lengths are constant and the drag coefficient is independent of wind speed, wind speed and eddy diffusivity can be represented by exponential functions of height (Inoue, 1963; Cionco, 1965). This condition would apply to the part of canopy with relatively uniform leaf area density. In forest windfiles, however, we find a bulge, where the wind speed gradient vanishes. Although in the Costa Rican tropical forest this effect could be attributed to a short fetch, this was not the case at other sites (Baumgartner, 1969, Denmead, 1969).

Allen (1968) found such a bulge in the wind profile for a larch plantation after the needles had fallen. He attributed it to the shorter fetch which allowed gusts to blow through the bottom, or to the occasional holes in the plantation area which allow gusts to penetrate at the bottom and spread from there through the stem zone. Millington & Peters (1969) observed an increase of eddy diffusivity beneath the main crown of a soybean canopy. They ascribed it to the space between rows which allowed considerable air movement.

Baumgartner (1969) presented a daily pattern of CO_2 distribution in a spruce forest in summer. It showed no bulge of CO_2 distribution in the daytime but the minimum concentration of CO_2 at any one time was in the lowest part of canopy. There was also a bulge of wind speed in the stem zone. He comments that parcels of air bring a higher momentum from the flow above the stand into the stem zone, and there raise the energy of air flow. Air with a lower CO_2 concentration is thus conveyed to the stem zone.

CO_2 flux within a canopy

At the immediate ground surface, CO_2 is transported upward by molecular diffusion within the boundary layer (Baumgartner, 1969). Within and under a plant canopy air flow is usually turbulent, although pseudo-laminar flow was observed at two to four metres above the ground in a larch stand (Ordway, 1969). Increasing turbulence reduces leaf-air boundary layer resistance (Kanemasu, Thurtell & Tanner, 1969). Hunt, Impens & Lemon (1968) indicated that turbulence in the field reduced the leaf–air boundary layer resistance of a large sunflower leaf much more than predicted from a laminar flow equation. The magnitude of turbulent transfer is several orders of magnitude greater than molecular diffusion even at levels deep within the crop (Wright & Lemon, 1966a; Baumgartner, 1969).

Inside a canopy there are short-term fluctuations of CO_2 content, and the amplitude of these fluctuations increased towards the ground (Lemon, Wright & Drake, 1969). Little small-scale turbulence could be detected with the CO_2 analyzer used. In the upper layers of the cornfield the amplitude was much less. As a result of cross-spectral analyses of turbulence in a mature corn crop, Isobe (1972) revealed that the characteristic components of wind in a frequency range of 0.11 to 0.18 Hz traveled upward and that the traveling speed increased with the mean wind speed in the crop. The lower part of the larch plantation was characterized by a peak in the eddy frequency of 0.05 Hz, which corresponds to a 100 m wavelength. Allen *et al.* (1972) concluded that the forest drag occurs because of low wind speed and the lack of small scale atmospheric turbulence in the forest.

When obtaining diffusivities under turbulent conditions, simultaneous transport of CO_2, water vapour, sensible heat and momentum is assumed, and the same diffusivity value is used. Denmead (1970) and Denmead & McIlroy (1971) have discussed fully the technical difficulties of obtaining correct diffusivity values. To estimate fluxes inside the canopy the energy balance method has mostly been used, though the eddy correlation method (Wright & Lemon, 1966b) and momentum balance approach (Lemon & Wright, 1969) have also been used. The experimental site of the Costa Rican tropical forest had some advective effect, but its characteristic CO_2 profile showed no variability (Allen *et al.*, 1972). With some assumptions made about the momentum balance approach, they were able to compute CO_2 fluxes in the main canopy and lower canopy separately (Lemon, Allen & Müller, 1970).

The numerical differentiation of CO_2 fluxes within a canopy provides us with a probable distribution pattern of the sink and source intensity of CO_2 within a plant canopy (Lemon, 1963; Wright & Lemon, 1966a,b; Uchijima, Kobayashi & Ito, 1966; Inoue et al., 1968; Lemon & Wright, 1969). However, the error associated with such computations might be enormous (Denmead, 1970; Lemon, 1970).

Theoretical approach to the CO_2 environment

With an assumption of constant eddy diffusivity within a canopy in the night-time, Inoue (1965) obtained a quadratic function which corresponds to the night-time profile of CO_2 concentration. Assuming that eddy diffusivity and light flux density in the daytime both decrease exponentially in relation to height within the canopy (Uchijima, 1962), Inoue derived an equation that shows CO_2 concentration to decrease exponentially in the upper part of the canopy. Next, by assuming a very low light flux density and constant diffusivity in the deep layers of canopy, as during the night, a typical daytime profile of CO_2 concentration was constructed. The profile has two characteristic points, one being the point of minimum concentration and the other the light compensation point which corresponds to the point of inflection of the profile curve. The latter point makes the profile curve convex upward at the lower layer of the canopy, as can sometimes be recognized in the field measurements (Inoue, Tani, Imai & Isobe, 1958a,b; Wright & Lemon, 1966a,b; Monteith, 1962) and in a simulated CO_2 profile without soil respiration (Uchijima & Inoue, 1970.)

The theoretical analysis of eddy diffusivity within a canopy is still in its infancy. Wind attributes in plant canopies have not been extensively analyzed in relation to foliage structure, although empirical generalization is also scanty. The Monte Carlo simulation method applied to this problem might suggest a new approach (Oikawa, 1973).

There are some simulation models dealing with CO_2 and radiation environment. For example, Uchijima & Inoue (1970) revealed the effects on the CO_2 profile of factors such as eddy diffusivity (or wind velocity) at the top of a canopy, soil CO_2 flux, leaf area density, incident radiation flux density and LAI, using a model with the assumption of linearly decreasing diffusivity within the canopy. Exponential decrease of wind and diffusivity in relation to cumulative LAI was also assumed by Goudriaan & Waggoner (1972). In order to simulate the effect of soil respiration or artificial CO_2 enrichment on the total CO_2 fixation of

313

stands, Allen, Jensen & Lemon (1971) proposed a simulation model, assuming certain aerodynamic boundary conditions above the canopy and on the soil surface.

Light and CO_2 as environmental factors

Strictly speaking, the distribution of CO_2 in plant stands tells us nothing more than itself. If eddy diffusivity is uniform and sufficiently high within a plant canopy, the CO_2 concentration in the canopy would accurately represent the actual CO_2 environment for photosynthesis. But this is not the case in real plant communities. The important CO_2 environment for photosynthesis is the potential rate of CO_2 flux on the leaf surface during the time that the leaf requires the supply of CO_2.

The leaf photosynthesis rate (p) is usually expressed as a function of PAR flux density (I) in a rectangular hyperbolic equation, $p = b\, p_{max} I / (p_{max} + bI)$, where p_{max} is the saturated rate of photosynthesis when I is large, and b the efficiency of PAR when I is close to zero. Assuming that CO_2 concentration in the photosynthetic centre in the leaf is zero when I is large, p_{max} is expressed in a simple form as follows (Gaastra, 1963): $p_{max} = C/(r_1 + r_a)$, where C is the atmospheric CO_2 concentration, r_1 the leaf resistance including stomatal, mesophyll and biochemical resistances, and r_a the sum of leaf–air boundary layer resistance and the resistance in eddy transport.

According to this equation, Oikawa (1973) suggested that p_{max} is an adequate expression of the CO_2 environment, because p_{max} is the potential CO_2 flux density when PAR is high and temperature is moderate. Although p_{max} in the above equation comprises a property of the leaf itself, environmental factors cannot be separated from leaf morphology and both function in interconnecting phases. He modified the above PAR–photosynthesis equation as follows: $p/bI + p/p_{max} = 1$. Here, bI is the potential photosynthetic rate when none of environmental factors other than I is limiting, and p_{max} is the potential photosynthesis rate (CO_2 flux density) when only CO_2 supply is limiting. Using this equation he could separate the relative limitations of PAR and the CO_2 environment quantitatively, and demonstrate graphically that the CO_2 limitation for photosynthesis is confined mostly to the upper part of leaf canopy, even under bright sunshine.

I am very grateful to Dr Uchijima, National Institute of Agricultural Sciences, Tokyo for information on some relevant literature.

References

Acock, B., Thornley, J. H. M. & Warren Wilson, J. (1970). Spatial variation of light in the canopy. In *Prediction and Measurement of Photosynthetic Productivity*, ed. I. Šetlík, pp. 91–102. Wageningen, PUDOC.

Allen, L. H. (1968). Turbulence and wind speed spectra within a Japanese larch plantation. *Journal of Applied Meteorology*, **7**, 73–8.

Allen, L. H., Jensen, S. E. & Lemon, E. R. (1971). Plant response to carbon dioxide enrichment under field conditions: A simulation. *Science*, **173**, 256–8.

Allen, L. H. & Lemon, E. R. (1972). Net radiation frequency distribution in a corn crop. *Boundary Layer Meteorology*, **3**, 246–54.

Allen, L. H., Lemon, E. R. & Müller, L. (1972). Environment of a Costa Rican forest. *Ecology*, **53**, 102–11.

Allen, W. A., Gayle, T. V. & Richardson, A. J. (1970). Plant-canopy irradiance specified by the Duntley equations. *Journal of the Optical Society of America*, **60**, 372–6.

Allen, W. A. & Richardson, A. J. (1968). Interaction of light with a plant canopy. *Journal of the Optical Society of America*, **58**, 1023–8.

Anderson, M. C. (1964). Studies of the woodland light climate. I. The photographic computation of light conditions. *Journal of Ecology*, **52**, 27–41.

Anderson, M. C. (1966). Stand structure and light interception. II. A theoretical analysis. *Journal of Applied Ecology*, **3**, 41–54.

Anderson, M. C. (1969). A comparison of two theories of scattering of radiation in crops. *Agricultural Meteorology*, **6**, 399–405.

Anderson, M. C. (1970a). Interpreting the fraction of solar radiation available in forest. *Agricultural Meteorology*, **7**, 19–28.

Anderson, M. C. (1970b). Radiation climate, crop architecture and photosynthesis. In *Prediction and Measurement of Photosynthetic Productivity*, ed. I. Šetlík, pp. 71–8. Wageningen, PUDOC.

Anderson, M. C. (1971). Radiation and crop structure. In *Plant Photosynthetic Production, Manual of Methods*, eds. Z. Šesták, J. Catský & P. G. Jarvis, pp. 412–66. The Hague, Junk.

Baumgartner, A. (1969). Meteorological approach to the exchange of CO_2 between the atmosphere and vegetation, particularly forest stands. *Photosynthetica*, **3**, 127–49.

Brown, K. W. & Covey, W. (1966). The energy-budget evaluation of the micrometeorological transfer processes within a cornfield. *Agricultural Meteorology*, **3**, 73–96.

Cionco, R. M. (1965). A mathematical model for air flow in a vegetative canopy. *Journal of Applied Meteorology*, **4**, 517–22.

Cowan, I. R. (1968). The interception and absorption of radiation in plant stands. *Journal of Applied Ecology*, **5**, 367–79.

Denmead, O. T. (1964). Evaporation sources and apparent diffusivities in a forest canopy. *Journal of Applied Meteorology*, **3**, 383–9.

Denmead, O. T. (1969). Comparative micrometeorology of a wheat field and a forest of *Pinus radiata*. *Agricultural Meteorology*, **6**, 357–71.

Denmead, O. T. (1970). Transfer processes between vegetation and air: Measurement, interpretation and modelling. In *Prediction and Measurement of Photosynthetic Productivity*, ed. I. Šetlík, pp. 149–64. Wageningen, PUDOC.

Denmead, O. T. & McIlroy, I. C. (1971). Measurement of carbon dioxide exchange in the field. In *Plant Photosynthetic Production, Manual of Methods*, eds. Z. Šesták, J. Catský & P. G. Jarvis, pp. 467–516. The Hague, Junk.

Duncan, W. G., Loomis, R. S., Williams, W. A. & Hanau, R. (1967). A model for simulating photosynthesis in plant communities. *Hilgardia*, **38**, 181–205.

Federer, C. A. (1971). Solar radiation absorption by leafless hardwood forests. *Agricultural Meteorology*, **9**, 3–20.

Federer, C. A. & Tanner, C. B. (1966). The spectral distribution of light in the forest. *Ecology*, **47**, 555–60.

Ford, E. D. & Newbould, P. J. (1971). The leaf canopy of a coppiced deciduous woodland. I. Development and structure. *Journal of Ecology*, **59**, 843–62.

Gaastra, P. (1963). Climatic control of photosynthesis and respiration. In *Environmental Control of Plant Growth*, ed. L. T. Evans, pp. 113–140. New York & London, Academic Press.

Gillespie, T. J. (1971). Carbon dioxide profiles and apparent diffusivities in corn fields at night. *Agricultural Meteorology*, **8**, 51–7.

Gillespie, T. J. & King, K. M. (1971). Night-time sink strengths and apparent diffusivities within a corn canopy. *Agricultural Meteorology*, **8**, 59–67.

Goudriaan, J. & Waggoner, P. E. (1972). Simulating both aerial microclimate and soil temperature from observations above the foliar canopy. *Netherland Journal of Agricultural Science*, **20**, 104–24.

Horie, T. & Udagawa, T. (1971). Canopy photosynthesis of sunflower plants. Its measurements and modeling. *Bulletin of National Institute of Agricultural Science (Japan)*, A **18**, 1–56.

Horn, H. S. (1971). *The Adaptive Geometry of Trees*, 144 pp. Princeton University Press.

Hunt, L. A., Impens, I. I. & Lemon, E. R. (1968). Estimates of the diffusion resistance of some large sunflower leaves in the field. *Plant Physiology*, **43**, 522–6.

Ino, Y. (1969). CO_2 fixation activity of cut leaf under intermittent illumination conditions. *JIBP/PP-Photosynthesis Level III Experiments* 1968, pp. 56–9.

Ino, Y. (1970). The effect of fluctuating light on photosynthesis. *JIBP/PP-Photosynthesis Level III Experiments* 1969, pp. 68–70.

Inoue, E. (1963). On the turbulent structure of airflow within crop canopies. *Journal of the Meteorological Society of Japan*, **41**, 317–26.

Inoue, E. (1965). On the CO_2-concentration profiles within crop canopies. *Journal of Agricultural Meteorology, Tokyo*, **20**, 137–40.

Inoue, E., Tani, N., Imai, K. & Isobe, S. (1958a). The aerodynamic measurement of photosynthesis over the wheat field. *Journal of Agricultural Meteorology, Tokyo*, **13**, 121–5.

Inoue, E., Tani, N., Imai, K. & Isobe, S. (1958*b*). The aerodynamic measurement of photosynthesis over a nursery of rice plants. *Journal of Agricultural Meteorology, Tokyo,* **14**, 45–53.

Inoue, E., Uchijima, Z., Udagawa, T., Horie, T. & Kobayashi, K. (1968). Studies of energy and gas exchange within crop canopies. (2) CO_2 flux within and above a corn plant canopy. *Journal of Agricultural Meteorology, Tokyo,* **23**, 165–76.

Isobe, S. (1969). Theory of light distribution and photosynthesis in canopies of randomly dispersed foliage area. *Bulletin of National Institute of Agricultural Science (Japan),* A **16**, 1–25.

Isobe, S. (1972). A spectral analysis of turbulence in a corn canopy. *Journal of Agricultural Meteorology, Tokyo,* **27**, 129–35.

Ito, A. (1969). Geometrical structure of rice canopy and penetration of direct solar radiation. *Proceedings of Crop Science Society of Japan,* **38**, 355–63.

Ito, K. (1971). Population photosynthesis in sugar beet plant under field conditions. *JIBP/PP-Photosynthesis Level III Experiments, 1971,* pp. 24–7.

Kanemasu, E. T., Thurtell, G. S. & Tanner, C. B. (1969). Design, calibration, and field use of a stomatal diffusion prometer. *Plant Physiology,* **44**, 881–5.

Kira, T., Shinozaki, K. & Hozumi, K. (1969). Structure of forest canopies as related to their primary productivity. *Plant and Cell Physiology,* **10**, 129–42.

Kriedemann, P. E. & Smart, R. E. (1971). Effects of irradiance, temperature, and leaf water potential on photosynthesis of vine leaves. *Photosynthetica,* **5**, 6–15.

Kriedemann, P. E., Törökfalny, E. & Smart, R. E. (1973). Natural occurrence and photosynthetic utilization of sunflecks by grapevine leaves. *Photosynthetica,* **7**, 18–27.

Kumura, A. (1968). Studies on dry matter production of soybean plant. 3. Photosynthetic rate of soybean plant population as affected by proportion of diffuse light. *Proceedings of Crop Science Society of Japan,* **37**, 570–82.

Kuroiwa, S. (1968*a*). A new calculation method for total photosynthesis of a plant community under illumination consisting of direct and diffuse light. In *Functioning of Terrestrial Ecosystem at the Primary Production Level,* ed. F. E. Eckardt, pp. 391–8. Paris, UNESCO.

Kuroiwa, S. (1968*b*). Theoretical analysis of light factor and photosynthesis in plant communities. (3) Total photosynthesis of a foliage under parallel light in comparison with that under isotropic light condition. *Journal of Agricultural Meteorology, Tokyo,* **24**, 75–90.

Kuroiwa, S. (1970). Total photosynthesis of a foliage in relation to inclination of leaves. In *Prediction and Measurement of Photosynthetic Productivity,* ed. I. Šetlík, pp. 79–89. Wageningen, PUDOC.

Kuroiwa, S. & Monsi, M. (1963*a*). Theoretical analysis of light factor and photosynthesis in plant communities. (1) Relationships between foliage

Radiant energy, CO_2 and community structure

structure and direct, diffuse and total solar radiations. *Journal of Agricultural Meteorology, Tokyo*, **18**, 143–51.

Kuroiwa, S. & Monsi, M. (1963*b*). Theoretical analysis of light factor and photosynthesis in plant communities. (2) Diurnal change of extinction coefficient and photosynthesis. *Journal of Agricultural Meteorology, Tokyo*, **19**, 15–21.

Květ, J., Svoboda, J. & Fialce, K. (1967). A simple device for measuring leaf inclinations. *Photosynthetica*, **1**, 127–8.

Laisk, A. (1965). Uso vershenstvovanny fotoplanimetr i prisposoblenie dlya opredeleniya orientatsii listev. [An improved photoplanimeter and a device for estimating leaf inclination.] In *Voprosy Radiatsionnogo Rezhima Rastitelnogo Pokrova*, pp. 102–113. Tartu, Akad. Naok Est. SSR.

Laisk, A. (1968). Statisticheskii Kharakter oslableniya rodatsii v rastitel'nom pokrove. [Statistical character of light extinction in plant communities.] In *Rezhim Solnechnoï Radiatsii v Rastitel'nom Pokrove*, pp. 81–111. Tartu, Akad. Nauk Est. SSR.

Landsberg, J. J. (1970). Discussion section 1: Structural characteristics of photosynthetic systems. In *Prediction and Measurement of Photosynthetic Productivity*, ed. I. Šetlík, pp. 143–4. Wageningen, PUDOC.

Lang, A. R. G. (1973). Leaf orientation of a cotton plant. *Agricultural Meteorology*, **11**, 37–51.

Lemon, E. R. (1960). Photosynthesis under field conditions. II. An aerodynamic method for determining the turbulent carbon dioxide exchange between the atmosphere and a corn field. *Agronomy Journal*, **52**, 697–703.

Lemon, E. R. (1963). Energy and water balance of plant communities. In *Environmental Control of Plant Growth*, ed. L. T. Evans, pp. 55–78. New York, Academic Press.

Lemon, E. R. (1970). Summary section 2. Mass and energy exchange between plant stands and environment. In *Prediction and Measurement of Photosynthetic Productivity*, ed. I. Šetlík, pp. 14–21. Wageningen, PUDOC.

Lemon, E., Allen, L. H., Jr & Müller, L. (1970). Carbon dioxide exchange of a tropical rain forest. Part II. *BioScience*, **20**, 1054–9.

Lemon, E. R. & Wright, J. L. (1969). Photosynthesis under field conditions. XA. Assessing sources and sinks of carbon dioxide in a corn (*Zea mays* L.) crop using a momentum balance approach. *Agronomy Journal*, **61**, 405–11.

Lemon, E. R., Wright, J. L. & Drake, G. M. (1969). Photosynthesisu nder field conditions. XB. Origins of short-time CO_2 fluctuations in a cornfield. *Agronomy Journal*, **61**, 411–3.

Loomis, R. S. & Williams, W. A. (1969). Productivity and the morphology of crop stands: Patterns with leaves. In *Physiological aspects of crop yield*, pp. 24–47. Madison, Wisconsin USA, American Society of Agronomy, Crop Science Society of America.

McCree, K. J. (1972). The action spectrum, absorptance and quantum yield of photosynthesis in crop plants. *Agricultural Meteorology*, **9**, 191–216.

Miller, E. E. & Norman, J. M. (1971*a*). A sunfleck theory for plant canopies. I. Length of sunlit segments along a transect. *Agronomy Journal*, **63**, 735–8.

Miller, E. E. & Norman, J. M. (1971*b*). A sunfleck theory for plant canopies II. Penumbra effect: Intensity distributions along sunfleck segments. *Agronomy Journal*, **63**, 739–43.

Millington, R. J. & Peters, D. B. (1969). Exchange (Mass transfer) coefficients in crop canopies. *Agronomy Journal*, **61**, 815–9.

Monsi, M. (1968). Mathematical models of plant communities. In *Functioning of Terrestrial Ecosystems at the Primary Production Level*, ed. F. E. Eckardt, pp. 131–49. Paris, UNESCO.

Monteith, J. L. (1962). Measurement and interpretation of carbon dioxide fluxes in the field. *Netherland Journal of Agricultural Science*, **10**, 334–46.

Monteith, J. L. (1965). Light distribution and photosynthesis in field crops. *Annals of Botany*, NS **29**, 17–37.

Monteith, J. L. (1969). Light interception and radiative exchange in crop stands. In *Physiological Aspects of Crop Yield*, pp. 89–91. Madison, Wisconsin, USA, American Society of Agronomy.

Monteith, J. L. & Szeicz, G. (1960). The carbon-dioxide flux over a field of sugar beets. *Quarterly Journal of Royal Meteorological Society*, **86**, 205–14.

Mototani, I. (1968). Horizontal distribution of light intensity in plant communities. *JIBP/P-Photosynthesis Level III Experiments, 1966–1967*, pp. 25–8.

Nichiporovich, A. A. (1961). O svoistvakh poserov rasteniikak opticheskoi sistemy. (Properties of plant crops as an optical system.) *Fysiologia Rastenii*, **8**, 536–46.

Niilisk, H. (1964). Spektral'nyï radiatsionnyï rezhim poseva kukuruzy i rasthet fotosinteticheski aktivnoï radiatsii (FAR). (Spectral radiation regime in a maize stand and calculation of photosynthetically active radiation.) *Iziv. Akad. Nauk Est. SSR. Ser. fiz-met. tech. Nauk*, **13**, 177–91.

Niilisk, H., Nilson, T. & Ross, J. (1970). Radiation in plant canopies and its measurement. In *Prediction and Measurement of Photosynthetic Productivity*, ed. I. Šetlík, pp. 14–21. Wageningen, PUDOC.

Nilson, T. (1968). Ob optimal'noï geometricheskoï strukture rastitel'nogo pokrova. (On the optimum geometrical arrangement of foliage in the plant cover.) In *Rezhim Solnechnoï Rodiatsii v Rastitel'nom Pokrove*, pp. 112–46. Tartu, Akad. Nauk Est. SSR.

Nilson, T. (1971). A theoretical analysis of gap frequency in plant stands. *Agricultural Meteorology*, **8**, 25–38.

Norman, J. M., Miller, E. E. & Tanner, C. B. (1971). Light intensity and sunfleck-size distributions in plant canopies. *Agronomy Journal*, **63**, 743–8.

Ogawa, H. (1969). Stand structure and light distribution in Ashiu beech forest. *JIBP/PT/F Report* **41**, 45–52.

Oikawa, T. (1973). ECODYPS, a simulator to examine the interrelationship

Radiant energy, CO_2 and community structure

between plant stands and environmental factors (In Japanese.) *JIBP/PP-Photosynthesis Level III Experiments 1972*, pp. 31–41.

Oikawa, T. & Saeki, T. (1972). *JIBP/PP-Photosynthesis Level III Experiments 1971*, pp. 105–16.

Ordway, D. E. (1969). An aerodynamicist's analysis of the Odum cylinder approach to net CO_2 exchange. *Photosynthetica*, **3**, 199–209.

Rabinowich, E. I. (1951). *Photosynthesis and related processes*, vol. II, part 1. New York, Wiley-Interscience.

Ross, Yu. (1972). Teoriya propuskaniya priamoï solnechnoï radiatsil v gorizontal'io neodnorodnom rastitel'nom pokrove. (A theory for penetration of direct solar radiation into the plant canopy.) In *Solnechnaya Radiatsiya i Productivnost' Rastitel'nogo Pokrova*, pp. 122–47. Tartu, Akad. Nauk Est. SSR.

Ross, Yu. & Nilson, T. (1965). Proposkanie pryamoï radiatsii solntsa sel'skokhozyaïstvennymi posevami. (Transmission of direct solar radiation in agricultural crops.). *Voprosy Radiatsionnogo Rezhima Rastitel'nogo Porkova Issled. Fiz. Atmos.* **7**, 25–64.

Ross, Yu. & Nilson, T. (1967). Radiatsionnyi rezhim rastitel'nogo pokrova gorizontal'nymi list'yami. (Radiation regime of plant communities with horizontal leaves.) In *Fitoaktivomet-richeskie Issledovanyia Rastitel'nogo Pokrova. Issled. Fiz. Atmos. Tartu*, **9**, 5–34.

Ross, Yu. & Nilson, T. (1968*a*). Matematicheskaya model' radiatsionnogo rezhima rastitel'nogo pokrova. (A mathematical model of radiation regime of the plant cover.) In *Aktinometriya i Optika Atmosfery*, pp. 263–81. Valgus, Tallin.

Ross, Yu. & Nilson, T. (1968*b*). Raschet fotosinteticheski akfivnoï radiatsii v rastitel'nom pokrove. (The calculation of photosynthetically active radiation in plant communities.) In *Rezhim Solnechnoi Radiatsii v Rastitel'nom Pokrove*, pp. 5–54. Tartu, Akad. Nauk Est. SSR.

Saeki, T. (1960). Interrelationships between leaf amount, light distribution and total photosynthesis in a plant community. *Botanical Magazine, Tokyo*, **73**, 55–63.

Shiman, L. M. (1967). Opredelenie orientatsii listev rasteny v prostranstve. (Determination of the orientation of plant leaves.) *Fysiologia Rastenii*, **14**, 381–3.

Shinozaki, K., Yoda, K., Hozumi, K. & Kira, T. (1964*a*). A quantitative analysis of plant form – the pipe model theory. I. Basic analyses. *Japanese Journal of Ecology*, **14**, 97–105.

Shinozaki, K., Yoda, K., Hozumi, K. & Kira, T. (1964*b*). A quantitative analysis of plant form – the pipe model theory. II. Further evidence of the theory and its application in forest ecology. *Japanese Journal of Ecology*, **14**, 133–9.

Shulgin, I. A. (1967), *Solnechnaya Radiatsiya i Rastenie*. (*Solar Radiation and Plants.*) 179 pp. Leningrad, Gidrometeorologicheskoe Isdatel'stvo.

Suits, G. H. (1972*a*). The calculation of the directional reflectance of a vegetative canopy. *Remote Sensing Environment*, **2**, 117–25.

Suits, G. H. (1972*b*). The cause of azimuthal variations in directional reflectance of vegetative canopies. *Remote Sensing Environment*, **2**, 175–82.

Suits, G. H. & Safir, G. R. (1972). Verification of a reflectance model for mature corn with applications to corn blight detection. *Remote Sensing Environment*, **2**, 183–92.

Tagayava, S. V. & Brandt, A. B. (1960). Study of the optical properties of leaves in relation to the angle of incidence of light. *Biofizika*, **5**, 308–17.

Tanaka, S. (1969). Estimation of sunlit leaf area in tobacco plant community by the Monte Carlo method. Estimation on direct sunlight. *JIBP/PP-Photosynthesis Level III Experiments 1968*, pp. 76–9.

Tanaka, S. (1970). Estimation of sunlit leaf area in tobacco community by the Monte Carlo method. Estimation of sky radiation. *JIBP/PP-Photosynthesis Level III Experiments 1969*, pp. 80–4.

Tanaka, T. (1972). Studies on the light-curves of carbon assimilation of rice plants. The interrelation among the light-curves, the plant type and the maximizing yield of rice. *Bulletin of the National Institute of Agricultural Sciences, Japan*, Ser. A, **19**, 1–100.

Uchijima, Z. (1962). Studies on the micro-climate within the plant communities. (1). On the turbulent transfer coefficient within plant layer. *Journal of Agricultural Meteorology, Tokyo*, **18**, 1–9.

Uchijima, Z., Kobayashi, K. & Ito, A. (1966). Preliminary report of studies on microclimate within a corn canopy. *Journal of Agricultural Meteorology, Tokyo*, **21**, 121–6.

Uchijima, Z., Udagawa, T., Horie, T. & Kobayashi, K. (1967). Studies of energy and gas exchange within crop canopies. (1). CO_2 environment in a corn plant canopy. *Journal of Agricultural Meteorology, Tokyo*, **23**, 99–108.

Uchijima, Z., Udagawa, T., Horie, T. & Kobayashi, K. (1968). Studies of energy and gas exchange within crop canopies. (4). The penetration of direct solar radiation into corn canopy and the intensity of direct radiation on the foliage surface. *Journal of Agricultural Meteorology, Tokyo*, **24**, 141–51.

Uchijima, Z. & Inoue, K. (1970). Studies of energy and gas exchange within crop canopies. (9). Simulation of CO_2 environment within a canopy. *Journal of Agricultural Meteorology, Tokyo*, **26**, 5–18.

Udagawa, T. & Uchijima, Z. (1969). Studies of energy and gas exchange within crop canopies. (5). Geometrical structure of barley canopies and the penetration of direct solar radiation into the canopy. *Proceedings Crop Science Society of Japan*, **38**, 364–75.

Warren Wilson, J. (1959). Analysis of the distribution of foliage area in grassland. In *The measurement of grassland productivity*, ed. J. D. Ivins, pp. 51–61. London, Butterworths.

Warren Wilson, J. (1960). Inclined point quadrats. *New Phytologist*, **59**, 1–8.

Warren Wilson, J. (1961). Influence of spatial arrangement of foliage area on light interception and pasture growth. *Proceedings 8th International Grassland Congress*, pp. 275–9.

Warren Wilson, J. (1965). Stand structure and light penetration. 1. Analysis by point quadrats. *Journal of Applied Ecology,* **2,** 383–90.

Warren Wilson, J. (1967). Stand structure and light penetration. III. Sunlit foliage area. *Journal of Applied Ecology,* **4,** 159–65.

de Wit, C. T. (1965). Photosynthesis of leaf canopies. *Agricultural Research Reports,* **663,** pp. 1–57, Wageningen, PUDOC.

Woolley, J. T. (1971). Reflectance and transmittance of light by leaves. *Plant Physiology,* **47,** 656–62.

Wright, J. L. & Lemon, E. R. (1966*a*). Photosynthesis under field conditions. VIII. Analysis of windspeed fluctuation data to evaluate turbulent exchange within a corn crop. *Agronomy Journal,* **58,** 255–61.

Wright, J. L. & Lemon, E. R. (1966*b*). Photosynthesis under field conditions. IX. Vertical distribution of photosynthesis within a corn crop. *Agronomy Journal,* **58,** 265–8.

Yim, Y. J., Ogawa, H. & Kira, T. (1969). Light interception by stems in plant communities. *Japanese Journal of Ecology,* **19,** 233–8.

Yocum, C. S., Allen, L. H. & Lemon, E. R. (1964). Photosynthesis under field conditions. VI. Solar radiation balance and photosynthetic efficiency. *Agronomy Journal,* **56,** 249–53.

14. The roles of nutrient cycling and radiant energy in aquatic communities

D. W. SCHINDLER & E. J. FEE

We have spent the last few years considering problems of nutrients, light, and their effects on photosynthesis and growth of freshwater phytoplankton, mainly, but not exclusively connected with studies of artificially eutrophied and natural lakes in the Experimental Lakes Area of northwestern Ontario. Our experience in working with these lakes taught us some rather bitter lessons about causal relationships. Although the more obvious and general changes occurring in a lake with an altered nutrient regime were easily perceived, the methods we were using did not allow us to unravel the complex series of underlying changes in function of the aquatic ecosystem, and we found ourselves devoting a large proportion of our time to development of methods suitable for studying the dynamics of causal factors (for example, Emerson, Broecker & Schindler, 1973; Fee, 1973a,b; Lean, 1973b; Schindler & Fee, 1973; Schindler et al., 1973).

An exhaustive survey of the literature confirmed that others, too, are having problems in interpreting and comparing data from different lakes. The reason was a very simple one; traditional limnological field methods have been observational, designed to *monitor*, rather than *predict*, changes in phytoplankton growth and production related to nutrient and light regimes. Data collected by such methods contain intolerable amounts of 'environmental noise', for example spurious correlations between environmental parameters, the random nature of cloud cover, and inaccurate or inappropriate chemical methods. Specific examples will be discussed below.

A second possibility for establishing relationships between nutrients, light and phytoplankton lay in the large body of laboratory work conducted under closely controlled conditions. Again, a number of factors made us extremely uneasy about extrapolating to field studies. A given species of algae may give entirely different responses in the laboratory and under natural conditions. Rodhe (1948) demonstrated how great this discrepancy can be for phytoplankton. Natural algal populations usually thrived at nutrient concentrations far below those

323

necessary in pure culture. Although laboratory populations of blue-green algae have demonstrated a need for high concentrations of sodium and potassium (Provasoli, 1969), species of *Lyngbya, Pseudoanabaena* and *Oscillatoria* at bloom concentrations lived quite happily as domi-nants in our artificially eutrophied Lakes 227 and 304, at concentrations of Na and K of less than 1 and 0.5 p.p.m., respectively (Schindler, Armstrong, Holmgren & Brunskill, 1971; Schindler *et al.*, 1973). Methods for resolving the analytical, physiological and genetical prob-lems which may be responsible for these differences do not yet exist, and we conclude that while valuable physiological information can frequently be obtained from laboratory studies, they do not provide a reliable quantitative basis for relating the effects of light and nutrients on mixed populations of phytoplankton under field conditions.

In what follows we shall, therefore, rely heavily upon experiments done in the Experimental Lakes Area, either under field conditions or in laboratories at lakeside, where natural populations are held for short periods. Such methods have not often been employed in studies of phytoplankton, nutrients and light.

Measuring the relationship between phytoplankton production and light

It has been known for some time that strong natural daylight inhibits phytoplankton photosynthesis, while at lower light intensities produc-tion is proportional to the total energy of visible light. Since light entering at a lake surface is attenuated approximately exponentially:

$$I_z = I_0 e^{-kz} \qquad (1)$$

the response of the photosynthetic community at any depth to a *linear* change in surface light is a *logarithmic* one. This fact has been established experimentally for homogenous water masses, and has been the basis for most previous primary production models (Talling, 1957; Vollen-weider, 1965; Fee, 1969, 1973a).

Difficulties were encountered when attempts were made to apply the above models in nature, due to the fluctuating, unpredictable nature of incident solar radiation. Fee (1969) provided a solution to this problem by measuring the photosynthetic response of natural algal communities at several light intensities in an incubator system in order to obtain instantaneous solutions for photosynthesis per unit of area (Fig. 14.1). Daily production estimates are obtained by digitizing entire daily light curves to obtain a set of instantaneous production versus depth integrals, which are themselves integrated. Agreement of results of this technique with *in situ* measurements is excellent (Fig. 14.2).

Because of the excellent agreement this incubator technique has several advantages over *in situ* measurements. Due to the random nature of cloud cover, predictability from results of the latter technique is poor i.e. results from two incubation periods will not be exactly comparable unless the solar radiation is equal in both *distribution over time* and *total*

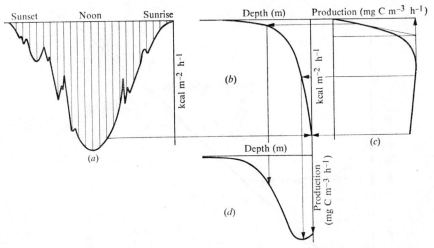

Fig. 14.1. The relationship between natural light (*a*), attenuation of irradiance in natural waters (*b*) production–light responses as obtained in an incubator (*c*), and in-situ production rate (*d*). Step-by-step procedures in the calculation are:

(1) Measure the photosynthetic response of the phytoplankton population in an incubator at several constant light intensities (represented in *c*).
(2) Measure the attenuation of vertical irradiance with depth (represented in *b*).
(3) Continuously measure the incident solar radiation at the lake surface using a pyrheliometer, followed by digitization of the entire daily light curve (*a*; horizontal lines intercepting daily light curve represent digital points).
(4) Integrate results from (*b*) and (*c*) for each digital light value on (*a*) to obtain instantaneous rates of production (*d*). Repeating the above process for all digital values from (*c*), then integrating over depth and time, give estimates of integral daily production.

The entire process is easily programmed for a digital computer. The figure is modified from Fee (1973*a*), with permission of the *Journal of the Fisheries Research Board of Canada*.

energy. Comparisons of photosynthesizing populations separated in time or space are therefore nearly impossible to make. In contrast, the constant light regime of the incubator makes comparisons possible between lakes, dates and depths. This gives powerful insight into mechanisms controlling photosynthetic systems (see below).

An added advantage is that samples can be speedily collected by aircraft or fast boats and delivered to a central station for incubation, so that synoptic data can be obtained for several lakes, or several stations in a large lake (Fee, 1971). The technique appears ideally suited for use on Great Lakes or oceanic cruises, where facilities are shared with non-biologists carrying out other programs and where returning to stations to pick up *in situ* production sets is not always possible. Moreover, with the new method, samples can be processed continuously, whereas the *in situ* method is restricted to bright daylight periods.

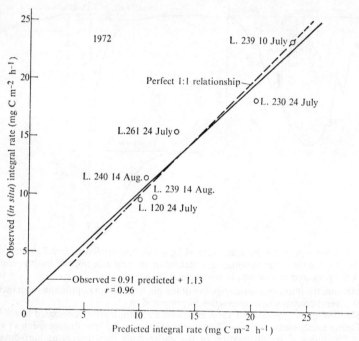

Fig. 14.2. Agreement between in-situ measurements of integral production and those predicted by Fee's incubator technique for several lakes in the Experimental Lakes Area. From Fee (1973*b*). Reprinted with permission of the *Journal of the Fisheries Research Board of Canada.*

A major shortcoming of Vollenweider's and Fee's models, as outlined in the above references, is that both depend on the assumption that phytoplankton are distributed homogenously with depth throughout the system studied. This is a severe disadvantage when studying clear, thermally stratified lakes, where considerable photosynthesis takes place below the thermocline; algal communities in the metalimnion and hypolimnion may differ greatly from those in the epilimnion. Recent work by Fee (1973*b*) has solved this problem by approaching the problem numerically instead of using complex mathematics. This work is an

326

extension of the earlier model, where the 'layers' of a complex ecosystem are treated as individual systems, applying the above techniques to all layers, then integrating the result.

For valid application of any sophisticated incubator technique, accurate measurements of photosynthetically active light are necessary, both at the surface and at several depths in the euphotic zone. Apparatus and techniques used for such measurements are often inadequate. Underwater light has typically been measured with some sort of simple irradiance meter, with or without filters. Such meters often read out in units which cannot be readily converted to photosynthetically available light, or the response of photocells include an unknown component of photosynthetically inactive wavelengths.

Surface light is typically measured with a pyrheliometer, which measures light energy for the total spectrum. A standard factor of 0.48–0.50 is usually used to convert output to photosynthetically active light.

Both underwater irradiance meters and pyrheliometers are generally too cumbersome to use for calibration of laboratory incubators, and the investigator is faced with having to interconvert data from three meters with different response to common units. The problems associated with such interconversions are discussed briefly by Tyler (1971).

The above problems have been overcome to some extent by recent developments in photocells, which measure light in quanta, and are less expensive than traditional equipment. These can be used both in and out of the water (for example Biggs *et al.*, 1972). Errors in interconversion of results can therefore be eliminated.

Little attention has been paid to the special optical problems of fresh water. It is generally recognized that a spherical (4π) collector would be best for measuring photosynthetically available light (Duntley, 1963), although in the sea, hemispherical (2π) collectors have proved to be a satisfactory substitute (Jerlov, 1968). Dissolved coloring matter and reflection of light from the bottom and from suspended particles are more important in typical freshwater systems. The special problems associated with measurement of underwater light field in fresh water need serious study in the near future, using modern instrumentation.

Limiting nutrients and phytoplankton production

Fertilization of Lake 227, in the Experimental Lakes Area, with phosphate and nitrate caused the standing crop of phytoplankton to increase

327

nearly two orders of magnitude (Schindler, Armstrong, Holmgren & Brunskill, 1971; Schindler *et al.*, 1973). In spite of this, little or no increase in primary production was found when mid-day exposures by the in-situ ^{14}C technique were compared for the first three years of fertilization. The reason for this paradox did not become apparent until studies of the diurnal variation of dissolved inorganic carbon (DIC) concentrations were made in 1972. We discovered that, although production has increased markedly due to fertilization, nearly all of the production took place during the first two to three hours of daylight each morning. After this time, DIC dropped to extremely low concentrations, severely limiting phytoplankton production (Fig. 14.3), as enrichment of ^{14}C bottles with DIC demonstrated (Fig. 14.4; see also Schindler, Lean & Fee, 1973).

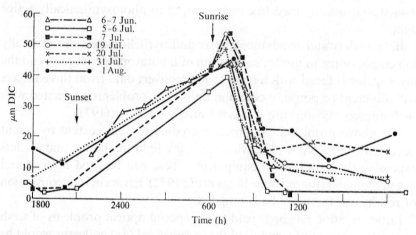

Fig. 14.3. Diurnal variation in dissolved inorganic carbon (DIC) at 0.5 m in Lake 227, summer, 1972. Note the regularity of the diurnal curves throughout the two months shown, even though both clear and cloudy days were included.

Phosphorus and carbon affected Lake 227 phytoplankton in quite different ways. The standing crop of algae appeared to be roughly a function of the amount of phosphorus added, as one would expect from the predictions of Vollenweider (1968) and Sakamoto (1966). Carbon governed the *rate* at which the phosphorus-determined standing crop was reached, since when sufficient carbon was present algal populations were able to photosynthesize at high rates for most of the daylight period, instead of only for a few hours in the morning (Schindler & Fee, 1973). The distinction between rate-limiting and standing crop-limiting

328

factors has been suggested by O'Brien (1972) although he used slightly different terminology. The distinction between these types of factors will not be apparent when low growth rates are combined with a high rate of depletion – for example in an oligotrophic lake with a fast water renewal time.

Other errors in production calculations occur when DIC concentrations are low. In Lake 227, net production at mid-day is limited nearly entirely by the amount of CO_2 supplied by invasion from the atmosphere As a result, bottle techniques, which allow no invasion, severely underestimate production in such lakes (Schindler & Fee, 1973).

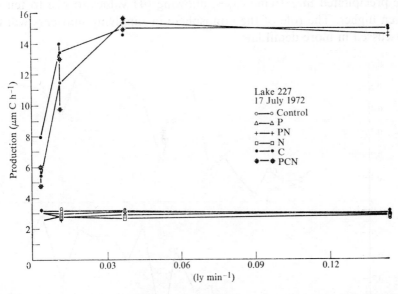

Fig. 14.4. Results of nutrient enrichment experiments with Lake 227 samples taken at mid-day in midsummer. Only carbon caused a stimulation of production (from Schindler & Fee, 1973). Reprinted by permission of the *Journal of the Fisheries Research Board of Canada*.

Undersaturation with gaseous CO_2 is characteristic of the epilimnions of productive lakes which receive large amounts of other nutrients (Schindler & Fee, 1973; Schindler & Comita, 1972; Jonasson & Mathiesen, 1959). In lakes of low alkalinity, such as Lake 227, hydroxide, silicic acids, humic acids and other titratable anions or even suspended clays, all of which are usually considered to be of minor chemical significance, form a major component of the total alkalinity. For example, in Lake 227, nearly 50% of the total alkalinity is furnished by

329

M

the hydroxyl ion as the pH approaches 10 and hydroxylation is probably the predominant reaction affecting invading CO_2:

$$CO_2 + OH^- \gtreqless HCO_3^-$$

Due to the rapidity of this equilibrium (Kern, 1960), partial pressure of CO_2 in the water is kept low, and the resulting invasion from the atmosphere is far higher than one would expect for chemically unreactive gases (Schindler *et al.*, 1972; Emerson, Broecker & Schindler, 1973).

On the other hand, in lakes with higher bicarbonate concentrations, $CaCO_3$ may precipitate, controlling pH values so that OH^- does not dominate the total alkalinity. Even in alkaline lakes, all the $CaCO_3$ may be precipitated in extreme cases, allowing pH values to rise to ten or even higher. The role of the atmosphere in supplying nutrients will be discussed in more detail later.

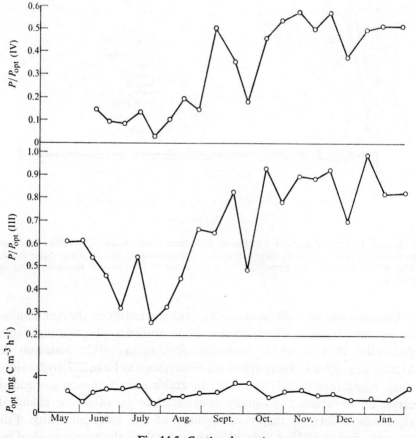

Fig. 14.5. *Continued opposite.*

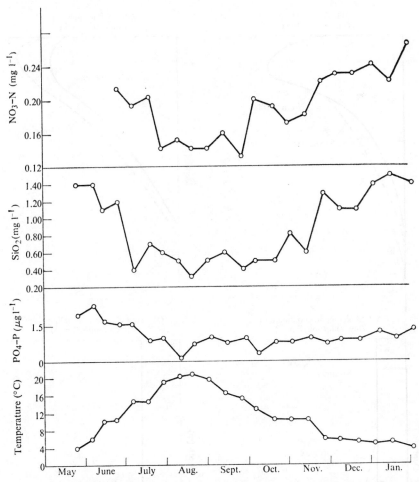

Fig. 14.5. Seasonal data for concentrations of several nutrients, temperature, P_{opt}, and P/P_{opt} in tanks III and IV (low light) for Lake Michigan.

Combined effects of light and nutrients

Because the extinction of light in water is exponential, and attenuation of inhibitory ultraviolet radiation with depth is rapid, most phytoplankton production occurs at suboptimal light levels. Algal communities may respond to a decreased supply of a limiting nutrient by either decreasing the maximum rate of production, or producing less efficiently at suboptimal irradiances. Although almost all emphasis in production studies has been placed on the former mechanism, in our work the latter has also proved to be important.

331

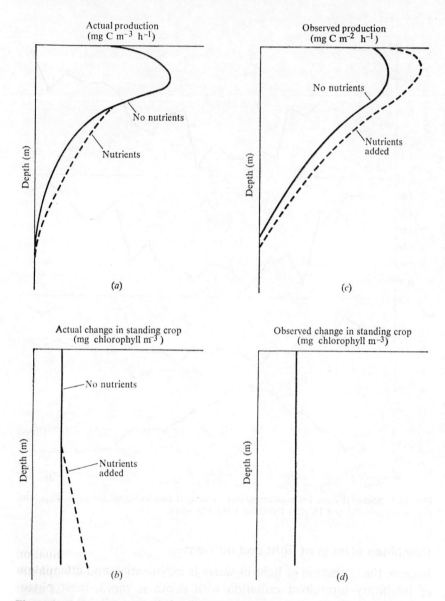

Fig. 14.6. The hypothesized interaction between photosynthesis and nutrient concentration in the Experimental Lakes Area as suggested by incubator results. (*a*) Nutrients actually stimulate production only at suboptimal light intensities. (*b*) If the euphotic zone were not freely circulating, one would expect to see an increase in standing crop at suboptimal light intensities. (*c*) and (*d*). In a well-mixed euphotic zone, the above features will not be detectable by ordinary in-situ techniques run on successive days. Phytoplankton produced at all depths are mixed together, so what is observed is an increase in production and standing crop throughout the euphotic zone.

In Lake Michigan, production at optimum light for a given station and time did not increase in response to increased concentrations of nutrients. Instead, P_{opt} remained relatively constant, while production at suboptimal light intensities (P) was enhanced (Fee, 1971). This is most easily seen when the ratio of submaximal to maximum production P/P_{opt}, as obtained in the incubator, is compared to nutrient concentrations (Fig. 14.5). The net result would be to increase production per unit area.

The above data may at first appear confusing, since the fact that P_{opt} is higher in lakes rich in nutrients is well known. It is, in fact, shown by Fee's own (1971) data. It is possible that such nutrient-induced changes in P_{opt} are a secondary effect, observed because increased production at suboptimal light (i.e. greater depths) increases the population at all light levels within a homogenous, freely circulating system such as the epilimnion of a lake (Fig. 14.6).

In contrast, Gächter (1972) and recent work at the Environmental Lakes Area (Fee, unpublished results) found that the major response of phytoplankton to nutrient addition is an increase in P_{opt}. Further investigation is required to explain such differences.

Relationships between inorganic nutrients and phytoplankton production

We believe there is reason to suspect that chemical *concentrations* may provide an imperfect means of assessing the importance of nutrients as stimuli for primary production. Brylinski & Mann (1973) found that latitude provided much more predictive information about the productivity of lakes than nutrient concentrations. Even in our example shown in Fig. 14.6, where variation in production due to fluctuating incident light has been eliminated by use of the light incubator, correlations between production and nutrient concentration are barely of statistical significance. On the other hand, Schindler & Fee (1974) found a good correlation between annual phytoplankton production and annual phosphorus input. They summarized some data suggesting that nutrient input might be inversely correlated with latitude. There are logical reasons for this. Grazing by zooplankton, water renewal via outflow and groundwater, sedimentation and concentrations of other nutrients may affect the velocity with which phosphorus is assimilated by plankton, recycled, or removed from the lake. It seems more logical to expect a good correlation between primary production and phosphorus input,

333

which are both rates, than between nutrient concentration and primary production.

A further complication exists in the measurement of concentrations of inorganic nutrients. For example, the popular molybdate method appears to overestimate phosphate in some natural waters. The exact amount of the discrepancy is unpredictable, with overestimates ranging from 10 to 500 times in oligotrophic lakes, while in more eutrophic lakes results appear to be roughly of the right order of magnitude (Rigler, 1966,1968; Schindler, unpublished data). Little work of the above sort has been done on other common phytoplankton nutrients.

A common practice is to calculate the demand of phytoplankton for nutrients by stoichiometry, i.e. by assuming that demands of algae for nutrients are in proportion to the relative concentrations of the nutrients in the algal cell (Hutchinson, 1957; Redfield, Ketchum & Richards, 1963; Stumm & Morgan, 1962). Such calculations applied to the production of algal blooms in lakes have caused great confusion. For example, Kuentzel (1969) used such logic to 'prove' that a supply of organic carbon was necessary to produce an algal bloom on Lake Sebasticook, Maine.

We do not believe that such calculations are valid. The proportions of nutrients in supply pools are not necessarily the ideal proportions in phytoplankton. In a series of radiotracer experiments in Lake 227, Lean & Schindler (unpublished data) found that an average phosphorus atom was recycled 1500 times between entering the lake and sedimenting with phytoplankton from the epilimnion, even though phosphate was being added at 10 μg P l^{-1} wk^{-1}. An average carbon atom was cycled only thirty times in its path through the epilimnion, in spite of the fact that no artificial additions of carbon were made. Yet the stoichiometric ratio of C to P in seston remained at about 120:1 by weight, and rates of sedimentation of both elements from the epilimnion, as a per cent of seston standing crop, were similar.

It is apparent that we are still far from having an intelligible picture of nutrient–phytoplankton interactions in lakes.

Input and output of nutrients from lakes

Other valid means of studying the effect of nutrients on aquatic systems have been developed and refined in the past few years. One of these, the measurement of nutrient input and output was first attempted by Mortimer (1939). Vollenweider (1968) amassed enough of such data to demonstrate that there was a general relationship between nutrient input and several indices of the productivity of aquatic systems. In a later paper (Vollenweider, 1969), he developed a preliminary model for the eutrophying effects of increased nutrient inputs, as well as for outflow and sedimentation. The compilation of a large body of nutrient input and output rates and phytoplankton standing crop and production data could provide a valuable basis for limnological predictions. Great care must be taken, however, to ensure that estimates of nutrient input are accurate. Because most drainage basins lie in geologically and culturally complicated basins, input measurements will prove to be of questionable accuracy, unless considerable funding and a variety of expertise can be applied to a lake. For example, a high proportion of nutrient input may enter some lakes via the flow of ground water (Lee, 1973) which is difficult and expensive to measure even in the simplest of systems. In other cases, atmospheric gases may contribute a considerable proportion of annual input (Schindler *et al.*, 1972,1973; Emerson, Broecker & Schindler, 1973).

The contribution of atmospheric gases to nutrient input budgets has been often neglected. Many studies (reviewed by Brezonik, 1972 and Horne & Goldman, 1972) have shown that fixation of atmospheric nitrogen can be a major portion of annual input for that element. As mentioned above, Lake 227 and other lakes developed an enormous deficit of CO_2 in midsummer, due chiefly to removal of dissolved inorganic carbon by photosynthesizing phytoplankton. Atmospheric invasion of CO_2 was sufficient to support massive blooms of phytoplankton. The atmosphere represents an almost uncontrollable source of nutrients, and the factors controlling such sources deserve serious study.

Utilization of organic substrates by phytoplankton

Much of the organic carbon and phosphorus in natural lake water is bound to large, colloid-size molecules (molecular weight 10^6-10^7; Lean, 1973*b*; Lean & Schindler, unpublished data). This 'pool' of large molecules is relatively constant in size throughout the year, and turns over very slowly, in both hard and soft waters (Wetzel, Rich, Miller & Allen, 1972; Schindler *et al.*, 1973). Uptake of carbon or phosphorus from this pool by phytoplankton is negligible (Lean & Schindler, unpublished data), although there are circumstances where orthophosphate is released from the pool at low rates by interaction between colloids and small molecular weight phosphorylated algal excretory products (Lean, 1973*b*).

335

Small molecular weight organic compounds are an entirely different matter. Usually these are algal excretory products of some sort. Concentrations are usually low, and turnover is extremely rapid, due in large part to microbial activity (Lean, 1973a; Wetzel, Rich, Miller & Allen, 1972).

Interpreting applied production problems in terms of nutrients and radiant energy

The lack of understanding of critical mechanisms in the nutrient–light–phytoplankton interaction has forced us to treat such problems as production of fishes in ponds or eutrophication as 'black boxes', i.e. we know that certain manipulations cause a desirable effect without really knowing why. While in some cases simple but effective management models have been constructed from such knowledge (Patalas & Zawisza, 1966), in order to precisely control the type and quantity of production we must, eliminate 'witchcraft' aspects of such problems. Much experimental research should therefore be devoted to such problems in the near future.

One poorly understood concept is the relationship between nutrient inflow and outflow to lakes, sedimentation, sedimentary return, and recycling within the water column. The relative importance of these events must be clearly understood by aquatic managers.

With respect to nutrient replacement via input and output, which depend to a large degree on the rate of water renewal, a body of fresh water may have replacement time ranging from instantaneous for fast-flowing rivers to thousands of years for lakes in arid regions. A survey of the literature, however, reveals that most of the lakes and ponds of concern have water renewal times and thus nutrient turnover time via outflow from several months to several decades.

In contrast, sedimentation of nutrients is relatively constant for most lakes, ranging from 1 to 3% of seston per day, when annual values are averaged (Gächter, 1968; Johnson, 1969; Vollenweider, 1969; Schindler *et al.*, 1973). Since seston usually contains from 50 to 95% of *total* nutrient concentration in the epilimnion of a lake, nutrient turnover times via sedimentation would usually be from 30 to 200 days. In many cases, sedimentation is therefore more important than outflow in altering nutrient concentrations in lakes. Yet sedimentation data are seldom collected in lake studies. Even less abundant are data on nutrient return from sediments. Seasonal data for rates of sediment return for

336

whole lakes are all but totally lacking in the limnological literature. In the studies which have been carried out, annual return of nutrients from sediments has proven negligible when compared to sedimentation (Burns & Ross, 1972; Megard, 1970; Schindler *et al.*, 1973).

As mentioned above, little information is available on recycling of nutrients within the water column of a lake. The works on phosphorus turnover discussed above suggest that this internal 'recycling' turnover is typically at least an order of magnitude more important than return from sediment as a nutrient source for phytoplankton. Excretion by phytoplankton and bacteria and grazing by zooplankton all appear to be important recycling mechanisms (Lean, 1973*a,b*; Peters, 1972; Peters & Lean, 1973; Haney, 1970). Recycling times for other nutrients may also be extremely fast in some circumstances. Schindler, Lean & Fee (1973) calculated that turnover times for CO_2 gas in Lake 227 in mid-summer was only a few seconds.

Two facts appear to be emerging from what data do exist. Regardless of other factors, phytoplankton production, degree of eutrophication, or yield of fishes, appear to be closely related to *input* of nutrients (Vollenweider, 1968; Winberg & Lyaknovich, 1965; Schindler & Fee, 1974). When inputs of critical nutrients such as phosphorus and nitrogen are increased, the affected water body responds very quickly by increasing algal production.

The effects of nutrient input, and also the recovery of a lake when nutrient inputs are reduced, appears to be related to the rate of *sedimentation*. In most cases, 75–99 % of incoming phosphorus or nitrogen leaves the lake by sedimentation. In reservoirs and lakes with extremely fast water renewal times, flushing via the outflow also will be of considerable importance in removal of nutrients from a lake (Uhlmann, 1972; Dillon, 1974).

Modelling of relationships between phytoplankton, nutrients and light

Dynamic modelling of aquatic systems, employing either multivariate or engineering (systems analysis) techniques, has recently become very popular. Elegant and successful models have been used to predict the dynamics of phytoplankton in chemostats and similar simple systems (for example, Williams, 1971). Attempts to use such methods on complex natural ecosystems have, however, met with very limited success. The few authors daring enough to attempt to verify such models have found

M*

that predictive powers were generally poor. For example, Schindler & Comita (1972) found poor agreement between observed phytoplankton production and that predicted by a multiple regression equation with regression coefficients based upon chemical, physical, and production measurements from another year.

One of the major shortcomings of the above techniques is that the mathematics is designed for steady-state systems, i.e. *coefficients* relating causal variables and production are *constants* (see, for example, Davidson & Clymer, 1966; Parker, 1968). While this is fine for a chemostat, to assume constant relationships between causal variables and phytoplankton responses in nature is not biologically realistic. Observational studies and laboratory batch cultures have shown that there are seasonal, spatial, species-specific and age-related factors affecting the response of phytoplankton to light and nutrients, as well as other factors. The net result of incorporating all of this variation, even if it could be measured, would undoubtedly be mathematical chaos.

Some of the constant coefficients commonly incorporated in models have no biological validity, even at steady state. For example, both Davidson & Clymer (1966) and Parker (1968) assumed that production is linearly related to light. The invalidity of this assumption will be obvious to those who have read the earlier part of this paper. Such models will be of use only if developed simultaneously with careful experimental work.

The Fee incubator technique measuring light–phytoplankton interactions is a modelling technique, in the broad sense. There are important differences from the type of models mentioned above.

First, the model can be verified. Results are repeatable, and good agreement is found between observations and predicted results.

Second, the technique requires only short-term steady-state conditions, since measurements last only a few hours.

Third, because the technique relies on frequent observations of the phytoplankton–light interaction, assumptions about constancy of relationships need not be made.

In comparison to the whole-ecosystem models mentioned above, this incubator technique appears naively simple. It deals with only a small portion of a total ecosystem. We conclude that a realistic model of phytoplankton–nutrient–light systems must be built up from such simple beginnings, with careful examination of the logical basis for the model each time an additional component is added.

Implications for the management of natural waters

Because of our poor knowledge of the phytoplankton–nutrient–light system, we are often tempted to construct management schemes based upon incomplete data in spite of great expense or potentially harmful environmental consequences. One such scheme proposed in the US is to remove all important nutrients from municipal effluents (Bueltman, 1969; Duthie, 1972). In studies of Lake 227, we have shown that it would be useless to remove carbon from effluents entering a lake, since any carbon needed to balance elemental input to phytoplankton can be drawn from the atmosphere (Schindler *et al.*, 1972,1973). Preliminary evidence from a number of studies (reviewed by Horne & Goldman, 1972; also Brezonik, 1972) indicates that N_2 fixation can contribute substantial amounts to the N input to lakes. Values reviewed range as high as 70% of total input, with values of 30–40% common.

Well-designed research on the roles of atmospheric reservoirs of nitrogen and carbon in lake nutrient cycles is critically needed. Should attempts to control phytoplankton by removal of carbon and nitrogen from effluents prove as futile as the above preliminary studies suggest, enormous amounts of time and money which could be devoted to other aspects of environmental control would be totally wasted. There is a rapidly growing body of evidence that control of phosphorus alone is sufficient to halt or even reverse the course of eutrophication in many cases (Edmondson, 1972; Mathiesen, 1971; Michalski & Conroy, 1973; Schindler, 1974; Schindler & Fee, 1974).

The role of aquatic science today can perhaps be likened to that of medicine in the seventeenth century. Based upon the then relatively complete science of comparative anatomy, the purposes of most of the body's major organs were precisely known, yet next to nothing was known about *why* the body functioned.

The solution to medical problems lay in the modern physiological approach to medicine, where a few compounds were found to exert fundamental chemical control over the functions of cells and organs of many sorts, greatly simplifying the understanding of the body. Examples are acetylcholine, adenosine triphosphate, nucleic acids and antigens. Progress was swift once these major changes in medical philosophy were made.

It appears that some equivalent drastic revision in approach to understanding the aquatic ecosystem may be necessary if solutions to a variety of environmental problems are to be obtained with confidence.

Radiant energy, CO_2 *and community structure*

Drs J. R. Vallentyne, K. Patalas, G. J. Brunskill and J. F. Talling provided helpful reviews of the manuscript. J. Shearer and V. E. Frost did much of the data analysis and figure construction.

References

Biggs, W. W., Edison, A. R., Eastin, J. D., Brown, K. W., Maranville, J. W. & Clegg, M. D. (1972). Photosynthesis light sensor and meter. *Ecology*, **52**, 125–31.

Brezonik, P. L. (1972). Nitrogen: Sources and transformations in natural waters. In *Nutrients in Natural Waters*, eds. H. E. Allen & J. R. K. Kramer, 50 pp. New York, John Wiley.

Brylinski, M. & Mann, K. H. (1973). An analysis of factors governing productivity in lakes and reservoirs. *Limnology and Oceanography*, **18**, 1–14.

Bueltman, C. G. (1969). Statement. In *Phosphates in Detergents and the Eutrophication of American Waters*, pp. 66–7. Washington D.C., United States Government Printing office, Superintendent of Documents.

Burns, N. M. & Ross, C. (1972). Oxygen–nutrient relationships within the central basin of Lake Erie. In *Project Hypo: An Intensive Study of the Lake Erie Central Basin Hypolimnion and Related Surface Water Phenomena*. Paper no. **6**, pp. 85–119. Ontario, Canada Centre for Inland Waters.

Davidson, R. S. & Clymer, A. B. (1966). The desirability and applicability of simulating ecosystems. *Annals, New York Academy of Science*, **128**, 790–4.

Dillon, P. J. (1974). The prediction of phosphorus and chlorophyll concentrations in lakes, 269 pp. Ph.D. Thesis, University of Toronto.

Duntley, S. Q. (1963). Light in the sea. *Journal of the Optical Society of America*, **53**, 214–33.

Duthie, J. R. (1972). Detergent developments and their impact on water quality. In *Nutrients in Natural Waters*, eds. H. E. Allen & J. R. Kramer, pp. 333–52. New York, John Wiley.

Edmondson, W. T. (1972). The present condition of Lake Washington. *Verhandlungen der Internationalen Vereinigung für theoretische und angewandte Limnologie*, **18**, 284–91.

Emerson, S., Broecker, W. & Schindler, D. W. (1973). Gas-exchange rates in a small lake as determined by the radon method. *Journal of the Fisheries Research Board of Canada*, **30**, 1475–84.

Fee, E. J. (1969). A numerical model for the estimation of photosynthetic production, integrated over time and depth, in natural waters. *Limnology and Oceanography*, **14**, 906–11.

Fee, E. J. (1971). A numerical model for the estimation of integral primary production and its application to Lake Michigan, 169 pp. Ph.D. Thesis, University of Wisconsin, Milwaukee.

Fee, E. J. (1973a). A numerical model for determining integral primary production and its application to Lake Michigan. *Journal of the Fisheries Board of Canada*, **30**, 1447–68.

Fee, E. J. (1973*b*). Modeling primary production in water bodies: a numerical approach that allows vertical inhomogeneities. *Journal of the Fisheries Research Board of Canada*, **30**, 1469–73.

Gächter, R. (1968). Phosphorhaushalt und planktische Primarproduktion im Vierwaldstättersee (Horwer Bucht). *Schweizerische Zeitschrift für Hydrologie*, **30**, 1–66.

Gächter, T. (1972). Die Bestimmung der Tagesraten der planktischen Primärproduktion. Modelle und in-situ Messungen. *Schweizerische Zeitschrift für Hydrologie*, **34**, 211–44.

Haney, J. F. (1970). Seasonal and spatial changes in the grazing rate of limnetic zooplankton, 117 pp. Ph.D. Thesis, University of Toronto.

Horne, A. J. & Goldman, C. R. (1972). Nitrogen fixation in Clear Lake, California. I. Seasonal variation and the role of heterocysts. *Limnology and Oceanography*, **17**, 678–92.

Hutchinson, G. E. (1957). *A Treatise on Limnology*, Vol. 1, *Geography Physics and Chemistry*, 1015 pp. New York, John Wiley.

Jerlov, N. G. (1968). *Optical Oceanography*, 194 pp. New York, Elsevier Publishing Co.

Johnson, M. (1969). Structure and production in benthic macroinvertebrate communities of Lake Ontario. Ph.D. Thesis, University of Toronto.

Jonasson, P. M. & Mathiesen, H. (1959). Measurements of primary production in two Danish eutrophic lakes, Esrom Sø and Furesø. *Oikos*, **10**, 137–67.

Kern, D. M. (1960). The hydration of CO_2. *Journal of Chemical Education*, **37**, 1–14.

Kuentzel, L. E. (1969). Bacteria, carbon dioxide, and algal blooms. *Journal of the Water Pollution Control Federation*, **41**, 1737–47.

Lean, D. R. S. (1973*a*). Phosphorus dynamics in lake water. *Science*, **179**, 678–80.

Lean, D. R. S. (1973*b*). Movements of phosphorus between its biologically important forms in lake water. *Journal of the Fisheries Research Board of Canada*, **30**, 1525–36.

Lee, G. F. (1973). The role of phosphorus in eutrophication and diffuse source control. *Water Research* **7**, 111–28.

Mathiesen, H. (1971). Summer maxima of algae and eutrophication. *Mitteilung der Internationalen Vereinigung für theoretische und angewandte Limnologie*, **19**, 161–81.

Megard, R. O. (1970). Lake Minnetonka: Nutrients, nutrient abatement, and the photosynthetic system of the phytoplankton. *Interim report no. 7, Limnological Research Center, University of Minnesota, Minneapolis*, 210 pp.

Michalski, M. F. P. & Conroy, N. (1973). The 'Oligotrophication' of Little Otter Lake, Parry Sound District. *Proceedings 16th Conference Great Lakes Research*, pp. 934–48.

Mortimer, C. H. (1939). The nitrogen balance of large quantities of water. *British Waterworks Association, Official Circular*, **21**, 154–62.

O'Brien, W. J. (1972). Limiting factors in phytoplankton algae. Their meaning and measurement. *Science*, **178**, 616–17.

Radiant energy, CO_2 and community structure

Parker, R. A. (1968). Simulation of an aquatic ecosystem. *Biometrics*, **24**, 803–21.

Patalas, K. & Zawisca, J. (1966). Limnological research in the fishery management of lakes in Poland. *Verhandlungen, Internationale Vereinigung für theoretische und angewandte Limnologie*, **18**, 1161–71.

Peters, R. H. (1972). Phosphorus regeneration by zooplankton, 205 pp. Ph.D. Thesis, University of Toronto.

Peters, R. H. & Lean, D. R. S. (1973). The characterization of soluble phosphorus released by limnetic zooplankton. *Limnology and Oceanography*, **18**, 270–9.

Provasoli, L. (1969). Algal nutrition and eutrophication. In *Eutrophication: Causes, Consequences, Correctives*, pp. 574–93. Washington D.C., National Academy of Sciences.

Redfield, A. C., Ketchum, B. H. & Richards, F. A. (1963). The influence of organisms on the composition of sea-water. In *The Sea*, ed. M. N. Hill, vol. **2**, pp. 26–77. New York, John Wiley.

Rigler, F. H. (1966). Radiobiological analysis of inorganic phosphorus in lakewater. *Verhandlungen, Internationale Vereiningung für Theoretische und Angewandte Limnologie*, **16**, 465–70.

Rigler, F. N. (1968). Further observations inconsistent with the hypothesis that the molybdenum blue method measures orthophosphate in lake water. *Limnology and Oceanography*, **13**, 7–13.

Rodhe, W. (1948). Environmental requirements of freshwater plankton algae. Experimental studies in the ecology of phytoplankton. *Symbolae botanicae opsalienses*, **10**, 1–149.

Sakamoto, M. (1966). The chlorophyll amount in the euphotic zone in some Japanese lakes and its significance in the photosynthetic production of phytoplankton community. *Botanical Magazine, Tokyo*, **79**, 77–88.

Schindler, D. W. (1974). Eutrophication and recovery in experimental lakes: Some implications for lake management. *Science*, **184**, 897–99.

Schindler, D. W., Armstrong, F. A. J., Holmgren, S. K. & Brunskill, G. J. (1971). Eutrophication of Lake 227, Experimental Lakes Area, Northwestern Ontario, by addition of phosphate and nitrate. *Journal of the Fisheries Research Board of Canada*, **28**, 1763–82.

Schindler, D. W., Brunskill, G. J., Emerson, S., Broecker, W. S. & Peng, T. H. (1972). Atmospheric carbon dioxide: Its role in maintaining phytoplankton standing crops. *Science*, **177**, 1192–4.

Schindler, D. W. & Comita, G. W. (1972). The dependence of primary production upon physical and chemical factors in a small, senescing lake, including the effects of complete winter oxygen depletion. *Archiv für Hydrobiologie*, **69**, 413–51.

Schindler, D. W. & Fee, E. J. (1973). Diurnal variation of dissolved inorganic carbon and its use in estimating primary production of CO_2 invasion in lake 227. *Journal of the Fisheries Research Board of Canada*, **30**, 1501–10.

Schindler, D. W. & Fee, E. J. (1974). Primary production in freshwater. *Proceedings 1st. International Congress of Ecology, The Hague, Sept. 1974*, pp. 155–8. Wageningen, PUDOC.

Schindler, D. W., Kling, H., Schmidt, R. V., Prokopowich, J., Frost, V. E. & Reid, R. A. (1973). Eutrophication of Lake 227. Experimental Lakes Area Northwestern Ontario, by addition of phosphate and nitrate. *Journal of the Fisheries Research Board of Canada*, **30**, 1415–45.

Schindler, D. W., Lean, D. R. S. & Fee, E. J. (1973). Nutrient cycling in freshwater ecosystems. *Proceedings, IBP Symposium on Productivity of World Ecosystems, Seattle, Washington, Sept. 1972*, ed. J. Franklin, in press.

Stumm, W. & Morgan, J. J. (1962). Stream pollution by algal nutrients. *Transactions, 12th Annual Conference on Sanitary Engineering*, University of Kansas, Lawrence, Kansas.

Talling, J. F. (1957). The phytoplankton population as a compound photosynthetic system. *New Phytologist*, **56**, 133–49.

Tyler, J. E. (1971). Marine ecology, Vol. 1. Environmental factors, part 1 (book review). *Limnology and Oceanography*, **16**, 841–2.

Uhlmann, D. (1972). Das Staugewässer als offenes System und als Reaktor. *Verhandlungen, Internationale Vereinigung für Theoretische und Angewandte Limnologie*, **18**, 781–6.

Vollenweider, R. A. (1965). Calculation models of photosynthesis-depth curves and some implications regarding day rate estimates in primary production measurements. *Memorie Instituto Dell'Italiano di Idrobiologia*, **18**, (suppl), 425–57. Also in *Primary Production in Aquatic Environments*, ed. C. Goldman, 464 pp. Berkeley, University of California Press.

Vollenweider, R. A. (1968). Scientific fundamentals of the eutrophication of lakes and flowing waters, with particular reference to nitrogen and phosphorus as factors in eutrophication. *Organization for Economic Cooperation and Development*, DAS/CSI/68, 27. 159 pp. + 34 figures + bibliography.

Vollenweider, R. A. (1969). Möglichkeiten und Grenzen elementarer Modelle der Stoffbilanz von Seen. *Archiv für Hydrobiologie*, **66**, 136.

Wetzel, R. G., Rich, P. H., Miller, M. C. & Allen, H. L. (1972). Metabolism of dissolved and particulate detrital carbon in a temperate hard-water lake. *Memorie, Dell'Istituto Italiano di Idrobiologia* 29 Suppl., in press.

Williams, F. M. (1971). Dynamics of microbial populations. In *Systems Analysis and Simulation in Ecology*, ed. B. C. Patten, vol. 1, pp. 198–267. New York, Academic Press.

Winberg, G. G. & Lyaknovich, V. P. (1965). Udobrenie prudov (*Fertilization of fishponds*). Moscow: Izdatel'stovo "Pishchevaya Promyshlennost". 271 pp. Fisheries Research Board of Canada Translation no. 1339 (1969) 482 pp.

15. Solar radiation and carbon dioxide in plant communities – conclusions

MARGARET C. ANDERSON

Life is thermodynamically unstable; to maintain it requires energy. The ultimate input for this energy in natural biological systems comes from the photosynthesis of carbon dioxide by plants, with the transformation of the kinetic energy of the sun. From the global scale to the microscopic, solar energy and carbon dioxide are closely coupled, through both biological and physical processes. These links are generally highly non-linear.

Solar energy transformations both in meteorological processes and in photosynthesis include a complex of variables which cannot readily be subsumed under a single figure. Simple descriptions of the relations between the two are therefore even more hard to find and can mislead the inexperienced. Frequently, refuge is taken in multiple regression or correlation between environmental factors and plant growth. These can describe a pre-existing situation, but only predict over the range of conditions already encountered. Above all, such relations do not explain.

When describing solar radiation available for photosynthesis, a single total over a period is often given. Particularly under natural light fields, this single figure can hide much potential physiological variation (Talling, 1971). First, the radiant flux can change with time, with changing solar altitude and the passage of clouds. Second, spectral composition may alter. It is fortunate that, under most conditions, the proportion of photosynthetically active radiation (PAR) does not alter greatly. However, despite repeated warnings (e.g. Gaastra, 1968), far too many experimenters, in both field and laboratory, still do not take account of the effects of different spectral composition, under canopy or from artificial sources, on the calibration of sensors (Federer & Tanner, 1966; McPherson, 1969). At the same time, particularly in the field, there are limitations in the time response of instruments measuring CO_2, as discussed in various chapters of the IBP Manual on photosynthetic production (Šesták, Čatský & Jarvis, 1971). We may thus be losing potential physiological and micrometeorological information.

At present, the global atmospheric concentration of CO_2 is increasing steadily (e.g. Machta, 1972; Sawyer, 1972). This could have considerable effects on climate, generally predicted to be warming through a 'greenhouse' effect. But Pearman & Garratt (1972) have already pointed out that the warming effect may be confounded by changes in albedo, atmospheric humidity and increasing turbidity of the atmosphere from dust and aerosols. Also, the oceans are a major reservoir of CO_2. We still know relatively little about the dynamics of physical and biological exchanges between oceans and atmosphere, or of the effects of upwelling of deep waters.

The increase of atmospheric CO_2 is normally attributed to man's increasing consumption of fossil fuels. Johnson (1970) estimated that burning fossil fuel released about 1.5×10^{16} g CO_2 yr^{-1}, about one-seventh of the CO_2 entering the photosynthetic cycle each year. This fossil fuel is the unoxidised remnant of previous photosynthetic activity. The gradual accumulation of photosynthetically produced oxygen in the atmosphere has occurred since Cambrian times (Berkner & Marshall, 1964). Estimates suggest that only about one part in 10^4 of photosynthetic products escape oxidation. Pearman & Garratt (1972) provide speculative figures for the possible effects of increased forest clearance on CO_2 release of 2.5×10^5 g yr^{-1}, equivalent to an increase of 0.3 p.p.m. yr^{-1} in the atmosphere. Perhaps the results of the PT and CT sections of IBP will enable us to improve on this figure. The ongoing Global Atmospheric Research Project may then enable us to assess their possible significance on climate. But even quite simple models of global CO_2 dynamics, reviewed by Young, Brenner & Tameel (1973), do not predict a continuing rise of atmospheric CO_2. It is up to biologists and ecologists to provide more definite rate constants for such models.

It is clear that the complex and non-linear relation between solar radiation and CO_2 concentration and uptake requires careful exploration at all levels. The turnover time between ocean–atmosphere is about five to seven years (e.g. Craig, 1957) compared with about twenty years for the atmospheric–land system (Pearman & Garrett, 1972). Understanding aquatic photosynthesis is therefore essential. As Talling (1961, 1971) and Vollenweider (1965,1970) have shown, equations similar to those developed by Monsi & Saeki (1953) and Russian workers (Nichiporovich, 1967) for terrestrial systems, can predict crop dry weight gain from radiant flux receipt. These relations are approximately logarithmic. This work, however, is difficult to relate to short-term measurements of CO_2 distribution in relation to sources and sinks in the vegetation. Such studies have largely been confined to terrestrial systems (Monteith, 1973a).

Radiation and carbon dioxide are coupled in plant communities by the requirement of energy balance:

$$R_n = H+LE+S+P-R, \qquad (1)$$

where R_n is net radiation, H sensible heat transfer, LE latent heat transfer, S energy storage in the system, P energy gain through photosynthesis and R metabolic energy loss. Quantum efficiency in absorbed PAR conversion is about 12.5% (Heath, 1969). But R_n includes longer wavelengths little absorbed by plants, so that P always remains a very small fraction of R_n. Specially cultured algae have achieved high rates (Tamiya, 1957), but few terrestrial communities have reached even 5% efficiency (Denmead, 1968; Warren Wilson, 1967a). It is because it is difficult to separate P and R, and together they are such a small fraction of the total energy balance, that most difficulties in measuring and interpreting community photosynthesis arise.

Early this century F. F. Blackman (1905) first foreshadowed the classic hyperbolic relation between CO_2 uptake and radiant flux density, by his suggestion that photosynthesis was light-limited at low flux receipts and CO_2-limited at high. This experiment with Matthaei (Blackman & Matthaei, 1905) showed that CO_2 concentration could affect maximum photosynthesis levels. This note appropriately appeared in the same volume of the Proceedings of the Royal Society in which Brown & Escombe (1905) first attempted an energy budget for a leaf. Later Blackman & Smith (1911) published response curves for the water plant *Elodea*, and it was not particularly difficult to show that algal mass cultures showed similar relations. McIntyre & Phinney (1965) showed that CO_2 concentration could limit ceiling levels of production in laboratory stream communities.

By following dry weight changes over time, terrestrial communities were also shown to show similar response patterns. In greenhouses, extensive CO_2 addition will increase production, even as Tamiya increased algal production. But under natural conditions we need to know far more about transfer round photosynthetic tissues. Lemon, Stewart & Shawcroft (1971) released CO_2 at soil level in normal and dense canopies of *Zea mays*; and studied the system by aerodynamic methods. Even with a 45-fold increase at soil level, there was little change in CO_2 concentration in the upper part of the canopy, and they estimated only a $10–20\%$ increase was possible with this heavy CO_2 manuring, because of vigorous mixing in the stand. However, Harper, Baker, Box & Hesketh (1973) obtained an increase of photosynthesis up to 26% in a stand of cotton (*Gossypium hirsutum*). This was achieved by adding a very large amount of CO_2 (222.7 kg ha^{-1} h^{-1}), and under high incoming radiation, CO_2 concentrations in the upper part of the canopy exceeded 400 p.p.m. Whether this photosynthetic increase is generally feasible agronomically is doubtful.

These transfer processes are partly governed by the pattern of airflow over the foliage. The components of the energy balance are coupled by the diffusion resistances, as Raschke (1956,1960) and Gaastra (1959) first showed. Despite the limitations of this electrical analogue treatment, it has greatly advanced our understanding of crop physiology. So far as I know, it has not been attempted in aquatic systems and might provide a useful approach. We can write:

$$H = \rho_a C_p \Delta T / \gamma_a^H$$
$$LE = \rho_a L \Delta q / (\gamma_a^w + \gamma_s^w) \qquad (2)$$
$$P = \Delta C / (\gamma_a^c + \gamma_s^c + \gamma_m),$$

where ρ_a is the bulk density of air, ΔT, Δq and ΔC the air foliage-bulk differences in temperature, specific humidity and carbon dioxide concentration, and γ_a, γ_s, γ_m the boundary layer, stomatal and mesophyll diffusion resistances. These differ for the different entities as indicated by superscripts.

The γ_a term is a function of leaf size, but it has been found by a number of workers in both field and laboratory that classical fluid dynamic relations for flat plates are inadequate and much lower resistances are found (e.g. Thom, 1968; Vogel, 1970; Schuepp, 1972; Parlange & Waggoner, 1972). However, as nineteenth-century travellers such as Haberlandt realised, leaf size is closely related to environment and has great ecological and physiological significance (Lewis, 1972).

Within the canopy, with decrease of exchanges of momentum and energy, boundary layer thickness and resistance will rise as turbulent intensity and diffusivity decrease with depth, though it may fluctuate widely over short periods (Cionco, 1972). In fact, exact knowledge of patterns of air flow within the canopy and around small finite irregular objects is still a major limitation to our understanding of crop photosynthesis. Bradley & Finnigan (1973) provide an excellent review of the aerodynamic problems.

By now we have many measurements of CO_2 profiles in terrestrial communities of various types, as reviewed by Monteith (1973a). It is not, however, the concentration, but flux distribution that is interesting and great care is needed in its estimation. There are few analogous aquatic systems, when it is more common to measure oxygen, and the CO_2–bicarbonate balance is affected by pH and other conditions. Also, aquatic measurements have largely been made inside sample bottles, which may well alter the local exchange conditions as does a cuvette round a leaf. As Denmead (1970) showed, on three successive days with identical incoming radiation, carbon dioxide uptake by a wheat crop differed substantially. These differences in crop photosynthetic activity were to some extent related to changes in ambient CO_2 above the crop. Increases in diffusive resistances on the lower part of the canopy probably accounted for a CO_2 uptake only 40% of the observed maximum, though variations in ambient and leaf temperature may have also had an effect. Many cuvette systems, which are necessarily air conditioned to prevent overheating, would have failed to detect these significant differences in photosynthetic activity under identical radiation conditions.

Besides coupling of processes through resistances, the radiation field affects stomatal and mesophyll resistances. There are a number of different effects of light on stomata, through both flux density and spectral quality (Meidner & Mansfield, 1968). Further feedback in the system is provided by effects of ambient CO_2 concentration on stomatal aperture. The mesophyll resistance is light-dependent, and varies with species, age and environmental history. In aquatic systems the complications of stomatal movement do not arise. Instead, plankton populations may be highly mobile as radiation conditions alter.

Because of many indirect effects of radiation on photosynthetic activity as well as on photosynthesis itself it is essential that we know the radiation receipt of photosynthetic organs. In general, terrestrial and aquatic ecologists have approached this in similar ways using a form of Beer's Law:

$$I = I_0 e^{-kx}, \tag{3}$$

where x is a measure of depth in the community (usually cumulative foliage area F in terrestrial systems) and k an extinction coefficient. The problems arise because k is not constant. Particularly in aquatic systems, it is wavelength-dependent (Talling, 1971; Yocum, Allen & Lemon, 1964). The spectral effect on photosynthetic organs is confounded by the presence of other parts, and in aquatic systems, of water with different spectral properties (Smith & Tyler, 1967). The change of spectral composition with depth makes it extremely difficult to intercept the amount of PAR measured with a sensor with a non-PAR spectral response. Technology of this problem has improved greatly during the past four years.

In terrestrial systems further problems arise, since there are separate extinction coefficients for diffuse and direct radiation (Anderson, 1964). This leads to severe sampling problems in actual measurement, which are frequently ignored (Anderson, 1971). Sampling with a large surface instrument will give an averaged extinction coefficient (Monteith, 1973*b*), but this is only valid for the period of measurement. Besides, as the photosynthesis/light response is non-linear, we need to know which parts of the canopy are sunlit (Warren Wilson, 1967*b*).

From the pioneering work of Monsi & Saeki (1953) terrestrial ecologists have managed to relate canopy structure and radiation penetration. The extinction coefficient is a function of foliage area, foliage inclination and angle of penetration. Several groups have developed the relations more or less independently. These are reviewed by Anderson (1971). The basic theory demands random distribution of foliage, which is unrealistic, as the mass of studies of real communities during IBP, particularly in Japan, have shown. Extinction coefficients both larger and smaller than theoretical maxima and minima have been found.

Nilson (1970) has provided a non-random model, which may partly overcome this problem. Miller & Norman (1971) and Norman, Miller & Tanner (1971) have attempted theoretical and practical analysis of sunfleck distribution and penumbral effects. The physiological effects of fluctuating levels of radiation are unclear and deserve close attention. For instance, Kriedemann, Törokfalvy & Smart (1973) have recently found that grapevines have a higher photosynthetic rate in fluctuating radiation than under a constant average flux.

The Weslaco, Texas group have already adopted another approach, based on the Duntley equations (Allen & Richardson, 1968; Allen, Gayle & Richardson, 1970). The spectral properties of the individual leaves are related to those of the canopy, an important point when remote sensing is rapidly gaining agricultural importance (Baumgardner, Leamer & Shay, 1970).

There remain two fundamental problems. Firstly, because of sampling difficulties in real canopies we cannot adequately test the different, sophisticated theories (Anderson, 1969). Yet we need these theories if, secondly, we are going to predict CO_2 uptake. No sensor is available with directional properties similar to those of real leaves, inclined at

350

various angles and pointing in many directions. We must calculate along the lines of de Wit (1965) or Duncan, Loomis, Williams & Hanau (1967). Also, measurements of leaf angle are very tedious, even with computerised procedures (Lang, 1972).

The interrelations of CO_2 and radiation are many and complex. Over the IBP working period, we have gained much information and some insight into the behaviour of the homeostatic mechanisms in a wide range of plant communities. We must now synthesise this information; but, as de Wit pointed out at the Třeboň meeting, we can only model two levels of complexity at a time. When seeking causal relations between climate and plant behaviour, let us remember Hooke's advice at the opening of *Micrographia*. 'As in geometry, the most natural way of beginning is from a Mathematical point; so is the same method in Observations and Natural history the most genuine, simple and instructive. We must first endeavour to make letters, and draw single strokes true, before we venture to write whole Sentences or draw large Pictures.'

IBP has greatly increased the alphabet; now for the next stage.

References

Allen, W. A., Gayle, T. V. & Richardson, A. J. (1970). Plant-canopy irradiance specified by the Duntley equations. *J. opt. Soc. Amer.* **60**, 372–6.

Allen, W. A. & Richardson, A. J. (1968). Interaction of light with a plant canopy. *J. opt. Soc. Amer.* **58**, 1023–8.

Anderson, M. C. (1964). Studies of the woodland light climate. I. The photographic computation of light conditions. *J. Ecol.* **52**, 27–41.

Anderson, M. C. (1969). A comparison of two theories of scattering of radiation in crops. *Agric. Meteorol.* **6**, 399–405.

Anderson, M. C. (1971). Radiation and crop structure. In *Plant Photosynthetic Production*, eds. Z. Šesták, J. Čatský & P. G. Jarvis, pp. 412–66. The Hague, Junk.

Baumgardner, M. F., Leamer, R. W. & Shay, J. R. (1970). Remote sensing techniques used in agriculture today. In *Aerospace Science and Agricultural Development*, ed. M. F. Baumgardner, pp. 9–26. Madison, Wisconsin, American Society of Agronomy, Spl Pub. 18.

Berkner, L. V. & Marshall, L. C. (1964). The history of the growth of oxygen in the earth's atmosphere. In *The Origin and Evolution of Atmospheres and Oceans*, eds. P. T. Brancazio & A. G. W. Cameron, pp. 102–26. New York, John Wiley.

Blackman, F. F. (1905). Optima and limiting factors. *Ann. Bot., Lond.* **19**, 281–95.

Blackman, F. F. & Mathaei, G. L. C. (1905). Experimental researches in vegetable assimilation and respiration. IV. A quantitative study of carbon dioxide assimilation and leaf-temperature in natural illumination. *Proc. Roy. Soc.* B **76**, 402–60.

Blackman, F. F. & Smith, A. M. (1911). On assimilation in submerged water-plants and its relation to the concentration of carbon dioxide and other factors. *Proc. Roy. Soc.* B **83**, 389–412.

Bradley, E. F. & Finnigan, J. J. (1973). Heat and mass transfer in the plant–air continuum. In *First Australasian Conference on Heat and Mass Transfer. Reviews*, pp. 57–78. Melbourne, Monash University.

Brown, H. T. & Escombe, F. (1905). Researches on some physiological processes of green leaves, with special reference to the interchange of energy between the leaf and its surroundings. *Proc. Roy. Soc.* B **76**, 29–111.

Cionco, R. M. (1972). Intensity of turbulence within canopies with simple and complex roughness elements. *Boundary Layer Meteorol.* **2**, 453–65.

Craig, H. (1957). The natural distribution of carbon dioxide and the exchange time of carbon dioxide between atmosphere and sea. *Tellus.* **9**, 1–17.

Denmead, O. T. (1968). Evaporation and photosynthesis in wheat and *Pinus radiata* – a study in micrometeorology. *Proc. ecol Soc. Aust.* **3**, 61–9.

Denmead, O. T. (1970). Transfer processes between vegetation and air: measurement, interpretation and modelling. In *Prediction and Measurement of Photosynthetic Productivity*, pp. 149–64. Wageningen, PUDOC.

Duncan, W. G., Loomis, R. S., Williams, W. A. & Hanau, R. (1967). A model for simulating photosynthesis in plant communities. *Hilgardia*, **38**, 181–205.

Federer, C. A. & Tanner, C. B. (1966). Sensors for measuring light available for photosynthesis. *Ecology*, **47**, 654–7.

Gaastra, P. (1959). Photosynthesis of crop plants as influenced by light, temperature, and stomatal diffusion resistance. *Meded. Landbhoogesch, Wageningen*, **59** (13), 1–68.

Gaastra, P. (1968). Radiation measurements for investigations of photosynthesis under natural conditions. In *Functioning of Terrestrial Ecosystems at the Primary Production Level*, ed. F. E. Eckardt, pp. 467–80. Paris, UNESCO.

Harper, L. A., Baker, D. N., Box, J. E. & Hesketh, J. D. (1973). Carbon dioxide and the photosynthesis of field crops: a metered carbon dioxide release in cotton under field conditions. *Agron. J.* **65**, 7–11.

Heath, O. V. S. (1969). *The Physiological Aspects of Photosynthesis*. London, Heinemann.

Johnson, F. S. (1970). The oxygen and carbon dioxide balance in the earth's atmosphere. In *Global Effects of Environmental Pollution*, ed. S. F. Singer. New York, Springer-Verlag.

Kriedemann, P. E., Törokfalvy, E. & Smart, R. E. (1973). Natural occurrence and photosynthetic utilization of sunflecks by grapevine leaves. *Photosynthetica*, **7**, 18–27.

Lang, A. R. G. (1972). Leaf orientation of a cotton plant. *Agric. Meteorol.* **11**, 37–51.

Lemon, E. Stewart, D. W. & Shawcroft, R. W. (1971). The sun's work in a cornfield. *Science*, **174**, 371–8.

Lewis, M. C. (1972). The physiological significance of variation in leaf structure. *Sci. Prog., Oxf.* **60**, 25–51.

Machta, L. (1972). Mauna Loa and global trends in air quality. *Bull. Amer. Meteorol. Soc.* **53**, 402–20.

McIntyre, C. D. & Phinney, H. K. (1965). Laboratory studies of penphyton production and community metabolism in lotic environments. *Ecol. Monogr.* **35**, 237–58.

McPherson, H. G. (1969). Photocell-filter combinations for measuring photosynthetically active radiation. *Agric. Meteor.* **6**, 347–56.

Meidner, H. & Mansfield, T. A. (1968). *Physiology of Stomata*, London, McGraw-Hill.

Miller, E. E. & Norman, J. M. (1971). A sunfleck theory for plant canopies. II. Penumbra effect: intensity distributions along sunfleck segments. *Agron. J.* **64**, 739–43.

Monsi, M. & Saeki, J. (1953). Über den Lichtfaktor in den Pflanzengesellschaften und seine Bedeuting für die Stoffproduktion. *Jap. J. Bot.* **14**, 22–52.

Monteith, J. L. (ed.) (1973*a*). *Vegetation and Atmosphere*, London, Academic Press.

Monteith, J. L. (1973*b*). *Principles of Environmental Physics*. London, Edward Arnold.

Nichiporovich, A. A. (ed.) (1967). *Photosynthesis of Productive Systems.* Jerusalem, Israel Program for Scientific Translations.

Nilson, T. (1971). A theoretical analysis of the frequency of gaps in plant stands. *Agric. Meteorol.* **8**, 25–38.

Norman, J. M. Miller, E. E. & Tanner, C. B. (1971). Light intensity and sunfleck-size distribution in plant canopies. *Agron. J.* **63**, 743–8.

Parlange, J.-Y. & Waggoner, P. E. (1972). Boundary layer resistance and temperature distribution on still and flapping leaves. II. Field experiments. *Plant Physiol.* **50**, 60–3.

Pearman, G. I. & Garratt, J. R. (1972). Global aspects of carbon dioxide. *Search*, **3**, 67–73.

Raschke, K. (1956). Über die physikalischem Beziehungen zwischen Wärme übergangszahl, Strahlungsaustausch, Temperatur und Transpiration eines Blattes. *Planta*, **48**, 200–37.

Raschke, K. (1960). Heat transfer between the plant and environment. *A. Rev. Pl. Physiol.* **11**, 111–26.

Sawyer, J. S. (1972). Man-made carbon dioxide and the 'greenhouse' effect. *Nature*, **239**, 23–6.

Schuepp, P. H. (1972). Studies of forced-convection heat and mass transfer of fluttering realistic leaf models. *Boundary Layer Meteorol.* **2**, 263–74.

Šesták, Z., Čatský, J. & Jarvis, P. G. (1971). *Plant Photosynthetic Production: Manual of Methods.* The Hague, Junk.

Smith, R. C. & Tyler, J. E. (1967). Optical properties of clear natural water. *J. Opt. Soc. Amer.* **57**, 589–95.

Talling, J. F. (1961). Photosynthesis under natural conditions. *A. Rev. Pl. Physiol.* **11**, 133–54.

Talling, J. F. (1971). The underwater light climate as a controlling factor on the production ecology of freshwater phytoplankton. *Mitt. Internat. Verein. Linnol.* **19**, 214–43.

Tamiya, H. (1957). Mass culture of algae. *A. Rev. Pl. Physiol.* **8**, 309–34.

Thom, A. S. (1968). The exchange of momentum, mass and heat between an artificial leaf and the airflow in a wind-tunnel. *Quart. J. Roy. Meteorol. Soc.* **94**, 44–55.

Vogel, S. (1970). Convective cooling at low airspeeds and the shape of leaves. *J. Exp. Bot.* **21**, 91–101.

Vollenweider, R. A. (1965). Calculation models of photosynthesis-depth curves and some implications regarding day rate estimates in primary production. *Mem. 1st Ital. Idrobiol.* **18**, Suppl. 425–57.

Vollenweider, R. A. (1970). Models for calculating integral photosynthesis and some implications regarding structural properties of the community metabolism of aquatic systems. In *Prediction and Measurement of Photosynthetic Productivity*, pp. 455–72. Wageningen, PUDOC.

Warren Wilson, J. (1967*a*). Ecological data on dry-matter product by plants and plant communities. In *The Collection and Processing of Field Data*, eds. E. F. Bradley & O. T. Denmead, pp. 77–123. New York, John Wiley.

Warren Wilson, J. (1967*b*). Stand structure and light penetration. III. Sunlit foliage area. *J. Appl. Ecol.* **4**, 159–65.

de Wit, C. T. (1965). Photosynthesis of leaf canopies. *Agric. Res. Rep. (Wageningen)*, **663**, 1–57.

Yocum, C. S., Allen, L. H. & Lemon, E. R. (1964). Photosynthesis under field conditions. VI. Solar radiation balance and photosynthetic efficiency. *Agron. J.* **56**, 249–53.

Young, J. W., Brenner, J. W. & Tameel, H. J. (1973). An engineering systems analysis of man's impact on the global carbon cycle. Appendix C in *Land Use, Energy Flow and Decision Making in Human Society*, eds. R. Boyd & J. Young. Paris, University of California.

PART IV

Photosynthetic activity of individual plants and tissues

16. Photosynthetic mechanisms in higher plants

J. H. TROUGHTON

The presence of higher plants in almost all ecological sites is evidence that they can accumulate carbon, even under apparently adverse environmental conditions. The mechanism of carbon accumulation is at least superficially similar for all higher plants, indicating the adaptability or flexibility of the photosynthetic process. The basic processes are the 'Z' scheme for the photoreactions and the C_3-pathway for carbon metabolism. Modifications of these processes occur which may be significant to the ecological aspects of the photosynthetic mechanism, and these include the variation in pigments used in light absorption and the C_4 and CAM carbon pathways. In spite of the similarities in the basic photosynthetic mechanism among higher plants, there are large variations in the capacity of the processes which can be modified both genetically and by the environment.

In spite of the complexity of the photosynthetic mechanism, the behaviour of the reaction can be thought of as a simple kinetic chemical reaction. The rate of the reaction will be regulated by the supply of substrate (CO_2), the level of the product and the environment. In photosynthesis the reaction rate is modified by the presence of enzymes, the utilisation of light as an energy source and the need for compartmentalization of some reactions.

Structure and the photosynthetic mechanism

Gross leaf anatomy

There is extensive variation in the organisation of cells in leaves of higher plants (Troughton & Donaldson, 1972). In many C_3-plants there are two distinct regions, the palisade mesophyll and the spongy mesophyll (Plate 16.1a) but even within a species the distribution of cells between these layers varies with age and pretreatment. Another distinct type of leaf anatomy in angiosperms is the Kranz type which is genetically determined, relatively independent of the environment and uniquely related to C_4-photosynthesis. It consists of two (sometimes more) concentric layers of cells surrounding the vascular bundle, an outer mesophyll layer and an inner parenchyma bundle sheath layer (Plate

357

Individual plants and tissues

16.1*b*). In some C$_4$-species a different arrangement occurs with the mesophyll and bundle sheath layer underlying the epidermis around the perimeter of the leaf (Björkman, Troughton & Nobs, 1973). The close association of mesophyll and bundle sheath cells (or their equivalent) is important for the success of C$_4$-photosynthesis and the association of these cells with the vascular bundle may enhance physiologically important access to the water in the xylem or to loading of carbon into the phloem.

The ultrastructure of chlorophyllous cells

The distribution of the chloroplasts, microbodies and mitochondria which are involved in carbon metabolism and the photosynthetic process in higher plants varies between species. In mesophyll cells these organelles occur in a thin strip of cytoplasm close to the cell wall. The large vacuole is conspicuous. In the bundle sheath cells of C$_4$-type plants the cytoplasm may occupy more than 50% of the volume of the cell. The chloroplasts in these cells may be randomly distributed in the cytoplasm or centripetally arranged (as in *Gomphrera globosa* and *Portulaca grandifolia*) or centrifugally arranged (as in *Zea mays* and *Chloris gayang*) (Downtown, 1971).

Some C$_4$-plants have dimorphic chloroplasts. The initial observation was that starch accumulated in the chloroplasts in bundle sheath cells in the light, but not in the mesophyll cells of maize and sorghum (Rhoades & Carvalho, 1944). This distinction applied to some members of the subfamily Panicoideae but not to wheat, oats and barley in the subfamily Paoideae (see also Bisalputra, Downton & Tregunna, 1969). An ultrastructural study in *Zea mays* L. provided evidence that the mesophyll cell chloroplasts contained grana but this feature was absent from chloroplasts in the bundle sheath cells (Hodge, McLean & Mercer, 1955). The dimorphic nature of chloroplast ultrastructure in C$_4$-plants has been well documented (Johnson & Brown, 1973; Weier, Stocking & Shumway, 1966; Laetsch, 1971; Osmond, Troughton & Goodchild, 1969; Bisalputra, Downton & Tregunna, 1969).

Light and the photosynthetic mechanism

Chlorophyll and photosynthesis

Many plant pigments intercept radiation involved in photosynthesis, but chlorophyll is of most importance. In fact, the use of chlorophyll content

358

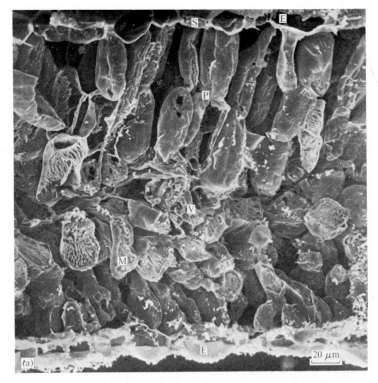

Plate 16.1. (a) Transverse view of a leaf of *Atriplex hastata* (C₃-plant) (SEM). Epidermis (E), stomata (S), palisade mesophyll (P), spongy mesophyll (M) and vascular tissue (V). (b) Transverse view of a leaf of *Atriplex spongiosa* (C₄-plant) (SEM). Epidermis (E), stomata (S), mesophyll cells (M), bundle sheath cells (B) and vascular tissue (V).

of leaves as an index of organic matter production (Brougham, 1960) implies that the chlorophyll content of leaves may limit photosynthesis. Variations in chlorophyll content may occur as a result of the genotype, nutrient or disease disorder, temperature lesions and stage of greening in etiolated leaves. The temperature sensitivity of chlorophyll synthesis may limit the distribution of some species, especially C_4-plants (Millerd, Goodchild & Spencer, 1969; McWilliam & Naylor, 1967).

There are many reports suggesting depressed photosynthetic rates due to reduced chlorophyll concentration (Heath, 1969; Šesták, Čatský & Jarvis, 1971), but in many natural communities the normal chlorophyll content of leaves is adequate to absorb the available photosynthetic flux (Anderson, 1967) and chlorophyll contents are likely to adjust to the flux available (Rabinowitch, 1951).

The content of the different forms of chlorophyll is similar in the leaves of most higher plants (French, 1971). The ratio of two of the more important chlorophyll pigments, chlorophylls *a* and *b*, varies with the genotype, environment, nutrition and position of leaves within the plant. The chlorophyll *a*/*b* ratio and chlorophyll concentration tends to be higher in C_4-plants than C_3-plants when grown under the same conditions (Chang & Troughton, 1972). In C_4-plants the chlorophyll *a*/*b* ratio varies within a leaf between the mesophyll and bundle sheath cells (Black & Mayne, 1970; Pyliotis, Woo & Downton, 1971; Bishop, Anderson & Smillie, 1971; Chang & Troughton, 1972).

Photon absorption and transfer

Absorption of photons by chlorophylls *a* and *b* and the carotenoids causes the pigments to pass from their lowest energy states to higher ones. Emerson & Arnold (1932) concluded that only about 0.1 % of the pigments were photoactive and energy not used must dissipate quickly or irreversible photo-oxidation of chlorophyll will occur. Much energy is lost as heat, little lost by fluorescence as the electron falls back to the ground state, some energy channelled by a triplet–triplet transfer to the carotenoids and some migrates to the reaction centre. De-activation in the carotenoids can occur rapidly (Wolff & Witt, 1969; Witt & Wolff, 1970) and is oxygen-dependent (Mathis & Galmiche, 1967). Chlorophyll in mutant cells without carotenoids is destroyed by light (Griffiths, Sistrom, Cohen-Bazire & Stanier, 1955) and mutants of *Euglena gracilis* with a block between the photosystems possess more carotenoids

359

(xanthophylls) than wild-type cells and this may protect the chlorophyll (Schwelitz, Dilley & Crane, 1972).

Photosynthetic electron transport

The current, and widely accepted, view of photosynthetic electron transport is that two photoacts, involving two pigment systems, are linked according to a 'Z-scheme' originally proposed by Hill & Bendall (1960). Details of the 'Z-scheme' are discussed elsewhere (Gregory, 1971; Arnon, 1971).

The system involves photosystem I (PSI) which is activated at wavelengths longer than 680 nm, has P700 as the trapping centre and reduces $NADP^+$, and photosystem II (PSII), which is activated by wavelengths less than 680 nm and has chlorophyll *a* II; P680 as the trapping centre. The Hill reaction involving the 'splitting' of water to produce O_2 is associated with PSII. The sequential operation of the two photosystems results in the production of ATP and NADP; the latter molecule is relatively small and capable of diffusing to sites of carbon reduction.

The availability of ATP and NADP to the cell will depend on both the efficiency of photon absorption and transfer, and on the capacity for electron flow. The latter feature has now been shown to vary depending on genetic and environmental factors, particularly light intensity (Grahl & Wild, 1972; Wild, Ke & Shaw, 1973).

Nutrient deficiency has often been used to investigate chloroplast structure and function. Mineral deficiency in tomatoes resulted in reduced Hill activity (Spencer & Possingham, 1960), while manganese deficiency inhibits photosystem II but induces stacking in *Chlamydomonas* (Teichler-Zallen, 1969). In maize, PSI activity was relatively unaffected by mineral deficiency but PSII was enhanced on a chlorophyll basis by the lack of N or S and was accompanied by granal stacking. These latter results suggest an increase in PSII with increased granal stacking (Baszynski *et al.*, 1972; Hall, Barr, Al-Abbas & Crane, 1972).

The quantum efficiency of photosynthesis

A quantum efficiency can be obtained from information about electron transport in the photosystems. The quantum requirement for the transfer of an electron from water to ferredoxin–NADP is two, i.e. two quanta

360

per electron or eight quanta per molecule of O_2. In PSI only one photoact is required and this has a theoretical quantum requirement of one quantum per electron.

Measurement of the quantum efficiency in intact plants necessitates the use of rate-limiting light levels, correction for the effects of photorespiration and dark respiration and the measurement of quanta absorbed by the tissue. McCree (1972) investigated the effect of leaf age, temperature, CO_2 concentration, growth conditions, species and photosynthetic pathway on the quantum yield at different wavelengths over the range 350–750 nm. The shape of the spectral quantum yield curves was similar for all species, with peaks at 440, 620 and 670 ± 10 nm. The absolute value of the quantum yield varied from 0.054 to 0.076 molecule of CO_2 per absorbed quantum, with a mean of 0.065. Increasing the temperature from 11 to 38 °C decreased the quantum yield in oats, increasing the CO_2 concentration from 200 to 600 v.p.m. doubled the quantum yield in sugar-beet, while species, leaf age, carbon pathway or growth conditions had smaller effects.

The carbon pathways of photosynthesis

The C₃-pathway

Virtually all carbon entering higher plants passes through the C_3-pathway, and for most plants this pathway includes the primary carboxylation event. Evidence for the pathway came initially from radiocarbon tracer studies on an alga, *Chlorella pyrenoidosa* (Calvin & Benson, 1948), in which most of the isotope label after a thirty-second feeding period appeared in phosphoglyceric acid (PGA) and triose phosphate.

The enzyme catalysing the CO_2-ribulose diphosphate reaction to produce PGA is ribulose-1,5-diphosphate carboxylase (RuDP carboxylase) (Quayle, Fuller, Benson & Calvin, 1954). This enzyme is widely distributed in plant tissues with 3-PGA as the first stable carbon compound, its activity correlates with photosynthetic activity, and it is present in the chloroplast. CO_2 has been established as the form of inorganic carbon used in the carboxylation reaction (Cooper, Filmer, Wishnik & Lane, 1969).

N

The C4-pathway

When sugar cane leaves are fed $^{14}CO_2$ as a pulse, the radioactivity appears initially in malic acid, aspartic acid and some unidentified compounds (Burr *et al.*, 1957). Kortschak, Hartt & Burr (1965) therefore proposed that in sugar cane the first stable products in photosynthesis were malate and aspartate and that these compounds are converted to sucrose via 3-phosphoglyceric acid (3-PGA) and hexosephosphates. Hatch & Slack (1966,1967,1968,1969,1970) provided extensive and well documented evidence for a C4-pathway of photosynthesis, which differs in many respects from that in C3-plants. The biochemistry of the pathways also correlates with differences in the CO_2 compensation point, oxygen sensitivity of net photosynthesis, the characteristics of CO_2 evolution into CO_2 free air or on transfer from light to dark, the shape of the light response curve and extent of isotope fractionation.

Specific biochemical evidence for the C4-pathway is given by the pattern of ^{14}C-labelling which indicates that the label initially enters the C-4 of the C4-dicarboxylic acids and subsequently the C-1 of 3-PGA in the C3-pathway (Hatch & Slack, 1966,1970; Hatch, Slack & Johnson, 1967; Osmond, 1967; Osmond, Troughton & Goodchild, 1969).

Substantial support for the new pathway also comes from the comparative enzymology of C3- and C4-plants, and differences in distribution between the mesophyll and bundle sheath cells of C4-plants (Slack & Hatch, 1967; Slack, 1969; Slack, Hatch & Goodchild, 1969; Björkman & Gauhl, 1969; Hatch & Slack, 1970; Kanai & Black, 1972) (Table 16.1). The high activities of phosphoenolpyruvate (PEP) carboxylase in C4-plants and its location in the mesophyll cells of C4-plants further supports evidence that it is involved in the primary carboxylation of these plants. Furthermore, Osmond & Avadani (1970) have shown that an inhibitor of PEP carboxylase inhibits CO_2 fixation in C4- but not C3-plants.

The compartmentation of the C4-reactions in the mesophyll cell and C3-reactions in the bundle sheath cells is important for the operation of C4-photosynthesis. This is demonstrated in a virescent mutant of maize (Chollet & Ogren, 1972) and hybrids between C3 and C4 *Atriplex* sp. (Björkman *et al.*, 1971).

A further variant of the C4-system lies in the particular C4-acid involved in the transport of carbon between mesophyll and bundle sheath cells. In many species (maize, *Digitaria* sp., sugar cane) there is malic enzyme in the bundle sheath cell and ^{14}C accumulates in malic acid immediately after labelling. In the *Panicum* group and *Amaranthus edulis, A. palmerii* and *Atriplex spongiosa*, PEP carboxykinase is present and aspartic or oxaloacetic is transported to bundle sheath cells. There is a third type (including bermudagrass) in which ^{14}C-label appears in aspartic, but the mode of decarboxylation is unknown (Kanai & Black, 1972).

Table 16.1. *Distribution of enzymes in mesophyll cells and bundle sheath cells of* Digitaria sanguinalis (Kanai & Black, 1972).

Enzyme	Mesophyll cell (μmol h^{-1} mg^{-1} chl.)	Bundle sheath cell
PEP carboxylase	740	54
Malic dehydrogenase (NADP$^+$)	103	–
Malic enzyme (NADP$^+$)	26	543
RuDP carboxylase	12	290
Ru5P kinase	76	1434
R5P isomerase	48	970
FDP aldolase	50	588
Pyrophosphatase	1820	2660
Adenylate kinase	1900	1500
Glyceraldehyde-3P dehydrogenase (NADP$^+$)	206	284
Glutamate-OAA transaminase	202	148
Phosphoglyceromutase	116	102
Enolase	16	16
Pyruvate-P$_i$-dikinase	85	393

Species that predominately produce malate have a reduction in granal stacking in the chloroplasts of bundle sheath cells and a reduction in photosystem II and photophosphorylation. A reduced capacity to generate NADPH from the light reactions may be compensated by its production from the oxidative decarboxylation of malic acid. Also, transfer of some 3-PGA from the bundle sheath to the mesophyll cells may also reduce the energy requirement of the bundle sheath cells. Overall, the C$_4$-pathway has a requirement for five moles of ATP and two moles of NADPH.

The active species of inorganic carbon utilised by PEP carboxylase has been investigated *in vitro* with enzymes from twelve- to fourteen-day old corn shoots (Cooper & Wood, 1971). The kinetics of the reaction indicate HCO$_3^-$ was the functional carboxylating species for PEP carboxylase.

Individual plants and tissues

Crassulacean acid metabolism

Many Crassulacean species, such as *Bryophyllum calycinum*, show a diurnal variation in the acid content of their tissue, and can often assimilate significant amounts of CO_2 in the dark (Ranson & Thomas, 1960). The accumulation of acids in the dark in leaves containing chloroplasts is the result of a carboxylation reaction involving PEP, PEP carboxylase and atmospheric CO_2 to yield malate (Vickery, 1952). This dark fixation of CO_2 has several similarities to the carboxylation processes in C_4-plants. The two main differences between the pathways are that PEP is formed from stored carbohydrates in CAM-plants and regenerated from photosynthetic intermediates in C_4-plants (Ting, 1971) and there is temporal (CAM) compared with intercellular (C_4) separation of the primary and secondary carboxylation.

The major organic acid showing diurnal fluctuation is 1-malate (Ting, 1971) though other acids, e.g. isocitrate, also accumulate and may form a substantial proportion of the acid content of the plants (Soderstrom, 1962). Other enzymes important to the operation of CAM are malate dehydrogenase, malic enzyme and aspartate amino transferase (Ting, 1971). There appears to be only one carboxylation step in the dark fixation of CO_2 (Sutton & Osmond, 1972).

CO_2 fixation in the dark and acid accumulation has often been shown to be greater at lower night temperatures (Neales, 1973*a,b*). Environmental regulation of CAM activity has been suggested by Brandon (1967) to be due to the balance in temperature dependence of two enzymes, malic enzyme and PEP carboxylase. It has also been shown that PEP carboxylase is inhibited by malic acid but this effect can be reversed by millimolar concentrations of glucose-6-phosphate (Ting & Osmond, 1973).

Malate fixed and stored in the dark is mobilised and decarboxylated to pyruvate in the light (Ranson & Thomas, 1960). Elevated temperatures favour the mobilisation and decarboxylation of the malate pool (Vickery, 1952) although decarboxylation is also influenced by the CO_2 concentration in the cell (Ranson & Thomas, 1960). It has also been shown that light-dependent deacidification depends on respiratory processes (Denius & Homann, 1972). The extent to which CO_2 decarboxylated from malate in the light is utilised and incorporated into the normal C_3-cycle will depend on the magnitude of the resistances (e.g. stomata) to CO_2 transport between the site of decarboxylation, the chloroplast and the atmosphere.

364

Dark fixation of CO_2 can be photoperiodically induced, with short days increasing the rate of dark fixation. There was no difference in the products of CO_2 fixation in the dark in long- or short-day plants (Kunitake, Saltman & Lang, 1957). Investigations of circadian rhythms in *Bryophyllum* leaves indicate that evolution of dark-fixed CO_2 is controlled by a pigment which absorbs light only at the red end of the spectrum (Wilkins, 1973). The characteristics of the spectra are consistent with the photoreceptor molecule being phytochrome but no red/far-red reversibility has been achieved.

Carbon isotope fractionation among higher plants

All higher plants have $\delta^{13}C$ values more negative than the CO_2 of the atmosphere they are grown in, but the outstanding feature is that there is a pronounced bimodel distribution of these values (Bender, 1971; Smith & Epstein, 1971; Troughton, 1971,1972) (Fig. 16.1). C_4-plants have values within one group with a mean of $-14\%_0$ while C_3-plants

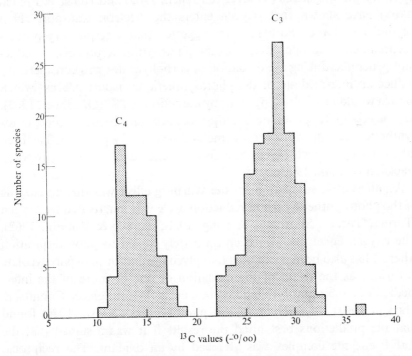

Fig. 16.1. The distribution of ^{13}C values for 240 species of higher plants (from results of Troughton, Card & Hendy). The group with a mean of $-14\%_0$ are C_4-plants and the group with a mean of $-27\%_0$ are C_3-plants. The species were chosen for analysis and the distribution does not necessarily represent the normal distribution for higher plants.

have values within a group with a mean of -27% CAM-plants cover both groups. This method therefore, provides a further technique of distinguishing between C_3- and C_4-plants which can be used for the rapid screening of large numbers of small samples, including dead material and non-photosynthetic organs.

Regulation of the photosynthetic mechanism
Oxygen effects on the photosynthetic mechanism

In 1920 Warburg reported that photosynthesis (oxygen evolution) in a green alga (*Chlorella pyrenoidosa*) was inhibited by oxygen. This phenomena became known as the Warburg effect and has been intensively investigated (Turner & Brittain, 1962).

Warburg originally suggested that oxygen might re-oxidise the primary photochemical product, thus competing with CO_2 for reducing power (Warburg, 1920) and this view has some support. Oxygen is taken up in the photosystems (Vidaver & French, 1965) and Heber & French (1968) have shown that oxygen enters the electron transport chain beyond PSI. Other workers have suggested that a respiratory process occurs in close co-operation with the photosynthetic process. A reductant generated during the oxidation of carbohydrates was considered to reduce an intermediate of the photosynthetic transport process which in turn would be oxidised by O_2 or by the action of PSI (Goedheer, 1963). The necessity to postulate multiple connections between the photosynthetic electron transport scheme and respiratory processes has been advanced by French (1966) and several schemes have been proposed (Jackson & Volk, 1970).

An alternative suggestion for the Warburg effect was that an enzyme of the photosynthetic carbon reduction cycle was inactivated by oxygen (Turner, Turner, Shortman & King, 1958; Turner & Brittain, 1962). The oxygen effect has also been intimately linked to photorespiration where it has also been postulated that glycolate and/or phosphoglycolate is formed as the result of the oxidation of one or more of the intermediates of the photosynthetic carbon cycle (Whittingham, Coombs & Marker, 1967). In a model of leaf photosynthesis Laisk (1970) found that the predictions best fitted the results if it was assumed that the RuDP–enzyme complex was attacked by an oxidant. The reciprocal competitive interactions of CO_2 and O_2 on the rates of CO_2 fixation and glycolate formation have also been observed in the lower plant *Chlamydomonas reinhardi* (Bowes & Berry, 1972). Ogren & Bowes (1971) observed an oxygen inhibition of RuDP carboxylase activity and suggested that RuDP is oxidised to phosphoglycolate and 3-phospho-glycerate. Andrews, Lorimer & Tolbert (1971) fed leaves $^{18}O_2$ and observed that the label was incorporated into the carboxyl groups of glycine and serine but there was no label in glycerate and phospho-glycerate. Subsequently these authors (Andrews, Lorimer & Tolbert, 1973; Lorimer, Andrews & Tolbert, 1973) showed that RuDP carboxy-lase *in vitro* catalysed the formation of phosphoglycolate and 3-phospho-glycerate from RuDP in the presence of oxygen but $^{18}O_2$ supplied as molecular oxygen only appeared in phosphoglycolate.

Regulation of CO_2 exchange

CO_2 exchange is widely used to monitor the rate of photosynthesis and so provide information on the effect of the environment and plant components on regulating the photosynthetic process.

In chloroplasts in the light there is a depletion of CO_2 (or HCO_3^-) concentration in the vicinity of the carboxylation reaction. CO_2 for the carboxylation reaction is provided from the atmosphere. The difference in CO_2 concentration between the two positions provides the driving force for gas transfer. Interpretation of gas exchange data requires associated biochemical and photochemical information if the kinetic results are to be adequately interpreted.

Transfer of CO_2 from the bulk atmosphere to the vicinity of the leaf is by a process of eddy exchange or turbulent mixing, while near surfaces there is a boundary layer, across which movement of CO_2 is by mole-cular diffusion. The magnitude of the boundary layer is often expressed as a resistance which can be obtained by knowing the concentration difference and flux of CO_2 across the segment (Cowan, 1972).

The cuticle and epidermis of leaves provide a major resistance to CO_2 transport and the stomata provide a regulatory mechanism to control CO_2 exchange (and water loss) across the epidermis. Resistances to CO_2 transfer across the cuticle and epidermis (excluding the stomata) are generally of the order 50–200 s cm^{-1} while that of the stomata is highly variable but between 0.5 and 50 s cm^{-1}. The structure, size and distribution of the stomatal apertures show large variation and are regulated by a variety of environmental and plant components including light, humidity, CO_2, O_2, plant water status, nutritional status and wind (Figs. 16.2, 16.3). The dynamic nature of stomata and their regulatory effect on photosynthesis through an effect on CO_2 supply is best illustrated by the oscillations in stomatal resistance that can occur (Troughton & Cowan, 1968; Troughton, 1969b; Barrs, 1971).

The internal cellular organisation of leaves shows wide variation between species (Troughton & Donaldson, 1972; Troughton & Sampson, 1973) and would be expected to contribute to differences in intercellular transport of CO_2 in the gaseous phase by molecular diffusion. Little regular relationship has been found between photosynthesis and leaf thickness in several genotypes (El-Sharkawy & Hesketh, 1965), although Wilson & Cooper (1967, 1969a,b,c,d) report a strong negative relationship between the mean cross-sectional area per mesophyll cell and

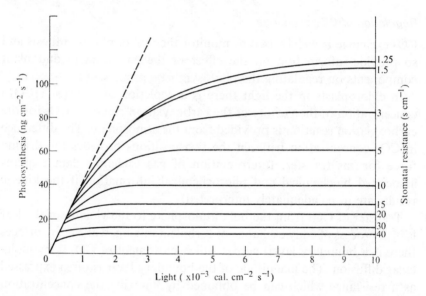

Fig. 16.2. The interaction between light level, stomatal resistance and photosynthesis for a characteristic C_3-type plant without respiration. Calculations made from the formulation of Monteith (1963).

apparent photosynthesis in *Lolium*. The most pronounced relationship between anatomy and cellular photosynthetic ability is that associated with Kranz leaf anatomy but this effect is associated with the intracellular resistance. Estimates of the intercellular resistance component vary from less than 0.5 s cm^{-1} (Milthorpe, 1961; Milthorpe & Penman, 1967; Jones & Slatyer, 1972) to 3 s cm^{-1} (Jarvis, Rose & Begg, 1967).

During transfer of CO_2 within the cell, CO_2 goes into solution at the cell wall and depending on the pH of the solution, cytoplasm and the chloroplast, moves as CO_2 or HCO_3^- to the site for carboxylation. Transport in solution may be by diffusion or may be activated (Kreuzer, 1970) and carbonic anhydrase may be involved in this process (Enns, 1967). The pathlength for transport into the chloroplast from the cell wall is highly variable and may be greater than the thickness of the wall. The transport path also includes the plasmalemma, the cytoplasm in the cell and, in the case of C_3-type plants, the outer membrane of the chloroplast.

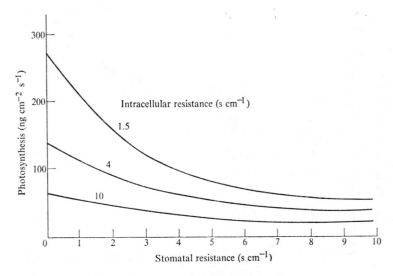

Fig. 16.3. The interaction of the stomatal resistance, intracellular resistance and photosynthesis. The lowest intracellular resistance is characteristic of a C_4-plant, the intermediate of a C_3-angiosperm and the highest of trees. Calculations were from the formulation of Monteith (1963), assuming saturating light levels.

Several cellular aspects of CO_2 fixation may contribute to differences in photosynthesis between C_3- and C_4-plant types. Firstly, PEP carboxylase is the primary carboxylation enzyme in C_4-plants and RuDP carboxylase in C_3-plants; secondly, the enzyme is outside the chloroplast in C_4-plants and inside in C_3-plants, which therefore affects the pathlength for diffusion, and thirdly, RuDP carboxylase utilises 'CO_2' whereas PEP carboxylase from maize shoots uses HCO_3^- (Cooper, Filmer, Wishnick & Lane, 1969; Cooper & Wood, 1971).

The CO_2 concentration at the mesophyll cell wall can be controlled and is a valuable parameter in interpreting cellular reactions because it is one of the reactants. By varying the CO_2 concentration it is possible

369

N*

to identify two features, an initial linear relationship between CO_2 concentration and CO_2 uptake and a second phase when CO_2 uptake is independent of CO_2 concentration. It is necessary to allow for a photo-respiration effect on the curve (Lake, 1967*a,b*) and for non-linearity in the relationship at low CO_2 concentrations (Holmgren & Jarvis, 1967; Heath & Orchard, 1968; Troughton & Slatyer, 1969).

The initial slope of the CO_2 response curve in cotton is sensitive to oxygen concentration, but relatively unaffected by temperature from

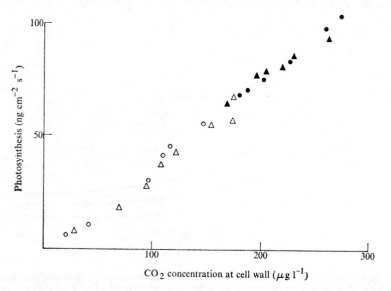

Fig. 16.4. Effects of relative water content (RLWC) on photosynthesis in cotton at 25 °C, when oxygen-free air was blown through the leaf. Data from Troughton & Slatyer (1969). (●) Leaf 1, RLWC = 92%; (○) leaf 1, RLWC = 56%; (▲) leaf 2, RLWC = 92%; (△) leaf 2, RLWC = 69%. The constant slope of the relationship between CO_2 concentration at the cell wall and photosynthesis suggests a lack of an effect of water stress on this aspect of photosynthesis under these conditions.

12 °C to 38 °C, by light level or by relative leaf water content from 56% to 92% (Figs. 16.4, 16.5 and 16.6) (Troughton, 1969*a*; Troughton & Slatyer, 1969). The relation between the initial slope of the CO_2 response curve in air and O_2-free air and at saturating light also differs between C_3- and C_4-plants as in *Atriplex hastata* (C_3) and *Atriplex spongiosa* (C_4) (Fig. 16.7) (Osmond, Troughton & Goodchild, 1969). The C_4-plant utilises cellular CO_2 more efficiently than C_3-plants and would therefore be expected to have a higher water-use efficiency than

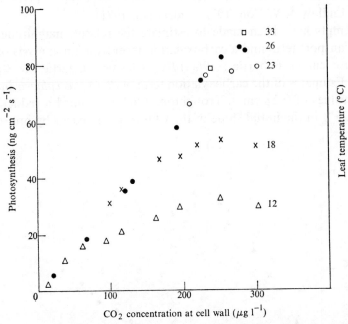

Fig. 16.5. CO_2 response curves determined for cotton at five temperatures when oxygen-free air was blown through the leaf. There was no effect of temperature from 12 to 33 °C on the initial slope of the CO_2 response curve but there were substantial effects on the maximum rate of photosynthesis at CO_2 concentration of 300 μg l^{-1}. Data from Troughton (1969b).

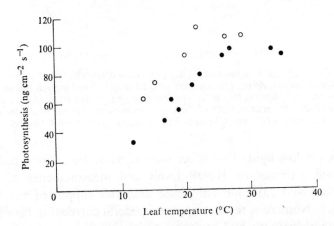

Fig. 16.6. Relationship between leaf temperature and the rate of photosynthesis for cotton and tobacco when oxygen-free air was blown through the leaf. The CO_2 concentration at the mesophyll cell wall was 300 μg l^{-1}. The difference in response for the two species may indicate differences in the temperature-sensitivity of the photosynthetic mechanism. Data from Troughton (1969b).

Individual plants and tissues

C_3-plants, as confirmed for several C_3- and C_4-type plants (Woolhouse, 1968; Ludlow & Wilson, 1972; Björkman, 1971).

Attempts have been made to estimate the relative magnitudes of a CO_2 transport term and a carboxylation term from an analysis of light response curves (Chartier, 1966,1970; Chartier, Chartier & Čatský, 1970). Estimates of the carboxylation term in *Phaseolus vulgaris* indicate small values of 0.2 s cm^{-1}. Troughton (1969a) obtained a reduction of up to 25% in the initial slope of the CO_2 response curve by pretreating

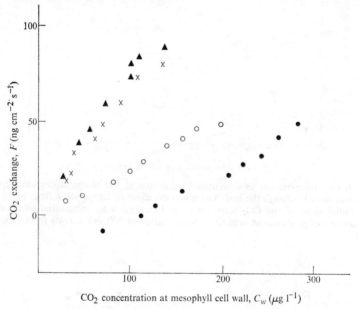

CO$_2$ concentration at mesophyll cell wall, C_w (μg l^{-1})

Fig. 16.7. CO_2 exchange as a function of the CO_2 concentration at the mesophyll cell wall for two *Atriplex* species. *Atriplex spongiosa* (C_4-plant) in air ($\times$) and oxygen-free air ($\blacktriangle$) and *Atriplex hastata* (C_3-plant) in air ($\bullet$) and oxygen-free air ($\bigcirc$). The effect of oxygen on CO_2 exchange and the difference in slope of the CO_2 response curve for the two plant types are characteristic features of C_3- and C_4-plants. From Osmond, Troughton & Goodchild (1969).

the leaves in low light. This effect may be associated with a reduction in enzyme activities or RuDP levels and measurements of RuDP carboxylase and carbonic anhydrase activities supported the former possibility. Numerous results support a general correlation between the rate of photosynthesis and enzyme activity.

Investigations into the distribution of RuDP carboxylase within the chloroplast suggest it may occupy specific binding sites on the chloroplast membranes (Kannangara, Van Wyk & Menke, 1970). It is possible that there is a correlation between chloroplast membrane development or area, photosynthetic enzyme activity and photosynthesis (Habig & Racusen, 1969; Chollet & Ogren, 1972).

Biochemical regulation of the photosynthetic mechanism

The most obvious biochemical regulation of photosynthesis is in the light–dark reactions. Inhibition of photosynthesis in the dark is generally attributed to the removal of electron flow and NADPH and ATP production. RuDP is necessary, although in isolated chloroplasts it has been shown that CO_2 fixation ceases within two minutes of darkness, but the RuDP level does not drop by more than 60% from the light value. When ATP was added to the chloroplasts, the level of RuDP was not influenced by darkness but CO_2 fixation stopped (Jensen & Bassham, 1966).

It has also been proposed that RuDP carboxylase activity is light-activated. This is unlikely to be a light effect on RuDP carboxylase synthesis, and it may be a result of variation in the ionic content (especially Mg^{2+}) of the chloroplasts (Bassham, 1971; Sugiyama, Nakayama & Akazawa, 1968). More direct activation of RuDP carboxylase by light has also been reported (Schacter, Gibbs & Champigny, 1971; Chu & Bassham, 1972).

Carbon accumulates within the photosynthetic cells during photosynthesis and the extent of accumulation depends on the relative rates of photosynthesis and translocation. Interconversion between sucrose and other carbon compounds will occur and may stabilise the levels of sucrose within the leaf. Conversion into the relatively chemically inactive starch may reduce feedback inhibition on photosynthetic reactions but may physically disrupt chloroplast membrane organisation. An accumulation of sucrose may depress CO_2 fixation (King, Wardlaw & Evans, 1967; Neales & Incoll, 1968; Medina, 1971).

Two enzymes of the C_4-pathway, PEP carboxylase and pyruvate P_i dikinase are inhibited by their reaction products, oxaloacetate and PEP, and AMP and P_i, respectively. Pyruvate P_i dikinase is also sensitive to light level (Slack, 1968; Hatch & Slack, 1970). Light also influences the synthesis of PEP carboxylase and pyruvate P_i dikinase in leaves (Hatch, Slack & Bull, 1969).

Carbonic anhydrase has often been implicated in photosynthesis (Burr, 1936). Carbonic anhydrase catalyses the reversible hydration of CO_2 and is widely distributed among the higher plants, with a

373

Individual plants and tissues

'dicotyledon' and 'monocotyledon' type (Atkins, Patterson & Graham, 1972a,b). Several functions for carbonic anhydrase have been proposed; that it facilitates CO_2 transport, that it increases the local availability of the CO_2 near the carboxylation enzyme, increases the affinity of the enzyme for CO_2 or influences the light-induced pH gradient in the chloroplasts (Graham *et al.*, 1971).

Photorespiration

The pathway of photorespiration

During photosynthesis some carbon enters the glycolate pathway and with the metabolism of glycolate to 3-phosphoglycerate there is a release of CO_2 during the condensation of glycine to serine (Tolbert, 1971a,b), although Zelitch (1971) suggests CO_2 is derived from a decarboxylation of glycolate. This potential source of CO_2 has been implicated as the cause of reduced CO_2 exchange in normal air in C_3-plants (Zelitch, 1971).

The glycolate pathway requires the co-operation of three subcellular organelles, the chloroplast, mitochondrion and microbody. The reaction sequence is initiated by the RuDP oxygenase catalysed oxidation of RuDP by molecular oxygen. Phosphoglycolate and 3-phosphoglycolate are formed and in the presence of P-glycolate phosphatase, glycolate is formed. Glycolate excreted by chloroplasts is converted to glyoxylate by glycolate oxidase in the microbodies. The glyoxylate may be converted to glycine in the microbody, or it may be slowly oxidised to oxalate or it may return to the chloroplast where it is reduced by NADP glyoxylate reductase to glycolate to complete the glycolate–glyoxylate cycle (Tolbert, 1971a,b). In the mitochondria there is conversion of two glycines to one serine and it is suggested that this conversion is a site for the CO_2 loss associated with photorespiration.

Methods used to estimate photorespiration

There is no currently available technique to quantitatively and unambiguously measure CO_2 evolved during photorespiration (Jackson & Volk, 1970; Ludlow & Jarvis, 1971). A CO_2 response curve technique and ^{14}C uptake method have been widely used and may reliably estimate CO_2 lost from the plant (Decker, 1957,1959a,b; McCree & Troughton, 1966a; Lake, 1967a,b; Heath & Orchard, 1968; Whiteman

374

and Koller, 1968; Troughton & Slatyer, 1969; Ludwig & Canvin, 1971; Jackson & Volk, 1970).

Other techniques are semi-quantitative and may be used to estimate the presence or absence of photorespiration. These include the carbon dioxide efflux into CO_2-free air (El-Sharkawy & Hesketh, 1965), CO_2 compensation point, CO_2 burst on transfer from light to dark (Decker, 1955) and the effect of O_2 on net photosynthesis (Forrester, Krotkov & Nelson, 1966a,b).

Magnitude of CO_2 evolution in the light

In assessing the role of photorespiration in plant productivity it is necessary to estimate the rate of CO_2 evolution from the leaf. Estimates using the CO_2 response curve method indicate it is about 25% of net photosynthetic rate (Troughton & Slatyer, 1969), which is similar to results using the ^{14}C technique (Ludwig & Canvin, 1971). The extent to which the oxygen effect on net photosynthesis is attributable to an effect on photorespiration is regarded as 50% in soyabean (Curtis, Ogren & Hageman, 1969), 32% in sunflower (Ludwig & Canvin, 1971), 40% in *Atriplex hastata* (Osmond, Troughton & Goodchild, 1969), 50% in cotton (Troughton & Slatyer, 1969) and 'probably a minor component' (Osmond & Björkman, 1972).

Most techniques suggest that C_4-plants have a reduced ability to evolve CO_2 in the light. The localisation of the C_3-reactions in the bundle sheath cells would enhance the possibility of refixation of respired CO_2, though there may also be variation in the enzymes associated with the glycolate cycle.

Environmental effects on photorespiration

Light and photorespiration are intimately linked, as are light and glycolate synthesis. This effect is likely to operate through the supply of ATP and $NADPH_2$ involved in the regeneration of RuDP. Photorespiration therefore is a 'dark' reaction. Blue light has been suggested to stimulate respiration but the action spectra of Bulley & Nelson (1968) do not support this for photorespiration. Björkman (1966) observed that the inhibitory effect of oxygen on CO_2 fixation in higher plants was greater at wavelengths which preferentially excite photosystem I.

Temperature stimulates both dark and photorespiration, with photorespiration showing a Q_{10} of about 2 (Decker, 1959a,b; Troughton &

Slatyer, 1969). CO_2 evolution occurs in oxygen-free air in cotton leaves at rates of 1.0 and 10.0 ng cm^{-2} s^{-1} at 25 °C and 35 °C, respectively (Troughton & Slatyer, 1969).

At low CO_2 concentrations photorespiration is apparently independent of CO_2 concentration (Ludwig & Canvin, 1971) but high CO_2 concentrations will inhibit photorespiration.

Oxygen stimulates photorespiration and some results suggest it is proportional to oxygen concentration (Fig. 16.8) (Forrester, Krotkov & Nelson, 1966*a,b*; Troughton & Slatyer, 1969).

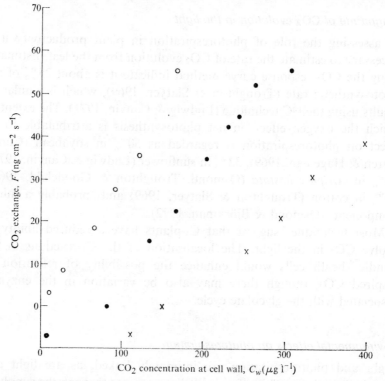

Fig. 16.8. The CO_2 response curve for cotton, with air blown through the leaf, for three levels of oxygen. (○) 0%; (●) 22%; (×) 44%. Leaf temperature was 25 °C and light level was 110 W m^{-2} (400–700 nm). From Troughton & Slatyer (1969).

Acclimation of the photosynthetic mechanism
Acclimation to the light regime

The effects of illuminance during growth on the metabolic performance of plants has been investigated in several studies. In white clover and in other plants the light response curves for photosynthesis were similar

376

for plants grown under a range of light levels but there was adaptation of respiration to illuminance (McCree & Troughton, 1966*a*,*b*; Ludwig, Saeki & Evans, 1965). However, in tall fescue and in *Lolium* plants grown under high illuminance had higher rates of apparent photosynthesis than plants grown under low illuminance (Woledge, 1971; Wilson & Cooper, 1969*d*). In *Atriplex patula* subsp. *hastata* plants grown under different illuminances indicate that adjustment in most components of the light reactions and gas exchange components to illuminance occurs (Björkman *et al.*, 1972).

Investigation of natural populations of *Dactylis glomerata* L. showed marked differences in the photosynthetic activity between populations at high light (Eagles & Treharne, 1969), while in *Solidago virgaurea* (Björkman & Holmgren, 1966) plants from shaded sites had lower photosynthesis at light saturation and lower photochemical activity than plants grown in unshaded sites.

Acclimation to thermal regimes

Ecotypes and species vary greatly in their temperature characteristics of photosynthesis. In general, photosynthesis is limited at low temperature through effects on chlorophyll synthesis, leaf area development and the reaction rates of chemical reactions, and at high temperature by inactivation and denaturation of enzymes (McWilliam & Naylor, 1967; Langridge & McWilliam, 1967).

Most plants possess a relatively broad temperature optimum (El-Sharkawy & Hesketh, 1965; Whiteman & Koller, 1967; Hofstra & Hesketh, 1969; Jolliffe & Tregunna, 1968; Troughton & Slatyer, 1969), which for C_4-plants is in the range 30–40 °C whereas for C_3-plants it is in the range 10–25 °C (Cooper & Tainton, 1968; Murata, Iyama & Honma, 1965; Downton & Slatyer, 1972).

The lack of a difference in the temperature characteristics in oxygen-free air may be due to the involvement of the C_3-reaction in both species.

In general, the optimum temperature for photosynthesis is correlated with the temperature conditions of the natural environment (Mooney & West, 1964; Treharne & Eagles, 1970), an extreme example being the desert species *Tidestromia oblongifolia* which has an optimum temperature of 47 °C (Pearcy, Björkman, Harrison & Mooney, 1971).

Conditions during growth would be expected to alter many anatomical and biochemical components of the photosynthetic pathway.

Individual plants and tissues

In *Lolium* sp. however, differences in light-saturated apparent photosynthesis in plants grown at different temperatures were not due to mesophyll or stomatal characteristics (Wilson & Cooper, 1969c). Björkman & Pearcy (1971) investigated the temperature-dependence of photosynthesis in *Atriplex patula* subsp. *spicata* and *A. rosea*. The activation energy (*Ea*) was unaffected by the temperature regime under which the plants were grown. In the same study it was shown that *Ea* was similar for a wide range of species, including liverworts, C$_3$- and C$_4$-plants from a wide range of habitats. *Ea* values of 79.5 kJ mol^{-1} (19.0 kcal mol^{-1}) for *Canchrus cilioris* and 75.4 and 134 kJ mol^{-1} (18 and 32 kcal mol^{-1}) for *Lolium* sp. have been reported (Charles-Edwards & Charles-Edwards, 1970) and 44 kJ mol^{-1} (10.5 kcal mol^{-1}) for *Zea mays* (Raschke, 1970).

Activation energies were similar for RuDP carboxylase from several C$_3$- and C$_4$-species grown under a range of temperatures and measured *in vitro* (Björkman & Pearcy, 1971). Discontinuities in the Arrhenius plot for RuDP carboxylase *in vitro* were observed in PEP carboxylase from maize (Phillips & McWilliams, 1971) and this effect was due to phase changes in membrane lipids associated with the enzymes.

Evolution of the photosynthetic mechanisms among higher plants

Evidence from many sources suggest that carbon compounds of a photosynthetic origin were in existence 3.3×10^9 years ago. Carbon isotope ratios of carbon in coal deposits up to 400 million years old and in present-day C$_3$-plants are similar, suggesting that the C$_3$-pathway was operating over this period (Troughton, 1971a).

The origins of the light reactions of photosynthesis are discussed by Olson (1970). It is likely that the photosystems as currently formulated were present in the early algae, with little further development in higher plants. The sequence of development in the photosynthetic bacteria and algae may have involved the presence of chlorophyll and a cyclic system of electron flow. The final steps may have been associated with the oxidation of water and the development of a respiratory mechanism based on oxygen. The eukaryotic organism may have then been initiated.

Both the photosystems and C$_3$-pathway may have been constant from earliest times. It has been suggested that 93% of all enzymes present in eukaryote types are also present in prokaryote types. This apparent constancy of the chemical components contrasts with the

378

dramatic variation in plant morphology that has occurred as different ecological sites have been exploited.

It is not possible yet to reconstruct the edaphic and aerial environmental conditions that may have led to the evolutionary development of higher plants, particularly with respect to the carbon pathways. Nevertheless, the development of plants from an aquatic environment onto dry land, and from swamps to deserts, is likely to have been determined by the availability of water, with the thermal and chemical characteristics of the environment and the concentration of O_2 and CO_2 in the air imposing further restrictions.

In considering specifically the development of the C_4-pathway, and assuming it developed later than the C_3-pathway, the criteria likely to be important in determining its occurrence are: (1) The potential for C_4-photosynthesis. The enzymic potential for this pathway was always present, as PEP carboxylase is present in bacteria and C_3-plants. The modified leaf anatomy may not have been necessary (e.g. CAM), but it was an advantage (C_4). However, leaf anatomy is a highly flexible component and the compartmentalization could be achieved in different ways. (2) That the carboxylation processes were compatible with the C_3-pathway. Carbon metabolism was based on the C_3-pathway and it is unlikely that a completely new carbon pathway would evolve *de novo*. (3) That the pathway was successful in both persistence and reproduction. Its success is likely to be greater if the pathway has an advantage in some conditions, and changes in the oxygen concentration of the atmosphere during geologic time and the extension of plants into more arid environments may have guaranteed the success of the C_4-pathway.

The RuDP carboxylase reaction would have evolved in an anaerobic atmosphere and therefore, during its evolution, oxygen concentration was not a factor influencing the competition between carboxylases. During geologic time, however, there was an increase in the oxygen concentration in the atmosphere which did not completely inhibit but reduced the activity of RuDP carboxylase. PEP carboxylase is not oxygen-sensitive and this effect allowed it to become more competitive with RuDP carboxylase as a carboxylation system. The higher carboxylation efficiency of PEP carboxylase would lead to its success as the primary carboxylation enzyme but its inability to process the carbon necessitated co-operation with the C_3-pathway. The apparent inability of the development of a transcarboxylation system necessitated compartmentalization if the higher carboxylation efficiency was to be realized. It was necessary that RUDP carboxylase fix CO_2 at the same rate as

PEP carboxylase, and this was only likely to be achieved if the CO_2 concentration was raised above the atmospheric level, hence a requirement for a compartment.

The higher carboxylation efficiency of cells containing PEP carboxylase had an advantage in water use efficiency and therefore, in exploiting arid environments (Osmond, Troughton & Goodchild, 1969). The results of Shantz & Piemeisel (1927) provide, in retrospect, evidence that C_4-type plants use half as much water as C_3-type plants, in producing the same amount of dry matter. CAM-plants provide a further modification in terms of water use efficiency by having the ability to accumulate CO_2 at night and to conserve water during conditions of high radiation load in the daytime, though its effectiveness is influenced by the environment, especially night temperatures (Neales, 1973a,b).

The ease with which the C_4-pathway arose is evidenced by its widespread occurrence in widely diverse families of both monocotyledons and dicotyledons. In the grasses (Brown & Smith, 1972) and in *Atriplex* (Hatch, Osmond, Troughton & Björkman, 1972) there is evidence that the pathway may have evolved several times.

References

Anderson, M. C. (1967). Photon flux, chlorophyll content and photosynthesis under natural conditions. *Ecology*, **48**, 1050–3.

Andrews, T. J., Lorimer, G. H. & Tolbert, N. E. (1971). Incorporation of molecular oxygen into glycine and serine during photorespiration in spinach leaves. *Biochemistry*, **10**, 4777–82.

Andrews, T. J., Lorimer, G. H. & Tolbert, N. E. (1973). Ribulose diphosphate oxygenase. I. Synthesis of phosphoglycolate by fraction-1 protein of leaves. *Biochemistry*, **12**, 11–18.

Arnon, D. I. (1971). The light reactions of photosynthesis. *Proceedings of the National Academy of Science, USA*, **68**, 2883–92.

Atkins, C. A., Patterson, B. C. & Graham, D. (1972a). Plant carbonic anhydrases. I. Distribution of types among species. *Plant Physiology, Lancaster*, **50**, 214–17.

Atkins, C. A., Patterson, B. C. & Graham, D. (1972b). Plant carbonic anhydrases. II. Preparation and some properties of monocotyledon and dicotyledon enzyme types. *Plant Physiology, Lancaster*, **50**, 218–23.

Barrs, H. D. (1971). Cyclic variations in stomatal aperture, transpiration, and leaf water potential under constant environmental conditions. *Annual Review of Plant Physiology*, **22**, 223–36.

Bassham, J. A. (1971). Photosynthetic carbon metabolism. *Proceedings National Academy Science, USA*, **68**, 2877–82.

Baszynski, T., Brand, J., Barr, R., Krogmann, D. W. & Crane, F. L. (1972). Some biochemical characteristics of chloroplasts from mineral-deficient maize. *Plant Physiology, Lancaster*, **50**, 410–11.

Bender, M. M. (1971). Variations in the $^{13}C/^{12}C$ ratios of plants in relation to the pathway of photosynthetic carbon dioxide fixation. *Photochemistry*, **10**, 1239–44.

Bisalpultra, T., Downton, W. J. S. & Tregunna, E. G. (1969). The distribution and ultrastructure of chloroplasts in leaves differing in photosynthetic carbon metabolism. I. Wheat, sorghum, and *Aristida* (*Gramineae*). *Canadian Journal of Botany*, **47**, 15–21.

Bishop, D. G., Anderson, K. S. & Smillie, R. M. (1971). Incomplete membrane-bound photosynthetic electron transfer pathway in agranal chloroplasts. *Biochemical and Biophysical Research Communications*, **42**, 74–81.

Björkman, O. (1966). The effect of oxygen concentration on photosynthesis in higher plants. *Physiologia Plantarum*, **19**, 618–33.

Björkman, O. (1971). Comparative photosynthetic CO_2 exchange in higher plants. In *Photosynthesis and Photorespiration*, eds. M. D. Hatch, C. B. Osmond & R. O. Slatyer, pp. 18–32. New York, Wiley-Interscience.

Björkman, O., Boardman, N. K., Anderson, J. M., Thorne, S. W., Goodchild, D. J. & Pyliotis, N. A. (1972). Effect of light intensity during growth of *Atriplex patula* on the capacity of photosynthetic reactions, chloroplast components and structure. *Carnegie Institution Year Book*, **71**, 115–35.

Björkman, O. & Gauhl, E. (1969). Carboxydismutase activity in plants with and without β-carboxylation photosynthesis. *Planta*, **88**, 197–203.

Björkman, O. & Holmgren, P. (1966). Photosynthetic adaptation to light intensity in plants native to shaded and exposed habitats. *Physiologia Plantarum*, **19**, 854–9.

Björkman, O., Nobs, M., Pearcy, R., Boynton, J. & Berry, J. (1971). Characteristics of hybrids between C_3- and C_4-species of *Atriplex*. In *Photosynthesis and Photorespiration*, eds. M. D. Hatch, C. B. Osmond & R. O. Slatyer, pp. 105–19. New York, Wiley-Interscience.

Björkman, O. & Pearcy, R. W. (1971). Effect of growth temperature on the temperature dependence of photosynthesis *in vivo* and on CO_2 fixation by carboxydismutase *in vitro* in C_3- and C_4-species. *Carnegie Institution Year Book*, **70**, 511–20.

Björkman, O., Troughton, J. H. & Nobs, M. A. (1973). Photosynthesis in relation to leaf structure. *Brookhaven Symposium in Biology*, **26**, in press.

Black, C. C. & Mayne, B. C. (1970). P700 activity and chlorophyll content of plants with different photosynthetic carbon dioxide fixation cycles. *Plant Physiology*, **45**, 738–41.

Bowes, G. & Berry, J. A. (1972). The effect of oxygen on photosynthesis and glycolate excretion in *Chlamydomonas reinhardtii*. *Carnegie Institution Year Book*, **71**, 148–58.

Brandon, P. C. (1967). Temperature features of enzymes effecting Crassulacean Acid Metabolism. *Plant Physiology*, **42**, 977–86.

Brougham, R. W. (1960). The relationship between critical leaf area, total chlorophyll content, and maximum growth rate of some pasture and crop plants. *Annals of Botany*, **24**, 463–74.

Individual plants and tissues

Brown, W. V. & Smith, B. N. (1972). Grass evolution, the Kranz syndrome, $^{13}C/^{12}C$ ratios, and continental drift. *Nature, London,* **239,** 345–6.

Bulley, N. R. & Nelson, C. D. (1968). Action spectra of photosynthesis and photorespiration in radish leaves. *Plant Physiology,* **43,** S-20.

Burr, G. O. (1936). Carbonic anhydrase and photosynthesis. *Proceedings of the Royal Society of London Series B,* **120,** 42–7.

Burr, G. O., Hartt, C. E., Brodie, H. W., Tanimoto, T., Kortschak, H. P., Takahashi, D., Ashton, F. M., & Coleman, R. E. (1957). The sugar cane plant. *Annual Review of Plant Physiology,* **8,** 275–8.

Calvin, M. & Benson, A. A. (1948). The path of carbon in photosynthesis. *Science,* **107,** 476–480.

Chang, F. H. & Troughton, J. H. (1972). Chlorophyll a/b ratios in C_3 and C_4-plants. *Photosynthetica,* **6,** 57–65.

Charles-Edwards, D. A. & Charles-Edwards, J. (1970). An analysis of the temperature response curves of CO_2 exchange in the leaves of two temperate and one tropical grass species. *Planta,* **94,** 140–51.

Chartier, P. (1966). Étude theorique de l'assimilation brute de la feuille. *Annales de Physiologie végétale* (Paris), **8,** 167–95.

Chartier, P. (1970). A model of CO_2 assimilation in the leaf. In *Prediction and Measurement of Photosynthetic Productivity,* pp. 307–15. Wageningen, PUDOC.

Chartier, P., Chartier, M. & Čatský, J. (1970). Resistances for carbon dioxide diffusion and for carboxylation as factors in bean leaf photosynthesis. *Photosynthetica,* **4,** 48–57.

Chollet, R. & Ogren, W. L. (1972). Greening in a virescent mutant of maize. II. Enzyme studies. *Zeitschrift für Pflanzenphysiologie,* **68,** 45–54.

Chu, D. K. & Bassham, J. A. (1972). Inhibition of ribulose-1,5-diphosphate carboxylase by 6-Phosphogluconate. *Plant Physiology,* **50,** 224–7.

Cooper, T. G., Filmer, D., Wishnick, M. & Lane, M. D. (1969). The active species of CO_2 utilized by ribulose diphosphate carboxylase. *Journal of Biological Chemistry,* **244,** 1081–83.

Cooper, J. P. & Tainton, N. M. (1968). Light and temperature requirements of the growth of tropical and temperate plants. *Herbage Abstracts,* **38,** 167–76.

Cooper, T. G. & Wood, H. G. (1971). The carboxylation of phosphoenol pyruvate and pyruvate. II. The active species of 'CO_2' utilized by phosphoenolpyruvate carboxylase and pyruvate carboxylase. *Journal of Biological Chemistry,* **246,** 5488–90.

Cowan, I. R. (1972). Mass and heat transfer in laminar boundary layers with particular reference to assimilation and transpiration in leaves. *Agricultural Meteorology,* **10,** 311–29.

Curtis, P. E., Ogren, W. L. & Hageman, R. M. (1969). Varietal effects in soybean photosynthesis and photorespiration. *Crop Science,* **9,** 323–7.

Decker, J. P. (1955). A rapid postillumination declaration of respiration in green leaves. *Plant Physiology,* **30,** 82–4.

Decker, J. P. (1957). Further evidence of increased carbon dioxide production accompanying photosynthesis. *Journal of Solar Energy and Scientific Engineering,* **1,** 30–3.

382

Decker, J. P. (1959*a*). Comparative responses of carbon dioxide outburst and uptake in tobacco. *Plant Physiology*, **34**, 100–2.

Decker, J. P. (1959*b*). Some effects of temperature and carbon dioxide concentration on photosynthesis of *Mimulus*. *Plant Physiology*, **34**, 103–6.

Denius, H. R. & Homann, P. H. (1972). The relation between photosynthesis, respiration, and Crassulacean Acid Metabolism in leaf slices of *Aloe arborescens* Mill. *Plant Physiology*, **49**, 873–80.

Downton, W. J. S. (1971). Adaptive and evolutionary aspects of C_4-photosynthesis. In *Photosynthesis and Photorespiration*, eds. M. D. Hatch, C. B. Osmond & R. O. Slatyer, pp. 3–17. New York, Wiley-Interscience.

Downton, J. & Slatyer, R. O. (1972). Temperature-dependence of photosynthesis in cotton. *Plant Physiology*, **50**, 518–22.

Eagles, C. F. & Treharne, K. J. (1969). Photosynthetic activity of *Dactylis glomerata* L., in different light regimes. *Photosynthetica*, **3**, 29–38.

El-Sharkawy, M. & Hesketh, J. (1965). Photosynthesis among species in relation to characteristics of leaf anatomy and CO_2 diffusion resistances. *Crop Science*, **5**, 517–21.

Emerson, R. & Arnold, W. (1932). The photochemical reaction in photosynthesis. *Journal of General Physiology*, **16**, 191–5.

Enns, T. (1967). Facilitation by carbonic anhydrase of carbon dioxide transport. *Science*, **155**, 44–7.

Forrester, M. L., Krotkov, G. & Nelson, C. D. (1966*a*). Effect of oxygen on photosynthesis, photorespiration and respiration in detached leaves. I. Soybean. *Plant Physiology*, **41**, 422–7.

Forrester, M. L., Krotkov, G. & Nelson, C. D. (1966*b*). Effect of oxygen on photosynthesis, photorespiration and respiration in detached leaves. II. Corn and other monocotyledons. *Plant Physiology*, **41**, 428–31.

French, C. S. (1966). Kinetics of oxygen evolution. In *Currents in Photosynthesis*, eds. J. B. Thomas & J. G. Goedheer, pp. 285–95. Rotterdam, Ad. Donker.

French, C. S. (1971). The distribution and action in photosynthesis of several forms of chlorophyll. *Proceedings of the National Academy of Sciences, USA*, **68**, 2893–7.

Goedheer, J. C. (1963). In *La Photosynthèse*, pp. 148–59. Paris, Centre National de la Recherche Scientifique.

Graham, D., Atkins, C. A., Reed, M. L., Patterson, B. D. & Smillie, R. D. (1971). Carbonic anhydrase, photosynthesis, and light-induced pH changes. In *Photosynthesis and Photorespiration*, eds. M. D. Hatch, C. B. Osmond & R. O. Slatyer, pp. 267–74. New York, Wiley-Interscience.

Grahl, H. & Wild, A. (1972). Die Variabilität der Grosse der Photosyntheseeinheit bei Licht-und Schattenpflanzen. Untersuchungen zur Photosynthese von experimentell induzierten Licht- und Schattentypen von *Sinapis alba*. *Zeitschrift Pflanzenphysiology*, **67**, 443–53.

Gregory, R. P. F. (1971). *Biochemistry of Photosynthesis*. London, Wiley-Interscience.

Griffiths, M., Sistrom, W. R., Cohen-Bazire, G. & Stanier, R. Y. (1955). Function of carotenoids in photosynthesis. *Nature*, **176**, 1211.

Individual plants and tissues

Habig, W. & Racusen, D. (1969). The effect of light on ribulose diphosphate carboxylase in corn leaves. *Canadian Journal of Botany*, **47**, 1051–4.

Hall, J. D., Barr, R., Al-Abbas, A. H. & Crane, F. L. (1972). The ultra-structure of chloroplasts in mineral-deficient maize leaves. *Plant Physiology*, **50**, 404–9.

Hatch, M. D., Osmond, C. B., Troughton, J. H. & Björkman, O. (1972). Physiological and biochemical characteristics of C_3- and C_4-*Atriplex* species and hybrids in relation to the evolution of the evolution of the C_4-pathway. *Carnegie Institution Year Book*, **71**, 135–44.

Hatch, M. D. & Slack, C. R. (1966). Photosynthesis by sugar-cane leaves. A new carboxylation reaction and the pathway of sugar formation. *Biochemical Journal*, **101**, 103–11.

Hatch, M. D. & Slack, C. R. (1967). The participation of phosphoenol-pyruvate synthetase in photosynthetic CO_2 fixation of tropical grasses. *Archives of Biochemistry and Biophysics*, **120**, 244–5.

Hatch, M. D. & Slack, C. R. (1968). New enzyme for the interconversion of pyruvate and phosphopyruvate and its role in the carbon(4)dicarboxylic acid pathway of photosynthesis. *Biochemical Journal*, **106**, 141–6.

Hatch, M. D. & Slack, C. R. (1969). Studies on the mechanism of activation and inactivation of pyruvate, phosphate dikinase. A possible regulatory role for the enzyme in the C_4-dicarboxylic acid pathway of photo-synthesis. *Biochemical Journal*, **112**, 549–58.

Hatch, M. D. & Slack, C. R. (1970). Photosynthetic CO_2 fixation pathways. *Annual Review of Plant Physiology*, **21**, 141–62.

Hatch, M. D., Slack, C. R. & Bull, T. A. (1969). Light-induced changes in the content of some enzymes of the C_4-dicarboxylic acid pathway of photo-synthesis and its effects on other characteristics of photosynthesis. *Phytochemistry*, **8**, 669–705.

Hatch, M. D., Slack, C. R. & Johnson, H. (1967). Further studies on a new pathway of photosynthetic carbon dioxide fixation in sugar-cane and its occurrence in other plant species. *Biochemical Journal*, **102**, 417–22.

Heath, O. V. S. (1969). *The physiological aspects of photosynthesis*. London, Heinemann.

Heath, O. V. S. & Orchard, B. (1968). Carbon assimilation at low carbon dioxide levels. II. The processes of apparent assimilation. *Journal of Experimental Botany*, **19**, 176–92.

Heber, U. & French, C. S. (1968). Effects of oxygen on the electron transport chain of photosynthesis. *Planta*, **79**, 99–112.

Highkin, H. R., Boardman, N. K. & Goodchild, D. J. (1969). Photosynthetic studies on a pea-mutant deficient in chlorophyll. *Plant Physiology*, **44**, 1310–20.

Hill, R. & Bendall, F. (1960). Function of the two cytochrome components in chloroplasts: A working hypothesis. *Nature*, **186**, 136–7.

Hofstra, G. & Hesketh, J. D. (1969). Effects of temperature on the gas exchanges of leaves in the light and dark. *Planta*, **85**, 228–37.

Hodge, A. J., McLean, J. D. & Mercer, F. V. (1955). Ultrastructure of the lamellae and grana in the chloroplasts of *Zea mays* L. *Journal of Biophysical and Biochemical Cytology*, **1**, 605–14.

Holmgren, P. & Jarvis, P. G. (1967). Carbon dioxide efflux from leaves in light and darkness. *Physiologia Plantarum*, **20**, 1045–51.

Jackson, W. A. & Volk, R. J. (1970). Photorespiration. *Annual Review of Plant Physiology*, **21**, 385–432.

Jarvis, P. G., Rose, C. W. & Begg, J. E. (1967). An experimental and theoretical comparison of viscous and diffusive resistances to gas flow through amphistomatous leaves. *Agricultural Meteorology*, **4**, 103–17.

Jensen, R. G. & Bassham, J. A. (1966). Photosynthesis by isolated chloroplasts. *Proceedings of the National Academy of Science, USA*, **56**, 1095–101.

Johnson, C. & Brown, W. V. (1973). Grass leaf ultrastructural variations. *American Journal of Botany*, **60**, 727–35.

Jolliffe, P. A. & Tregunna, E. B. (1968). Effect of temperature, CO_2 concentration, and light intensity on oxygen inhibition of photosynthesis in wheat leaves. *Plant Physiology*, **43**, 902–6.

Jones, H. G. & Slatyer, R. O. (1972). Effects of intercellular resistances on estimates of the intracellular resistance to CO_2 uptake by plant leaves. *Australian Journal of Biological Sciences*, **25**, 443–53.

Kanai, R. & Black, C. C. (1972). Biochemical basis for net CO_2 assimilation in C_4-plants. In *Net Carbon Dioxide Fixation in Higher Plants*, ed. C. C. Black, pp. 75–105. North Carolina, Cotton.

Kannangara, C. G., Van Wyk, D. & Menke, W. (1970). Immunological evidence for the presence of latent Ca^{2+} dependent ATPase and carboxydismutase on the thylakoid surface. *Zeitschrift für Naturforschung*, **25b**, 613–18.

King, R. W., Wardlaw, I. F. & Evans, L. T. (1967). Effect of assimilate utilization on photosynthetic rate in wheat. *Planta*, **77**, 261–76.

Kortschak, H. P., Hartt, C. E. & Burr, G. O. (1965). Carbon dioxide fixation in sugar cane leaves. *Plant Physiology*, **40**, 209–13.

Kreuzer, F. (1970). Facilitated diffusion of oxygen and its possible significance; a review, *Respiration Physiology*, **9**, 1–30.

Kunitake, G. M., Saltman, P. & Lang, A. (1957). The products of CO_2 dark fixation in leaves of long- and short-day treated *Kalanchoe blossfeldiana*. *Plant Physiology, Lancaster*, **32**, 201–3.

Laisk, A. (1970). A model of leaf photosynthesis and photorespiration. In *Prediction and Measurement of Photosynthetic Productivity*, pp. 295–306. Wageningen, PUDOC.

Laetsch, W. M. (1971). Chloroplast structural relationships in leaves of C_4-plants. In *Photosynthesis and Photorespiration*, eds. M. D. Hatch, C. B. Osmond & R. O. Slatyer, pp. 323–49. New York, Wiley-Interscience.

Lake, J. V. (1967*a*). Respiration of leaves during photosynthesis. I. Estimates from an electrical analogue. *Australian Journal of Biological Science*, **20**, 487–93.

Lake, J. V. (1967*b*). Respiration of leaves during photosynthesis. II. Effects on the estimation of mesophyll resistance. *Australian Journal of Biological Science*, **20**, 495–9.

Langridge, J. & McWilliam, J. R. (1967). Heat responses of high plants. In *Thermobiology*, ed. A. H. Rose, pp. 231–92. London, Academic Press.

Lorimer, G. H., Andrews, T. J. & Tolbert, N. E. (1973). Ribulose diphosphate oxygenase. II. Further proof of reaction products and mechanism of action. *Biochemistry*, **12**, 18–23.

Ludlow, M. M. & Jarvis, P. G. (1971). Methods for measuring photorespiration in leaves. In *Plant Photosynthetic Production. Manual of Methods*, eds. Z. Šesták, J. Čatský & P. G. Jarvis, pp. 294–315. The Hague, Junk.

Ludlow, M. M. & Wilson, G. L. (1972). Photosynthesis of tropical pasture plants. IV. Basis and consequences of differences between grasses and legumes. *Australian Journal of Biological Science*, **25**, 1133–45.

Ludwig, L. J. & Canvin, D. T. (1971). The rate of photorespiration during photosynthesis and the relationship of the substrate of light respiration to the products of photosynthesis in sunflower leaves. *Plant Physiology*, **48**, 712–9.

Ludwig, L. J., Saeki, T. & Evans, L. T. (1965). Photosynthesis in artificial communities of cotton plants in relation to leaf area. I. Experiments with progressive defoliation of mature plants. *Australian Journal of Biological Science*, **18**, 1103–18.

McCree, K. J. (1972). The action spectrum, absorptance and quantum yield of photosynthesis in crop plants. *Agricultural Meteorology*, **9**, 191–216.

McCree, K. J. & Troughton, J. H. (1966*a*). Prediction of growth rate at different light levels from measured photosynthesis and respiration rates. *Plant Physiology*, **41**, 559–66.

McCree, K. J. & Troughton, J. H. (1966*b*). Non-existence of an optimum leaf area index for the production rate of white clover grown under constant conditions. *Plant Physiology, Lancaster*, **41**, 1615–22.

McWilliam, J. R. & Naylor, A. W. (1967). Temperature and plant adaption. I. Interaction of temperature and light in the synthesis of chlorophyll in corn. *Plant Physiology, Lancaster*, **42**, 1711–15.

Mathis, P. & Galmiche, J. M. (1967). Action des gaz paramagnetiques sur un état transitoire induit par un éclair laser dans une suspension de chloroplasts. *Comptes rendus hebdomadaires Sèances Academie Sciences, Paris*, Ser. D, **264**, 1903–7.

Medina, E. (1971). Effect of nitrogen supply and light intensity during growth on the photosynthetic capacity and carboxydismutase activity of leaves of *Atriplex patula* ssp. *hastata. Carnegie Institution Year Book*, **70**, 551–9.

Millerd, A., Goodchild, D. J. & Spencer, D. (1969). Studies on a maize mutant sensitive to low temperature. II. Chloroplast structure, development, and physiology. *Plant Physiology, Lancaster*, **44**, 567–83.

Milthorpe, F. L. (1961). Plant factors involved in transpiration. *Arid Zone Research*, **16**, 107–15.

Milthorpe, F. L. & Penman, H. C. (1967). The diffusive conductivity of the stomata of wheat leaves. *Journal of Experimental Botany*, **18**, 422–57.

Monteith, J. L. (1963). Gas exchange in plant communities. In *Environmental Control of Plant Growth*, ed. L. T. Evans, pp. 95–112. New York & London, Academic Press.

Mooney, H. A. & West, M. (1964). Photosynthetic acclimation of plants of diverse origin. *American Journal of Botany*, **51**, 825–7.

Murata, Y., Iyama, J. & Honma, T. (1965). Studies on the photosynthesis of forage crops. IV. Influence of air-temperature upon the photosynthesis and respiration of alfalfa and several southern type forage crops. *Proceedings of the Crop Science Society of Japan*, **34**, 154–8.

Neales, T. F. (1973*a*). Effect of night temperature on the assimilation of carbon dioxide by mature pineapple plants, *Ananas comosus* (L.) Merr. *Australian Journal of Biological Science*, **26**, 539–46.

Neales, T. F. (1973*b*). The effect of night temperature on CO_2 assimilation, transpiration, and water use efficiency in *Agave americana* L. *Australian Journal of Biological Sciences*, **26**, 705–14.

Neales, T. F. & Incoll, L. D. (1968). The control of leaf photosynthesis rate by the level of assimilate concentration in the leaf: A review of the hypothesis. *Botanical Review*, **34**, 107–25.

Ogren, W. L. & Bowes, G. (1971). Ribulose diphosphate carboxylase regulates soybean photorespiration. *Nature, New Biology*, **270**, 159–60.

Olson, J. M. (1970). The evolution of photosynthesis. *Science*, **168**, 438–46.

Osmond, C. B. (1967). β-carboxylation during photosynthesis in *Atriplex*. *Biochimica et Biophysica Acta*, **141**, 197–9.

Osmond, C. B. & Avadhani, P. N. (1970). Inhibition of the β-carboxylation pathway of CO_2 fixation by bisulfite compounds. *Plant Physiology, Lancaster*, **45**, 228–30.

Osmond, C. B. & Björkman, O. (1972). Simultaneous measurements of oxygen effects on net photosynthesis and glycolate metabolism in C_3 and C_4-species of *Atriplex*. *Carnegie Institution Year Book*, **71**, 141–8.

Osmond, C. B., Troughton, J. H. & Goodchild, D. J. (1969). Physiological, biochemical and structural studies of photosynthesis and photo-respiration in two species of *Atriplex*. *Zeitschrift für Pflanzenphysiologie*, **61**, 218–37.

Pearcy, R. W., Björkman, O., Harrison, A. T. & Mooney, H. A. (1971). Photosynthetic performance of two desert species with C_4-photo-synthesis in Death Valley, California. *Carnegie Institution Year Book*, **70**, 540–51.

Phillips, P. J. & McWilliam, J. R. (1971). Thermal responses of the primary carboxylating enzymes from C_3- and C_4-plants adapted to contrasting temperature environments. In *Photosynthesis and Photorespiration*, eds. M. D. Hatch, C. B. Osmond & R. O. Slatyer, pp. 97–104. New York, Wiley-Interscience.

Pyliotis, N. A., Woo, K. C. & Downton, W. J. S. (1971). Thylakoid aggrega-tion correlated with chlorophyll *a*/chlorophyll *b* ratio in some C_4-species. In *Photosynthesis and Photorespiration*, eds. M. D. Hatch, C. B. Osmond & R. O. Slatyer, pp. 406–12. New York, Wiley-Interscience.

Quayle, J. R., Fuller, R. C., Benson, A. A. & Calvin, M. (1954). Enzymatic carboxylation of ribulose diphosphate. *Journal of the American Chemical Society*, **76**, 3610–11.

Individual plants and tissues

Rabinowitch, E. L. (1951). *Photosynthesis and related processes*, vol. 2. New York, Interscience.

Ranson, S. L. & Thomas, M. (1960). Crassulacean acid metabolism. *Annual Review of Plant Physiology*, **11**, 81–110.

Raschke, K. (1970). The temperature-dependence of CO_2 assimilation and stomatal aperture in leaf sections of *Zea mays*. *Planta*, **91**, 336–63.

Rhoades, M. M. & Carvalho, A. (1944). The function and structure of the parenchyma sheath plastids of the maize leaf. *Bulletin of the Torrey Botanical Club*, **71**, 335–46.

Schacter, B. Z., Gibbs, M. & Champigny, M. (1971). Effect of actinomycin A on photosynthesis of intact spinach chloroplasts. *Plant Physiology, Lancaster*, **48**, 443–6.

Schmid, G. H. & Gaffron, H. (1971). Fluctuating photosynthetic units in higher plants and fairly constant units in algae. *Photochemistry and Photobiology*, **14**, 451–64.

Schwelitz, F. D., Dilley, R. A. & Crane, F. L. (1972). Structural characteristics of a photosynthetic mutant of *Euglena gracilis* blocked in photosystem II. *Plant Physiology, Lancaster*, **50**, 166–70.

Šesták, Z., Čatský, J. & Jarvis, P. G. (1971). Criteria for the selection of suitable methods. In *Plant Photosynthetic Production. Manual of methods*, eds. Z. Šesták, J. Čatský & P. G. Jarvis, pp. 1–48. The Hague, Junk.

Shantz, H. L. & Piemeisel, L. N. (1927). The water requirements of plants at Akron, Colorado. *Journal of Agricultural Research*, **34**, 1093–190.

Slack, C. R. (1968). The photoactivation of a phosphopyruvate synthase in leaves of *Amaranthus palmeri*. *Biochemistry and Biophysical Research Communications*, **30**, 483–8.

Slack, C. R. (1969). Localization of certain photosynthetic enzymes in mesophyll and parenchyma sheath chloroplasts of maize and *Amaranthus palmeri*. *Photochemistry*, **8**, 1387–91.

Slack, C. R. & Hatch, M. D. (1967). Comparative studies on the activities of carboxylases and other enzymes in relation to the new pathway of photosynthetic carbon dioxide fixation in tropical grasses. *Biochemical Journal*, **103**, 660–5.

Slack, C. R., Hatch, M. D. & Goodchild, D. J. (1969). Distribution of enzymes in mesophyll and parenchyma-sheath chloroplasts of maize leaves in relation to the C_4-dicarboxylic acid pathway of photosynthesis. *Biochemical Journal*, **114**, 489–98.

Smith, B. N. & Epstein, S. (1971). Two categories of $^{13}C/^{12}C$ ratios for higher plants. *Plant Physiology, Lancaster*, **43**, 380–4.

Soderstrom, T. R. (1962). The isocitric acid content of crassulaceae plants and a few succulent species from other families. *American Journal of Botany*, **49**, 850–5.

Spencer, D. & Possingham, J. V. (1960). The effect of nutrient deficiencies on the Hill reaction of isolated chloroplasts from tomatoes. *Australian Journal of Biological Science*, **15**, 599–610.

Sugiyama, T., Nakayama, N. & Akazawa, T. (1968). Structure and function of chloroplast proteins. V. Homotropic effect of bicarbonate on RuDP carboxylase reaction and the mechanism of activation by magnesium ions. *Archives of Biochemistry and Biophysics*, **126**, 737–45.

Sutton, B. G. & Osmond, C. B. (1972). Dark fixation of CO_2 by crassulacean plants. Evidence for a single carboxylation step. *Plant Physiology, Lancaster*, **50**, 366–70.

Teichler-Zallen, D. (1969). The effect of manganese on chloroplast structure and photosynthetic ability of *Chlamydomonas reinhardi*. Manganese deficiency inhibits photosystem II but induces stacking. *Plant Physiology, Lancaster*, **44**, 701–10.

Ting, I. P. (1971). Non-autotrophic CO_2 fixation and crassulacean acid metabolism. In *Photosynthesis and Photorespiration*, eds. M. D. Hatch, C. B. Osmond & R. O. Slatyer, pp. 169–85. New York, Wiley-Interscience.

Ting, I. P. & Osmond, C. B. (1973). Activation of plant P-enolpyruvate carboxylases by glucose-6-phosphate: a particular role in crassulacean acid metabolism. *Plant Science Letters*, **1**, 123–8.

Tolbert, N. E. (1971a). Leaf peroxisomes and photorespiration. In *Photosynthesis and Photorespiration*, eds. M. D. Hatch, C. B. Osmond & R. O. Slatyer, pp. 458–71. New York, Wiley-Interscience.

Tolbert, N. E. (1971b). Microbodies – peroxisomes and glyoxysomes. *Annual Review of Plant Physiology*, **22**, 45–74.

Treharne, K. J. & Eagles, C. F. (1970). Effect of temperature on photosynthetic activity of climatic races of *Dactylis glomerata* L. *Photosynthetica*, **4**, 107–17.

Troughton, J. H. (1969a). Regulation of carbon dioxide exchange in plants. Ph.D. Thesis, Australian National University.

Troughton, J. H. (1969b). Plant water status and carbon dioxide exchange of cotton leaves. *Australian Journal of Biological Science*, **22**, 289–302.

Troughton, J. H. (1971). Aspects of the evolution of the photosynthetic carboxylation reaction in plants. In *Photosynthesis and Photorespiration*, eds. M. D. Hatch, C. B. Osmond & R. O. Slatyer, pp. 124–9. New York, Wiley-Interscience.

Troughton, J. H. (1972). Carbon isotope fractionation by plants. In *Proceedings of the 8th International Conference on Radiocarbon Dating*, pp. E39–E57.

Troughton, J. H. & Cowan, I. R. (1968). Carbon dioxide exchange in cotton. Some anomalous fluctuation. *Science*, **161**, 281–3.

Troughton, J. H. & Donaldson, L. A. (1972). *Probing Plant Structure*. Wellington & Sydney, A. H. & A. W. Reed.

Troughton, J. H. & Sampson, F. B. (1973). *Plants: A Scanning Electron Microscope Survey*. Sydney, Wiley.

Troughton, J. H. & Slatyer, R. O. (1969). Plant water status, leaf temperature, and the calculated mesophyll resistance to carbon dioxide of cotton leaves. *Australian Journal of Biological Science*, **22**, 815–27.

Turner, J. S. & Brittain, E. G. (1962). Oxygen as a factor in photosynthesis. *Biological Reviews*, **37**, 130–70.

Turner, J. S., Turner, J. F., Shortman, K. D. & King, J. E. (1958). The

389

inhibition of photosynthesis by oxygen. II. The effect of oxygen on glyceraldehyde phosphate dehydrogenase from chloroplasts. *Australian Journal of Biological Science*, **11**, 336–42.

Vickery, H. B. (1952). The formation of starch in leaves of *Bryophyllum calycinum* cultured in darkness. *Plant Physiology, Lancaster*, **27**, 231–9.

Vidaver, W. & French, C. S. (1965). Oxygen uptake and evolution following monochromatic flashes in *Ulva* and an action spectrum for system 1. *Plant Physiology, Lancaster*, **40**, 7–12.

Warburg, O. (1920). Über die Geschwindigkeit der photochemischen Kohlensäurezersetzung in lebenden Zellen. *Biochemical Journal*, **103**, 188–217.

Weier, T. E., Stocking, C. R. & Shumway, L. K. (1966). The photosynthetic apparatus in chloroplasts of higher plants I. *Brookhaven Symposium in Biology*, **19**, 353–74.

Whiteman, P. C. & Koller, D. (1967). Interactions of carbon dioxide concentration, light intensity and temperature on plant resistances to water vapour and carbon dioxide diffusion. *New Phytologist*, **66**, 463–73.

Whiteman, P. C. & Koller, D. (1968). Estimation of mesophyll resistance to diffusion of carbon dioxide and water vapour. In *Functioning of Terrestrial Ecosystems at the Primary Production Level*, ed. F. E. Eckardt, pp. 415–19. Paris, UNESCO.

Whittingham, C. P., Coombs, J. & Marker, A. F. H. (1967). The role of glycolate in photosynthetic carbon fixation. In *Biochemistry of Chloroplasts*, ed. T. W. Goodwin, vol. II, pp. 155–73. New York, Academic Press.

Wild, A., Ke, B. & Shaw, E. R. (1973). The effect of light intensity during growth of *Sinapis alba* on the electron transport components. *Zeitschrift für Pflanzenphysiologie*, **69**, 344–50.

Wilkins, M. B. (1973). An endogenous circadian rhythm in the rate of CO_2 output of *Bryophyllum*. VI. Action spectrum for the induction of phase shifts by visible radiation. *Journal of Experimental Biology*, **24**, 488–96.

Wilson, D. & Cooper, J. P. (1967). Assimilation of *Lolium* in relation to leaf mesophyll. *Nature*, **214**, 989–92.

Wilson, D. & Cooper, J. P. (1969a). Effect of light intensity and CO_2 on apparent photosynthesis and its relationship with leaf anatomy in genotypes of *Lolium perenne* L. *New Phytologist*, **68**, 627–44.

Wilson, D. & Cooper, J. P. (1969b). Apparent photosynthesis and leaf characters in relation to leaf position and age, among contrasting *Lolium* genotypes. *New Phytologist*, **68**, 645–55.

Wilson, D. & Cooper, J. P. (1969c). Effect of temperature during growth on leaf anatomy and subsequent light saturated photosynthesis among contrasting *Lolium* genotypes. *New Phytologist*, **68**, 1115–23.

Wilson, D. & Cooper, J. P. (1969d). Effect of light intensity during growth on leaf anatomy and subsequent light saturated photosynthesis among contrasting *Lolium* genotypes. *New Phytologist*, **68**, 1125–35.

Witt, K. & Wolff, C. H. (1970). Rise time of the absorption changes in chlorophyll *a*, and carotenoids in photosynthesis. *Zeitschrift für Naturforschung*, **25b**, 387–9.

Woledge, J. (1971). The effect of light intensity during growth on the subsequent rate of photosynthesis of leaves of tall fescue (*Festuca arundinacea* Schreb.) *Annals of Botany*, **35,** 311–22.

Wolff, C. H. & Witt, H. T. (1969). On metastable states of carotenoids in primary events of photosynthesis. *Zeitschrift für Naturforschung*, **246,** 1031–7.

Woolhouse, H. W. (1968). Leaf age and mesophyll resistance as factors in the rate of photosynthesis. *Hilger Journal*, **11,** 7–12.

Zelitch, I. (1971). *Photosynthesis, photorespiration and plant productivity.* New York, Academic Press.

17. Photosynthesis in mosses and lichens

P. KALLIO & L. KÄRENLAMPI

The role of lichens and mosses as primary producers varies much in different biomes. These groups are relatively most important in Antarctica, where there are approximately 400 lichens (Lamb, 1970) in contrast with two (rare) vascular plant species, and hence almost the whole terrestrial ecosystem is based on primary production of these lower plants (Gannutz, 1970). As regards the whole circumpolar tundra area, the Arctic is the centre of ecosystems dominated by lichens and bryophytes (Wielgolaski, 1971). Thus in the three million km² Soviet tundra area half of the total phytomass consists of mosses, and in many ecosystems more than half (Schamurin, Polozova & Khodachek, 1971; Ignatenko, Knorre, Lovelius & Norin, 1971). In the European southern subarctic mosses make up 37.3 %, while the role of reindeer lichens in the area is 8.5 % (Andreev, 1971). In addition to these polar areas, the significance of the bryophytes and lichens is notable in many forest areas, particularly in the oceanic 'mossy forests' (Steere, 1954) and in the dry areas of heaths dominated by the reindeer lichen (Ahti & Hepburn, 1967). The mosses and lichens dominate in mountain areas and particularly in the highest belts (Forman, 1969). The most important genera in these key areas of lichens and mosses are *Cladonia*, *Cetraria*, *Aulacomnium*, *Dicranum*, *Polytrichum*, *Rhacomitrium* and *Hylocomium*. In the subarctic area around Kevo in Finnish Lapland, where the Finnish IBP Tundra work has taken place, the following proportions of ground vegetation are formed by different groups – *low alpine heath:* vascular plants 81.6 %, mosses 1.6 %, and lichens 16.8 %; *fjeld birch forest:* vascular plants 93.5 %, mosses 4.1 %, and lichens 2.4 %; *pine forest:* vascular plants 79.3 %, mosses 3.6 %, and lichens 17.1 % (L. Kärenlampi, in preparation). In these calculations, the below-ground parts of vascular plants are included. If there is no grazing by reindeer, the percentage of lichen biomass in dry ecosystems may be as much as 50 % of the total above-ground vegetation biomass.

Mosses and lichens differ from vascular plants (amongst other things) in that photosynthetic activity and productivity are mostly lower. The reason for this is mainly the low chlorophyll content (Ahmadjian, 1967; Hale, 1967) and the poikilohydric water economy which restricts the

o

season of activity. Rapid drying is a mechanism of adaptation to high light and temperature conditions. Their relatively slow growth rate may also be regarded as a homeostatic mechanism for the bryophytes and lichens. The most important characteristics determining their distribution in the areas described above include both resistance adaptation and capacity adaptation to low temperature conditions. In addition to stress resistance to temperature extremes and water deficiency, there is an ability for rapid reactivation without a lag phase. Both lichens (Kappen & Lange, 1970,1972) and mosses (the work of Kevo IBP group; Kallio & Heinonen, 1973) are able to take advantage of very short periods of temperatures suitable for photosynthesis. For their water economy, lichens and mosses are better adapted than vascular plants to use dew and the water vapour of the air (Bertsch, 1966; Büttner, 1971). Bryophytes and lichens are also better adapted than vascular plants to use the aerial supply of macro- and micronutrients (Tamm, 1953; Rastorfer, 1972) which may be their only or main nutrient source. The lack of nutrients may in some conditions limit photosynthetic activity. In some particular conditions (as in the desert; Lange & Evenari, 1971) the activity of lichens as well as of mosses (as in some very oceanic or in very arctic conditions; Tallis, 1964) may reach the same activity as the vascular plants adapted to the same conditions.

Before evaluating the growth rates of mosses and lichens one should consider the rate of functioning of the ecosystems in which they play the role of primary producers. A higher growth rate of reindeer lichens would necessitate higher decomposition rate or higher consumption rate in northern ecosystems, otherwise the lichen biomass would be accumulating continuously, and one can imagine the unbalanced situation which would follow this higher growth rate of lichens. It seems to us that rates of photosynthesis and production of lichens and mosses although low by certain standards are in good balance with other rates of functioning of their ecosystems. The whole ecosystems obviously have lower rates of functioning towards polar areas.

Ecophysiological studies of mosses and lichens have been started somewhat later than those of vascular plants. In the Antarctica the impetus was given by the IGY (International Geophysical Year; Greene, 1967), and in the subarctic–arctic zone the establishment of field stations and the IBP acted as a stimulus. The literature, particularly from the last few years, contains much information about photosynthesis and its relationship to ecology in mosses and lichens. Rapid methods of measuring CO_2 exchange, especially, have increased the amount of data.

Our present purpose is to give a general view of the ecological features important in the role of mosses and lichens as a component of terrestrial ecosystem. Laboratory and field work must be combined and suitable methods elaborated for modelling the CO_2 exchange of mosses and lichens. The examples and the main ecological background in this discussion are mostly taken from the subarctic and temperate zones, owing to the location of the Kevo Subarctic Research Station in Finnish Lapland where our own work was carried out. The biomes that are dominated by lichen and moss occur in these zones. The literature concerning the ecology of lichens and mosses also refers mainly to the temperate and polar zones.

The maximal photosynthetic capacity in mosses and lichens

In only a few cases in the literature are photosynthetic rates of mosses given on a comparable (dry weight) basis. The concept of the 'whole moss' is not standardized over all studies, and the laboratory measurements on area basis (of the stand) are subject to still greater variability. The 'optimal conditions' in both methods depend on so many variables that they are seldom analysed satisfactorily. Measurement on the segment basis has therefore been recommended for IBP studies. Variation based on acclimation and adaptation is a further source of great variability.

In Table 17.1 some 'maximal' net photosynthetic rates for mosses are given. Corresponding values for lichens are given in Table 17.2. The concept 'maximal' should not be taken too strictly. It means neither a single 'record value' reached in laboratory experiments nor the 'record value' observed in the field. The values are rather 'highest values given' by the authors of the papers to which we refer, and they are intended to show the approximate level of the upper limit of net photosynthetic rate.

Büttner (1971) has given gross photosynthetic rates for many lichens from dry heath forests, Germany. When the estimated respiration rate is taken into consideration, his values show somewhat higher net photosynthetic rates than those reported by Stålfelt (1938) (Table 17.2), and a grouping into an active *Cetraria* group and a less active *Cladonia* group is justified.

The mean for the lichens is lower than for the mosses and apparently both are lower than the values 1.77 and 2.28 mg CO_2 g^{-1} h^{-1} respectively reported by Stålfelt (1938). When compared on an area basis (mg CO_2 dm^{-2} h^{-1}) the values for the more or less crustaceous lichens (Lange,

Individual plants and tissues

Schulze & Koch, 1970*b*), 0.7 in *Lecanora farinosa*, 2.1 in *Caloplaca ehrenbergii*, and 2.2 in *Xanthoria isidioides*, do not differ very much from the value for *Peltigera aphthosa*, which was 1.5 in our experiments (also Ried, 1960*a*).

Table 17.1. *Some maximal values for net photosynthetic rate in mosses*

Author Ecological group and locality	Species	Net photo- synthetic rate (mg CO_2 g^{-1} h^{-1})	Notes
Stålfelt (1937) Forest mosses South Sweden	*Pleurozium schreberi*	2.0	⎡1.63
	Hylocomium proliferum	3.2	Youngest 2.26
	H. squarrosum	3.5	segments in 2.20
	Ptilium crista-castrensis	3.4	autumn for all ⎬2.70
	Rhytidiadelphus triquetrus	2.5	species Mean 2.20
	Sphagnum girgensohnii	3.0	⎣1.50
Hosokawa *et al.* (1964) Epiphytes Japan	*Thuidium cymbifolium*	0.6	⎫
	T. toyamae	1.4	⎮
	Hylocomium cavifolium	0.6	⎬Stump species
	Homaliodendron scabellifolium	0.6	⎮
	Leucobryum neilgherrense	1.4	⎭
	Anomodon giraldi	0.9	⎫
	Pterobryum arbuscula	1.5	⎮
	Macrosporiella scabriseta	0.9	⎮
	Boulaua mittenii	0.9	⎬Trunk species
	Neckera konoi	1.0	⎮
	Macromitrium gynostomum	1.3	⎭
	Ulota crispula	1.2	Crown species
Rastorfer (1972) Antarctica	*Drepanocladus uncinatus*	0.9	⎫
	Polytrichum strictum	0.7	Estimated from the
	Pohlia nutans	0.9	values given
	Calliergon austrostramineum	1.0	⎭
Own measurements (cf. also Kallio & Heinonen, 1973) Strains from different parts of the globe	*Rhacomitrium lanuginosum*	0.4–0.8	In optimum conditions in autumn, 1 cm from top
Own measurements Subarctic Finland Spitsbergen	*Dicranum elongatum*	0.9	⎫As above
	Drepanocladus uncinatus	0.8	⎭
Own measurements South Finland	*Pleurozium schreberi*	1.1	⎫
	Hylocomium proliferum	2.5	⎮As above
	Polytrichum juniperinum	1.6	⎮
	Pohlia drummondii	2.0	⎭

In comparison with the leaves of vascular plants, the maximal photosynthetic rate of lichens is much lower both on an area and on a dry weight basis (Smith, 1962; Stålfelt, 1938,1960). The values for the most active lichens are some 10% of those for the vascular plants of tundra (Zalenskij, Shvetsova & Voznessenskij, 1971).

396

Table 17.2. *Some maximal values for net photosynthetic rate in lichens*

Author Ecological group and locality	Species	Net photo- synthetic rate $(mg\ CO_2\ g^{-1}\ h^{-1})$	Notes
Stålfelt (1938) Forest species South Sweden	*Cladonia alpestris*	1.0	
	Cladonia silvatica	0.8	
	Cladonia digitata	0.8	
	Peltigera aphthosa	2.5	
	Umbilicaria pustulata	0.9	
	Cetraria islandica	1.0	In optimum
	Ramalina farinacea	3.4–3.9	condition in autumn
	R. fraxinea	1.1	
	Cetraria glauca	1.3	
	Evernia prunastri	2.5	
	Parmelia physodes	2.4	
	Usnea dasypoga	2.5	
Butin (1954)	*Peltigera praetextata*	0.65	
Bliss & Hadley (1964) North America	*Cladonia rangiferina*	0.4	Total specimen
	Cetraria nivalis	0.4	
Lange (1965) Different origins and ecology	*Cladonia elongata*	0.5	The Alps
	Cladonia alcicornis	0.3	Middle Europe
	Stereocaulon alpinum	0.3	The Alps
	Parmelia encausta	0.2	
	Parmelia coreyi	1.4	Antarctica
	Parmelia pachyderma	0.3	Brazil
	Parmelia magna	0.3	
	Letharia vulpina	0.4	The Alps
Bertsch (1966)	*Ramalina farinacea*	2.1	
	Ramalina thrausta	2.8	From the graphs
	Evernia prunastri	1.8	
	Evernia divaricata	1.9	
Gannutz (1967)	*Xanthoria mawsoni*	0.2	Antarctica
	Stereocaulon sp.	0.7	New Zealand
Schulze & Lange (1968) Central Europe	*Parmelia physodes*	2.8	
Kärenlampi (1970)	*Cladonia alpestris*	0.8	Young specimens
Lange et al. (1970b) Israel	*Ramalina maciformis*	1.8	Desert
	Teloschistes lacunosus	0.4	
Adams (1971a,b)	*Cladonia rangiferina*	0.5	
Harris (1971)	*Parmelia sulcata*	0.8	
	Parmelia physodes	0.8	
Kallio & Heinonen (1971) and partly unpublished material of Kevo			Total specimens in optimum conditions
	Cetraria nivalis	0.3	Subarctic terricolous
	Nephroma arcticum	0.6	
	Solorina crocea	0.6	
	Stereocaulon paschale	0.3	
	Umbilicaria vellea	0.6	Subarctic saxicolous
	Parmelia olivacea	0.4	Subarctic epiphytic
	Parmelia physodes	0.9	S. Finland epiphytic
	Ramalina farinacea	1.0	
	Ramalina fraxinea	0.3	
	Evernia prunastri	1.5	
	Peltigera aphthosa	0.5	S. Finland terricolous
Own measurements Kevo	*Cladonia alpestris*	0.3–0.4	Total specimens
	Cetraria nivalis	0.3–0.4	

Schulze & Lange (1968) have shown that the maximal photosynthetic rate of *Hypogymnia physodes* (which is one of the most active lichens) is about 20% that of coniferous leaves and some cultivated plants. In the list compiled by Gabrielsen (1960), the corresponding value was near 10% when *Umbilicaria pustulata* and *Parmelia tinctorum* were compared with cultivated vascular plants. On the other hand, no great differences are seen when *Oxalis acetosella* is compared to these lichens.

The relationship is, however, quite different when the total plants are compared. The green parts form only 5–15% of the woody vascular plants, for instance, in the Kevo area. It seems to us that there are no significant differences in the net assimilation rate (NAR) on a total dry matter basis. The genetically determined size and structure seem to be the key aspects.

In lichens, the tops of the fruticose thalli and the margins of the foliose thalli are the most active parts. Measurements of the whole thalli give lower and more varying values (Ried, 1960*c*; Smith, 1962; Godish & Schein, 1966; Kärenlampi, 1970). The values for crustaceous lichens are not strictly comparable, because most of the measurements have been made on an area basis. The variability in the maximal photosynthetic rate in lichens is great, and the most active lichens (mostly epiphytes) show higher values than the most active mosses. The comparison of the tops shows that even the rather slowly growing lichens *Cladonia alpestris* and *Cetraria nivalis* are equal or more active than *Rhacomitrium lanuginosum* and *Dicranum elongatum*, which are very well adapted to the northern conditions. When the photosynthetic rate was measured on three different segments of *Hylocomium proliferum* (growth from the previous summer, the year before that and the rest) the following values were found: 1.5, 0.9 and 0.4 mg CO_2 g^{-1} h^{-1}, respectively (13 000 lx, $+5$ °C).

In *Cetraria nivalis*, 1-cm long top parts may have a maximal photosynthetic rate of about 0.8–1.0 mg CO_2 g^{-1} h^{-1} (measurements of the Kevo IBP groups), whereas the total living thallus has a maximum mean value of approximately 0.4 (a value similar to that given by Bliss & Hadley, 1964). Fig. 17.1 shows some results of a study on *Cetraria nivalis*. The length of the specimen used has a strong effect on the results obtained. The highest photosynthetic rate is found in the 1-cm long part from the top. Correspondingly, when measuring chlorophyll content, the length of the specimens used should be given (Kärenlampi, 1970). On the other hand, our experiments on fruticose epiphytic *Ramalina*

398

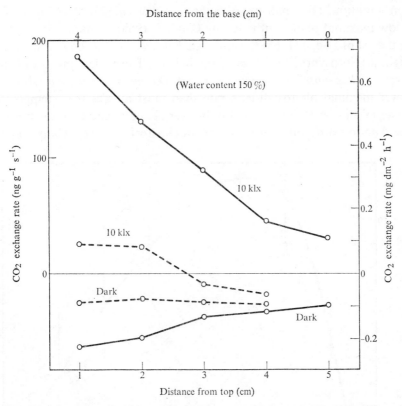

Fig. 17.1. CO_2 exchange rate of apical and basal parts of *Cetraria nivalis*. Dashed lines refer to basal parts and solid lines to apical parts.

farinacea and *Evernia prunastri* show no or only slight differences in photosynthetic rate between top parts and total thalli.

The results of the Kevo IBP group show (Fig. 17.1) that the top parts of the thallus have a higher respiration rate then the lower parts. This should be remembered when 'gross photosynthetic rate' is estimated. The respiration rate in the bases that belong to the 'standing dead material' is no higher than in old live parts. This is in accordance with the low decomposition rate of the dead lichen bases.

The significance of local adaptation and acclimation for maximal photosynthetic rate

Although 'each world climatic region is inhabited by lichens adapted to that particular region' (Gannutz, 1970), the great variation among mosses and lichens in each region is an aspect which must be taken into consideration. The small size of antarctic lichens may be correlated with a low maximal photosynthetic rate (Dodge, 1965; Gannutz, 1967), but in the list of Lange (1965) the antarctic *Parmelia coreyi* shows one of the highest photosynthetic values of the lichens. The typical mosses of the Arctic, *Rhacomitrium lanuginosum* and *Dicranum elongatum*, show a lower maximal photosynthetic rate than most mosses from temperate zones (Kallio & Heinonen, 1973), but very high values are known from the Antarctica in different moss genera (Rastorfer, 1972). Many widely

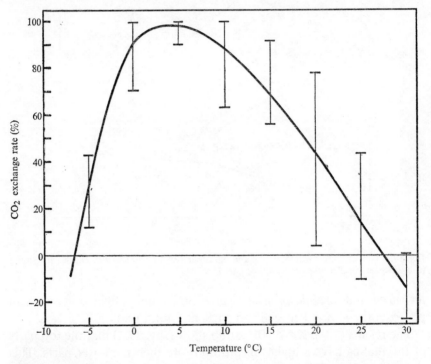

Fig. 17.2. Relation of CO_2 exchange rate to temperature for 9 different 'provenances' of *Rhacomitrium lanuginosum* (Arctic, Antarctic and temperate areas). The maximum value is plotted as 100 and the other values are given as percentages of the maximum.

distributed lichens and mosses (Scholander, Flagg, Walters & Irving, 1952; Lange, 1965; Biebl, 1968; Kappen & Lange, 1972; Kallio & Heinonen, 1971,1973) are 'preadapted' to different temperature and light zones and have not developed local 'provenance' adaptations. The freezing tolerance of tropical lichens and the same optimum temperature of photosynthesis in all the measured *Rhacomitrium lanuginosum* strains (cf. Fig. 17.2) round the globe illustrate this point.

The high capacity of many epiphytic and desert lichens is seen as an adaptational response to the short daily and/or yearly periods suitable for dry matter production (Stålfelt, 1937; Schulze & Lange, 1968; Lange, Schulze & Koch, 1970a,b; Lange & Evenari, 1971). The adaptation and/or acclimation to light, moisture and mineral nutrient supply conditions under the canopy of trees is seen also in the photosynthetic capacity of forest mosses and lichens (Tamm, 1974; Büttner, 1971; Kershaw & Rouse, 1971b).

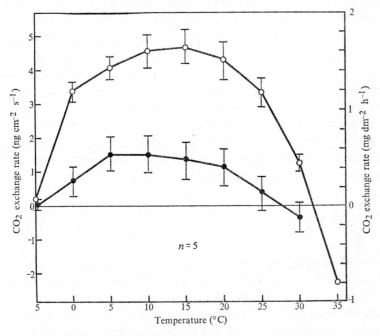

Fig. 17.3. Dependence of net photosynthetic rate on temperature in *Pleurozium schreberi*. The upper curve = S. Finland strain, the lower curve = Kevo strain.

Adams (1971a,b) has shown that there are ecophysiological differences in *Cladonia rangiferina*, and this seems to be the case also in our lichen transplantation cultures at Kevo, as when the S. Finnish and Kevo strains of *Cladonia alpestris* are compared. In our experiments no differences were found in the photosynthetic capacity of *Nephroma arcticum* from different localities in S. and N. Finland.

Local physiological variations among mosses have been shown, for instance, by Bazzaz, Paolillo & Jagels (1970) in *Polytrichum juniperinum* from forest and alpine populations. Clear differences in the photosynthetic capacity of *Pleurozium schreberi* are seen in S. Finnish and

Individual plants and tissues

Lapland populations (Kallio & Heinonen, 1973; see Fig. 17.3). Some typical differences are also seen in different strains of *Rhacomitrium lanuginosum*, particularly when the polar strains are compared with strains from S. Finland or from the Alps.

It is still impossible to say to what extent the photosynthetic (and productivity) capacities of the taxonomical units of mosses and lichens are the same in different areas, so that the values obtained for instance, in one IBP site could be transferred to the models of another site. However, it is apparent that in the circumpolar tundra zone the differences will not be great. The values for the 'total' thallus of *Cetraria nivalis* are the same in the works of Bliss & Hadley (1964), Kallio & Heinonen (1971) and in the later Kevo works (in all the maxima are between 0.34 and 0.38 mg g^{-1} h^{-1}). Even the values for *Cladonia* spp. from different sites agree well. In *Rhacomitrium lanuginosum* the 'variation gradient' seems to proceed longitudinally.

The annual rhythm of capacity stressed by Stålfelt (1938) and later reported by different authors (e.g. Atanasiu, 1971a,b) – showing in principle a different response in mosses and lichens (Gannutz, 1970) – complicates the comparisons between the different data.

Light response

Lichens

The compensation point for net photosynthesis in lichens depends both on genetical constitution and on ecological factors. In optimal temperature and nearly saturated moisture conditions, the compensation point varied between 400 lx in *Usnea dasypoga* and 2000 lx in *Umbilicaria pustulata* and *Ramalina farinacea* (Stålfelt, 1938), indicating typical values for shade and light lichens. Similar values are given by Smyth (1934), where *Peltigera* shows a compensation point of 500 lx, at a CO_2 concentration of 0.6%, by Butin (1954) and by Hosokawa, Odani & Tagawa (1964). The forest lichens in Germany show values between 600 and 1000 lx (Büttner, 1971). In lower temperature ranges all the values are lower. At 0 °C the compensation point in our measurements is 400 lx in *Nephroma arcticum* and 150 lx in *Cetraria nivalis*. The compensation values are, of course, very dependent on the water content and on the length of the specimen used. Longer parts and drier specimens need higher illumination for compensation. In some antarctic species, the compensation point at −8 °C is still 500 lx (Ahmadjian, 1970).

402

The optimum light range, where the photosynthetic rate is not very sensitive to changes in illuminance, begins in most species between 10 and 20 klx (Smyth, 1934; Stålfelt, 1938; Butin, 1954; Bliss & Hadley, 1964; Bazzaz, Paolillo & Jagels, 1970; Kallio & Heinonen, 1971). Often, however, and particularly in short-period exposures, it may rise to much higher values. Bliss & Hadley (1964) have shown higher values for maximal photosynthetic rate in *Cladonia rangiferina*; values up to 50 klx are mentioned in epiphytes (Hosokawa, Odani & Tagawa, 1964). Ahmadjian (1970) notices a saturation value over 48 klx at $+5\,°C$ in the antarctic *Neuropogon*, and Schulze & Lange (1968) report about 25–35 klx for some desert lichens. When the time factor is included, however, this high illuminance can be detrimental (Godish & Schein, 1966). In *Nephroma arcticum*, particularly in low temperatures, a continuous illuminance of 15 klx lowers the net photosynthetic rate more than 50% in four days, while no change is seen in activity in the same light alternating with a twelve-hour night. Recovery after inactivation caused by continuous light take place in a period of one week.

The seasonal rhythm of activity (Stålfelt, 1938; Godish & Schein, 1966; Harris, 1971; Gannutz, 1970) seems to depend mainly on the variation in chlorophyll content (Verseghy, 1972).

Lichens show both acclimation and adaptation to environmental differences in light (Ertl, 1951; Butin, 1954; Buttner, 1971; Adams, 1971a; Rundel, 1972). A mechanism for this may be, in addition to the differences in chlorophyll content, the regulation in cortical absorption (Ertl, 1951; Smith, 1962), particularly by means of quantitative variation in usnic acid (Rundel, 1969).

Mosses

The light compensation values of mosses for net photosynthesis do not differ much from those of lichens. At optimum temperatures they are often around 400 lx (Hosokawa, Odani & Tagawa, 1964; Rastorfer & Higinbotham, 1968; Paolillo & Bazzaz, 1968). Stålfelt (1937) gives values of 300–700 lx for the forest mosses, and Miyata & Hosokawa (1961) over 1000 lx for heliophilous mosses. In the very heliophilous *Rhacomitrium lanuginosum*, the compensation point is usually over 2000 lx, but it is able to change to about 1000 lx in a few days (Kallio & Heinonen, 1973). The relationship of light compensation values to temperature is seen in Fig. 17.4.

The light saturation level is similar to that in lichens (in optimum temperature), being mostly between 10 and 20 klx, the maxima being up to 40 to 50 klx in some epiphytes (Miyata & Hosokawa, 1961) and 4 klx in some forest mosses, such as *Funaria hygrometrica* and *Polytrichum juniperinum* (Paolillo & Bazzaz, 1968).

Bazzaz *et al.* (1970) have described different adaptation types of *Polytrichum juniperium* in Washington and Indiana populations, the differences appearing both in saturation and in compensation values. There are also differences which are correlated with the season. High

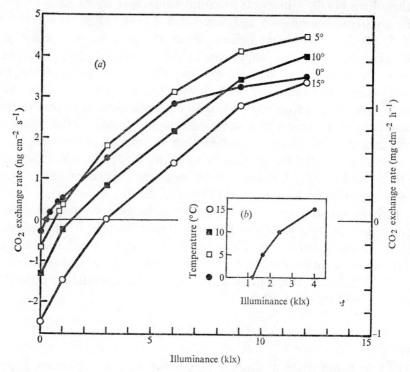

Fig. 17.4. (*a*) Relation of net photosynthetic rate to illuminance, (*b*) light compensation points in relation to temperature, both in *Hypnum cupressiforme* (S. Finland).

illuminances often have a detrimental effect on mosses as shown by Stålfelt (1936) in *Hylocomium triquetrum* and *Ptilium crista-castrensis*, and observed also in antarctic *Bryum antarcticum* by Rastorfer (1970). In different strains of *Rhacomitrium lanuginosum*, continuous low illuminance causes lowering of activity, particularly in the arctic strains – from Kevo and Spitsbergen – the strain from the Alps being more tolerant. *Pleurozium schreberi* is still more sensitive to continuous light (Kallio & Heinonen, 1973) while *Dicranum elongatum* is less sensitive.

404

The light rhythm is significant also for reproductive development in mosses (Clarke & Greene, 1971). In ecological studies and particularly in production studies, the changes in the light response curve with acclimation and seasonal and genetical variation must be taken into consideration, but the differences are not very great. Apparently damage caused by high illuminance is not so significant in nature as in the laboratory. In nature, high light values are correlated with desiccation and high temperatures, and the daily rhythm of activity may be sufficient to prevent light damage in arctic conditions.

Temperature response

Lichens

Lichens have a net photosynthetic rate which is typically adapted to a wide temperature range; this makes them flexible as regards the climatic zones and local habitats, both at the species level and at the whole-group level (Smith, 1962; Ahmadjian, 1970; Kappen & Lange, 1970). Gannutz (1970) showed some particular adaptation features in his comparison of the temperature responses of lichens from Antarctica, New Zealand and Brazil. Lichens from the tropics may show tolerance against freezing stress, and some lichens in polar regions may have rather a high optimum temperature for net photosynthetic rate (Lange, 1965; Ahmadjian, 1970). Respiration rate shows some zonal regularities – the arctic species having higher values than the tropical ones (Scholander, Flagg, Walters & Irving, 1952).

Apparently an optimal temperature range round 10–15 °C is usual in temperate areas, e.g. for *Cladonia rangiferina*, *Cetraria islandica*, *C. crispa*, *Cornicularia muricata* and *C. aculeata* (Bliss & Hadley, 1964; Büttner, 1971; Adams, 1971*a*), and for *Ramalina farinacea*, *R. fraxinea*, and *Peltigera aphtosa* (observations of the Kevo group). Stålfelt (1938) gives the average values for some forest lichens in S. Sweden as 14.1 °C in winter and 18.4 °C in summer. The alpine species or strains of *Cladonia elongata*, *C. alcicornis*, *Stereocaulon alpinum*, *Letharia vulpina*, and *Parmelia encausta* have a lower optimum range – between 0 °C and 10 °C (Lange, 1965). Some subarctic and arctic lichens have almost the same optimum range (round +10 °C): including *Cetraria nivalis*, *Parmelia olivacea*, *Nephroma arcticum*, *Solorina crocea* (Kallio & Heinonen, 1971; Kallio, P., 1973), *Coriscium viride* (Heikkilä & Kallio, 1966), and the antarctic *Parmelia coreyi* (Lange, 1965). The lowest

known optimum values are close to 0 °C in *Stereocaulon paschale*
Kevo strain, S. *alpinum* Ny Ålesund strain (Lange, 1965) and *Neuropogon* sp. from the Antarctica (Ahmadjian, 1970). The highest values
are from tropical species *Parmelia pachyderma* and *Umbilicaria mammulata*, both over 20 °C (Lange, 1965). From the USA, *Parmelia
conspersa* has an optimum at 20 °C and *Umbilicaria mammulata* at
25 °C (Godish & Schein, 1966). Some endolithic desert species may
show still higher values (Lange, Schulze & Koch, 1970*b*), and high
values of 10–20 °C are known in *Xanthoria mawsonii* in the Antarctica.

The temperature response shows adaptational variation, e.g. in
Cladonia rangiferina (Adams, 1971*a*), and acclimation is known in
different lichens (Büttner, 1971).

The minimum temperatures at which CO_2 influx is observable are
lowest in lichens. Lange (1965) has given a list of thirty species with
minima below 0 °C. In half of these the minima are below −10° C.
These include species from Middle Europe, the Alps and Antarctica,
but *Usnea livida* from Congo rain forests and *U. ochrophora* from
Cameroon also show positive net assimilation at −8 °C. In the subarctic zone of Finland the following minima are known: *Nephroma
arcticum* −10 °C (in some circumstances −20 °C), *Cetraria nivalis*
−20° C, *Cladonia alpestris* −10 °C (−15° C), *Parmelia olivacea* −10 °C,
Solorina crocea −7 °C, *Hypogymnia physodes* −10° C, *Xanthoria
parietina* from central Finland −18° C. Atanasiu (1969*a,b*; 1971*a,b*) has
given values between −8 and −12 °C for five epiphytic lichens.

The lichens are known to need little time for activation after freezing,
which indicates adaptation to great daily variations of temperature
around 0 °C. This is important during a season 'potentially the most
dangerous during the year' (Longton, 1972; Rudolph, 1965). Recovery –
which apparently is an active process because vigorous respiration
surges are usually connected with it – take place in a few minutes or at
most a couple of hours, *e.g.* in *Cetraria nivalis, Nephroma arcticum,
Peltigera aphthosa, Solorina crocea, Cladonia alpestris, Parmelia olivacea*
and *Hypogymnia physodes* (Lange, 1962; Kallio & Heinonen, 1971). In
most cases, no clear correlations are seen between this feature and the
local climate, so a preadaptational feature is involved. Some sensitive
lichens, however, are also known, e.g. *Roccella fucoides* which is
sensitive to temperatures below −10 °C (cf. Kappen & Lange, 1972).
Damage in temperatures at −17 °C are noted in some antarctic lichens
(Ahmadjian, 1970).

The temperature maxima at which CO_2 influx is still observable are low in lichens, and in many species the values for the compensation point given by Lange (1965) are between 18 °C and 26 °C; in our studies the values in *Nephroma arcticum* varied between 25 °C and 30 °C. The same values are given from S. Sweden by Stålfelt (1938) in different lichens. High temperatures (over 30 °C) can damage many species, the lichens being the most sensitive terrestrial organisms. There is always a time factor involved in the high temperature responses (Lange, 1966). Again, one should remember that the length of the specimen used has a strong effect on the maximum temperature for positive net photosynthetic rate, i.e. for CO_2 influx. Top parts have higher maximum temperatures and they seem to have a 'temperature response curve' with steeper slope. On the other hand, one must remember that higher temperatures in the field are reached only in fairly dry lichens, where water content is the factor with strongest effect on the rate of photosynthesis (see Fig. 17.7).

Mosses

The optimum values of temperature for mosses are almost the same as for lichens. In forest mosses at high illuminances in Sweden values between 15° C and 20 °C are typical (Stålfelt, 1937; cf. Fig. 17.4). For *Polytrichum juniperinum* 10 °C is given by Bazzaz *et al.* (1970) and the same value for *Homalothecium sericeum* by Romose (1940). In the antarctic *Bryum sandbergii*, a high value of 20 °C is known, while in *B. antarcticum* a low value of 5–10 °C is given by Rastorfer (1970). In the Kevo *Dicranum elongatum* the average optimum is 10° C. As regards the response to temperature, *Rhacomitrium lanuginosum* is a good example of a moss which is able to react homeostatically to very different local climatic conditions without having formed any physiological races. Samples from the Arctic, S. Finland, W. Norway, Great Britain, the Alps and Antarctica have the same optimum of about 5 °C.

The temperature minima for net photosynthesis in mosses are somewhat higher than those of the lichens (Gannutz, 1970) Rastorfer & Higinbotham (1968) have recorded −5 °C for *Bryum sandbergii* from the Antarctica, and Atanasiu (1971a) −8 °C to −9 °C for *Camptothecium philippeanum, Isothecium viviparum* and *Brachythecium gehebii.* All strains of *Rhacomitrium lanuginosum* in our experiments have minima near −10 °C, and the same value has been measured in *Dicranum elongatum* and *Pleurozium schreberi.*

Like lichens, mosses reactivate very rapidly after freezing. All provenances of *Rhacomitrium lanuginosum* activate 60% in one hour after having been frozen for ten to fifteen hours at −30 °C (Fig. 17.5). Almost the same rate of reactivation has been measured in *Pleurozium schreberi*, *Dicranum elongatum*, and *Hypnum cupressiforme* in our experiments.

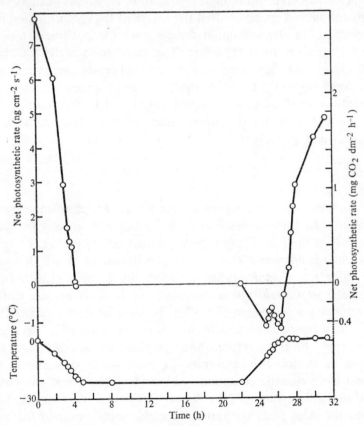

Fig. 17.5. Response of *Rhacomitrium lanuginosum* to freezing and thawing. Temperature indicated by the lower curve, net photosynthetic rate by the upper curve. The respiration surge associated with thawing, followed by rapid activation, is well shown.

It is known that mosses, like lichens, are sensitive to high temperatures when hydrated. Temperatures between 32 °C and 34 °C lasting an hour are detrimental for some species (Lange, 1966). Ecologically this has only a minor significance because the highest temperatures, particularly in temperate and arctic areas, are connected with dessication.

A seasonal rhythm of activity, probably due to temperature and light rhythms, is known in mosses (Stålfelt, 1937; Tamm, 1953; Romose, 1940; Kujala, 1962; Atanasiu, 1969a), the early spring and autumn being the most active seasons in the temperate zones. In *Dicranum elongatum* the optimum temperature is highest in autumn and lowest in winter with a difference of 5–10 °C.

Response to moisture

Low moisture content is apparently the most important limitation to photosynthesis in the poikilohydric plants. In wide areas of the temperate zone the moisture supply shows a clear seasonal rhythm, the most favourable season being the winter. Many adaptational mechanisms such as winter activity are known to respond to this situation (Smyth, 1934; Butin, 1954; Smith, 1962; Schulze & Lange, 1968). The xerothermic desert areas show additional adaptation responses (Lange, Schulze & Koch, 1970a,b; Verseghy, 1971). In particular, the crustaceous lichens are very resistant to high degrees of desiccation (Reid, 1953; Lange, 1953; Stålfelt, 1960). *Umbilicaria pustulata* tolerates desiccation for more than a year (Lange, 1953), and in our experiments, *Coriscium viride* activated in a few hours after having been in the herbarium for over four months.

Most of the lichens have optimal moisture values at approximately 100–200 (300)% of dry weight – the maximum water capacity values of 400–500% are supraoptimal for photosynthesis (cf. however, Ellée, 1939). When measured as a percentage of the saturation value, Lange & Bertsch (1965) give an optimum figure of 80% for *Ramalina maxiformis*, Kershaw & Rouse (1971a) 10–60% for *Cladonia alpestris*, and Smyth (1934) 30–90% for *Peltigera polydactyla* (see also the literature cited in Adams, 1971b). Moisture optimum seems to depend on illuminance (see Fig. 17.7). At high illuminance maximal net photosynthetic rate is reached at a lower moisture content than it is a low illuminance.

Water supply from atmospheric humidity is enough to activate some lichen species even to near the optimum level (Butin, 1954; Lange & Bertsch, 1965; Bertsch, 1966; Heatwole, 1966; Ahmadjian, 1970; Gannutz, 1970; Lange, Schulze & Koch, 1970a,b; Buttner, 1971; Verseghy, 1971). The water content of *Cladonia* spp. is 60–70% when the relative humidity of the air is near 100%, but only 20% in a relative humidity of 75% (Heatwole, 1966). In epiphytic *Cetraria* spp. and *Evernia* spp. an air humidity of 80–85% is sufficient to allow the photosynthetic compensation point to be reached (Bertsch, 1966). Acclimation and adaptation in many lichen groups are indicated by the correlation between desiccation resistance (measured in terms of photosynthesis) and the water stress of the habitat (Lee & Stewart, 1971; Harris, 1971; Verseghy, 1971).

The poikilohydric water economy described may be regarded as an adaptational homeostatic mechanism for avoiding high temperature damage (Lange, 1953; Heatwole, 1966; Ahmadjian, 1967). This mechanism functions, however, only if the loss or gain of water is sufficiently rapid. Similar observations have been made by several investigators, the hygroscopic action taking a matter of a few minutes (Ellée, 1939; Butin, 1954; Ried, 1960a,b; Verseghy, 1971) and the reactivation of photosynthesis several hours (Ellée, 1939; Ried, 1953; Lange, 1969; Lange et al., 1970a,b). In some species reactivation takes place still more rapidly, as in *Parmelia physodes* (Ensgraber, 1954).

The ecology of mosses is also based on poikilohydric physiology. The optimum water content for net photosynthetic rate was mostly at 200–300 (400)% in our experiments (Stålfelt, 1937; Tallis, 1959), but in some bryophytes it is higher, for instance in *Conocephalum conicum* (Ensgraber, 1954). Reactivation after desiccation can take several hours (Stålfelt, 1937), or only half an hour (McKay, 1935). Great variation in their ability to recover after desiccation is typical of mosses (Lee & Stewart, 1971). Mosses are also able to take a considerable amount of water from air moisture. Different species vary much in this respect, however (Lange, 1969). Some species, such as *Barbilophozia hatcheri*, reactivate very well in high air humidity (98%), while some others do not reactivate at all (*Mnium punctatum*) or only to a small extent (*Pohlia nutans* and *Polytrichum piliferum*). As a group, mosses lie between lichens and cormophytes in their relation to atmospheric moisture supply. Acclimation and adaptation of water economy are also known in mosses (Lee & Stewart, 1971).

The relations between nitrogen fixation rate and photosynthetic rate

Lichens form an important group of nitrogen fixers, particularly in drier tundra ecosystems. The most important species are *Stereocaulon* spp., *Nephroma arcticum*, *Peltigera* spp., *Solorina crocea*, studied especially by Dr Alexander in Alaska and by the Swedish, Norwegian and Finnish IBP groups. The ecology of these lichens has also been surveyed by Kallio, Suhonen & Kallio (1972) and Kallio, S. (1973). It is evident that nitrogenase activity is not well adapted to the arctic temperature conditions. Fixation takes place only at temperatures over 0 °C (sometimes over 5° C), while the optimum is at +15 °C (sometimes 20 °C); i.e. the temperatures required are higher than those for net photosynthesis in the same lichens (Fig. 17.6). The nitrogenase activity is dependent directly on the energy from photosynthesis, but the short and comparatively light summer night in the subarctic (Kevo area) allows continuous nitrogen fixation when the moisture is over about 50 % and the temperature over 5 °C.

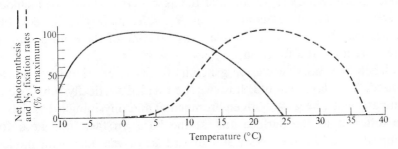

Fig. 17.6. Temperature response curves for net photosynthetic rate (continuous line) and nitrogen fixation rate (broken line) of *Stereocaulon paschale* from Kevo.

Although the temperature optimum of nitrogenase activity is higher than that of net photosynthesis, it is possible that both are most active (in the Kevo area) at the same time. The rainy days in July offer favourable conditions for both processes. During rain the temperature goes down to 10–15 °C, which is not too high for photosynthesis and not too low for nitrogenase. Illuminance is high enough for a high photosynthetic rate, and moisture is optimal for both. These rainy days in the middle of summer obviously are of great importance in the gain of both carbon and nitrogen.

The low nitrogen content typical of the arctic zones (Russell, 1940; Sørensen, 1941) may be correlated with the ecology of nitrogen fixation. This low nitrogen content is also a pre-requisite for nitrogen fixation; in *Stereocaulon paschale* one dip in 0.1 % KNO_3 stops the activity. On the other hand, the low nitrogen content may limit photosynthesis in mosses. At Kevo this is very clearly seen in *Pleurozium schreberi* but not in *Rhacomitrium lanuginosum*. The adaptation to different levels of nitrogen supply may have some zonal climatic basis, as emphasized by Sörensen (1941).

411

Brief word model of CO_2 exchange

A computer model seems to be the only realistic way for integrating CO_2 exchange over longer periods. Calculating production on the basis of CO_2 exchange data, therefore, requires the building of a computer model. The work by Kershaw & Harris (1971*a,b*) on epiphytic lichens seems to be, so far, the only completed simulation of the photosynthesis of multicellular lower plants. The Kevo IBP group has tried to develop multiple regression models for the integration of the CO_2 gain of reindeer lichens. In the following paragraphs we attempt to give a word model in which we briefly consider the aspects that should be included in a fairly complete dynamic model. We refer mainly to lichens, but mosses may be treated in a similar way, in spite of their more complicated structure and function.

Lichen and moss vegetation generally forms a very thin layer on the ground. This layer should, however be divided vertically into several compartments, because both environmental and physiological variables are different at the surface and at the base. In fact, this need for compartmentalization is very similar to that of vascular plant models (cf. the levels in the canopy of the model of Miller & Tieszen, 1972). The model should simulate the changes in the water content at different levels, as indicated by Büttner (1971) and Kershaw & Rouse (1971*a*). Correspondingly, temperature and light should also be simulated differently at different levels. As regards the light profiles, the work by Kershaw & Harris (1971*c*) should be noted. In addition, the model should include interactions between inclination and geometric structure of the thallus.

Different levels of the ground vegetation have, of course, different photosynthetic activities. The work by the Kevo IBP group has shown that the form of response to the environmental factors at different levels may also be different: the high CO_2 uptake rate and typical environmental factor responses of the top parts gradually change into the CO_2 output of the basal parts with their own environmental responses.

The interactions, such as translocation of photosynthates, between the levels are probably not critical in lichens. The highest photosynthetic activity in reindeer lichens seems to occur in the same layer as the maximum growth activity (Kärenlampi, 1970). Mosses are obviously more complicated, at least those species that show clearly defined growth bursts and rich development of reproductive organs.

Lag effects are easily simulated in a computer model. The after-

412

effects of dry and cold periods have already been discussed in this chapter. The model should be able to simulate changes in the physiological state of the plant as a function of environment. For instance, changes of the chlorophyll content should be included, though they need to be studied and quantified more clearly.

Carbon dioxide exchange models are obviously most easily developed for ecosystems with only one dominant species or group in the ground layer, such as reindeer lichen mats, because different species in the group have fairly similar environmental responses, and competition between the species is not complicated. However, the differences in the behaviour of individuals that have grown under a canopy and in open woodland must be kept in mind (Kershaw, 1972).

One possibility for modelling the environmental factors is the use of real values obtained with automatic recorders. A more realistic approach is probably to generate the moisture, temperature, and illumination of a lichen or moss first from the standard climatic variables (like radiation and precipitation), secondly from the time of the day, and thirdly from other vegetation (shading tree or dwarf shrub canopy, etc.).

For the CO_2 exchange model to be more meaningful as regards the functioning of the whole ecosystem, it should also include the effects of grazing. In an ungrazed state there are thick layers of dead bases, which greatly change the temperature and moisture conditions. Grazing and decomposition of dead bases should therefore be included in the simulation model of reindeer lichen dynamics (Bunnell, Kärenlampi & Russell, 1973). This model uses one week as the interval over which the changes are updated. The advantages of longer or shorter intervals remain to be considered. Long interval models may be more appropriate for general ecosystem purposes and short interval models may prove most useful in special studies. Modelling the CO_2 exchange of multi-cellular lower plants offers a challenging task to scientists aiming at a synthesis of IBP results.

Multiple regression model of CO_2 exchange

The Kevo IBP group has been developing multiple regression models to describe CO_2 exchange as a function of environmental factors. In the past physiologists usually changed only one environmental factor in each gas-exchange experiment. The results of such experiments were easily presented, and it was a matter of routine to fit curves to the observed points. In the work done at Kevo, we have tried to make

413

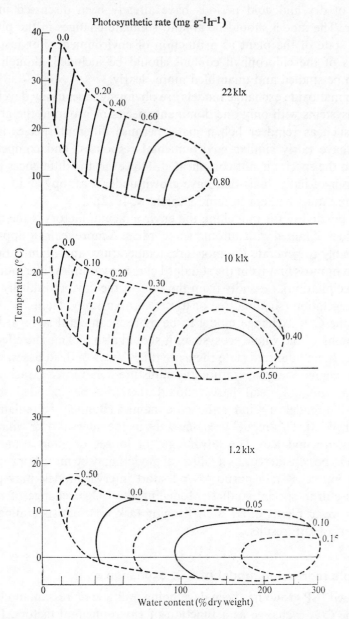

Fig. 17.7. Net photosynthetic rate 2-cm long parts from the top of *Cetraria nivalis*, in terms of the output from the multiple regression model. The CO_2 exchange (mg CO_2 g^{-1} h^{-1}) is shown at three illuminances in relation to temperature and water content of the thallus. The combinations of temperature and water content shown are those generally occurring during summer at the given illuminances.

factorial experiments using all combinations of moisture, illuminance and temperature that occur during the summer. Treatment of such observations necessitates the use of some method such as multiple regression analysis. The values predicted by the regression model may be presented in relation to a single environmental factor within its range, or an attempt may be made to present CO_2 exchange in relation to several factors simultaneously. In Fig. 17.7 some results are given of the study on *Cetraria nivalis* (2-cm long top parts). The photosynthetic rates F (mg CO_2 g^{-1} h^{-1}) were predicted using the following model:

$$F = A + B_1 d_2 D_3 (K/100)^2 + B_2 (d_2)^2 (d_3)^2 + \\ + B_3 (d_1)^2 d_3 + B_4 (d_2)^2 (D_3)^2,$$

where

$d_1 = $ (temperature in °C) $\times 10^{-2}$

$d_2 = $ (illuminance in lx) $\times 10^{-4}$

$d_3 = $ (moisture content in per cent of dry weight) $\times 10^{-3}$

$D_3 = d_3/(d_3 + 100)$

$K = $ temperature in kelvins, K.

Regression models of the form shown above explain about 86–93% of the variation. The usefulness of such models remains to be considered further, because they may not be sensitive enough to include all the special features such as moisture curves presented by Kershaw (1972).

CO_2 exchange in relation to dry matter production of reindeer lichens

In the following paragraphs, we present some calculations comparing the production estimates obtained from CO_2 exchange integration with values obtained from simple weighings. The material of the analysis is 2-cm long top parts of *Cetraria nivalis*. The assumption is made that the organic carbon content of the lichen is 36% of the dry weight. During the summer of 1971, these lichens grew by 0.258% of their weight per day (for a period of 110 days). One gram of lichen thus produced 2.58 mg per day, including 0.93 mg carbon, which means that the CO_2 gain must have been 3.44 mg. In 1969, the relative growth rate was 0.63% per day (i.e. 9.33 mg CO_2 per g lichen) during a rainy and relatively cold period at the end of July. During dry and warm periods, the growth was only 0.03% per day (i.e. 0.40 mg CO_2). Are these estimates in accordance with the CO_2 exchange calculations?

The Kevo group has proceeded as follows. The environmental factors to which the lichen was exposed were computed through the summer from the standard meteorological variables. The CO_2 exchange responses to these combinations of environmental factors were computed using three-hour intervals, and the daily CO_2 gains were computed using linear interpolation. One should remember that the models for the CO_2 exchange responses were based on experiments made in the laboratory in cuvettes, where the light falls vertically, whereas in the field, the light is not unidirectional and interacts with the thallus structure. In a cuvette, water is probably more evenly distributed throughout the lichen, whereas the tips (with the highest activity) are the first to become moist or dry in the field. Correspondingly, temperature is probably less variable in a lichen in the cuvette than in the field. Nevertheless, fairly small pieces of lichen have given consistent results.

When snow is melting in the spring, there are a few days that are favourable for photosynthesis. Lichens are moistened by the melting snow; the illuminance is high (no snow cover, low cloudiness, long day), and temperatures are close to zero or slightly above it. The photosynthetic CO_2 gain is fairly high at this time, and we estimate that it is enough to compensate for the respiration losses during winter.

June is generally very dry at Kevo. At noon and during the first two or three hours of the afternoon, lichens are very warm (30–45 °C) and very dry (water content 5–6 % of dry weight). Illuminance in the very sparse pine heaths is 40–50 klx on an average. In such conditions, only very slight CO_2 output takes place, about 0.02 mg CO_2 g^{-1} h^{-1}. At midnight, the illuminance decreases to about 1.5 klx and the temperature to about 7 °C. Relative humidity becomes high at the soil surface, and the lichen may reach a water content of 30–40 % of dry weight. Illuminance begins to increase while the lichens are still a little moist, and the CO_2 uptake may be about 0.10–0.15 mg CO_2 g^{-1} h^{-1} for a few hours. The moisture compensation point seems to be very low in the top parts of *Cetraria nivalis*, and positive CO_2 balance, therefore, continues for a fairly long time. The total gain of one dry June day may be about 0.4–0.6 mg CO_2 g^{-1}, which is in good accordance with the weight growth data.

July seems to be the rainiest month at Kevo (Kärenlampi, 1972). Illuminance is still high and temperature during rain is not too high. The ample moisture causes very high daily CO_2 gains at this time. At noon, the uptake rate may be 0.40–0.60 mg CO_2 g^{-1} h^{-1} for several hours. At midnight there is negative CO_2 balance (about 0.10–0.15 mg CO_2 g^{-1} h^{-1}), but the daily gain may still be about 7.0–8.0 mg CO_2 g^{-1}. This is not so much as the estimate (9.33) based on weight growth, but fairly close to it. These figures are about three times higher than the estimated average for the summer.

Towards the end of August and September, dewy and foggy nights become more frequent. Nights are dark for several hours, but the respiratory losses are compensated by the moist morning hours. CO_2 gains equalling the mean for the whole summer occur, but values considerably higher than the mean are reached when there is some rain during the day. Towards the end of September, illuminance begins to be a limiting factor. The dark period is long, and especially on cloudy days, the illuminance may be only of about 5–6 klx, but this is compensated by the advantageous moisture and low temperature. An average date for the formation of a stable snow cover is 20 October (Kärenlampi, 1972). Plants are under the snow for about seven months, and only slow respiration occurs during this period.

Lichen pasture management

In an ungrazed lichen-bearing area, the biomass of lichens may be as high as 200–300 g m^{-2} (L. Kärenlampi & E. Pulliainen, unpublished data). The yearly production, in such a case, is about 10% of the biomass and is almost equalled by transfer to decomposing litter base. The yearly CO_2 gain may be estimated to be then about 26–40 g m^{-2}, which means 7–11 g organic carbon. In a normal, fairly strongly grazed stand, the biomass of lichens is only 15–30 g m^{-2}. Productivity is now higher (25–30% yearly), and nearly all primary production is used by the consumer food chain. In a strongly grazed stand, there is a tendency for the ground vegetation to become 'worn-out' to such an extent that the ground surface becomes very xeric, which is unfavourable for the growth of lichens. At the same time, the growing biomass is reduced, resulting in a strong decrease in productivity. It is a generally known phenomenon that too high a grazing pressure lowers the carrying capacity of the grazing land. The problem is how to find the correct grazing pressure and grazing policy in order to keep the producing biomass satisfactorily high, but still young and productive, and to keep it in good environmental conditions. We may theorize that good lichen land management implies a good regulation of lichen photosynthesis.

References

Adams, M. S. (1971*a*). Temperature response of carbon dioxide exchange of *Cladonia rangiferina* from the Wisconsin pine barrens, and comparison with an Alpine population. *American Midland Naturalist*, **86**, 224–7.

Individual plants and tissues

Adams, M. S. (1971*b*). Effects of drying at three temperatures on carbon dioxide exchange of *Cladonia rangiferina* (L.) Wigg. *Photosynthetica*, **5**, 124–7.

Ahmadjian, V. (1967). In *The lichen symbiosis*, p. 152. Mass., Toronto & London, Blaisdell Publishing Co.

Ahmadjian, V. (1970). Adaptations of Antarctic terrestrial plants. In *Antarctic Ecology*, ed. M. W. Holdgate, vol. 2, pp. 801–11. London & New York, Academic Press.

Ahti, T. & Hepburn, R. L. (1967). Preliminary studies on woodland caribou range, especially on lichen stands, in Ontario. *Research Report (Wildlife), Ontario*, **74**, 1–134.

Andreev, V. N. (1971). Methods of defining overground phytomass on vast territories of the Subarctic. *Reports from the Kevo Subarctic Research Station*, **8**, 3–11.

Atanasiu, L. (1969*a*). Photosynthesis and respiration of some lichens during winter. *Revue Roumaine de Biologie, Ser. Bot.* **14**, 165–8.

Atanasiu, L. (1969*b*). La photosynthése et la respiration chez les Mousses et les Lichens pendant l'hiver. *Revue Bryologique et Lichénologique* **36**, 747–53.

Atanasiu, L. (1971*a*). Photosynthesis and respiration of three mosses at winter low temperatures. *Bryologist*, **74**, 23–7.

Atanasiu, L. (1971*b*). Photosynthesis and respiration in some lichens in relation to winter low temperatures. *Revue Roumaine de Biologie, Ser. Bot.* **16**, 105–10.

Bazzaz, F. A., Paolillo, D. J. & Jagels, R. H. (1970). Photosynthesis and respiration of forest and alpine populations of *Polytrichum juniperinum*. *Bryologist*, **73**, 579–85.

Bertsch, A. (1966). Über den CO_2-Gaswechsel einiger Flechten nach Wasserdampfaufnahme. *Planta*, **68**, 157–66.

Biebl, R. (1968). Über Wärmehaushalt und Temperaturresistenz arktischer Pflanzen in Westgrönland. *Flora*, **157**, 327–54.

Bliss, L. C. & Hadley, E. B. (1964). Photosynthesis and respiration of alpine lichens. *American Journal of Botany*, **51**, 870–874.

Bunnel, F., Kärenlampi, L. & Russel, D. (1973). A simulation model of the lichen – Rangifer interactions in northern Finland. *Reports from the Kevo Subarctic Research Station*, **10**, 1–8.

Butin, H. (1954). Physiologisch-ökologische Untersuchungen über den Wasserhaushalt und die Photosynthese bei Flechten. *Biologisches Zentralblatt*, **73**, 459–502.

Büttner, R. (1971). Untersuchungen zur Okologie und Physiologie des Gasstoffwechsels bei einigen Strauchflechten. *Flora*, **160**, 72–99.

Clarke, G. C. S. & Greene, S. W. (1971). Reproductive performance of two species of *Pohlia* from temperate and subantarctic station under controlled environmental conditions. *Transactions of the British Bryological Society*, **6**, 278–95.

Dodge, C. W. (1965). Lichens. In *Biogeography and ecology in Antarctica*, ed. J. van Mieghem, P. van Oye & J. Schell. *Monographiae Biologicae*, **15**, 194–200. The Hague.

Ellée, O. (1939). Über die Kohlensäureassimilation von Flechten. *Beiträge zur Biologie der Pflanzen*, **26**, 250–87.

Ensgraber, A. (1954). Über den Einfluss der Antrocknung auf die Assimilation und Atmung von Moosen und Flechten. *Flora*, **141**, 432–75.

Ertl, L. (1951). Über die Verhältnisse in Laubflechten. *Planta*, **39**, 245–70.

Forman, R. T. T. (1969). Comparison of coverage, biomass, and energy as measures of standing crop of bryophytes in various ecosystems. *Bulletin of the Torrey Botanical Club*, **96**, 582–591.

Gabrielsén, E. K. (1960). Beleuchtungsstärke und Photosynthese. In *Handbuch der Pflanzenphysiologie*, ed. W. Ruhland, vol. 5, part 2, pp. 27–48. Berlin, Göttingen & Heidelberg, Springer-Verlag.

Gannutz, T. P. (1967). Effects of environmental extremes on Lichens. *Société Botanique de France, Colloque sur les Lichens*, pp. 169–79.

Gannutz, T. P. (1970). Photosynthesis and respiration of plants in the Antarctic Peninsula area. *Antarctic Journal of the United States*, **5**, 49–51.

Godish, T. & Schein, R. D. (1966). The eco-physiology of lichens: assimilation and respiration. *Plant Physiology, Lancaster*, **41** (suppl.) 37.

Greene, S. W. (1967). The changing pattern of antarctic botanical studies. *Proceedings of the Symposium on Pacific–Antarctic Sciences Jare Scientific Reports*, special issue, **1**, 236–44.

Hadley, E. B. & Bliss, L. C. (1964). Energy relationships of alpine plants on Me. Washington, New Hampshire. *Ecological Monographs*, **34**, 331–57.

Hale, M. E. (1967). In *The Biology of Lichens*, pp. 1–176. London, Edward Arnold Ltd.

Harris, G. P. (1971). The ecology of corticolous lichens. II. The relationship between physiology and the environment. *Journal of Ecology*, **59**, 441–52.

Heatwole, H. (1966). Moisture exchange between the atmosphere and some lichens of the genus *Cladonia*. *Mycologia*, **58**, 148–56.

Heikkilä, H. & Kallio, P. (1966). On the problem of subarctic basidiolichens I. *Reports from the Kevo Subarctic Research Station*, **3**, 48–74.

Hosokawa, T., Odani, N. & Tagawa, H. (1964). Causality of the distribution of corticolous species in forests with special reference to the physio-ecological approach. *Bryologist*, **67**, 396–411.

Ignatenko, IV., Knorre, A. V., Lovelius, N. V. & Norin, B. N. (1971). Standing crop in plant communities at the station Ari-Mas. *IBP Tundra Biome, Proc. IV International Meeting in Leningrad on the Biological Productivity of Tundra*, eds. F. E. Wielgolaski & Th. Rosswall, pp. 140–9, Tundra Biome Steering Committee, Stockholm.

Kallio, P. (1973). Nitrogen fixation in subarctic lichens. *Oikos*, **25**, 1–5.

Kallio, P. & Heinonen, S. (1971). Influence of short-term low temperature on net photosynthesis in some subarctic lichens. *Reports from the Kevo Subarctic Research Station*, **8**, 63–72.

Kallio, P. & Heinonen, S. (1973). Ecology of photosynthesis in *Rhacomitrium lanuginosum* (Hedw.) Brid. *Reports from the Kevo Subarctic Research Station*, **10**, 43–54.

Individual plants and tissues

Kallio, P., Suhonen, S. & Kallio, H. (1972). The ecology of nitrogen fixation in *Nephroma arcticum* and *Solorina crocea*. *Reports from the Kevo Subarctic Research Station*, **9**, 7–14.

Kallio, S. (1973). The ecology of nitrogen fixation in *Stereocaulon paschale*. *Reports from the Kevo Subarctic Research Station*, **10**, 34–42.

Kappen, L. & Lange, O. L. (1970). Kälteresistenz von Flechten aus verschiedenen Klimagebieten. *Deutsche Botanische Gesellschaft, Neue Folge*, **4**, 61–5.

Kappen, L. & Lange, O. L. (1972). Die Kälteresistenz einiger Makrolichenen. *Flora*, **161**, 1–29.

Kershaw, K. A. (1972). The relationship between moisture content and net assimilation rate of lichen thalli and its ecological significance. *Canadian Journal of Botany*, **50**, 543–55.

Kershaw, K. A. & Harris, G. P. (1971*a*). Simulation studies and ecology. A simple defined system and model. *Proceedings of the International Symposium of Statistical Ecology*, **3**, 1–21.

Kershaw, K. A. & Harris, G. P. (1971*b*). Simulation studies and ecology – use of the model. *Proceedings of the International Symposium Statistical Ecology*, **3**, 22–42.

Kershaw, K. A. & Harris, G. P. (1971*c*). A technique for measuring the light profile in a lichen canopy. *Canadian Journal of Botany*, **49**, 609–11.

Kershaw, K. A. & Rouse, W. R. (1971*a*). Studies on lichen-dominating systems. I. The water relations of *Cladonia alpestris* in spruce-lichen woodland in northern Ontario. *Canadian Journal of Botany*, **49**, 1389–99.

Kershaw, K. A. & Rouse, W. R. (1971*b*). Studies on lichen-dominated systems. II. The growth pattern of *Cladonia alpestris* and *Cladonia rangiferina*. *Canadian Journal of Botany*, **49**, 1401–10.

Kujala, V. (1962). Die Dicke der Moosschicht in den Heidewäldern Finnlands. *Communicationes ex Instituto Quaestionum Forestalium Finlandiae*, **55**, 1–6.

Kärenlampi, L. (1970). Distribution of chlorophyll in the lichen *Cladonia alpestris*. *Reports from the Kevo Subarctic Research Station*, **7**, 1–8.

Kärenlampi, L. (1972). Comparisons between the microclimates of the Kevo ecosystem study sites and the Kevo Meteorological Station. *Reports from the Kevo Subarctic Research Station*, **9**, 50–65.

Lamb, M. (1970). Antarctic terrestrial plants and their ecology. In *Antarctic Ecology*, ed. M. W. Holdgate, vol. 2, pp. 733–51. London and New York, Academic Press.

Lange, O. L. (1953). Hitze- und Trockenresistenz der Flechten in Beziehung zu ihrer Verbreitung. *Flora*, **140**, 39–97.

Lange, O. L. (1954). Einige Messungen zum Wärmehaushalt poikilohydrer Flechten und Moose. *Archiv für Meteorologie, Geophysik, Bioklimatologie*, B **5**, 182–90.

Lange, O. L. (1962). Die Photosynthese der Flechten bei tiefen Temperaturen und nach Frostperioden. *Berichte der Deutschen Botanischen Gesellschaft*, **75**, 351–52.

Lange, O. L. (1965). Der CO_2-Gaswechsel von Flechten bei tiefen Temperaturen. *Planta*, **64**, 1–19.

Lange, O. L. (1966). Der CO_2-Gaswechsel von Flechten nach Erwärmung im feuchten Zustand. *Berichte der Deutschen Botanischen Gesellschaft*, **78**, 441–54.

Lange, O. L. (1969). CO_2-Gaswechsel von Moosen nach Wasserdampfaufnahme aus dem Luftraum. *Planta*, **89**, 90–4.

Lange, O. L. & Bertsch, A. (1965). Photosynthese der Wüstenflechte *Ramalina maciformis* nach Wasserdampfaufnahme aus dem Luftraum. *Naturwissenschaften*, **25**, 215–6.

Lange, O. L. & Evenari, M. (1971). Experimentell-ökologische Untersuchungen an Flechten der Negev-Wüste. IV. Wachstumsmessungen an *Caloplaca aurantia* (Pers.) Hellb. *Flora*, **160**, 100–4.

Lange, O. L., Schulze, E. D. & Koch, W. (1968). Photosynthese von Wüstenflechten am natürlichen Standort nach Wasserdampfaufnahme aus dem Luftraum. *Naturwissenschaften*, **55**, 658–9.

Lange, O. L., Schulze, E-D. & Koch, W. (1970a). Experimentell-ökologische Untersuchungen an Flechten der Negev-Wüste II. CO_2-Gaswechsel und Wasserhaushalt von *Ramalina maciformis* (Del.) Bory am natürlichen Standort während der sommerlichen Trockenperiode. *Flora*, **159**, 38–62.

Lange, O. L., Schulze, E-D. & Koch, W. (1970b). Experimentell-ökologische Untersuchungen an Flechten der Negev-Wüste III. CO_2-Gaswechsel und Wasserhaushalt von Krusten- und Blattflechten am natürlichen Standort während der sommerlichen Trockenperiode. *Flora*, **159**, 525–8.

Lee, J. A. & Stewart, G. R. (1971). Desiccation injury in mosses I. Intraspecific differences in the effect of moisture stress on photosynthesis. *New Phytologist*, **70**, 1061–8.

Longton, R. E. (1972). Reproduction of antarctic mosses in the genera *Polytrichum* and *Psilopilum* with particular reference to temperature. *British Antarctic Survey Bulletin*, **27**, 51–96.

McKay, E. (1935). Photosynthesis in *Grimmia montana*. *Plant Physiology, Lancaster*, **10**, 803–9.

Miller, P. C. & Tieszen, L. (1972). A preliminary model of processes affecting primary production in the arctic tundra. *Arctic and Alpine Research*, **4**, 1–18.

Miyata, I. & Hosokawa, T. (1961). Seasonal variations of the photosynthetic efficiency and chlorophyll content of epiphytic mosses. *Ecology*, **42**, 766–75.

Paolillo, D. J. & Bazzaz, F. A. (1968). Photosynthesis in sporophytes of *Polytrichum* and *Funaria*. *Bryologist*, **71**, 335–43.

Quispel, A. (1959). Lichens. In *Handbuch der Pflanzenphysiologie*, ed. W. Ruhland, Vol. 11, pp. 577–604. Berlin, Göttingen & Heidelberg, Springer-Verlag.

Rastorfer, J. R. (1970). Effects of light intensity and temperature on photosynthesis and respiration of two East Antarctic mosses, *Bryum argenteum* and *Bryum antarcticum*. *Bryologist*, **73**, 544–56.

Rastorfer, J. R. (1972). Comparative physiology of four West Antarctic

Individual plants and tissues

mosses. In *Antarctic Terrestrial Biology*, ed. G. A. Llano, *Antarctic Research Series*, **20**, 143–61.

Rastorfer, J. R. & Higinbotham, N. (1968). Rates of photosynthesis and respiration of the moss *Bryum sandbergii* as influenced by light intensity and temperature. *American Journal of Botany*, **55**, 1225–9.

Ried, A. (1953). Photosynthese und Atmung xerostabilen und xerolabilen Krustenflechten in der Nachwirkung vorausgegangener Entquellungen, *Planta*, **41**, 436–8.

Ried, A. (1960*a*). Stoffwechsel und Verbreitungsgrenzen von Flechten. *Flora*, **149**, 345–85.

Ried, A. (1960*b*). Nachwirkungen der Entquellung auf den Gaswechsel von Krustenflechten. *Biologisches Zentralblatt*, **79**, 657–78.

Ried, A. (1960*c*). Thallusbau und Assimilationshaushalt von Laub- und Krustenflechten. *Biologisches Zentralblatt*, **79**, 129–51.

Romose, V. (1940). Ökologische Untersuchungen über *Homalothecium sericeum*, seine Wachstumsperioden und seine Stoffproduktion. *Dansk Botaniske Arkiv*, **10**, 1–134.

Rudolph, E. D. (1965). Antarctic lichens and vascular plants: Their significance. *BioScience*, **15**, 285–7.

Rundel, P. W. (1969). Clinal variation in the production of usnic acid in *Cladonia subtenuis* along light gradients. *Bryologist*, **72**, 40–4.

Rundel, P. W. (1972). CO_2 exchange in ecological races of *Cladonia subtenuis*. *Photosynthetica*, **6**, 13–7.

Russell, R. S. (1940). Physiological and ecological studies on an arctic vegetation. II. The development of vegetation in relation to nitrogen supply and soil micro-organisms on Jan Mayen island. *Journal of Ecology*, **28**, 269–88.

Schamurin, V. F., Polozova, T. G. & Khodachek, E. A. (1971). Plant biomass of main plant communities at the Tareya station (Taimyr). In *IBP Tundra Biome Proceedings IV. International Meeting on the Biological Productivity of Tundra, Leningrad USSR*, eds. F. E. Wielgolaski & Th. Rosswall, pp. 1–320. Tundra Biome Steering Committee, Stockholm.

Scholander, P. F., Flagg, W., Walters, V. & Irving, L. (1952). Respiration in some arctic and tropical lichens in relation to temperature. *American Journal of Botany*, **39**, 707–13.

Schulze, E-D. & Lange, O. L. (1968). CO_2 Gaswechsel der Flechte *Hypogymnia physodes* bei tiefen Temperaturen im Freiland. *Flora*, **158**, 180–4.

Smith, D. C. (1962). The biology of lichen thalli. *Biological Reviews*, **37**, 537–70.

Smyth, E. S. (1934). A contribution to the physiology and ecology of *Peltigera canina* and *P. polydactyla*. *Annals of Botany*, **38**, 781–818.

Steere, W. C. (1954). Bryophytes. *Botanical Reviews*, **20**, 425–50.

Stålfelt, M. G. (1936). Über die Beziehung zwischen den Assimilations- und Atmungsgrössen. *Svensk Botanisk Tidskrift*, **30**, 343–54.

Stålfelt, M. G. (1937). Der Gasaustausch der Moose. *Planta*, **27**, 30–60.

Stålfelt, M. G. (1938). Der Gasaustausch der Flechten. *Planta*, **29**, 11–31.

Stålfelt, M. G. (1960). Flechten und Moose. In *Handbuch der Pflanzen-physiologie*, ed. W. Ruhland, vol. 5, part 2, pp. 364–75. Berlin, Göttingen & Heidelberg, Springer-Verlag.

Sørensen, T. (1941). Temperature relationship and phenology of the north-east Greenland flowering plants. *Meddelelser om Grønland*, **125**, 1–305.

Tallis, J. H. (1959). Studies in the biology and ecology of *Rhacomitrium lanuginosum* Brid. II. Growth, reproduction and physiology. *Journal of Ecology*, **47**, 325–350.

Tallis, J. H. (1964). Growth studies on *Rhacomitrium lanuginosum*. *Bryologist*, **67**, 417–22.

Tamm, C. O. (1953). Growth, yield and nutrition in carpets of a forest moss (*Hylocomium splendens*). *Meddelanden från Statens Skogsforskning Inst.* **43**, 1–140.

Tamm, C. O. (1964). Growth of *Hylocomium splendens* in relation to tree canopy. *Bryologist*, **67**, 423–7.

Verseghy, K. (1972). Saisonale Veränderung des Chlorophyllgehaltes einiger zerothermen Flechtenarten. *Botanikai Közlemenyek*, **59**, 109–17.

Willis, A. J. (1964). Investigations to the physiological ecology of *Tortula ruraliformis*. *Transactions of the British Bryological Society*, **4**, 668–83.

Wielgolaski, F. E. (1971). Vegetation types and primary production in Tundra. In *IBP Tundra Biome Proceedings IV. International Meeting on the Biological Productivity of Tundra, Leningrad USSR*, eds. F. E. Wielgolaski & Th. Rosswall, pp. 9–34. Tundra Biome Steering Committee, Stockholm.

Zalenskij, O. V., Shvetsova, V. M. & Voznessenskij, V. L. (1971). Photosynthesis in some plants of Western Taimyr. In *IBP Tundra Biome Proceedings IV. International Meeting on the Biological Productivity of Tundra, Leningrad USSR*, eds. F. E. Wielgolaski & Th. Rosswall, pp. 182–6. Tundra Biome Steering Committee, Stockholm.

18. Photosynthetic systems – conclusions

Ph. CHARTIER & J. ČATSKÝ

The knowledge of the photosynthetic activity of plant organs and assimilatory tissues, and of its response to environmental factors forms the basis for any detailed study of the photosynthetic rate and/or primary production of a crop stand. In the last decades, the role of the carbon dioxide uptake of individual leaves in total crop photosynthesis has been studied in detail, and various more or less sophisticated models and procedures have been proposed for calculating and predicting crop photosynthetic rates and primary production (Šetlík, 1970). The importance of this research was recognised by the creation of the PP section of the International Biological Programme, and also by the development of leaf photosynthesis research in many agricultural and ecological projects.

On the other hand, a leaf as a part of the whole plant organism cannot be considered as an isolated unit. The biological control of its photosynthetic activity by other organs, operating through sink effects, growth regulators, etc. may play a decisive role at certain periods of its life (Penning de Vries, Chapter 20; Wareing & Patrick, Chapter 21; Evans, Chapter 22). The photosynthetic activity of the leaf can also be markedly influenced by such stress factors as water deficit, extremes of temperature or shortage of soil nutrients (Slavík, Chapter 23; Nátr, Chapter 24; Bauer, Larcher & Walker, Chapter 25; Koller, Chapter 26).

The last two decades have seen an increasing interest in the theoretical analysis of carbon dioxide exchange by the leaf. This approach has stimulated the studies of relationships between the elementary processes of photosynthesis and photorespiration and CO_2 uptake by the leaf. The transfer conductances for carbon dioxide, the rates of photochemical reactions, the activities of photosynthetic enzymes in vivo, and the role of certain structural features, are the main examples of the elementary processes involved in CO_2 uptake by the leaf. A large amount of experimental data on these processes and relationships has recently become available and is reviewed in the present volume.

The present chapter will simply summarise some of the specific topics arising from the discussions at the Aberystwyth IBP meeting, particularly those concerned with the characterisation of CO_2 exchange

425

P

processes and with the relative importance of transfer and carboxylation resistances in leaf photosynthesis.

Characterisation of CO_2 exchange processes

One of the important methodological problems in photosynthesis research lies in developing appropriate methods of characterising the CO_2 exchange process in the laboratory, in particular its response to environmental factors, and relating this information to performance in the field.

The following types of measurement, for instance, have been used by Jarvis, Neilson & Ludlow (p. 691) in studying the response of photosynthesis to the environment in Sitka spruce (*Picea sitchensis*):

(i) light response curves, combined with transpiration measurements, which can provide estimates of photochemical efficiency, dark respiration, maximum rate of photosynthesis at 300 v.p.m., stomatal resistance as influenced by light, and intracellular resistance;

(ii) [CO_2] response curves combined with transpiration measurements, which can provide estimates of CO_2 compensation concentration in air, presence and magnitude of photorespiration, and stomatal resistance as influenced by CO_2 concentration in air;

(iii) influence of temperature on dark respiration, maximum rate of photosynthesis at 300 v.p.m., stomatal and intracellular resistances, CO_2 compensation concentration in air and magnitude of photorespiration;

(iv) influence of leaf–air vapour pressure difference on the maximum rate of photosynthesis at 300 v.p.m. and on the stomatal resistance;

(v) influence of oxygen concentration on the maximum rate of photosynthesis at 300 v.p.m. CO_2, the CO_2 compensation concentration in air, the magnitude of photorespiration and the stomatal and intracellular resistances.

Such measurements can then be related to records of photosynthetic behaviour in the field, where Jarvis *et al.* (p. 691), for instance, have used an energy balance method to measure the overall photosynthesis of the canopy, and a $^{14}CO_2$ technique to study the distribution of photosynthetic activity within the canopy.

Although the $^{14}CO_2$ method is often used to determine the gross flux of CO_2 in the leaf, this method of estimating gross photosynthesis is probably not completely accurate because the $^{14}CO_2$ within the leaf will be diluted by internally recycled CO_2 derived from respiratory processes. The specific activity of the $^{14}CO_2$ fixed in photosynthesis will therefore be lower than that in the external air. Furthermore, there is likely to be some discrimination against $^{14}CO_2$ fixation. The measurements may therefore provide only a minimal estimate of gross photosynthesis (see Voznesenskii, 1965).

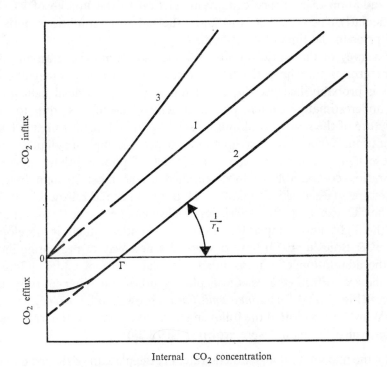

Fig. 18.1. Carbon dioxide exchange rates as influenced by the concentration of CO_2 in the intercellular spaces: *Gross* (1) and *net* (2) photosynthetic rates, and CO_2 uptake rate in air with a very low oxygen concentration (3). r_i – internal resistance.

A comparison of the influence of the internal CO_2 concentration on *gross* and *net* photosynthesis using this method could help to resolve the problem (as illustrated in Fig. 18.1). For a C_3-plant in which photorespiration occurs, the usual response curve (2) is obtained. Theoretically, if photorespiration were suppressed, the response curve would be shifted into position (1). If the experimental curves (1) and (2) are parallel, and curve (1) passes through the origin, it seems reasonable to assume that the determinations using $^{14}CO_2$ are giving a good estimate

427

of *gross* photosynthesis. (In practice, if photorespiration is suppressed by lowering the oxygen concentration, curve 3 rather than curve 1 is usually obtained.)

In such characterisation of the CO_2 process in relation to environmental factors, it is also important to make sure that measurements are made of the environment actually experienced by the plant. Jarvis *et al.* (p. 691), for instance, have emphasised the difficulty of measuring the radiation in a spruce canopy in relation to the uptake of $^{14}CO_2$, particularly since one needs to know the radiation conditions both at and prior to the time of measurement.

A survey of the world literature shows that conifers are among the plant groups that have the lowest measured rates of photosynthesis. This is probably because the use of unidirectional artificial light gives an underestimate of their photosynthetic efficiency as, due to the structure of the needles and mutual shading, it is difficult to reach light saturation. When, however, methods to provide high irradiance with diffuse light are used, conifers show rates of photosynthesis at light saturation comparable to those reached in the most efficient broad-leaved trees (Żelawski, Szaniawski, Dybczynski & Piechurowski, 1973).

The CO_2 exchange characteristics of a leaf can be markedly influenced by the light and temperature conditions under which it develops. Prioul & Bourdu (1973) have developed a new way of presenting data on the adaptation of photosynthesis in plants grown under different irradiances. From the classical photosynthesis irradiance response curves (Fig. 18.2*a*) for *Lolium multiflorum* grown under 16, 45, 85 and 110 W m^{-2}, they plotted the following parameters against the irradiance under which the plants were grown (Fig. 18.2*b*):

(1) the maximal photosynthetic rate, i.e. the plateau of the irradiance response curve,
(2) the CO_2 uptake rate at the irradiance under which the plants were grown,
(3) the initial slope of the curve relating CO_2 uptake rate to irradiance.

The extent and the nature of adaptation in plants to increasing irradiance are shown by the slope of these curves. The extent of possible adjustment to short periods of increase in irradiance for instance, is given by the distance between curves 1 and 2. This characteristic may be useful for plants growing in cloudy climates with short sunlit periods.

An example of structural regulation of photosynthetic activity in *Teucrium scorodonia* under different light regimes has been presented by

428

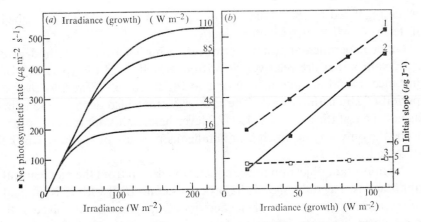

Fig. 18.2. Carbon dioxide exchange rates as influenced by irradiance or radiation regime during the growth period of *Lolium multiflorum* (Prioul & Bourdu, 1973). See text for details.

Mousseau (p. 692). For instance, the chlorophyll content per unit area of leaf is similar in shaded and non-shaded stands. However, the number of chloroplasts per unit leaf area is twice as high for non-shaded leaves but the concentration of chlorophyll per chloroplast is higher for shaded leaves; the chloroplasts of shaded leaves contain more grana and less granal discs.

The relative importance of transfer and carboxylation resistances in C₃-plants

The internal resistances to CO_2 fixation are the transfer resistance r_m and the carboxylation resistance r_x. Chartier, Chartier & Čatský (1970) and other workers, by measuring gas exchange and subsequent modelling, obtained a ratio of r_m/r_x in the order of five to ten or more, indicating that the main resistance to CO_2 assimilation is that of transfer to the sites of carboxylation rather than carboxylation itself. In contrast, Björkman (1968), Treharne (1972) and other workers using biochemical techniques obtained very good correlations between activity of the carboxylation enzyme and the net assimilation of CO_2 suggesting that r_x is the highest resistance.

A possible objection to the first conclusion lies in the assumptions made in the model, since the shape of the CO_2 fixation curve at the carboxylation site and the way it is influenced by irradiance and CO_2 concentration at that site may be queried. Considered in another way, the problem is to know if the activity of RuDP carboxylase in situ,

429

when regulated by the whole Calvin cycle, can be adequately described in terms of Michaelis–Menten kinetics.

Other experimental results, however, using Chartier's method give r_m/r_x values that are relatively low. Sunderland & Elston (p. 692), for instance, found a value of one or two for leaves of *Vicia faba* over a period of about thirty days. The ratio r_m/r_x may also depend upon the age of the leaf (Šesták *et al.*, 1974). Nevertheless, this approach appears to be the only way in which a simultaneous measure of r_x and r_m can be obtained.

An important objection to the conclusion drawn from the biochemical approach is that only one of the processes concerned with r_x is studied *in vitro* and no estimation of the activity of the processes involved with r_m is given. The conclusion is drawn only from the high correlation between carboxylation enzyme activity *in vitro* and net CO_2 exchange by the leaf. As many processes are involved and correlated *in vivo*, it is perhaps dangerous to extrapolate results obtained from enzymological studies on one enzyme to those existing in whole leaves. One could imagine for instance, that the activity of the carboxylating enzyme is governed by the rate of CO_2 fixation itself or by other parts of the whole process.

To solve this problem, Chartier proposes to examine the possible physiological basis for r_m. The overall transfer resistance r_m for example, could be divided into two parts: (i) r_{m_1}, the resistance along the path from the intercellular spaces to the sites where CO_2 from photorespiration is evolved in the cytoplasm. r_{m_1} accounts for the resistance due to the cellular membranes and transfer through the cytoplasm; (ii) r_{m_2}, the resistance along the path from the sites where photorespiratory CO_2 is evolved to the sites of carboxylation inside the chloroplast. r_{m_2} involves the resistance due to the chloroplast membranes, the stroma and chloroplast lamellae.

Experiments in CO_2-limiting conditions show that the recycling of respiratory CO_2 is low. This could mean that the resistance to CO_2 transfer between the sites of photorespiration and the sites of carboxylation could be high. Hence, if one assumes that the carboxylation resistance is low, the main resistance is r_{m_2}, i.e. the main resistance to transfer is at the level of the chloroplast.

Some work supports this view. Under conditions of very low irradiance (lower than 50 W m^{-2}), there is an increased development of internal structures in the chloroplasts of *Lolium*. This is associated with an increase in r_m (Prioul, 1973). However, this relationship is no longer valid at higher irradiance. Similarly, for nine strains of three cultivated species of *Brassica*, Kariya & Tsunoda (1972) found a good relationship between the chloroplast area index (CAI), i.e. the ratio of chloroplast area to leaf area, and the rate of photosynthesis at 50 klx and 30 °C. If the chloroplast envelope provides the main resistance to CO_2 transfer this result might be predicted, as the resistance is inversely proportional to the area available for CO_2 uptake. This effect might also explain the high net CO_2 exchange found in leaves that are not fully expanded, as the CAI decreases with leaf expansion.

Another consideration is that the conversion of CO_2 to HCO_3^- may be important in the transfer and fixation of carbon. The permeability of artificial lipoprotein membranes, for example, is higher for CO_2 than for HCO_3^-. However, the concentration of HCO_3^- in the stroma of chloroplasts is higher than the concentration of CO_2 and increases with increasing pH (Werdan & Heldt, 1972), even though the substrate for RuDP carboxylase is CO_2 (Cooper, Filmer, Wishnick & Lane, 1969).

The importance of carbonic anhydrase in regulating the CO_2/HCO_3^- ratio at different sites in the chloroplast can be considered in relation to the above findings. A range of correlations have been found between the carbonic anhydrase activity and the rate of photosynthesis (Everson, 1970; Graham & Reed, 1971; Downton & Slatyer, 1972), and significant correlations might be expected if the r_m value were high. Randall & Bouma (1973), however, suggest that carbonic anhydrase does not affect the diffusion of CO_2.

Comparison of the CO_2 response curves for photosynthesis in C_3-plants at normal and low O_2 concentrations shows that at low O_2 concentrations photorespiration is suppressed (see Fig. 18.1) and the CO_2 curve passes through the origin. Moreover, the internal resistance is also decreased as shown by the change in slope of the CO_2 response curve.

However, studying CO_2 exchange alone does not indicate whether it is the transfer or the carboxylation resistance which is affected. Bio-chemical studies indicate that the carboxylation step also is affected by O_2 concentration, although if r_m is much higher than r_x, O_2 must also affect the process of transfer, for instance, by an effect on carbonic anhydrase activity.

Conclusions

In spite of the extensive comparative studies on photosynthetic systems in higher plants, particularly the comparisons between plants with the

431

C₃-, C₄- or CAM(Crassulacean Acid Metabolism)-systems, there remain many important ecological and physiological topics which require further investigation.

It is usually found, for instance, that C_4-plants have a higher optimum temperature for photosynthesis than C_3-plants, and also a greater maximum photosynthetic rate at light saturation (Cooper & Tainton, 1968; Troughton, Chapter 16). There is, however, increasing evidence that among C_3-plants there exists a range of temperature optima from low to fairly high, and that this may depend on the previous history of the plant. Sunflower and cotton, for instance, although possessing a C_3-system have temperature optima within the usual C_4-range. Furthermore, certain C_3-species, such as sunflower, do not reach light saturation until comparatively high irradiances, and exhibit maximum photosynthetic rates similar to those of many C_4-species.

The isotope ratio of $^{13}C/^{12}C$ can be used for distinguishing between the C_3- and C_4-pathways (Troughton, Chapter 16), but applying this technique to CAM-plants shows a bimodal distribution, possibly suggesting that some CAM-plants are in fact capable of assimilating CO_2 directly through the C_3-pathway in the light, or directly through the C_4-pathway in the dark or both under certain conditions. The work of Osmond *et al.* (1973) shows that in *Kalanchoe* it is possible to convert a plant which fixes CO_2 in the light through the C_3-pathway to a plant which fixes its CO_2 by the C_4-pathway in the dark. Changing night temperatures or daylength can achieve this conversion.

Finally, although most comparative ecological and physiological studies in photosynthesis have been carried out on higher plants, in arctic, subarctic and alpine zones, and in many desert areas, mosses or lichens are important producers of organic matter. Photosynthetic studies on mosses and lichens have already provided important information on the effects of freezing and dehydration (Oechel & Collins, p. 692; Kallio & Kärenlampi, Chapter 17), but many of the methods which have been developed for the study of photosynthesis have not yet been fully utilised for studies in these lower plants.

References

Björkman, O. (1968). Further studies on differentiation of photosynthetic properties in sun and shade ecotypes of *Solidago virgaurea*. *Physiologia Plantarum*, **21**, 84–99.

Chartier, P., Chartier, M. & Čatský, J. (1970). Resistances for carbon dioxide diffusion and for carboxylation as factors in bean photosynthesis. *Photosynthetica*, **4**, 48–57.

Cooper, J. P. & Tainton, N. M. (1968). Light and temperature requirements for the growth of tropical and temperate grasses. *Herbage Abstracts*, **38**, 167–76.

Cooper, T. G., Filmer, D., Wishnick, M. & Lane, M. D. (1969). The active species of 'CO$_2$' utilized by ribulose diphosphate carboxylase. *Journal of Biological Chemistry*, **244**, 1081–3.

Downton, J. & Slatyer, R. O. (1972). Temperature dependence of photosynthesis in cotton. *Plant Physiology*, **50**, 518–22.

Everson, R. G. (1970). Carbonic anhydrase and CO$_2$ fixation in isolated chloroplasts. *Phytochemistry*, **9**, 25–32.

Graham, D. & Reed, M. L. (1971). Carbonic anhydrase and the regulation of photosynthesis. *Nature New Biology*, **231**, 81–3.

Kariya, K. & Tsunoda, S. (1972). Relationship of chlorophyll content, chloroplast area index and leaf photosynthesis rate in *Brassica*. *Tohoku Journal of Agricultural Research*, **23**, 1–14.

Osmond, C. B., Allaway, W. G., Sutton, B. G., Troughton, J. H., Querioz, O., Lüttge, U. & Winter, K. (1973). Carbon isotope discrimination in photosynthesis of CAM plants. *Nature*, **246**, 41–2.

Prioul, J. L. (1973). Eclairment de croissance et infrastructure des chloroplastes de *Lolium multiflorum*, Lmk. Relation avec les résistances au transfert de CO$_2$. *Photosynthetica*, **7**, 373–81.

Prioul, J. L. & Bourdu, R. (1973). Graphical display of photosynthetic adaptability to irradiance. *Photosynthetica*, **7**, 405–7.

Randall, P. J. & Bouma, D. (1973). Zinc deficiency, carbonic anhydrase and photosynthesis in leaves of spinach. *Plant Physiology*, **52**, 229–32.

Šesták, Z., Čatský, J., Solárová, J., Strnadová, H. & Tichá, I. (1974). Carbon dioxide transfer and photochemical activities as factors of photosynthesis during ontogenesis of primary bean leaves. In *Genetic Aspects of Photosynthesis*, eds. Yu. S. Nasyrov & Z. Šesták. The Hague, Junk.

Šetlik, I. (ed.) (1970). *Prediction and Measurement of Photosynthetic Production*. Wageningen, PUDOC.

Treharne, K. J. (1972). Biochemical limitations to photosynthetic rates. In *Crop Processes in Controlled Environments*, eds. A. R. Rees, K. E. Cockshull, D. W. Hand & R. G. Hurd, pp. 285–303. London & New York, Academic Press.

Voznesenskiï, V. L. (1965). [On the possibility of investigating gas exchange of plants in closed systems with help of ^{14}CO$_2$.] In Russian. *Fiziologiya Rastenii*, Moscow, **12**, 746–9.

Werdan, K. & Heldt, H. W. (1972). Accumulation of bicarbonate in intact chloroplasts following a pH gradient. *Biochimica et Biophysica Acta*, **283**, 430–41.

Żelawski, W., Szaniawski, R., Dybczyński, W. & Piechurowski, A. (1973). Photosynthetic capacity of conifers in diffuse light of high illuminance. *Photosynthetica*, **7**, 351–7.

P*

PART V

Use of assimilates for maintenance, growth and development

19. Biochemical pathways in unicellular plants

G. E. FOGG

A unicellular alga shows remarkable flexibility as a photosynthetic system. According to its physiological state and the conditions to which it is exposed, newly fixed carbon may appear almost exclusively in protein, on the one hand, or mainly in reserve products such as carbohydrate or fat, on the other. This situation has been discussed by Myers (1949) and Fogg (1959). To develop this theme and to consider the distribution of photosynthate among all the various biochemical pathways involved in maintenance, growth and development has become an impossibly large task. However, at a much earlier stage in the photosynthetic fixation of carbon there is bifurcation into pathways, one of which leads to synthesis of cell material, the other to loss of photosynthate from the cell, which appears to be of particular importance for studies of primary productivity in aquatic habitats. It is with this one stage, at which glycollate is formed as a product of photosynthesis, that this paper is concerned.

The biosynthesis of glycollate

Since Tolbert & Zill (1956) observed that glycollate may be excreted from photosynthesizing *Chlorella* cells, the metabolism of this substance has been the subject of much investigation. The present picture of its metabolic interrelations is summarized in Fig. 19.1. It appears that ribulose-1,5-diphosphate (RuDP), the 5-carbon acceptor substance in the Calvin–Benson carbon fixation cycle, may either participate in the cycle by reacting with carbon dioxide under the influence of RuDP carboxylase to yield two molecules of phosphoglycerate or react with oxygen. The latter reaction yields one molecule of phosphoglycerate and one molecule of phosphoglycollate from which glycollate is formed by phosphatase action.

The enzyme catalyzing the oxidative cleavage of RuDP may be regarded as a RuDP oxygenase but Bowes & Berry (1972) consider that this is an alternative reaction catalyzed by RuDP carboxylase. Experiments with $^{18}O_2$ confirm RuDP as the precursor since the tracer is incorporated, both in an *in vitro* reaction mixture and *in vivo*, into the

437

The use of assimilates

carboxyl group of phosphoglycollate but not into phosphoglycerate. If H_2 ^{18}O is supplied then the carboxyl group of phosphoglycerate is labelled (Tolbert, 1974). Such evidence appears to rule out the operation of another mechanism for glycollate formation, by peroxidation of α,β-dihydroxyethylthiamine pyrophosphate, which has been demonstrated *in vitro* (Gibbs, 1971) but not *in vivo*. Some glycollate may,

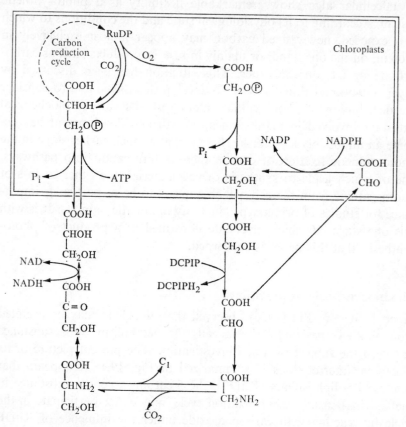

Fig. 19.1. The glycollate pathway (after Tolbert, 1974). RuDP, ribulose-1,5-diphosphate; NAD, nicotinamide adenine dinucleotide; NADP, nicotinamide adenine dinucleotide phosphate; DCPIP, dichlorophenol-indophenol.

however, be produced by reduction of glyoxylate formed during photo-assimilation of certain organic substrates (Marker & Whittingham, 1966; Merrett & Goulding, 1968).

As would be expected from the hypothesis that RuDP is its precursor, glycollate formation is strongly influenced by the relative concentrations of oxygen and carbon dioxide. Coombs & Whittingham (1966) using

Chlorella, and Bidwell (1972) using *Acetabularia* chloroplasts have shown that increase in pO_2 increases glycollate formation during photosynthesis. Pritchard, Griffin & Whittingham (1962), Nalewajko, Chowdhuri & Fogg (1963) and Watt & Fogg (1966) working with *Chlorella* strains and Gimmler, Ullrich, Domanski-Kaden & Urbach (1969) with *Ankistrodesmus* found maximum glycollate excretion at low carbon dioxide concentrations. In experiments in which both pO_2 and pCO_2 were varied, Bowes & Berry (1972) found that with *Chlamydomonas reinhardtii* glycollate excretion, in terms of the percentage of the total carbon fixed in this form, depended on the ratio of oxygen to carbon dioxide (but see below, this page).

The amount of glycollate produced will also depend on the amount of precursor available. Watt & Fogg (1966) found that, following transfer of *Chlorella* to conditions favouring release, the rate of glycollate production fell after 50–100 minutes and the amount liberated per cell by the end of this period was found to increase exponentially with the relative growth rate of the material used. A similar relationship of amount of extracellular products of photosynthesis to the relative growth rate of the diatom, *Stephanodiscus hantzschii*, was found by Watt (1969). These findings are consistent with the idea that glycollate is formed from a precursor, such as RuDP, the amount of which is limited and proportional to photosynthetic activity and which accumulates in excess when the rate of carbon dioxide fixation is reduced (such accumulation of RuDP is shown clearly in the experiments of Bassham *et al.*, 1954). Of course, very low concentrations of carbon dioxide will prevent the regeneration of RuDP by the Calvin–Benson cycle and so reduce the formation of glycollate. Bowes & Berry (1972) found this in their experiments with *Chlamydomonas*, the maximum excretion rate occurring in 2 mM bicarbonate at all the pO_2 levels tested and suppression of glycollate excretion taking place only at concentrations higher than this.

Among other factors which may affect glycollate production directly is pH. Nalewajko, Chowdhuri & Fogg (1963) found that although the maximum rate of photosynthesis of *Chlorella pyrenoidosa* occurred in medium of pH 5.5 to 7.0, glycollate excretion was at a maximum at pH 8.5. Bidwell (1972) found with isolated *Acetabularia* chloroplasts that the fixation of ^{14}C into glycollate and its derivatives increased as pH was increased to 9.5. At limiting and saturating light intensities the rate of glycollate excretion more or less parallels the rate of photosynthesis but at inhibitory intensities there is an increase in the proportion of the total carbon fixed appearing in this form (Fogg, Nalewajko & Watt, 1965; Bowes & Berry, 1972).

The glycollate pathway

In higher plants it has been established that glycollate, after oxidation to glyoxylate, is transformed successively to glycine, serine and glycerate (Fig. 19.1). It was suggested by Hess & Tolbert (1967) that algae lack glycollic oxidase and are thus unable to carry out the first step in this sequence, this being the reason for the excretion of glycollate. Lord & Merrett (1968) found, indeed, that a strain of *Chlorella pyrenoidosa*, which does not excrete glycollate, does contain this enzyme or, more strictly speaking, glycollate : dichlorophenolindophenol oxidoreductase (Lord & Merrett, 1971a). It appears, however, that the algal glycollate oxidoreductase or dehydrogenase is widely distributed. It is, for example, present in *Euglena gracilis* (Codd & Merrett, 1970) and in *Chlamydomonas reinhardtii* (Cooksey, 1971). Although, because of its lability and low activity it has not been fully purified, its properties seem similar to those of higher plant glycollate oxidase, except that its action is not associated with the presence of excess catalase (Tolbert, 1974) and it cannot use oxygen itself as a hydrogen acceptor. The specific activity of this enzyme in *Chlamydomonas reinhardtii* is related to the pCO_2. Cells grown in 1% carbon dioxide in air metabolized little of the glycollate produced in photosynthesis but liberated it into the medium whereas cells grown in air showed high glycollate dehydrogenase activity and did not excrete glycollate (Nelson & Tolbert, 1969). Similar results were obtained with *Euglena gracilis* (Lord & Merrett, 1971b) but Kowallik & Schmid (1971) found no such effect with *Chlorella vulgaris*, *C. pyrenoidosa*, *Ankistrodesmus convolutus* and *A. braunii*. They concluded that closely related species of green algae showed widely differing levels of glycollate dehydrogenase activity and that external factors have only slight modifying effects on these levels.

The operation of the glycollate pathway has been demonstrated in *Chlorella pyrenoidosa* (Lord & Merrett, 1970) and in *Euglena gracilis* (Codd & Merrett, 1971). Enzymes for conversion of glyoxylate to glycine and serine but not that for conversion between serine and hydroxypyruvate have been reported as present in various algae (Tolbert, 1974). Hydroxypyruvate reductase (D-glycerate dehydrogenase) has been found in *Chlorella* and other algae (Lord & Merrett, 1970; Tolbert, 1974) and although the presence of glycerate kinase, necessary

440

for the final step in the cycle, conversion of glycerate to 3-phospho-glycerate, has not been reported for algae there is no reason to suppose that it is absent. 3-Phosphoglycerate may then re-enter the carbon reduction cycle and its carbon be used in biosynthesis in the usual ways. In higher plants glycollate oxidase, certain other enzymes of the glycollate pathway and catalase are localized in vesicular structures which have been called peroxisomes. Similar structures appear to be present in algae (Lord & Merrett, 1971*b*; Gergis, 1971; Codd, Schmid & Kowallick, 1972)

The utilization of glycollate as a substrate for growth

Glycollate does not support the heterotrophic growth of many algae (Danforth, 1962; Droop & McGill, 1966) but it has been shown to be photoassimilated by several species. Concentrations of the order of 1 mg glycollate per litre increase considerably the relative growth rate at limiting but not at saturating, light intensities, of a planktonic strain of *Chlorella pyrenoidosa* (Sen & Fogg, 1966) and of *Skeletonema costatum* (Pant, 1973), neither of which can use it as a substrate in the dark. This suggests that glycollate is photoassimilated by these algae and Pant (1973) has shown that carbon from glycollate supplied in the light is incorporated into the cell fraction containing polysaccharide and protein. *Euglena gracilis*, which can grow heterotrophically in the dark on a variety of organic substrates, can also utilize glycollate as sole carbon source, but only in the light. Since this assimilation is inhibited by 3-(3,4 dichlorophenyl)-1,1-dimethyl urea it appears that it is dependent on photochemical reactions in the chloroplast (Murray, Giovanelli & Smillie, 1971). Blue-green algae have also been shown to assimilate glycollate in the light (Miller, Chang & Colman, 1971; Lex, Silvester & Stewart, 1972), but with some other algae significant uptake of this substrate has not been demonstrated (Tolbert, 1974).

Utilization of glycollate in growth would be expected to depend on the operation of the glycollate pathway (Fig. 19.1) and for *Chlorella pyrenoidosa* (Lord & Merrett, 1970) and for *Euglena gracilis* (Codd & Merrett, 1971; Murray, Giovanelli & Smillie, 1971) this has been shown to be so. Glycollate assimilation would therefore be expected to be related to glycollate dehydrogenase activity, which seems to vary considerably from one algal species to another (p. 440), and to photo-respiration.

Experiments with *Scenedesmus obliquus* in synchronous culture have shown that this alga, which excretes glycollate, can also assimilate it, as indicated by stimulation of oxygen consumption when it is supplied, both heterotrophically and by photoassimilation. Such assimilation occurs, however, only at the time of cell division, when excretion is at a minimum (Nelson, Tolbert & Hess, 1969).

The presence of an active enzyme system for glycollate assimilation in *Euglena gracilis* appears to depend on cells being photosynthetic. Codd & Merrett (1970) found that the greening of cells grown in the dark was accompanied by synthesis *de novo* of glycollate dehydrogenase and phosphoglycollate phosphatase. The former enzyme was present only at a low level in cells growing heterotrophically even when these were supplied with glycollate.

The consumption of glycollate in photorespiration

Investigations in higher plants have shown that the mechanism of photorespiration is one of glycollate formation followed by its metabolism as discussed in the previous section. Uptake of oxygen may occur at three points; during glycollate production in the chloroplast, during oxidation of glycollate to glyoxylate in the peroxisome and during glycine oxidation and conversion to serine in the mitochondrion. Carbon dioxide is evolved in the conversion of glycine to serine.

The reactions of photorespiration would be expected to occur in algae as in higher plants. This has been demonstrated for *Nitella flexilis* by Downton & Tregunna (1968). Photorespiration is favoured by low carbon dioxide and high oxygen concentrations; many investigators have not examined algae under these conditions and, consequently, demonstration of photorespiration has often been equivocal (Tolbert, 1974). However, Bunt, Owens & Hoch (1966) using ^{18}O as a tracer found consistent light-stimulated uptake of oxygen by a diatom *Fragilaria sublinearis* and recently Lex, Silvester & Stewart (1972) have carried out a thorough study of the phenomenon in the blue-green alga, *Anabaena cylindrica*. The rate of uptake of oxygen in photorespiration was found to be up to twenty times that in dark respiration and at its maximum almost balanced the output in photosynthesis. It was highest at the CO_2 compensation point and was completely inhibited at a pCO_2 of 0.02 atm. Its rate was increased linearly with rising pO_2. These characteristics are similar to those of higher plant photorespiration but although glycollate is assimilated by this alga, supply of this substrate had no effect on the respiration rate nor did addition of hydroxyethane

442

sulphonate, an inhibitor of glycollate oxidase, have any effect. Other workers have reported limited output of carbon dioxide during photo-respiration by algae (for references see Tolbert, 1974). Döhler (1972), in a study of carbon dioxide uptake transients in *Anacystis nidulans*, obtained results consistent with the hypothesis that glycollate was acting as substrate for photorespiration.

In a study of *Chlamydomonas reinhardtii*, Bowes & Berry (1972) found that in addition to reacting with RuDP carboxylase, oxygen also inhibits it competitively with respect to carbon dioxide. This is indicated by the absence of photorespiratory carbon dioxide release concurrent with low rates of glycollate production by intact cells. The algal RuDP carboxylase *in vitro* was competitively inhibited by oxygen in a manner similar to that of the higher plant enzyme.

The excretion of glycollate

The escape of glycollate from a cell will depend on the intracellular concentration, as determined by the relative rates of production and consumption in the reactions described above, the permeability of the cell membranes and the extracellular concentration, which will depend on the rate of glycollate liberation by this and other cells, its rate of consumption or adsorption and the turbulence of the medium (Fogg, 1966). The evidence is broadly in agreement with the idea that the cell membranes are freely permeable to glycollate and that the amount excreted is determined by an equilibrium between intra- and extra-cellular concentrations. Factors that would be expected to diminish the assimilation of glycollate, e.g. absence of the necessary enzymes, inhibitors (see above) and nutrient deficiency (see Ignatiades, 1972), as we have seen, increase glycollate excretion. The amount of glycollate excreted per cell increased as the concentration of cells was decreased in experiments with *Chlorella* (Nalewajko, Chowdhuri & Fogg, 1963) and with *Skeletonema* (Ignatiades, 1972). When small numbers of cells of algae such as *Chlorella pyrenoidosa* (Sen & Fogg, 1966), *Nitzschia closterium* (Tokuda, 1966) or *Ditylum brightwellii* (Paredes, 1967–8) are inoculated into fresh medium and exposed to low light intensity there is a lag of one or two days before increase in cell number begins. This lag can be largely abolished by adding 1 mg glycollate per litre to the medium, suggesting that before carbon fixed by photosynthesis can be used for growth an equilibrium concentration of glycollate must first be established in the vicinity of the cells. This idea is borne out by the finding that addition of alumina, which adsorbs glycollate, prolongs the lag phase of *Skeletonema* indefinitely although growth in the same medium takes place if the alumina is removed by decantation (Pant, 1973). The lack of agreement between observations of glycollate excretion by *Chlorella* and a simple mathematical model based on the assumption of equilibrium between intra- and extracellular concentrations (Watt & Fogg, 1966) is most probably to be ascribed to steady-state conditions not being established in the algal cultures. Furthermore, although the escape of glycollate from the cell may be a process of simple diffusion, uptake may be an active process (Lord & Merrett, 1971*a*). However, although Pant (1973) found higher rates of glycollate uptake by *Skeletonema costatum* in the light as compared with the dark, the results of a kinetic study, which according to Hobbie & Wright (1965) differentiates between diffusive and active uptake, yielded ambiguous results.

It appears from work discussed above (p. 440) that the original hypothesis of Hess & Tolbert (1967) is broadly true and that excretion of glycollate in quantity by a particular species depends primarily on it not possessing an active glycollate dehydrogenase. However, activities of this and other enzymes concerned in the production and consumption of glycollate would be expected to vary during the cell division cycle, with corresponding changes in the excretion of this substance. The observations of Nelson, Tolbert & Hess (1969) on variations in glycollate uptake during the cell cycle of *Scenedesmus obliquus* have already been noted (p. 442). Chang & Tolbert (1970) studied *Ankistrodesmus braunii* in synchronous culture and found that cells at the end of the growing phase, after 10 h of a 16-h light phase, excreted nearly 35 % of the total carbon fixed as glycollate. Dividing cells from the dark phase, when tested in the light, excreted only 4 % as much glycollate. These dividing cells also excreted mesotartrate and isocitrate lactone in the dark as well as in the light. *Euglena gracilis* strain Z was found by Codd & Merrett (1971) to excrete maximum quantities of glycollate in synchronized cultures at the end of the dark phase when the cells had just divided; thereafter excretion declined and was minimal in the early dark phase. In unsynchronized cultures glycollate excretion varied widely with growth conditions and was found to be inversely related to the activity of glycollate dehydrogenase in the cells. In the synchronous cultures, however, the amount of this enzyme was found to be sufficient at all stages to oxidize the glycollate being produced and it was concluded that glycollate oxidation was limited by the availability of hydrogen acceptor. This agrees with the observation that maximum glycollate excretion takes place when rates of biosynthesis in the cells are minimal. At other stages in the cell cycle the glycollate pathway is fully operative and ^{14}C supplied as carbon dioxide appears rapidly in glycine, serine and glycerate.

External conditions may also alter the balance between production and consumption of glycollate. Lord, Codd & Merrett (1970) found that with a strain of *Chlorella pyrenoidosa* which does not normally release glycollate, this substance was excreted after addition of α-hydroxy-sulphate in red light but not in blue light. Döhler (1972) has observed a similar effect of wavelength on glycollate excretion by *Anacystis nidulans*. This may be an effect of blue light stimulating photorespiration. Döhler (1972) has also observed a marked effect of temperature on glycollate excretion by *Anacystis nidulans* with a maximum at 15 °C and a fall to zero at about 27 °C.

Much of the work on glycollate excretion has been done with *Chlorella* spp. and the question arises as to how far these are typical of other unicellular algae. Since the mechanism of the photosynthetic fixation of carbon dioxide appears to be basically the same in all plants it would be expected that glycollate would occupy a similar key position in the metabolism of other algae. Glycollate has been detected amongst the extracellular products of a variety of different kinds of phytoplankton (for references see Fogg, 1971). More recently it has been reported as being excreted by the blue-green alga *Anacystis nidulans* and the red algae *Porphyridium cruentum* and *P. aerugineum* (Döhler, 1972). In many studies, total extracellular products of photosynthesis have been deter-mined, using ^{14}C as a tracer, rather than glycollate itself but the general kinetics have usually been found to be consistent with the idea that glycollate or some closely related substance is the main component of the fraction being estimated (for references see Fogg, 1971). Nalewajko, Chowdhuri & Fogg (1963) using *Chlorella pyrenoidosa* and Bowes & Berry (1972) using *Chlamydomonas reinhardtii* showed that indirect determinations by the ^{14}C method agreed well with direct colorimetric estimates of glycollate in culture filtrates. However, it now seems clear that although all unicellular algae tested liberate extracellular products of photosynthesis, glycollate is not invariably detectable among these. Watt (1969) from his own observations and a review of published evidence, concluded that there are two major types of excretion during photosynthesis, one, represented by *Chlorella* spp. and the diatom *Stephanodiscus hantzschii*, with glycollate as the principal extracellular product and another, represented by *Synedra acus* and possibly the most common type, in which polysaccharides predominate. Barker (1972) has found that the common freshwater plankton diatom *Asterionella formosa* belongs to this second type. The marine forms *Dunaliella tertiolecta* (Huntsman, 1972) and *Phaeocystis poucheti* (Guillard & Hellebust, 1971) also liberate little glycollic acid during photosynthesis.

Indication that even when glycollate itself is not excreted the kinetics of excretion of photosynthetic products remain broadly the same suggests that these other products may be metabolically closely related to glycollate. Thus glycerol, which appears to be the main extracellular product of *Dunaliella tertiolecta* (Hellebust, 1965), is readily derived from glycerate, a component of the glycollate pathway. The polysaccharides which are excreted by many species are however less obviously related to glycollate.

The excretion of glycollate under natural conditions

Conditions such as high pO_2, low pCO_2, high light intensity and nutrient deficiency, which have been shown in laboratory experiments to favour glycollate excretion, are frequently found in natural waters and species known to liberate glycollate as their main extracellular product are often abundant in both fresh water and the sea. The expectation that glycollate is liberated by natural populations of algae appears to be borne out by the finding that liberation of extracellular products of photosynthesis is of normal occurrence in aquatic habitats. The results of experiments *in situ* (Table 19.1) show that liberation of extracellular products by algae is always appreciable and sometimes substantial, occurring both in fresh water and the sea and regardless of water type, climate, season or type of alga. The organic matter found in solutions does not appear to originate from cells damaged during filtration (Fogg, 1971). Most determinations have been made by a method in which the appearance of ^{14}C-labelled organic matter in filtrates from samples allowed to photosynthesize in the presence of [14]CO$_2$ is taken as a measure of excretion. The techniques used have recently been greatly improved (Thomas, 1971) and observations made by quite different methods (Antia *et al.*, 1963) confirm that loss of organic matter from photosynthesizing cells does take place.

Release of extracellular products of photosynthesis was found by Fogg, Nalewajko & Watt (1965) to proceed linearly with time for up to eight hours during daylight. Thomas (1971) found in half-day

446

Table 19.1. *The liberation of extracellular products of photosynthesis (as percentage of the total carbon fixed) by natural populations of algae. Results were obtained by the* ^{14}C *method unless otherwise stated*

Location	Water type	Month	Algal type	Extracellular products	Reference
Torneträsk 68°25'N., 18°50'E.	Oligotrophic freshwater	Aug.	Nannoplankton	11	Fogg, 1958
Lake Erken 59°50'N., 18°34'E.	Eutrophic freshwater	Aug.– Sept.	Planktonic Cyanophyceae	1.5–2.4	Fogg, 1958
Departure Bay 49°20'N., 123°50'W.	Inshore 125 m³ plastic bag	June– July	Mainly diatoms	35–50*	Antia et al., 1963
Windermere 54°20'N., 2°55'W.	Oligotrophic freshwater	March– Oct.	Varied phytoplankton	7–50	Fogg, Nalewajko & Watt, 1965
Blelham Tarn 54°25'N., 2°57'W.	Oligotrophic freshwater	July	Mixed phytoplankton	38	Fogg, Nalewajko and Watt, 1965
North Sea 53°40'N., 2°00'E.	Shallow sea, eutrophic	June	Diatoms, dinoflagellates	7.8	Fogg, Nalewajko & Watt, 1965
North Sea 52°20'N., 3°00'E.	Shallow sea, eutrophic	June	Diatoms	5.8	Fogg, Nalewajko & Watt, 1965
Tring Reservoirs 51°45'N., 0°40'W.	Eutrophic freshwater	Feb.– Oct.	Varied phytoplankton	1.5–33	Watt, 1966
Indian Ocean	Oceanic	June	Not stated	5–32	Jitts, 1967
Lake Ontario 43°30'N., 79°0'W.	Oligotrophic		Mainly Stephanodiscus tenuis	23–76	Nalewajko & Marin, 1969
Weddell Sea 60°43'S., 45°36'W.	Productive inshore water	Jan.	Diatoms	<2	Horne, Fogg & Eagle, 1969
Lake 5 Signy Island 60°43'S., 45°38'W.	Oligotrophic freshwater	Feb.	Chlorophycean Nannoplankton	43	Fogg & Horne, 1970
Gravel Pond Massachusetts 42°30'N., 71°W.	Eutrophic freshwater	Aug.	Not stated	7.9	Wright, 1970
NE. Pacific Ocean 45–49°N. 124–129°W.	Eutrophic	July	Not stated	7	Anderson & Zeutschel, 1970
	Oligotrophic	July	Not stated	49	Anderson & Zeutschel, 1970
Cochin Backwater 9°58'N., 76°15'E.	Shallow brackish, eutrophic	Jan.– Feb.	Various phytoplankton	5–19	Samuel, Shah & Fogg, 1971
Georgia estuaries 31°30'N., 81°0'W.	Estuarine Eutrophic	Aug.	Not stated	<7	Thomas, 1971
SE. USA coastal waters 29–33°30'N., 77°45'–81°30'W.	Coastal	Sept.	Not stated	<21	Thomas, 1971
Sargasso sea 36°30'N., 74°50'W. 35°00'N., 73°0'W.	Oligotrophic Oceanic	Nov.	Not stated	<44	Thomas, 1971
Loch Etive 56°40'N., 5°20'W.	Sheltered inshore brackish	March– Oct.	Mainly Skeletonema costatum	3.5–46	Ignatiades, 1972

* Determined as difference between inorganic carbon removed from water and organic carbon appearing in cells.

447

experiments that although the absolute amount of extracellular products released remained about the same, particulate fixation decreased in the second half of the day so that the percentage extracellular release increased. Successive two-hour experiments sometimes showed a progressive decrease in liberation of extracellular products but increases in percentage release with time were also found (Thomas, 1971).

The absolute amount of extracellular products released in any given situation is approximately proportional to the amount of photosynthesis but when release in different situations is compared it is evident that it does not bear a linear relation to biomass or primary productivity but becomes proportionately greater as these become less. This was first observed by Watt (1966) for fresh waters and is evident in the data given in Table 19.1. Anderson & Zeutschel (1970) found for sea areas in the northern Pacific Ocean that percentage extracellular release ranged from one for the most eutrophic waters to forty-nine for oligotrophic waters. They summarized their results in the following expression relating x (dissolved organic matter release in the euphotic zone in mg C m^{-2} $\frac{1}{2}$ d^{-1}) to y (particulate fixation in the euphotic zone in mg C m^{-2} $\frac{1}{2}$ d^{-1})

$$\log x = 0.66 \log y + 0.03 \qquad r = 0.932,$$

r being the correlation coefficient between $\log x$ and $\log y$. Samuel, Shah & Fogg (1971) found in tropical estuarine waters that percentage extracellular release rose from 5.0 at 117 mg chlorophyll a m^{-3} to 18.9 at 0.54 mg chlorophyll a m^{-3}. This situation may be a consequence of a tendency to equilibrium between intracellular and extracellular concentrations of the substances concerned, so that proportionately more is released from the fewer cells in oligotrophic waters, or it may be an effect of nutrient limitation. Probably both these effects are involved.

Another general feature is that the relative amount of extracellular material liberated increases when photosynthesis is inhibited in bright sunlight near the water surface. Extracellular release amounting to as much as 95 % of the total carbon fixation has been reported as occurring at the surface of lakes on bright days when the extent of release lower down in the water column was of the order of 10 % or less (Fogg, Nalewajko & Watt, 1965; Watt, 1966; Fogg, 1966). The extent of release increases with the extent of inhibition of photosynthesis. A similar phenomenon has been reported in the sea (Thomas, 1971). Surface inhibition of phytoplankton photosynthesis appears to be due

448

to both visible and ultraviolet light and it is possible that the increased excretion could result from the damage to the systems consuming photosynthetic intermediates being greater than that to those producing them. However, it is to be noted that oxygen often reaches super-saturating concentrations near the surface of water under conditions favouring photosynthesis so that, at least in part, both the inhibition of photosynthesis and greater relative release of glycollate, if this is indeed the substance concerned, could be direct effects of oxygen as described in earlier sections.

Watt (1966) showed, by chromatography of filtrates from samples of a freshwater plankton population, dominated by *Stephanodiscus hantzschii*, supplied with high activity [^{14}C]bicarbonate and incubated *in situ*, that 92% of the total radioactivity in extracellular products was in the form of glycollate. However, in a population containing princi-pally *Scenedesmus* and *Ankistrodesmus* the corresponding value was 10%, and in one comprised mainly of *Nitzschia palea* the figure was 13%. In these latter two examples the principal component was poly-saccharide.

Glycollate has been shown to be sometimes present in natural waters in appreciable concentrations. Fogg, Eagle & Kinson (1969) separated glycollate from lake water by a two-stage ion exchange process, monitoring its recovery by means of added [^{14}C]glycollate, and finally estimated it by the Calkins colorimetric method. Using this method, it was found that the glycollate concentration in Windermere, English Lake District, varied from 0.00 up to 0.06 mg per litre in the 0–30-m water layer during the period from the end of February to the beginning of June. Determinations by an entirely different method based on enzyme kinetics gave the upper limit, not the actual value, for the glycollate concentration in Gravel Pond, eastern Massachusetts, as between 0.05 to 0.20 mg per litre in the summer (Wright, 1970). Values reported for sea water from the northeast Pacific, obtained after chloro-form extraction, ranged up to 1.4 mg per litre but the evidence indicated that the major part of this was derived by breakdown of high molecular weight organic compounds (Koyama & Thompson, 1964). Recently an improved method for analysing sea water, in which glycollate is concentrated by adsorption on alumina and then estimated colorimetri-cally after elution with mineral acid, has been described (Shah & Fogg, 1973). Using this method Pant (1973) found concentrations up to 0.06 mg per litre in water off Anglesey (53° 15′ N., 4° 10′ W.).

The utilization of glycollate in the natural environment

Glycollate and other labile extracellular products of photosynthesis are likely to be removed rapidly from the water, particularly by bacteria. Wright (1970) isolated twenty bacterial strains able to use glycollate as sole carbon source, from fresh waters and found in plate counts of lake water samples on glycollate media that the numbers of glycollate-utilizing colonies were as high as 950 ml^{-1} and always amounted to 75% or more of the total visible colonies. He also made a study of the uptake of glycollate by natural populations of micro-organisms in Gravel Pond, Massachusetts using [^{14}C]glycollate as a tracer. Uptake during the summer was highest in the epilimnion and decreased sharply with increasing depth and lower temperatures. Rates of glycollate uptake were of the same order as those for acetate and glucose but uptake of these latter two compounds was high at depths below 10 m where glycollate uptake was negligible. The depth distribution of glycollate uptake paralleled that of photosynthesis, a good correlation being found between the rates of glycollate uptake and the liberation of extracellular products of photosynthesis. Glycollate-utilizing bacteria have also been isolated from marine habitats (R. A. Lewin, personal communication) but no estimates of their numbers and distribution appear to have been made.

It is not clear whether phytoplankton utilize excreted glycollate to any appreciable extent. As we have seen (p. 441) many species have been shown to be capable of photoassimilating this substance and it may be imagined that such assimilation would be biologically advantageous towards the bottom of the photic zone. Uptake of glycollate by natural populations of phytoplankton has been demonstrated (Hobbie & Wright, 1965; Watt, 1966; Pant, 1973) but it is not established that bacteria associated with the algae were not mainly responsible. Hobbie & Wright (1965) proposed a method of analysis of the kinetics of uptake of organic substrates which they believed could distinguish between active uptake (by bacteria) and diffusive uptake (by algae). They concluded that, at least under purely heterotrophic conditions, planktonic algae compete poorly with bacteria for the low concentrations of substrates present in natural waters. However, in the hands of other workers (Bunt, 1969; Pant, 1973) this method has yielded ambiguous results and Hobbie & Wright (1965) did not do experiments in the light, in which algal uptake would be expected to be more vigorous. Watt (1966) found no difference in rate of glycollate uptake by fresh-

450

water phytoplankton populations in the light and the dark but used unnaturally high glycollate concentrations (1–11 mg l^{-1}). Pant (1973), using natural populations of *Skeletonema costatum*, which has been shown to photoassimilate glycollate under laboratory conditions (see p. 441), found that light-stimulated uptake from a concentration of 1 mg per litre. This indicates that photoassimilation of glycollate by algae may sometimes be appreciable under natural conditions. If the activity of glycollate dehydrogenase is the main factor controlling excretion or assimilation of glycollate then it might follow that the species assimilating glycollate are different from those liberating it.

The finding that glycollate is strongly adsorbed on to alumina (Shah & Fogg, 1973) suggests that in natural waters it could be adsorbed on to particulate matter such as flocs of ferric hydroxide and in this form contribute appreciably to animal diets.

Conclusions

The biochemical evidence shows that RuDP is at a particularly sensitive point in the pathway of photosynthetic carbon fixation at which, according to external conditions, fixed carbon may be directed into synthesis of cell material or into channels which lead to its loss from the cell. Oxygen both inhibits and reacts with RuDP carboxylase. In the former case the total fixation of carbon is reduced. In the latter case RuDP is broken down yielding phosphoglycerate and glycollate. Glycollate may then be excreted from the cell, or, if an active glycollate pathway is present, it will be photorespired, one quarter of its carbon being lost as carbon dioxide and the rest being used in biosynthesis or re-entering the carbon reduction cycle.

Tolbert (1974) sees this system as having three functions; (1) the formation, as intermediates in the glycollate pathway, of glycine and serine, which are essential for various biosynthetic pathways; (2) glycollate formation may be an unavoidable reaction of photosynthesis occurring in the presence of high oxygen concentrations and the glycollate pathway may represent a means of salvaging part of its carbon; (3) the production of glycollate may be a means of regulating cellular growth by disposing of excess carbon. If glycollate is metabolized rather than lost from the cell, the glycollate–glyoxylate shuttle is envisaged as disposing of excess reducing capacity of the chloroplasts, permitting further ATP synthesis without involving a cyclic photophosphorylation process.

These hypotheses are not mutually exclusive but the third seems most relevant at present for our understanding of primary productivity in aquatic environments. A phytoplankton cell appears to have no means of regulating the rate of the primary reactions of photosynthesis save by alteration in its content of photosynthetic pigments, which is a relatively long-term process. Therefore it must often happen that in the upper parts of the photic zone, where there is severe limitation by nutrient deficiency, that these reactions proceed much more rapidly than is needed to maintain growth. The excess assimilatory power may be used for synthesis of carbohydrate or fat, but the necessary enzyme systems for this may not be active. It seems that some overflow mechanism is essential and the formation of glycollate seems to provide for this need. Photorespiration of glycollate and excretion of glycollate appear to be two successive mechanisms of increasing effectiveness for disposing of excess primary products of photosynthesis. If it is assumed that the extracellular products of photosynthesis detected by the ^{14}C method comprise glycollate and compounds metabolically closely related to it then the data obtained in in-situ experiments support this hypothesis very well: the highest relative rates of liberation of extracellular products of photosynthesis are found in oligotrophic waters and near the surface in bright sunshine, in both of which situations photosynthesis may be expected to be in excess of growth requirements.

Whether or not the main substance concerned is glycollate, the fact of the liberation of extracellular products of photosynthesis has important implications for the measurement of primary productivity in aquatic habitats. In the standard ^{14}C method of Steemann Nielsen as described in Vollenweider (1974) carbon fixation in particulate matter only is determined and therefore the method estimates net photosynthesis as far as this is concerned (but this leaves open the question of whether early products of photosynthesis are preferentially used in dark respiration). Carbon in liberated glycollate will not be included either but obviously, since it represents potential chemical energy, should be allowed for in an estimate of net primary productivity. Methods of determining fixation in extracellular products have been described by Watt (1966), Fogg (in Vollenweider, 1974), and Thomas (1971). However, these have not yet been applied extensively and until they are, guesses of average values must be used in estimates of total primary productivity. Vallentyne (1965) in estimating the total primary productivity of the marine environment used a factor of 1.25 to correct values of particulate fixation for loss of extracellular products. This may be on the low side since higher excretion rates are found in the oligotrophic waters which cover most of the earth's surface. Thomas (1971) considers that estimates for oceanic waters based on particulate fixation only may, in some cases, be under by 50%. The liberation of quantities of glycollate or other labile organic matter clearly provides a major pathway, making organic matter produced in photosynthesis available to heterotrophic organisms, which must be taken into account in discussion of trophic relations. Most probably bacteria are the major consumers of this organic matter and in turn support a greater amount of secondary production than has hitherto been thought possible. This would account for the apparent inadequacy of the cell production of phytoplankton in providing for zooplankton, which has been pointed out both for freshwater (Nauwerck, 1963) and marine (Steele, 1964) situations.

References

Anderson, G. C. & Zeutschel, R. P. (1970). Release of dissolved organic matter by marine phytoplankton in coastal and offshore areas of the northern Pacific Ocean. *Limnology and Oceanography*, **15**, 402–7.

Antia, N. J., McAllister, C. D., Parsons, T. R., Stephens, K. & Strickland, J. D. H. (1963). Further measurements of primary production using a large-volume plastic sphere. *Limnology and Oceanography*, **8**, 166–83.

Barker, G. M. (1972). Studies on extracellular production by freshwater phytoplankton. Ph.D. thesis, University of London.

Bassham, J. A., Benson, A. A., Kay, L. D., Harris, A. Z., Wilson, A. T. & Calvin, M. (1954). The path of carbon in photosynthesis. XXI. The cyclic regeneration of carbon dioxide acceptor. *Journal of the American Chemical Society*, **76**, 1760–70.

Bidwell, R. G. S. (1972). Products of photosynthesis by *Acetabularia* chloroplasts: possible control mechanisms. In *Proceedings of the IInd International Congress on Photosynthesis Research*, eds. G. Forti, M. Avron & A. Melandri, vol. 3, pp. 1927–34. The Hague, Junk.

Bowes, G. & Berry, J. A. (1972). The effect of oxygen on photosynthesis and glycolate excretion in *Chlamydomonas reinhardtii*. *Carnegie Institution Year Book*, **71**, 148–58.

Bunt, J. S. (1969). Observations on photoheterotrophy in a marine diatom. *Journal of Phycology*, **5**, 37–42.

Bunt, J. S., Owens, O. van H. & Hoch, G. (1966). Exploratory studies on the physiology and ecology of a psychrophilic marine diatom. *Journal of Phycology*, **2**, 96–100.

Chang, W. & Tolbert, N. E. (1970). Excretion of glycolate, mesotartrate and isocitrate lactone by synchronized cultures of *Ankistrodesmus braunii*. *Plant Physiology*, **46**, 377–85.

The use of assimilates

Codd, G. A. & Merrett, M. J. (1970). Enzymes of the glycollate pathway in relation to greening in *Euglena gracilis*. *Planta*, **95**, 127–32.

Codd, G. A. & Merrett, M. J. (1971). The regulation of glycolate metabolism in division synchronized cultures of *Euglena*. *Plant Physiology*, **47**, 640–3.

Codd, G. A., Schmid, G. H. & Kowallik, W. (1972). Enzymic evidence for peroxisomes in a mutant of *Chlorella vulgaris*. *Archiv für Mikrobiologie*, **81**, 264–72.

Cooksey, K. E. (1971). Glycolate : dichlorophenolindophenol oxidoreductase in *Chlamydomonas reinhardtii*. *Plant Physiology*, **48**, 267–9.

Coombs, J. & Whittingham, C. P. (1966). The effect of high partial pressures of oxygen on photosynthesis in *Chlorella*. I. The effect on end products of photosynthesis. *Phytochemistry*, **5**, 643–51.

Danforth, W. F. (1962). Substrate assimilation and heterotrophy. In *Physiology and Biochemistry of Algae*, ed. R. A. Lewin, pp. 99–123. New York & London, Academic Press.

Döhler, G. (1972). Induction phenomena in CO_2 exchange and glycollate metabolism of the blue-green alga *Anacystis* and the red alga *Porphyridium*. In *Proceedings of the IInd International Congress on Photosynthesis Research*, eds. G. Forti, M. Avron & A. Melandri, vol. 3, pp. 2071–6. The Hague, Junk.

Downton, W. J. S. & Tregunna, E. B. (1968). Photorespiration and glycolate metabolism: a re-examination and correlation of some previous studies. *Plant Physiology*, **43**, 923–9.

Droop, M. R. & McGill, S. (1966). The carbon nutrition of some algae: the inability to utilize glycollic acid for growth. *Journal of the Marine Biological Association of the United Kingdom*, **46**, 679–84.

Fogg, G. E. (1958). Extracellular products of phytoplankton and the estimation of primary production. *Rapport et procès-verbaux des réunions. Conseil permanent international pour l'exploration de la Mer*, **144**, 56–60.

Fogg, G. E. (1959). Nitrogen nutrition and metabolic patterns in algae. *Symposia of the Society for Experimental Biology*, **13**, 106–25.

Fogg, G. E. (1966). The extracellular products of algae. *Oceanography and Marine Biology Annual Review*, **4**, 195–212.

Fogg, G. E. (1971). Extracellular products of algae in freshwater. *Archiv für Hydrobiologie*, **5**, 1–25.

Fogg, G. E., Eagle, D. J. & Kinson, M. E. (1969). The occurrence of glycollic acid in natural waters. *Verhandlungen der Internationalen Vereinigung für theoretische und angewandte Limnologie*, **17**, 480–4.

Fogg, G. E. & Horne, A. J. (1970). The physiology of Antarctic freshwater algae. In *Antarctic Ecology*, ed. M. W. Holdgate, vol. 2, pp. 632–8. London & New York, Academic Press.

Fogg, G. E., Nalewajko, C. & Watt, W. D. (1965). Extracellular products of phytoplankton photosynthesis. *Proceedings of the Royal Society*, B **162**, 517–34.

Gergis, M. S. (1971). The presence of microbodies in three strains of *Chlorella*. *Planta*, **101**, 180–4.

Gibbs, M. (1971). Biosynthesis of glycolic acid. In *Photosynthesis and Photo-*

respiration, eds. M. D. Hatch, C. B. Osmond & R. O. Slatyer, pp. 433–41. New York, Wiley-Interscience.

Gimmler, H., Ullrich, W., Domanski-Kaden, J. & Urbach, W. (1969). Excretion of glycolate during synchronous culture of *Ankistrodesmus braunii* in the presence of disalicylidenepropanediamine or hydroxy-pyridinemethanesulfonate. *Plant and Cell Physiology, Tokyo*, **10**, 103–12.

Guillard, R. R. L. & Hellebust, J. A. (1971). Growth and the production of extracellular substances by two strains of *Phaeocystis poucheti. Journal of Phycology*, **7**, 330–8.

Hellebust, J. A. (1965). Excretion of some organic compounds by marine phytoplankton. *Limnology and Oceanography*, **10**, 192–206.

Hess, J. L. & Tolbert, N. E. (1967). Glycolate pathway in algae. *Plant Physiology*, **42**, 371–9.

Hobbie, J. E. & Wright, R. T. (1965). Competition between planktonic bacteria and algae for organic solutes. *Memorie dell Instituto Italiano di Idrobiologia*, **18**, Suppl. 175–85.

Horne, A. J., Fogg, G. E. & Eagle, D. J. (1969). Studies *in situ* of the primary production of an area of inshore Antarctic sea. *Journal of the Marine Biological Association of the United Kingdom*, **49**, 393–405.

Huntsman, S. A. (1972). Organic excretion by *Dunaliella tertiolecta. Journal of Phycology*, **8**, 59–63.

Ignatiades, L. (1972). Studies on the factors affecting the release of organic matter by a marine diatom. Ph.D. thesis, University of London.

Jitts, H. R. (1967). Productivity. *CSIRO Division of Fisheries and Oceanography Annual Report* (1966–7), p. 36.

Kowallik, W. & Schmid, G. H. (1971). Zur Glycolatoxydation einzelliger Grünalgen. *Planta*, **96**, 224–37.

Koyama, T. & Thompson, T. G. (1964). Identification and determination of organic acids in sea water by partition chromatography. *Journal of the Oceanographical Society of Japan*, **20**, 209–20.

Lex, M., Silvester, W. B. & Stewart, W. D. P. (1972). Photorespiration and nitrogenase activity in the blue-green alga, *Anabaena cylindrica. Proceedings of the Royal Society*, B **180**, 87–102.

Lord, J. M., Codd, G. A. & Merrett, M. J. (1970). The effect of light quality on glycolate formation and excretion in algae. *Plant Physiology*, **46**, 855–6.

Lord, J. M. & Merrett, M. J. (1968). Glycollate oxidase in *Chlorella pyrenoidosa. Biochimica et biphysica acta*, **159**, 543–4.

Lord, J. M. & Merrett, M. J. (1969). The effect of hydroxymethanesulphonate on photosynthesis in *Chlorella pyrenoidosa. Journal of Experimental Botany*, **20**, 743–50.

Lord, J. M. & Merrett, M. J. (1970). The pathway of glycollate utilization in *Chlorella pyrenoidosa. Biochemical Journal*, **117**, 929–37.

Lord, J. M. & Merrett, M. J. (1971*a*). The growth of *Chlorella pyrenoidosa* on glycolate. *Journal of Experimental Botany*, **22**, 60–9.

Lord, J. M. & Merrett, M. J. (1971*b*). The intracellular localization of glycollate oxidoreductase in *Euglena gracilis. Biochemical Journal*, **124**, 275–81.

Marker, A. F. H. & Whittingham, C. P. (1966). The photoassimilation of glucose in *Chlorella* with reference to the role of glycollic acid. *Proceedings of the Royal Society*, B **165**, 473–85.

Merrett, M. J. & Goulding, K. H. (1968). The glycollate pathway during the photoassimilation of acetate by *Chlorella*. *Planta*, **80**, 321–7.

Miller, A. G., Chang, K. H. & Colman, B. (1971). The uptake and oxidation of glycolic acid by blue-green algae. *Journal of Phycology*, **7**, 97–100.

Murray, D. R., Giovanelli, J. & Smillie, R. M. (1971). Photometabolism of glycolate by *Euglena gracilis*. *Australian Journal of Biological Sciences*, **24**, 23–33.

Myers, J. (1949). The pattern of photosynthesis in *Chlorella*. In *Photosynthesis in Plants*, eds. J. Franck & W. E. Loomis, pp. 349–64. Iowa, Iowa State College Press.

Nalewajko, C., Chowhuri, N. & Fogg, G. E. (1963). Excretion of glycollic acid and the growth of a planktonic *Chlorella*. In *Studies on Microalgae and Photosynthetic Bacteria. Japanese Society of Plant Physiologists*, pp. 171–83. Tokyo, University of Tokyo Press.

Nalewajko, C. & Marin, L. (1969). Extracellular production in relation to growth of four planktonic algae and of phytoplankton populations from Lake Ontario. *Canadian Journal of Botany*, **47**, 405–13.

Nauwerck, A. (1963). Die Beziehungen zwischen zooplankton und phytoplankton im See Erken. *Symbolae Botanicae Upsalienses*, **17**, (5), 1–163.

Nelson, E. B. & Tolbert, N. E. (1969). The regulation of glycolate metabolism in *Chlamydomonas reinhardtii*. *Biochimica et biphysica acta*, **184**, 263–70.

Nelson, E. B., Tolbert, N. E. & Hess, J. L. (1969). Glycolate stimulation of oxygen evolution during photosynthesis. *Plant Physiology*, **44**, 55–9.

Pant, A. (1973). Uptake of an Extracellular Product, Glycollic Acid, by a Neritic Photosynthesizing Species *Skeletonema costatum* (Grev) Cleve, in Culture and in the Sea. Ph.D. thesis, University of London.

Paredes, J. F. (1967–8). Studies on cultures of marine phytoplankton. I. Diatom *Ditylum brightwellii* West. *Memórias do Instituto de investigacão cientifica de Moçambique*, A **9**, 157–83.

Pritchard, G. G., Griffin, W. J. & Whittingham, C. P. (1962). The effect of carbon dioxide concentration, light intensity and *iso*nicotinyl hydrazide on the photosynthetic production of glycollic acid by *Chlorella*. *Journal of Experimental Botany*, **13**, 176–84.

Samuel, S., Shah, N. M. & Fogg, G. E. (1971). Liberation of extracellular products of photosynthesis by tropical phytoplankton. *Journal of the Marine Biological Association of the United Kingdom*, **51**, 793–8.

Sen, N. & Fogg, G. E. (1966). Effects of glycollate on the growth of a planktonic *Chlorella*. *Journal of Experimental Botany*, **17**, 417–25.

Shah, N. M. & Fogg, G. E. (1973). The determination of glycollic acid in sea water. *Journal of the Marine Biological Association of the United Kingdom*, **53**, in press.

Steele, J. H. (1964). Some problems concerning production estimates for the northern North Sea. In *Tenth International Botanical Congress: Abstracts of Papers*, pp. 252–3, Edinburgh.

Thomas, J. P. (1971). Release of dissolved organic matter from natural populations of marine phytoplankton. *Marine Biology*, **11**, 311–23.

Tokuda, H. (1966). On the culture of a marine diatom, *Nitzschia closterium*. In *Cultures and Collections of Algae; Proceedings of the US – Japan Conference, Hakone, September 12–15, 1966. Japanese Society of Plant Physiologists*, pp. 53–8. Tokyo, University of Tokyo Press.

Tolbert, N. E. (1974). Photorespiration by algae. In *Algal Physiology and Biochemistry*, ed. W. D. P. Stewart, pp. 474–504. Oxford & Edinburgh, Blackwell.

Tolbert, N. E. & Zill, L. P. (1956). Excretion of glycolic acid by algae during photosynthesis. *Journal of Biological Chemistry*, **222**, 895–906.

Vallentyne, J. R. (1965). Net primary productivity and photosynthetic efficiency in the biosphere. *Memorie dell Instituto Italiano di Idrobiologia*, **18**, Suppl. 309–11.

Vollenweider, R. A. (ed.) (1974). *A Manual on Methods for Measuring Primary Production in Aquatic Environments*. IBP Handbook no. 12, 2nd ed. Oxford & Edinburgh, Blackwell.

Watt, W. D. (1966). Release of dissolved organic material from the cells of phytoplankton populations. *Proceedings of the Royal Society* B, **164**, 521–51.

Watt, W. D. (1969). Extracellular release of organic matter from two freshwater diatoms. *Annals of Botany*, **33**, 427–37.

Watt, W. D. & Fogg, G. E. (1966). The kinetics of extracellular glycollate production by *Chlorella pyrenoidosa*. *Journal of Experimental Botany*, **17**, 117–34.

Wright, R. T. (1970). Glycollic acid uptake by planktonic bacteria. In *Symposium on Organic Matter in Natural Waters*, ed. D. W. Hood, Institute of Marine Science Occasional Publication no. 1, 1970, pp. 521–36.

Q

20. Use of assimilates in higher plants

F. W. T. PENNING DE VRIES

This chapter explains briefly how to compute the quantitative relation between substrate consumption, dry matter production and respiration, when substrate and product are chemically well-defined. To compute dry matter increase of plants, the chemical composition of the end product must be determined analytically and the quality and amount of substrate specified. Analysis of phloem contents shows that the organic substrate for growth consists mainly of sucrose and amino acids, whose biosynthesis is closely linked. Thus, total plant CO_2 assimilation alone is not a sufficient base from which to compute growth, and nitrate reduction, amino acid synthesis and other processes must also be considered: neglecting these may underestimate the yield from a given amount of CO_2 assimilated by up to 30%. These subjects are elaborated, and the consequences for the interpretation of CO_2 assimilation light response curves are discussed. Maintenance of biomass and translocation of assimilates through phloem vessels also use assimilates, but will not be considered here, mainly for reasons of uncertainty about the underlying mechanisms.

An experimental approach to the relation of CO_2 assimilation to growth

From the 'molecular formula' of the biomass produced the relation of net CO_2 assimilation to biomass increase is easily obtained: when the 'molecular formula' is $C_{86}H_{160}O_{45}N_7$, for instance, it follows from the 'molecular weight' and the fraction of carbon that 1.00 g biomass is formed from 1.88 g CO_2. The net carbon assimilation corresponds with the dry weight increase, irrespective of the nature and efficiency of the processes that occur. The efficiency of carbon utilization appears to be 100%, because CO_2 losses are masked.

This procedure is very simple in the case of algae continuously exposed to sufficient light. When periods of light and darkness alternate, the CO_2-assimilation in the light and dissimilation in darkness must be measured to determine the daily net CO_2 uptake. Again, from this value and the elementary composition of the biomass the weight produced can be calculated. In higher plants the site of CO_2 assimilation is removed from the sites where growth occurs, and the period for substrate production (CO_2 assimilation) is shorter than that for substrate consumption in growth. Nevertheless, the rate of dry matter increase can be calculated from the daily net CO_2 uptake and the elementary composition, but this knowledge is of little practical value. Empirical equations may be used to calculate the biomass yield and respiration from the gross assimilation, but since the underlying mechanisms are not known such equations cannot be applied in other conditions or to other species (McCree, 1970). To obtain an insight into the relation between gross assimilation and biomass yield and respiration in different situations a more fundamental approach is required.

The term 'biosynthesis' will be used to refer to formation of dry matter, and 'growth' to total dry weight increase, including biosynthesis and maintenance.

A biochemical approach to plant biosynthesis

Detailed analysis of the biochemical and cellular processes occurring in growing cells enables computation of yield and gas exchange for the conversion of glucose into plant dry matter in darkness. Both yield and gas exchange depend on the chemical composition of the end product (Table 20.1). Energy requirements for the maintenance of enzyme activity and uptake of molecules through membranes are not known, but the results of such computations are often little affected by rough estimates of these costs (Penning de Vries, Brunsting & van Laar, 1974).

Table 20.1. *Values characterizing the conversion of glucose into the main chemical fractions of plant dry matter in darkness. Each fraction consists of a natural mixture of different molecules*

Chemical fraction	Yield (g product g^{-1} glucose)	Oxygen consumed (g O_2 g^{-1} glucose)	Carbon dioxide produced (g CO_2 g^{-1} glucose)	Note
Nitrogenous compounds (consisting of amino acids,	0.616	0.137	0.256	$+NH_3$
proteins and nucleic acids)	0.404	0.174	0.673	$+NO_3^-$
Carbohydrates	0.826	0.082	0.102	
Lipids	0.330	0.116	0.530	
Lignin	0.465	0.116	0.292	
Organic acids	1.104	0.298	-0.050	

The substrate for growth in plants consists of mono- and disac-charides, amino acids, organic acids and other specific compounds (e.g. Kursanov, 1963). This makes computation of the yield and gas exchange of growth more complicated, but does not add a major difficulty as long as the substrate composition is known, and the most efficient use of the substrate is made. For biosynthesis of 1.00 g leaf dry matter, 1.36 g of a mixed organic substrate is required; formation of organs with different chemical compositions requires other amounts, examples of which are given in Table 20.2. It is important to note that the numbers given in Tables 20.1 and 20.2 are independent of tempera-ture and species, and are determined only by the compositions of substrate and end product.

Table 20.2. *Requirements for the biosynthesis of* 1.00 g *dry matter of tissues with different chemical compositions. The composition stated refers to per cent of nitrogenous compounds, carbohydrates, lipids, lignin and minerals, respectively*

Nature of biomass	Composition	Sucrose (g)	Amino acids (g)	CO_2 produced (g)	O_2 consumed (g)
Leaves	25; 66.5; 2.5; 4; 2	1.055	0.305	0.333	0.150
Non-woody stem	12.5; 74; 2.5; 8; 2	1.153	0.153	0.278	0.135
Woody stem	5; 45; 5; 40; 5	1.515	0.061	0.426	0.176
Bean seeds	35; 55; 5; 2; 3	1.011	0.427	0.420	0.170
Rice seeds	5; 90; 2; 1; 2	1.135	0.061	0.186	0.110
Peanut seeds	20; 21; 50; 6; 3	1.915	0.245	1.017	0.266
Bacteria	60; 25; 5; 2; 8	0.804	0.732	0.573	0.208

Translocation of substrate in the phloem is an active process. Only a negligible fraction of the translocated assimilates is consumed to provide energy for translocation over short distances (Kursanov, 1963; Weather-ley & Johnson, 1968; Aikman & Anderson, 1971), but the integrated costs for transport over several metres may not be negligible. Costs of translocation within the phloem are not considered here. Loading and unloading the phloem will be treated separately.

It is concluded that the rate of biosynthesis can be predicted from the rate of substrate supply to growing points and the chemical composition of the biomass formed. The rate of substrate production by leaves is easily obtained from the CO_2 assimilation light response curve and incident light intensity to a 10% accuracy level, but a precise calculation presents some difficulties.

A plant physiological – biochemical approach to biosynthesis

CO_2 assimilation and photosynthesis

In growth simulation models it is generally assumed that all assimilated CO_2 molecules are converted into glucose, and that glucose plus minerals are the only substrates for growth. This is an over-simplification, because in irradiated leaves very often other energy-consuming processes occur simultaneously with CO_2 reduction. The reduction of NO_3^-, the subsequent formation of amino acids, and the loading of the phloem are the most important of these processes, which are not detected by measuring CO_2 uptake. Most of the NO_3^- reduction of agricultural crop plants occurs in the light in green leaves (Beevers & Hageman, 1969; Bornkamm, 1970; Hewitt, 1970). In these cases photosynthesizing cells consume more energy than is calculated from reduction of the assimilated CO_2 to glucose. Still, not all assimilated CO_2 is reduced: for each molecule of reduced NO_3^- one organic acid molecule is formed by carboxylating pyruvate. The salts of these acids remain in the leaves in some species, but about half are transported to the roots in others (Ben Zioni, Vaadia & Lips, 1971; Dijkshoorn & Ismunadji, 1972), where the organic acid is converted into pyruvate and the CO_2 re-formed is exchanged with NO_3^- from the root medium, NO_3^- reduction being accompanied by a CO_2 flux through the plant.

Determination of energy absorption by leaves via measurement of O_2 evolution is better than via CO_2 uptake, because it accounts for NO_3^- reduction and carboxylation. But, for instance, loading of the phloem consumes energy without exchange of molecules with the environment, and cannot be detected by measuring gas exchange (Ried, 1970). Even if it were possible to determine accurately leaf energy absorption in chemical processes (including transport processes) by measuring the total energy absorption and subtracting the energy lost by thermal reradiation and transfer of sensible and evaporative heat loss, the actual energy absorption would still not be measured. Firstly, because in primary chlorophyll reactions more energy is absorbed than is retained in glucose, but since glucose is the starting point for biochemical conversion calculations there is no need to consider energy lost before this point. Secondly, because the energy retained in processes that occur in addition to CO_2 reduction is smaller than the amount of energy required to execute them. Simultaneous energy-consuming processes in the leaf are probably competitive, so that at low light intensities the rate of CO_2 reduction is reduced when the rate of NO_3^-

reduction increases, as shown experimentally by Bongers (1956) with algae. At high light intensities, where the rate of CO_2 diffusion limits the assimilation rate, these additional energy consuming processes occur free of cost for the plant. It was shown by Dijkshoorn & Ismunadji (1972) that rice plants supplied with NO_3^- at high light intensities grow as fast as with NH_3, but such experiments must be interpreted with care, since the plant composition may be changed, thereby changing the relation between CO_2 fixation and dry matter increase.

Such considerations indicate that photosynthesis, CO_2 assimilation and conversion processes must be considered in their physiological context. Only when the information is available as to which processes occur in the leaf and at what rate can the measured CO_2 assimilation light response curve be extrapolated to a range of conditions in which it was not established. CO_2 assimilation light response curves are fairly well known for many species, especially agricultural plants, but little information is available on the rate of NO_3^- reduction and substrate export from leaves throughout the day in field situations or in particular experiments. An average rate of NO_3^- reduction during the day can be obtained analytically, but the actual rate may vary with light intensity (e.g. Bongers, 1956) and incubation period (e.g. Travis, Huffaker & Key, 1970). At present, only in steady-state conditions when the rate of all processes can be derived from the CO_2 uptake rate, can calculations be performed with some accuracy.

Photorespiration decreases the net CO_2 reduction rate of an irradiated leaf. It does not contribute to any substrate production, and does not provide energy to any active process that cannot be otherwise performed (Beevers & Björkman, in Canvin, 1970). On a cellular level, photo-respiration may be useful in providing reduction equivalents to the cytoplasm, where these are used instead of mitochondrial products (Tolbert, 1971). For growth predictions photorespiration can be seen as a factor that diminishes the rate of CO_2 assimilation, like low temperatures or low atmospheric CO_2 concentrations.

Assimilation and dissimilation in a steady-state condition

A particular steady-state condition may be considered in order to verify the predicted dissimilation rate against a measured rate of CO_2 assimilation (substrate production). Maize plants were grown on a nutrient solution at 20–25 °C and at a light level of 70 J m^{-2} s^{-1}. During the first day of the experiment, whole plants of ten to twenty-four days age received three periods of seven hours light of one intensity, each followed by one hour darkness at a relative humidity of 85%. During four subsequent days light intensities of up to $300 \, J \, m^{-2} \, s^{-1}$ were applied. The rate of CO_2 assimilation was monitored continuously with the assembly described by Louwerse & Van Oorschot (1969). As indicated by preliminary experiments, at the end of the third period the rates of net assimilation and dissimilation, measured in the next hour, are in 'equilibrium', unless the rates in the old and the new 'steady-state' are very different. In this 'steady-state' the amount of carbon assimilated in seven hours is equal to the amount of carbon utilized in eight hours for conversion, transport and maintenance. The relation between the amounts of CO_2 assimilated, dry matter produced and CO_2 formed in these processes for this particular 'steady-state' experiment will be computed below. Essentially similar experiments have been reported elsewhere (Penning de Vries, 1972), but some improvements have been introduced and the range of experiments extended. The biomass formed was composed as indicated in the small rectangles in Fig. 20.1; the numbers refer to the weight of each fraction per 1000 g of biomass. The arrows represent conversion and dissimilation processes, and the numbers beside them the amounts of glucose and CO_2 involved. O_2 was not considered, but the amounts involved can be found from data published elsewhere (Penning de Vries, Brunsting & van Laar, 1973). From Table 20.1 and other data the amounts of glucose needed to synthesize lipids, lignin and carbohydrates were derived. The latter fraction was assumed to consist of cellulose, while the other fractions consist of a natural mixture of molecules. It was also assumed that half of the lignin is formed in mature leaves. The amino acid composition of the protein was chosen to be that of zein (Spector, 1956). The composition of the transported amino acids, in Fig. 20.1 characterized as AA_t, was derived from zein by assuming that the amino acids that can be formed from aspartic and glutamic acid are formed from them, and that cysteine is transported as such. This composition was also used in Table 20.2. The other amino acids present were assumed to be synthesized from glucose, the ammonia being carried in amides (glutamine and asparagine). The resulting mixture consists of aspartic acid 41% (by weight), glutamic acid 37%, asparagine 7%, glutamine 15% and cysteine 0.6%.

Uptake of minerals, glucose and amino acids are active processes. On the basis of a little quantitative information (Kaback, 1970; Oxender, 1972) it is estimated that both uptake of one mole of carbo-

464

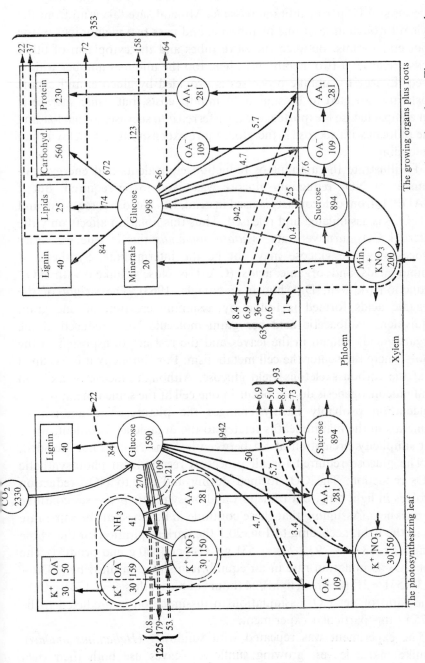

Fig. 20.1. A schematic representation of assimilation of carbon and nitrogen and their utilization in maize plants. The rectangles indicate end products, the circles intermediates. Double lines indicate processes occurring during photosynthesis only, single lines conversions or translocations, and dashed lines CO₂ formation. The numbers give the corresponding weights of material.

hydrates and three moles of salts or amino acids requires the energy of one mole ATP per membrane passage. Minerals are taken up from the xylem through at least one membrane, and pass two membranes of the root endodermis. Between the sieve tubes and the cytoplasm of other cells are at least two membranes; here too the minimal number will be used. Energy for uptake processes is provided by glucose, and export costs are expected to be similar to import costs, but while sucrose is taken up, glucose is exported and transferred into sucrose, so that loading the phloem with sucrose is therefore more expensive (eq. 4, below) than unloading.

To illustrate the amount of reduction equivalents and energy consumed for NO_3^- reduction, glucose was taken to be required. But if $NADPH_2$ from chloroplasts is used instead, less glucose is required, and less CO_2 is assimilated and released. Thus this notation affects only the internal CO_2 turnover rate. *Mutatis mutandis* this is true for other processes where glucose may not be the intermediate. Synthesis of amino acids and organic acids (OA^-) is closely linked with NO_3^- reduction (de Wit, Dijkshoorn & Noggle, 1963). The weight of the organic acids formed is found by assuming creation of one gram equivalent oxaloacetic acid per gram molecule NO_3^- reduced. Some organic acids remain in the leaves and the rest are transported to the roots where they enter the cell metabolism. For simplicity it is assumed that the carbon skeletons yield glucose. Although glucose breakdown and gluconeogenesis do not occur in one cell at the same time, a precise calculation probably hardly changes the picture. The amount of minerals in the mature leaf is related to the organic acid content, while for simplicity circulation of K^+ between leaf and roots is not included.

The glucose required for all processes results from photosynthetic CO_2 reduction. The CO_2 formed during and due to NO_3^- reduction evolves in light only, but transport and biosynthetic processes continue in darkness. Assuming that these continue in darkness at the same rate as in the light, according to Fig. 20.1 the dark respiration for the whole plant is $(353+63+93+22) = 531$ g CO_2 per 1000 g end product. The net CO_2 assimilation rate in an equilibrium situation must be $(2330-125-531 \times 21)$ (hours in light)/24 (hours of biosynthesis) $= 1741$ g CO_2. The ratio of net CO_2 assimilation to dissimilation is predicted to be 3.75 in this particular experiment.

The experiment was repeated with sunflower (*Helianthus annuus*). Unlike maize leaves, growing sunflower leaves use both their own assimilates and those supplied by other leaves. Less transportation costs

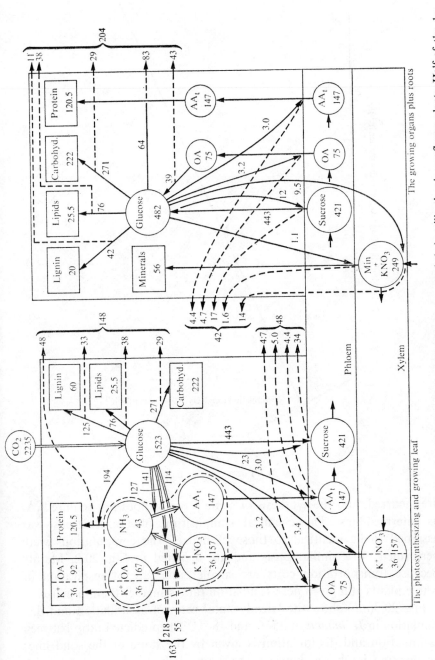

Fig. 20.2. A schematic representation of assimilation of carbon and nitrogen and their utilization in sunflower plants. Half of the dry matter increase occurs in photosynthesizing leaves. For explanation see legend to Fig. 20.1.

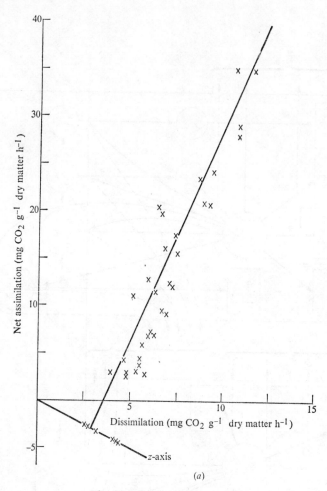

(a)

Fig. 20.3. For legend see p. 470.

are incurred, and the synthesis of some proteins does not require AA_t as intermediates. The chemical composition of the fractions was assumed to be identical to those of maize. The computations were performed on a similar basis and are depicted in Fig. 20.2. Mainly because transportation costs are smaller, the rate of respiration of whole plants at a given net assimilation rate is smaller than in maize.

Fig. 20.3(a,b) show the 'steady-state' rates of assimilation and dissimilation in *H. annuus* at 25 °C and 18 °C. The predicted ratio between assimilation and dissimilation is given by the slope of the solid line; its position is chosen between the actual values. The intercept with the z-axis, which has a 1 : 1 relation to x- and y-axes, represents the

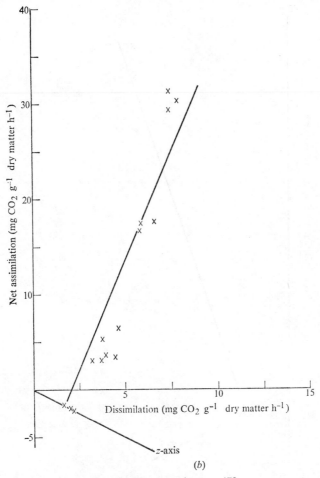

(b)

Fig. 20.3. For legend see p. 470.

rate of maintenance respiration. There is a good agreement between the position of the measured points and the computed slope over a wide range of assimilation rates, and there is no indication that the lower temperature decreases the slope. Treatment with dilute nutrient solution decreased the nitrogen content of the biomass produced to 2.4%. A calculation similar to previous ones showed that this should increase the slope by 28%. Fig. 20.3(c) shows that under these conditions this efficiency is maintained, and that the rate of maintenance respiration was not increased (Semikatova, 1970). Similar experiments on maize were performed at 25, 18 and 33 °C, and the results are presented in Fig. 20.4(a–c). Except at the lowest light intensities there is a good

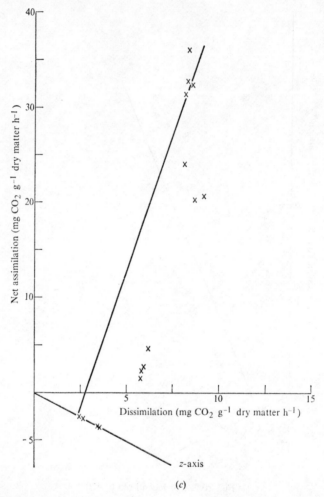

(c)

Fig. 20.3. (a) The relation between assimilation and dissimilation in a steady-state situation in whole sunflower plants at 25 °C.

(b) The relation between assimilation and dissimilation in a steady-state situation in whole sunflower plants at 18 °C.

(c) The relation between assimilation and dissimilation in a steady-state situation in whole sunflower plants at 25 °C. Plants were grown and measured at a diluted nutrient solution.

agreement between the position of the points and the calculated slope of the line at the three temperatures. It is concluded that these experiments confirm the value of this approach and support the hypothesis that the efficiency of biochemical processes in higher plants is independent of temperature in the range normally encountered. It was suggested earlier (Penning de Vries, 1972) that a low relative humidity could induce some

470

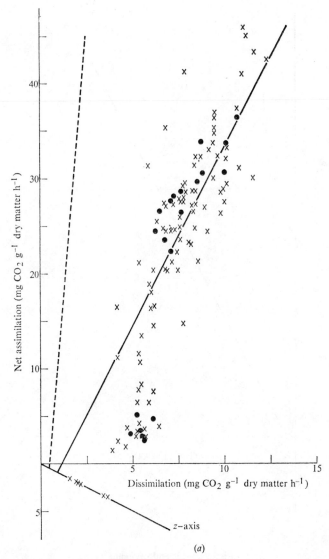

Fig. 20.4. For legend see p. 473.

waterstress in the light period, eliminating the steady-state character of the experiment. To check this the experiment at 25 °C was repeated at a relative humidity of about 50%. The results are included in Fig. 20.4(*a*) and demonstrate that no water-stress developed. McCree (1970) obtained results similar to those in the Figs. 20.3 and 20.4 by plotting daily totals of dissimilation versus gross assimilation of white clover plants.

471

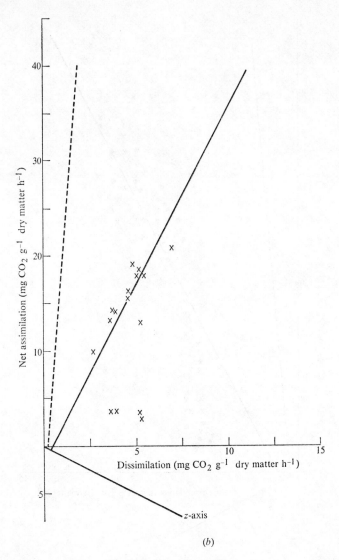

(*b*)

Fig. 20.4. Legend opposite.

The dashed lines in Fig. 20.4 indicate the ratios of net assimilation of the photosynthesizing leaves to their dissimilation, which were not measured. Their intercepts with the *z*-axis are found by multiplying the plant maintenance respiration rate by the dry weight of the mature leaves over the total dry weight. The solid lines in Figs. 20.3(*a,b*) and 20.4(*a–c*) have different intercepts with the *z*-axis, indicating that the rate of maintenance respiration depends upon temperature. The inter-

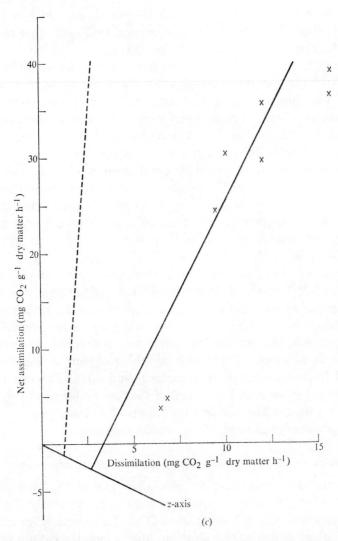

Fig. 20.4. (*a*) The relation between assimilation and dissimilation in a steady-state situation in whole maize plants at 25 °C and at 85% (×) and 50% (●) relative humidity.

(*b*) The relation between assimilation and dissimilation in a steady-state situation in whole maize plants at 18 °C.

(*c*) The relation between assimilation and dissimilation in a steady-state situation in whole maize plants at 33°C.

(The dashed lines in (*a*)–(*c*) indicate the ratios of net assimilation of the photosynthesizing leaves to their dissimilation: for details see text.)

cept with the z-axis in *H. annuus* suggests that its maintenance respiration is about three times larger than that in maize, which is an unexpected result. The rate for maize compares well with other observations (McCree, 1970; Penning de Vries, 1972).

In maize the rate of leaf appearance does not depend on light intensity above 50–70 J m^{-2} s^{-1} (Grobbelaar, 1962; Gallagher & Lof, unpublished results). A minimal specific leaf weight combined with a constant rate of leaf production leads to a minimal rate of formation biomass. It is suggested that at light levels below 60 J m^{-2} s^{-1} this minimal rate of about 0.15 g leaves per g plant per day could not be supported by photosynthesis, but is sustained by breakdown of biomass and translocation from older organs, causing a relatively high respiration rate. This process continues for a few days at a diminishing rate. Fig. 20.3(*a*) suggests that in sunflower, unlike maize, there is no minimal rate of formation of structural material. This was also found in leaves of lettuce (Bensink, 1971).

These experiments exclude the presence of wasteful respiration (Beevers, 1970; Tanaka, 1972), except at a low and constant rate, which would appear similar to maintenance respiration. The scatter of the measurements in all experiments is fairly large, and may cover an error in the approach, but can also be interpreted as changes of the rate of biosynthesis. Research on rates of biosynthesis of plant biomass and its chemical fractions in relation to external and internal factors is still largely *terra incognita*. A key to one of the first problems of this field, the measurement of the rate of biosynthesis of an intact plant, may be the measurement of the rate of conversion respiration.

Interpretation of CO_2 assimilation light response curves of leaves

Steady-state conditions are exceptional. The rate of CO_2 assimilation and other energy-consuming processes changes continuously. To use a CO_2 assimilation light response curve (CO_2–a.l.c.) correctly for calculations of plant assimilate production, the external conditions (CO_2 concentration and temperature) and internal conditions (rate of NO_3^- reduction and assimilate export) prevailing during the measurement and at the moment for which the curve is used must be considered. To assess the relative importance of CO_2 assimilation and other energy-consuming processes some widely different examples will be studied. That the CO_2–a.l.c. is not a constant but subject to stresses and adaptations is not important in this context, where the maximum rate of CO_2 assimilation is measured and used as an input for further calculations.

EXAMPLE 1. *During measurements of the CO_2–a.l.c. the leaf only reduces the assimilated CO_2 to glucose*
In this case photosynthesis in C_3-plants may be represented by

$$6\ CO_2 + 12\ NADPH_2 + 18\ ATP \rightarrow$$
$$C_6H_{12}O_6 + 12\ NADP + 18\ ADP + 18\ P_i \quad (1)$$

The energy absorption per assimilated C atom is 2 $NADPH_2$ molecules plus 3 ATP molecules, expressing energy absorption in reduction equivalents and ATP units. Slightly more ATP is used in C_4-plants (Mayne, Edwards & Black, 1971).

EXAMPLE 2. *During measurement of the CO_2–a.l.c. the leaf reduces the assimilated CO_2 to glucose and forms cellulose or starch or exports sucrose.*
Recognizing that glucose-6-P or fructose-6-P is the photosynthesis product, these processes can be characterized by

$$n \text{ glucose-6-P} + 2n\ ATP \rightarrow \text{starch} \quad (2)$$

$$n \text{ glucose-6-P} + 3n\ ATP \rightarrow \text{cellulose} \quad (3)$$

$$2 \text{ glucose-6-P}_{cell} + 4\ ATP \rightarrow \text{sucrose}_{phloem} \quad (4)$$

Synthesis of cellulose is more expensive than starch synthesis since the monomers must be exported through one cell membrane. For equation 4 it was assumed that export of each fructose and glucose molecule requires 1 ATP molecule, the coupling of both to sucrose a third, while another ATP molecule is required for uptake of sucrose into the phloem. Assuming that formation of 1 $NADPH_2$ molecule from NADP uses 7.5 times more light energy than 1 ATP molecule from ADP, it follows that in these cases 1.9–2.8% more energy is absorbed per assimilated C atom than calculated according to equation 1. It is also assumed that the ratio of photosynthetically produced $NADPH_2$ and ATP can vary according to the requirements, as suggested by Ried (1970). Photorespiration may help to achieve this (Tolbert, 1971).

The cell cannot use energy stored in starch other than in glucose molecules, since its hydrolysis does not yield ATP. From the point of view of energy conservation starch and glucose formation are equal. The energy spent to export sucrose (equation 4) corresponds with 1.9% of the energy needed to synthesize glucose, but with 5.3% of the energy stored in it (since 38 ATP molecules can be formed per glucose molecule). Thus 5.6% more glucose remains when the processes described in equation 4 occur during photosynthesis, as compared with glucose formation in daylight and sucrose export in darkness. The latter percentage represents the undervaluation of the yield of bio-synthesis when photosynthesis is considered to be merely glucose formation, and is given in Table 20.3.

These cases apply to many laboratory and field conditions: often the CO_2-a.l.c. is measured when NO_3^- reduction does not occur and in some field situations lack of NO_3^- reduction in leaves has been reported. When a leaf forms starch only and exports sucrose in darkness, the conversion calculations described above can be applied directly.

Table 20.3. *The hydrogen and energy requirements during photosynthesis, the additional energy assimilation and the yield undervaluation for the different examples discussed in the text*

Example	Requirements per assimilated CO_2 molecule		Additional energy assimilation (%)	Undervaluation dry matter yield (%)	Calculated from equation nos.
	NADPH$_2$	ATP			
1	2.00	3.00	0	0	–
2	2.00	3.33	2	0	2
	2.00	3.33	2	6	4
3	2.74	5.65	46	−28	5, 6+7
4	2.47	3.75	21	20	9, 8
5	2.53	3.80	27	30	10, 10+11

If the CO_2-a.l.c. is measured in conditions in which equation 1 applies but sucrose is exported, the CO_2-a.l.c. can be constructed from an initial slope, equal to the slope of the original curve divided by the energy absorption in equation 4 relative to equation 1, and the maximum rate of CO_2 diffusion, causing a maximum rate of energy fixation.

EXAMPLE 3. *During measurement of the CO_2-a.l.c. the leaf stores the CO_2 assimilated as lipids*

This occurs in algae under conditions where growth is restricted (van Oorschot, 1955) and possibly in leaves of higher plants when oil droplets are formed. When the starting point is phosphoglyceric acid (PGA) the equation can be derived

$$31.7 \text{ mgmol PGA} + 2.5 \text{ mgmol NADPH}_2 + 146.0 \text{ mgmol ATP} \rightarrow$$
$$1.0 \text{ g lipids} + 1.342 \text{ g } CO_2 \qquad (5)$$

The energy consumed per C atom in the lipid fraction is about 46% more than in equation 1 and under these conditions the slope of the CO_2–a.l.c. is considerably lowered. Sucrose or glucose are used for transport of carbon and energy between cells, and although slightly more chemical energy per gram C is present in lipids (4.56 10^4 J) than in starch (3.86 10^4 J), in the conversion of lipids into glucose some 28% of the C gets lost. This reduces the yield of lipids considerably:

$$1.47 \text{ g CO}_2 \rightarrow 0.52 \text{ g lipids} \rightarrow 0.72 \text{ g glucose} \tag{6}$$

$$1.47 \text{ g CO}_2 \rightarrow 0.90 \text{ g starch} \rightarrow 1.00 \text{ g glucose} \tag{7}$$

Storage of lipids may be advantageous when low weight is important, as in some seeds, or when the specific characteristics are useful. The high costs of glucose synthesis from lipids may be the major reason that lipids are not used for short-term storage in leaves.

EXAMPLE 4. *During the measurement of the CO_2–a.l.c. the leaf reduces NO_3^- and forms amino acids; CO_2 is reduced only to provide carbon skeletons for the acids*
NO_3^- reduction, amino acid and organic acid formation can be described by

$$1.785 \text{ g glucose} + 0.535 \text{ g NO}_3^- \rightarrow$$
$$1.00 \text{ g amino acids} + 0.567 \text{ g organic acids} + 0.447 \text{ g CO}_2 \tag{8}$$

and by

$$49.3 \text{ mgmol CO}_2 + 119 \text{ mgmol NADPH}_2 + 181 \text{ mgmol ATP} +$$
$$8.62 \text{ mgmol NO}_3^- \rightarrow 1.00 \text{ g amino acids} + 0.567 \text{ g organic acids} \tag{9}$$

In the processes described by equation 9, 21.0% more energy is consumed per assimilated C atom than in equation 1. If it were supposed that only glucose was formed photosynthetically and amino acid synthesis occurred in darkness, the conversion calculations would underestimate the yield of the photosynthesis process by 19.8%. Nine per cent of the assimilated CO_2 still remains unreduced and is exported in organic acids to the roots and excreted.

Like starch formation during photosynthesis, storage of amino acids as proteins increases the energy fixation per assimilated C atom (to 24.1%) but this is lost during protein hydrolysis. Export of the amino acids is relatively cheap and when it occurs during photosynthesis the energy assimilation per C atom is increased only to 21.3%.

The use of assimilates

EXAMPLE 5. *During the measurement of the CO_2–a.l.c. the leaf increases in biomass, but does not export or import assimilates*
In this example photosynthesis can be described by

$$38.2 \text{ mgmol } CO_2 + 96.5 \text{ mgmol } NADPH_2$$
$$+ 145 \text{ mgmol ATP}$$
$$+ 0.092 \text{ g minerals}$$
$$+ 0.157 \text{ g } NO_3^- \rightarrow 1.00 \text{ g plant biomass} \quad (10)$$

Equation 10 was obtained by modifying Fig. 2 such that all growth occurred in the photosynthesizing part, and it is concluded that the energy absorption per C atom is 26.7% more than that calculated from equation 1. This result depends on the chemical composition of the biomass, which in this example is very rich in minerals. For biosynthesis from glucose in darkness the equation is

$$1.49 \text{ g glucose} + 0.150 \text{ g } O_2 + 0.157 \text{ g } NO_3^- + 0.092 \text{ g minerals} \rightarrow$$
$$1.00 \text{ g plant biomass} + 0.502 \text{ g } CO_2 \quad (11)$$

Performing the processes described by equation 10 during photosynthesis yields 30% more dry matter than performing those of equation 1, with those of equation 11 occurring in darkness!

Leaves of bean and sunflower plants go through this stage, but generally most of the growth occurs in darkness or in organs that do not photosynthesize. For leaves growing from their own assimilates the efficiency of C utilization, expressed as the percentage of assimilated CO_2 molecules retained in the plant twenty-four hours after application, must be between 100% (equation 10) and 70% (equation 11 plus equation 1). When leaves send their assimilates to mature organs, such as lower leaves to roots, these assimilates are used for maintenance exclusively, and thus the C utilization is 0%, although some labelled C may be retained due to exchange in turnover processes. It can be estimated that some 70% of the assimilated C is retained in the plant permanently at relative growth rates of 0.3 g g^{-1} d^{-1} and higher, about 50% at a relative growth rate of 0.03, and about 30% at a relative growth rate of 0.01. Estimating the fractions of substrate consumed for maintenance and biosynthesis gives the key for these predictions.

The author is indebted to Dr Ir. C. T. de Wit for reading the manuscript critically and to Miss H. H. van Laar and Mr W. van der Zweerde for carrying out the experiments. The chemical analyses were done by the IBS chemical laboratory.

478

References

Aikman, D. P. & Anderson, W. P. (1971). A quantitative investigation of a peristaltic model for phloem translocation. *Annals of Botany*, **35**, 761–72.

Beevers, H. (1970). Respiration in plants and its regulation. In *Prediction and Measurement of Photosynthetic Productivity*, ed. I. Šetlík, pp. 209–14. Wageningen, PUDOC.

Beevers, L. & Hageman, R. H. (1969). Nitrate reduction in higher plants. *Annual Review of Plant Physiology*, **20**, 495–522.

Ben-Zioni, A., Vaadia, Y. & Lips, S. H. (1971). Correlations between nitrate reduction, protein synthesis and malate accumulation. *Physiologia Plantarum*, **23**, 1039–47.

Bensink, J. (1971). On morphogenesis of lettuce leaves in relation to light and temperature. *Mededelingen Landbouwhogeschool, Wageningen*, **71** (15), 1–93.

Bongers, L. H. J. (1956). Aspects of nitrogen assimilation by cultures of green algae. *Mededelingen Landbouwhogeschool, Wageningen*, **56** (15), 1–52.

Bornkamm, R. (1970). Dunkel-Assimilation von Nitrat bei *Lemna minor* L. *Planta*, **92**, 50–6.

Canvin, D. T. (1970). Losses in energy transformation in relation to the use of photosynthates for growth and maintenance of photosynthetic systems. In *Prediction and Measurement of Photosynthetic Productivity*, ed. I. Šetlík, pp. 251–7, Wageningen, PUDOC.

Dijkshoorn, W. & Ismunadji, M. (1972). Nitrogen nutrition of rice plants measured by growth of nutrient content in pot experiments. 3. Change during growth. *Netherlands Journal of Agricultural Science*, **20**, 133–44.

Grobbelaar, W. P. (1962). The growth of maize pretreated at various soil temperatures. *Jaarboek Instituut voor Biologisch en Scheikundig Onderzoek van Landbouwgewassen*, pp. 33–8.

Hewitt, E. J. (1970). Physiological and biochemical factors which control the assimilation of inorganic nitrogen supplies by plants. In *Nitrogen nutrition of the plant*, ed. E. A. Kirkny, pp. 78–103. Leeds, Waverley Press.

Kaback, H. R. (1970). Transport. *Annual Review of Biochemistry*, **39**, 561–98.

Kursanov, A. L. (1963). Metabolism and transport of organic substances in the phloem. *Advances in Botanical Research*, **1**, 209–79.

Louwerse, W. & von Oorschot, J. L. P. (1969). An assembly for routine measurements of photosynthesis, respiration and transpiration of intact plants under controlled conditions. *Photosynthetica*, **3**, 305–15.

Mayne, B. C., Edwards, G. E. & Black, C. C. (1971). Light relations in C_4 photosynthesis. In *Photosynthesis and Photorespiration*, eds. M. D. Hatch, C. B. Osmond & R. O. Slatyer, pp. 361–71. New York, Wiley-Interscience.

McCree, K. J. (1970). An equation for the rate of respiration of white clover plants grown under controlled conditions. In *Prediction and Measurement of Photosynthetic Productivity*, ed. I. Šetlík, pp. 221–9, Wageningen, PUDOC.

479

Oorschot, J. L. P. van (1955). Conversion of light energy in algal cultures. *Mededelingen Landbouwhogeschool, Wageningen,* **55** (5), 225–76.

Oxender, D. L. (1972). Membrane transport. *Annual Review of Biochemistry,* **41**, 777–814.

Penning de Vries, F. W. T. (1972). Respiration and growth. In *Crop processes in controlled environments,* eds. A. R. Rees, K. E. Cockshull, D. W. Hand & R. G. Hurd, pp. 327–47, London, Academic Press.

Penning de Vries, F. W. T., Brunsting, A. & van Laar, H. H. (1974). Products, requirements and efficiency of biosynthesis; a quantitative approach. *Journal of Theoretical Biology,* **45**, 339–77.

Ried, A. (1970). Energetic aspects of the interaction between photosynthesis and respiration. In *Prediction and Measurement of Photosynthetic Productivity,* ed. I. Šetlík, pp. 231–46, Wageningen, PUDOC.

Semikatova, O. A. (1970). Energy efficiency of respiration under unfavourable conditions. In *Prediction and Measurement of Photosynthetic Productivity,* ed. I. Šetlík, pp. 247–50, Wageningen, PUDOC.

Spector, W. S. (ed.) (1956). *Handbook of Biological Data,* 584 pp. Philadelphia, W. B. Saunders Co.

Tanaka, A. (1972). Efficiency in respiration. In *Proceedings Symposium Rice Breeding, IRRI, Los Banos, Philippines,* pp. 483–98.

Tolbert, N. E. (1971). Leaf peroxisomes and photorespiration. In *Photosynthesis and Photorespiration,* eds. M. D. Hatch, C. B. Osmond & R. O. Slatyer, pp. 458–71. New York, Wiley-Interscience.

Travis, R. L., Huffaker, R. C. & Key, J. L. (1970). Light-induced development of polyribosomes and the induction of nitrate reductase in corn leaves. *Plant Physiology,* **46**, 400–5.

Weatherley, P. E. & Johnson, R. P. C. (1968). The form and function of the sieve tube; a problem in reconciliation. *International Review of Cytology,* **24**, 149–92.

Wit, C. T. de, Dijkshoorn, W. & Noggle, J. C. (1963). Ionic balance and growth of plants. *Agricultural Research Reports,* **69** (15), Wageningen, PUDOC.

21. Source – sink relations and the partition of assimilates in the plant

P. F. WAREING & J. PATRICK

The manner in which dry matter is partitioned between the different parts of the plant is clearly of great importance both in natural vegetation and in crop plants. Indeed, the possibilities of changing the distribution of assimilates in crops, either by chemical growth regulators or by breeding, offer some of the most promising ways of increasing agricultural productivity.

Normally, the regions of assimilate production (the leaves) are separate from the regions of consumption (the growing regions or storage organs.) However, a developing leaf may both produce assimilates itself and import them from other parts of the plant. These regions of production and consumption are referred to as 'source' and 'sink' for assimilates, respectively. Thus assimilates move from source to sink via the transport system of the plant.

As Warren Wilson (1972) has pointed out, the terms 'source' and 'sink' are often used rather loosely and in several different senses, namely:

(1) in relation to the direction of transport – sources are regions that export assimilates, while sinks import them.

(2) Because mature leaves tend to be associated with production and export of assimilate, whereas other parts (roots, meristems, fruits, and storage organs) tend to be associated with import and utilization of assimilates, the terms source and sink are applied, in a morphological sense, to particular parts of the plant.

(3) Because sources produce assimilates by photosynthesis or by mobilization of stored materials, while sinks utilize assimilate in respiration and growth, it is possible to define source and sink in metabolic terms.

The use of these terms in these different senses is liable to cause confusion and Warren Wilson (1972) suggests that sources and sinks should be defined in terms of losses and gains of a particular substance in a particular plant part.

481

The change in dry weight (W) of a plant or a plant part can be considered as being due to exchange of matter across its physical boundary by various processes, and can be expressed as

$$W = P - R - T - D,$$

where P = gain in dry weight due to photosynthesis or import of photosynthates; R = losses due to respiration; T = loss due to translocation to other parts of plant; D = loss by death. On the other hand, the use of this matter within the plant can be resolved into growth (G), i.e. permanent gain in essential plant structure, and storage (S), i.e. gain in material held in reserve but not yet incorporated as structural material.

Thus, $\qquad\qquad W = G + S - D.$

Hence $\qquad\qquad (G + S) = P - R - T,$

or the dry matter balance may be analysed into its three components:

$$(P - R) = (G + S) - T.$$

This equation can be applied at any level – cell, organ, plant or stand – and the quantities can be expressed as amounts or rates.

Warren Wilson has further suggested the introduction of the terms 'source strength' and 'sink strength' that are defined as follows:

$$\text{source strength} = \text{source size} \times \text{source activity}, \qquad (1)$$

i.e. rate of assimilation per plant = leaf area × rate of assimilation per unit leaf area.

$$\text{Sink strength} = \text{sink size} \times \text{sink activity}, \qquad (2)$$

where sink activity may be defined as the rate of uptake or incorporation of assimilates per unit weight of sink tissue. In terms of total dry matter, this relation corresponds to the equation:

absolute growth rate = dry weight × relative growth rate.

Opinions differ as to whether 'sink strength' should apply only to the utilization of assimilates for structural material (G) or whether it should include also incorporation of dry matter into storage materials (S), but the latter assumption will be adopted here.

Whilst this approach is conveniently amenable to experimental measurement, it is debatable whether it provides meaningful estimates of sink strength for the reasons outlined below. Most importantly, dry matter data do not account for respiratory losses of assimilate imported into sinks and consequently only *net* sink strength may be derived from

482

such information. Respiratory losses of recently imported carbon have been found to be as high as 40–50% of total accumulation (Ryle, 1972) and presumably these losses could vary considerably according to the metabolic state of the sink (e.g. storage versus growth). Therefore, if sink activity is a measure of the rate of uptake of assimilates per unit weight of sink tissue then estimates of respiratory losses should be incorporated to determine total uptake. Furthermore, implicit in this definition of sink activity is the assumption that assimilate uptake is non-limited by supply and unaffected by neighbouring sinks – a situation rarely attained in practice (cf. Maggs, 1963; and other references cited in the section on Competition for assimilates, p. 492).

Thus, in most circumstances, dry matter accumulation (net gain plus respiratory losses) provides some indication of the *competitive ability* of a sink to 'attract' assimilates relative to other sink regions rather than an estimate of the potential capacity to accumulate assimilates. Even under competitive conditions within whole plants, the ability of certain sinks to attract assimilates may not depend entirely upon their capacity to accumulate these compounds. For instance, in wheat, the supply of assimilates to developing leaf primordia may be limited by the absence of a differentiated transport channel linking the apex with the more mature parts of the plant (Williams, 1960; Patrick, 1972*a,b*). Therefore, there is a need to explore other possible ways of obtaining more satisfactory estimates of sink strength. Perhaps one approach would be to devise methods of determining sink strength in isolation from other plant processes, such as incubating tissues in sucrose solutions and determining sucrose uptake (Patrick & Wareing, 1970; Patrick & Wareing, in preparation). Nevertheless measurements of dry matter import by various plant parts have proved a valuable basis from which source–sink relations may be examined. However, for the reasons outlined above, it is considered that the term 'sink strength' should refer to the *potential* capacity of a sink to accumulate assimilate, whereas *mobilizing ability* would seem a more applicable term to describe the resultant accumulation of dry matter by a sink within the competitive framework of a whole plant system.

The approach to the problem of assimilate partition will depend upon whether one is concerned with (1) total dry matter production and utilization within the whole plant; (2) partition, as between the whole shoot and the whole root, or (3) partition of assimilates within the individual parts of the shoot, namely leaves, stems and fruits, and the subject will be discussed separately under these three headings.

483

The use of assimilates

Total assimilate accumulation within the whole plant

It is clear that total *net* production and *net* consumption (i.e. in growth and storage) of assimilates within the whole plant must be in balance. Two possible situations may be envisaged: (1) the actual rate of assimilate production is *less* than the potential maximum rate of consumption, or (2) the potential rate of production is *greater* than the actual rate of consumption. Thus, the overall rate of assimilate accumulation in (1) is determined by the rate of production (source limitation), and in (2) by the rate of consumption (sink limitation). These models assume that assimilate movement between source and sink is non-limiting under all conditions. In most cases this assumption would appear to be valid (cf. Milthorpe & Moorby, 1969) but several reports suggest that, at least in some circumstances, the transport system may restrict transfer of assimilates from source to sink (Geiger, Saunders & Cataldo, 1969; Jenner & Rathjen, 1972). In terms of the hypothetical models described above, any limitation imposed by the vascular system would be indistinguishable from the 'sink-limited' situation.

The sink strength of the whole plant depends upon the capacity to convert assimilates into both structural material (G) and/or storage material (S). In most studies of changes in dry matter, growth and storage components are not separated and the total gain is commonly referred to as 'growth'. While this practice may be justified if sink strength is assumed to include both G and S, Warren Wilson (1972) has pointed out that, for certain purposes, it is necessary to distinguish sink activity for structural growth (R_G) from the relative growth rate derived from total dry weight (R_W). Where a plant contains a negligible proportion of storage materials, the leaf area ratio (F_A), i.e. leaf area/plant dry weight, can be regarded as the ratio of source size to sink size. However, in most cases, plants contain stored assimilates and sink activity should be represented by R_G (the relative growth rate of structural material), and the source–sink ratio by leaf area/plant structural dry weight. Limiting values of this ratio can be expected at which stored material is at a minimum (source-limiting) or is at a maximum concentration at which further accumulation is not possible (sink-limiting).

The sink strength of whole plants exhibits considerable elasticity. For instance, growth and branching patterns of shoots and roots of whole plants are usually indeterminate, thus offering an array of competing sinks which may be expected to readily absorb any increases

484

in assimilate production. Furthermore, if conversion to structural components is reduced (e.g. cessation of shoot growth with the onset of dormancy), assimilate consumption can be diverted into the accumulation of food reserves. At first sight, therefore, it would seem unlikely that overall accumulation is limited by sink strength. However, under field conditions assimilate utilization may be limited by various external factors, including temperature and the supply of water and mineral elements. Low temperature reduces the rate of G more than the rate of $(P-R)$, and hence the total sink strength of the plant may become limiting. Indeed, Warren Wilson (1966) found that when plants of *Oxyria digyra* L. were grown in the Arctic, storage carbohydrate levels were 2- to 3-fold higher compared to those for plants grown in England in summer. The Arctic-grown plants exemplify the situation mentioned above where carbohydrate levels are at a maximum concentration at which further accumulation is not possible (i.e. 'sink-limiting'). Deficiencies in the supply of either water or mineral nutrients may have a similar effect on the rate of assimilate utilization. A well documented instance of mineral nutrient levels regulating sink strength is the effect of nitrogen on leaf growth. High levels of N tend to promote excessive leaf production and low levels of starch reserve, whilst low levels of N cause the reverse (e.g. in potatoes). It would seem that the old concept of carbon/nitrogen ratio contained an element of truth – a high C/N ratio indicates that overall utilization of assimilates is limited by N deficiency (sink limitation), while a low C/N ratio indicates a 'source-limited' situation. Hence, it frequently happens, both under natural conditions and under cultivation, that dry matter accumulation by the plant is sink-limited rather than source-limited.

Source–sink relations have been examined extensively using plants grown under optimal environmental conditions, in which external restraints acting on the expression of potential 'sink strength' presumably would be minimized. Most of these studies have involved the removal of plant parts and, as such, a certain degree of caution must be attached to the interpretation of the experimental results obtained. Source–sink ratios may be altered by (1) reducing the leaf area by partial defoliation or shading (i.e. decreasing the source–sink ratio); (2) removing physiological sinks such as fruits, apices or root tips (i.e. increasing the source–sink ratio). When source–sink ratios of whole plants are decreased, net photosynthetic and net assimilation rates of the remaining leaves increase (Maggs, 1964,1965; Sweet & Wareing, 1966), suggesting that assimilate accumulation is operating below its maximum potential.

Increasing source–sink ratios tends to reduce the rate of assimilate accumulation (Sweet & Wareing, 1966), whilst, at least in some cases, the growth of remaining sinks (especially fruits, cf. Maggs, 1963) has been observed to increase. The latter observation may be indicative of a 'source-limited' situation, but an equally adequate proposal is that sink strength was controlled by competition for some other factor in limiting supply. Indeed, this alternative explanation may also be applied to conditions of reduced source–sink ratios, especially when it is achieved by partial defoliation (Wareing, Khalifa & Treharne, 1969). Thorne & Evans (1964) explored source–sink relations by several grafting experiments between sugar-beet and spinach beet. It was shown that leaves of spinach beet grafted onto sugar-beet roots (which constitute a larger sink than spinach beet roots) had a higher net assimilation rate than spinach beet leaves grafted onto spinach beet roots. These studies provide some evidence (although far from being unequivocal) suggesting that even when plants were grown under optimal environmental conditions, assimilate production was below its potential maximum and that assimilate accumulation was probably sink-limited.

Assuming that the proportionate rates of respiratory loss of assimilates are largely unaffected by changes in absolute rates of accumulation (but cf. Milthorpe & Moorby, 1969), then under conditions where the potential rate of production exceeds the rate of consumption, there must be some 'feedback' mechanism whereby the rate of assimilation is regulated to meet the demand. The nature of such a feedback control is not known but may, in part, depend upon the attainment of threshold levels of sucrose and other soluble assimilates in the source leaves (see review by Neales & Incoll, 1968). However, it would seem that the assimilation rate is not invariably dependent upon carbohydrate levels in leaves of some plants (cf. Little & Loach, 1973). There is some evidence that both stomatal movement and levels of certain photosynthetic enzymes are affected by the supply of plant hormones to the leaves (Meidner, 1970; Wareing, Khalifa & Treharne, 1969). Therefore, whilst perhaps being a more tenuous proposition, it is possible that photosynthetic rate may be under some control by hormonal factors synthesized in the sink regions and transported to the leaves.

Shoot–root balance

The partition of assimilates between shoot and root is obviously of fundamental importance. For maximum rate of production of dry matter within the plant as a whole it is important that as high a proportion of assimilates as possible should be 'ploughed back' into leaf tissue, which will still further increase the productive capacity of the plant and that 'expenditure of dry matter on the rest of the plant (stems, petioles, roots) should be no more than is required to support the leaves in an efficient arrangement and supply sufficient mineral nutrients and water' (Watson, 1971).

The overall rate of utilization of assimilates in leaf production will depend upon: (1) the rate of new leaf initiation; (2) the rate of leaf growth and final leaf size; and (3) the branching habit, i.e. the number of active shoot apices.

It seems unlikely that, in the majority of dicotyledonous species growing under adequate conditions of soil moisture and mineral nutrition, assimilate accumulation will be limited by the total sink capacity of the shoots, which shows considerable elasticity (p. 484). However, Warren Wilson (1967) has shown for young plants of *Brassica napus*, grown under wide spacing and high light intensity, that the relative growth rate was directly proportional to the rate of leaf production at the apex. The same relationship was found for *Helianthus annuus*, suggesting that for these species the sink strength may be limiting under certain conditions. Similarly, in young conifer seedlings, in which the leaves are small and there is little branching, it seems likely that the sink capacity of the shoots may limit the overall growth rate (Wareing, 1970). However, this limitation probably does not apply to the older stages of conifers, in which a high degree of branching (i.e. a large number of shoot apices) allows a higher rate of leaf area increase.

As is well known, environmental factors and mineral nutrient conditions markedly affect the root–shoot ratio. Thus, high nitrogen levels (which lead to a high overall growth rate and tend to deplete carbohydrate levels) promote shoot growth as against root growth, as do also low light intensities. It would appear that when there is keen competition between shoot and root for assimilates, the shoot system has the advantage.

Under any given set of environmental conditions, the root–shoot balance of a species is remarkably stable and if it is disturbed, for example by partial defoliation, the partition of assimilates for the next one to two weeks changes so that a high proportion are incorporated into new leaf tissue at the expense of root growth and so the original root–shoot balance is rapidly restored (Wareing, 1970). Evidently, there is some homeostatic mechanism maintaining a given root–shoot balance under any given set of conditions and this, in turn, implies an interplay between growth in root and shoot. Since roots supply water and mineral nutrients to the shoot and the latter supply carbohydrates to the roots, the possibility of such an interplay is immediately apparent. However, it is known that there is an interdependence between shoot and root in respect of other metabolites also, the roots supplying hormonal factors (e.g. cytokinins) and certain species of amino acids to the shoots, while the latter supply vitamins, including thiamin, to the roots, and these other metabolites may also be involved in the regulation of shoot–root balance.

Since there is frequently an allometric relation between shoot weight (S) and root weight (R) of the form $S = cR^k$ where c and k are constants, the commonly used root–shoot ratio will vary with the size of the plant (except where $k = 1$) and a better index of the balance between root and shoot growth is the relative growth coefficient, k (Pearsall, 1927). Differentiation of the allometric growth equation gives

$$\frac{\mathrm{d}s}{\mathrm{d}t}\frac{1}{S} = \frac{k\,\mathrm{d}R}{\mathrm{d}t\,R}$$

which indicates that there is a constant ratio between the relative growth rates (RGR) of shoot and root. Since RGR is a measure of sink activity (p. 482), there is thus a constant ratio between the sink activities of root and shoot.

Nelder (1963) has pointed out that in the case of *exponential* growth the growth equation would be given by

$$\frac{\mathrm{d}w}{w\,\mathrm{d}t} = a$$

where a is a constant, and suggests that this implies that the growth of any part is primarily limited by demand and not supply. Thus, if the supply of photosynthates is divided between shoots and roots in direct proportion to their sizes, this would imply that k, the relative growth coefficient, must be unity; demand-limited growth shows no such restriction. Since values of k other than unity are common, the demand-limited situation is suggested. However, it is not difficult to envisage that, even where there is supply limitation, and there is competition between root and shoot, assimilate partition will be determined by the relative sink strengths of shoot and root (assuming the pressure flow theory of translocation) which in turn will be a function of their respective sink activities as well as of their size. Hence, it seems questionable whether supply limitation and demand limitation can be distinguished quite as simply as Nelder (1963) suggests.

Thornley (1972*b*) has constructed a model based upon the interdependence of root and shoot for the supply of carbon and nitrogen, respectively (Fig. 21.1). It is assumed that growth and partitioning of assimilates depend upon two processes: transport and utilization. It is further assumed that the rate of transport of carbon or nitrogen is proportional to a concentration difference divided by a resistance, and that the utilization of the two substrates for growth is described by an equation appropriate to bi-substrate enzyme kinetics. The equations describing the model were solved for a plant undergoing steady-state

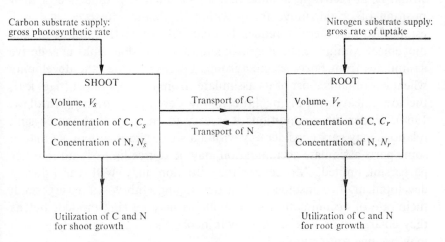

Fig. 21.1. Model of interdependence of root and shoot for the supply of carbon and nitrogen (from Thornley, 1972*b*).

exponential growth. One result which emerges from the model is that the total 'activities' of the root and shoot are in constant ratio to one another. Secondly, in the model a large change in specific activity of the root or shoot results in a proportionately much smaller change in the specific growth rate; that is, the plant automatically adjusts its growth pattern so that the total activities of the shoot and root are in balance, a result which again agrees closely with the experimental observations described above.

A different approach to the partition of assimilates between root and shoot is adopted in the simulation model of de Wit, Brouwer & Penning de Vries (1970).

R

Partition within the shoot system

Although it may be useful, for certain purposes, to consider whether dry matter accumulation within the plant as a whole is source-limited or sink-limited, or to consider partition between the whole shoot system and the root system, for other purposes it may be more pertinent to consider partition between the various parts of the shoot, namely leaves, stems, and fruits, particularly if it is the accumulation of assimilate within one specific plant part, e.g. seeds and fruits, which constitutes the harvested crop or the part consumed by animals in a natural ecosystem.

As a first approximation in understanding assimilate distribution, it would be attractive to assume that all assimilates, irrespective of their position of origin, move freely within the plant. However, it is well established that there is frequently a characteristic pattern of assimilate movement within the shoot system and that individual sinks may derive assimilates from fairly specific groups of leaves. Thus, the developing wheat ear obtains most of its assimilates from the uppermost (flag) leaf, the lower leaves supplying little to the developing grains (Wardlaw, 1968). Under these conditions it is easy to envisage that source–sink relations may vary considerably within a single shoot system, so that in some parts assimilate accumulation may be source-limited and in other parts sink-limited. Moreover, the situation may well vary during development. For instance, when developing embryos are very small their rate of accumulation of assimilates may be sink-limited, but as they enlarge their sink strength will increase so that ultimately growth may become source-limited.

The movements of the products of carbon fixation to and from each leaf changes continually as it and the plant develop. A very young leaf obtains assimilates required for growth from older leaves; as it expands it enters a phase when it may be exporting assimilates although still a *net* importer, and then it becomes a net exporting organ with virtually no import. In most dicotyledonous plants studied, net export commences when the leaf has reached between one-third and one-half its final area (Wardlaw, 1968). Factors that may influence the transition from import to export of assimilates in an expanding leaf are not fully understood. The availability of assimilates for export does not appear to be a decisive factor (Kocher & Leonard, 1971); perhaps the differentiation of vein-loading structures may determine the switch from import to export (Gunning & Pate, 1972). Whatever the mechanism,

490

once export commences, even adverse physiological conditions do not appear to reverse the flow of assimilates in either attached or detached leaves (Thrower, 1964; Hartt & Kortschak, 1964).

Initially, most of the assimilate exported from a young leaf is transported to the adjacent shoot apex. However, with time and the development of leaves above it, an increasingly greater proportion of its assimilates move to the roots. Thus, a fairly universal pattern of assimilate distribution within whole plants has emerged from the many investigations of this process (cf. Wardlaw, 1968). That is, the lower leaves act as the main source of assimilates for roots, whereas the upper leaves supply the shoot apex and leaves in an intermediate position may supply assimilates in both directions. Defoliation experiments suggest that the pattern of assimilate movement is the net result of a complex interaction between the many sources and sinks (Thaine, Ovenden & Turner, 1959; Thrower, 1962). Furthermore, the physiological state of the source leaf influences the direction of assimilate movement in the stem; for example, both light and ATP treatment of leaves have been shown to increase the proportion of exported assimilate moved basipetally (Moorby, 1964; Shiroya, 1968).

Over and above the partitioning of exported assimilates into acropetal and basipetal moving streams, it has been found that assimilates from any one leaf are distributed amongst the competing sinks in strict patterns. Thus, in tobacco, there appears to be preferential transport between leaves on the same orthostichy (Jones, Martin & Porter, 1959; Shiroya, Lister, Nelson & Krotkov, 1961); in wheat, the main source of assimilate imported by a young expanding leaf comes from the leaf two nodes below (Doodson, Manners & Myers, 1964; Patrick, 1972*a,b*). These apparent restrictions on assimilate distribution are considered to be imposed by the vascular geometry of the plant, but manipulative experiments have demonstrated that these limitations are overcome readily when 'sink' demand is increased (Wardlaw, 1968). Nevertheless, this canalizing effect of the vascular system could have an important function in influencing the degree of competition between neighbouring sinks. Therefore, the control of partitioning of exported assimilate is complex, being influenced by factors within and beyond the source leaf.

Whilst there is much empirical information on assimilate distribution within whole plants, quantitative measurements are rather scant. Indeed, an appreciation of the relative importance of successive source leaves as donors of assimilate depends upon obtaining estimates of *absolute* quantities of carbon exported from each leaf. Recently, by combining measurements of ^{14}C distribution with those of photosynthetic rate, Ryle (1972) demonstrated that in seedlings of *Lolium temulentum* L. the youngest leaves supplied some two- to five-times more carbon than the lower, old leaves. These observations are consistent with the concept that assimilate export and photosynthetic activity of a leaf are closely linked (Hofstra & Nelson, 1969). Perhaps attempts to describe assimilate partition by model simulation (de Wit, Brouwer & Penning de Vries, 1971; Thornley, 1972*a*) will provide the necessary impetus and direction for future investigations to strive for quantitative measurements of carbon distribution. Therefore, of particular interest is the quantitative model developed by Thornley (1972*a*) to account for partitioning of assimilates between leaf, stem and root. This model is based upon similar assumptions to those for the shoot–root interaction referred to above (p. 489) namely (1) that the transport of substances between two points in the plant is given by the substrate concentration difference divided by a resistance factor, and (2) that utilization of substrate for growth depends upon the local substrate concentration according to the Michaelis–Menten equation for enzyme kinetics. The partitioning of assimilates was shown to agree reasonably with that found in real plants. This type of approach is, as yet, only in its infancy, but it holds out considerable promise for elucidating the problem of assimilate partition within whole plants.

Competition for assimilates

That there is frequently competition for assimilates between the different growing regions within the plant is almost self-evident. Thus, everyday horticultural experience shows that pruning, disbudding, and fruit-thinning normally lead to increased growth of the remaining shoot, flowers and fruits. Moreover, plant physiological literature provides many examples of competition for assimilates between different regions. Reference has already been made to the fact that roots seem to show a low competitive ability against shoots when the supply of assimilates is low. Thus, in pine seedlings, root growth ceases during the period of rapid shoot elongation in the spring, and recommences when shoot elongation ceases (Nelson, 1963).

On the other hand, there are many observations indicating that developing flowers and fruits have high competitive ability and that with the transition from vegetative to reproductive development there is frequently a marked change in the pattern of assimilate distribution (Wardlaw, 1968). A developing fruit has a priority of demand on assimilates from neighbouring leaves and frequently can draw on assimilates from more distant regions of the shoot. Other evidence of the ability of developing fruits to monopolize available assimilates is provided by the fact that the cessation of vegetative and root growth frequently associated with the onset of reproduction can be reversed by fruit removal. Storage organs, such as potato tubers and root stocks also appear to dominate vegetative growth in a similar manner to fruits (Wardlaw, 1968).

There may be competition between meristematic regions in close proximity, e.g. between shoot apex, developing leaves and growing stem tissue. In cereals, the expanding stem internodes may compete with the developing ear primordia. Indeed, it has been suggested that one of the reasons for larger ear size in semi-dwarf wheat may be reduced competition from the stem initials at the stage of spikelet initiation (Bingham, 1970).

While it is no doubt true that in many instances the observed competition is for assimilates, it is not difficult to imagine a situation in a shoot system in which the overall status is one of sink limitation, and yet there is still competition between sinks for the available mineral nutrients or organic substances, such as amino acids or hormones, supplied by the roots (see earlier discussion p. 488). Therefore, when we consider competition between sinks, it would seem important to determine first whether the status of the shoot system is one of source or sink limitation, i.e. whether the competition is for assimilates or for some other factor.

The mechanism of assimilate partition

The picture which emerges from the considerations discussed in the preceding section is that the various growth and storage centres of the plant actively compete for assimilates and that each centre has a certain competitive or 'mobilizing ability', whereby it can 'pull' or 'attract' assimilates, against the effects of other centres. What determines competitive ability of a growth centre, and what is the relation between mobilizing ability and sink strength? As we have seen, the 'mobilizing ability' of a sink is a measure of its ability to import assimilates and is given by the absolute growth rate of the whole plant or plant part under investigation. The mobilizing ability will vary depending upon

493

the rate of supply of assimilates and will reach its maximum potential value only under conditions of non-limiting supply.

Moreover, the concept of 'mobilizing ability' as defined above makes no assumptions as to whether the role of the sink in transport is a purely passive one (i.e. an active transport system would determine the potential maximum rate of assimilate movement to the sink; under these conditions, the only control the sink may exert on transport is if its capacity to accumulate assimilates is less than the potential rate of movement) or whether it directly influences the rate and pattern of assimilate movement (i.e. movement depends upon the relative capacities of the sinks to withdraw assimilates from the transport system). This question cannot be answered fully until the mechanism of phloem transport is understood.

The most generally accepted theory of phloem transport is the Pressure Flow (or 'Mass Flow') Theory, according to which the flow of dissolved organic substances depends upon a turgor pressure gradient along the path of transport. The maintenance of this turgor pressure difference between the source and the sink will depend upon continual 'loading' of sucrose into the phloem at the source, and its removal at the sink, either by metabolism or by compartmentation into storage materials.

On this hypothesis, it seems less likely that the loading of assimilates into the phloem at the source would be under direct control of the sink, but in so far as uptake at the sink ensures continued flow of assimilates towards it, the sink may be said to 'attract' assimilates. Such a mechanism would ensure that assimilate is transported to a sink at a rate which is proportional to the rate of its consumption in growth and/or the storage of reserve materials, i.e. is proportional to its 'sink strength'. Furthermore, where there is competition between sinks it is assumed that the *competitive ability* of any given growth centre will depend upon its sink strength; that is to say, in terms of the Pressure Flow Theory, the '*mobilizing ability*' of a sink is determined by its capacity to accumulate assimilates.

There appear to have been few studies aimed directly at testing this hypothesis, namely, whether mobilizing ability is proportional to capacity to accumulate assimilate, but it would not appear difficult to devise suitable experiments. However, caution would be required in interpreting the results of such an investigation, especially if a linear relationship was found to exist between sink strength and mobilizing ability. Such information could be accounted for by either (1) an

494

active transport mechanism being limited by the rate of assimilate withdrawal at the sink, or (2) assimilate uptake by the sink 'driving' transport.

Apart from the commonly accepted concept of sink activity in relation to the Pressure Flow Hypothesis, there is an increasing body of evidence suggesting that the hormone content of a growth centre may affect its mobilizing ability for assimilates. However, despite many investigations, the relationship between endogenous hormone level and the rate of dry matter import remains unclear. This situation is not all that surprising when consideration is given to the number of variable factors which influence assimilate movement, together with the problem of dealing with a bulk hormone extract only part of which may contain the active component. Nevertheless, investigations in which hormones have been applied to certain plant parts (e.g. detached leaves, Mothes & Engelbrecht, 1961; decapitated stems, Booth *et al.*, 1962) have consistently substantiated the tentative conclusions drawn from studies on endogenous hormones. That is, assimilates move towards regions of high hormone concentration and that amounts mobilized depend upon the concentration of hormone applied (Patrick & Woolley, 1973). This phenomenon has been commonly referred to in the literature as hormone-directed transport.

Central to the context of the present discussion, these observations raise the question as to the mechanism of hormone action in stimulating assimilate movement to the sink regions. One possibility (and perhaps currently the most widely accepted) is that hormones influence assimilate mobilization by regulating sink strength (Seth & Wareing, 1967; Mullins, 1970). Moorby (1968) suggested a number of ways in which hormones might affect sink strength. Indeed, several studies have shown that when indolyl-acetic acid (IAA) was applied to tissue segments, rates of metabolite accumulation (i.e. sink strength) were enhanced (Sacher & Glasziou, 1962; Ilan & Reinhold, 1963). Unfortunately, the relationship between sink strength and mobilizing ability was not examined within the same experimental system (cf. p. 483). Furthermore, whilst estimates of metabolic activity may provide some qualitative prediction of sink strength (Mullins, 1970), these types of observation need to be substantiated by estimates of metabolite accumulation before being of much value in exploring the relationship between sink strength and mobilizing ability. A number of studies have shown that increased assimilate movement into *non-growing* internodes of decapitated plants may be detected within six hours of applying IAA to the cut surfaces of

495

the stumps (Booth *et al.*, 1962; Davies & Wareing, 1965). On the premise that metabolic activity of mature stems may take longer than six hours to respond to IAA, these authors suggested, for their system, that enhanced mobilization may occur without any concomitant change in sink strength. Recently, this possibility has received further support from experiments designed to measure sink strength of non-growing internodes of decapitated bean seedlings (Patrick & Wareing, 1973). Although assimilate mobilization was promoted in those stems treated with IAA, Patrick & Wareing (1973) were unable to detect any alteration in either the metabolic state (respiration, protein synthesis, sucrose metabolism) or the capacity to accumulate sucrose of these internodes compared to the controls. These results redirect attention to the relatively neglected proposition that IAA may be acting more directly on the transport process and, in particular, on longitudinal movement in the phloem of the treated stems (Davies & Wareing, 1965; Hew, Nelson & Krotkov, 1967). It must be stressed, however, that these studies do not preclude sink strength as a regulator of assimilate movement, but do emphasize that it may not be the only factor involved.

The precise mechanism of these 'hormone-directed transport' phenomena remains obscure and, indeed, future work should concentrate more on relating observations obtained from the rather artificial system of decapitating plants back to the whole-plant situation. However, it remains a possibility that high endogenous hormone content of growing organs may play an important role in their mobilizing ability.

References

Bingham, J. (1970). The physiological determinants of yield in cereals. *Agric. Progr.* **44**, 30–42.

Booth, A., Moorby, J., Davies, C. R., Jones, H. & Wareing, P. F. (1962). Effects of indolyl-3-acetic acid on the movement of nutrients within plants. *Nature*, **194**, 204–5.

Davies, C. R. & Wareing, P. F. (1965). Auxin-directed transport of radio-phosphorous in stems. *Planta*, **65**, 139–56.

Doodson, J. K., Manners, J. G. & Myers, A. (1964). The distribution of [14]carbon assimilated by the third leaf of wheat. *J. Exp. Bot.* **15** (43), 96–103.

Geiger, D. R., Saunders, M. A. & Cataldo, D. A. (1969). Translocation and accumulation of translocate in the sugar beet petiole. *Plant Physiol.* **44**, 1657–65.

Gunning, B. E. S. & Pate, J. S. (1972). Transfer cells. In *Dynamic Aspects of Plant Ultrastructure*, ed. A. W. Robards. London, McGraw-Hill.

Hartt, E. & Kortschak, H. P. (1964). Sugar gradients and translocation of sucrose in detached blades of sugar cane. *Plant Physiol.* **39** (3), 460–74.

Hew, C. S., Nelson, C. D. & Krotkov, G. (1967). Hormonal control of translocation of photosynthetically assimilated ^{14}C in young soybean plants. *Amer. J. Bot.* **54**, 252–6.

Hofstra, G. & Nelson, C. D. (1969). A comparative study of translocation of assimilated ^{14}C from leaves of different species. *Planta,* **88**, 103–12.

Ilan, K. & Reinhold, L. (1963). Analysis of the effects of indole-3-acetic acid on the uptake of monovalent cations. *Physiol. Plant.* **16**, 596–603.

Jenner, C. F. & Rathjen, A. J. (1972). Limitations to the accumulation of starch in the developing wheat grain. *Ann. Bot.* **36**, 743–54.

Jones, H. Martin, R. V. & Porter, H. K. (1959). Translocation of ^{14}carbon in tobacco following assimilation of $^{14}CO_2$ by a single leaf. *Ann. Bot.* **23**, 493–508.

Kocher, H. & Leonard, O. A. (1971). Translocation and metabolic conversion of ^{14}C-labelled assimilates in detached and attached leaves of *Phaseolus vulgaris* L. in different phases of leaf expansion. *Plant Physiol.* **47**, 212–16.

Little, C. H. A. & Loach, K. (1973). Effect of changes in carbohydrate concentration on the rate of net photosynthesis in mature leaves of *Abies balsamea. Can. J. Bot.* **51**, 751–8.

Maggs, D. H. (1963). The reduction in growth brought about by fruiting. *J. Hort. Sci.* **38**, 119–28.

Maggs, D. H. (1964). Growth rates in relation to assimilate supply and demand. I. Leaves and roots as limiting region. *J. Exp. Bot.* **15**, 574–84.

Maggs, D. H. (1965). Growth rates in relation to assimilate supply and demand. II. The effect of particular leaves and growing regions in determining dry matter distribution in young apple trees. *J. Exp. Bot.* **16**, 387–404.

Meidner, H. (1970). Effects of photoperiodic induction and debudding in *Xanthium pennsylvanicum* and of partial defoliation in *Phaseolus vulgaris* on rates of net photosynthesis and stomatal conductances. *J. Exp. Bot.* **21**, 164–9.

Milthorpe, F. L. & Moorby, J. (1969). Vascular transport and its significance in plant growth. *Ann. Rev. Plant Physiol.* **20**, 117–38.

Moorby, J. (1964). The foliar uptake and translocation of caesium. *J. Exp. Bot.* **15**, 457–69.

Moorby, J. (1968). The effect of growth substances on transport in plants. In *Transport of Plant Hormones*, ed. Y. Varder, pp. 192–206. Amsterdam, North-Holland.

Mothes, K. & Engelbrecht, L. (1961). Kinetin-induced directed transport of substances in excised leaves in the dark. *Phytochem.* **1**, 58–62.

Mullins, M. G. (1970). Hormone-directed transport of assimilates in decapitated internodes of *Phaseolus vulgaris* L. *Ann. Bot.* **34**, 897–909.

Neales, T. F. & Incoll, L. D. (1968). The control of leaf photosynthesis rate by the level of assimilate concentration in the leaf: a review of the hypothesis. *Bot. Rev.* **34**, 107–25.

Nelder, J. (1963). Quantitative genetics and growth analysis. In *Statistical*

R*

Genetics and Plant Breeding, pp. 445–54. Washington, National Academy of Sciences.

Nelson, C. D. (1963). Effect of climate on the distribution and translocation of assimilates. In *Environmental Control of Plant Growth*, ed. L. T. Evans, pp. 149–74. New York & London, Academic Press.

Patrick, J. W. (1972*a*). Vascular system of the stem of the wheat plant. II. Development. *Aust. J. Bot.* **20**, 65–78.

Patrick, J. W. (1972*b*). Distribution of assimilate during stem elongation in wheat. *Aust. J. Biol. Sci.* **25**, 455–67.

Patrick, J. W. & Wareing, P. F. (1970). Experiments on the mechanism of hormone-directed transport. In *Plant Growth Substances*, ed. D. J. Carr. Berlin, Springer-Verlag.

Patrick, J. W. & Woolley, D. J. (1973). Auxin physiology of decapitated stems of *Phaseolus vulgaris* L. treated with indol-3yl-acetic acid. *J. Exp. Bot.*, in press.

Pearsall, W. H. (1927). Growth studies. VI. On the relative sizes of growing plant organs. *Ann. Bot.* **41**, 64–73.

Ryle, G. J. A. (1972). A quantitative analysis of the uptake of carbon and of the supply of ^{14}C-labelled assimilates to areas of meristimatic growth in *Lolium temulentum*. *Ann. Bot.* **36**, 497–512.

Sacher, J. A. & Glasziou, K. T. (1962). Regulation of invertase levels in sugar cane by an auxin and carbohydrate mediated control system. *Biochem. Biophys. Res. Commun.* **8**, 280–2.

Seth, A. & Wareing, P. F. (1967). Hormone directed transport of metabolites and its possible role in plant senescence. *J. Exp. Bot.* **18**, 67–77.

Shiroya, M. (1968). Comparison of upward and downward translocation of ^{14}C from a single leaf of sunflower. *Plant Physiol.* **43**, 1605–10.

Shiroya, M., Lister, G. R., Nelson, C. D. & Krotkov, G. (1961). Translocation of ^{14}C in tobacco at different stages of development following assimilation of ^{14}CO$_2$ by a single leaf. *Can. J. Bot.* **39**, 855–64.

Sweet, G. B. & Wareing, P. F. (1966). Role of plant growth in regulating photosynthesis. *Nature*, **210**, 77–9.

Thaine, R., Ovenden, S. L. & Turner, J. S. (1959). Translocation of labelled assimilate in the soybean. *Aust. J. Biol. Sci.* **12**, 349–72.

Thorne, G. N., Evans, A. F. (1964). Influence of tops and roots on net assimilation rate of sugar-beet and spinach beet and grafts between them. *Ann. Bot.* **28**, 499–508.

Thornley, J. H. M. (1972*a*). A model to describe the partitioning of photosynthate during vegetative growth. *Ann. Bot.* **36**, 419–30.

Thornley, J. H. M. (1972*b*). A balanced quantitative model for root: shoot ratios in vegetative plants. *Ann. Bot.* **36**, 431–41.

Thrower, L. (1962). Translocation of labelled assimilates in the soybean. II. The pattern of translocation in intact and defoliated plants. *Aust. J. Biol. Sci.* **15**, 629–50.

Thrower, L. (1964). Translocation of labelled assimilates in the soybean. In Translocation and other factors affecting leaf growth. *Aust. J. Biol. Sci.* **17**, 412–27.

Wardlaw, I. F. (1968). The control and pattern of movement of carbohydrates in plants. *Bot. Rev.* **34**, 79–105.

Wareing, P. F. (1970). Growth and its coordination in trees. In *Physiology of Tree Crops*, eds. L. C. Luckmill & C. W. Cutting, pp. 1–21. London & New York, Academic Press.

Wareing, P. F., Khalifa, M. M. & Treharne, K. J. (1969). Rate limiting processes in photosynthesis at saturating light intensities. *Nature*, **220**, 453–7.

Wilson, J. Warren (1966). An analysis of plant growth and its control in arctic environments. *Ann. Bot.* **30**, 383–402.

Wilson, J. Warren (1967). Ecological data on dry-matter production by plants and plant communities. In *The Collection and Processing of Field Data*, eds. E. F. Bradley & O. T. Denmead, pp. 77–123. New York: Interscience.

Wilson, J. Warren (1972). Control of crop processes. In *Crop Processes in Controlled Environments*, eds. A. R. Rees *et al.*, pp. 7–30. London & New York, Academic Press.

Watson, D. J. (1971). Size structure and activity of the productive system of crops. In *Potential Crop Production*, eds. P. F. Wareing & J. P. Cooper, pp. 76–88. London, Heinemann.

Williams, R. F. (1960). The physiology of growth in the wheat plant. 1. Seedling growth and pattern of growth at the shoot apex. *Aust. J. Biol. Sci.*, **13**, 401–28.

Wit, de C. T., Brouwer, R. & Penning de Vries, F. W. T. (1971). A dynamic model of plant and crop growth. In *Potential Crop Production*, eds. P. F. Wareing & J. P. Cooper, pp. 117–42. London, Heinemann.

22. Beyond photosynthesis — the role of respiration, translocation and growth potential in determining productivity

L. T. EVANS

All biomass production depends on photosynthesis. Nevertheless, neither the rate nor the extent of production need bear a close relation to photosynthetic rate, or be determined by it as is perhaps implied in the title of this book. The processes that follow photosynthesis, such as respiration and translocation, or other limitations on the capacity of plants to grow and utilize photosynthate, can be major determinants of productivity. This is evident, for example, in the communities of algae growing in oligotrophic waters, which Fogg has described (Chapter 19). For many of these, growth and productivity are limited to such an extent by nutrient supply that the algae cannot utilize most of their photosynthetic assimilate, and may excrete up to 90% of it. In higher plants such surplus photosynthate tends to be stored rather than excreted, particularly under conditions where water or nutrient stress or low temperatures restrict the capacity for growth more than they limit photosynthesis (e.g. Wardlaw, 1969; Boyer, 1970). In such cases the accumulated assimilates may exert a feedback inhibition on photosynthetic rate to the extent that it then matches the environmentally determined capacity of the plant to grow.

The mechanisms by which photosynthates are distributed in plants, and the extent to which assimilates are invested in new growth, especially of leaves, are as important determinants of productivity as is photosynthetic capacity. Growth in plants is open-ended, as pointed out by Wareing & Patrick (Chapter 21), and active growth at all potential meristems could result in photosynthesis being the limiting process, but many potential sinks for photosynthate are restricted by environmental or correlative inhibitions.

Respiration

We shall not consider 'photorespiration' as it is to a large degree a feature of photosynthesis itself, and of the oxygenase activity of carboxydismutase (Andrews, Lorimer & Tolbert, 1973; Lorimer, Andrews & Tolbert, 1973) rather than of the cellular work represented by dark respiration.

Loss of photosynthate by dark respiration can be substantial, particularly in communities with a large biomass, and growing under high temperature conditions. In the forests of Thailand and Cambodia, for example, Kira (Chapter 2) estimates that about three-quarters of the carbon assimilated is lost by dark respiration.

Given the potential magnitude of dark respiration losses, much greater understanding of them is required not only for the purposes of simulating the productive processes of plants, but also to assess the possibilities for their reduction. Early simulation models for the growth of plant communities assumed that respiration losses were proportional to accumulated dry weight and leaf area index (see, for example, Davidson & Philip, 1958), and therefore concluded that there was a pronounced optimum leaf area index and stand structure, and much effort was given to defining these. However, crop respiration was subsequently shown to increase asymptotically with increase in leaf area index (Ludwig, Saeki & Evans, 1965; McCree & Troughton, 1966), and to be proportional to photosynthesis rather than to accumulated dry weight, although influenced by temperature. At the IBP symposium in Třeboň, McCree (1970) suggested that respiration by plant communities should be considered as a sum of two terms. The first is a basal or metabolic respiration, related to accumulated dry weight, but strongly dependent on temperature. The second term is the respiratory cost of growth or synthesis, which should be independent of temperature, provided respiration remains coupled, and proportional to gross photosynthesis.

In the intervening years Penning de Vries has explored this synthesis respiration term and has developed a rational basis for it, by examining the respiratory cost of conversion from glucose to the various groups of compounds found in plants (Penning de Vries, 1972). In Chapter 20 he extends his analysis to allow for conversion from the nitrogenous compounds and organic acids formed in photosynthesizing leaves and translocated in the phloem to growing tissues. He also allows for the cost of nitrate reduction in the leaves and for the loading and unloading of organic compounds into the vascular system, and compares his estimates with experimental results from young plants of high relative growth rate. For both maize and sunflower the agreement is excellent, and he has shown that synthesis respiration is independent of temperature and species, although it obviously depends on the composition of the plants, which must be known if his estimations are to be used in modelling crop respiration. Maintenance (i.e. metabolic) respiration in his experiments was not only dependent on temperature, but also on species, being much larger in sunflower than in maize. In the young, rapidly growing plant material examined by Penning de Vries the synthesis respiration term is the dominant one, whereas in communities of plants which have accumulated considerable dry weight and age the maintenance respiration term may be the larger one, particularly at high temperatures.

It is not altogether clear what we mean by maintenance respiration as against synthesis respiration, because the distinction is merely operational and implies no differences between them in either biochemical pathway or products. To a large extent maintenance respiration probably derives from the turnover of enzymes and membrane proteins, and we urgently need more data on actual turnover rates, even of that most abundant protein of all, carboxydismutase. In wheat and tobacco leaves, Hellebust & Bidwell (1964) estimated turnover rates to be 0.2–0.5% per hour in expanding leaves, but considerably lower in fully grown leaves. The two species differed substantially, and the dependence of turnover on temperature, and on the availability of photosynthate requires clarification. Maintenance respiration for protein turnover may be coupled tightly in the biochemical sense, but not necessarily in the physiological sense in that the rate of turnover may be dependent on substrate levels.

If maintenance respiration is due primarily to protein turnover, it is unsatisfactory to attempt to relate it to accumulated dry weight. The wood of trees, the cellulose of cotton crops, or the starch of cereals may have very low turnover, and it may be better to relate maintenance respiration to total protein rather than to dry weight.

Translocation and distribution of assimilates

When plant community processes are being modelled for productivity, the first steps are to estimate stand photosynthesis and respiration loss, leading to the problem of how the net assimilate is to be allocated among the various plant organs to give the pattern of growth and storage on which the next round of photosynthesis estimations is based. It is here that our understanding is weakest, and so long as the mechanism of transport remains unknown it is difficult to see how satisfactory models can be developed.

Several IBP programmes have provided extensive data on the partitioning of dry matter at various stages of the life cycle, and in a range of conditions, for many varieties and species. Monsi & Murata (1970) have reviewed some of the extensive data collected under the Japanese IBP programmes in this context.

From such data it is possible to derive allocation ratios for photosynthate at any one stage of growth, and to develop expressions for progressive changes in these as growth proceeds. Patefield & Austin (1971) have developed such an empirical expression for the modelling of growth in beet, and for the time being this may be the only satisfactory approach until we understand more of the mechanisms of translocation. However, the pattern of assimilate distribution is very sensitive to environmental conditions, as well as to genotype, and even small variations in allocation ratio can, over time, result in large differences in growth pattern.

An alternative approach has been developed by Thornley (1972) in which he assigns resistances to the various parts of the translocation pathway. Such resistances can be derived empirically from existing data, but I very much doubt whether this will prove to be a satisfactory approach, and we have little evidence to indicate what the magnitude of the resistance to translocation in the phloem is compared with those for the loading and unloading of assimilates into and from the vascular system. Peel & Ho (1970) examined the influence of aphid colonies of various sizes on the translocation of labelled sugars through willow bark, and I have done similar experiments on wheat plants with two ears containing differing numbers of grains, and found that the size of the sink is the major determinant of the distribution of assimilates. In these experiments the pathways to the two competing sinks were identical, and presumably therefore of equal resistance, yet distribution was biassed towards the larger sink far more than would be expected from the relative sink sizes. Thus, it is the characteristic of the sink rather than the resistance of the translocation pathway to it that is likely to govern assimilate distribution, and perhaps our most urgent task is to understand the processes involved in unloading at the various kinds of sink. Thornley's model assumes much lower concentrations of assimilates at the sink than in the source, but this is unlikely to be the case for a number of potent sinks, where storage may occur against a concentration gradient, as in sugar cane and beet. Sufficiently steep gradients in sugar concentration to drive translocation by diffusion between source and sink may develop only over short distances, in which case the sink organs must be close to the source of assimilates for rapid translocation to occur (Canny, 1971).

By sinks we mean regions of net import, usually but not always converting soluble compounds from the phloem into less soluble and more complex storage, structural and enzymatic components. Such sinks are of several different kinds, and different mechanisms for unloading may prevail in them. Meristematic sinks are characterized by active cell division, and possibly by high endogenous production of cytokinins. Elongation sinks are characterized mainly by cell wall synthesis and rapid water uptake, and possibly by high endogenous levels of gibberellins. Storage sinks are of two kinds, one characterized by conversion of the soluble phloem components to insoluble polymers, as in the cereal grain, the other by extremely high levels of soluble sugars which may be loaded against a gradient in concentration. Clearly, very different mechanisms of attraction and demand are likely to be involved at these different sinks, and until these are understood more fully it will be difficult to develop a coherent explanation of the pattern of distribution of assimilates in plants. Geiger & Christy's (1971) experiments on the effects of anoxia of the sink leaf on translocation in sugar beet plants show clearly that although ATP-dependent active transport in the sink augments the driving force for translocation, effects on the permeability and metabolic activity of the sink leaf are also important.

Nor do we clearly understand how sinks compete, and how one may dominate over another. Warren Wilson (1972) has suggested that sink strength equals sinks size × sink activity. However, size and activity may not be independent variables, and moreover, sinks of small strength by such a definition may nevertheless have an apparently high priority in obtaining assimilates. Consider the shoot apex, for example. It may have a dry weight of only a few micrograms and a low relative growth rate and metabolic activity, yet, at least in the grass *Lolium temulentum*, it continues to receive a stable supply of assimilates regardless of the stresses placed on the plant. Although of low sink strength in Warren Wilson's terminology it must nevertheless be a sink of high priority.

Similarly, the experiments of Peel & Ho (1970) with aphid colonies of various sizes, and my comparable experiments on wheat plants with two ears containing different numbers of grains, both indicate that distribution among two sinks of equal activity is not merely in proportion to the relative size of the two sinks, but is heavily biassed towards proportionally greater distribution to the larger sink. Thus, Warren Wilson's expression for sink strength seems unlikely to provide a satisfactory way of partitioning assimilates among several competing sinks.

Besides the problem of how assimilates are allocated there is also that of whether the capacity of the phloem for translocation is always adequate to match the capacity of photosynthesis in generating assimilates and that of growth in consuming them. In spite of the much higher maximum photosynthetic rate of the C_4-grasses compared with their C_3-counterparts, the amount of phloem per unit of supply leaf area in them does not appear to be greater (Lush & Evans, 1974). Transport through the phloem in C_4-grasses may well be faster, however, as suggested by Troughton and Currie (p. 693) who recorded speeds of assimilate movement of 3.2 cm s^{-1} in maize, which is considerably higher than the speeds usually found in C_3-grasses. In agreement with this, we have found that the rate of assimilate transfer per unit cross-sectional area of phloem is three or more times as high in leaves of grasses with C_4-photosynthesis as in those with the C_3-pathway. The speed of movement appears to be responsive to the demand for assimilates, as shown earlier by Wardlaw (1965), and by Moorby, Troughton & Currie (p. 692), emphasizing again that the characteristics of the sink may have a controlling influence on the speed and distribution of assimilates, as also on photosynthetic rate.

Future progress will depend to a very considerable extent on clarification of the characteristics of the many kinds of growth centres in plants, and of the mechanisms by which they attract and unload assimilates, as emphasized by Wareing & Patrick (Chapter 21), and our understanding of productivity in plants will depend as much on that as on increased insight into their photosynthetic mechanisms.

References

Andrews, T. A., Lorimer, G. H. & Tolbert, N. E. (1973). Ribulose diphosphate oxygenase. I. Synthesis of phosphoglycolate by fraction-1 protein of leaves. *Biochem.* **12**, 11–8.

Boyer, J. S. (1970). Leaf enlargement and metabolic rates in corn, soybean and sunflower at various leaf water potentials. *Plant Physiol.* **46**, 233–5.

Canny, M. J. (1971). Translocation: mechanisms and kinetics. *Ann. Rev. Plant Physiol.* **22**, 237–60.

Davidson, J. L. & Philip, J. R. (1958). Light and pasture growth. In *Arid Zone Research: Climatology and Microclimatology*, pp. 181–7. Paris, UNESCO.

Geiger, D. R. & Christy, A. L. (1971). Effect of sink region anoxia on translocation rate. *Plant Physiol.* **47**, 172–4.

Hellebust, J. A. & Bidwell, R. G. S. (1964). Protein turnover in attached wheat and tobacco leaves. *Canad. J. Bot.* **42**, 1–12.

Lorimer, G. H., Andrews, T. A. & Tolbert, N. E. (1973). Ribulose diphosphate oxygenase. II. Further proof of reaction products and mechanism of action. *Biochem.* **12**, 18–23.

Ludwig, L. J., Saeki, T. & Evans, L. T. (1965). Photosynthesis in artificial communities of cotton plants in relation to leaf area. *Aust. J. biol. Sci.* **18**, 1103–18.

Lush, W. M. & Evans, L. T. (1974). Translocation of photosynthetic assimilate from grass leaves, as influenced by environment and species. *Aust. J. Plant Physiol.* **1**, 417–31.

McCree, K. J. (1970). An equation for the rate of respiration of white clover plants grown under controlled conditions. In *Prediction and Measurement of Photosynthetic Productivity*, pp. 221–9. Wageningen, PUDOC.

McCree, K. J. & Troughton, J. H. (1966). Non-existence of an optimum leaf area index for the production rate of white clover grown under constant conditions. *Plant Physiol.* **41**, 1615–22.

Monsi, M. & Murata, Y. (1970). Development of photosynthetic systems as influenced by distribution of matter. In *Prediction and Measurement of Photosynthetic Productivity*, pp. 115–29. Wageningen, PUDOC.

Patefield, W. M. & Austin, R. B. (1971). A model for the simulation of the growth of *Beta vulgaris* L. *Ann. Bot.* **35**, 1227–50.

Peel, A. J. & Ho, L. C. (1970). Colony size of *Tuberolachnus salignus* (Gmelin) in relation to mass transport of ^{14}C-labelled assimilates from the leaves in willow. *Physiol. plant.* **23**, 1033–8.

Penning de Vries, F. W. T. (1972). Respiration and growth. In *Crop Processes in Controlled Environments*, eds. A. R. Rees, K. E. Cockshull, D. W. Hand & R. G. Hurd, pp. 327–46. London, Academic Press.

Thornley, J. H. M. (1972). A model to describe the partitioning of photosynthate during vegetative plant growth. *Ann. Bot.* **36**, 419–30.

Wardlaw, I. F. (1965). The velocity and pattern of assimilate translocation in wheat plants during grain development. *Aust. J. biol. Sci.* **18**, 269–81.

Wardlaw, I. F. (1969). The effect of water stress on translocation in relation to photosynthesis and growth. *Aust. J. biol. Sci.* **22**, 1–16.

Warren Wilson, J. (1972). Control of crop processes. In *Crop Processes in Controlled Environments*, eds. A. R. Rees, K. E. Cockshull, D. W. Hand & R. G. Hurd, pp. 7–30. London, Academic Press.

PART VI

Influence of stress factors and the use of assimilates

23. Water stress, photosynthesis and the use of photosynthates

B. SLAVÍK

The term 'water stress' is taken here to mean internal water deficit induced by external stresses such as soil water stress and/or atmospheric stress. Although the term water strain (*sensu* Weatherley, 1965) might be appropriate in this respect, it has not been widely accepted.

The excellent reviews by Crafts (1968) and Slatyer (1969, 1973) cover a similar although broader field. The present Chapter will therefore concentrate on reviewing recent advances in this topic, in both IBP and other projects.

The development of water deficit

It is generally accepted that water deficit in leaves is a result of excess water loss by transpiration over the simultaneous water supply. In this connection the concept of a time lag of absorption behind transpiration is frequently expressed, suggesting that such a time lag is the primary cause of the resulting water deficit. However, several recent studies, based on pioneer work by Gradmann (1928) and van den Honert (1948), have indicated a different concept. Water flux through the plant from the root–soil interface to the plant–air interface, to replace the amount of water simultaneously transpired, is driven by the gradients of water potential or, generally speaking, by the overall difference in water potential between absorbing root surfaces and transpiring aerial plant surfaces, mainly in the leaves. Resistance to liquid water flux along these pathways is overcome by a driving force, namely by the difference in water potential, which is brought about by the decrease of leaf water potential, i.e. development of a leaf water deficit. Theoretically, any water loss due to transpiration results in a decrease of leaf water potential and hence in a water potential gradient, causing an immediate water supply from plant parts with higher water potential, such as roots or cut leaf petiole immersed in water (as has been dramatically shown by Raschke (1970*a,b*) in the case of epidermis turgor). Nevertheless, during rapid transpiration, the concomitant water supply to the leaf can only be achieved by development of water potential gradients, i.e. by decrease of leaf water potential. This means that, at

511

constant resistances, the water deficits in leaves, resulting from transpiration, would be determined by their transpiration rate.

Thus leaf water deficit is primarily due to the resistances of plant structures to the water flux through them, from the water 'source' in the soil surrounding the roots to the 'sink' in the atmosphere surrounding the leaves.

The decrease of leaf water potential is also a function of the relationship between water potential and relative water content. This relationship, different in different leaves and taxa (Slavík, 1969), is also a function of the rate of the development of the deficit, being generally steeper with the rapid increase of water deficit (Jordan & Ritchie, 1971; Pospíšilová, 1973). The steeper the dependence of water potential on the relative water content, the greater is the drought resistance assumed to be (e.g. Sanchez-Diaz & Kramer, 1971).

When the water potential of the water 'source' in the soil is decreased a further decrease in leaf water potential must take place in order to re-establish the water potential gradient required to maintain the supply of water to the leaves at the necessary level. Moreover, a local decrease in soil moisture content in the soil boundary layer surrounding the roots may also develop as a result of rapid water absorption by the roots. This leads to a decrease in hydraulic conductivity of this soil layer which, in turn, slows down the water supply at the given water potential gradient (from more recent papers, e.g. Tinklin & Weatherley, 1968; Lang & Gardner, 1970).

Leaf mesophyll resistance increases with water deficit (Pospíšilová, 1970). The total calculated plant resistance was found to decrease with increasing water flux (Janes, 1970; Stoker & Weatherley, 1971; Barrs, 1973) apparently because of changes in root resistance. An abrupt decrease in leaf water potential was found to be a probable result of higher local resistance between stem xylem and petiole xylem (Begg & Turner, 1970). Boyer (1969) estimated the ratio of resistances in root, stem and leaf of sunflower to be about 2:1:1. On the other hand, Passioura (1972) reported that increasing the total root xylem resistance of wheat plants by leaving only one seminal root had a favourable influence on yield in plants growing on stored soil water. He also found surprisingly high pressure gradients in roots (0.03–0.1 bar mm^{-1}).

Thus we may conclude that leaf water deficit is caused by the existence of resistances to liquid water flux in the pathways of water supply and is determined primarily by these resistances and by the transpiration rate.

Water deficit and photosynthetic carbon dioxide uptake

The dependence of photosynthetic CO_2 uptake on water deficit was reconfirmed in recent years. Thus Suzuki, Kaneko & Torikata (1969) found a high negative correlation between saturation water deficit and net photosynthesis in Satsuma orange trees. A linear relationship was found between relative growth rate and stomatal resistance in beans (Kanemasu & Tanner, 1969). In *Pinus contorta* seedlings net photosynthetic CO_2 uptake was reduced as soil water potential was lowered to -3 bar and ceased entirely at -9 bar (Morris & Tranquillini, 1969). A distinct relationship between the relative water content of soybean leaves (measured by the beta gauge technique) and net photosynthesis was found by Chen, Mederski & Curry (1971). Ghorashy *et al.* (1971) found highly significant correlations between net photosynthesis and leaf water potential of soybean (measured by the pressure chamber technique). These correlations were different in different ontogenetic stages. A linear relationship between photosynthesis (and respiration) in *Pinus silvestris* seedlings and soil moisture content was described by Schultz & Gatherum (1971). On the other hand, Kaul & Crowle (1971) found no significant correlation between either leaf water potential or stomatal conductivity, and dry matter production in wheat varieties.

Generally there are two main groups of processes in photosynthesis: the first group is involved in CO_2 transfer from the bulk atmosphere above the plant surface to the carboxylation centres in the chloroplasts of photosynthesizing tissues. Here the problem is the relationship between the CO_2 flux rate, the CO_2 concentration gradients as the driving force of the CO_2 flux, and the resistance to CO_2 transport along the pathway. The second group (which will be dealt with later) is involved in biochemical processes of photosynthesis, rather than in CO_2 transport.

A part of the pathway of CO_2 influx is common with that of the water vapour efflux: transfer in the boundary air layer adhering to the leaf surface (boundary-layer diffusive resistance r_a), diffusion in air through the stomatal apertures (stomatal diffusive resistance, r_s) and across the mesophyll intercellular spaces (internal diffusive resistance r_i). These parts of the pathway are in the gaseous phase, the diffusion of CO_2 and water vapour being also determined by their diffusion coefficients in air or their empirical relationship. The remaining portions of the pathway are in the liquid phase and differ for CO_2 and for water. Very often all resistances to CO_2 (or its dissolved forms) in the liquid phase

513

are summarily treated as an intracellular resistance, r_m, which because of the methodological approach, may also include a component corresponding to part of the biochemical photosynthetic processes.

Water deficit and stomatal resistance

Changes in stomatal resistance are the most obvious mechanism by which leaf water deficits affect photosynthetic CO_2 uptake in higher plants. Stomatal aperture increases, i.e. stomatal resistance decreases, when turgor pressure of the guard cells sufficiently exceeds turgor pressure of the neighbouring epidermal cells (see also Koeppner, 1970). Light-induced increase in turgor of guard cells is primarily due to water uptake which results from a decrease in osmotic potential brought about by ATP-dependent intake of cations, mostly K^+ (Fischer, 1968; Sawhney & Zelitch, 1969; Willmer & Mansfield, 1969; Humble & Hsiao, 1970; Humble & Raschke, 1971; Pallas & Dilley, 1972), and only in the second place by synthesis of soluble carbohydrate in the guard cells themselves (Shaw & Maclachlan, 1954; Mansfield & Willmer, 1969). These are the hydroactive and photoactive movements respectively of the guard cells.

A passive (hydropassive) closure of stomata is caused by excess turgor in epidermal cells, which thus mechanically press the guard cells together. This is expressed by a decrease of net photosynthesis in fully water-saturated leaves, as observed for instance in kale (Čatský, 1965). The direct sensitivity of stomatal closure to air humidity (closure with dry air) found by Lange, Lösch, Schulze & Kappen (1971) and by Schulze *et al.* (1972) suggests a possible feedback regulation of stomatal transpiration due to a local, peristomatal transpiration (Seybold, 1961–2) by guard cells and subsidiary cells. Such decrease in water potential (turgor pressure) of the guard cells is brought about by transpiration loss coupled with an insufficient water supply, due on the one hand to the hydraulic isolation of the guard cells by subjacent subepidermal intercellular spaces and on the other hand to the high resistance to liquid water transport in the epidermis. This peristomatal decrease in turgor potential would induce closure even before water potential of the leaf mesophyll decreased. This feedback control of transpiration flux forms a water vapour parallel to the CO_2 feedback suggested by Raschke (1966). Even the thermoactive closure of stomata due to the increase in temperature in a given range (Whiteman & Koller, 1964, 1967; Hofstra & Hesketh, 1969; Schulze, Lange & Koch, 1972) may be associated with water relations. Wuenscher & Kozlowski

\(1971) calculated that the experimentally found increase in total resistance to water vapour diffusion with rising leaf temperature between 20 °C and 40 °C (*Quercus, Acer*) compensates to a high degree for the increase in the leaf/air water vapour gradient resulting from increased leaf temperature.

Kanemasu & Tanner (1969) found a linear relationship between turgor potential and stomatal conductance (see Fig. 23.6), while Turner (p. 693) reports a curvilinear dependence of leaf resistance on turgor

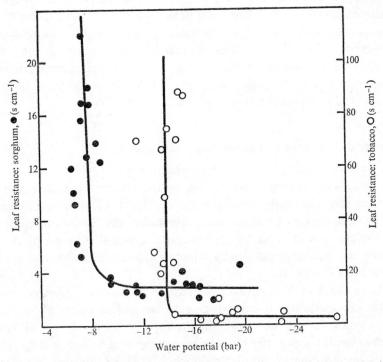

Fig. 23.1. Dependence of leaf resistance in sorghum and tobacco on leaf water potential in field conditions (Turner, see p. 693).

potential as well as on total water potential in sorghum and tobacco (Fig. 23.1). Čatský, Chartier & Djavanchir (1973), working with maize under field conditions, found a hysteresis loop in the dependence of stomatal resistance on the water saturation deficit over a twenty-four-hour period, which interfered with photoactive changes of the stomatal aperture. These discrepancies are probably due to non-equilibrium versus equilibrium situations during the changes of water deficit in leaves.

Induced periodic changes in stomatal aperture, detected mostly indirectly by gas exchange measurement in leaves of many plants (review by Barrs, 1971, and also in Hopmans, 1971) may also be used when looking for the dependence between stomatal resistance and net photosynthetic CO_2 uptake (e.g. Troughton, 1969; Kriedemann, 1971). Two types of oscillations may be distinguished (Apel, 1967; Raschke, 1967; Barrs, 1971): (1) water-based cycling with longer periods of cycle (10 to 50 min) induced mostly by rapid changes in air humidity and hence by rapid changes in leaf water content, and (2) CO_2-based cycling with periods of 2–5 min, mostly induced by a change in CO_2 concentration, or a short interval of darkness. Water-based oscillations were observed to be often in phase (synchronous) throughout the whole plant. Such oscillations, which result in pronounced cyclic changes in photosynthetic CO_2 uptake may represent a special influence of water stress in photosynthesis even under field conditions.

Water deficit and intracellular resistances

The role of stomatal resistance in photosynthesis has to some extent been over-emphasized, probably due to a more direct correlation of the transpiration rate with stomatal aperture. But it is just these differences in the dependence of transpiration rate and of net photosynthetic rates on the changes of stomatal aperture, that prove that stomatal closure is not the only mechanism by which water deficit influences photosynthetic CO_2 uptake.

As far back as 1951, Scarth & Shaw found that at equivalent porometer conductivities (corresponding to equivalent stomatal aperture) photosynthetic rate was lower in the rapidly wilting leaves of *Pelargonium* (with temporarily reopened stomata) than in non-wilting leaves (with open stomata). Similarly Souchon (1971) found an increase in transpiration rate connected with a decrease in photosynthetic rate when the wilting leaves of *Cardamine pratensis* reopened their stomata. Boyer (1965) found an unchanged transpiration rate with decreased CO_2 uptake after the addition of salt to the root medium of cotton. Shimshi (1963) observed a non-parallel decrease of the photosynthetic and transpiration rates of maize as soil moisture content was lowered.

On the other hand, Barrs (1968) found a direct correlation between net photosynthesis and transpiration, indirectly correlated with the relative water content of the leaves of sunflower, pepper and cotton during oscillations of stomatal aperture.

516

The greatest role in this respect is ascribed to the resistance to CO_2 in liquid phase, a resistance which is usually summarized as intracellular (mesophyll) resistance, r_m. This is often calculated as the residual resistance, after subtracting the boundary-layer and stomatal resistances (computed from transpiration, or evaporation rates respectively, and the water vapour concentration gradient). Hence this intracellular resistance includes not only the transport resistances of carbon dioxide in the liquid phase from the mesophyll cell wall to the carboxylation centres in its chloroplasts, but also the reaction rates of biochemical pathways of photosynthesis, expressed, not quite consistently, in terms of transfer resistance.

In order to estimate the participation of intracellular resistance in CO_2 transfer, it is necessary to eliminate the stomatal (and boundary layer) resistances or to keep them constant. One possibility is to use plant material without stomata:

In leaf discs of *Valerianella locusta* var. *oleracea* with stripped epidermis, Bertsch (1967) found a 50% decrease in net photosynthetic rate at a water potential even as low as −69 bar and a 90% decrease at −190 bar (when compared with full saturation). These results were comparable with data obtained in the crustaceous lichen *Evernia prunastri*.

The results found in lower green plants must, however, be treated with some caution if they are to be applied as analogous to the conditions in higher plants. In the aerophilic green alga *Apatococcus lobatus* net photosynthesis decreased to 50% of the rate at full water saturation at the low water potential of −152 bar, and stopped at −520 bar (Bertsch, 1966). Lichens are capable of maintaining active CO_2 exchange down to very low water content values: net photosynthesis of the desert lichen *Ramalina maciformis* was positive down to 18% relative water content, respiration ceasing at about 16% relative water content (Lange & Bertsch, 1965). In fruticose lichens (*Cladonia, Cetraria, Cornicularia*) photosynthesis and respiration were positive during water vapour uptake, starting with the low water content of 10–25% and 5–15%, respectively, of values at full saturation and were almost unaffected by water content between those two extremes (Büttner, 1971). Photosynthetic rate of the hepatic *Conocephalum conicum* was found to be linearly proportional to the osmotic potential in the range from 100% down to 20% relative water content (Slavík, 1965).

In the poikiolhydrous fern with stomata, *Polypodium polypodioides*, Stuart (1968) found net photosynthesis to be inversely linearly proportional to the relative water content in the range from 20–100%.

Troughton & Slatyer (1969) found no effect of relative water content (in the range 56–92%) on mesophyll resistance of cotton leaves in oxygen-free air. Meidner (1962,1967) and Heath & Meidner (1961) described an increase in the CO_2 compensation points in maize, wheat and *Phoenix reclinata* leaves with water deficit induced by immersing petioles in mannitol solutions.

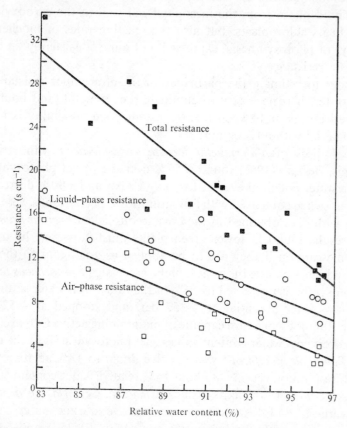

Fig. 23.2. Relationship between relative water content and the total, liquid-phase and air-phase resistance in tobacco leaves (Redshaw & Meidner, 1972).

Comparing maize and soybean, Boyer (1970*a*) found that while the sum of leaf resistances to CO_2 increased progressively with the decreasing water potential of leaves, intracellular resistance was much less affected.

Redshaw & Meidner (1972) found that gaseous phase resistance in *Nicotiana tabacum* leaves was small in proportion to the residual resistance at high relative water content and rose to about 45% with decreasing relative water content (Fig. 23.2). The authors conclude that the reduction in net photosynthetic CO_2 uptake with decrease in relative water content of the leaf is most probably due to an increase in biochemical components of the intracellular resistance.

In *Citrus sinensis*, Kriedemann (1971) induced changes in the measured leaf resistance to CO_2, either by water deficit, or by induced oscillations of stomatal aperture. At low resistance values (< 10 s cm^{-1}) the ratio of transpiration to net photosynthesis decreased with stomatal closure, thus indicating a looser dependence of transpiration that of net photosynthesis on stomatal aperture, whereas at high resistances (> 10 s cm^{-1}) transpiration and net photosynthesis were linearly dependent. Nevertheless a high positive correlation was found between r_m and total leaf resistance.

Okanenko, Gulyaev & Manuilskii (1969) found in sugar beet leaves that up to a water saturation deficit of 30%, stomatal resistance was slightly increased, to about 4 s cm^{-1}, while intracellular resistance remained almost unchanged, ranging between 5 and 10 s cm^{-1}, but both resistances increased sharply with further increase in water saturation deficit. Gloser (p. 693) reports an increase in the average stomatal resistance and a simultaneous decrease in the intracellular resistance in grasses grown under soil water stress.

It may be concluded that the problem of the relative contribution of stomatal and intracellular resistances to CO_2 transport during water stress is still far from being solved. Most results indicate that low water deficit has some slight effect on intracellular resistance which, even in higher plants, does not become high until the relative water content (or the water potential) is very low.

Water deficit and biochemical processes in photosynthesis

As far as carboxylation is concerned, part of the dependence of biochemical processes in photosynthesis on water stress is included in the value of intracellular resistance, although separable as carboxylation resistance r_x by the procedure described by Chartier (1966,1972) and by Chartier, Chartier & Čatský (1970). The influence of water deficit on this carboxylation resistance has not yet been studied.

Santarius (1967), Santarius & Heber (1967) and Santarius & Ernst (1967) found when working with either isolated chloroplasts or leaf lamina segments that ATP (adenosine triphosphate) synthesis, the

519

reduction of NADP (nicotinamide adenine dinucleotide phosphate) and that of PGA (phosphoglyceric acid) were decreased only at a very high water deficit (relative water content of leaves less than 50%). Boyer & Bowen (1970) determined oxygen evolution in chloroplasts isolated from leaves of pea and sunflower under a water stress. Oxygen evolution was decreased by previous water potentials of below −12 bar (pea) and −8 bar (sunflower) and was linearly proportional to previous water potential below these values (Fig. 23.3). The authors conclude from the parallel measurement of photosynthetic rate in intact leaves, that a moderate decrease of leaf water potential also affects photosynthesis by the inhibition of oxygen evolution, in addition to the known effect of stomatal closure.

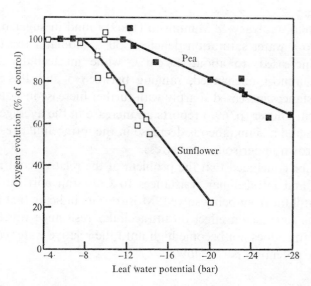

Fig. 23.3. Oxygen evolution by pea and sunflower chloroplasts isolated from leaf tissue desiccated immediately prior to isolation to various water potentials (Boyer & Bowen, 1970).

A pronounced decrease in photosynthesis during desiccation was observed in mosses (Lee & Stewart, 1971; Hinshiri & Proctor, 1971). It was therefore surprising that Stewart & Lee (1972) found only a very small decrease in the activity of ten enzymes studied in one of these species (*Acrocladium cuspidatum*). It was suggested that the decline in photosynthesis may be explained in part by the oxidation of sulfhydril residues essential for the catalytic activity of the NADP+–glyceraldehyde 3-phosphate dehydrogenase.

A relevant question is whether there are any differences between C_3- and C_4-plants with respect to their sensitivity to water stress. Laetsch (1968) suggested that plants with the C_4-pathway may be less sensitive to periods of desiccation. Slatyer (1970) compared two species of *Atriplex: A. spongiosa* (C_4) and *A. hastata* (C_3). Net photosynthetic CO_2 uptake was higher in the C_4-species, which also had a higher stomatal resistance (1.0 to 2.6 s cm^{-1} in comparison to 0.7 to 0.8 s cm^{-1} in the C_3-species), a lower transpiration rate and hence a higher water-use efficiency. The C_4-species had lower intracellular resistance (0.4–1.5 s cm^{-1} in comparison to 2.5–2.9 s cm^{-1} in the C_3-species). Boyer (1970*a*) found that in soybean (a C_3-plant) net photosynthesis was not decreased until leaf water potential dropped down to -10 to -11 bar, while in maize (a C_4-plant), this critical value was -3.5 bar. With a further decrease to leaf water potential, net photosynthesis decreased in parallel with increasing stomatal resistance to -16 bar (soybean) and -10 bar (maize). It may be concluded that maize, in spite of having (even during desiccation) a higher absolute rate of photosynthesis, was more sensitive to decreased leaf water potential than soybean.

Recovery of photosynthesis after water deficit

Recovery depends primarily on the degree of the preceding deficit. If this deficit was too high, incomplete recovery may be expected, as far as water content is concerned. The resaturation deficits may be expressed either as the difference in relative water content after resaturation and at full saturation previous to the deficit (Rychnovská, 1967), or as the analogous difference in water potential (Weinberger, Romero & Oliva, 1972).

A temporary after-effect on photosynthesis was found even after full recovery from a smaller deficit that was not accompanied by any resaturation deficits. Fischer (1970) and Fischer, Hsiao & Hagan (1970) describe a slow recovery of stomatal opening after the closure due to water stress. Similar results were obtained by Boyer (1971). Photosynthetic CO_2 uptake in leaves of sunflower in high irradiance (where stomata seem to be the limiting factor) did not fully recover from a water deficit of -12 bar for one to two days after resaturation (Fig. 23.4), while in low irradiance the photosynthetic rate recovered completely even after a decrease of leaf water potential to -17 bar. (Water potential recovered after a decrease to -15 bar.)

An analogy may also be found in experiments with mitochondria

521

and/or chloroplasts isolated from plants with a water deficit. Though the isolation procedure itself equalizes their hydration, an after-effect of previous dehydration may be experimentally proved. As an example, the results of Boyer & Bowen (1970) could be mentioned again.

Ziegler & Vieweg (see Walter & Kreeb, 1970) described a rapid recovery of photosynthetic CO_2 uptake after rehydration in the poikilo-hydrous desert shrub *Myrothamnus flabellifolia*, which had previously been completely desiccated. Most poikilohydrous higher plants (i.e. plants the hydration of which changes over a wide range according to the humidity conditions of the habitat, and are capable of reviving even after a long period of 'complete' desiccation) have a common feature: central vacuoles which solidify when dehydrated.

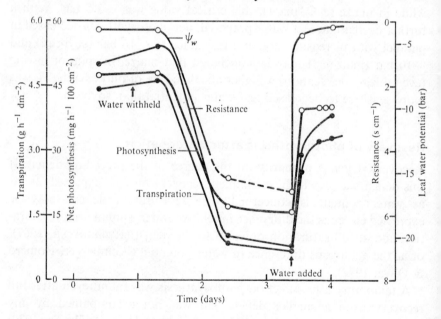

Fig. 23.4. Recovery of photosynthetic and transpiration rates, resistance (cube root of the time lapse in a pressure-drop porometer measurement) and leaf water potential after desiccation to −16 bar water potential in sunflower leaves (Boyer, 1971).

An extreme example of photosynthetic activity during high water stress was described by Kappen *et al.* (1972) in the desert plant *Artemisia herba-alba* during the dry season. With morning values of xylem pressure potential around −100 bar and an osmotic potential of xylem sap −50 bar, it was still photosynthetically active for two hours in the morning.

522

Leaf water deficit and growth

The term growth is here used collectively for the different processes
resulting in an enlargement of the plant which is directly connected with
the results of photosynthetic activity.

Water deficit causes surprisingly rapid changes in cell microstructure,
primarily in membrane ultrastructures (endoplasmic reticulum, membranes of mitochondria), and causes disintegration of the polysomes
(Hsiao, 1970). It is supposed (Nir, Poljakoff-Mayber & Klein, 1970)
that loss of messenger RNA synthesis is one of the first results of water
stress, leading to a decrease of amino acid incorporation after the
disintegration of polysomes. Interruption of protein synthesis is a very
general result of water stress. While DNA synthesis was found to be
significantly reduced only at severe water stress, levels of RNA were
lowered even at smaller water deficits, probably due more to accelerated
degradation than to a slower synthesis rate. An increase of proline
content by water stress (Pálfi & Juhász, 1971; Gates, Williams & Court,
1971) has been suggested as a test of water stress resistance (Pálfi &
Juhász, 1971).

Cell division is very sensitive to water deficit. Terry, Waldron &
Ulrich (1971) found a very high sensitivity in mitotic activity in the leaf
tissue of *Beta vulgaris*. Initiation and differentiation of leaf primordia
are also influenced by relatively small water deficits. There is some
evidence that mitotic activity is resumed very quickly when water stress
is removed.

Extension growth also seems to be very sensitive to internal water
deficit. It has been frequently suggested that it is the decrease of the
turgor component of water potential which is responsible for the
depression of cell enlargement (Lockhart, 1965; Oertli, 1968,1969;
Lawlor, 1970). Wardlaw (1969) found similar sensitivity for both
extension growth and photosynthesis in leaves of *Lolium temulentum*.
A decrease in extension growth even with a very small depression of
leaf water potential was found by Hsiao, Acevedo & Henderson (1970).
Boyer (1968) compared the sensitivity of leaf growth (extension
growth) to lowered leaf water potential in sunflower, tomato, papaya
and *Abutilon*, and suggested that extension growth is more sensitive
than photosynthetic CO_2 uptake. In his recent paper, Boyer (1970*b*)
confirmed this opinion by further experimental data on maize, soybean
and sunflower. Leaf enlargement (measured in plants transferred for
24 h in a dark humid chamber) was strongly inhibited by a water

523

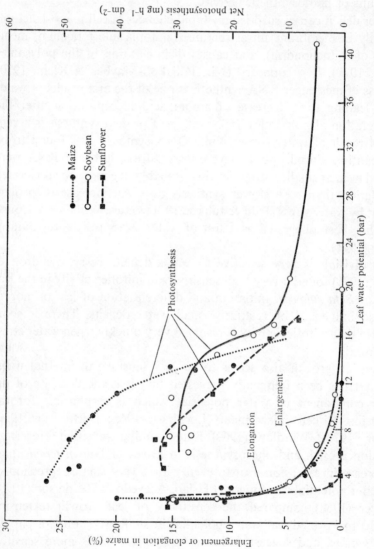

Fig. 23.5. Leaf enlargement and net photosynthesis rate of maize, soybean and sunflower at various leaf water potential (Boyer, 1970b).

potential of about −2 bar and practically stopped at values as high as −4 (sunflower) and −8 and −12 bar (maize and soybean respectively) (Fig. 23.5). The decrease in photosynthetic rate with decreasing water potential started at lower water potential values and was less steep, as did the decrease in dark respiration. Taking into account the values of osmotic potential in well watered plants, the minimal turgor values for extension growth were 7, 1 and 6 bar in maize, soybean and sunflower, respectively.

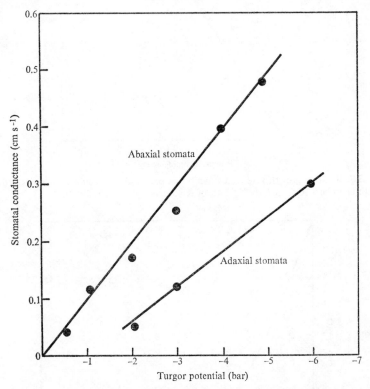

Fig. 23.6. Average stomatal conductance of bean leaves as a function of leaf turgor pressure under field conditions (Gardner, 1973; data of Kanemasu & Tanner, 1969).

Kanemasu & Tanner (1969) measured the relationship between relative growth rate and leaf water potential of snap beans in a growth chamber. Zero relative growth rate was found at about −12 bar with a probable maximum growth at zero (?) water potential.

Three growth characteristics (net assimilation rate, relative growth rate and relative leaf growth rate) in maize, bean, cotton and *Lolium perenne* decreased with the decreasing osmotic potential of the root

525

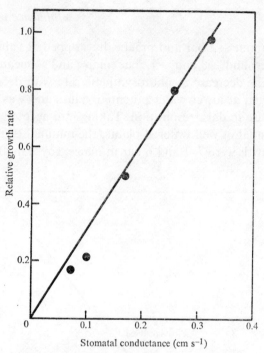

Fig. 23.7. Relative growth rate as a function of stomatal conductance in beans grown in growth chambers (Gardner, 1973; data of Kanemasu & Tanner, 1969).

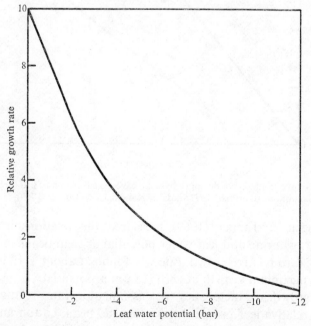

Fig. 23.8. Relative growth rate as a function of leaf water potential in beans grown in growth chambers (Gardner, 1973; data of Kanemasu & Tanner, 1969).

medium (polyethylene glycols added). A slight decrease in leaf water potential resulted in subsequent partial adaptation: the increase in growth was connected with increased turgor pressure (Lawlor, 1970).

The influence of water stress on growth is usually more pronounced in rapidly growing tissues (Slatyer, 1969,1973). This is probably the rationale for studying the so-called sensitive periods in the ontogeny of crops.

The influence of water stress on growth is an important factor in photosynthesis, since it determines the quantity and ontogenetical quality of the area of photosynthesizing surfaces. The plastochron, the relative leaf area of subsequently developing leaves, their senescence and replacement, all affect the photosynthetic productivity of the total plant leaf area.

General remarks on the mechanisms of the influence of water stress

Although great efforts have often been made to find out the mechanism by which water deficit affects different physiological processes and their components, not much is yet known.

In recent years there has been discussion as to whether it is the water potential of the cell, or its osmotic, or matric, component that is the factor of hydration of colloidal protoplasmic ultrastructures co-determining the enzymatic activity in the cell. According to Walter & Kreeb (1970), the relative degree of imbibition of protoplasmic structures – being equivalent to their matric potential, which, in turn (in vacuolated cells in equilibrium), is always equal to the osmotic potential in the vacuole – is independent of the superimposed turgor pressure. It may therefore be expressed by the osmotic potential or relative water vapour pressure (Walter's term 'Hydratur'). Results of Flowers & Hanson (1969) support this idea, showing that the enzymatic activity of isolated mitochondria was not influenced by the changes of hydrostatic pressure. Opponents of this view assume that it is the chemical potential of water, which is pressure-dependent, that is the physiologically effective factor resulting from hydration.

As far as the general biochemical activity of cellular protoplasmic ultrastructures is concerned, direct experimental proofs are still lacking. Total water potential or its individual components (osmotic, matric and pressure potentials) may play different roles insofar as they affect different physiological processes: There is no doubt that it is the total

527

water potential which decides the water transport phenomena in the plant, although in some cases it may be only its component (e.g. pressure in xylem conducting elements).

It is highly probable that it is the turgor pressure (the pressure component of water potential) which directly influences extension growth, at least its mechanical component, and probably affects cell division as well. Turgor pressure is certainly the last immediate cause of stomatal opening or closing, and the chief factor in the mechanical support of the plant body.

Cell osmotic potential is no doubt a measure of the not easily measurable cytoplasmic matric potential in equilibrium with it within the protoplast, but not of the matric potential in the cell wall. According to Walter and also Oertli (1968,1969) it is a measure of protein hydration. In some cases it is not the potential but the gradient (or difference) in potential which is responsible, as for instance in the guard cells.

Conclusions

It is obvious that water deficit decreases photosynthetic CO_2 uptake by limiting CO_2 transport to the chloroplasts in the gaseous phase and in the liquid phase, and by restricting the biochemical activity in the chloroplasts. The relative importance of these limiting factors, usually summed up in the form of transport resistance (including the biochemical 'resistances' of carboxylation and excitation), changes at different water deficit levels.

Although the mechanism controlling stomatal aperture is fairly well understood, stomatal movement in response to external factors such as light, CO_2 and water vapour pressure, and to internal factors, including feedback and interactions, is extremely complex. Hydroactive and hydropassive changes in stomatal aperture and hence changes in stomatal resistance may therefore be obscured by other factors. Nevertheless, stomatal resistance generally seems to change fairly linearly with decrease in leaf water potential, probably more directly with the turgor potential pressure component, or with the turgor pressure difference between guard and surrounding epidermal cells. This means that stomatal resistance is exponentially increasing with increasing water saturation deficit.

At low values of water deficit the dependence of intracellular resistance (including biochemical resistances) in leaf water deficit was found not to be steep in most cases. This is in good agreement with direct measurement of photosynthetic activity in water-stressed chloroplasts and in material lacking stomata, which was substantially decreased only at very low values of water potential. Intracellular resistance, including the biochemical components, is usually from three to about ten times as high as simultaneous values of stomatal resistance at mild water deficits. C_4-plants were found to have relatively lower intracellular resistance, which resulted in higher photosynthetic CO_2 uptake in spite of a higher mean stomatal resistance.

The overall photosynthesis of plants is also strongly determined by growth. Both mitotic activity and extension growth seem to be very sensitive to water deficit. Growth decreases even at very low levels of water deficit, probably depending on turgor pressure, but is mostly resumed very rapidly after rehydration. This feature seems to be very general and very significant, as recovery after a more severe water deficit often depends on ability to form new leaves and shoots, respectively.

Evaluation of the influence of water stress on plant photosynthetic production is generally very complex, especially owing to the long chain of individual relationships which are involved. Even if the individual relationships were quantitatively known with reasonable precision, we would scarcely be able to formulate a general statement of the overall relationship. Nevertheless, the time has probably come to try to determine such chains of empirical relationships in some plant species, in the form of logical models which would enable us to formulate questions more precisely. Gardner (1973) made an extremely interesting attempt to follow quantitatively the causal chain of relationships starting with the soil/leaf water potential gradient, the water flux through the plant, leaf water and turgor potentials, stomatal conductivity and ending with the relative growth rate. Some of the resulting relationships (based mainly on the paper by Kanemasu & Tanner, 1969) are shown in Figs. 23.6, 23.7 and 23.8. The procedure exemplified by Gardner may serve as a stimulating example in this field.

References

Apel, P. (1967). Über rhythmisch verlaufende Änderungen in der CO_2-Aufnahme von Blättern. *Berichte der Deutschen botanischen Gesellschaft*, **80**, 3–9.

Barrs, H. D. (1968). Effect of cyclic variations in gas exchange under constant environmental conditions on the ratio of transpiration to net photosynthesis. *Physiologia Plantarum*, **21**, 918–29.

529

s*

Barrs, H. D. (1971). Cyclic variations in stomatal aperture, transpiration, and leaf water potential under constant environmental conditions. *Annual Review of Plant Physiology*, **22**, 223–36.

Barrs, H. D. (1973). Controlled environment studies of the effects of variable atmospheric water stress on photosynthesis, transpiration and water status of *Zea mays* L. and other species. In *Plant Response to Climatic Factors*, ed. R. O. Slatyer, pp. 249–58. Paris, UNESCO.

Begg, J. E. & Turner, N. C. (1970). Water potential gradients in field tobacco. *Plant Physiology*, **46**, 343–6.

Bertsch, A. (1966). CO₂-Gaswechsel und Wasserhaushalt der aerophilen Grünalge *Apatococcus lobatus*. *Planta*, **70**, 46–72.

Bertsch, A. (1967). CO₂-Gaswechsel, Wasserpotential und Sättigungsdefizit bei der Antrockung epidermisfreier Blattscheiben von *Valerianella*. *Naturwissenschaften*, **54**, 204.

Boyer, J. S. (1965). Effects of osmotic water stress on metabolic rates of cotton plants with open stomata. *Plant Physiology*, **40**, 229–34.

Boyer, J. S. (1968). Relationship of water potential to growth of leaves. *Plant Physiology*, **43**, 1056–62.

Boyer, J. S. (1969). Free-energy transfer in plants. *Science*, **163**, 1219–20.

Boyer, J. S. (1970*a*). Differing sensitivity of photosynthesis to low leaf water potentials in corn soybean. *Plant Physiology*, **46**, 236–9.

Boyer, J. S. (1970*b*). Leaf enlargement and metabolic rates in corn, soybean, and sunflower at various leaf water potentials. *Plant Physiology*, **46**, 233–5.

Boyer, J. S. (1971). Recovery of photosynthesis in sunflower after a period of low leaf water potential. *Plant Physiology*, **47**, 816–20.

Boyer, J. S. & Bowen, B. L. (1970). Inhibition of oxygen evolution in chloroplasts isolated from leaves with low water potentials. *Plant Physiology*, **45**, 612–15.

Büttner, R. (1971). Untersuchungen zur Ökologie und Physiologie des Gasstoffwechsels bei einigen Strauchflechten. *Flora*, **160**, 72–99.

Čatský, J. (1965). Water saturation deficit and photosynthetic rate as related to leaf age in the wilting plant. In *Water Stress in Plants*, ed. B. Slavík, pp. 203–9. The Hague, Junk.

Čatský, J., Chartier, P. & Djavanchir, A. (1973). Assimilation nette, utilisation de l'eau et microclimat d'un champ de mais. IV. Evolution diurne de la résistance stomatique et du déficit de saturation des feuilles: conséquences sur la fixation du CO₂. *Annales agronomiques*, **24**, 287–305.

Chartier, P. (1966). Étude théorique de l'assimilation brute de la feuille. *Annales de Physiologie végetale*, **8**, 167–95.

Chartier, P. (1972). Net assimilation of plants as influenced by light and carbon dioxide. In *Crop Processes in Controlled Environments*, eds. A. R. Rees, K. E. Cockhull, D. W. Hand & R. G. Hurd, pp. 203–16. New York, Academic Press.

Chartier, P., Chartier, M. & Čatský, J. (1970). Resistances for carbon dioxide diffusion and for carboxylation as factors in bean leaf photosynthesis. *Photosynthetica*, **4**, 48–57.

Chen, L. H., Mederski, H. J. & Curry, R. Bruce (1971). Water stress effects on photosynthesis and stem diameter in soybean plants. *Crop Science*, **11**, 428–31.

Crafts, A. S. (1968). Water deficits and physiological processes. In *Water Deficits and Plant Growth*, ed. T. T. Kozlowski, vol. 2, pp. 85–133. New York, Academic Press.

Fischer, R. A. (1968). Stomatal opening: role of potassium uptake by guard cells. *Science*, **160**, 784–5.

Fischer, R. A. (1970). After-effect of water stress on stomatal opening potential. II. Possible causes. *Journal of Experimental Botany*, **21**, 386–404.

Fischer, R. A., Hsiao, T. C. & Hagan, R. M. (1970). After-effect of water stress on stomatal opening potential. I. Techniques and magnitude. *Journal of Experimental Botany*, **21**, 371–85.

Flowers, T. J. & Hanson, J. B. (1969). The effect of reduced water potential on soybean mitochondria. *Plant Physiology*, **44**, 939–45.

Gardner, W. R. (1973). Internal water status and response in relation to the external water regime of plants. In *Plant response to climatic factors*, ed. R. O. Slatyer, pp. 221–5. Paris, UNESCO.

Gates, C. T., Williams, W. T. & Court, R. D. (1971). Effect of droughting and chilling on maturation and chemical composition of Townsville stylo (*Stylosanthes humilis*). *Australian Journal of Agricultural Research*, **22**, 369–81.

Ghorashy, S. R., Pendleton, J. W., Peters, D. B., Boyer, J. S. & Beuerlein, J. E. (1971). Internal water stress and apparent photosynthesis with soybeans differing in pubescence. *Agronomy Journal*, **63**, 674–6.

Gradmann, H. (1928). Untersuchungen über die Wasserverhältnisse des Bodens als Grundlage des Pflanzenwachstums. *Jahrbuch für wissenschaftliche Botanik*, **69**, 1–100.

Heath, O. V. S. & Meidner, H. (1961). The influence of water strain on the minimum intercellular space CO_2 concentration, Γ, and stomatal movement in wheat leaves. *Journal of Experimental Botany*, **12**, 226–42.

Hinshiri, H. M. & Proctor, M. C. F. (1971). The effect of desiccation on subsequent assimilation and respiration of the bryophytes *Anomodon viticulosus* and *Porella platyphilla*. *New Phytologist*, **70**, 527–38.

Hofstra, G. & Hesketh, J. D. (1969). The effect of temperature on stomatal aperture in different species. *Canadian Journal of Botany*, **47**, 1307–10.

van den Honert, T. H. (1948). Water transport in plants as a catenary process. *Discussions of Faraday Society*, **3**, 146–53.

Hopmans, P. A. M. (1971). Rhythms in stomatal opening of bean leaves. *Mededelingen Landbouwhogeschool Wageningen*, **71**-3, 1-86.

Hsiao, T. C. (1970). Rapid change in levels of polyribosomes in *Zea mays* in response to water stress. *Plant Physiology*, **46**, 281–5.

Hsiao, T. C., Acevedo, E. & Henderson, D. W. (1970). Maize leaf elongation: continuous measurements and close dependence on plant water status. *Science*, **168**, 590–1.

Humble, G. D. & Hsiao, T. C. (1970). Light-dependent influx of potassium of guard cells during stomatal opening and closing. *Plant Physiology*, **46**, 483–7.

Humble, G. D. & Raschke, K. (1971). Stomatal opening quantitatively related to potassium transport. *Plant Physiology*, **48**, 447–53.

Janes, B. E. (1970). Effect of carbon dioxide, osmotic potential of nutrient solution, and light intensity on transpiration and resistance to flow of water in pepper plants. *Plant Physiology*, **45**, 95–103.

Jordan, W. R. & Ritchie, J. T. (1971). Influence of soil water stress on evaporation, root absorption, and internal water status of cotton. *Plant Physiology*, **48**, 783–8.

Kanemasu, E. T. & Tanner, C. B. (1969). Stomatal diffusion resistance of snap beans. I. Effect of leaf water potential. *Plant Physiology*, **44**, 1547–52.

Kappen, L., Lange, O. L., Schulze, E.-D., Evenari, M. & Buschbom, U. (1972). Extreme water stress and photosynthetic activity of the desert plant *Artemisia herba-alba* Asso. *Oecologia*, **10**, 177–82.

Kaul, R. & Crowle, W. L. (1971). Relations between water status, leaf temperature, stomatal aperture, and productivity of some wheat varieties. *Zeitschrift für Pflanzenzüchtung*, **65**, 233–43.

Koeppner, T. (1970). Osmotische Gradienten in der Epidermis in Verlauf der Spaltöffnungsbewegung. *Protoplasma*, **69**, 389–403.

Kriedemann, P. E. (1971). Photosynthesis and transpiration as a function of gaseous diffusive resistances in orange leaves. *Physiologia Plantarum*, **24**, 218–25.

Laetsch, W. M. (1968). Chloroplast specialization in dicotyledons possessing the C_4-dicarboxylic acid pathway of photosynthetic CO_2 fixation. *American Journal of Botany*, **55**, 875–83.

Lang, A. R. G. & Gardner, W. R. (1970). Limitation to water flux from soils to plants. *Agronomy Journal*, **62**, 693–5.

Lange, O. L. & Bertsch, A. (1965). Photosynthese der Wüstenflechte *Ramalina maciformis* nach Wasserdampfaufnahme aus dem Luftraum. *Naturwissenschaften*, **52**, 215–6.

Lange, O. L., Lösch, R., Schulze, E.-D. & Kappen, L. (1971). Responses of stomata to changes in humidity. *Planta*, **100**, 76–86.

Lawlor, D. W. (1970). Absorption of polyethylene glycols by plants and their effects on plant growth. *New Phytologist*, **69**, 501–13.

Lee, J. A. & Stewart, G. R. (1971). Desiccation injury in mosses. I. Intraspecific difference in the effect of moisture stress. *New Phytologist*, **70**, 1061.

Lockhart, J. A. (1965). Cell extension. In *Plant Biochemistry*, eds. J. Bonner & J. E. Varner, pp. 826–49. New York, Academic Press.

Mansfield, T. A. & Willmer, C. M. (1969). Stomatal responses to light and carbon dioxide in the hart's-tongue fern, *Phyllitis scolopendrium* Newm. *New Phytologist*, **68**, 63–6.

Meidner, H. (1962). The minimum intercellular-space CO_2 concentration (Γ) of maize leaves and its influence on stomatal movements. *Journal of Experimental Botany*, **13**, 284–93.

Meidner, H. (1967). Further observations on the minimum intercellular space carbon dioxide concentration (*Γ*) of maize leaves and the postulated role of 'photorespiration' and glycollate metabolism. *Journal of Experimental Botany*, **18**, 177–85.

Morris, J. Y. & Tranquillini, W. (1969). Über den Einfluss des osmotischen Potentiales des Wurzelsubstrates auf die Photosynthese von *Pinus contorta*- Sämlingen im Wechsel der Jahreszeiten. *Flora*, B **158**, 277–87.

Nir, I., Poljakoff-Mayber, A. & Klein, S. (1970). The effect of water stress on the polysome population and the ability to incorporate amino acids in maize root tips. *Israel Journal of Botany*, **19**, 451–62.

Oertli, J. J. (1968). Effects of components of water potential on the water content of plant cells. *Zeitschrift für Pflanzenphysiologie*, **59**, 340–52.

Oertli, J. J. (1969). Discussion to the paper by Slatyer, R. O.: Physiological significance of internal water relations to crop yield. In *Physiological Aspects of Crop Yield*, eds. J. D. Eastin, F. A. Haskins, C. Y. Sullivan & C. H. M. Van Bavel, pp. 85–8. Madison, Wisconsin, Amer. Soc. Agron.

Okanenko, A. S., Gulyaev, B. I. & Manuilskii, V. D. (1969). Diffusive resistance for CO_2 and water vapour in a sugar-beet leaf under different water status. *Dopovidi Akademii Nauk Ukr. RSR*, **1969B**, 161–6.

Pálfi, G. & Juhász, J. (1971). The theoretical basis and practical application of a new method of selection for determining water deficiency in plants. *Plant Soil*, **34**, 503–7.

Pallas, J. E. Jr. & Dilley, R. A. (1972). Photophosphorylation can provide sufficient adenosine $5'$-triphosphate to drive K^+ movements during stomatal opening. *Plant Physiology*, **49**, 649–50.

Passioura, J. B. (1972). The effect of root geometry on the yield of wheat growing on stored water. *Australian Journal of Agricultural Research*, **23**, 745–52.

Pospíšilová, J. (1970). The relationship between the resistance to water transport and the water saturation deficit in leaf tissue of kale and tobacco. *Biologia Plantarum*, **12**, 78–80.

Pospíšilová, J. (1973). Water potential–water saturation deficit relationship during dehydration and resaturation of leaves. *Biologia Plantarum*, **15**, 290–3.

Raschke, K. (1966). Die Reaktionen des CO_2-Regelsystems in den Schliesszellen von *Zea mays* auf weisses Licht. *Planta*, **68**, 111–40.

Raschke, K. (1967). Zur Steuerung der Transpiration durch die Photosynthese. *Berichte der Deutschen botanischen Gesellschaft*, **80**, 138–44.

Raschke, K. (1970*a*). Leaf hydraulic system: rapid epidermal and stomatal responses to changes in water supply. *Science*, **167**, 189–91.

Raschke, K. (1970*b*). Stomatal responses to pressure changes and interruptions in the water supply of detached leaves of *Zea mays* L. *Plant Physiology*, **45**, 415–23.

Redshaw, A. J. & Meidner, H. (1972). Effects of water stress on the resistance to uptake of carbon dioxide in tobacco. *Journal of Experimental Botany*, **23**, 229–40.

Rychnovská, M. (1967). The relationship between sublethal water saturation deficit and the dynamics of soil moisture in some xerophilous grasses. *Biologia Plantarum*, **9**, 135–41.

Sanchez-Diaz, M. F. & Kramer, P. J. (1971). Behavior of corn and sorghum under water stress and during recovery. *Plant Physiology*, **48**, 613–6.

Santarius, K. A. (1967). Das Verhalten von CO_2-Assimilation, NADP-und PGS-Reduktion und ATP-Synthese intakter Blattzellen in Abhängigkeit vom Wassergehalt. *Planta*, **73**, 228–42.

Santarius, K. A. & Ernst, R. (1967). Das Verhalten von Hill-Reaktion und Photophosphorylierung isolierter Chloroplasten in Abhängigkeit vom Wassergehalt. I. Wasserentzug mittels konzentrierter Lösungen. *Planta*, **73**, 91–108.

Santarius, K. A. & Heber, U. (1967). Das Verhalten von Hill-Reaktion und Photophosphorylierung isolierter Chloroplasten in Abhängigkeit vom Wassergehalt. II. Wasserentzug über $CaCl_2$. *Planta*, **73**, 109–37.

Sawhney, B. L. & Zelitch, I. (1969). Direct determination of potassium ion accumulation in guard cells in relation to stomatal opening in light. *Plant Physiology*, **44**, 1350–4.

Scarth, G. W. & Shaw, M. (1951). Stomatal movement and photosynthesis in *Pelargonium*. II. Effects of water deficit and of chloroform: photosynthesis in guard-cells. *Plant Physiology*, **26**, 581–97.

Schultz, R. C. & Gatherum, G. E. (1971). Photosynthesis and distribution of assimilate of Scotch pine seedlings in relation to soil moisture and provenance. *Botanical Gazette*, **132**, 91–6.

Schulze, E.-D., Lange, O. L., Buschbom, U., Kappen, L. & Evenari, M. (1972). Stomatal responses to changes in humidity in plants growing in the desert. *Planta*, **108**, 259–70.

Schulze, E.-D., Lange, O. L. & Koch, W. (1972). Ökophysiologische Untersuchungen an Wild- und Kulturpflanzen der Negev-Wüste. II. Die Wirkung der Aussenfaktoren auf CO_2-Gaswechsel und Transpiration am Ende der Trockenzeit. *Oecologia*, **8**, 334–55.

Seybold, A. (1961/62). Ergebnisse und Probleme pflanzlicher Transpirationsanalysen. *Jahrbuch der Heidelberger Akademie der Wissenschaften*, 1961/62, pp. 5–8.

Shaw, M. & Maclachlan, G. A. (1954). The physiology of stomata. I. Carbon dioxide fixation in guard cells. *Canadian Journal of Botany*, **32**, 784–94.

Shimshi, D. (1963). Effect of soil moisture and phenylmercuric acetate upon stomatal aperture, transpiration, and photosynthesis. *Plant Physiology*, **38**, 713–21.

Slatyer, R. O. (1969). Physiological significance of internal water relations to crop yield. In *Physiological Aspects of Crop Yield*, eds. J. D. Eastin, F. A. Haskins, C. Y. Sullivan & C. H. M. Van Bavel, pp. 53–83. Madison, Wisconsin, Amer. Soc. Agron.

Slatyer, R. O. (1970). Comparative photosynthesis, growth and transpiration of two species of *Atriplex*. *Planta*, **93**, 175–89.

Slatyer, R. O. (1973). The effect of internal water status on plant growth, development and yield. In *Plant Response to Climatic Factors*, ed. R. O. Slatyer, pp. 177–91. Paris, UNESCO.

Slavík, B. (1965). The influence of decreasing hydration level on photosynthetic rate in the thalli of the hepatic *Conocephalum conicum*. In *Water Stress in Plants*, ed. B. Slavík, pp. 195–201. The Hague, Junk.

Slavík, B. (1969). Relationship between water potential and relative water content. *XI. International Botanical Congress* (Seattle, Wash.) Abstracts, 202.

Souchon, Ch. (1971). Réouverture des stomates au cours de la fanaison de feuilles coupées chez le *Cardamine pratensis* L.; relations avec la transpiration et la photosynthèse. *Comptes rendus Academie Sciences (Paris) Sér. D.* **272**, 2892–5.

Stewart, G. R. & Lee, J. A. (1972). Desiccation injury in mosses. II. The effect of moisture stress on enzyme levels. *New Phytologist*, **71**, 461–6.

Stoker, R. & Weatherley, P. E. (1971). The influence of the root system on the relationship between the rate of transpiration and depression of leaf water potential. *New Phytologist*, **70**, 547–54.

Stuart, T. S. (1968). Revival of respiration and photosynthesis in dried leaves of Polypodium polypodioides. *Planta*, **83**, 185–206.

Suzuki, T., Kaneko, M. & Torikata, H. (1969). Studies on the water balance in Satsuma orange trees. II. On the estimation methods of water saturation deficit (W.S.D.) of leaves, and the effects of soil moisture and fertilizer supply on the W.S.D. and the apparent photosynthetic rate of leaves. *Journal of Japanese Society of Horticultural Science*, **38**, 1–8.

Terry, N., Waldron, L. J. & Ulrich, A. (1971). Effects of moisture stress on the multiplication and expansion of cells in leaves of sugar beet. *Planta*, **97**, 281–9.

Tinklin, R. & Weatherley, P. E. (1968). The effect of transpiration rate on the leaf water potential of normal and soil rooted plants. *New Phytologist*, **67**, 605–15.

Troughton, J. H. (1969). Plant water status and carbon dioxide exchange of cotton leaves. *Australian Journal of Biological Science*, **22**, 289–302.

Troughton, J. H. & Slatyer, R. O. (1969). Plant water status, leaf temperature, and the calculated mesophyll resistance to carbon dioxide of cotton leaves. *Australian Journal of Biological Science*, **22**, 815–27.

Walter, H. & Kreeb, K. (ed.) (1970). *Die Hydratation und Hydratur des Protoplasmas der Pflanzen und ihre öko-physiologische Bedeutung.* Protoplasmatologia II. C-6. Wien & New York, Springer-Verlag.

Wardlaw, I. F. (1969). The effect of water stress on translocation in relation to photosynthesis and growth. II. Effect during leaf development in *Lolium temulentum* L. *Australian Journal of Biological Science*, **22**, 1–16.

Weatherley, P. E. (1965). Discussion on terminology. In *Water Stress in Plants*, ed. B. Slavík, pp. 305–7. The Hague, Junk.

Weinberger, P., Romero, M. & Oliva, M. (1972). Ein methodischer Beitrag zur Bestimmung des subletalen (kritischen) Wassersätigungsdefizits. *Flora*, **161**, 555–61.

Whiteman, P. C. & Koller, D. (1964). Saturation deficit of the mesophyll evaporating surfaces in a desert halophyte. *Science*, **146**, 1320–1.

Whiteman, P. C. & Koller, D. (1967). Interactions of carbon dioxide concentration, light intensity and temperature on plant resistances to water vapour and carbon dioxide diffusion. *New Phytologist*, **66**, 463–73.

Willmer, C. M. & Mansfield, T. A. (1969). Active cation transport and stomatal opening: a possible physiological role of sodium ions. *Zeitschrift für Pflanzenphysiologie*, **61**, 398–400.

Wuenscher, J. E. & Kozlowski, T. T. (1971). The response of transpiration resistance to leaf temperature as a desiccation resistance mechanism in tree seedlings. *Physiologia Plantarum*, **24**, 254–9.

24. Influence of mineral nutrition on photosynthesis and the use of assimilates

L. NÁTR

A great number of studies carried out during the last fifty years show that the rate of photosynthesis may be decreased by a deficiency in any one of the essential mineral elements (Nátr, 1972). Recently, Bottrill, Possingham & Kriedemann (1970) followed the influence of all macro- and nearly all micronutrient elements on the rate of CO_2 fixation in spinach plants. The effect of the following elements was investigated: N, P, K, Mg, S, Ca, Fe, Mn, Cu, B, Zn, Mo. Deficiency of any nutrient depressed the rate of photosynthesis, based on chlorophyll content or on fresh weight. This was in agreement with earlier data by Possingham and his fellow-workers (Possingham, 1970), showing that the photochemical activities of chloroplasts isolated from mineral-deficient plants were inhibited.

Thus there is no doubt about the inhibitory effect of mineral deficiencies on photosynthesis, but a better description of the individual steps of the mechanism of these inhibitory effects is needed. Also, the description of the quantitative relationship between mineral nutrition and photosynthesis is still unsatisfactory.

One of the first tabular schemes showing the effects of mineral nutrients on photosynthesis was presented in the review by Pirson (1958). He distinguished four ways in which minerals influence photosynthesis:

(1) Interference with the previously formed assimilatory apparatus, without being incorporated in it.
(2) Incorporation into pigments or enzymes of photosynthesis.
(3) Involvement in the formation of structures or substances that are necessary for photosynthesis.
(4) Influencing conditions outside the plastids that affect photosynthesis.

This scheme demonstrates very clearly the multi-faceted and complex nature of the effects of mineral nutrients on photosynthesis.

The survey by Keller (1967) is based on recent data. Summarizing his own experiences and results, he concludes that minerals exert a direct or indirect influence by

(1) forming part of pigments or enzymes involved in photosynthesis;
(2) acting as catalysts in the synthesis and/or activity of such pigments and enzymes;
(3) influencing the permeability of membranes;
(4) regulating stomatal behaviour;
(5) altering the size and number of leaves and their anatomical structure;
(6) affecting the life-span of photosynthetic tissues.

These modes of action interact, as do the various nutrients with each other.

Such schemes may help us to formulate the questions to be answered by a particular experiment and to obtain an improved, or more detailed interpretation of the results obtained. At present, we are far from having a complete picture of how the different nutrients act and interact at the various levels of plant structure (chloroplast, cell, tissue, organ, plant, canopy) under different external and internal conditions. Such a picture can only be achieved by the accumulation of more extensive experimental data on mineral nutrition, photosynthesis and on their mutual relationship. In this, the use of the computer will be indispensable. This picture should include the causal sequence of processes induced by changes in mineral nutrients in the root substrate and followed by changes in the amount of absorbed and translocated minerals and other substances from the roots to the leaves and finally expressed by changes in structure and function of the photosynthesizing apparatus.

As such a picture cannot as yet be drawn, I have chosen to restrict the present discussion to the following aspects of the effect of mineral nutrition on photosynthesis:

(1) Effects on CO_2 uptake, considered as a diffusion process.
(2) Effects on structure and activity of chloroplasts.
(3) The relation between nitrogen content of the assimilatory tissue and photosynthesis.
(4) Effects of nutrients on translocation of assimilates.

I have tried to summarize preferentially papers not included in the recently published review (Nátr, 1972).

Influence of deficiencies in mineral nutrients on rate of photosynthesis and on diffusion resistances to CO_2 transfer

The analysis of photosynthesis as a process of CO_2 diffusion introduced by Gaastra (1959) has proved extremely useful, not only for a better understanding of photosynthesis, but also for studying the effects of external conditions, including mineral nutrients, on rates of photosynthesis.

A deficiency in N, P or K induces a decrease in the rate of CO_2 absorption and the effect of nitrogen deficiency is especially pronounced (Fig. 24.1). A typical example is provided by Nevins & Loomis (1970), who measured the light-response curves of the rate of photosynthesis of

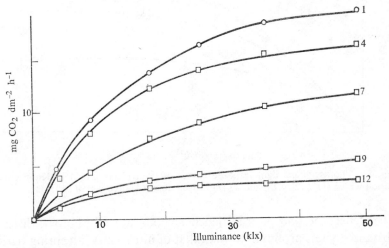

Fig. 24.1. Photosynthetic light response curves of a mature sugar-beet leaf 1, 4, 7, 9 and 12 days after the plant was transferred to nitrogen-free nutrient solution (Nevins & Loomis, 1970).

sugar-beet leaves at different times after the plants had been transferred into a nitrogen-free culture solution. Similar results were obtained with bean (Fig. 24.2) by Andreeva *et al.* (1971), with wheat by Osman & Milthorpe (1971), and with barley by Nátr (1970). In a series of experiments with forest trees Keller (1968*a,b*;1970) demonstrated a remarkable effect of nitrogen deficiency on rate of photosynthesis.

Changes in diffusion resistances to CO_2 transfer induced by nitrogen deficiency have been clearly demonstrated (Fig. 24.3) by Ryle & Hesketh (1969). The inhibition of photosynthesis in nitrogen-deficient plants was accompanied by an increase in mesophyll resistance and to a lesser

539

extent by an increase in stomatal resistance. In our own experiments with barley (Nátr, 1970), nitrogen deficiency induced an increase in mesophyll resistance, to the same degree (relative to control plants) at both low and high illuminances. On the other hand, the increase in stomatal resistance, relative to values in control plants, depended on illuminance. The quantitative data vary not only among plant species but also among varieties of the same species (Nátr, 1971).

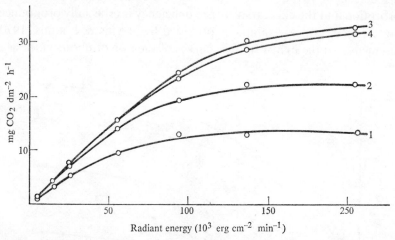

Fig. 24.2. Photosynthetic light response curves of bean plants grown in Knop culture solution with $\frac{1}{8}$ (1), $\frac{1}{4}$ (2), 1 (3) and 3 (4) nitrogen doses (Andreeva *et al.*, 1971).

The effect of phosphorus deficiency on rate of photosynthesis is substantially less pronounced than that of nitrogen. With spring barley, a short absence of phosphorus from the culture solution did not inhibit photosynthesis, even though the phosphorus concentration of leaves was considerably decreased (Nátr & Purš, 1970). Photosynthesis did decrease during prolonged phosphorus deficiency (Fig. 24.4). Andreeva & Persanov (1970) also obtained light curves of the rate of photosynthesis that were not influenced by a relatively high phosphorus deficiency. Only a very strong decrease in phosphorus content of leaves depressed photosynthesis and the depression was higher at higher illuminance. The authors explain the decrease in dry matter production under a slight phosphorus deficiency as resulting from a reduction in leaf area. Analysing the effect of phosphorus deficiency of sugar-beet, Okanenko, Bershteïn, Manuil'skiï & Il'yashuk (1972) found a depression in the initial slope and in the saturation plateau of the photosynthesis light curve. This depression was closely related to an increase in the meso-phyll resistance to CO_2 transfer.

The effect of potassium deficiency on rate of photosynthesis was less than that of phosphorus or nitrogen deficiencies (Okanenko *et al.*, 1972). Potassium deficiency decreased diffusion resistance of stomata. This finding is in agreement with those of Brag (1972) which showed

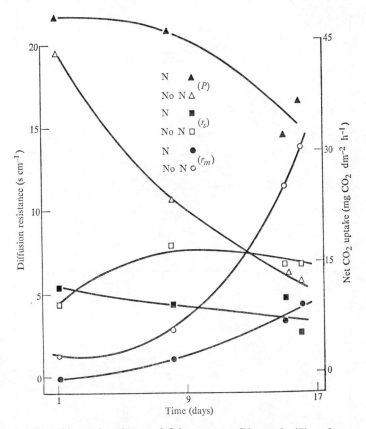

Fig. 24.3. Effect of increasing nitrogen deficiency on net CO_2 uptake (*P*), and on mesophyll (r_m) and stomatal (r_s) resistances to CO_2 transfer in maize (Ryle & Hesketh, 1969).

that wheat and pea plants with the highest potassium content had the lowest transpiration rates. Okanenko *et al.* (1972) suggested that potassium deficiency impaired the regulatory function of stomata. This suggestion fits in with recent data showing that the opening mechanism of stomata depends on active accumulation of potassium by guard cells (Fischer, 1968; Thomas, 1970*a,b*; 1971).

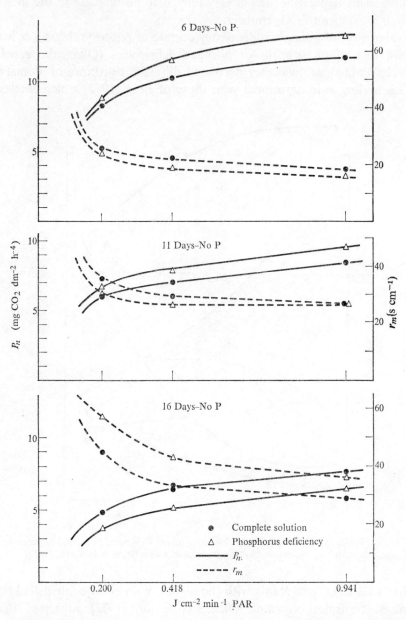

Fig. 24.4. Effect of phosphorus deficiency on the rate of net-photosynthesis (P_n) and on mesophyll resistance to CO_2 transfer (r_m) of young barley plants cv. Valtický. The plants were grown for 6, 11 and 16 days on a phosphorus-free culture solution (Nátr & Vu Van Vu, unpublished results).

542

There have been only few studies on the influence of deficiencies in other elements on the rate of CO_2 absorption and on the diffusion resistances, and comprehensive data are not available. It may be concluded that deficiencies in either nitrogen, or phosphorus, or potassium induce an inhibition of CO_2 uptake that is accompanied by an increase in stomatal and/or in mesophyll resistances to CO_2 transfer. The degree of photosynthetic inhibition and of the increase in resistances depends on many factors and may vary quite considerably. Analysis of diffusion resistances alone cannot explain the mechanism of the inhibitory effect of such deficiencies of mineral nutrients. Nevertheless, this analysis supplies information on the basis of which it is possible to distinguish effects at the stomatal level from those in the mesophyll. In other words, this analysis makes it possible to show whether a particular deficiency exerts its effects on photosynthesis only, predominantly, or not at all via the stomatal mechanism.

Changes in structure and activity of chloroplasts induced by deficiencies in mineral elements

In experiments dealing with the relationship between mineral nutrition and photosynthesis, the attention paid to different minerals has been very different. For example, in addition to nitrogen, phosphorus and potassium, a great deal of attention has been paid to manganese and iron, but substantially less is known about the effect of sulphur on photosynthesis. For many plant species the influence on photosynthesis of almost any mineral nutrient may be found in the literature. An increasing number of papers describe experiments at the chloroplast level, but even a complete survey of our present knowledge would fail to give a clear picture of the effect of minerals on structure and functions of chloroplasts. Certain examples of the effects of elements other than N, P and K, however, provide some conclusions which may possibly be generalized.

Lin & Nobel (1971), on a basis of literature data and their own experiments, indicated how photosynthesis is regulated by Mg^{2+}. They confirmed experimentally that chloroplasts isolated from illuminated plants contain substantially more Mg^{2+} (0.45 μmol mg^{-1} chlorophyll) than chloroplasts isolated from leaves taken from dark-grown plants (0.35 μmol mg^{-1}). In plant cells, changes in magnesium level occur *in vivo*. Light causes an increase in magnesium concentration in chloroplasts, firstly, by light-induced decrease in the volume of the aqueous compartments within the chloroplasts and, secondly, by an actual

543

increase in the amount of magnesium in the chloroplasts. In the dark, magnesium moves into the cytoplasm, where it may be involved in certain magnesium-dependent biosynthetic reactions. The increase in magnesium concentration in the chloroplast upon illumination is therefore considered to be a regulatory mechanism by which light controls photosynthetic activity. These results may be considered as an example of fundamental knowledge about the function of a mineral nutrient in photosynthesis, on at least one level.

Deficiencies in nearly any macro-, or micronutrient, except iron, reduced Hill-activity of isolated chloroplasts (Spencer & Possingham, 1960). The exception of iron cannot be taken as generally valid, because chloroplasts in iron-deficient leaves were characterized by absence of the chlorophyll–protein complexes (Machold, 1972). Of course, the effects of different mineral nutrients at the chloroplast level may differ. Thus, Bottrill & Possingham (1969) found that deficiencies in manganese, iron, sulphur and potassium reduced chlorophyll content per chloroplast, but in manganese- or iron-deficient plants there were the same amounts of nitrogen per chloroplast as in the control plants. On the other hand, chloroplasts from sulphur- or potassium-deficient plants had less chlorophyll and nitrogen than control plants.

According to Bottrill & Possingham (1969) the dry weight, nitrogen and chlorophyll content per chloroplast range between about $10–20 \times 10^{-12}$ g, $1–2 \times 10^{-12}$ g and $0.1–1.0 \times 10^{-12}$ g, respectively. Such data may in the future be used to characterize certain aspects of the internal structure of the assimilatory tissue. Possingham & Saurer (1969) published data on changes in chloroplast number per cell during leaf development in spinach. By combining both groups of data, i.e. chlorophyll and nitrogen content per chloroplast and chloroplast number per cell, it could be shown that the structure of the assimilatory apparatus may differ even when chlorophyll, or nitrogen content per unit leaf area or per unit leaf dry weight are the same. Furthermore, such a description of the photosynthesizing organs, together with data on rate of photosynthesis and diffusion and other resistances would improve our understanding of the relationship between structure and photosynthetic activity of the leaf.

Rate of photosynthesis and nitrogen content in the assimilatory tissue

As emphasized many times, nitrogen occupies a special position among all the nutrients involved in photosynthesis. Nichiporovich, Nguyen &

Andreeva (1972), for instance, state that during photosynthesis in chloroplasts, not only carbohydrates but also amino acids, proteins and other substances are being synthesized. Consequently, not only water and carbon dioxide, but also simple compounds of other elements, especially nitrogen, must be included among the substrates needed for this synthesis. Nitrogen enters the chloroplast in the form of nitrate ions or amino acids and is incorporated during photosynthesis into a number of other organic compounds. Among these transformations, light-dependent nitrate reduction and light-dependent reductive amination of organic acids should be included. Furthermore, the special importance of nitrogen in photosynthesis is indicated by the very high nitrogen content of the chloroplast. According to Stocking & Ongun (1962) about 75% of the nitrogen content of green cells is located in their chloroplasts.

The evidence indicated above is reflected in the large number of papers dealing with the relationship between nitrogen content in assimilatory tissue and rate of photosynthesis. Some papers show the relationship between rate of photosynthesis and the content of other mineral nutrients in leaves or shoots (e.g. Keller, 1970), but most attention has been devoted to nitrogen content, and its quantitative relationship to rate of photosynthesis has frequently been demonstrated.

Ojima & Kawashima (1968) investigated varietal differences in rates of photosynthesis in soyabean and found that the correlation coefficients (r) between rate of photosynthesis and nitrogen content per unit leaf area ranged between 0.61 and 0.83. Later, Ojima, Kawashima & Mikoshiba (1969) measured photosynthesis in plants of F_1 and F_2 generations. They concluded that in the group of plants with high nitrogen content per unit leaf area there were individuals with both high and low rate of photosynthesis, while in the group of plants with low nitrogen content there were few individuals with a high rate of photosynthesis.

An increase in nitrogen concentration from 2.22% to 4.76% on a dry weight basis in leaves of bean plants, brought about by higher nitrogen concentration in the culture solution, was associated with a considerable increase in the rate of photosynthesis (Oda & Kawata, 1970).

A correlation coefficient of 0.847 was found by Khan & Tsunoda (1970a) between rate of photosynthesis and nitrogen content in cultivated wheat species and their wild relatives, the rates of photosynthesis ranging from 15 to 40 mg CO_2 dm^{-2} h^{-1} and nitrogen contents from

17 to 30 mg dm^{-2}. In a further analysis of six commercial wheat varieties the same authors (Khan & Tsunoda, 1970*b*) found $r = 0.574$ for the relationship between photosynthesis and nitrogen content, the rates of photosynthesis ranging from 25 to 40 mg CO_2 dm^{-2} h^{-1} and nitrogen contents from 18 to 28 mg dm^{-2}.

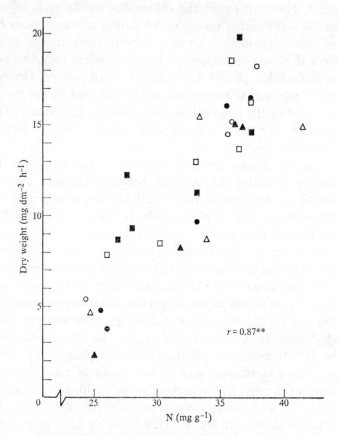

Fig. 24.5. Relationship between rate of photosynthesis (mg dry weight dm^{-2} h^{-1}) and nitrogen content (mg N g^{-1} dry weight) of flag leaves of winter wheat varieties grown in a field experiment. Correlation coefficient $r = 0.87$ (calculated from unpublished data of Kousalová, Cereal Research Institute, Kroměříž).

A good correlation was found between the rate of photosynthesis (from 12 to 15 mg CO_2 dm^{-2} h^{-1}) and nitrogen content of black poplar leaves (from 1.0% to 3.5% of dry weight) (Keller, 1970). A similar close relationship was indicated by Sasahara (1971) in some *Brassica* spp. and by Keller (1971) in spruce needles. In our Institute, a close relationship was found between rate of photosynthesis and nitrogen content of

546

flag leaves of winter wheat grown in field experiments (Fig. 24.5). A significant correlation was also found between photosynthesis and nitrogen content of young spring barley plants cultivated in growth chambers under different illuminances, temperatures and nutrient deficiencies (Fig. 24.6). The lack of relationship between rate of photosynthesis and phosphorus content in the experiment with spring barley is shown in Fig. 24.7 for comparison.

Numerous data have also been obtained with rice. Watanabe & Yoshida (1970) induced change in nitrogen content and in rate of photosynthesis of *Oryza sativa* by varying nitrogen concentration in the

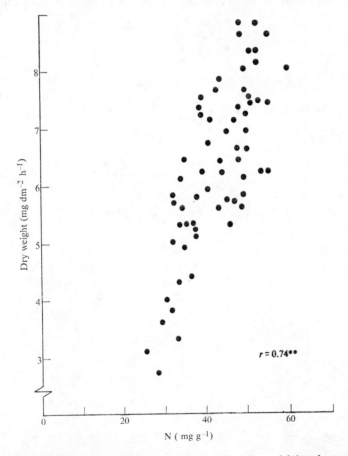

Fig. 24.6. Relationship between nitrogen content (mg N g⁻¹ dry weight) and rate of photosynthesis (mg dry weight dm⁻² h⁻¹) of leaves of young barley plants cultivated in a growth chamber under different illuminances, temperatures and mineral nutrient deficiencies ($r = 0.74**$). (Nátr, unpublished data).

culture solution. In leaves containing 2.43, 3.54, 4.00 and 6.16%
nitrogen (on a dry weight basis) the rate of photosynthesis was 25, 34,
37 and 48 mg CO_2 dm^{-2} h^{-1}, respectively. Takano & Tsunoda (1971)
found a good relationship between nitrogen content and the photosynthetic rate per unit leaf area in strains of *Oryza* spp. (Fig. 24.8). They
expressed it by the equation for a quadratic regression

$$y = -14.375 + 4.8846x - 0.10691x^2$$

where x is nitrogen content per unit leaf area (mg dm^{-2}) and y is rate of
photosynthesis (mg CO_2 dm^{-2} h^{-1}) (see also Kishitani, Takano &
Tsunoda, 1972). Tsunoda (1972), summarizing previous results, suggested that a high nitrogen content per unit leaf area was connected with

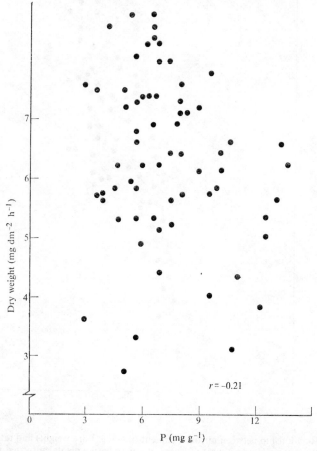

Fig. 24.7. Relationship between phosphorus content and rate of photosynthesis in the
experiments shown in Fig. 24.6 ($r = -0.21$ NS). (Nátr, unpublished data).

high rates of photosynthesis per unit leaf area, but this was also coupled with a decrease in leaf area.

Watanabe & Yoshida (1970) conclude from their experiments that the effect of nitrogen on photosynthesis is mediated by chlorophyll. Takano & Tsunoda (1970) deduce from their measurements of light reflection, transmission and absorption of rice leaves in relation to the chlorophyll and nitrogen contents, that the close relationship between rate of photosynthesis and nitrogen content seems to be of an indirect nature.

On the other hand, Andreeva, Nguyen, Vlasova & Nichiporovich (1972) presented results showing that the decrease in the rate of photosynthesis of bean leaves as induced by N deficiency, was coupled with a decrease in fraction I protein. In another paper, Andreeva *et al.* (1971) demonstrate a correlation between rate of photosynthesis at light saturation and amount of fraction I protein. They came to the important

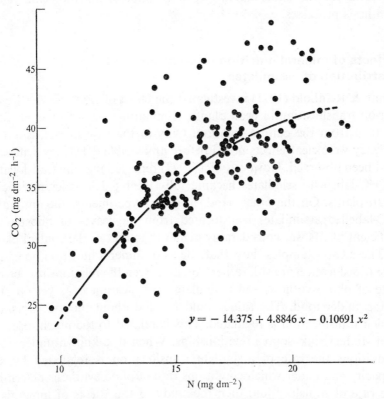

$$y = -14.375 + 4.8846\,x - 0.10691\,x^2$$

Fig. 24.8. Relationship between nitrogen content (mg N dm^{-2}) in rice leaves and rate of photosynthesis (mg $CO_2\ dm^{-2}\ h^{-1}$) (Takano & Tsunoda, 1971).

conclusion that changes in the synthesis and in the activity of ribulose diphosphate carboxylase may effectively regulate rate of photosynthesis. This is supported by Wareing, Khalifa & Treharne (1968), who deduced from experiments with partial defoliation that under normal field conditions the rate of photosynthesis may be limited by levels of carboxylating enzymes. Similarly, Björkman & Björkman (1968) suggested the existence of a strong relationship between the light-saturated rate of photosynthesis and the specific activity of carboxydismutase.

This quantitative relationship between rate of photosynthesis and nitrogen content seems to be very important and widespread. The concept that nitrogen affects photosynthesis mainly, or at least in many cases, through changes in the level and activity of ribulose diphosphate carboxylase, is also a very useful one. This concept can be expected to stimulate further research in this field, bringing new experimental results of value for the understanding of both mineral nutrition and photosynthesis processes.

Effects of mineral nutrition on transport and distribution of assimilates

Amir & Reinhold (1971) investigated the effect of K, P, S, Mg, Fe and Ca on translocation in bean plants, eliminating each of these elements in turn from the culture solution. Only in the case of potassium deficiency were clear effects noted before any visible deficiency symptoms had been observed. However, Gej (1972) reported that the translocation of ^{14}C-labelled assimilates became fully inhibited in calcium-deficient bean plants. On the other hand, in Gej's experiments, the amount of ^{14}C-labelled assimilates translocated from the leaves of phosphorus-deficient plants was considerably higher than that of the control plants.

These two examples show that effects of mineral nutrition on assimilate translocation are still rather obscure. Even the relationship between rate of photosynthesis and assimilate translocation is as yet far from being understood. The same could be said about the mechanism by which translocation is regulated. This is related to the much discussed and studied sink–source relationships. When it is known under which conditions the rate of assimilate translocation is regulated by sink capacity and under which conditions rate of photosynthesis determines the rate of translocation, then the study of the effects of minerals on assimilate translocation will be much more effective and the results obtained less ambiguous. Thus, for instance, Il'yashuk & Okanenko (1970) found that potassium (K_2SO_4) enhanced assimilate transport out of the leaves of sugar-beet plants. Detailed analysis of the results enabled the authors to deduce that the enhancement of ^{14}C-assimilate translocation by potassium was due to accumulation of large amounts of ^{14}C-labelled assimilates which resulted from enhanced photosynthesis. However, an opposite conclusion was reached by Hartt (1969,1970) on the basis of her experiments, namely that the effect of potassium deficiency in decreasing translocation is direct and primary and not secondary to the other effects of potassium deficiency. Her results showed a high sensitivity of translocation rate to potassium supply: translocation was inhibited earlier and to a greater extent than rate of photosynthesis and before symptoms of potassium deficiency become visible.

By supplying labelled sucrose to the primary leaf of the bean plant, Amir & Reinhold (1971) studied the effect of potassium deficiency on sucrose translocation. They found significant interaction between the effect of added sugar and potassium deficiency on [14]CO_2 fixation and presented the following scheme for explaining these results: exogenous sugar and photosynthetic sugar mix in the 'translocation pool'. Potassium plays a role in reversible intermediate steps between photosynthesis and the entry of the sugar derived into the translocation pool. Hence, potassium deficiency has no effect when photosynthetic sugar is not being translocated, and reduces transport only when photosynthetic sugar is being translocated. On the basis of this scheme, the authors conclude that potassium deficiency inhibits translocation of assimilates by decreasing, or stopping, their transport from the sites of assimilation to the hypothetical 'translocation pool'.

Gej (1972) also confirmed that potassium deficiency considerably decreased the amounts of assimilates translocated from the leaves to the nonassimilating organs of the bean plant.

As mentioned above, there are only few data about the effect of individual mineral nutrients on the rate of assimilate translocation. But the problem of the effects of mineral nutrition on assimilate translocation could be considered from another point of view, i.e. one may follow the changes in assimilate distribution in the whole plant as brought about by changes in mineral nutrition. Here, the following general conclusions were reached by Brouwer (1962), taking into account the fact that roots are the most important organs for supplying minerals and water, and the shoot for supplying carbohydrates:

Since the shoots depend on the roots for their supply of minerals and water, and since the shoots are further away from the region of supply than the roots, it would seem that these essential materials limit shoot growth more often than root growth. If this is the case, any treatment that increases the uptake of minerals and moisture is likely to increase shoot growth relative to root growth. When other growth-limiting factors are eliminated, shoot growth continues at a rate that depends on the minerals and moisture supplied by the roots. Root growth continues at a rate depending on the carbohydrates supplied by the shoot. In most cases there is an interaction between the two processes.

Dr G. N. Thorne helped in translating this paper into English. I wish to express my deep gratitude for her effort, making many valuable suggestions to the manuscript.

References

Amir, S. & Reinhold, L. (1971). Interaction between K-deficiency and light in ^{14}C-sucrose translocation in bean plants. *Physiologia Plantarum*, **24**, 226–31.

Andreeva, T. F., Avdeeva, T. A., Vlasova, M. P., Nguyen-Thyu-Thyok & Nichiporovich, A. A. (1971). Vliyanie azotnogo pitaniya rasteniĭ na strukturu i funkciyu fotosinteticheskogo apparata. (Effect of nitrogen nutrition of plants on structure and function of the photosynthetic apparatus.) *Fiziologiya rasteniĭ*, **18**, 701–7.

Andreeva, T. F., Nguyen-Thyu-Thyok, Vlasova, M. P. & Nichiporovich, A. A. (1972). Vliyanie azotnogo pitaniya na fotosinteticheskuyu aktivnost' list'ev razlichnych yarusov i na produktivnost'rasteniĭ konskich bobov. (Effect of nitrogen nutrition on photosynthetic activity in the leaves of different tiers and on the productivity of horse bean plants.) *Fiziologiya rasteniĭ*, **19**, 265–72.

Andreeva, T. F. & Persanov, V. M. (1970). Vliyanie prodolzhitel'nosti fosfornogo golodaniya na intensivnost' fotosinteza i rost list'ev v svyazi s produktivnost'yu konskich bobov. (Effect of duration of phosphorus deficiency on rate of photosynthesis and growth of leaves in connection with plant productivity.) *Fiziologiya rasteniĭ*, **17**, 478–84.

Björkman, O. & Björkman, M. (1968). Carboxydismutase activity in sun and shade ecotypes of *Solidago*. *Carnegie Institute, Department of Plant Biology Annual Report*, **66**, 216–20.

Bottrill, D. E. & Possingham, J. V. (1969). The effect of mineral deficiency and leaf age on the nitrogen and chlorophyll content of spinach chloroplasts. *Biochimica et Biophysica Acta*, **189**, 80–4.

Bottrill, D. E., Possingham, J. V. & Kriedemann, P. E. (1970). The effect of nutrient deficiencies on photosynthesis and respiration in spinach. *Plant and Soil*, **32**, 424–38.

Brag, H. (1972). The influence of potassium on the transpiration rate and stomatal opening in *Triticum aestivum* and *Pisum sativum*. *Physiologia Plantarum*, **26**, 250–7.

Brouwer, R. (1962). Nutritive influences on the distribution of dry matter in the plant. *Netherlands Journal of Agricultural Science*, **10**, 399–408.

Fischer, R. A. (1968). Stomatal opening: Role of potassium uptake by guard cells. *Science*, **160**, 784–5.

Gaastra, P. (1959). Photosynthesis of crop plants as influenced by light, carbon dioxide, temperature and stomatal diffusion resistance. *Mededelingen Landbouwhogeschool Wageningen*, **59**, 1–68.

Gej, B. (1972). The leaf uptake of $^{14}CO_2$ and translocation of ^{14}C-assimilates in bean plants grown under conditions of P-, Ca- or K-deficiency. *Bulletin de l'Académie Polonaise des Sciences, Série des sciences biologiques* Cl. II., **20**, 803–8.

Hartt, C. E. (1969). Effect of potassium deficiency upon translocation of ^{14}C in attached blades and entire plants of sugar-cane. *Plant Physiology*, **44**, 1461–9.

Hartt, C. E. (1970). Effect of potassium deficiency upon translocation of ^{14}C in detached blades of sugarcane. *Plant Physiology*, **45**, 183–7.

Il'yashuk, E. M. & Okanenko, A. S. (1970). Vliyanie kaliya na peredvizhenie fotosinteticheski assimilirovannoï $^{14}CO_2$ u sakharnoï svyokly. (Effect of potassium on translocation of photosynthetically assimilated $^{14}CO_2$ in sugar beet plants.) *Fiziologiya rastenïï*, **17**, 445–51.

Keller, T. (1967). The influence of fertilization on gaseous exchange of forest tree species. *Proceedings of the Colloquium on Forest Fertilization, Jyväskylä/Finland*, pp. 65–79.

Keller, T. (1968a). The influence of mineral nutrition on gaseous exchange by forest trees. *International Superphosphate Manufacturers' Association Ltd. Agricultural Committee, Paris, "Phosphorus in Agriculture" Bull. Doc. No. 50*, June, 1968, pp. 1–11.

Keller, T. (1968b). Nettoassimilation, Spross- und Wurzelatmung junger Pappeln bei unterschiedlicher Ernährung. Klimaresistenz Photosynthese und Stoffproduktion. *Tagungsberichte Nr. 100 der Deutschen Akademie der Landwirtschaftswissenschaften zu Berlin, DDR*, pp. 233–44.

Keller, T. (1970). Gaseous exchange – a good indicator of nutritional status and fertilizer response of forest trees. *Proceedings of the 6th International Colloquium on Plant Analysis and Fertilizer Problems (ISHS), Tel Aviv*, pp. 669–78.

Keller, T. (1971). Der Einfluss der Stickstoffernährung auf den Gaswechsel der Fichte. *Allgemeine Forst und Jagdzeitung*, **142**, 89–93.

Khan, M. A. & Tsunoda, S. (1970a). Leaf photosynthesis and transpiration under different levels of air flow rate and light intensity in cultivated wheat species and its wild relatives. *Japanese Journal of Breeding*, **20**, 305–14.

Khan, M. A. & Tsunoda, S. (1970b). Differences in leaf photosynthesis and leaf transpiration rates among six commercial wheat varieties of west Pakistan. *Japanese Journal of Breeding*, **20**, 344–50.

T

Stress factors and assimilates

Kishitani, S., Takano, Y. & Tsunoda, S. (1972). Optimum leaf-areal nitrogen content of single leaves for maximizing the photosynthesis rate of leaf canopies: A simulation in rice. *Japanese Journal of Breeding*, **22**, 1–10.
Lin, D. C. & Nobel, P. S. (1971). Control of photosynthesis by Mg^{2+}. *Archives of Biochemistry and Biophysics*. **145**, 622–32.
Machold, O. (1972). Lamellarproteine grüner und chlorotischer Chloroplasten. *Biochemie und Physiologie der Pflanzen (BPP)*, **163**, 30–41.
Nátr, L. (1970). Gas exchange of barley leaves as influenced by mineral nutrient deficiency. *Scientia Agriculturae Bohemoslovaca*, **2**, 211–8.
Nátr, L. (1971). Odrůdové rozdíly v působení deficitu minerálních živin na intenzitu fotosyntézy a transpirace (Varietal differences in the effect of the deficiency of mineral nutrients on the rate of photosynthesis and transpiration). *Rostlinná výroba*, **17**, 411–8.
Nátr, L. (1972). Influence of mineral nutrients on photosynthesis of higher plants. *Photosynthetica*, **6**, 80–99.
Nátr, L. & Purš, J. (1970). The relation between rate of photosynthesis and N, P, K concentration in barley leaves. II. Phosphorus absent from the nutrient solution. *Photosynthetica*, **4**, 31–7.
Nátr, L., Purš, J. & Bezděk, V. (1971). Intenzita fotosyntézy po aplikaci minerálních živin postřikem na list u jarního ječmene (Photosynthesis rate after leaf application of sprayed mineral nutrients in spring barley). *Rostlinná výroba*, **17**, 519–28.
Nevins, D. J. & Loomis, R. S. (1970). Nitrogen nutrition and photosynthesis in sugar beet (*Beta vulgaris* L.). *Crop Science*, **10**, 21–5.
Nichiporovich, A. A., Nguyen-Thyu-Thyok & Andreeva, T. F. (1972). Sravnitel'naya ocenka vzaimosvyazi mezhdu fotosintezom i nekotorymi osobennostyami azotnogo metabolizma u kukuruzy i bobov. (Comparative evaluation of the correlation between photosynthesis and some peculiarities of nitrogen metabolism in maize and bean plants.) *Fiziologiya rasteniĭ*, **19**, 1066–73.
Oda, Y. & Kawata, K. (1970). Effect of carbon dioxide concentrations on dry matter accumulation in bean leaves measured by an improved half-leaf method. *Bulletin of University of Osaka Prefecture, Series B*, **22**, 39–47.
Ojima, M. & Kawashima, R. (1968). Studies on the seed production of soybean. 5. Varietal differences in photosynthetic rate of soybean. *Proceedings of the Crop Science Society of Japan*, **37**, 667–75.
Ojima, M. Kawashima, R. & Mikoshiba, K. (1969). Studies on the seed production of soybean. 7. The ability of photosynthesis in F_1 and F_2 generations. *Proceedings of the Crop Science Society of Japan*, **38**, 693–9.
Okanenko, A. S., Bershteĭn, B. J., Manuil'skiĭ, V. D. & Il'yashuk, E. M. (1972). Narushenie gazoobmena list'ev sacharnoĭ svyokly v usloviyach deficita kaliya, fosfora i azota. (Effect of deficiency of K, P and N on gas exchange in sugar beet leaves.) *Fiziologiya rasteniĭ*, **19**, 1132–8.
Osman, A. M. & Milthorpe, F. L. (1971). Photosynthesis of wheat leaves in relation to age, illuminance and nutrient supply. II. Results. *Photosynthetica*, **5**, 61–70.

Pirson, A. (1958). Mineralstoffe und Photosynthese. In *Encyclopedia of Plant Physiology*, ed. W. Ruhland, vol. 4, pp. 355–74. Berlin, Göttingen & Heidelberg: Springer-Verlag.

Possingham, J. V. (1970). Some effects of mineral nutrient deficiencies on the chloroplasts of higher plants. *Proceedings of the 6th International Colloquium on Plant Analysis and Fertilizer Problems* (*ISHS*), *Tel Aviv*, pp. 155–65.

Possingham, J. V. & Saurer, W. (1969). Changes in chloroplast number per cell during leaf development in spinach. *Planta*, **86**, 186–94.

Ryle, G. J. A. & Hesketh, J. D. (1969). Carbon dioxide uptake in nitrogen-deficient plants. *Crop Science*, **9**, 451–4.

Sasahara, T. (1971). Genetic variation in cell and tissue forms in relation to plant growth. II. Total cell surface area in the palisade parenchyma and total cell surface area: Total nitrogen content ratio in relation to photosynthetic activity in *Brassica*. *Japanese Journal of Breeding*, **21**, 61–8.

Spencer, D. & Possingham, J. V. (1960). The effect of nutrient deficiencies on the Hill reaction of isolated chloroplasts from tomato. *Australian Journal of Biological Sciences*, **13**, 441–55.

Stocking, C. R. & Ongun, A. (1962). The intracellular distribution of some metallic elements in leaf. *American Journal of Botany*, **49**, 284–9.

Takano, Y. & Tsunoda, S. (1970). Light reflection, transmission and absorption rates of rice leaves in relation to their chlorophyll and nitrogen contents. *Tohoku Journal of Agricultural Research*, **21**, 111–7.

Takano, Y. & Tsunoda, S. (1971). Curvilinear regression of the leaf photosynthetic rate on leaf nitrogen content among strains of *Oryza* species. *Japanese Journal of Breeding*, **21**, 69–76.

Thomas, D. A. (1970*a*). The regulation of stomatal aperture in tobacco leaf epidermal strips. I. The effect of ions. *Australian Journal of Biological Sciences*, **23**, 961–79.

Thomas, D. A. (1970*b*). The regulation of stomatal aperture in tobacco leaf epidermal strips. II. The effect of ouabain. *Australian Journal of Biological Sciences*, **23**, 981–9.

Thomas, D. A. (1971). The regulation of stomatal aperture in tobacco leaf epidermal strips. III. The effect of ATP. *Australian Journal of Biological Sciences*, **24**, 689–707.

Tsunoda, S. (1972). Photosynthetic efficiency in rice and wheat. *Rice Breeding*. The International Rice Research Institute, Los Banos, Philippines, pp. 471–482.

Wareing, P. F., Khalifa, M. M. & Treharne, K. J. (1968). Rate-limiting processes in photosynthesis at saturating light intensities. *Nature*, **220**, 453–7.

Watanabe, H. & Yoshida, S. (1970). Effects of nitrogen, phosphorus and potassium on photophosphorylation in rice in relation to the photosynthetic rate of single leaves. *Soil Science and Plant Nutrition*, **16**, 163–6.

25. Influence of temperature stress on CO_2-gas exchange

H. BAUER, W. LARCHER & R. B. WALKER

The temperature dependence of net photosynthesis in higher plants follows the well known optimum curve. There is an optimal range, dependent upon species and conditions, within which net CO_2 fixation is highest. As temperatures increase, or decrease beyond this range, net fixation becomes steadily smaller, until finally limits are reached where CO_2 output equals intake. These are the heat- or cold-limits of net photosynthesis, respectively. If these limits are exceeded, then net CO_2 evolution occurs even in the light. How far these temperature limits are from those temperatures which cause lethal damage varies with species, conditions, and time of year (Fig. 25.1).

Extreme temperatures may not only inhibit CO_2 uptake during their operation, but may also have after-effects which inhibit subsequent

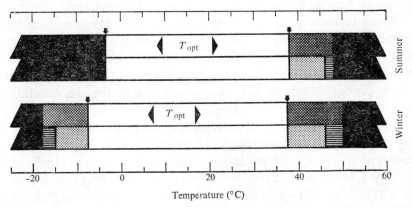

Fig. 25.1. CO_2-gas exchange in light of *Abies alba* in summer and winter during and following different temperatures.

Upper section of each block: CO_2-gas exchange at different temperatures. *Clear area:* net CO_2 uptake; ◀ T_{opt} ▶ : optimal temperature range for net-photosynthesis. *Vertical arrows:* heat and cold limit of net-photosynthesis; *shaded area:* CO_2 evolution in light (at lower temperatures respiration approaches zero); *black area:* necrotic damage (after Lingl-Kemnitzer, 1964).

Lower section of each block: CO_2-gas exchange at 15–20 °C following the temperatures given in the abscissa. *Clear area:* no after-effect on photosynthesis; *dotted area:* photosynthetic capacity partially and temporarily reduced; *hatched area:* gross photosynthesis completely but reversibly blocked; *black area:* gross photosynthesis irreversibly blocked. Duration of frost treatments: 12 h; duration of heat treatments: 30 min. (After Pisek & Kemnitzer, 1968; Bauer, 1970.)

557

photosynthesis at optimal temperatures. Depending on the intensity of the stress (temperature and duration) photosynthesis may be only partially reduced, or in extreme instances, may be completely halted. Such complete cessation may be reversible or irreversible, with death of the affected tissue usually ensuing if the effect is irreversible (Larcher, 1973, Fig. 25.1). These effects and after-effects are ecologically important. Therefore, it is not sufficient to measure the photosynthetic depression only during the stress but it is especially important in evaluating production decreases which result from stress temperatures, to know how long the impairment of photosynthesis had lasted.

Heat stress

CO_2-*gas exchange during high temperatures*

Physiological principles. The high temperature limit of net CO_2 uptake (=temperature maximum of net photosynthesis, or heat compensation point) is a resultant of two counteracting temperature-dependent processes. One involves the dark reactions of photosynthesis, the rates of which increase with rise in temperature in the lower and medium temperature range, but are strongly inhibited by high temperatures. The other is respiration, which increases rapidly with rising temperature almost to the lethal point, then finally collapses. A limit is thus reached where photosynthesis is just able to compensate for the respiratory CO_2 evolution.

There is little in the literature regarding the temperature response of the carboxylation enzymes (ribulose diphosphate (RuDP) and phospho-enolpyruvic (PEP)-carboxylase): Treharne & Cooper (1969) and Phillips & McWilliam (1971) noted little difference between the activities of RuDP- and PEP-carboxylase at optimal and higher temperatures. However, Tieszen & Sigurdson (1973) found that activity of RuDP-carboxylase in C_3- and C_4-grasses increased with rising temperatures up to 50 °C, but activity of PEP-carboxylase declined above 40 °C. Nevertheless, in general, C_4-plants show a higher temperature limit for CO_2 uptake than C_3-plants. A possible reason can be the greater carboxylating capacity of PEP-carboxylase at high temperatures. As a result the CO_2 compensation point of C_4-plants remains low at high temperatures, while in C_3-plants it rises substantially (Zelitch, 1971). Because of this the respiratory CO_2 can be reassimilated better. According to Charles-Edwards & Charles-Edwards (1970) the decline in net photosynthesis at high temperatures in C_3-grasses is due to the enormous increase in respiration, while in C_4-grasses it is caused by heat denaturation of the photosynthetic enzymes.

There are various reports concerning the temperature-dependence of respiration in light and in the dark. In *Atriplex hastata, Glycine max, Beta vulgaris* (Hofstra & Hesketh, 1969), *Glycine max, Canavalia ensiformis, Solanum melangena, Citrullus vulgaris* and *Helianthus annuus* (Hew, Krotkov & Canvin, 1969) CO_2 evolution above 35 °C is higher in light and in CO_2-free air than in the dark. Zelitch (1971) states that dark respiration has a higher Q_{10} than photorespiration in the range 20–30 °C (see also Troughton, Chapter 16). Moreover, it is conceivable that CO_2-gas exchange is hindered at high temperatures by closing of the stomata. Information on the direct effect of heat on stomatal opening is most desirable for understanding gas exchange under heat stress. However, there are several methodological difficulties in such experimentation. First, as temperature increases the CO_2 compensation point rises greatly (especially with C_3-plants), resulting in an increase in intercellular CO_2 concentration (Heath & Orchard, 1957; Meidner & Mansfield, 1968; Zelitch, 1971), which could lead to a closing of the stomata (Meidner & Mansfield, 1968). Second, the excessive heat increases transpiration so much that leaf water deficit may rapidly become so severe that stomata may close as a result of water-stress. These methodological difficulties may explain the very different results found in the literature (compare Stålfelt, 1962; Wuenscher & Kozlowski, 1971; Schulze *et al.*, 1973, and others).

Specific heat limits of net photosynthesis. The heat limits of net photosynthesis of higher plants are distributed over a temperature span of more than 25 °C (Table 25.1). For all plants within this group, a relationship can be recognized between the heat limit and the thermal stress of the habitat.

In certain species the heat limit of photosynthesis comes more or less close to the heat-killing temperature of the leaves. However, in all species which have been investigated, net CO_2 uptake ceases before necrosis becomes evident. The span between the heat limit and the thermal death point is greatest in the northern conifers and in the southern oaks (9–12 °C), while in most plants it is 4–8 °C. *Leucojum vernum* and *Alnus viridis* show positive assimilation up to 2–3 °C below the death point (Pisek, Larcher, Pack & Unterholzner, 1968; Hellmuth, 1971).

Stress factors and assimilates

Table 25.1. *Heat limits for net photosynthesis* (Ph$_n$) *of higher plants*

Temp. range of heat limit for Ph$_n$ (°C)	Plants	References
35–39	Conifers of boreal forests	Pisek, Larcher, Pack & Unterholzner, 1968
	Alpine and arctic herbs	Pisek, Larcher, Pack & Unterholzner, 1968; Billings, Godfrey, Chabot & Bourque, 1971
	Grasses of Alaskan tundra	Tieszen, 1970
40–46	Conifers from maritime climates	Pharis & Woods, 1960; Helms, 1965; Krueger & Ferrell, 1965; Negisi, 1966; Pisek, Larcher, Pack & Unterholzner, 1968
	Deciduous broad-leaved trees from temperate zones	Nomoto, 1964; Pisek, Larcher, Pack & Unterholzner, 1968; Bauer, 1972
	Shrubs of atlantic origin	Pisek, Larcher, Pack & Unterholzner, 1968
	Arctic and alpine dwarf shrubs	Pisek, Larcher, Pack & Unterholzner, 1968
	Forage-grasses from temperate zones	Winkler & Pregenzer, 1970
43–48	Broad-leaved evergreen trees from Southern Europe and South Japan	Kusumoto, 1957, 1961; Pisek, Larcher, Pack & Unterholzner, 1968
	Cultivated trees and herbs from warmer countries	Pisek & Winkler, 1959; El-Sharkawy & Hesketh, 1964; Kriedemann, 1968; Hofstra & Hesketh, 1969; Schulze, Lange & Koch, 1972
49–55	Trees and shrubs from semi-arid and arid regions of Australia	Hellmuth, 1967, 1971
	Desert plants	Björkman, Pearcy, Harrison & Mooney, 1972; Schulze, Lange & Koch, 1972
	Tropical pasture legumes	Begg & Jarvis, 1968; Ludlow & Wilson, 1971
	Cotton	El-Sharkawy & Hesketh, 1964
55–61	Tropical C$_4$-grasses	El-Sharkawy & Hesketh, 1964; Ludlow & Wilson, 1971

Variability of the heat limit of net photosynthesis within a species. Although the heat limit of net photosynthesis of various plants can differ appreciably (Table 25.1), little is known of the variability of this limit within a single species. In maize this variability is remarkably great, as the heat limit can range from 44 to 50 °C, depending on the variety and culture conditions (Hofstra & Hesketh, 1969; Raschke, 1970; H. Bauer, unpublished data). It is not possible to distinguish to what extent these different limits can be attributed to temperature adaptation or to genetically fixed characteristics. In addition, the stage of development has an effect on the heat limit of net photosynthesis. In this, the higher respiratory activity of growing tissues and the decline of this activity with age plays a role. Thus, Winkler (1961) showed that heat limits of net

560

photosynthesis of young, not yet fully differentiated leaves of potato varieties were about 2 °C lower than those of mature leaves, which had a low dark respiration.

Influence of heat adaptation and heat stress on the heat limit of net photosynthesis. A number of studies have been concerned with the influence of temperature during growth and development on the temperature-dependence of net photosynthesis. Most of these refer only to the optimum range. Strain & Chase (1966) also determined the heat limits of four woody desert species, grown for four months at 15 °C, 30 °C and 40 °C, respectively: The warm-adapted plants showed a 3–4 °C higher heat limit of net photosynthesis than did the cool-adapted specimens, which clearly respired more intensively. Billings, Godfrey, Chabot & Bourque (1971), using seventeen populations of *Oxyria digyna*, showed very impressively the influence of acclimatization on the value of the heat limit of net photosynthesis. Plants which had been held for five to six months at 32 °C day/21 °C night temperature showed a heat limit of net photosynthesis of 36–42 °C (average 39 °C) while those held at 12 °C day/4 °C night compensated at a temperature between 32 °C and 37 °C (average 35 °C). Furthermore, the cold-adapted plants respired appreciably more at temperatures above 25 °C.

It is also of ecological significance to know whether or not a short exposure to heat (from a few hours to a day) can raise the heat limit of net photosynthesis. In one study, ten days after a thirty-minute exposure to 44 °C, needles of *Abies alba* showed a heat limit about three degrees higher than before the heat-treatment. Preliminary trials with other plants suggest that such heat-treatment can be effective only where a sufficient difference exists between the heat limit of net photosynthesis and the lethal temperature (Bauer, 1972). Lyutova (1963*b*) did not find a rise in the heat limit of net photosynthesis in *Tradescantia fluminensis* leaves in response to heat-treatment.

Dependence of the heat limit for net photosynthesis on light intensity and water supply. The heat limit of net photosynthesis rises with light intensity up to saturated values of the photosynthetic process itself (Larcher, 1969).

There have been almost no experiments on the influence of water supply on the heat limit of net photosynthesis. In one study, Hellmuth (1967,1971) found a higher value in *Acacia acuminata* under soil

т*

moisture stress than when water supply was optimal. However, the possibility of thermal adaptation can not be ruled out here.

Dark respiration at high temperatures. Dark respiration certainly appears to be one of the most heat-stable of life functions (review: Alexandrov, Lomagin & Feldman, 1970; Larcher, 1973). Nevertheless exposures to excessive temperatures (above about 40 °C) result in a clear depression of CO_2 release (as well as O_2 uptake) within a few hours (Fig. 25.2; Semikhatova & Denko, 1960; Kinbacher & Sullivan, 1967; review: Levitt, 1972). Whether this represents heat inactivation of enzymes, or exhaustion of food reserves is not clear.

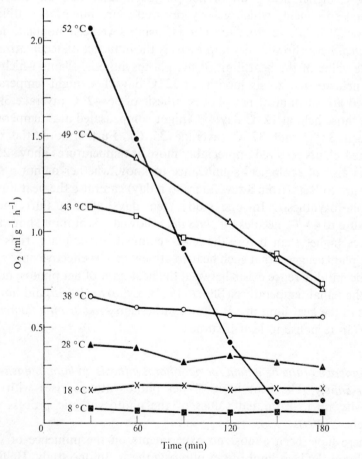

Fig. 25.2. Time-course of dark respiration of *Citrullus colocynthis* at various temperatures (after Semikhatova, 1968).

CO_2-gas exchange following heat stress

Photosynthesis following heat stress. The after-effect of previous temperature on the subsequent photosynthetic rate at favourable temperatures was investigated in maize by Raschke (1970). The resulting regression curve (Fig. 25.3) shows that CO_2 assimilation at 25 °C was not significantly affected by previous temperatures between 10 and 35 °C, but that exposure to high, i.e. stress, temperatures sharply diminished subsequent CO_2 uptake. Heat thus not only reduces CO_2 fixation while it is in operation but also causes reduction as an after-effect.

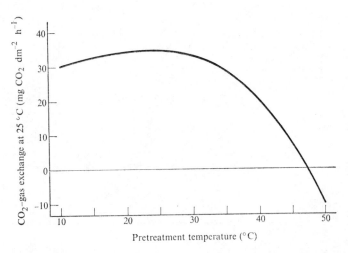

Fig. 25.3. Regression curve for CO_2-gas exchange of *Zea mays* at 279 W m^{-2} and 25 °C. Leaf samples were exposed for about 1 h to temperatures given in the abscissa, then transferred to 25 °C for measurement. The curve was drawn according to the regression equation (based on the measurements):

$$Ph_{25} = 27 + 0.04T_p^2 - 0.0011\,T_p^3.$$

Ph_{25} – photosynthetic rate at 25 °C; T_p – pretreatment temperature (after Raschke, 1970).

Photosynthesis following heat-stress was investigated in detail using *Abies alba* and *Acer pseudoplatanus* (Bauer, 1972). Photosynthetic capacity was reduced in *Abies* after a thirty-minute exposure to 38 °C and above and in *Acer* to 42 °C and above (Fig. 25.4). These temperatures of 38 °C and 42 °C are also the heat limits for CO_2 uptake in these two species. As stress temperature increased, the magnitude of the subsequent depression also increased greatly, so that after about 46 °C in *Abies* and 47 °C in *Acer* the photosynthetic process (gross photosynthesis) was completely blocked. In *Acer* such heating causes necrosis, while in *Abies* needles this occurs only if the temperature is 2 °C higher. Although the fir needles are thus more resistant to tissue damage, their photosynthetic apparatus is more sensitive to heat. Both species can fully recover their photosynthetic capacity as long as no necrosis has occurred, but the time required for recovery becomes longer as stress temperature is increased. Further, if the fir plants are exposed to a

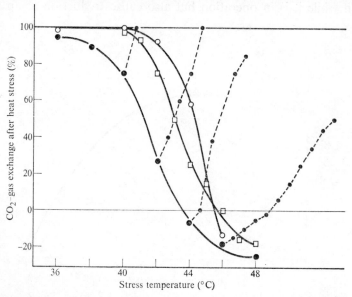

Fig. 25.4. CO_2-gas exchange (as percentage of rate before treatment) at 10 klx and 20 °C, 1–2 h after 30 min heating at the temperatures given in the abscissa. ●—● *Abies alba*, after one heat treatment (each dot on the broken lines represents recovery on the days following treatment). □—□ *Acer pseudoplatanus*, after one heat treatment. ○—○ *Abies alba*, after two heat treatments at the same temperature (after Bauer, 1970).

second heat stress, their photosynthesis is affected less than after the first exposure (Fig. 25.4), and recovery is also appreciably faster. Lyutova (1958,1962) also showed the effectiveness of an eighteen-hour heat-hardening at about 36–38 °C in increasing heat tolerance of photosynthesis in a number of herbaceous plants. The effectiveness of a heat stress depends not only on the temperature level but also on the duration of exposure (Fig. 25.5, Semikhatova, 1964).

In Table 25.2 the photosynthetic capacity of various plants after heat stress is presented. Heat stability of photosynthesis of the species listed shows only small differences, except for cotton, which is somewhat more heat-tolerant. Unfortunately, plants from very warm regions have not been studied.

A number of studies have been concerned with structural and bio-chemical changes of the photosynthetic apparatus of higher plants following heat stress. Daniell, Chappell & Couch (1969) observed a swelling of the chloroplasts of *Elodea canadensis* after sublethal heat stress, and a loss of chlorophyll at lethal temperatures. Lyutova (1963a) suggested that the binding of chlorophyll to protein was increasingly disrupted with rising temperature. Heat-hardening should then involve

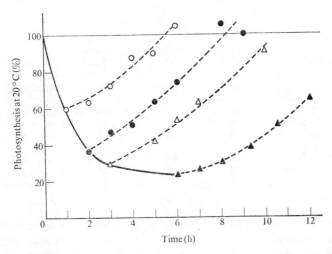

Fig. 25.5. Depression (solid line) and recovery in time (broken lines) of photosynthesis (as percentage of untreated controls) of *Zea mays* at 20°C following exposure to 38–39 °C for 1, 2, 3 and 6 h (after Semikhatova, 1964).

a stabilization of chlorophyll–protein complexes. Ageeva & Lyutova (1971) investigated photosynthesis and photochemical reactions after heat stress in heat-hardened and untreated pea leaves. The Hill reaction, photoreduction of NADP (nicotinamide adenine dinucleotide phos-phate) and cyclic phosphorylation were more heat-stable than were non-cyclic phosphorylation and the overall photosynthetic CO_2 uptake. In heat-hardened leaves all reactions were somewhat more heat-resistant. Tieszen & Sigurdson (1973) investigated the heat-stability of RuDP- and PEP-carboxylase in C_3- and C_4-grasses. A thirty-minute heat-stress at 40 °C had no after-effect on the activity of either enzyme. Exposure of leaves to 50 °C resulted in a loss of RuDP-carboxylase activity in the arctic C_3-grasses, but in the C_4-grasses *Sorghum vulgare* and *Andropogon gerardi* this enzyme retained 50% of its initial activity after the 50 °C stress. In both C_3- and C_4-grasses, PEP-carboxylase was more heat-stable than RuDP-carboxylase. No clear statement can be made on the behaviour of stomata after heating (cf. different results in the paper by Raschke, 1970, depending on the evaluation method). Stomatal resistance apparently scarcely changes following heating (Drake & Salisbury, 1972).

Table 25.2. *Depression of photosynthetic rate of some cormophytes following heat-stress*

Species	Heat-stress		Depression of photosynthesis (% of unstressed controls)	Reference
	Duration (min)	Temperature (°C)		
Zea mays	60	38–39	40	Semikhatova, 1964
Pulmonaria obscura				
spring leaves	10	42	100	Kamensteva, 1969
autumn leaves	10	42	50	Kamensteva, 1969
Pisum sativum	10	42	86	Ageeva & Lyutova, 1971
Abies alba	30	42	70	Bauer, 1972
Polygonum sachalinense	90	42	88	Semikhatova, Saakov & Gorbacheva, 1962
Caragana arborescens	5	44	70	Feldman, 1968
Acer pseudoplatanus	30	44	75	Bauer, 1972
Zea mays	c. 60	44	c. 60	Raschke, 1970
Podophyllum peltatum	5	46	99	Lyutova, 1962
Campanula persicifolia	5	46	97	Lyutova, 1962
Phaseolus vulgaris	5	46	95	Lyutova, 1962
Polygonum sachalinense	5	46	95	Lyutova, 1962
Tradescantia fluminensis	5	46	85	Lyutova, 1958
Hepatica nobilis	5	46	82	Lyutova, 1962
Gossypium hirsutum	15	46	c. 40	Esipova, 1959
Nicotiana rustica	2	48	60	Ben Zioni & Itai, 1972

Dark respiration following heat stress. Following sublethal heat stress, dark respiration shows no appreciable changes (Lyutova, 1962; Wagenbreth, 1965*a,b*; Bauer, 1972). Only when at least a part of the cells have been killed does a drastic decrease in CO_2 release occur (Wagenbreth, 1965*a,b*; Daniell *et al.*, 1969; Kamentseva, 1969). However, CO_2 release can rise enormously immediately before death (Wagenbreth, 1965*a*). The rise in 'post-heating' respiratory rate reported by Parker (1971) probably represents such a premortal increase.

Chilling at temperatures above 0°C

Plants sensitive to chilling

CO_2-*gas exchange at temperatures from 0° to 10°C.* Various plants of tropical origin are damaged lethally if exposed for several hours to temperatures from 0 °C to 5 °C, and sometimes even to 10 °C. Net photosynthesis of plants sensitive to chilling ceases several degrees above the freezing point (Ludlow & Wilson, 1971; and others). Photosynthesis is already affected by low temperature before the cold limit of CO_2 uptake is reached. If cold-sensitive plants (such as *Sorghum* hybrid NK-145, *Zea mays* hybrid 575, *Paspalum dilatatum*) are cooled from 25 °C to 10 °C and exposed to strong light, their photosynthetic rates

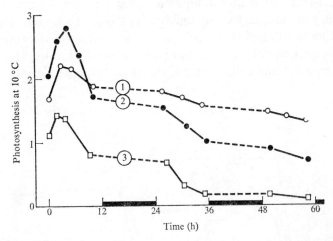

Fig. 25.6. Photosynthesis (relative scale) of the youngest mature leaves of some tropical grasses during 3 days chilling at 10 °C. Irradiance 170 W m⁻²; black bars: dark period. (1) *Paspalum dilatatum;* (2) *Zea mays,* hybrid Wisc. 575; (3) *Sorghum,* hybrid NK145 (after Taylor & Rowley, 1971).

drop to a low value, which gradually declines further (Fig. 25.6; Taylor & Rowley, 1971). The chloroplasts undergo ultrastructural changes with chilling temperatures: membranes of the individual thylakoids move closer together, reducing the space between them, while the chloroplast as a whole begins to swell (Taylor & Craig, 1971).

With respect to temperature-dependence of the activation energy of PEP-carboxylase, in chilling sensitive plants (millet, maize) there is an abrupt rise in Q_{10} at about 10–12 °C, whereas in chilling-resistant species the activation energy increases uniformly from 25 °C down to 5 °C (Phillips & McWilliam, 1971).

Respiration of cotton leaves is sharply reduced at temperatures under 15 °C (Amin, 1969). An extraordinarily strong depression of respiratory activity was observed between 10 °C and 0 °C in fruits of a group of chilling-sensitive plants (review: Larcher, 1973). Under 10 °C the Q_{10} for succinate oxidation by isolated mitochondria of chilling-sensitive plants (sweet potato roots, tomato fruits, cucumber fruits) increases from a normal range of 1.3–1.6 up to values of 2.2–6.3. In chilling-resistant tissue (beet roots, potato tubers, cauliflower buds) the Q_{10} for succinate oxidation remains between 1.7 and 1.8 over the entire tempera-ture range of 25 °C to 1.5 °C (Lyons & Raison, 1970).

CO_2-*gas exchange following chilling stress.* If *Sorghum* leaves are kept at 10° C (with 170 W m^{-2} illumination) for 1.5 days, then warmed to 25 °C, they are able to fix only one-half as much CO_2 on the succeeding day as they could before the cold treatment, while on the second day this CO_2-fixation falls to one-third of the original value (Fig. 25.7). Following a 2.5-day chilling stress, leaves of *Sorghum* become necrotic

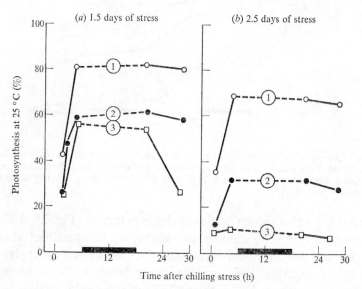

Fig. 25.7. Recovery of photosynthesis (as percentage of rate before stress; at 25 °C and 170 W m^{-2}) of the youngest mature leaves of some tropical grasses following chilling-stress at 10 °C.

(*a*) Photosynthesis after 1.5 days chilling-stress.
(*b*) Photosynthesis after 2.5 days chilling-stress.

Black bars: dark period. (1) *Paspalum dilatatum*; (2) *Zea mays*, hybrid Wisc. 575; (3) *Sorghum*, hybrid NK 145 (after Taylor & Rowley, 1971).

and photosynthetically inactive. Leaves of maize and *Paspalum dilatatum* are less sensitive, being able to photosynthesize at one-third to two-thirds of the control value after 2.5 days exposure to 10 °C (Taylor & Rowley, 1971).

Fig. 25.8 shows the respiratory rates at 25 °C of leaves and roots of cotton which have been subjected for varying periods to 2.8 °C (Amin, 1969). After a stress period lasting twelve to twenty-four hours, respiration is sharply increased over the values before treatment. However, if the chilling-stress lasted too long, severe damage results, so that respiration at 25 °C falls far below the levels before treatment. Maize seedlings treated for thirty-six hours at 0.3 °C showed higher O_2 uptake (at 21 °C) than untreated controls (Creencia & Bramlage, 1971). Increases in respiration following chilling stress have also been observed in sensitive fruits (review: Larcher, 1973).

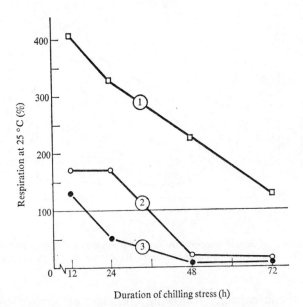

Fig. 25.8. Respiration rate (as percentage of rate before treatment) of tissue fractions of *Gossypium hirsutum* at 25 °C following chilling-stress at 2.8 ± 1 °C as affected by duration of stress. (1) Roots; (2) old leaves; (3) young leaves (after Amin, 1969).

Chilling-resistant plants

In chilling-resistant species, the photosynthetic rates under 10° C are more or less reduced, and this corresponds to the reduced carboxylating capacity, especially of PEP-carboxylase (Treharne & Cooper, 1969), and also to the increased gaseous diffusion resistance of the leaves (Fig. 25.9; Ludlow & Jarvis, 1971; Drake & Salisbury, 1972; and others).

The effect of low temperatures higher than 0 °C on the start of photosynthetic activity after illumination has been studied by Pharis, Hellmers & Schuurmans (1967). *Pinus ponderosa* seedlings show normal photosynthetic behavior for some weeks at 3 °C. They attain full photosynthetic activity within one to two hours after the start of the light period. However, after four months of 3 °C treatment, rate of photosynthesis does not reach its full value after six hours of light. In contrast, photosynthesis of cold-adapted *Pseudotsuga menziesii* seedlings is not influenced even by a four-month cold-treatment.

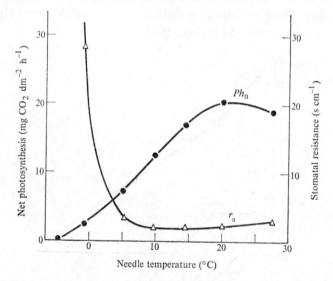

Fig. 25.9. Influence of needle temperature on net photosynthesis (Ph_n) and on stomatal resistance to CO_2 transfer (r_s) of *Picea sitchensis*. Irradiance, 240 W m^{-2} (after Ludlow & Jarvis, 1971).

Photosynthetic capacity following chilling was studied by Pharis, Hellmers & Schuurmans (1972). When *Pinus ponderosa* seedlings were exposed for only one to four days to 3 °C, then returned to 23 °C, they rapidly regained the original level of photosynthesis. However, if they were exposed to 3 °C for seventeen days, they attained at 23 °C only about one-half of the initial level of the photosynthetic capacity (see also Neilson, Ludlow & Jarvis, 1972). This reduction of photosynthesis is probably not a direct effect of cold, but could be a result of winter dormancy, which occurs in many plants when exposed to short days and temperatures lower than 5 °C (review on dormancy induction: Perry, 1971). A number of studies (Bourdeau, 1959; Parker, 1961; Bamberg, Schwarz & Tranquillini, 1967; Bauer, 1970) have demonstrated that the photosynthetic capacity might decline due to the onset of winter dormancy even without the direct effect of low temperature. It remains to be seen whether under such conditions the photosynthetic mechanism itself operates at a lower rate, or whether CO_2-gas exchange is depressed by stomatal closure as a result of increased concentration of abscisic acid, or of other inhibitors. Stomatal influence is indicated by Christerson's (1972) observations that the transpiration rates of frost-hardened seedlings of *Pinus sylvestris* and *Picea abies* were only about one-half that of unhardened plants, and that they increased with dehardening.

Frost

CO_2-*gas exchange during freezing temperatures*

Physiological principles. From all previous experience, CO_2 uptake in higher plants ceases abruptly if the assimilating organs freeze (Pisek, *et al.*, 1967). In contrast to higher plants, many lichens and mosses are able to fix some CO_2 in the frozen state. Furthermore, after thawing their photosynthesis rapidly reaches its full capacity (see Kallio & Kärenlampi, Chapter 17). Possible causes for the cold limit of photosynthesis at freezing in higher plants could be: (i) frost-induced closure of the stomata; (ii) abrupt increase in diffusion resistance in the mesophyll through ice formation in the intercellular spaces; (iii) the effect of extracellular freezing on enzyme activity and ultrastructure of the chloroplasts (Heber, 1967). Further studies on the effect of freezing on the various processes concerned with photosynthesis and CO_2 flux are urgently needed.

Structural changes in plastids and mitochondria below 0°C. After about four-hour exposure of seedlings of *Agropyron glaucum* and *Triticum aestivum* to 0 °C their plastids stretch and assume irregular forms, mostly spindle shapes. Gradually all starch grains disappear. At -4 °C the plastids round up, begin to expand, and develop an inflexible coat (Kwiatkowska, 1970*b*).

In epidermal cells of coleoptiles of seedlings of these two cereals the mitochondria change in form and size in two steps when cooled below 0 °C. Exposure to -4 °C for five to twenty minutes causes elongation of

571

the mitochondria and decrease in their number. Longer exposure at −4 °C (60–120 min) causes the mitochondria to round up and swell at the beginning of extracellular ice formation. Ultrastructural changes are first visible after about a week at 0 °C to −4 °C, and involve clarification of the matrix and reduction of cristae. If the seedlings are returned again to warm temperatures, the mitochondria resume their original condition (Kwiatkowska, 1970*a,b*). Similar observations, have been reported frequently in the literature (review: Kwiatkowska, 1970*a*).

Specific cold limits of photosynthesis. In all chilling-resistant higher plants photosynthesis ceases a few degrees below 0 °C (Zeller, 1951; Tranquillini, 1957; Pisek & Rehner, 1958; Larcher, 1961; Polster & Fuchs, 1963; Keller, 1965; Negisi, 1966; Pisek, Larcher & Unterholzner, 1967; Pharis, Hellmers & Schuurmans, 1970; Ludlow & Jarvis, 1971; reviews by Pisek, 1960, and Kozlowski & Keller, 1966).

Table 25.3 summarizes the cold-limits of CO_2 uptake at 3 klx of a number of chilling-resistant species (Pisek *et al.*, 1967). An intermediate chilling-sensitive plant is illustrated by *Citrus*, in which photosynthesis in summer ceases at −1 °C, probably before the leaves freeze. During the vegetation period, photosynthesis in almost all the species investigated (northern conifers, deciduous and evergreen trees of temperate and warm temperate zones, alpine dwarf shrubs and shrubs of atlantic origin) ceases between −3 ° and −5 °C. A somewhat lower minimum is characteristic for the subarctic and high-alpine herbs *Oxyria digyna* and *Ranunculus glacialis* (not, however, for the alpine *Geum reptans*), and the spring geophyte *Leucojum vernum*. Various plants from the alpine timberline, which even in summer are frequently exposed to freezing temperatures, show a minimum only 1–2 °C lower than the same species from the valley sites.

During the vegetation period, herbaceous plants and the foliage of the woody plants will not survive ice formation. Photosynthesis ceases with appearance of necrosis injury (tissue disruption) in the leaves. In winter the temperature minimum for photosynthesis falls to values 3–4 °C below those of summer, but never reaches the low temperatures which frost-resistant leaves can undergo without injury. Especially striking is the low temperature minimum shown by Mediterranean species as *Olea europaea* subsp. *sativa*, *Laurus nobilis*, and *Citrus limon* which do not acquire frost tolerance in winter, but rather an increased frost avoidance through effective lowering of the freezing point (Larcher, 1961,1963*a*).

The temperature minima for CO_2 uptake, insofar as they coincide with ice formation in the tissues, appear to be independent of external factors such as light (Pisek, Larcher & Unterholzner, 1967).

Table 25.3. *Cold limits for* CO_2 *uptake* (Ph_n) *and ranges of tiss* : *freezing temperatures of some cormophytes* (from Pisek, Larcher Unterholzner, 1967)

Species	Summer Cold limit of Ph_n (°C)	Summer Tissue-freezing temp. (°C)	Winter Cold limit of Ph_n (°C)	Winter Tissue-freezing temp. (°C)
Coniferous trees				
Pinus sylvestris	−3.5	(−3.0 to −4.4)	−7.0	(−6.1 to −7.0)
Abies alba	−3.5	(−3.0 to −4.4)	−7.5	(−5.9 to −7.8)
Picea abies	−4.1	(−3.8 to −5.0)	−6.5	(−5.6 to −7.2)
Taxus baccata	−4.9	(−3.6 to −5.2)	−8.0*	(−4.2 to −6.8)
Pinus cembra	−5.0			
Larix decidua	−5.1	(−4.5 to −5.6)		
Dicotyledonous trees				
Deciduous trees				
Alnus viridis	−3.5	(−3.2 to −4.2)		
Betula pendula	−3.9	(−3.2 to −4.1)		
Fagus sylvatica, shade leaves	−5.0			
Evergreen trees				
Citrus limon	−1.3	(−3.2 to −4.2)	−7.0	(−5.6 to −7.2)
Laurocerasus officinalis	−4.0	(−3.0 to −4.0)	−6.0	(−4.3 to −6.0)
Pittosporum tobira	−4.0	(−3.5 to −4.3)	−7.5*	(−4.5 to −6.3)
Arbutus unedo	−4.5	(−3.5 to −4.7)		
Quercus ilex			−4.9	(−5.0 to −6.0)
Olea europaea subsp. *sativa*			−8.0	
Shrubs				
Viscum album	−3.0	(−2.6 to −4.2)	−7.0	(−6.0 to −8.2)
Hedera helix	−3.0	(−2.2 to −3.8)	−7.1*	(−4.5 to −5.6)
Vaccinium vitis-idaea	−3.5	(−3.0 to −4.2)		
Vaccinium myrtillus	−3.7	(−3.2 to −4.2)		
Herbs				
Geum reptans	−3.0	(−1.5 to −4.0)		
Leucojum vernum (March)	−5.5*	(−3.1 to −4.7)		
Oxyria digyna	−6.0*	(−3.0 to −3.9)		
Ranunculus glacialis	−6.0*	(−3.0 to −3.9)		

* Leaves undercooled some degrees below their freezing point during experiment; no CO_2 uptake when leaves were frozen.

Dark respiration. Dark respiration continues at temperatures below the tissue freezing point, although at much lower intensities. CO_2 release can be demonstrated down to −6 °C (Polster & Fuchs, 1963; Keller, 1965) and even to −10 °C (Zeller, 1951; Rakitina, 1960; and others), even when the plants are frozen (cf. Pisek *et al.*, 1967).

After-effect of frost on CO_2-gas exchange

Field experiments. In autumn, the CO_2 uptake during the day decreases progressively with increasing intensity and duration of night-frost and ceases entirely after a close succession of frost nights, even though the daytime temperatures are a few degrees above zero (Fig. 25.10; Tranquillini, 1957). After short and not too sharp frosts photosynthesis is strongly reduced, but recovers gradually after thawing of the assimilatory organs (Tranquillini, 1957; Polster & Fuchs, 1963; Keller, 1965; Negisi, 1966). In extreme frost periods, during which temperatures fall below the freezing point of the leaves each night, photosynthesis remains blocked even when it is mild and frost-free during the day. Only winter annuals such as *Hordeum vulgare, Triticum vulgare, Spinacea oleracea,* and *Valerianella locusta* maintain a positive daily CO_2-balance during the entire winter, as long as daytime temperatures rise above the freezing point of the leaves (Zeller, 1951).

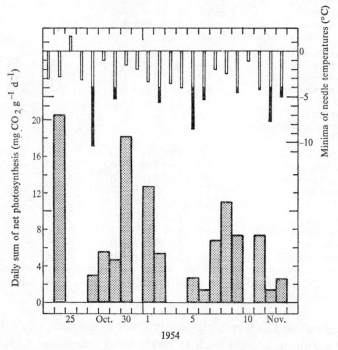

Fig. 25.10. Daily sum of net photosynthesis of *Pinus cembra* in the field at the alpine timberline in autumn on clear days, and minimum needle temperature during the previous night. Temperatures below -4 °C (i.e. freezing point of the needles, Tranquillini & Holzer, 1958) are marked by black area (after Tranquillini, 1957).

After-effect of frost on photosynthesis of field-growing plants as measured under standard conditions. The after-effect of freezing temperatures can be clearly shown by measuring photosynthetic capacity of field grown plants in the laboratory under constant conditions (Pisek & Winkler, 1958; Saeki & Nomoto, 1958; Bourdeau, 1959; Larcher, 1961; Negisi, 1966; Bamberg *et al.*, 1967; Zelawski & Kucharska, 1967; Schwarz, 1971; Tranquillini & Machl-Ebner, 1971; and others). The photosynthetic capacity of *Picea abies* from the valley and the alpine timberline, measured at 12 °C and 10 klx from autumn to spring is presented in Fig. 11, in relation to the air temperature minimum at the habitat (Pisek & Winkler, 1958). Photosynthetic capacity was severely reduced as soon as sharp frosts occurred in the valley at the end of November. The effective temperature threshold again proved to be the freezing or undercooling temperature of the needles (-5 °C to -7 °C in *Picea abies*, Pisek, Larcher & Unterholzner, 1967). In December, with temperature minima above -5 °C the photosynthesis reached about two-thirds of the summer capacity. At the end of January and in the first half of February minimum air temperatures remained almost constantly below -10 °C, and CO_2 uptake at 12 °C was fully blocked. In plants from the alpine timberline, however, photosynthesis was blocked from end of November to mid-April. It then required several days at room temperature before the photosynthetic capacity could recover to some extent. There are plants such as *Rhododendron ferrugineum*, *Pseudotsuga menziesii*, and *Picea glauca*, whose photosynthesis can be activated very quickly and to a high level by warm temperature, but species like *Pinus cembra* and *Pinus contorta* recover very slowly and incompletely (Schwarz, 1971). The depth of winter dormancy must play a role in the ability to recover (Pisek & Winkler, 1958; Schwarz, 1971), while temperature during the recovery period is of less importance (Tranquillini & Machl-Ebner, 1971).

Photosynthesis following experimental frost treatments. The after-effect of frost can be best evaluated in the laboratory with defined cold treatments (Pisek & Kemnitzer, 1968; Bauer, Huter & Larcher, 1969; Pharis, Hellmers & Schuurmans, 1970; Neilson, Ludlow & Jarvis, 1972). *Abies alba* has been intensively studied using such techniques (Fig. 25.12): In October, when the fir is not yet fully frost-hardened, photosynthesis is depressed more severely by frost than in December (cf. Neilson, Ludlow & Jarvis, 1972). Temperatures above the freezing point of the needles (in October about -4 °C, in December about

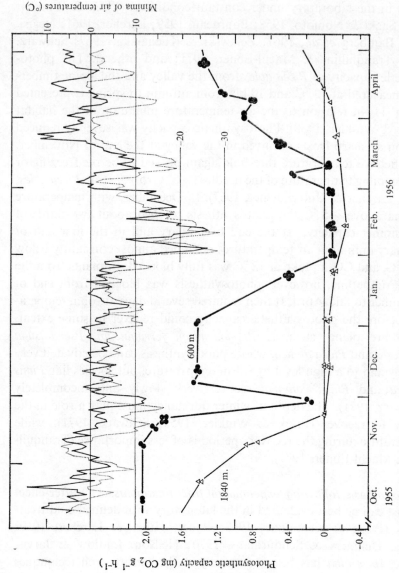

Fig. 25.11. Photosynthetic capacity (at 12 °C and 10 klx) of sun twigs of *Picea abies* from the valley (600 m) and from the alpine timberline (1840 m) from October to April, and daily minima of air temperatures (upper curves) at an elevation of 580 m (solid line) and 1909 m (dotted line) (after Pisek & Winkler, 1958).

−8 °C) have no effect on photosynthetic capacity as measured at 15 °C with 10 klx. Only when the needles freeze is a post-treatment reduction in CO_2 uptake observed. Ice formation in the leaves thus results not only in cessation of CO_2 fixation during treatment, but also restricts the subsequent photosynthetic capacity. With increasing sharpness of frost the extent of the subsequent depression increases: photosynthesis is entirely stopped in October following −8 °C and in December following −15 °C. However, as long as no necrosis occurs, the photosynthetic apparatus can always fully recover.

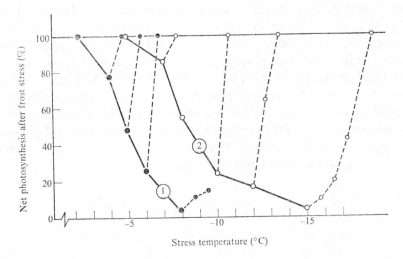

Fig. 25.12. Depression of photosynthesis (solid lines; measured at 15 °C and 10 klx; expressed as per cent of controls) of needles of *Abies alba* after 12 h exposure to various frost temperatures, and recovery (broken lines) during the following days. (1) Measurements in October; (2) measurements in December (after Pisek & Kemnitzer, 1968).

Causes for depression of net photosynthesis following frost. It is not possible to decide to what extent the reduction in CO_2 uptake following frost is due to inactivation of enzymes involved in the photosynthetic processes or to a frost-related paralysis of the stomata. Thus, net CO_2 uptake of leaves of *Hedera helix* is strongly reduced following frost, but no change was observed in the Hill reaction with ferricyanide and 2,6-dichloro-phenolindophenol (Albrecht, 1972). Decisive experiments on the activity of RuDP-carboxylase following frost are yet to be made.

CO_2 uptake may also be hindered by stomatal closure. This is indicated by the observation that a reduction in CO_2 uptake after frost is accompanied by a reduction in transpiration rate to the cuticular level

577

(Parker, 1963; review: Larcher, 1972). Stomatal closure may be caused by a high level of CO_2 in the mesophyll, when CO_2 fixation is reduced and respiratory CO_2 release is enhanced (Christerson, 1972; Drake & Salisbury, 1972). In the field, stomatal closure in winter might also be a result of water stress in the leaves. On warmer days the plants may transpire appreciably, while the soil still remains frozen, so that water uptake and conduction are interrupted (reviews: Kozlowski, 1961; Larcher, 1963*b*; Havranek, 1972).

Dark respiration after frost. In the recovery phase after frost, dark respiration shows an overshoot (Pisek & Winkler, 1958; Larcher, 1961; Rakitina, 1960; Weise & Polster, 1962; Terumoto, 1965; Pisek & Kemnitzer, 1968; Bauer, Huter & Larcher, 1969; and others). This intensive increase in respiration may lead to a marked impairment of the CO_2 balance during short warm periods in winter. In such cases there may be strong CO_2 release even in light, because photosynthesis is inactive. Bauer, Huter & Larcher (1969) investigated the respiratory behaviour of *Abies alba* following a two-hour frost exposure at different temperatures (Fig. 25.13). A stimulation of dark respiration at 20°C following frost was found, but only if the needles had frozen hard during

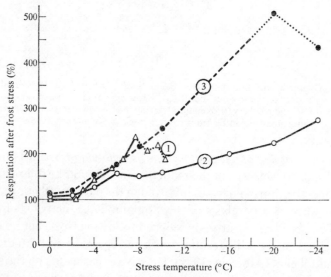

Fig. 25.13. Dark respiration of shoots of *Abies alba* at 20 °C (expressed as per cent of rate before treatment) following 2 h exposure to the frost temperatures given in the abscissa. (1) Measurements in late summer; (2) measurements in winter, field grown plants; (3) measurements in winter, greenhouse grown plants; dotted part of the lines represents respiration after necrotic damage of the needles (from Bauer, Huter & Larcher, 1969).

the cold treatment. (During the intensive growth in spring and early summer the needles showed necrosis from the frost treatment, thus a stimulation of respiration from frost in these periods could not be proved.) The extent and duration of the respiratory rise increase with the sharpness of the frost treatment. However, the needles become partially necrotic, respiration increases to a lesser extent, because of the reduced mass of living respiring tissue. The peak of CO_2 release is reached four to twelve hours after thawing, depending on the frost temperature. The respiratory enhancement attains a maximum of 250% in field-growing plants in winter, and of 500% in greenhouse plants, as compared with respiration before frost. Furthermore, in late summer the respiration of the plants reacted more sensitively. (Frost hardy provenances of *Picea abies* and *Pseudotsuga menziesii* showed a stronger respiratory overshoot after 3 days frost treatment at $-11\,°C$ than did the less frost hardy material used by Weise & Polster (1962).) If the frost was not lower than $-6\,°C$, the respiratory overshoot disappears after ten to twelve hours; after treatment at still lower temperatures, respiration did not normalize until several days had passed.

Summary

This chapter reviews the temperature-dependent limits of net photosynthesis in higher plants, and the alterations in their CO_2-gas exchange following temperature stresses. Depending on species, the heat limits of net photosynthesis range from $35\,°C$ to $61\,°C$. There is also a reduction in CO_2 uptake as an after-effect of heat stress; the degree and duration of this depression become larger with increasing stress (both in temperature and in duration). In chilling-sensitive plants, CO_2 uptake is blocked even at temperatures a few degrees above $0\,°C$. Furthermore, the photosynthetic activity of sensitive plants declines gradually when they are kept for an extended period at temperatures some degrees above the cold limit of their net photosynthesis; after returning such plants to optimal temperatures their photosynthesis never regains the original value. With chilling-tolerant cormophytes, ice formation in photosynthetic tissue (occurring a few degrees below $0\,°C$) has a very decisive influence on their CO_2-gas exchange. Upon freezing, photosynthesis is abruptly stopped and remains depressed after thawing. The severity of this depression depends on the depth and frequency of the frost. On the other hand, after thawing, dark respiration shows a strong overshoot for some hours.

Stress factors and assimilates

References

Ageeva, O. G. & Lyutova, M. I. (1971). Vliyanie teplovogo zakalivaniya gorokha *Pisum sativum*. L. na fotosintez i fotokhimicheskie reaktsii. (The influence of heat hardening of peas *Pisum sativum* L. on photosynthesis and photochemical reactions.) *Botanitcheskii Zhurnal*, **56**, 1365–73.

Albrecht, A. (1972). CO_2-Gaswechsel und Hill-Aktivität von *Hedera helix* L. im Jahresverlauf unter Berücksichtigung klimatischer Faktoren. *Photosynthetica*, **6**, 240–6.

Alexandrov, V. Ya., Lomagin, A. G. & Feldman, N. L. (1970). The responsive increase in thermostability of plant cells. *Protoplasma*, **69**, 417–58.

Amin, J. V. (1969). Some aspects of respiration and respiration inhibitors in low temperature effects of the cotton plant. *Physiologia Plantarum*, **22**, 1184–91.

Bamberg, S., Schwarz, W. & Tranquillini, W. (1967). Influence of daylength on the photosynthetic capacity of stone pine (*Pinus cembra* L.). *Ecology*, **48**, 264–9.

Bauer, H. (1970). Hitzeresistenz und CO_2-Gaswechsel nach Hitzestress von Tanne (*Abies alba* Mill.) und Bergahorn (*Acer pseudoplatanus* L.). Ph.D. thesis, Innsbruck.

Bauer, H. (1972). CO_2-Gaswechsel nach Hitzestress bei *Abies alba* Mill. und *Acer pseudoplatanus* L. *Photosynthetica*, **6**, 424–34.

Bauer, H., Huter, M. & Larcher, W. (1969). Der Einfluß und die Nachwirkung von Hitze- und Kältestress auf den CO_2-Gaswechsel von Tanne und Ahorn. *Berichte der Deutschen Botanischen Gesellschaft*, **82**, 65–70.

Begg, J. E. & Jarvis, P. G. (1968). Photosynthesis in Townsville lucerne (*Stylosanthes humilis* H.B.K.). *Agricultural Meteorology*, **5**, 91–109.

Ben Zioni, A. & Itai, C. (1972). Short- and long-term effects of high temperatures (47–49 °C) on tobacco leaves. I. Photosynthesis. *Physiologia Plantarum*, **27**, 216–99.

Billings, W. D., Godfrey, F. J., Chabot, B. F. & Bourque, D. P. (1971). Metabolic acclimation to temperature in arctic and alpine ecotypes of *Oxyria digyna*. *Arctic and Alpine Research*, **3**, 277–89.

Björkman, O., Pearcy, R. W., Harrison, A. T. & Mooney, H. (1972). Photosynthetic adaptation to high temperatures: A field study in Death Valley, California. *Science*, **175**, 786–9.

Bourdeau, Ph. F. (1959). Seasonal variations of the photosynthetic efficiency of evergreen conifers. *Ecology*, **40**, 63–7.

Charles-Edwards, D. A. & Charles-Edwards, J. (1970). An analysis of the temperature response curves of CO_2 exchange in the leaves of two temperate and one tropical grass species. *Planta*, **94**, 140–51.

Christerson, L. (1972). The transpiration rate of unhardened, hardened and dehardened seedlings of spruce and pine. *Physiologica Plantarum*, **26**, 258–63.

Creencia, R. P. & Branlage, W. J. (1971). Reversibility of chilling injury to corn seedlings. *Plant Physiology*, **47**, 389–92.

Daniell, J. W., Chappell, W. E. & Couch, H. B. (1969). Effect of sublethal and lethal temperatures on plant cells. *Plant Physiology*, **44**, 1684–9.

Drake, B. G. & Salisbury, F. B. (1972). Aftereffects of low and high temperature pretreatment on leaf resistance, transpiration, and leaf temperature in *Xanthium*. *Plant Physiology*, **50**, 572–5.

El-Sharkawy, M. A. & Hesketh, J. D. (1964). Effects of temperature and water deficit on leaf photosynthetic rates of different species. *Crop Science*, **4**, 515–18.

Esipova, I. V. (1959). Posledeistvie vysokikh i nizkikh temperatur na fotosintez khlopchatnika. (After-effects of high and low temperatures on the photosynthesis of the cotton plants). *Fiziologiya rastenii*, **6**, 104–6.

Feldman, N. L. (1968). The effect of heat hardening on the heat resistance of some enzymes from plant leaves. *Planta*, **78**, 213–25.

Havranek, W. (1972). Über die Bedeutung der Bodentemperatur für die Photosynthese und Transpiration junger Forstpflanzen und für die Stoffproduktion an der Waldgrenze. *Angewandte Botanik*, **46**, 101–16.

Heath, O. V. S. & Orchard, B. (1957). Temperature effects on the minimum intercellular space carbon dioxide concentration 'Γ'. *Nature*, **180**, 180–1.

Heber, U. (1967). Freezing injury and uncoupling of phosphorylation from electron transport in chloroplasts. *Plant Physiology*, **42**, 1343–50.

Hellmuth, E. O. (1967). A method of determining true values for photosynthesis and respiration under field conditions. *Flora*, B **157**, 265–86.

Hellmuth, E. O. (1971). Eco-physiological studies on plants in arid and semiarid regions in Western-Australia. III. Comparative studies on photosynthesis, respiration and water relations of ten arid zone and two semi-arid zone plants under winter and late summer climatic conditions. *Journal of Ecology*, **59**, 225–59.

Helms, J. A. (1965). Diurnal and seasonal patterns of net assimilation in douglas-fir, *Pseudotsuga menziesii* (Mirb.) Franco, as influenced by environment. *Ecology*, **46**, 698–708.

Hew, C.-S., Krotkov, G. & Canvin, D. T. (1969). Effects of temperature on photosynthesis and CO_2-evolution in light and darkness by green leaves. *Plant Physiology*, **44**, 671–7.

Hofstra, G. & Hesketh, J. D. (1969). Effects of temperature on the gas exchange of leaves in the light and dark. *Planta*, **85**, 228–37.

Kamentseva, I. E. (1969). Teploustoichivost fotosinteza i dykhaniya vesennikh i zetnikh listev *Pulmonaria obscura* Dumort. (Heat resistance of photosynthesis and respiration of spring and summer leaves of *Pulmonaria obscura* Dumort). *Doklady Akademiya Nauka SSSR*, **186**, 968–70.

Keller, T. (1965). Über den winterlichen Gaswechsel der Koniferen im schweizerischen Mittelland. *Schweizerische Zeitschrift für Forstwesen*, **116**, 719–29.

Kinbacher, E. J. & Sullivan, C. Y. (1967). Effect of high temperature on the respiration rate of *Phaseolus* sp. *Proceedings of the American Society for Horticultural Science*, **90**, 163–8.

Kozlowski, T. T. (1961). The movement of water in trees. *Forest Science*, **7**, 177–92.

Kozlowski, T. T. & Keller, T. (1966). Food relations of woody plants. *Botanical Review*, **32**, 293–382.

Kriedemann, P. E. (1968). Photosynthesis in vine leaves as a function of light intensity, temperature, and leaf age. *Vitis*, **7**, 213–20.

Krueger, K. W. & Ferrell, W. K. (1965). Comparative photosynthetic and respiratory responses to temperature and light by *Pseudotsuga menziesii* var. *menziesii* and var. *glauca* seedlings. *Ecology*, **46**, 794–801.

Kusumoto, T. (1957). Physiological and ecological studies on the plant production in plant communities, III. *Japanese Journal of Ecology*, **7**, 126–30.

Kusumoto, T. (1961). An ecological analysis of the distribution of broad-leaved evergreen trees, based on the dry matter production. *Japanese Journal of Botany*, **17**, 307–31.

Kwiatkowska, M. (1970*a*). Cold induced changes in the morphology of mitochondria in coleoptiles of corn of different frost-resistance. *Acta Societas Botanicorum Poloniae*, **39**, 347–60.

Kwiatkowska, M. (1970*b*). Cytological changes connected with the process of adaptation to low temperatures in the coleoptile epidermis of *Agropyron glaucum*. *Acta Societas Botanicorum Poloniae*, **39**, 361–71.

Larcher, W. (1961). Jahresgang des Assimilations- und Respirationsvermögens von *Olea europaea* L. ssp. *sativa* Hoff. et Link., *Quercus ilex* L. und *Quercus pubescens* Willd. aus dem nördlichen Gardaseegebiet. *Planta*, **56**, 575–606.

Larcher, W. (1963*a*). Zur Frage des Zusammenhanges zwischen Austrocknungsresistenz und Frosthärte bei Immergrünen. *Protoplasma*, **57**, 569–87.

Larcher, W. (1963*b*). Zur spätwinterlichen Erschwerung der Wasserbilanz von Holzpflanzen an der Waldgrenze. *Berichte des Naturwissenschaftlich-Medizinischen Vereins in Innsbruck*, **53**, 125–37.

Larcher, W. (1969). The effect of environmental and physiological variables on the carbon dioxide gas exchange of trees. *Photosynthetica*, **3**, 167–98.

Larcher, W. (1972). Der Wasserhaushalt immergrüner Holzpflanzen im Winter. *Berichte der Deutschen Botanischen Gesellschaft*, **85**, 315–27.

Larcher, W. (1973). Limiting temperatures for life functions. In *Temperature and Life*, eds. H. Precht, J. Christopherson, H. Hensel & W. Larcher, pp. 195–231. Berlin, Springer-Verlag.

Levitt, J. (1972). *Responses of plants to environmental stresses*. New York, Academic Press.

Lingl-Kemnitzer, R. (1964). Der Einfluß der Temperatur auf Nettoassimilation und Atmung der Tanne im Zusammenhang mit Kälte- und Hitzeresistenz. Ph.D. thesis, University of Innsbruck.

Ludlow, M. M. & Jarvis, P. G. (1971). Photosynthesis in Sitka spruce (*Picea sitchensis* (Bong.) Carr.). I. General Characteristics. *Journal of Applied Ecology*, **8**, 925–53.

Ludlow, M. M. & Wilson, G. L. (1971). Photosynthesis of tropical pasture plants. I. Illuminance, carbon dioxide concentration, leaf temperature, and leaf-air vapour pressure difference. *Australian Journal of Biological Science*, **24**, 449–70.

Lyons, J. M. & Raison, J. K. (1970). Oxidative activity of mitochondria isolated from plant tissues sensitive and resistant to chilling injury. *Plant Physiology*, **45**, 386–9.

Lyutova, M. I. (1958). Izuchenie fotosinteza na kletkakh s eksperimentalno povyshennoi ustoichivostyu. (Studying photosynthesis in cells with experimentally increased resistance). *Botanitcheskii Zhurnal*, **43**, 283–7.

Lyutova, M. I. (1962). Vliyanie teplovoi zakalki na fotosintez i dykhanie listev. (The effect of heat hardening on photosynthesis and respiration of leaves of higher plants). *Botanitcheskii Zhurnal*, **47**, 1761–74.

Lyutova, M. I. (1963a). Prochnost svyazi khlorofilla s belkom u rastenii s povyshennoi teploustoichivostyu. (The strength of the bond between chlorophyll and protein in plants endowed with high resistance). *Doklady Akademiya Nauka SSSR*, **149**, 1206–8.

Lyutova, M. I. (1963b). Temperaturnaya zavisimost fotosinteza zakalennykh nagrevom listev tradeskantsii. (Temperature dependence of photosynthesis of heat hardened *Tradescantia* leaves). *Botanitcheskii Zhurnal*, **48**, 890–3.

Meidner, H. & Mansfield, T. A. (1968). *Physiology of stomata*. London, McGraw-Hill.

Negisi, K. (1966). Photosynthesis, respiration and growth in 1-year-old seedlings of *Pinus densiflora*, *Cryptomeria japonica* and *Chamaecyparis obtusa*. *Bulletin of the Tokyo University Forests*, **62**, 1–115.

Neilson, R. E., Ludlow, M. M. & Jarvis, P. G. (1972). Photosynthesis in Sitka spruce (*Picea sitchensis* (Bong.) Carr.). II. Response to temperature. *Journal of Applied Ecology*, **9**, 721–45.

Nomoto, N. (1964). Primary productivity of beech forest in Japan. *Japanese Journal of Botany*, **18**, 385–421.

Parker, J. (1961). Seasonal trends in carbon dioxide absorption, cold resistance, and transpiration of some evergreens. *Ecology*, **42**, 372–80.

Parker, J. (1963). Causes of the winter decline in transpiration and photosynthesis in some evergreens. *Forest Science*, **9**, 158–66.

Parker, J. (1971). Heat resistance and respiratory response in twigs of some common tree species. *Botanical Gazette*, **132**, 228–73.

Perry, T. O. (1971). Dormancy of trees in winter. *Science*, **171**, 29–36.

Pharis, R. P., Hellmers, H. & Schuurmans, E. (1967). Kinetics of the daily rate of photosynthesis at low temperatures for two conifers. *Plant Physiology*, **42**, 525–31.

Pharis, R. P., Hellmers, H. & Schuurmans, E. (1970). Effects of subfreezing temperatures on photosynthesis of evergreen conifers under controlled environment conditions. *Photosynthetica*, **4**, 273–79.

Pharis, R. P., Hellmers, H. & Schuurmans, E. (1972). The decline and recovery of photosynthesis of Ponderosa pine seedlings subjected to low, but above freezing temperatures. *Canadian Journal of Botany*, **50**, 1965–70.

Pharis, R. P. & Woods, F. W. (1960). Effects of temperature upon photosynthesis and respiration of Choctawhatchee sand pine. *Ecology*, **41**, 797–9.

Phillips, P. J. & McWilliam, J. R. (1971). Thermal responses of the primary carboxylating enzymes from C_3 and C_4 plants adapted to contrasting temperature environments. In *Photosynthesis and Photorespiration*, ed. M. D. Hatch, C. B. Osmond & R. O. Slatyer, pp. 97–104. New York, Wiley-Interscience.

Pisek, A. (1960). Immergrüne Pflanzen. In *Handbuch der Pflanzenphysiologie*, ed. W. Ruhland, vol. 5, part II, pp. 415–59. Berlin, Springer-Verlag.

Pisek, A. & Kemnitzer, R. (1968). Der Einfluß von Frost auf die Photosynthese der Weißtanne (*Abies alba* Mill.). *Flora*, B **157**, 314–26.

Pisek, A., Larcher, W., Pack, I. & Unterholzner, R. (1968). Kardinale Temperaturbereiche der Photosynthese und Grenztemperaturen des Lebens der Blätter verschiedener Spermatophyten. II. Temperaturmaximum der Netto-Photosynthese und Hitzeresistenz der Blätter. *Flora*, B **158**, 110–28.

Pisek, A., Larcher, W. & Unterholzner, R. (1967). Kardinale Temperaturbereiche der Photosynthese und Grenztemperaturen des Lebens der Blätter verschiedener Spermatophyten. I. Temperaturminimum der Nettoassimilation, Gefrier- und Frostschadensbereiche der Blätter. *Flora*, B **157**, 239–64.

Pisek, A. & Rehner, G. (1958). Temperaturminima der Netto-Assimilation von mediterranen und nordisch-alpinen Immergrünen. *Berichte der Deutschen Botanischen Gesellschaft*, **71**, 188–93.

Pisek, A. & Winkler, E. (1958). Assimilationsvermögen und Respiration der Fichte (*Picea excelsa* Link.) in verschiedener Höhenlage und der Zirbe (*Pinus cembra* L.) an der alpinen Waldgrenze. *Planta*, **51**, 518–43.

Pisek, A. & Winkler, E. (1959). Licht- und Temperaturabhängigkeit der CO_2-Assimilation von Fichte (*Picea excelsa* Link.), Zirbe (*Pinus cembra* L.) und Sonnenblume (*Helianthus annuus* L.). *Planta*, **53**, 532–50.

Polster, H. & Fuchs, S. (1963). Winterassimilation und -atmung der Kiefer (*Pinus silvestris* L.) im mitteldeutschen Binnenlandklima. *Archiv für Forstwesen*, **12**, 1011–23.

Rakitina, Z. G. (1960). Vliyanie temperaturykh vozdeistvii na prozess dykhaniya drevesnykh rastenii. (The influence of previous temperatures on the respiratory process of woody plants.) In *Physiology of Hardiness of Plants*, pp. 278–84, Moscow, Nauka.

Raschke, K. (1970). Temperature dependence of CO_2-assimilation and stomatal aperture in leaf sections of *Zea mays*. *Planta*, **91**, 336–63.

Saeki, T. & Nomoto, N. (1958). On the seasonal change of photosynthetic activity of some deciduous and evergreen broadleaf trees. *The Botanical Magazine, Tokyo*, **71**, 235–41.

Schulze, E.-D., Lange, O. L., Kappen, L., Buschbom, U. & Evenari, M. (1973). Stomatal responses to changes in temperature at increasing water stress. *Planta*, **110**, 29–42.

Schulze, E.-D., Lange, O. L. & Koch, W. (1972). Ökophysiologische Untersuchungen an Wild- und Kulturpflanzen der Negev-Wüste. II. Die Wirkung der Außenfaktoren auf CO_2-Gaswechsel und Transpiration am Ende der Trockenzeit. *Oecologia*, **8**, 334–55.

Schwarz, W. (1971). Das Photosynthesevermögen einiger Immergrüner während des Winters und seine Reaktivierungsgeschwindigkeit nach scharfen Frösten. *Berichte der Deutschen Botanischen Gesellschaft*, **84**, 585–94.

Semikhatova, O. A. (1964). Intensivnost i dinamika fotosinteza molodykh listev kukuruzy posle razlitchnoi dlitelnosti vyderzhivaniya ukh pri vysokoi temperature. (The rate and dynamics of photosynthesis in young leaves of *Zea mays* after high temperature treatment of different duration.) In *Cytological aspects of adaption of plants to the environmental factors*, pp. 55–9, Moscow, Nauka.

Semikhatova, O. A. (1968). (Indices of respiratory gas exchange of plants). *Botanitcheskii Zhurnal*, **53**, 1069–84.

Semikhatova, O. A. & Denko, E. I. (1960). O vozdeistvii temperatury na dykhanie listev rastenii. (The effect of temperature on the respiration of leaves.) *Eksperimentalnaya Botanika, Moskva*, **14**, 112–37.

Semikhatova, O. A., Saakov, V. S. & Gorbacheva, G. I. (1962). Izuchenie posledeistviya temperatury na intensivnost i dinamiku fotosinteza *Polygonum sachalinense*. (Studies on the after-effect of temperature on the rate and dynamics of photosynthesis of *Polygonum sachalinense*). *Eksperimentalnaya Botanika, Moskva*, **15**, 25–42.

Stålfelt, M. G. (1962). The effect of temperature on opening of the stomatal cells. *Physiologia plantarum*, **15**, 772–9.

Strain, B. R. & Chase, V. C. (1966). Effect of past and prevailing temperatures on the carbon dioxide exchange capacities of some woody desert perennials. *Ecology*, **47**, 1043–5.

Taylor, A. O. & Craig, A. S. (1971). Plants under climatic stress. II. Low temperature, high light effects on chloroplast ultrastructure. *Plant Physiology*, **47**, 719–25.

Taylor, A. O. & Rowley, J. A. (1971). Plants under climatic stress. I. Low temperature, high light effects on photosynthesis. *Plant Physiology*, **47**, 713–18.

Terumoto, I. (1965). Respiration activity in the lake ball with special reference to the effect of freezing on respiration. *Low Temperature Science*, Ser. B, **23**, 1–10.

Tieszen, L. L. (1970). A report on the photosynthesis and primary production at Barrow intensive site. *Tundra Biome Meeting*, Kevo, pp. 1–4.

Tieszen, L. L. & Sigurdson, D. C. (1973). Effect of temperature on carboxylase activity and stability in some Calvin cycle grasses from the Arctic. *Arctic and Alpine Research*, **5**, 59–66.

Tranquillini, W. (1957). Standortsklima, Wasserbilanz und CO_2-Gaswechsel junger Zirben (*Pinus cembra* L.) an der alpinen Waldgrenze. *Planta*, **49**, 612–61.

Tranquillini, W. & Holzer, K. (1958). Über das Gefrieren und Auftauen von

U

Coniferennadeln. *Berichte der Deutschen Botanischen Gesellschaft*, **71**, 143–56.

Tranquillini, W. & Machl-Ebner, I. (1971). Über den Einfluß von Wärme auf das Photosynthesevermögen der Zirbe (*Pinus cembra* L.) und der Alpenrose (*Rhododendron ferrugineum* L.) im Winter. *Report of Kevo Subarctic Research Station*, **8**, 158–66.

Treharne, K. J. & Cooper, J. P. (1969). Effect of temperature on the activity of carboxylases in tropical and temperate gramineae. *Journal of Experimental Botany*, **20**, 170–5.

Wagenbreth, D. (1965a). Durch Hitzeschocks induzierte Vitalitätsänderungen bei Laubholzblättern. *Flora*, A **156**, 63–75.

Wagenbreth, D. (1965b). Das Auftreten von zwei Letalstufen bei Hitzeeinwirkung auf Pappelblätter. *Flora*, A **156**, 116–26.

Weise, G. & Polster, H. (1962). Untersuchungen über den Einfluß von Kältebelastungen auf die physiologische Aktivität von Forstgewächsen. II. Stoffwechselphysiologische Untersuchungen zur Frage der Frostresistenz von Fichten- und Douglasienherkünften (*Picea abies* (L.) Karst. und *Pseudotsuga taxifolia* (Poir.) Britton). *Biologisches Zentralblatt*, **81**, 129–43.

Winkler, E. (1961). Assimilationsvermögen, Atmung und Ertrag von Kartoffelsorten im Tal und an der Waldgrenze bei Innsbruck und Vent. *Flora*, **151**, 621–62.

Winkler, E. & Pregenzer, E. (1970). Stoffproduktion in Dauerwiesen in Abhängigkeit von Lufttemperatur, Bewässerung und Düngung in Höhenlagen von 600 und 900 m. *Die Bodenkultur*, **21**, 22–44.

Wuenscher, J. E. & Kozlowski, T. T. (1971). The response of transpiration resistance to leaf temperature as a desiccation resistance mechanism in tree seedlings. *Physiologia Plantarum*, **24**, 254–9.

Zelawski, W. & Kucharska, J. (1967). Winter depression of photosynthetic activity in seedlings of scots pine (*Pinus silvestris* L.). *Photosynthetica*, **1**, 207–13.

Zelitch, I. (1971). *Photosynthesis, photorespiration, and plant productivity*. New York & London, Academic Press.

Zeller, O. (1951). Über Assimilation und Atmung der Pflanzen im Winter bei tiefen Temperaturen. *Planta*, **39**, 500–26.

26. Effects of environmental stress on photosynthesis – conclusions

D. KOLLER

Apart from a shortage of photosynthetically active radiation, the major environmental stresses which impair productivity of plants via effects on their net photosynthesis are those which result from unfavourable temperature regimes, an inadequate water balance or nutrient deficiencies.

Information on the nature of the effect of stress on photosynthesis is obtainable in a variety of forms, depending on the method of study. Direct effects on the reaction-site itself can be determined from gas-exchange studies with intact leaves under controlled conditions of light, atmospheric humidity, temperature and mesophyll intercellular CO_2 concentration. This indicates whether the affected apparatus is the one concerned with transduction of light energy, with incorporation of CO_2, or with photorespiration. Studies with the particulate fractions of leaf homogenates can indicate adverse effects on the permeability of biological membranes, resulting in faulty separation of electrical charges and of soluble reactants and from loss of metabolites through leakage. Changes in concentration of the photosynthetic pigments can easily be determined by extraction and are common consequences of stress, although it is often hard to separate effects on the level of the pigment itself from those on the chromophore or on the membrane system to which the pigments are attached. Such data are derived to a certain extent from ultrastructural studies of chloroplast morphology in general and of thylakoid organization in particular. Finally, effects on particular enzymes can be studied *in vitro* to indicate changes affecting enzyme kinetics (V_{max} and K_m) and activation energy.

A major site for indirect effects of stress on photosynthesis resides in the control of CO_2 supply. In vascular phanerogams, the supply of CO_2 may be affected by stress, at various steps along its pathway from the free atmosphere to the photosynthetic reaction site. The most sensitive step in this respect is in the stomatal aperture. Leaf water potential, which may be reduced by adverse temperature as well as by plant water stress itself, affects relative water content of the guard cells. In this respect, the role of specific components of leaf water potential in regulating guard-cell turgor potential, is far from clear. Stress conditions in the leaf and roots, respectively, may affect stomatal aperture by modifying levels of abscisic acid and kinetin. Conditions which exert relatively slight, but differential effects on gross photosynthesis and photorespiration may cause comparatively large changes in stomatal aperture by modifying substomatal CO_2 concentration. The response of guard cells may also be strongly modified by the availability of certain mineral ions, particularly K^+, as well as by factors which modify the supply of metabolic energy for active ion uptake by guard cells.

Two additional steps, other than the stomata, which are susceptible to modification by stress (mainly water and temperature stresses) are in the intercellular spaces in the mesophyll and the liquid phase between the liquid–air interface and the reaction site within the chloroplast (this latter step is present in all green plants).

Other indirect effects of stress on photosynthesis are exerted by changing the posture of the leaf and the shoot. Interception of radiant energy, and to a lesser extent the uptake of CO_2, are modified by stress-induced changes in the orientation of leaves, leaflets and shoot, as well as by folding and rolling of leaf blades.

Finally, there is the possibility of indirect effects of stress by means of its direct effects on assimilate translocation. Effects of stress can be expected on the viscosity of the fluids moving along the sieve tubes, as well as on the supply of energy required to move them. There are also indications that sugar-loading, which is energy-driven, may be affected by stress. Similarly, sink-strength of meristems and storage organs is determined by their growth activities and those are most susceptible to stress. It remains to be seen to what extent translocation from the leaf determines its assimilation rate.

Stress may exert delayed effects, for instance by accelerating senescence. This in turn may express itself by increased production of abscisic acid and ethylene and by depressing the levels of kinetin, thereby affecting stomatal aperture and the integrity of the photosynthetic apparatus. Delayed effects become lethal when leaf proteins denature (e.g. heat stress), when mechanical damage is caused to the integrity of cellular organelles and membranes (e.g. frost), and when toxic by-products of abnormal metabolism accumulate. In a different category are delayed effects of stress which influence the development of the photosynthetic organs and organelles. On the organismic level, stress affects the plastochrone, the rate and extent of leaf expansion, leaf morphology and anatomy and spatial distribution and orientation of new leaves. On the subcellular level, stress may affect the development of proplastids into chloroplasts, and the synthesis of chlorophyll, photosynthetic membranes and enzymes.

Certain effects of stress may last only as long as the stress lasts. Others may have relaxation-times ranging from minutes to weeks. The fact that a certain dependence is sometimes observed between the relaxation time and the product of duration and intensity (or sensitivity) of stress is suggestive, but not explanatory. Recovery from stress is in some cases only partial.

The response of the plant to stress may be strongly modified by conditioning. Age of the leaf, as well as that of the whole plant and the nutritive status (organic and inorganic) play an important, but ill-understood role. The same applies to the developmental status of the plant (vegetative, reproductive, actively growing, or dormant).

The effect of stress on photosynthesis may be strongly modified by a variety of 'hardening' and 'softening' treatments. The mode of action still awaits clarification, though there are indications of physical changes in the cytoplasm and of formation of isozymes.

Very little is known regarding effects of stress on partitioning of assimilates. One possible effect is via differential effects on respiratory rates of the various components of the producer–consumer complex. Differential effects of stress on growth and activity of various consumers may have a similar result. This is particularly true for flowering, seed- and fruit-set.

Finally, stress may induce the plant to direct assimilates to structural defense strategies.

In summary, it is clear that the basic nature of the photosynthetic process and its central role in almost all aspects of plant growth and development make it susceptible to attack by stress in a variety of ways and at numerous points within the plant. The elucidation of the primary process which is affected by each stress is of vital importance for understanding of how productivity can be helped to cope with stress.

PART VII

Actual and potential production in photosynthetic systems

27. Control of photosynthetic production in terrestrial systems

J. P. COOPER

Photosynthetic production can be regarded as a biological input–output system in which the basic climatic limitations are set by the seasonal input of light energy, water and CO_2, but the use of these inputs by the plant can be modified by high- or low-temperature stress or by the availability of soil nutrients (Eastin, Haskins, Sullivan & van Bavel, 1969; Nichiporovich, 1969,1970; Loomis, Williams & Hall, 1971; Moss & Musgrave, 1971). The required outputs vary greatly; in wild species they are primarily concerned with features which confer survival and reproductive advantage, but in managed crop systems they usually consist of human or animal foodstuffs or industrial raw materials. The agronomist and plant breeder can attempt to control such photo-synthetic systems, both by modifying the available inputs or constraints, and by improving the efficiency with which the crop converts these inputs. Such an approach involves the following operational sequence:

(i) identify and, where possible, quantify the input limitations and constraints in particular environments,
(ii) assess the potential production of current crop varieties, and hence their efficiency of conversion of light energy,
(iii) examine the variation in those features of the crop which determine its efficiency, and
(iv) assess the possibility of improving this efficiency by management and/or by selection and breeding.

Input-output relationships

Input limitations and constraints

The available energy input in any environment is determined by the seasonal distribution of solar radiation, which varies with latitude and with cloud cover (Black, 1956; Trewartha, 1968; Cooper, 1970). This energy input is comparatively uniform through the year in equatorial regions, often with 1600–2000 J cm^{-2} d^{-1} (382–473 cal cm^{-2} d^{-1}), but

593

Table 27.1. *Annual and seasonal energy inputs and estimated potential production in different climatic regions*

| | | Total radiation* | | | Dry matter from 3% conversion of incoming light (t/ha)† | | | |
| | | Annual input ($kJ\ cm^{-2}\ yr^{-1}$) | Seasonal variation (lowest month) ($J\ cm^{-2}\ d^{-1}$) | Seasonal variation (highest month) ($J\ cm^{-2}\ d^{-1}$) | Whole year (total) | Whole year (50% allocation to economic yield) | Best 4 months (total) | Best 6 weeks (total) |
	Latitude							
Temperate								
Aberystwyth, UK	52° N.	350	210	1880	27	13	15.2	6.1
Berlin, Germany	53° N.	400	170	2010	30	15	17.2	6.9
Tokyo, Japan	36° N.	420	630	1510	31	15	11.8	5.0
Wellington, New Zealand	41° S.	480	500	1970	37	18	18.0	7.2
Madison, Wisconsin, USA	43° N.	500	540	2220	38	19	19.6	7.7
Subtropical								
Deniliquin, Australia	36° S.	650	880	2930	49	25	26.7	10.9
Davis, California, USA	39° N.	670	750	2720	51	25	19.6	9.4
Algiers, Algeria	37° N.	690	880	2800	52	26	25.1	10.1
Brisbane, Australia	28° S.	710	1250	2720	54	27	22.0	9.2
Imperial Valley, California, USA	33° N.	730	1130	2760	56	28	24.2	9.4
Tropical								
Manila, Philippines	15° N.	540	1130	1920	41	20	15.6	6.4
Hawaii	21° N.	650	1340	2180	49	24	18.9	7.4
Singapore	1° N.	650	1670	2010	43	25	17.5	6.9
Puerto Rico	18° N.	670	1550	2130	51	26	18.7	7.3
Townsville, Australia	19° N.	750	1670	3590	57	29	16.5	8.8

* From Black (1956). † Assuming 1 g dry matter = 17.8 kJ.

shows an increasing seasonal amplitude with increasing latitude (Table 27.1). The highest annual radiation inputs, over 710 kJ cm^{-2} yr^{-1} (170 kcal cm^{-2} yr^{-1}), are found in subtropical regions, with little cloud cover, while most north temperate regions have a comparatively low annual input, about 400 kJ cm^{-2} yr^{-1} (96 kcal cm^{-2} yr^{-1}), but can receive daily inputs of over 2000 J cm^{-2} (478 cal cm^{-2}) in mid-summer.

The period over which this energy can be used by the crop can be limited by two other important climatic constraints, temperature stress and water shortage. In both temperate and subtropical climates, seasonal extremes of temperatures can limit both photosynthesis and the use of assimilates for growth, though the optimum and limiting temperatures differ with species and variety, (Cooper & Tainton, 1968; Downton, 1971; Bauer, Larcher & Walker, Chapter 25). Water shortage for a large part of the year can be an even more important limitation to production, particularly in subtropical climates, since such water stress is often associated with periods of high energy input, while even where temperature and water shortage are not limiting, photosynthetic production is often restricted by the availability of soil nutrients, particularly nitrogen (Cooper, 1970; Nátr, Chapter 24).

From the appropriate climatic data, it should be possible to quantify, firstly, the potential growing season, as limited by the climatic constraints of low temperature and water stress, and, secondly, the energy input during that growing season. The choice of a suitable temperature threshold for delimiting the growing season will depend on the crop species concerned, while the limits set by water shortage are usually estimated from water balance calculations, such as those of Penman (1963) or Thornthwaite & Mather (1955), though the limiting soil-water deficit will differ with the crop and its stage of growth (Slatyer, 1969). Potential evapotranspiration is often used as a convenient measure of radiation input and hence of potential crop production, while actual evapotranspiration takes into account the effects of seasonal moisture stress. In Australia, for instance, Fitzpatrick & Nix (1970) have developed a series of thermal and moisture indices based on the known environmental responses of temperate and tropical crop species, which can be used to delimit the effective growing season, and in conjunction with records of the light energy input, to predict potential seasonal growth rate of the crop. For both temperature and water regimes, seasonal fluctuations from year to year must be taken into account in quantifying these environmental constraints (Finlay & Wilkinson, 1963).

Table 27.2. *Crop growth rates of some agricultural crops in different climatic regions*

		Crop growth rate (g m⁻² d⁻¹)	Total radiation* (J cm⁻² d⁻¹)	Conversion of light energy* (%)	Reference
I. TEMPERATE					
C₃-species:					
Tall fescue (*Festuca arundinacea*)	UK	43	2201	7.8	Sheehy & Cooper, 1973
Cocksfoot (*Dactylis glomerata*)	UK	40	2201	7.3	Sheehy & Cooper, 1973
Ryegrass (*Lolium perenne*)	UK	28	1983	5.6	Rhodes (personal commun.)
	Netherlands	20	(1880)	(4.2)	Alberda, 1968
Red Clover (*Trifolium pratense*)	New Zealand	19	(2130)	(3.5)	Brougham, 1960
Potato (*Solanum tuberosa*)	New Zealand	23	(2010)	(4.3)	Brougham, 1960
Sugar Beet (*Beta vulgaris*)	Netherlands	23	(1670)	(5.4)	Sibma, 1968
	UK	31	1230	9.5	Blackman & Black, 1959
Kale (*Brassica oleracea*)	Netherlands	21	(1460)	(5.6)	Sibma, 1968
	UK	21	1598	4.9	Blackman & Black, 1959
Barley (*Hordeum vulgare*)	New Zealand	16	(2130)	(2.9)	Brougham, 1960
	UK	23	2025	4.0	Blackman & Black, 1959
Wheat (*Triticum vulgare*)	Netherlands	18	(1880)	(3.7)	Sibma, 1968
	Netherlands	18	(1880)	(3.7)	Sibma, 1968
Rice (*Oryza sativa*)	Japan	36	—	7.1	Loomis & Gerakis (Chapter 6)
Soybean (*Glycine max*)	Japan	27	—	9.8	Loomis & Gerakis (Chapter 6)
Peas (*Pisum sativum*)	Netherlands	20	(1880)	(4.2)	Sibma, 1968
C₄-species:					
Maize (*Zea mays*)	UK	24	(1250)	(7.6)	Adelana & Milbourne, 1972
	Netherlands	17	(1460)	(4.6)	Sibma, 1968
	New Zealand	29	(1880)	(6.1)	Brougham, 1960
	Japan	52	—	10.2	Loomis & Gerakis (Chapter 6)
	New York, USA	52	(2090)	(9.8)	Wright & Lemon, 1966
	Kentucky, USA	40	(2090)	(7.6)	Ragland, Hatfield & Benoit, 1965

II. SUB-TROPICAL

C3-species:

Alfalfa (*Medicago sativa*)	California, USA	23	(2850)	(3.2)	Loomis & Williams, 1963
Potato	California, USA	37	(2850)	(5.1)	Loomis & Gerakis (Chapter 6)
Cotton (*Gossypium hirsutum*)	Georgia, USA	27	(2300)	(4.6)	Blackman & Black, 1959
Rice	S. Australia	23	2720	3.0	Boerema, 1973

C4-species:

Sudan grass (*Sorghum sp.*)	California, USA	51	2887	6.7	Loomis & Williams, 1963
	California, USA	52	3079	6.4	Williams, Loomis & Lepley, 1965
Maize	California, USA	38	2694	5.6	Loomis, Williams & Hall, 1971

III. TROPICAL

C3-species:

Cassava (*Manihot esculenta*)	Sierra Leone	15	(1590)	(3.7)	Enyi, 1972a,b
	Tanzania	17	(1800)	(3.7)	Enyi, 1973
	Malaysia	18	(1670)	(4.5)	Williams, 1972
Oil palm (*Elaeis guineensis*)	Malaysia	11†	1590	3.3	Corley, 1973
Rice	Philippines	27	(1670)	(6.4)	Chandler, 1969

C4-species:

Pennisetum typhoides	NT, Australia	54	2134	9.5	Begg, 1965a
Pennisetum purpureum	El Salvador	39	(1674)	(9.3)	Watkins & Lewy-van Severen, 1951
Sugar cane (*Saccharinum sp.*)	Hawaii	37	1678	8.4	Stewart, 1970
Maize	Thailand	31	(2090)	(5.9)	Stewart, 1970

* Values in brackets estimated from radiation data in Black (1956), using conversion factor of 1 g dry matter = 17.8 kJ.   † Over whole year.
(For further discussion, see Blackman & Black, 1959; Cooper, 1970; Stewart, 1970; Loomis, Williams & Hall, 1971; and Loomis & Gerakis, Chapter 6).

Efficiency of energy conversion

The efficiency of conversion of incoming light energy by the crop, i.e. output–input, can be expressed on several bases. The energy input may refer to the total input over the year, irrespective of other climatic constraints; it may refer to the input during the growing season, or it may refer solely to the period during which photosynthesis is contributing directly to the economic end product, i.e. during the filling of the grain, or bulking of the tubers. Similarly, the output, i.e. the energy fixed, may be expressed on the basis of the dry matter produced by the whole crop over the year *or* during the growing season, or solely in terms of the energy fixed in the economic end product (Holliday, 1966; Sibma, 1968,1970; Cooper, 1970; Stewart, 1970; Loomis, Williams & Hall, 1971).

The short-term crop growth rates and associated efficiencies of energy conversion recorded in different environments are illustrated in Table 27.2. In temperate environments, with maximum summer inputs of up to 2000 J cm^{-2} d^{-1} (478 cal cm^{-2} d^{-1}), closed canopies of most C$_3$-crops usually provide maximum values of about 20 g m^{-2} d^{-1}, corresponding to 3–4 % conversion of the incoming light energy, although higher values of up to 40 g m^{-2} and up to 9.5 % conversion have been reported. In cool temperate environments, C$_4$-species, such as maize, show summer crop growth rates little higher than C$_3$-species, but where summer temperatures are higher, values of over 50 g m^{-2} d^{-1} have been reported.

In subtropical environments, with higher energy inputs of up to 3000 J cm^{-2} d^{-1} (717 cal cm^{-2} d^{-1}), such C$_4$-species as maize and sorghum often shown higher crop growth rates (of over 40 g m^{-2} d^{-1}) and higher energy conversions than C$_3$-crops, while the highest daily rate yet reported is that of 54 g m^{-2} d^{-1} for the C$_4$-grass *Pennisetum typhoides* in N. Australia (Begg, 1965*a*).

In the wet tropics, with steady inputs of 1600–2000 J cm^{-2} d^{-1} (382–478 cal cm^{-2} d^{-1}) for most of the year, rates of about 20 g m^{-2} d^{-1} are commonly found for such C$_3$-crops as cassava, oil palm and rice, and, in the absence of limitations of water or soil nutrients, these rates may be maintained throughout the year.

It would appear, therefore, that in a closed crop canopy, provided water and soil nutrients are not limiting, C$_3$-plants may be expected to convert at least 3–4 % of the incoming light energy and C$_4$-plants 5–6 % or more, provided temperatures are adequate (Loomis & Gerakis, Chapter 6). The reported values of over 9 % conversion for both C$_3$- and

C_4-species, however, suggest considerable scope for improvement by breeding and/or management.

Such short-term efficiencies cannot necessarily be maintained over the whole year or growing season (Table 27.3), since the photosynthetic production of the whole crop will be influenced both by the length of the possible growing season, and by the extent to which a closed crop canopy can be maintained during that growing season. Furthermore, efficiency in terms of economic yield will also depend on the proportion of assimilates transferred to the economic end product, and the duration of such transfer.

In Northern Europe, for instance, a perennial canopy of a C_3 forage grass or of a young evergreen forest can produce over 20 t ha^{-1} of harvestable dry matter/annum, corresponding to about 3% conversion of incoming light energy (Blackman & Black, 1959; Cooper, 1970) while for tropical C_4 forage grasses, such as *Pennisetum purpureum*, growing in higher light regimes, over 80 t ha^{-1} yr^{-1} have been reported, corresponding to about 5% conversion (Cooper, 1970).

In tropical environments, without seasonal limitations of temperature or water stress, many plantation crops can maintain a closed photosynthetic surface throughout the year, and, once established, allocate a fairly constant proportion of their assimilates to the economic end product. In the C_4 sugar-cane in Hawaii, a total dry matter production of up to 64 t/ha has been reported, corresponding to about 4% conversion of light energy, with about 40–45% of the energy fixed in the form of sugar (Burr *et al.*, 1957). Similarly in the C_3-tropical tuber crop, cassava, 50–60% of the assimilates can be steadily transferred to the tubers; in Tanzania, for instance, a total dry matter yield of 31 t ha^{-1} in 330 days has been obtained, including 16 t ha^{-1} in the tubers (Enyi, 1973). Similarly, in the C_3 oil palm in Malaya, an annual total of up to 40 t ha^{-1} yr^{-1} has been recorded, of which about 30% by weight is in the fruit bunches and about 12% by weight and 25% by energy in the palm oil itself (Corley, 1973).

For determinate crops, however, such as grain or tuber crops with a restricted growing season, a more relevant consideration is the conversion of light energy during the period when assimilates are being transferred to the particular economic sink. In a cereal crop in Britain, a grain yield of 6 t ha^{-1} converts only about 0.7% of the annual input of light energy, but 2% of the energy received during the period from ear emergence to ripening (Thorne, 1971). Similarly the high grain yields of rice of over 9 t ha^{-1} recorded in high insolation environments such as

Table 27.3. *Productivity and energy conversion in agricultural crops in different environments*

Crop		Location	Latitude	Product	Yield† (t ha⁻¹)	Growing period (days)	% Conversion of light energy‡		Reference	Notes
							Year	Growing period		
I. TEMPERATE										
A. Forage crops										
Perennial ryegrass (*Lolium perenne*)	C₃	UK	52° N.	Forage	25	365	(3.0)	(3.0)	Cooper, 1970	
Perennial ryegrass	C₃	Netherlands	52° N.	Forage	22	365	2.4	2.4	Alberda, 1968	
Kale (*Brassica oleracea*)	C₃	UK	54° N.	Forage	21	140	2.4	3.8	Gibbon, Holliday, Mattei & Luppi, 1970	
Sorghum (*Sorghum* sp.)	C₄	Illinois, USA	40° N.	Forage	16	140	1.2	2.2	Burger & Hittle, 1967	
	C₄	Netherlands	52° N.	Forage	15	88*	–	4.4*	Sibma, 1968	Period with closed crop cover*
	C₄	Ottawa, Canada	45° N.	Forage	19	–	1.6	3.0	Milbourne, 1973	
	C₄	UK	51° N.	Forage	17	160	1.9		Adelana & Milbourne, 1972	
	C₄	Japan	35° N.	Total dm	26	–	2.5	–	Loomis & Gerakis (Chapter 6)	
Maize (*Zea mays*)	C₄	Kentucky, USA	38° N.	Total dm	22	129	1.7	3.4	Ragland, Hatfield & Benoit, 1965	
	C₄	Iowa, USA	42° N.	Total dm	16	141	1.1	2.8	Eik & Hanway, 1966	
	C₄	Italy	45° N.	Total dm	40	140	3.2	(6.4)	Gibbon, Holliday, Mattei & Luppi, 1970	
B. Tubers and roots										
Potato (*Solanum tuberosum*)	C₃	UK	52° N.	Tubers	11	164	1.1	1.6	Watson, 1971	
	C₃			Tubers	12	122*	–	2.4*	Thorne, 1971	Period of bulking only*
	C₃	Netherlands	52° N.	Total dm	18	162	1.9	2.8	Bodlaender & Reestman, 1968	
				Total dm	22	162	2.3	3.4		
Sugar beet (*Beta vulgaris*)	C₃	UK	52° N.	Sugar	8	217	0.8	1.0	Watson, 1971	
				Sugar	8	153*	–	(1.5)*	Thorne, 1971	Period of bulking only*
				Roots	13	217	1.4	1.7	Watson, 1971	
				Roots	14	153*	–	(2.5)*	Thorne, 1971	Period of bulking only*
				Total dm	23	217	2.5	3.0	Watson, 1971	
	C₃	Washington, USA	46° N.	Sugar	14	230	1.0	1.2*	Loomis & Gerakis (Chapter 6)	Assuming growing period of Feb.–Sept.*
				Roots	(26)	230	2.1	2.4*		
				Total dm	(32)	230	2.5	3.0*		
C. Cereals										
Wheat (spring) (*Triticum vulgare*)	C₃	UK	52° N.	Grain	5	160	0.5	0.7	Watson, 1971	Period with closed crop cover*
	C₃	Netherlands	52° N.	Grain	6	153*	–	(1.1)*	Sibma, 1970	
	C₃	Washington, USA	47° N.	Total dm	12	69*	0.9	3.7*	Sibma, 1968	
				Grain	12	–	2.4	–	Loomis & Gerakis (Chapter 6)	
				Total dm	(30)	–	0.7	–		
Barley (*Hordeum vulgare*)	C₃	UK	52° N.	Grain	7	148	0.7	1.1	Watson, 1971	Period of grain filling only*
				Grain	6	61*	–	(2.0)*	Thorne, 1971	

		Location	Latitude						Reference	Notes
Rice (*Oryza sativa*)	C3	Japan	37° N.	Grain	7	123	0.7	1.6	Evelyn et al., 1969	
	C4	UK	51° N.	Grain	5	160	0.5	1.1	Adelana & Milbourne, 1972	
	C4	Japan	35° N.	Grain	14	–	1.3	–	Loomis & Gerakis (Chapter 6)	
Maize	C4	Kentucky, USA	38° N.	Grain	10	127	0.7	(1.4)	Duncan, Shaver & Williams, 1973	Assuming growing period of May–Sept.*
	C4	Iowa, USA	42° N.	Grain	9	141	0.6	1.6	Eik & Hanway, 1966	
II. SUB-TROPICAL (including Mediterranean)										
A. Forage Crops										
Coastal Bermuda grass (*Cynodon dactylon*)	C4	Georgia, USA	31° N.	Forage	27	365	1.8	1.8	Burton, Jackson & Knox, 1959	
Alfalfa (*Medicago sativa*)	C3	California, USA	38° N.	Forage	33	250	2.1	–	Loomis & Williams, 1963	Assuming growing period of Jan.–Aug.*
Sudan grass (*Sorghum* sp.)	C4	California, USA	38° N.	Forage	30	160	1.9	3.4*	Loomis & Williams, 1968	
Sorghum	C4	California, USA	33° N.	Forage	47	210	2.6	3.6	Worker & Marble, 1968	
B. Tubers and Roots										
Potato	C3	California, USA	38° N.	Tubers	(20)	–	1.2	–	Loomis & Gerakis (Chapter 6)	
				Total dm	(22)	–	1.4	–		
Sugar-beet	C3	California, USA	36° N.	Sugar	19	240	1.1	1.4*	Loomis & Gerakis (Chapter 6)	
				Roots	(35)	240	2.1	2.9*		
				Total	(42)	240	2.6	3.5*		
C. Cereals										
Wheat	C3	Syria	33° N.	Grain	8	–	0.4	–	CIMMYT, 1970	
	C3	California, USA	38° N.	Grain	7	–	0.4	–	CIMMYT, 1970	
	C3	Mexico	27° N.	Total dm	(18)	–	1.0	–	Loomis & Gerakis (Chapter 6)	
Rice	C3	California, USA	38° N.	Grain	11	–	0.7	–	Loomis & Gerakis (Chapter 6)	
				Total dm	(22)	–	1.4	–		
	C3	NSW, Australia	32° S.	Grain	14	190	0.8	(1.1)	Boerema, 1965	Assuming sown mid-April*
	C4	California, USA	38° N.	Grain	13	130	0.8	1.5*	Loomis & Gerakis (Chapter 6)	
Maize	C4	Colorado, USA	39° N.	Total dm	(26)	130	1.7	3.3*	Loomis & Gerakis (Chapter 6)	
				Total dm	27	117	1.7	3.7*		
	C4	Egypt	30° N.	Grain	12	–	0.5	–	Loomis & Gerakis (Chapter 6)	Assuming growing period May–Aug.*
				Total dm	(29)	–	1.4	–		
III. TROPICAL										
A. Forage crops										
Napier grass (*Pennisetum purpureum*)	C4	El Salvador	14° N.	Forage	85	365	5.4	5.4	Vicente-Chandler, Silva & Figarella, 1959	
	C4	Puerto Rico	18° N.	Forage	85	365	4.9	4.9	Watkins & Lewy-van Severen, 1951	
Bulrush millet (*Pennisetum typhoides*)	C4	NT, Australia	14° S.	Forage	22	112	1.1	3.8	Begg, 1965b	

601

Table 27.3 – continued

Crop		Location	Latitude	Product	Yield† (t ha^{-1})	Growing period (days)	% Conversion of light energy‡ Year	Growing period	Reference	Notes
III. TROPICAL (continued)										
B. Cane crops										
Sugar cane (*Saccharum* sp.)	C₄	Hawaii	21° N.	Sugar	22	365	1.2	1.2	Burr *et al.*, 1957	
				Total dm	64	365	4.0	4.0	Burr *et al.*, 1957	
C. Tree crops										
Oil palm (*Elaeis guineensis*)	C₃	Malaysia	3° N.	Oil	5	365	(0.8)	(0.8)	Corley, 1973	
				Fruit	11	365	(1.1)	(1.1)	Corley, 1973	
				Total dm	40	365	(3.2)	(3.2)	Corley, 1973	
D. Roots and tubers										
Sugar beet (two crops per year)	C₃	Hawaii	21° N.	Sugar	14	365	0.8	0.8	Younge & Butchart, 1963	
				Total dm	(31)	365	1.9	1.9	Younge & Butchart, 1963	
	C₃	Tanzania	7° S.	Tubers	16	330	0.9	1.0	Enyi, 1973	
Cassava (*Manihot esculenta*)				Total dm	31	330	1.7	2.0	Enyi, 1973	
	C₃	Malaysia	3° N.	Tubers	22	270	1.4	1.9	Williams, 1972	
				Total dm	38	270	2.5	3.8	Williams, 1972	
E. Cereals										
Wheat	C₃	Sudan	17° N.	Grain	7	–	0.3	–	CIMMYT, 1970	
	C₃	NT, Australia	15° S.	Grain	11	125	0.5	(1.5)	Stewart, 1970	
	C₃	Philippines (dry season)	15° N.	Grain	10	122	0.5	(1.8)	Stewart, 1970	
Rice	C₃	Philippines (wet season)	15° N.	Grain	7	115	0.4	(1.5)	Stewart, 1970	
	C₃	Peru	7° S.	Grain	12	205	0.8	(1.3)	Sanchez, Ramirez & de Calderon, 1973	
				Total dm	22	205	1.5	(2.6)	Sanchez, Ramirez & de Calderon, 1973	
Sorghum	C₄	Philippines	15° N.	Grain	7	80	0.4	1.8	Stewart, 1970	
	C₄	Thailand	15° N.	Total dm	7	103	0.4	1.2	Stewart, 1970	
Maize	C₄	Peru	12° S.	Grain	16	103	1.0	2.7	Stewart, 1970	
				Grain	10	–	0.7	–	Loomis & Gerakis (Chapter 6)	
				Total dm	(26)	–	1.7	–		
F. Multiple cropping										
Rice	C₃	Philippines	15° N.	Grain	5	115	–	–		
+Sorghum	C₄	Philippines	15° N.	Grain	6	90	–	–		
+Sorghum (ratoon)	C₄	Philippines	15° N.	Grain	7	80	–	–	Stewart, 1970	
+Sorghum (ratoon)	C₄	Philippines	15° N.	Grain	5	80	–	–		
Total for year	–	Philippines	15° N.	Grain	23	365	1.6	1.6		

For further discussion, see Blackman & Black (1959); Cooper (1970); Stewart (1970); Loomis, Williams & Hall (1971); and Loomis & Gerakis (Chapter 6).
† Values in brackets estimated from standard partition factors; (see Loomis & Gerakis, Chapter 6).
‡ Values in brackets based on radiation data in original paper, remainder estimated from values given by Black (1956) using conversion factors of 1 g dry matter = 17.8 kJ for total dry matter; 1 g dry matter = 16.7 kJ for grain or tubers; 1 g dry matter = 15.8 kJ for sugar.
dm = dry matter

Peru (Sanchez, Ramirez & de Calderon, 1973) or the Philippines (Chandler, 1969) represent 2–3% conversion of incoming light energy during the effective assimilation period. For the C_4 maize, growing with high insolation in California, even higher grain yields of 13–14 t ha^{-1} have been reported, due in part to the longer period over which assimilates can be transferred to the grain in this crop. Although a single determinate cereal crop may not be particularly efficient in terms of annual conversion, where a multiple cropping system is possible, as in certain tropical and subtropical regions, the annual output can be greatly increased. In the Philippines, for instance, double cropping with rice can provide an annual total of 28 t ha^{-1} dry matter of which 15 t ha^{-1} is grain (Chandler, 1969), while a sequence of one rice crop, followed by three sorghum crops has provided 22.6 t ha^{-1} of grain in the year (Stewart, 1970).

In tuber or root crops, such as the potato or sugar beet, transfer of assimilates to the storage organ can continue over a much longer period than in a determinate cereal crop, and hence usually results in a greater annual energy conversion. In the potato crop in NW. Europe, for instance, a good yield of 12–15 t dry matter in the tubers represents a conversion of about 1% of the annual energy input, but about 2.5% of that received during the period of bulking of the tubers (Thorne, 1971; Watson, 1971). Similarly in the sugar-beet, a good yield of 14 t ha^{-1} dry matter in the roots (of which 8 t ha^{-1} may be sugar) corresponds to about 2.5% conversion to roots and 1–2% to sugar during the period of bulking.

In general, during the period of active assimilation and transfer to the economic end product, values of about 3% light energy conversion may be expected for most C_3-crops, while for C_4-species, growing in high insolation environments, values of up to 5% may be obtained. A general indication of the dry matter production to be expected in different environments can be obtained from Table 23.1, which provides estimates, on the basis of 3% conversion, for four different types of crop;

  (i) a closed canopy through the year (as in a grass or forest crop)
 (ii) a closed canopy through the year, but with 50% allocation of energy to the economic end product (as in cassava or sugar cane)
(iii) allocation of most or all of assimilates to the economic yield during the four months of greatest energy input (as in the potato in W. Europe)

(iv) allocation of most or all of assimilates to the economic yield during the six weeks of greatest energy input (as in a cereal in NW. Europe).

These estimates can, of course, be modified to allow of the higher energy conversions expected from C_4-species, or of the effects of low temperature or water stress in limiting the effective assimilation period to a particular season of the year.

Components of energy conversion

The next step is to identify those physiological or morphological features which determine the potential production and energy conversion of the crop, and to assess the amount of genetic variation available for their improvement (Wallace, Ozbun & Munger, 1972). Such genetic variation can be conveniently discussed under three main headings: (i) crop photosynthesis; (ii) distribution of assimilates; (iii) response to climatic or other environmental stresses.

Crop photosynthesis

Crop photosynthesis will be influenced not only by variation in the photosynthetic activity of the individual leaf, but also by the pattern of light distribution over the leaves in the crop canopy.

Photosynthesis of the individual leaf. The photosynthetic responses of the individual leaf to light intensity and to temperature, as well as to water and nutrient stress, have been discussed earlier (Troughton, Chapter 16; Slavík, Chapter 23; Nátr, Chapter 24; Bauer, Larcher & Walker, Chapter 25). In crop plants, the major difference lies between species with the C_3- and C_4-pathways, the C_4-plants having a greater maximum photosynthetic rate (60–100 mg CO_2 dm^{-2} h^{-1}) associated with little or no apparent photorespiration, compared with 10–33 mg CO_2 dm^{-2} h^{-1} in most C_3-plants, provided temperatures are high enough (Hatch & Slack, 1970; Downton, 1971).

Although certain genera, such as *Panicum* and *Atriplex*, contain both C_3- and C_4-species, there appears to be little possibility of finding individual genotypes with the C_4-pathway within such C_3-crop species as wheat, barley and soybean (Moss & Musgrave, 1971), and crosses between C_4- and C_3-species in *Atriplex* (Björkman *et al.*, 1971) indicate independent though complex genetic control of the various aspects of the C_4-syndrome.

Even so, some C_3-species, such as sunflower, cotton, and *Typha* appear to have maximum photosynthetic rates approaching those of the C_4-group (Downton, 1971), while marked varietal or genotype differences in maximum photosynthetic rate have been reported in many C_3-crops, including cotton, soybean, rice, barley, *Phaseolus*, wheat, oats, alfalfa and the forage grasses, *Phalaris* and *Lolium* (for references see Wallace, Ozbun & Munger, 1972) as well as in the C_4-crops, maize (Duncan & Hesketh, 1968; Heichel & Musgrave, 1969) sugar-cane (Irvine, 1967) and *Cenchrus ciliaris* (Treharne, Pritchard & Cooper, 1971). The physiological basis of these differences is not always clear, nor whether they are associated with changes in the stomatal, mesophyll or biochemical resistances (Wallace, Ozbun & Munger, 1972; Wilson, 1973).

The photosynthetic rate of a leaf can, of course, be modified by the conditions under which it develops. Growing plants at high light intensities and comparatively low temperatures usually increases their maximum photosynthetic rate, but species and varieties differ in such acclimation responses (Björkman, 1970; Wilson & Ludlow, 1970; Dunstone, Gifford & Evans, 1973; Wilson, 1973).

Considerable variation also occurs in the response of photosynthetic rate to temperature. The major difference appears between most C_3-plants with a broad optimum around 15–20° C, and C_4-plants with an optimum at 30–35° C (Hatch & Slack, 1970; Downton, 1971), but some C_3-crops such as sunflower, tobacco, cotton and many tropical legumes (Wilson & Ludlow, 1970) have temperature optima as high as the C_4-group, suggesting that this difference in temperature response may be related to past climatic selection rather than to basic differences in the photosynthetic pathway (Downton, 1971). Even so, local populations of the same species can differ markedly in their photosynthetic activity at low temperatures (5–10 °C), as in the C_3 forest trees (Bauer, Larcher & Walker, Chapter 25) and temperate grasses (Treharne & Eagles, 1970).

In general, however, photosynthesis appears less sensitive to changes in temperature than does the use of assimilates for active extension growth and the lower limits of the thermal growing season (about 5 °C for temperate species and 15 °C for tropical) are usually set by the requirements for active extension growth rather than for photosynthesis.

Variation has also been reported in the response of photosynthesis to water stress, often, as in douglas fir (Zavitkovski & Ferrell, 1970) or range grasses (Gloser, 1967) associated with differences in stomatal resistance to water vapour transfer (Slatyer, 1969; Slavík, Chapter 23). In both barley (Misken, Rasmusson & Moss, 1972) and *Panicum antidotale* (Dobrenz *et al.*, 1969) a lower stomatal frequency was associated with a lower transpiration, without corresponding changes in the photosynthetic rate.

The significance of such variation in photosynthesis of the individual leaf in determining either crop photosynthesis or agronomic yield, is however, far from clear. In many cases, differences in crop growth rate appear to be determined rather by changes in the use of assimilates, particularly their investment in increased leaf area or partitioning to the economic sink (Evans, Chapter 22; Wareing & Patrick, Chapter 21). Even the greater maximum photosynthetic rates of C_4- compared with C_3-species may be compensated by a lower partition to leaf area and so may not inevitably lead to greater crop growth rates (Slatyer, 1970, 1971; Bull, 1971).

Canopy structure. Most crops, however, do not consist of isolated leaves fully exposed to the incoming light, but of a more or less closed canopy of leaves, and variation in canopy structure, operating through the pattern of light distribution, appears to be rather more important than individual leaf photosynthesis in determining varietal differences in crop photosynthesis. As discussed in earlier chapters (Saeki, Chapter 13; Loomis & Gerakis, Chapter 6), an erect leaf arrangement, with a low extinction coefficient, results in the distribution of incoming light energy over a greater leaf area and, hence, might be expected to provide a greater potential crop photosynthesis and crop growth rate (Donald, 1968; Duncan, Loomis, Williams & Hanau, 1967; Brown & Blaser, 1968; Anderson & Denmead, 1969; Monteith, 1969).

In many crops, including maize (Pendleton, Smith, Winter & Johnston, 1968) rice (Chandler, 1969), soybean (Tsunoda, 1959; Hicks, Pendleton, Bernard & Johnston, 1969) and forage grasses (Rhodes, 1971; Sheehy & Cooper, 1973), varieties with more erect leaves, lower extinction coefficients, and hence higher critical leaf area indices, do appear to show higher photosynthetic rates (or crop growth rates) and in some cases greater economic yield, though these effects can be modified by density of planting or nitrogen application (Tanaka, Kawano & Yamaguchi, 1966; Stoskopf, 1967; Hayashi, 1968,1969).

This advantage of an erect leaf arrangement however, applies only to a closed or nearly closed crop cover. During early establishment, before complete ground cover is established, which may take several years in a tree canopy (Wareing & Matthews, 1972), production will be limited by the amount of light which can be intercepted by the crop, and during this stage, a rapid ground cover produced by fairly flat prostrate leaves will be more advantageous (Rhodes, 1971). In many annual crops, as in the potato and sugar-beet in Britain (Watson, 1971) the rate of attainment of a closed canopy can be a serious limitation to production, and selection for rapid expansion of leaf surface, particularly at low temperatures, can be an important breeding objective (Wareing, 1971).

Distribution of assimilates

Few crops, however, consist solely of young vegetative canopies and the most important determinant of economic yield is often not *total* crop photosynthesis, but the way in which assimilates are distributed within the plant, either for continued vegetative growth or for accumulation in particular sinks, such as storage organs, seeds or fruit (Donald, 1968; Nichiporovich, 1969,1970). It is often not clear how far such assimilation is limited by the supply of assimilates (i.e. source strength), by the ability of the sink to make use of them or by the rate of translocation; or indeed how far sink strength can itself influence photosynthetic rate (Neales & Incoll, 1968; Monsi and Murata, 1970; Warren Wilson, 1972; Evans, Chapter 22; Wareing & Patrick, Chapter 21).

Even in an annual vegetative crop, grown for total above-ground production, the relative distribution of assimilates can be important. As already mentioned, during early establishment, rapid expansion of leaf surface is usually desirable, and this can be aided by an increased shoot to root partition and by a greater area to weight ratio of the leaves themselves (Wilson & Cooper, 1969). At the same time, sufficient root development is necessary to obtain adequate water and soil nutrients; although with high fertilizer and water inputs, such root development may become less important.

In a perennial vegetative crop, such as a forage grass, which is utilized over several harvests, the partition of assimilates between continued leaf production, development of new vegetative buds, or storage can greatly influence the rate of regrowth after each harvest and hence the continued production of the crop (Brown & Blaser, 1968; Jewiss, 1972). The partition of assimilates between extension of new vegetative tissue and storage can also be important for survival of seasonal temperature or water stress. In short days and low temperatures, for instance, many winter-hardy north European populations of forage grasses continue active photosynthesis, but transfer most of their assimilates to the base of the shoot, whereas Mediterranean populations use their assimilates for continued active extension growth with associated sensitivity to frost damage (Treharne & Eagles, 1970; Eagles & Østgård, 1971).

In many crops the economic end product consists not of the leaves themselves but of vegetative storage organs such as roots or tubers, as in potatoes or sugar-beet, or enlarged stem, as in marrow-stemmed kale or sugar-cane. In such crops, once a closed canopy has been established, further leaf growth is required only to maintain that canopy, and the maximum amount of assimilates should be transferred to the relevant storage sink. In the potato crop, extensive genetic variation occurs for the date of initiation of tubers, and also for the rate and duration of bulking (Milthorpe, 1963; Milthorpe & Moorby, 1967; Simmonds, 1971), while in the tropical tuber crop, cassava, Williams (1972) reports marked varietal differences in the rate of bulking and the proportion of assimilates transferred to the tubers. The distribution of assimilates is also important in forest trees, where the appropriate partition is necessary between rapid attainment of a closed leaf canopy and its maintenance, the development of an adequate root system, and the necessary stem extension growth and cambial activity to provide quantity and quality of timber over several years (Wareing & Matthews, 1972).

Many important crop products, however, consist of seeds or fruit and hence involve the use of assimilates for reproductive rather than vegetative development. While in many vegetative crops the transfer of assimilates from source to sink can often proceed over a long or almost indefinite period, the duration of seed or fruit development is often restricted, particularly in crops of determinate habit. In the temperate small grains, for instance, most of the assimilates contributing to grain formation are derived from photosynthesis in the flag leaf and in the ear over the comparatively short period (6–8 weeks) from anthesis to grain ripening (Lupton & Kirby, 1968; Evans & Rawson, 1970). The main function of the vegetative canopy is to provide an appropriate crop structure on which to carry the optimum number and size of developing ears (Bingham, 1969; Rawson, 1970). In such crops, the mutual adjustment of sink and source strength is particularly important (Evans & Dunstone, 1970; Evans, Dunstone, Rawson & Williams, 1970). Selection for more rapid initial grain growth on the one hand and for increased longevity of the photosynthetic tissue on the other may therefore be of value (Thorne, 1966,1971; Lupton & Kirby, 1968; Bingham, 1969; Watson, 1971).

The total sink strength of the crop may be increased by maximizing the proportion of ear-bearing tillers, in the extreme case by growing a 'uniculm' variety (Donald, 1968), but also by increasing the number of grain sites per ear, possibly through selecting for earlier initiation, but slower development of the inflorescence (Bunting & Drennan, 1966; Bingham, 1969; Rawson, 1970).

In maize, on the other hand, there can be considerable translocation of assimilates from the stem into the grain, particularly at lower radiation inputs, and the period over which crop photosynthesis can contribute to grain yield is correspondingly larger (Daynard, Tanner & Hume, 1969; Adelana & Milbourne, 1972). The length of the grain-filling period, rather than the rate of filling, seems to be an important determinant of varietal differences in grain yield (Daynard, Tanner & Duncan, 1971).

For such determinate seed or fruit crops, it is important to synchronize the timing of seed and fruit development with a period of reasonably high light energy input, consonant with the avoidance of seasonal limitations of temperature stress or water shortage. In most crops, the onset of reproductive development is based on environmental responses to temperature and photoperiod, and the timing of the life cycle is a result of past natural or human selection. Natural selection has usually favoured a reproductive cycle which avoids extreme climatic limitations of cold or water stress, while agronomic requirements have often superimposed selection for a range of maturity dates to fit particular farming systems (Cooper, 1963; Kirby, 1969).

The type of farming system also determines the most effective growth habit for the crop (Donald, 1968). In the temperate cereals, for instance, under less advanced farming systems, which involve intense competition with weeds and even between genotypes within a heterogenous crop, a tall, rapidly growing crop has an important competitive advantage, and varieties grown under such a system tend to be long-strawed. On the other hand, under more advanced farming systems of comparatively weed-free cultivation and the use of uniform varieties, the competitive advantage of long-strawed types is outweighed by possible competition for assimilates between internode elongation and ear development (Bingham, 1969), and by the dangers of lodging. Many modern cereal breeding programmes have involved a reduction in straw length, as in the development of the semi-dwarf Mexican wheats (Reitz & Salmon,

1968; Borlaug, 1968; Syme, 1970) and the IR 8 series of rice varieties (Chandler, 1969). In addition many of these cereal varieties are relatively daylength-insensitive, and hence adapted to a range of latitudes and growing seasons, particularly in the absence of seasonal water stress.

By contrast, in some crops, such as sugar-beet and many brassicas, flowering is disadvantageous, and in beet, selection for a higher winter vernalization requirement has made it possible to sow earlier in the spring, without danger of diversion of assimilates away from the required vegetative sink (Bell, 1963).

In addition to the efficient distribution of assimilate to particular sinks, in many crops the nutritional or processing quality of the end product is important, such as baking or brewing quality in the cereals, cooking quality in potatoes, or the characteristics which make for efficient processing in quick-frozen vegetables. Similarly in forage grasses, which are processed through the ruminant, the digestibility of the herbage and those chemical and physical features which affect intake can be important breeding objectives (Raymond, 1969; Cooper, 1973).

Furthermore, certain crops are grown to produce specific chemical constituents, such as sugar, rubber, palm oil and other vegetable oils. These chemical requirements impose yet a further step in the breeding programme, as in selection for increased sugar content but a low concentration of such impurities as sodium, potassium, amino-nitrogen and betaine in sugar-beet (Bell, 1963) while recent breeding programmes in oil palm have involved the incorporation of a major gene difference controlling shell thickness in the fruit (Hardon, 1969).

Response to climatic stress

Cultivated crops and wild populations can become adapted to periods of temperature and water stress in several ways (Levitt, 1972; Slavík, Chapter 23; Bauer, Larcher & Walker, Chapter 25). In the first place, they may be able to develop life cycles which avoid the period of stress. In a Mediterranean environment for instance, many grain and forage crops germinate with the autumn rains, grow actively through the winter, and flower and produce seed in the spring before the summer drought stops further growth (Donald, 1960; Cooper, 1963; Finlay & Wilkinson, 1963). By contrast, to avoid frost damage in north temperate or north continental climates, many annual crops, such as the spring cereals, are spring-sown and harvested in late summer or early autumn, while others, such as potatoes or sugar-beet, though potentially biennial or perennial, are grown as spring-planted annuals.

Secondly, the plant may possess the necessary degree of winter or summer dormancy to survive the unfavourable season. Both deciduous and evergreen trees in north temperate latitudes, for instance, show such seasonal dormancy, in terms of cessation of extension growth, accompanied by leaf fall in the deciduous species. The initiation and breaking of such dormancy in locally adapted populations is often related to the length and severity of the winter (Wareing, 1956,1969; Perry, 1971; Bauer, Larcher & Walker, Chapter 26). Similar seasonal dormancy patterns, often associated with considerable cold hardiness, are shown by forage crops or winter cereals adapted to higher latitudes (Smith, 1964; Levitt, 1971). In environments with seasonal water stress, perennial species often become dormant during the period of stress, as in *Phalaris tuberosa, Hordeum bulbosum* and other perennial grasses in the Mediterranean environment (McWilliam, 1968; McWilliam & Kramer, 1968; Koller, 1969).

Both the initiation and breaking of dormancy are often brought about by response to other climatic factors, thus enabling the plant to become dormant before the particular stress becomes too severe. In forest trees and forage grasses, decreasing photoperiods often play an important part (Wareing, 1956,1969; Østgård & Eagles, 1971) while in the dormancy of Mediterranean grasses, increased temperatures together with long days are often involved (Laude, 1953; Koller, 1969).

The above mechanisms involve the avoidance of exposure to stress, either in the form of seed or of dormant vegetative material. In certain cases, however, the plant is able to continue photosynthesis or even active growth during moderate exposure to stress. Evergreen conifers, for instance, can continue to photosynthesize, although at a low rate, during the low temperatures of the northern or alpine winter, even though extension growth and cambial activity cease (Bauer, Larcher & Walker, Chapter 25).

Such mechanisms, which allow of continued photosynthesis or active growth under stress, appear to be more highly developed in regions of water shortage, accompanied by high insolation. One obvious means is to reduce transpiration by closing the stomata at moderate water stress, as in alfalfa compared to cotton (van Bavel, 1967) while, as mentioned earlier, in both barley and *Panicum antidotale* a low stomatal frequency can lead to lower transpiration, without any necessary reduction in photosynthetic rate. Even so, although C_4-plants appear to have developed mainly in regions with intense solar radiation, high day temperatures and seasonal dry periods (Downton, 1971; Wallace, Ozbun & Munger, 1972), i.e. in conditions where carbon loss by photorespiration becomes substantial in C_3-plants, their greater water use efficiency compated with C_3-plants seems to be based on a greater photosynthetic rate, rather than reduced transpiration, though C_4-plants may have somewhat higher stomatal resistances (Downton, 1971).

Water stress may also be avoided by the development of a deeper root system, to tap water reserves at lower levels in the soil as in bulrush millet compared with sorghum (Wetselaar & Norman, 1960) although this may well involve diversion of assimilates from harvestable yield. In the wild and cultivated wheats marked variation in the degree of root development has been reported (Khan & Tsunoda, 1970), while the summer dormancy of the Mediterranean grasses, *Hordeum bulbosum* (Koller, 1969) and *Phalaris tuberosa* (McWilliam, 1968), is associated with a deep root system.

Useful genetic variation thus exists for many of the morphological and physiological characteristics which determine the net photosynthesis of the crop canopy, the distribution of assimilates to the required economic end products, and the response of the crop to climatic stresses of low temperature or water shortage (Wallace, Ozbun & Munger, 1972). It should therefore be possible for the agronomist and plant breeder to make use of this variation to develop improved varieties whose physiological performance is specifically tailored to convert the seasonal input of light energy most efficiently over as long a growing period as possible.

Conclusions

Photosynthetic production, considered as a biological input–output system in terms of energy and nutrient conversion can be studied and modified by the agronomist and plant breeder according to the following sequence:

(i) Identify and quantify the relevant environmental inputs and constraints in a particular environment, particularly the length of the possible growing season as limited by temperature or water supply, and the energy input during that growing season.

(ii) Assess the potential production of particular crops in that environment, either by a general estimate of 3% light energy conversion for

C_3-species (or 5% for C_4-species in high radiation environments) during the period of effective assimilation, by simple models, such as the use of the thermal, moisture and light indices of Fitzpatrick & Nix (1970), or by more complex models, such as those of de Wit (1965), Duncan, Loomis, Williams & Hanau, (1967) and de Wit, Brouwer & Penning de Vries (1970). Such models have so far been developed largely for whole crop photosynthesis, but are currently being extended to incorporate the distribution and use of assimilates by the crop (Monsi & Murata, 1970; Warren Wilson, 1972; Rees & Thornley, 1973). These estimates of potential production can then be compared with the current production of existing varieties of the crop, to indicate the possible extent of further improvement.

(iii) Identify those physiological and morphological components of the crop which determine its efficiency of energy conversion, and assess the amount of genetic variation available. These may include such features as:

(*a*) the rapid establishment of a closed leaf canopy;

(*b*) efficient canopy photosynthesis, including both canopy structure and individual leaf photosynthesis;

(*c*) effective distribution of assimilates to the relevant economic sinks for as long a period as possible;

(*d*) avoidance or tolerance of other environmental constraints such as temperature and water stress.

On the basis of such knowledge of the seasonal input limitations and constraints, and of the genetic variation available for those features of the crop which determine response to these inputs, it should be possible to set up appropriate crop models which can be used by the breeder and agronomist to develop improved varieties and/or management systems specifically tailored to particular input–output systems.

References

Adelana, B. O. & Milbourne, G. M. (1972). The growth of maize. II. Dry matter partition in three maize hybrids. *J. agric. Sci., Camb.* **78**, 73–8.

Alberda, T. (1968). Dry matter production and light interception of crop surfaces. IV. Maximum herbage production as compared with predicted values. *Neth. J. agric. Sci.* **16**, 142–53.

Anderson, M. C. & Denmead, O. T. (1969). Short wave radiation on inclined surfaces in model plant communities. *Agron. J.* **61**, 867–72.

van Bavel, C. H. M. (1967). Changes in canopy resistance to water loss from alfalfa induced by soil water depletion. *Agric. Meteor.* **4**, 165–76.

Begg, J. E. (1965*a*). High photosynthetic activity in a low latitude environment. *Nature*, **205**, 1025–6.

Begg, J. E. (1965*b*). The growth and development of a crop of bulrush millet (*Pennisetum typhoides* S and H). *J. agric. Sci., Camb.* **65**, 341–9.

Bell, G. D. H. (1963). Developments in sugar beet breeding. *J. natn. Inst. agric. Bot.* **9**, 435–44.

Bingham, J. (1969). The physiological determinants of grain yield in cereals. *Agric. Prog.* **44**, 30–42.

Björkman, O. (1970). Characteristics of the photosynthetic apparatus as revealed by laboratory measurements. In *Prediction and Measurement of Photosynthetic Productivity*, ed. I. Šetlík, pp. 267–82. Wageningen, PUDOC.

Björkman, O., Nobs, M., Pearcy, R., Boynton, J. & Berry, J. (1971). Characteristics of hybrids between C_3- and C_4-species of *Atriplex*. In *Photosynthesis and Photorespiration*, eds. M. D. Hatch, C. B. Osmond & R. O. Slatyer, pp. 105–19. New York, Wiley-Interscience.

Black, J. N. (1956). The distribution of solar radiation over the earth's surface. *Arch. Met. Geophys. Bioklim.* **B7**, 165–89.

Blackman, F. G. & Black, J. N. (1959). Physiological and ecological studies in the analysis of plant environment. 12. The value of the light factor in limiting growth. *Ann. Bot.* **23**, 131–45.

Bodlaender, K. B. A. & Reestman, A. J. (1968). The interaction of nitrogen supply and plant density in potatoes. *Neth. J. agric. Sci.* **16**, 165–76.

Boerema, E. (1965). Sod-seeding of rice in New South Wales. *Aust. J. exp. Agric. Anim. Husb.* **5**, 475–8.

Boerema, E. (1973). Rice cultivation in Australia. *Riso*, **22**, 131–50.

Borlaug, N. E. (1968). Wheat breeding and its impact on world food supply. *Proc. 3rd Int. Wheat Genet. Symp.* pp. 1–39.

Brougham, R. W. (1960). The relationship between the critical leaf area, total chlorophyll content and maximum growth rate of some pasture and crop plants. *Ann. Bot.* **24**, 463–74.

Brown, R. H. & Blaser, R. E. (1968). Leaf area index in pasture growth. *Herb. Abstr.* **38**, 1–9.

Bull, T. A. (1971). The C_4-pathway related to growth rates in sugar cane. In *Photosynthesis and Photorespiration*, eds. M. D. Hatch, C. B. Osmond & R. O. Slatyer, pp. 68–75. New York, Wiley-Interscience.

Bunting, A. H. & Drennan, D. S. H. (1966). Some aspects of the morphology and physiology of cereals in the vegetative stage. In *The Growth of Cereals and Grasses*, eds. F. L. Milthorpe & J. D. Ivins. *Proc. 12th Easter Sch. Agric. Sci. Univ. Nott.*, pp. 20–38. London, Butterworths.

Burger, A. W. & Hittle, C. N. (1967). Yield, protein, nitrate and prussic acid content of sudan grass, sudan grass hybrids and pearl millets harvested at two cutting frequencies and two stubble heights. *Agron. J.* **59**, 259–62.

Burr, G. O., Hartt, C. E., Brodie, H. W., Tanimoto, T., Kortschak, H. P., Takahashi, D., Ashton, F. M. & Coleman, R. E. (1957). The sugar cane plant. *Ann. Rev. Pl. Physiol.* **8**, 275–309.

Burton, G. W., Jackson, J. E. & Knox, F. E. (1959). The influence of light reduction upon the production, persistence and chemical composition of Coastal Bermuda grass (*Cynodon dactylon*). *Agron. J.* **51**, 537–42.

Chandler, R. F. (1969). Plant morphology and stand geometry in relation to nitrogen. In *Physiological Aspects of Crop Yield*, eds. J. D. Eastin, F. A. Haskins, C. Y. Sullivan & C. H. M. van Bavel, pp. 265–85. Madison, American Society of Agronomy.

Cooper, J. P. (1963). Species and population differences in climatic response. In *The Environmental Control of Plant Growth*, ed. L. T. Evans, pp. 381–403. London & New York, Academic Press.

Cooper, J. P. (1970). Potential production and energy conversion in temperate and tropical grasses. *Herb. Abstr.* **40**, 1–15.

Cooper, J. P. (1973). Genetic variation in herbage constituents. In *Chemistry and Biochemistry of Herbage*, eds. G. W. Butler & R. W. Bailey, vol. 2, pp. 379–417. London and New York, Academic Press.

Cooper, J. P. & Tainton, N. M. (1968). Light and temperature requirements for the growth of tropical and temperate grasses. *Herb. Abstr.* **38**, 167–76.

Corley, R. H. V. (1973). Effects of plant density on growth and yield of oil palm. *Exp. Agric.* **9**, 169–80.

CIMMYT. (1970). *Preliminary Yield Summary of the 5th International Spring Wheat Yield Nursery, 1968–69*, 8 pp. Mexico, Cimmyt.

Daynard, T. B., Tanner, J. W. & Duncan, W. G. (1971). Duration of grain-filling period and its relation to grain yield in corn. *Crop Sci.* **11**, 45–8.

Daynard, T. B., Tanner, J. W. & Hume, D. J. (1969). Contribution of stalk soluble carbohydrates to grain maize in corn (*Zea mays* L.). *Crop Sci.* **9**, 831–4.

Dobrenz, A. K., Wright, L. N., Humphrey, A. B., Massengale, M. A. & Kneebone, W. R. (1969). Stomate density and its relationship to water-use efficiency of blue panic-grass (*Panicum antidotale* Retz.). *Crop Sci.* **9**, 354–7.

Donald, C. M. (1960). The influence of climatic factors on the distribution of subterranean clover in Australia. *Herb. Abstr.* **30**, 81–90.

Donald, C. M. (1968). The breeding of crop ideotypes. *Euphytica* **17**, 385–403.

Downton, W. J. S. (1971). Adaptive and evolutionary aspects of C_4 photosynthesis. In *Photosynthesis and Photorespiration*, eds. M. D. Hatch, C. B. Osmond & R. O. Slatyer, pp. 3–17. New York, Wiley-Interscience.

Duncan, W. G. & Hesketh, J. D. (1968). Net photosynthetic rates, relative leaf growth rates and leaf numbers of 22 races of maize grown at eight temperatures. *Crop Sci.* **8**, 670–4.

Duncan, W. G., Loomis, R. S., Williams, W. A. & Hanau, R. (1967). A model for simulating photosynthesis in plant communities. *Hilgardia*, **38**, 181–205.

Duncan, W. G., Shaver, D. L. & Williams, W. A. (1973). Insolation and temperature effects on maize growth and yield. *Crop Sci.* **13**, 187–91.

Dunstone, R. L., Gifford, R. M. & Evans, L. T. (1973). Photosynthetic characteristics of modern and primitive wheat species in relation to ontogeny and adaptation to light. *Aust. J. biol. Sci.* **76,** 795–808.

Eagles, C. F. & Østgård, O. (1971). Variation in growth and development in natural populations of *Dactylis glomerata* from Norway and Portugal. I. Growth analysis. *J. appl. Ecol.* **8,** 367–82.

Eastin, J. D., Haskins, F. A., Sullivan, C. Y. & van Bavel, C. H. M. (eds.) (1969). *Physiological Aspects of Crop Yield*, 396 pp. Madison, American Society of Agronomy.

Eik, K. & Hanway, J. J. (1966). Leaf area in relation to yield of corn grain. *Agron. J.* **58,** 16–18.

Enyi, B. A. C. (1972*a*). The effect of spacing on growth, development and yield of single and multishoot plants of cassava (*Manihot esculenta* Kranz). I. Root tuber yield and yield attributes. *E. Afr. agric. For. J.* **38,** 23–6.

Enyi, B. A. C. (1972*b*). The effects of spacing on growth, development and yield of single and multishoot plants of cassava (*Manihot esculenta* Kranz). II. Physiological factors. *E. Afr. agric. For. J.* **38,** 27–34.

Enyi, B. A. C. (1973). Growth rates of three cassava varieties (*Manihot esculenta* Kranz) under varying population densities. *J. agric. Sci., Camb.* **81,** 15–28.

Evans, L. T. & Dunstone, R. L. (1970). Some physiological aspects of evolution in wheat. *Aust. J. biol. Sci.* **23,** 725–42.

Evans, L. T., Dunstone, R. L., Rawson, H. M. & Williams, R. F. (1970). The phloem of the wheat stem in relation to requirements for assimilate by the ear. *Aust. J. biol. Sci.* **23,** 743–52.

Evans, L. T. & Rawson, H. M. (1970). Photosynthesis and respiration by the flag leaf and components of the ear during grain development in wheat. *Aust. J. biol. Sci.* **23,** 245–54.

Evelyn, S. H., Padmanabhan, S. Y., Matsuo, T., Hsieh, S. C., El-Mak, M. G. & Adair, C. R. (1969). *Preliminary Report on the Results of the International Rice Adaptation Experiments, 1968*. Special Committee for Rice Adaptation. IBP/UM/Gene Pools, 32 pp.

Finlay, K. W. & Wilkinson, G. N. (1963). An analysis of adaptation in a plant breeding programme. *Aust. J. agric. Res.* **14,** 742–54.

Fitzpatrick, E. A. & Nix, H. A. (1970). The climatic factor in Australian grassland ecology. In *Australian Grasslands*, ed. R. M. Moore, pp. 3–26. Canberra, Australian National University Press.

Gibbon, D., Holliday, R., Mattei, F. & Luppi, G. (1970). Crop production potential and energy conversion efficiency in different environments. *Expl. Agric.* **6,** 197–204.

Gloser, J. (1967). The dependance of CO_2 exchange on density of irradiation, temperature and water saturation deficit in *Stipa* and *Bromus*. *Photosynthetica*, **1,** 171–8.

Hardon, J. J. (1969). Developments in oil palm breeding. *Proc. 2nd Malaysian Oil Palm Conf.* pp. 13–24.

Hatch, M. D. & Slack, C. R. (1970). Photosynthetic CO_2 fixation pathways. *Ann. Rev. Pl. Physiol.* **21,** 141–62.

Hayashi, K. (1968). Response of net assimilation rate to differing intensity of sunlight in rice varieties. *Proc. Crop Sci. Soc. Japan*, **37**, 528–33.

Hayashi, K. (1969). Efficiencies of solar energy conversion and relating characteristics in rice varieties. *Proc. Crop Sci. Soc. Japan*, **38**, 495–500.

Heichel, G. H. & Musgrave, R. B. (1969). Varietal differences in net photosynthesis of *Zea mays* L. *Crop Sci.* **9**, 483–6.

Hicks, D. R., Pendleton, J. W., Bernard, R. L. & Johnston, J. J. (1969). Response of soybean plant types to planting patterns. *Agron. J.* **61**, 290–3.

Holliday, R. (1966). Solar energy consumption in relation to crop yield. *Agric. Progr.* **41**, 24–34.

Irvine, J. E. (1967). Photosynthesis in sugar cane varieties under field conditions. *Crop Sci.* **7**, 297–300.

Jewiss, O. R. (1972). Tillering in grasses – its significance and control. *J. Br. Grassld Soc.* **27**, 65–82.

Khan, M. A. & Tsunoda, S. (1970). Growth analyses of cultivated wheat species and their wild relatives with special reference to dry matter distribution among different plant organs and to leaf area expansion. *Tohoku J. agric. Res.* **21**, 47–59.

Kirby, E. J. M. (1969). The effects of daylength on the development of wheat, barley and oats. *Fld Crop Abstr.* **22**, 1–7.

Koller, D. (1969). The physiology of dormancy and survival of plants in desert environments. *Symp. Soc. exp. Biol.* **23**, 449–70.

Laude, H. M. (1953). The nature of summer dormancy in perennial grasses. *Bot. Gaz.* **114**, 284–92.

Levitt, J. (1972). *Responses of plants to environmental stresses*. Physiological Ecology Monographs, 697 pp. New York & London, Academic Press.

Loomis, R. S. & Williams, W. A. (1963). Maximum crop productivity – an estimate. *Crop Sci.* **3**, 67–72.

Loomis, R. S., Williams, W. A. & Hall, A. E. (1971). Agricultural productivity. *Ann. Rev. Pl. Physiol.* **22**, 431–68.

Lupton, F. G. H. & Kirby, E. J. M. (1968). Applications of physiological analyses to cereal breeding. *Rep. Pl. Breed. Inst. Cambridge for 1967*, pp. 5–26.

McWilliam, J. R. (1968). The nature of the perennial response in Mediterranean grasses. II. Senescence, summer dormancy and survival in *Phalaris*. *Aust. J. agric. Res.* **19**, 397–410.

McWilliam, J. R. & Kramer, P. J. (1968). The nature of the perennial response in Mediterranean grasses. I. Water relations and summer survival in *Phalaris*. *Aust. J. agric. Res.* **19**, 381–96.

Milbourne, G. M. (1973). The agronomy and physiology of grain maize. *Agric. Dev. Adv. Serv. Quart. Rev.* **9**, 24–30.

Milthorpe, F. L. (1963). Some aspects of plant growth. In *The Growth of the Potato*, eds. J. D. Ivins & F. L. Milthorpe, *Proc. 10th Easter Sch. agric. Sci. Univ. Nott*, pp. 3–16, London, Butterworths.

617

Milthorpe, F. L. & Moorby, J. (1967). The growth of the potato. *Proc. 3rd trienn. Conf. Eur. Ass. Potato Res.* 51–70.

Misken, K. E., Rasmusson, D. C. & Moss, D. N. (1972). Inheritance and physiological effects of stomatal frequency in barley. *Crop Sci.* **12**, 780–4.

Monsi, M. & Murata, Y. (1970). Development of photosynthetic systems as influenced by distribution of matter. In *Prediction and Measurement of Photosynthetic Productivity*, ed. I. Šetlík, pp. 115–30. Wageningen, PUDOC.

Monteith, J. L. (1969). Light interception and radiative exchange in crop stands. In *Physiological Aspects of Crop Yields*, eds. J. D. Eastin, F. A. Haskins, C. Y. Sullivan & C. H. M. van Bavel, pp. 89–111. Madison, American Society of Agronomy.

Moss, D. N. & Musgrave, R. B. (1971). Photosynthesis and crop production. *Adv. Agron.* **23**, 317–36.

Neales, T. F. & Incoll, L. D. (1968). The control of leaf photosynthesis rate by the level of assimilate concentration in the leaf: a review of the hypothesis. *Bot. Rev.* **34**, 107–25.

Nichiporovich, A. A. (1969). The role of plants in the bioregenerative systems. *Ann. Rev. Pl. Physiol.* **20**, 185–208.

Nichiporovich, A. A. (1970). Biological bases of plant productivity. In *Die Kulturpflanze*, ed. H. Stubbe, pp. 73–108. Berlin, Akademie–Verlag.

Østgård, O. & Eagles, C. F. (1971). Variation in growth and development in natural populations of *Dactylis glomerata* from Norway and Portugal. II. Leaf development and tillering. *J. appl. Ecol.* **8**, 383–92.

Pendleton, J. W., Smith, G. E., Winter, S. R. & Johnston, T. J. (1968). Field investigations of the relationships of leaf angle in corn (*Zea mays*) to grain yield and apparent photosynthesis. *Agron. J.* **60**, 422–4.

Penman, H. L. (1963). Vegetation and hydrology. *Tech. Commun Commonw. Bur. Soil Sci.* **53**, 1–124.

Perry, T. O. (1971). Dormancy of trees in winter. *Science*, **171**, 29–36.

Ragland, J. L., Hatfield, A. L. & Benoit, G. R. (1965). The growth and yield of corn. I. Microclimate effects on the growth rate. *Agron. J.* **57**, 217–20.

Rawson, H. M. (1970). Spikelet number, its control and relation to yield per ear in wheat. *Aust. J. biol. Sci.* **23**, 1–15.

Raymond, W. F. (1969). The nutritive value of forage crops. *Adv. Agron.* **21**, 2–108.

Rees, A. R. & Thornley, J. H. M. (1973). A simulation of tulip growth in the field. *Ann. Bot.* **37**, 121–32.

Reitz, L. P. & Salmon, S. C. (1968). Origin, history and use of Norin 10 wheat. *Crop Sci.* **8**, 686–9.

Rhodes, I. (1971). The relationship between productivity and some components of canopy structure in ryegrass (*Lolium* spp). II. Yield, canopy structure and light interception. *J. agric. Sci., Camb.* **77**, 283–92.

Sanchez, P. A., Ramirez, G. E. & de Calderon, M. V. (1973). Rice responses to nitrogen under high solar radiation and intermittent flooding in Peru. *Agron. J.* **65**, 523–9.

Sheehy, J. E. & Cooper, J. P. (1973). Light interception, photosynthetic activity and crop growth rate in canopies of six temperate forage grasses. *J. appl. Ecol.* **10**, 239–50.

Sibma, L. (1968). Growth of closed green crop surfaces in the Netherlands. *Neth. J. agric. Sci.* **16**, 211–16.

Sibma, L. (1970). Relation between total radiation and yield of some field crops in the Netherlands. *Neth. J. agric. Sci.* **18**, 125–31.

Simmonds, N. W. (1971). The potential of potatoes in the tropics. *Trop. Agric.* **48**, 291–300.

Slatyer, R. O. (1969). Physiological significance of internal water relations to crop yield. In *Physiological Aspects of Crop Yield*, eds. J. D. Eastin, F. A. Haskins, C. Y. Sullivan & C. H. M. van Bavel, pp. 53–83. Madison, American Society of Agronomy.

Slatyer, R. O. (1970). Comparative photosynthesis, growth and transpiration of two species of *Atriplex. Planta*, **93**, 175–89.

Slatyer, R. O. (1971). Relationship between plant growth and leaf photosynthesis in C_3- and C_4-species of *Atriplex*. In *Photosynthesis and Photorespiration*, eds. M. D. Hatch, C. B. Osmond & R. O. Slatyer, pp. 76–81. New York, Wiley-Interscience.

Smith, D. (1964). Winter injury and the survival of forage plants. *Herb. Abstr.* **34**, 203–9.

Stewart, G. A. (1970). High potential productivity of the tropics for cereal crops, grass forage crops and beef. *J. Aust. Inst. agric. Sci.* **36**, 85–101.

Stoskopf, N. C. (1967). Yield performance of upright leaved selections of winter wheat in narrow row spacings. *Can. J. Pl. Sci.* **47**, 597–601.

Syme, J. R. (1970). A high yielding Mexican semi-dwarf wheat and the relationship of yield to harvest index and other varietal characteristics. *Aust. J. exp. Agric. Anim. Husb.* **10**, 350–3.

Tanaka, A., Kawano, K. & Yamaguchi, J. (1966). Photosynthesis, respiration and plant type of the tropical rice plant. *Int. Rice Res. Inst. Tech. Bull.* **7**,

Thorne, G. N. (1966). Physiological aspects of grain yield in cereals. In *The Growth of Cereals and Grasses*, eds. F. L. Milthorpe & J. D. Ivins, *Proc. 12th Easter Sch. agric. Sci. Univ. Nott.*, pp. 88–105. London, Butterworths.

Thorne, G. N. (1971). Physiological factors limiting the yield of arable crops. In *Potential Crop Production*, eds. P. F. Wareing & J. P. Cooper, pp. 143–58. London, Heinemann.

Thornthwaite, C. W. & Mather, J. R. (1955). The water balance. *Publs Clim. Drexel Inst. Technol.* **8**, 1–104.

Treharne, K. J. & Eagles, C. F. (1970). Effect of temperature on photosynthetic activity of climatic races of *Dactylis glomerata* L. *Photosynthetica*, **4**, 107–17.

Treharne, K. J., Pritchard, A. J. & Cooper, J. P. (1971). Variation in photosynthesis and enzyme activity in *Cenchrus ciliaris* L. (Buffel grass). *J. exp. Bot.* **22**, 227–38.

Trewartha, G. T. (1968). *An introduction to climate.* New York, McGraw-Hill.

Tsunoda, S. (1959). A developmental analysis of yielding ability in varieties of field crops. II. The assimilation system of plants as affected by the form, direction and arrangement of single leaves. *Jap. J. Breed.* **9**, 237–44.

Vicente-Chandler, J., Silva, S. & Figarella, J. (1959). The effect of nitrogen fertilization and frequency of cutting on the yield and composition of three tropical grasses. *Agron. J.* **51**, 202–6.

Wallace, D. H., Ozbun, J. L. & Munger, H. M. (1972). Physiological genetics of crop yield. *Adv. Agron.* **24**, 97–146.

Wareing, P. F. (1956). Photoperiodism in woody plants. *An. Rev. Pl. Physiol.* **7**, 191–214.

Wareing, P. F. (1969). The control of bud dormancy in seed plants. *Symp. Soc. exp. Biol.* **23**, 241–62.

Wareing, P. F. (1971). Potential crop production in Britain – some conclusions In *Potential Crop Production*, eds. P. F. Wareing & J. P. Cooper, pp. 362–78. London, Heinemann.

Wareing, P. F. & Matthews, J. (1972). Physiological and genetic factors determining productivity in species of forest trees. *Cong. int. Un. Forest Res. Org.* 136–43.

Warren Wilson, J. (1972). Control of crop processes. In *Crop Processes in Controlled Environments*, eds. A. R. Rees, K. E. Cockshull, D. W. Hand & R. G. Hurd, pp. 7–32. London, Academic Press.

Watkins, J. M. & Lewy-van Severen, M. (1951). Effect of frequency and height of cutting on the yield, stand and protein content of some forages in El Salvador. *Agron. J.* **43**, 291–6.

Watson, D. J. (1971). Size, structure and activity of the productive system of crops. In *Potential Crop Production*, eds. P. F. Wareing & J. P. Cooper, pp. 76–88. London, Heinemann.

Wetselaar, R. & Norman, M. J. T. (1960). Recovery of available soil nitrogen by annual fodder crops at Katherine, Northern Territory. *Aust. J. agric. Res.* **11**, 693–704.

Williams, C. N. (1972). Growth and productivity of tapioca (*Manihot utilissima*). III. Crop ratio, spacing and yield. *Expl. Agric.* **8**, 15–23.

Williams, W. A., Loomis, R. S. & Lepley, C. R. (1965). Vegetative growth of corn as affected by population density. I. Productivity in relation to interception of solar radiation. *Crop Sci.* **5**, 211–15.

Wilson, D. (1973). Physiology of light utilization by swards. In *Chemistry and Biochemistry of Herbage*, eds. G. W. Butler & R. W. Bailey, vol. 2, pp. 57–101. London & New York, Academic Press.

Wilson, D. & Cooper, J. P. (1969). Assimilation rate and growth of *Lolium* populations in the glasshouse in contrasting light intensities. *Ann. Bot.* **33**, 951–66.

Wilson, G. L. & Ludlow, M. M. (1970). Net photosynthetic rates of tropical grass and legume leaves. *Proc. XIth Int. Grassld Congr.* 534–8.

de Wit, C. T. (1965). Photosynthesis of leaf canopies. *Agric. Res. Rep.* **663**, 1–57.

de Wit, C. T., Brouwer, R. & Penning de Vries, F. W. T. (1970). The simulation of photosynthetic systems. In *Prediction and Measurement of*

Photosynthetic Productivity, ed. I. Šetlík, pp. 47–70. Wageningen, PUDOC.

Worker, G. F. & Marble, V. L. (1968). Comparison of sorghum forage types as to yield and chemical composition. *Agron. J.* **60,** 669–72.

Wright, J. L. & Lemon, E. R. (1966). Photosynthesis under field conditions. 9. Vertical distribution of photosynthesis within a corn crop. *Agron. J.* **58,** 265–9.

Younge, O. R. & Butchart, D. H. (1963). Irrigated sugarbeet production in Hawaii. *Haw. Agric. Expt. Stn Bull.* **52,** 36 pp.

Zavitkovski, J. & Ferrell, W. K. (1970). Effect of drought upon rates of photosynthesis, respiration and transpiration of seedlings of two ecotypes of Douglas fir. II. Two-year old seedlings. *Photosynthetica,* **4,** 58–67.

28. Crop simulation and experimental evaluation – a case study

H. VAN KEULEN, W. LOUWERSE, L. SIBMA &
TH. ALBERDA

Once the significance of photosynthesis was understood, a large number of scientists tried to make an estimate of the total amount of dry matter that is produced yearly on our planet. The first to carry out such a calculation was Liebig (1840), who supposed that all the land surface of the earth consisted of one closed green grass surface, producing 5 tons of dry matter per ha each year. On this basis he calculated a total production of 3×10^{10} tons of organic carbon per year. His attempts were later followed by others, who usually found lower amounts, for instance Schroeder (1919a,b) who separated the land area into woods, farmlands, steppes and deserts and who arrived at a total amount of 1.63×10^{10} tons of organic carbon per year.

These calculations, however, are not directly related to the process of photosynthesis but are based on practical experience of primary production in different climatic areas around the world.

A different approach is to relate the production of a crop or of vegetation or the total global production to the amount of incoming light energy and to calculate the efficiency with which this energy is used to produce organic material. The low efficiency values found as compared to the photosynthetic efficiency of a single leaf led to speculations as to the possible causes of these differences, the main causes being the wastage of light during the phase when the vegetation is not closed, and the often suboptimal supply of minerals and/or water (Gaastra, 1958).

The next step was then to calculate the potential production rate, i.e. the growth rate of a crop or vegetation in which all the incoming light is intercepted by healthy green plant material and in which water and minerals are supplied in optimal amounts. In 1959 de Wit proposed a model to calculate the photosynthesis rate of a leaf canopy from the photosynthesis–light response curve and the optical properties of individual leaves, the crop architecture and the measured global radiation. Later (de Wit, 1965), this model was refined and the calculations were performed on a computer. This was, however, still a stationary model, which did not account for the dynamic behaviour of photosynthesis as a result of changes in weather and crop properties. With the development of high-speed computers and high-level simulation languages, which made it easy to handle dynamic systems, the attention shifted towards non-stationary models, like ELCROS (de Wit, Brouwer & Penning de Vries, 1969). As the knowledge of basic processes increased, this model was further expanded and is at present in a stage, where under a range of circumstances, good agreement is obtained between predicted and observed productivity.

The crux of this approach is that the simulation program contains as much basic data as possible on the photosynthetic capacity of individual leaves, respiration values, leaf position, dry matter distribution patterns between different organs and the factors governing these patterns, as well as the meteorological data. To make these programs not too complicated and to make a check on these programs possible, they are up to now best restricted to a closed crop of a single plant species, in its vegetative state, and supplied optimally with water and minerals. The production actually obtained under these conditions can then serve as an independent control. Once a simulation program works reasonably well it can be used for other purposes. The effect of different plant characteristics, which are though to influence production, can be studied by varying them one by one and then calculating their effect on dry matter production. Such factors include the light response curve of individual leaves, leaf position, or the dry matter distribution between different plant organs. Furthermore the program can gradually be extended to fit situations in which the water supply or any other environmental factor is limiting production. For instance, after checking against the appropriate field experiments at one place, the program can be used to predict productivity in other arid zones.

Instead of calculating and measuring dry matter production, it is also possible to construct the model in such a way that it calculates the rate of photosynthesis of a crop or a vegetation and then to compare this value with actual photosynthesis measurements under comparable conditions. As photosynthesis measurements can be carried out without destruction of the crop these programs can be used more easily than with measurements of dry matter production to study the effects of variations, in such climatic factors as light intensity, temperature and water availability, or in other features such as crop structure and mineral deficiency.

In this chapter a survey will be given of comparisons of actual and calculated production of a grass sward grown with optimal supply of water and minerals, and of the measured and calculated photosynthesis rate of such a sward. This survey will illustrate how the experimental results can influence the model, and how the calculations with the model may lead to new investigations into the background of crop production. A short description will also be given of the simulation program and of the apparatus used to measure photosynthesis in the field.

Simulation of crop growth

Introduction

Simulation may be defined as the building of models and the study of their behaviour. A model is a schematic representation of a limited part of reality. The building of a model requires the integration of detailed knowledge into the whole of a working system. Reality is always simplified in a model, partly because our understanding of basic processes is limited, partly because this enables us to handle the model. Hence a model is the reflection of our opinion about how the system works. It also means that the purpose of the simulation is limited. This purpose determines the boundaries of the chosen system, and thus which processes should be part of the model and which processes may be introduced as forcing functions. This determines at the same time which outputs can be used for validation of the model.

Detailed information on physical, physiological and chemical properties of plants can be collected under controlled conditions and then used to simulate the field situation. When such information is not available reasonable estimates may be used. The relative importance of such estimated parameters can be tested by 'sensitivity analysis', i.e. running the program with different values (or relations) and comparing the output.

Another possibility is to describe the relevant physiological processes on basis of biochemical knowledge and to incorporate this into the model. This introduces, however, a large amount of detail. Moreover the relaxation time – that is the time to recover from small changes – of the extreme processes in the model may differ by a factor of 10000. In that case it may be only possible to execute the model in time increments of 1/10000 or less of the total time span. Computer time and budget will then become the limiting factors. It is virtually impossible to build multi-level models in which the relaxation times of the extremes may differ up to a factor of 10^7.

625

x*

Actual and potential production

In the crop production model, an hierarchical approach is used, that is, more basic processes are incorporated via the outcome of separate models. Such models, for example, those for respiration (Penning de Vries, Chapter 20) and for microclimate (Goudriaan & Waggoner, 1972) comprise only part of the system and describe the relevant processes in more detail.

To check on the validity of our opinion, a model should be tested properly. This means on the one hand, that the same data are not used in both the construction and the evaluation of the model. On the other hand agreement should not be reached by adjusting the parameters and functions. That would lead to a most dangerous method of curve-fitting. The proper procedure, in cases where discrepancies between simulation and experiment exist, is to examine the relevant processes and to improve their description.

If good agreement exists between simulated and measured values, the model may be used to predict productivity under different environmental conditions, i.e. to extrapolate knowledge to other areas.

Simulation, if combined with experimentation, is a useful tool in testing the validity of our opinion, in pointing out weak areas in our knowledge and so designing new experiments, and in the extrapolation of our knowledge.

The crop growth model

The present model has many inputs, consisting of physical, physiological and chemical plant properties, as well as macrometeorological data from standard weather stations. These data are summarized in Table 28.1. The model calculates the increase in dry weight and the transpiration of a plant or a canopy.

A relational diagram of the model is shown in Fig. 28.1. The rectangles represent quantities, the valves represent rates, while the circles represent intermediate variables.

The growth of the canopy, defined as the increase in dry weight of the structural material, is dependent on the amount of reserves present in the crop, whereby the influence of the temperature and the water status of the crop can be taken into account. A functional balance, governed by the water status (Brouwer & de Wit, 1969), determines the division of the newly formed material between shoot and root.

The amount of reserves, consisting of soluble carbohydrates, is calculated from the rate of photosynthesis of the crop and the respiration

626

Meteorological		Physiological		Physical		Chemical
Variable	Units	Variable	Units	Variable	Units	Variable
Total global radiation	$J\ m^{-2}\ d^{-1}$	P (net photosynthesis) [graph: $kg\ CO_2\ ha^{-1}\ h^{-1}$ vs PAR, $J\ m^{-2}\ s^{-1}$]		Leaf area index	–	Composition of material
Dew point	°C			Leaf angle distribution	–	
Maximum temp.	°C	Stomatal resistance ($s\ m^{-1}$) [graph: vs RWC, $g\ g^{-1}$]		Average width of the leaves	m	
Minimum temp.	°C	Stomatal resistance [graph: vs PAR, $J\ m^{2}\ s^{-1}$]		Scattering coefficient of leaves	–	
Wind speed	$m\ s^{-1}$	Internal resistance ($s\ m^{-1}$) and Root conductivity ($kg\ H_2O\ m^{-2}\ d^{-1}\ (bar\ m^{-1})^{-1}$) [graph: vs Temperature]				

PAR—photosynthetically active radiation. RWC—relative water content

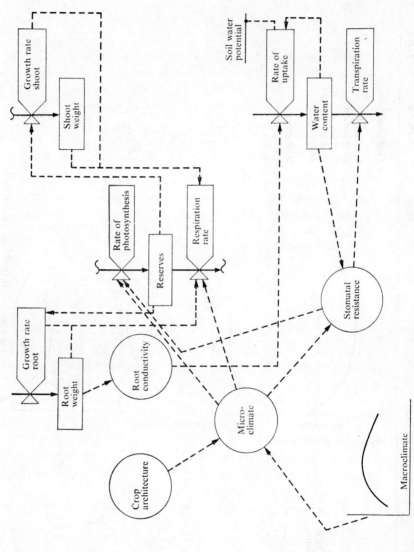

Fig. 28.1. Relational diagram of the simulation model.

rate. The respiration is the total of maintenance respiration, which is a function of the amount of material present, and respiration associated with growth, which depends on both the growth rate and the chemical composition of the structural material that is formed. Allowance is made for the influence of crop temperature on both respiratory processes.

Crop photosynthesis is calculated by adding the photosynthetic rates of a number of leaf layers, each with a certain leaf area, into which the total leaf area of the crop is divided. The photosynthetic rate of each layer is derived from the photosynthesis–light response curve of individual leaves and is dependent on the light intensity, the concentrations of CO_2 and the resistance for diffusion of CO_2 from the atmosphere towards the active sites.

The intensity of the visible light in each layer is calculated from the measured global radiation, taking into account reflection and assuming an exponential extinction with depth in the canopy. Allowance is made to distinguish between direct and diffuse light and between sunlit and shadowed leaves. The extinction and reflection coefficients are calculated from the leaf angle distribution of the crop, the scattering coefficients of the leaves, and the direction of the incident light.

The concentration of CO_2 is assumed to be constant throughout the canopy. The resistance for diffusion of CO_2 includes (i) a turbulent resistance above the canopy, dependent on the windspeed and the stability of the atmosphere; (ii) a resistance of the laminar layer around the leaves, which is a function of wind velocity and of the size of the leaves; (iii) a stomatal resistance and (iv) an internal resistance (mesophyll resistance). The stomatal resistance is governed by either the incident light intensity or the water status of the crop. (At present the working hypothesis is adopted that the stomatal resistance depends on the concentration of CO_2 in the stomatal cavity rather than on incident light intensity.) The internal resistance is a function of the leaf age and the temperature, and allowance can therefore be made for adaptation of the plant to different temperature regimes.

The water status of the plants is assumed to be constant throughout the canopy and is determined by the balance between transpiration and the water uptake from the soil. Transpiration is found by adding the transpiration rates of the various leaf layers. These rates are calculated from the absorbed radiation in each layer, the stomatal resistance, the resistance of the laminar layer, the turbulent resistance above the canopy and the humidity of the ambient air. The latter is again assumed

629

to be constant throughout the canopy. This calculation also computes the temperature in the leaf layer from the heat balance. These temperatures are used in the photosynthesis calculation and can also be averaged to give the average crop temperature that influences growth and respiration.

Water uptake from the soil is determined by the conductivity of the root system and the difference in water potential between plant and soil,

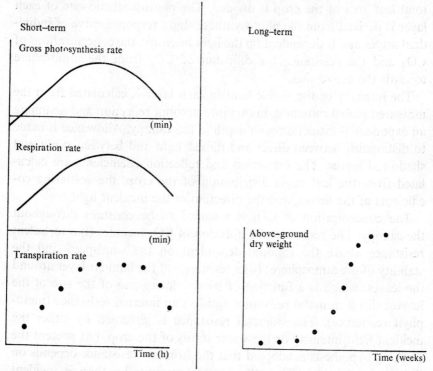

Fig. 28.2. The outputs of the short-term and the long-term simulation model, together with their time scale.

assuming the latter to be optimal (i.e. 0.1 bar). The conductivity is derived from the weight of the roots, assuming a ratio between weight and conductivity, that is dependent on soil temperature and on the degree of suberization of the roots. The growth of the roots is governed by the crop water status and the amount of available reserves. The temperature of the root zone is assumed to be constant with depth and follows the air temperature with a delay of four hours, taking into account a decrease in amplitude.

630

Some of the processes mentioned have a very short relaxation time and their dynamic behaviour can only be tested in short-term experiments, while other processes need long-term experiments for checking.

Two types of experiments are used to validate the model: short-term experiments with crop enclosures in which the measured and calculated rates of CO_2 exchange (or rates of photosynthesis and respiration) and the transpiration rates are compared, and long-term experiments with periodic harvest where a comparison is made between the measured and calculated above ground rate of biomass production. The outputs used for validation and their time scale are shown in Fig. 28.2.

Determination of crop growth and photosynthesis

As has been explained in the preceding paragraph, it is necessary to test the model either by the measurement of photosynthetic performance of a plant or a crop in short-term experiments, or by the determination of dry matter increase over longer periods. The latter method has already been used in testing an earlier simulation model, devised by de Wit (1959) by measuring the rate of dry herbage production of a closed sward of perennial rye-grass (Alberda & Sibma, 1968). From this comparison it appeared that, apart from periods in early spring and late autumn when the temperature was too low, there was a good agreement between the actual and simulated growth rate of a young sward during the greater part of the growth period under the assumption that the herbage production amounts to 60% of the total dry matter production. There were, however, two situations in which there was a discrepancy between the two values. Firstly, the actual growth rate lagged behind the simulated one from the second half of August onwards, and, secondly, there was a rather sudden decline in the rate of dry herbage production as the sward became older, a decline that cannot be explained by a relative increase in the rate of respiration (Alberda & Sibma, 1968).

In trying to get some more information about the latter discrepancy, an experiment was designed in which the following items were measured at four-weekly intervals throughout the season: (i) the rate of dry herbage production of a grass sward of an age of three to four weeks, seven to eight weeks and eleven to twelve weeks; (ii) the rate of photosynthesis of the same swards measured by putting a 2 m² enclosure over them; (iii) the rate of photosynthesis of just fully expanded leaves of these swards at different light intensities. A short description of each technique will be given here, with references to more detailed information.

The field experiment was carried out on a permanent pasture, consisting mainly of perennial rye-grass (*Lolium perenne*) mixed with some timothy (*Phleum pratense*). In the absence of nitrogen fertilizer there was hardly any growth. A rapid growth of a particular experimental strip could be started by nitrogen application. By choosing the appropriate times, it could be arranged that at four-weekly intervals there was one week for measurements in which closed swards were available which were three, seven and eleven weeks old, respectively at the beginning of the week. The growth rate of the herbage was measured by cutting an area of 8 m² at the beginning and the end of the measuring week and calculating the difference in dry weight. A more detailed description of the technique is given elsewhere (Alberda, 1962).

The rate of photosynthesis was determined by placing a 2 m² iron frame in the sward before fertilizer application and by putting a transparent enclosure over this frame during the measurement week. The rate of net photosynthesis was measured with a mobile installation, similar to that described by Stiles & Leafe (1969). Details of our method are given elsewhere (Louwerse & Eikhoudt, 1975). Usually a measurement on a particular sward took one or two 24-hour periods. On each measuring day two swards of different age were always compared by measuring them simultaneously.

The light response curve of individual leaves was measured in a laboratory set-up, described by Louwerse & van Oorschot (1969). To bring the leaves into the laboratory blocks of an area of 20 cm × 20 cm and 40 cm deep were dug out of the sward. These blocks were placed in a plastic bucket of the same shape, well watered and placed beside the leaf chamber. A sufficient number of just fully expanded leaves was placed between thin nylon wires in the leaf chamber and exposed to a series of light intensities.

Experimental results

The rate of herbage growth

The results of the growth rate measurements are presented in Fig. 28.3 in which the dry herbage weights are plotted against time. As was found earlier (Alberda, 1962), the growth curves are somewhat irregular and, therefore, growth rates calculated from weight differences between the successive cuts show usually rather large variations. These calculated growth rates during the measuring week are given in Table 28.2, columns 6, 11 and 15.

The rate of photosynthesis

An example of the measurement of the rate of canopy photosynthesis during a period of a little over twenty-four hours is presented in Fig. 28.4. In the upper half of the figure the course of temperature and light intensity are plotted against time, and in the lower half the same is done for the rate of photosynthesis of two swards of different age, calculated from the air speed and the difference in ingoing and outgoing carbon dioxide concentration. The sharp depression in light intensity and

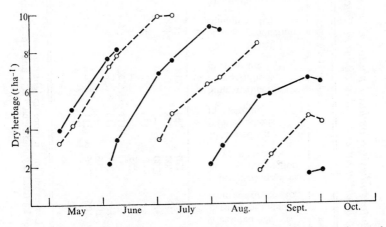

Fig. 28.3. Measured dry herbage weights at different stages of uninterrupted growth of closed swards at successive periods during the growing season.

photosynthesis during the first light period is caused by artificial darkening of the enclosure to measure the rate of respiration during the day. The temperature inside the enclosure was always kept at ambient. The younger and older swards show a very large difference both in net photosynthesis during the day and in respiration during the night. From these curves the net dry matter production during a 24-hour period can be calculated, as shown in the figure, and that of the eleven weeks old sward proves to be only about one-eighth of that of the three weeks old sward. For each measuring week, a few days with a rather regular distribution of light intensity during the day have been selected, and the net dry matter production over a 24-hour period, calculated from this data, is presented in Table 28.2, columns 3, 8 and 12, together

Table 28.2. *Comparison of measured photosynthesis, simulated photosynthesis, measured dry herbage production and calculated dry herbage production of different age and at different times during the season*

		Age 3–4 weeks					Age 7–8 weeks				Age 11–12 weeks			
Date	Radiation ($J\ cm^{-2}\ d^{-1}$)	Measured net photosynthesis in enclosure	Simulated net photosynthesis in enclosure	Calculated net herbage production column 3×0.6	Measured net herbage production from sward growth	Calculated mean net herbage production of young swards	Measured net photosynthesis in enclosure	Simulated net photosynthesis in enclosure	Calculated net herbage production column 8×0.6	Measured net herbage production from sward growth	Measured net photosynthesis in enclosure	Simulated net photosynthesis in enclosure	Calculated net herbage production column 12×0.6	Measured net herbage production from sward growth
1	2	3	4	5	6	7	8	9	10	11	12	13	14	15
7 May	1782	262	225	157	133	170	264	218	158	148	–	–	–	–
4 June	2845	359	–	215	312	200	238	181	143	148	–	–	–	–
6 June	2356	325	–	195	312	200	–	–	–	–	–	–	–	–
2 July	2569	–	–	–	–	–	130	–	78	101	144	129	86	117
4 July	2351	321	300	193	190	185	111	72	67	37	41	–	25	6
30 July	971	–	–	–	–	–	113	–	68	37	39	12	23	6
1 Aug.	1648	238	–	143	136	147	–	–	–	–	33	–	20	–21
28 Aug.	858	123	–	73	106	116	111	–	67	–	–	–	–	–21
29 Aug.	1276	184	–	110	106	116	74*	–	67	–	25	–	14	n.d.
24 Sept.	849	–	50	–	–	–	88†	49	44	19	–	–	–	–
26 Sept.	611	73	–	43	27	66	11	–	–	–47	11	11	7	–20

* Rather prostrate leaves.   † Leaves put into a more upright position.   n.d., not determined.

(Units for columns 3, 4, 8, 9, 12, 13: kg CH_2O or kg total dry matter $ha^{-1}\ d^{-1}$; units for columns 5, 6, 7, 10, 11, 14, 15: kg dry matter above cutting level $ha^{-1}\ d^{-1}$.)

with the total radiation (column 2). The large differences in the rate of net photosynthesis between swards of different age are evident.

From the data as presented in Fig. 28.4 the relation between light intensity and photosynthesis can also be constructed. This is done in Fig. 28.5 for a number of measurements, and again shows the large difference in photosynthetic performance between swards of different age, except at the beginning of the season (5 May). At this date a real difference in age was not yet established because the oldest sward only started to grow at the beginning of April and was therefore only four to five weeks old at the time of measurement, although nitrogen had already been applied much earlier.

The rate of photosynthesis of individual leaves

The detailed measurements of the rate of photosynthesis of individual leaves are not presented here. In all cases, the light response curves had approximately the same size and shape, whether the leaves were taken early or late in the season or from a young or an old sward. The saturation level was always around 80 μl CO_2 cm^{-2} h^{-1}, a value much lower than is found for leaves of plants grown on nutrient solution in the climate room. This lack of variation in light response curves of plants taken from the field is also at variance with data obtained on individual leaves *in situ* (Deinum, personal communication). These measurements showed that the saturation level of leaves *in situ* in young swards was similar to that found for leaves of plants grown in climate rooms, and that it dropped progressively with age. Calculations with the simulation program, using the light response curve of individual leaves taken from the field as found by us, gave values much lower than those calculated from photosynthesis measurements in the corresponding enclosure. For this reason, the aim to simulate the daily growth rate from the light response curve of a single leaf taken from the field failed. The alternative possibility was to simulate the daily growth rate of a young sward using the light response curve, as found for leaves of growth room plants on nutrient solution, to compare the outcome with the values calculated from the data obtained for photosynthesis and respiration in the enclosure and, if these agreed well, to vary the plant parameters in the simulation program within reasonable limits and to compare the outcome with the photosynthesis data obtained from the older swards. This should provide information on the factors that are most likely to be responsible for the ageing effect in swards.

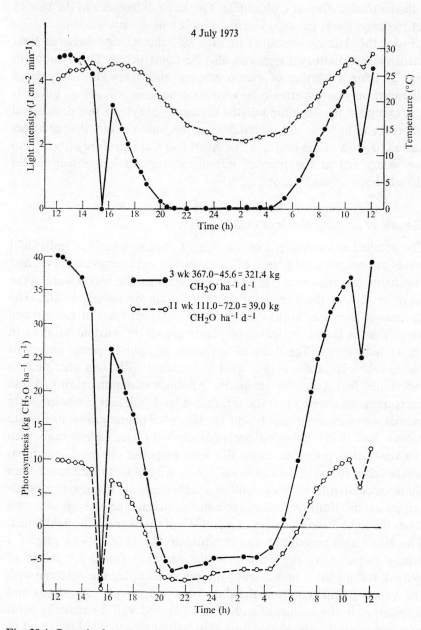

Fig. 28.4. Record of temperature and light intensity over a 24-h period (4 July 1973) together with the measured net photosynthesis values of two swards of different age.

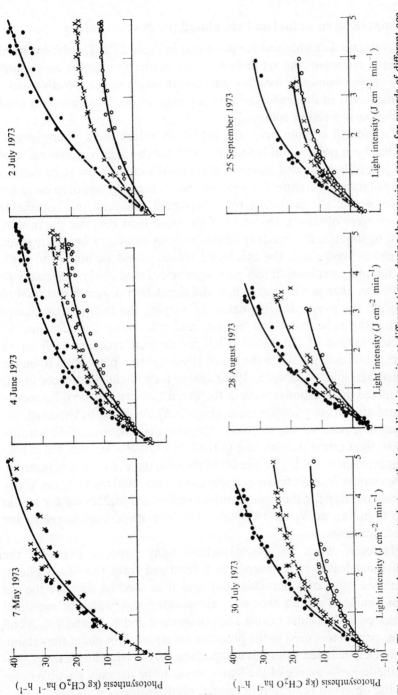

Fig. 28.5. The relation between net photosynthesis and light intensity at different times during the growing season for swards of different age. (●) 3–4 weeks old sward; (×) 7–8 weeks old sward; (○) 11–12 weeks old sward.

Comparison of actual and simulated production values

The relevant data obtained are presented in Table 28.2. The third vertical column represents the net daily total dry matter production on a sunny day at approximately monthly intervals throughout the growth season, as measured in the enclosure with a young sward. The measured total radiation is given in column 2.

The fourth column gives the simulated values for a young sward. As has been pointed out before, the data for the light response curve of the just fully expanded leaves of that sward were too low to be used in the program. Therefore, for a young sward, the light response curve for leaves grown in the climate room was used, and with this reasonable values were obtained. However, if the same light response curve were used to simulate the net daily photosynthesis of swards which are seven or eleven weeks old, the calculated values would be much too high. As the measurements of leaf photosynthesis failed methodologically to show any change with sward age, the simulation program was used to indicate the most plausible cause by varying the factors that change during the experiment one by one, and calculating the effect on net photosynthesis of the sward. Changes in crop architecture from an erectophile canopy, when the sward is young, to a planophile when the sward gets older (Alberda, 1966) create only slight differences in the simulated light response curve of the sward and virtually no difference in cumulative gross photosynthesis (Fig. 28.6). As might be expected, the planophile position was more advantageous than the erectophile position at low light intensities, because of the low altitude of the sun, but at high light intensities, i.e. high altitudes of the sun, the situation was reversed.

A change in maintenance respiration from 50.0 mg CO_2 per g dry matter per day for the young protein-rich sward to 22.5 mg for an old one (Penning de Vries, 1974) also led to a negligible change in net photosynthesis.

However, when the photosynthesis–light response curve of the individual leaves of a sward was determined from the sward photosynthesis curve of a particular day and then used to simulate the net photosynthesis on another day, close agreement with the measured values could be found (Table 28.2, columns 8 and 9, 12 and 13). As all other parameters used in the program are equal throughout the season, it can be concluded from this comparison that a reduction in the photosynthetic performance of the leaves seems to be the only possible cause for the observed reduction in canopy photosynthesis with age.

Although the leaf position has no effect on the daily photosynthesis of a sward, a sudden change in leaf position during measurement has a distinct influence. Bringing upright leaves into a more flat position by means of a wide-meshed gauze resulted in a reduction in photosynthesis of up to 40%, leaving respiration unaffected. When the rate of photosynthesis is simulated with a sward of the same leaf area index but with all the leaves in a horizontal position and in separate layers, each with a leaf area index of 1, a reduction in photosynthesis of about 40% as compared with normal positions is also obtained. As the photosynthesis of the individual leaves in unaffected by the manipulation, because nearly normal values were obtained when the leaves were returned to their normal position, it can reasonably be assumed that using the gauze a practically horizontal leaf position was achieved.

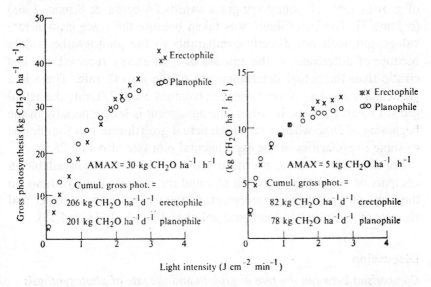

Fig. 28.6. The relation between gross photosynthesis and light intensity, simulated for a sward with planophile and erectophile leaf positions and for different saturation values (AMAX) of the single leaf photosynthesis.

Changing the rather flat leaves of an older sward into a more upright position, also by means of a wide meshed gauze, had no effect. This fits quite well with the results of the simulation program in which a shift in leaf position over the observed range had also no influence on total photosynthesis during the day (Fig. 28.6). If, however, during ageing of a sward the leaves were kept in an upright position, the diminution in photosynthesis was less than with a normal sward, the difference

639

being nearly 20% (see Table 28.2, column 8 for 24 Sept.). This suggests that it is the effect of micro-climatological influences on the photosynthetic performance of lower leaves rather than canopy structure that reduces the rate of photosynthesis with age. More insight into the effect of lodging on leaf performance and crop architecture is needed before any definite conclusions can be drawn.

The fifth column in Table 28.2 gives the dry herbage production calculated from column 3 by multiplying it with 0.6, on the assumption that the herbage weight is 60% of the total plant weight, a proportion found in many growth room experiments. This growth rate can then be compared with that calculated from the herbage yield difference between the beginning and the end of the measuring week (column 6), and also with the mean daily growth rate calculated from five-year measurements of growth rates of young rye-grass swards (Alberda & Sibma, 1968) (column 7). The latter figure was taken because the *mean* growth rate values, although not directly comparable to the photosynthesis data because of differences in the amount of light energy received, are less erratic than the actual determinations of the growth rate. There is a particularly good agreement between columns 5 and 7. Using the actual growth measurements, however, the agreement is less, especially in the beginning of June when a very high actual growth rate was found, due to some irregularities in the experimental plot (see also Fig. 28.3).

For the older swards, no mean growth rate data are available; a comparison between the growth rate and the rate of photosynthesis on the same plot shows less agreement, as the yields become smaller and thereby more uncertain (compare columns 10 and 11, 14 and 15).

Discussion

Comparison between the rate of growth and the rate of photosynthesis

The calculated rate of dry herbage production fitted reasonably well with the mean growth rates for the first two experimental periods, and with both mean and actual growth rate for the rest of the season. When the sward grows older both the growth rate and the rate of photosynthesis drop, but the smaller the production values, the larger the inaccuracy and the more difficult the comparison. When growth rates of herbage are below 100 kg ha^{-1} d^{-1}, a comparison becomes impossible. Nevertheless the experimental evidence clearly indicates that the reduction in growth rate with age of the sward is caused by a reduction in the rate of net photosynthesis and not by an increase in the rate of respiration, as has been suggested in the conception of optimum growth rate and ceiling value (Donald, 1961; see also McCree & Troughton, 1966).

Fig. 28.4 clearly indicates the large differences in net photosynthesis as compared to respiration. As the dry weight increases the respiration per g dry weight decreases, as can be seen when the respiration data are related to the dry herbage weight at the end of the measuring week:

Age of sward (wks)	Wt of dry herbage (kg ha⁻¹)	Respiration rate (kg CH₂O ha⁻¹ d⁻¹)	Respiration rate (g kg⁻¹ d⁻¹)
4	3400	45.6	13.41
11	8130	72.0	8.86

The role of the simulation model in analysing crop production factors

The aim of the present study was to gain a better insight into the performance of a closed grass sward of different ages throughout the season, and especially to analyse the factors that are responsible for the observed reduction in the rate of dry herbage production of the sward with age. For this purpose the increase in dry weight over a certain period, and the rate of crop photosynthesis, were determined. The photosynthetic performance of the youngest fully expanded leaves of that sward was also measured to use in the simulation program in order to test the validity of the program. To analyse the relative importance of the yield-determining factors the crop simulation model was used to calculate either the daily crop growth rate or the daily photosynthesis rate. For crop parameters, basic physiological knowledge was used together with known data on leaf density and leaf position and their change with age of the sward. Using the prevailing weather data, it was then possible to compare the actual and calculated values. A reasonable agreement between measured and simulated dry matter production and measured and simulated photosynthesis rate under varying outdoor conditions and at different ages of the sward, would indicate that the simulation model could now be used satisfactorily to predict the effect of various climatic and canopy factors on dry matter production.

Unfortunately, the present measurements of leaf photosynthesis on plants removed from the sward failed to demonstrate any influence of the season or the age of the sward on the light response curve, and, in addition, all measurements were much lower than those found for plants grown in growth rooms on nutrient solution, or than field measurements of individual leaves *in situ*. It must be concluded that the removal of small swards from the field to the laboratory has influenced the photosynthetic performance of the leaf. When, however, the light response curve of leaves of plants grown indoors was used in the simulation program, the agreement between calculated and measured sward photosynthesis was reasonably good. For older swards, the simulated values based on the values for leaf photosynthetic capacity estimated as described earlier, also agree well with the actual values determined under a range of climatic conditions. It can therefore be concluded that it is the reduction in leaf photosynthetic performance with age that is mainly responsible for the reduction in photosynthesis and growth rate of the sward with age, and also that the simulation program developed so far is able to calculate the rate of dry matter production with reasonable accuracy under various conditions of climate and sward architecture.

References

Alberda, Th. (1962). Actual and potential production of agricultural crops. *Neth. J. agric. Sci.* **10**, 325–33.

Alberda, Th. (1966). Responses of grasses to temperature and light. In *The Growth of Cereals and Grasses*, ed. F. L. Milthorpe & J. D. Ivins. *Proc. 12th Easter Sch. Agric. Sci. Univ. Nott.* pp. 200–12. London; Butterworths.

Alberda, Th. & Sibma, L. (1968). Dry matter production and light interception of crop surfaces. III. Actual herbage production in different years as compared with potential values. *J. Brit. Grassl. Soc.* **23**, 206–16.

Brouwer, R. & de Wit, C. T. (1969). A simulation model of plant growth with special attention to root growth and its consequences. In *Root Growth*, ed. W. J. Whittington. *Proc. 15th Easter Sch. Agric. Sci. Univ. Nott.* pp. 224–44. London, Butterworths.

Donald, C. M. (1961). Competition for light in crops and pastures. *Symp. Soc. exp. Biol.* **15**, 282–313.

Gaastra, P. (1958). Light energy conversion in field crops in comparison with the photosynthetic efficiency under laboratory conditions. *Meded. Landb. Hogesch. Wageningen*, **58**(4), 12 pp.

Goudriaan, J. & Waggoner, P. E. (1972). Simulating both aerial microclimate and soil temperature from observations above the foliar canopy. *Neth. J. agric. Sci.* **20**, 104–24.

Liebig, J. (1840). *Chemie in ihrer Anwendung auf Agrikultur und Physiologie*, Vieweg, Braunschweig.

Louwerse, W. & Eikhoudt, J. W. (1975). A mobile laboratory for measuring photosynthesis, respiration and transpiration of field crops. *Photosynthetica*, in press.

Louwerse, W. & van Oorschot, J. L. P. (1969). An assembly for routine measurements of photosynthesis, respiration and transpiration of intact plants under controlled conditions. *Photosynthetica*, **3**, 305–15.

McCree, K. J. and Troughton, J. H. (1966). Non-existence of an optimum leaf area index for the production rate of white clover grown under constant conditions. *Plant Physiol.* **41**, 1615–22.

Penning de Vries, F. W. T. (1974). The cost of maintenance processes in plant cells. *Ann. Bot.*, in press.

Schroeder, H. (1919*a*). Die jahrliche Gesamt produktion der grunen Pflanzendecke der Erde. *Naturwissenschaften*, **7**, 8.

Schroeder, H. (1919*b*). Quantitatives Untersuchungen über die Verwendung der solaren Energie auf Erden. *Naturwissenschaften*, **7**, 976.

Stiles, W. & Leafe, E. L. (1969). Measurement of photosynthesis and respiration in the field. *Rep. Grassld Res. Inst. 1969*, pp. 127–35.

Wit, C. T. de (1959). Potential photosynthesis of crop surfaces. *Neth. J. agric. Sci.* **7**, 141–9.

Wit, C. T. de (1965). Photosynthesis of leaf canopies. *Agric. Res. Rep.* **663**, 60 pp. Wageningen, PUDOC.

Wit, C. T. de, Brouwer, R. & Penning de Vries, F. W. T. (1969). The simulation of photosynthetic systems. In *Prediction and Measurement of Photosynthetic Productivity*, ed. I. Šetlík, pp. 47–70. Wageningen, PUDOC.

29. Control of photosynthetic production in aquatic ecosystems[*]

E. STENGEL & C. J. SOEDER

This chapter concentrates essentially on the control of pelagic aquatic production by external factors. The better our knowledge of these factors and their interactions is (Soeder & Stengel, 1974), the better is our chance to conserve or to manage aquatic ecosystems.

Our experimental work relies to a large extent on unsterile, unialgal, open mass cultures of planktonic freshwater algae at saturating nutrient concentrations. The culture units resemble oxidation ponds (raceways) in which flow and turbulence are generated by paddlewheels (Stengel, 1971). The average depth of the suspension layer is 10–15 cm. As a typical example of the biomass produced in our cultures, some values for *Scenedesmus acutus* ($=S.$ *obliquus*) can be mentioned. The dry weight of this alga contains 55 % of crude protein (Soeder *et al.*, 1970) and represents a caloric value of about 5.5 kcal g^{-1} or 6.1 kcal g^{-1} on an ashfree basis (Komárek & Přibil, 1968).

Yields of natural and artificial planktonic vegetations

Due to the wide scattering of productivity in natural waters (Table 29.1) estimates of average yields for oceans (Platt & Subba Rao, 1973) and for inland waters (Rodhe, 1965; Talling, 1965a,b,1970; Westlake, 1963) can hardly be calculated. On the other hand, average yields of natural planktonic vegetations are definitely lower than the maximal yields obtained under favourable conditions.

As is to be expected, the average yields of outdoor mass cultures of algae (Table 29.2) surpass the average production of natural waters considerably. The highest yields obtained so far by algal cultures are the ones by Vendlová (1969). At an average of 22.8 g m^{-2} d^{-1} for the period May to July, the mean efficiency of photosynthetic active radiation (PAR) conversion was 4.8 % (Vendlová, 1969). Other figures on PAR conversion by algae are summarized by Nichiporovich (1967) and Miller *et al.* (1968). Already Wassink, Kok & van Oorschot (1953)

[*] Dedicated to Professor Dr Hans-Joachim Elster on the occasion of his 65th birthday.

stated that the energetic efficiency of photosynthesis is, at optimal density of the algal suspension, inversely related to light intensity and may at very strong light limitation, become as high as 20%.

Algal suspensions theoretically offer the advantage over stands of higher plants that they can *continuously* be kept at areal densities which make optimal use of all available unreflected PAR. This requires the proper adjustment of *areal density* in terms of algal chlorophyll (Nichiporovich, 1967) or algal biomass (Soeder *et al.*, 1970) per unit of

Table 29.1. *Approximate average and maximum production in natural waters*

Type of water	Region	Net yield (dry matter) ($g\ m^{-2}\ d^{-1}$)	($t\ ha^{-1}\ yr^{-1}$)	Authors
Average temperate lakes	Europe; US	0.3–0.6	1–2	Talling (1970)
Average oceanic sites	–	0.4	2	Platt & Subba Rao (1973)
Eutrophic warm lakes	Africa	2.7–5.5	10–20	Talling (1965*a,b*)
Upwelling zone	Off Peru	20	?	Platt & Subba Rao (1973)

Table 29.2. *Yields of outdoor mass cultures of microalgae*

Alga	Site	Net yield (dry matter) ($g\ m^{-2}\ d^{-1}$)	($t\ ha^{-1}\ yr^{-1}$)	Operation ($d\ yr^{-1}$)	Authors
Scenedesmus	Rupite	35*	–	–	Vendlová (1969)
Scenedesmus	Rupite	23†	~45	200	Vendlová (1969)
Scenedesmus	Dortmund	11†	~25	240	Soeder *et al.* (1970)
Scenedesmus	Bangkok	15†	~55	365	
Scenedesmus	Bangkok	47‡	~170	365	Payer
Uronema	Bangkok	22†	80	365	(unpublished data)
Spirulina	Bangkok	15†	55	365	

* Maximal average over 7 days.
† Average over total period of operation.
‡ Mixed culture in sewage medium.

irradiated surface. The optimum curve by which areal yield and areal density are interrelated resembles the general light response curve of photosynthesis and seems to follow a hyperbolic function (Tamiya *et al.*, 1953; Talling, 1957,1970; Šetlík, Sůst & Malek, 1970; Soeder *et al.*, 1970).

At the areal density giving maximal yields per unit surface, the growth rate of any alga is much below its maximum, since the latter requires

maximal photosynthesis per cell. For *Scenedesmus acutus* the maximal
daily increment factor (i.e. the number of daughter cells per mother
cell during one 16:8 h light-and-dark cycle) is 18–30 in light-saturated
laboratory cultures. Growing the same strain outdoors at optimal
areal density, we obtain at best a 30% daily increase of biomass per
day, i.e. a doubling of biomass in at least three days. Almost any
planktonic algae should be capable of reaching this growth rate.

In order to test the assumption that algae of high potential growth
rate are not necessary to establish high yields per unit surface, *Euglena*

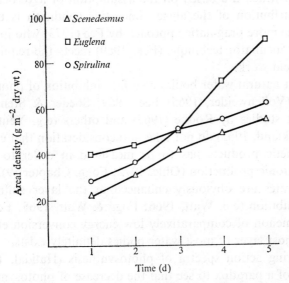

Fig. 29.1. Increase of areal density (g m^{-2}) in parallel cultures of *Euglena gracilis, Scenedesmus acutus* (strain 276–3a), and *Spirulina platensis* (strain Compère) in continuously
illuminated greenhouse ponds (raceway type, 2.7 m^2 net surface each; 30 klx; 20±1.5 °C;
7 l h^{-1} CO$_2$ per pond). Dry weights were determined daily at the same time.

gracilis and *Spirulina platensis* were cultivated in greenhouse ponds in
parallel to *Scenedesmus acutus*. The minimal doubling times of biomass
of these algae are about 16.4 h (Buetow, 1968), 6.0 h and 3.0 h, respectively. Nevertheless, the two algae with the lower growth potentials
grew under strong light limitation and at comparable areal densities at
least as well as did *Scenedesmus* (Fig. 29.1). Evidently, cell size or
specific cellular surface has little influence upon photosynthetic production per unit of illuminated surface, if light is the limiting factor of
production.

Light limitations

Among the external factors controlling aquatic production, light intensity has received the most extensive attention. In his latest papers on the subject Talling (1970,1971) gives a clear picture of what is known about the underwater light climate as determined by incident radiation and the optical properties of the medium. The theoretical analysis of the light-dependent profiles of pelagic photosynthesis is far advanced. The theoretical problems consisting in the integration of production values over space and time are solved by the equations of Vollenweider (1965,1970) which are based on the assumption of a vertically homogenous distribution of the algae. Since this condition is usually not fulfilled, the more pragmatic approach by Fee (1973) who introduced a convenient incubator technique (Fee, 1969) meets the requirements of practical field work.

For most natural water bodies a surface inhibition of photosynthesis is typical (Vollenweider, 1965; Fee, 1969; Soeder & Stengel, 1974). The classic studies by Rodhe (1965) and others (e.g. Yentsch, 1962, 1965; Strickland, 1965) do not take into consideration that excretion of photosynthetic products has to be measured in order to determine total planktonic production (Ohle, 1972; Fogg, Chapter 19). Although excretion rates are obviously enhanced at the layer suffering from surface inhibition (e.g. Watt, 1966; Fogg & Watt, 1965; Fogg, 1971), the phenomenon of comparatively low energy conversion efficiency in the uppermost layer of most water bodies definitely exists.

Considering action spectra of photosynthesis (Halldal, 1970), it is somewhat of a paradox to see that the decrease of photosynthesis with depth in the lower part of the profile parallels the attenuation of the green range of the visible spectrum (Rodhe, 1965). Whether this is indeed a dependence on the green light intensity, or a function of the sum of the photosynthetically more active intensities of blue and red light, has not yet been studied in detail.

An additional and probably very important regulatory mechanism of offshore photosynthesis consists in the daily rhythm of vertical migration of phytoflagellates which may in certain cases even be the dominant component of the photosynthetic canopy (Talling, 1970,1971; Tilzer, 1972).

The underwater light climate is clearly the factor setting the *upper threshold* of productivity at a given site. That rates of actual production in natural waters are almost always far below the production potential offered by the radiation energy input, is due to the limitation by factors other than light. The importance of these other factors can be ruled out to a large extent in artificial systems such as mass cultures of algae (cf. Table 29.2).

Since most of the incident light energy is transformed into heat, temperature conditions are usually dependent on the light regime (Hutchinson, 1957).

Temperature

If temperature is experimentally set to be the limiting factor of photosynthesis, we find an exponential increase of production over a fairly wide temperature range in mesophilic algae (Fig. 29.2; cf. also Slobodskoi *et al.* (1968) for a theoretical treatment of photosynthesis versus temperature). Only a few degrees above the optimum the temperature maximum is reached, and the system breaks down. The decrease of temperature-dependence with increasing limitation by other factors is important for natural ecosystems as well as for mass cultures of algae. For example, the Q_{10} is inversely related to the degree of light limitation (Fig. 29.2). We can with a high degree of certainty expect similar interactions if factors other than light input are limiting productivity. This is almost commonplace in the light of the general theory of crop yields (Nichiporovich, 1969).

The decrease of temperature effects in systems limited by nutrient supply and/or light intensity makes it plausible that the temperature profile has not to be taken into consideration in the theoretical treatment of offshore production profiles (Vollenweider, 1965,1970).

There is also an interrelationship between the temperature level and the concentrations of many essential nutrients, since the remineralization rate due to bacterial degradation of biomass is definitely temperature-dependent. Finally, the increasing sensitivity of algae to high light intensities at suboptimal or supraoptimal temperatures may be of ecological significance (e.g. Sorokin & Krauss, 1962; Šetlík *et al.*, 1970).

Mass cultures of algae can at times heat up considerably under intense irradiation. For example at Bangkok the water temperature may reach 42 °C in the early afternoon (H. D. Payer, unpublished observations). Such transitory temperature extremes are surprisingly well tolerated by mesophilic algae like *Scenedesmus acutus* for which the upper temperature limit under *thermoconstant* laboratory conditions was found to be 34–35 °C (Fig. 29.2). This observation demonstrates that a certain temperature hardiness as determined under constant conditions is not necessarily a true image of hardiness in an ecological situation where there are daily changes of temperature.

A daily change of water temperature occurs not only in shallow streams (e.g. Eckel & Reuther, 1950) but also in astatic standing waters (Eriksen, 1966). Such shallow waters may be as productive as are tidal rockpools, and it is this type of condition for which our mass cultures of algae provide an experimental model. The preliminary comparison

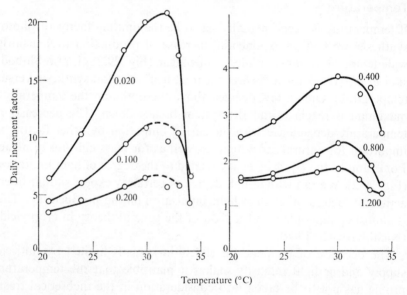

Temperature (°C)

Fig. 29.2. Daily increment factors of *Scenedesmus acutus* (276–3*a*) on a dry weight basis as a function of temperature and suspension density. Optimal temperature, constant laboratory conditions (Soeder *et al.*, 1967); 30 °C, light-and-dark cycle 16:8 h, gassing with 1 % in air. The numbers in the graph indicate the optical densities ($\lambda = 546$ nm) of the suspensions after dilution of the beginning of each cycle. The points represent averages of 3–4 cycles after adaptation. Synchrony was complete at o.d. < 0.1, but only partial at o.d. > 0.1 (after E. Hegewald, unpublished data).

between the mesophilic *Scenedesmus acutus* and the thermophilic *Spirulina platensis* (temperature optimum at 40 °C; Zarrouk, 1966) displays a striking dissimilarity of the daily rhythm of photosynthesis, for which the oxygen concentration in the medium is taken as an indirect measure (Fig. 29.3). It is clear from the data that the production in *Scenedesmus* follows the daily course of light intensity, whereas the production curve of *Spirulina* coincides with the daily changes of temperature.

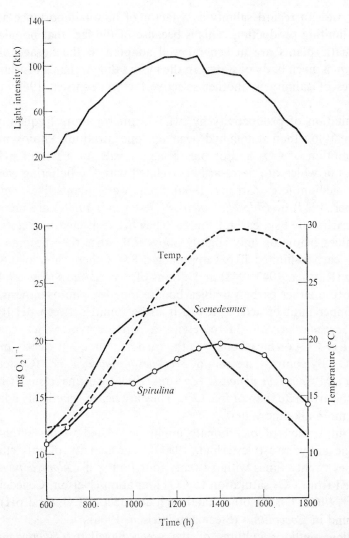

Fig. 29.3. Changes of total incident light intensity, water temperature and dissolved oxygen concentration during one summer day in two identical experimental outdoor ponds at Dortmund. One of the ponds contained *Scenedesmus acutus* (276–3*a*), the other one *Spirulina platensis* (strain Compère).

Salinity, pH and carbon dioxide

Only under extreme conditions, i.e. in hypersaline waters, does salinity seem to become the limiting factor of productivity. Although geographical distribution of algae is definitely determined by their degree of halophilic or halophobic reaction (Lund, 1965; Soeder & Stengel,

1974), we can regard salinity as a factor of minor importance among those limiting production. This is because of the fact that populations of aquatic plants are in general well adapted to the dosage of this factor in a given body of water. In the more saline waters a resistance to changes of salinity is another selective factor (Yentsch, 1962; Lund, 1965).

Limitation of productivity by pH is probably more frequently important at low than at high hydrogen ion concentrations. Photosynthetic consumption of CO_2 and/or bicarbonate results in a rise of pH, the kinetics of which are necessarily correlated with the buffering capacity of the medium (e.g. Zarrouk, 1966). Some water plants like *Fontinalis* (Ruttner, 1947) or *Chlorella vulgaris* (Oesterlind, 1950a) are unable to use bicarbonate as a carbon source. They are restricted to waters with pH values below or only slightly above 7.0, since they become completely carbon-limited if pH approaches 8.0. Other water plants like *Elodea* (Ruttner, 1947,1948) and strains of *Scenedesmus* (Fig. 29.4) are able to use either carbon or bicarbonate ions for photosynthesis, and their upper limit of active growth is to be found between pH 10 and 11.5. *Scenedesmus* 276–3a represents a reaction type which can use either free CO_2 or bicarbonate as the carbon source but clearly prefers free CO_2. By contrast, a strain of *Scenedesmus quadricauda* (Oesterlind, 1950a) and *Spirulina platensis* (Zarrouk, 1966) can make much better use of bicarbonate than of free CO_2. They are hence genetically adapted to the more alkaline waters.

The utilization of bicarbonate might be related to the activity of carbonic anhydrase (Oesterlind, 1950b). The activity of this enzyme increases twenty times within twenty-four hours, if *Chlamydomonas* is switched from CO_2 saturation to CO_2 limitation (Nelson, Cenedella & Tolbert, 1969). On the other hand such an effect of CO_2 (and pH) was not found in *Coccolithus* (Steemann Nielsen, 1966).

Shallow outdoor cultures of the green flagellate *Chlamydomonas* which were neither agitated nor aerated yielded at pH 6.5–7.0 up to 4.4 g m^{-2} d^{-1} (average 3.2 g m^{-2} d^{-1}) in Romania (Salageanu, 1967). The production in this system, depending essentially on the rate of CO_2 transport across the boundary between the atmosphere and the water surface, compares well with maximal values reported from warm eutrophic lakes (Table 29.1). Provided that the other nutrients are available in sufficient amounts, we have to consider the rate of CO_2 transport from the atmosphere as the major resistance in aquatic production, especially in deep waters. By comparison with the enormous

652

production potential of dense stands of terrestrial crop plants (Mattei & Gibbon, p. 694, Loomis & Gerakis, Chapter 6, Cooper, Chapter 28), one appreciates the gain in productivity in the course of evolution which has led, among other accomplishments, to an enormous increase in the CO_2-absorbing surface of terrestrial plants.

Carbon dioxide limitation is most likely to occur in waters of low alkalinity (Schindler & Fee, Chapter 14) where the liberation of CO_2 by bacterial degradation of sewage-borne organic substrates may result in an escalation of eutrophication (Lange, 1970, 1971; cf. Lund, 1971).

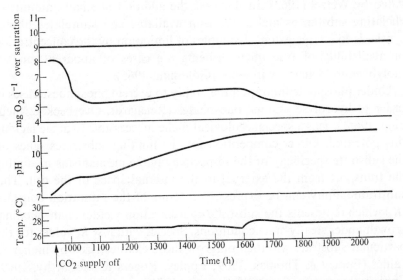

Fig. 29.4. Changes in oxygen supersaturation (as an indicator of photosynthetic rate) and pH, subsequent to a cessation of CO_2 supply in a culture of *Scenedesmus acutus* (276–3*a*). The culture (average density ~0.5 g l⁻¹) was kept in a greenhouse pond (cf. legend to Fig. 29.1) and continuously illuminated at ~60 klx.

A further ecologically relevant action of pH concerns the solubility and hence the availability of polyvalent cations, such as Fe (Wetzel, 1965; Lund, 1965; Stumm, 1972).

Waters of extremely high hydrogen ion concentrations are not common, and there are specialists among the algae which tolerate low pH values and are able to thrive in acid waters. An extreme case is *Chlamydomonas acidophila* (Fott & McCarthy, 1964) which is able to grow at pH 1.0, the corresponding extreme for *Chlorella saccharophila* being pH 2.0 (Kessler, 1965).

Minerals

The limitation of aquatic productivity by inorganic nutrients other than CO_2 is the normal situation in unpolluted aquatic ecosystems, both freshwater (Lund, 1965,1971) and marine (Yentsch, 1962; Strickland, 1965). Inorganic phosphate is the nutrient most frequently found to control aquatic production prior to the onset of eutrophication of inland waters, and it seems that nitrogen limitation is more typical for polluted standing waters. After the development of dense diatom crops, silica depletion often limits further growth (Lund, 1965). Limitation by iron characterizes waters of high alkalinity like the marl lakes investigated by Wetzel (1965). In this case the addition of small amounts of chelating substances makes the iron available and stimulates photosynthesis to a large extent. Examples of limitation by the concentration or availability of true microelements are cases of apparent zinc or molybdenum deficiency in lakes (Goldman, 1965).

Under phosphate limitation the ability to excrete phosphoesterases in order to hydrolyse organic phosphates (Reichardt, Overbeck & Steubing, 1968) opens a special ecological niche inaccessible to algae lacking this potential. Direct competition for the limiting substrates relies on the substrate specificity of the respective uptake mechanisms mediating the transport from the external to the internal space of the cell. This substrate affinity can be expressed in terms of the saturation constant (K_s) which represents the substrate concentration yielding half-maximal growth under steady-state conditions. Species with low K_s values for the particular substrate will then outgrow those characterized by higher K_s values (Eppley & Thomas, 1969; Eppley, Rogers & McCarthy, 1969; Eppley, Rogers, McCarthy & Sournia, 1971).

Organic substances

In the context of productivity control, the role of chelators has mainly been seen in connection with the alleviation of iron limitation. A noteworthy case is the limitation of production by a chelator deficiency in the Cromwell Current Upwelling in the Pacific Ocean (Barber & Ryther, 1969). The most important chelators in waters belong to the group of humic compounds (Stumm, 1972). However, it is known that excreted photosynthates, amino acids, dicarbonic and tricarbonic acids (Chang & Tolbert, 1970; Fogg, 1971) may also contribute to the solubilization of polyvalent cations like iron.

Many planktonic algae are auxotrophic with respect to certain vitamins, i.e. they grow only if the medium contains sufficient amounts of one or more vitamins which the organism is unable to synthesize by itself (Droop, 1962). Although some very interesting information was obtained by growing microalgae under vitamin-limiting conditions (Droop, 1966, 1970), cases where this type of limitation has clearly been proven for a natural system (Schwarz, 1972) are still rare, although limitation by vitamin concentration might very well exist in fresh or marine waters.

The excretion of organic acids such as glycollate by various algae (Fogg, 1971) has been interpreted in the sense that certain concentrations of organic compounds in the medium may be an essential prerequisite for optimal production and growth (Droop, 1966; Sen & Fogg, 1966; Fogg, Chapter 19). The concentration of such soluble organic substrates may be changed by the activities of bacteria or other algae. This could be an additional mechanism of productivity control.

Judging from laboratory experiments, limitation by autoinhibitors which are especially known to be excreted by diatoms (von Denffer, 1948; Harris, 1970; Fogg, 1971) might affect the growth of water blooms. In addition, there are antibiotic or synergistic interactions between different species of planktonic algae. For example, desmids are killed by excretion products of *Microcystis flosaquae* (Lefevre, 1964; Tassigny & Lefevre, 1971). *Pandorina morum* inhibits or kills *Volvox tertius* (Harris, 1971) and *Monoraphidium griffithsii* inhibits *Scenedesmus acutus* (W. Kottenmeier, unpublished observations). An impressive set of synergistic effects is seen in mixed cultures of two to three auxotrophic marine flagellates of which each excretes one or several vitamins which are needed by one or both of its partners (Carlucci & Bowes, 1970).

Conclusion and summary

Aquatic production in natural ecosystems, as well as in artificial models thereof, is in most cases far below its theoretical potential. The major factors limiting production are nutrient concentrations such as phosphate, nitrate or carbon dioxide. Light, temperature or pCO_2 become more important at the higher levels of nutrient supply. The relevance of dissolved organic compounds for the control of aquatic production is stressed.

Recent experiments by the authors demonstrate that a high potential

655

growth rate and/or a high specific surface per cell are not a prerequisite of high yields per unit surface of algal suspension. This is shown by comparative experiments with *Euglena, Scenedesmus* and *Spirulina*. The temperature dependence of algal production decreases with increasing limitation by light. The daily course of photosynthesis in shallow cultures of *Scenedesmus* follows the changes in light intensity, whereas the course of photosynthesis in the thermophilic *Spirulina* coincides with the daily course of temperature. A strain of *Scenedesmus acutus* is shown to use both free CO_2 and HCO_3^- as carbon sources but preferentially the former. This is the opposite situation to that in *Spirulina* (Zarrouk, 1966).

The experiments reported in this paper were financed by the Bundesministerium für Forschung und Technologie (grant NT 34) and by the Landesamt für Forschung des Landes NRW. Our thanks are also due to Miss B. Pamp, Miss M. Weltermann and Mr J. Reckermann for their contributions to the experimental work.

References

Barber, R. T. & Ryther, J. H. (1969). Organic chelators: factors effecting primary production in the Cromwell current upwelling. *J. Exp. Mar. Biol. Ecol.* **3**, 191–9.

Buetow, D. E. (ed.) (1968). In *The biology of Euglena*, vol. 1, pp. 1–361. New York & London, Academic Press.

Carlucci, A. F. & Bowes, P. M. (1970). Vitamin production and utilization by phytoplankton in mixed cultures. *J. Phycol.* **6**, 393–400.

Chang, W. H. & Tolbert, N. E. (1970). Excretion of glycollate, mesotartrate and isocitrate lactone by synchronized cultures of *Ankistrodesmus braunii. Plant Physiol.* **46**, 377–85.

von Denffer, D. (1949). Die planktische Massenkultur pennater Grunddiatomeen. *Arch. Mikrobiol.* **14**, 159–202.

Droop, M. R. (1962). Organic micronutrients. In *Physiology and Biochemistry of Algae*, ed. R. A. Lewin, pp. 141–59. New York & London, Academic Press.

Droop, M. R. (1966). Vitamin B_{12} and marine ecology. III. An experiment with a chemostat. *J. Mar. Biol. Assoc. UK*, **46**, 659–71.

Droop, M. R. (1970). Vitamin B_{12} and marine ecology. V. Continuous culture as an approach to nutritional kinetics. *Helg. Wiss. Meeresunters.* **20**, 629–36.

Eckel, O. & Reuther, H. (1950). Zur Berechnung des sommerlichen Wärmeumsatzes in Flußläufen. *Geogr. Annal. 1950*, pp. 188–209.

Eppley, R. W. & Thomas, W. H. (1969). Comparison of half-saturation constants for growth and nitrate uptake of marine phytoplankton. *J. Phycol.* **5**, 375–9.

Eppley, R. W., Rogers, J. N. & McCarthy, J. J. (1969). Half-saturation constants for uptake of nitrate and ammonium by marine phytoplankton. *Limnol. Oceanogr.* **14**, 912–20.

Eppley, R. W., Rogers, J. N., McCarthy, J. J. & Sournia, A. (1971). Light–dark periodicity in nitrogen assimilation of the marine phytoplankters *Skeletonema costatum* and *Coccolithus huxleyi* in N-limited chemostat cultures. *J. Phycol.* **7**, 150–4.

Eriksen, C. H. (1966). Diurnal limnology of two highly turbid puddles. *Verh. Internat. Limnol.* **16**, 507–14.

Fee, E. J. (1969). A numerical model for the estimation of photosynthetic production, integrated over time and depth, in natural waters. *Limnol. Oceanogr.* **14**, 906–11.

Fee, E. J. (1973). Modeling primary production in water bodies: a numerical approach that allows vertical inhomogeneities. *J. Fish. Res. Bd. Canada*, **30**, 1447–68.

Fogg, G. E. (1971). Extracellular products of algae in freshwater. *Ergebn. Limnol.* **5**, 1–25.

Fogg, G. E. & Watt, W. D. (1965). The kinetics of release of extracellular products of photosynthesis by phytoplankton. *Mem. Ist. Ital. Idrobiol.* **18**, Suppl., 165–74.

Fott, B. & McCarthy, J. J. (1964). Three acidophilic flagellates in pure culture. *J. Protozool.* **11**, 116–20.

Goldman, C. R. (1965). Micronutrient limiting factors and their detection in natural phytoplankton communities. *Mem. Ist. Ital. Idrobiol.* **18**, Suppl., 121–35.

Halldal, P. (ed.) (1970). *Photobiology of Micro-organisms*, 489 pp. New York & London, John Wiley.

Harris, D. O. (1970). An autoinhibitory substance produced by *Platydorina caudata* Kofoid. *Plant Physiol.* **45**, 210–14.

Harris, D. O. (1971). Growth inhibitors produced by green algae (Volvocaceae). *Arch. Mikrobiol.* **76**, 47–50.

Hutchinson, G. E. (1957). *A Treatise on Limnology*, 1015 pp. New York & London, John Wiley.

Kessler, E. (1965). Physiologische und biochemische Beiträge zur Taxonomie der Gattung *Chlorella* I. Säureresistenz als taxonomisches Merkmal. Arch. Mikrobiol. **52**, 291-96.

Komárek, J. & Přibil, S. (1968). Heat of combustion in the biomass of the alga *Scenedesmus quadricauda* during its ontogenetic cycle. *Nature*, **219**, 635–6.

Lange, W. (1970). Cyanophyta–bacteria systems: effects of added carbon compounds or phosphate on algal growth at low nutrient concentrations. *J. Phycol.* **6**, 230–4.

Lange, W. (1971). Enhancement of algal growth in Cyanophyta-bacteria systems by carbonaceous compounds. *Can. J. Microbiol.* **17**, 303–14.

Lefevre, M. (1964). Extracellular products of algae. In *Algae and Man*, ed. D. F. Jackson, pp. 337–67. New York, Plenum Press.

Lund, J. W. G. (1965). The ecology of freshwater phytoplankton. *Biol. Rev.* **40**, 231–93.

Y*

Lund, J. W. G. (1971). Eutrophication. In *The Scientific Management of Animal and Plant Communities*, eds. E. Duffy & A. S. Watt, pp. 225–40. Oxford & London, Blackwell.

Miller, R. L., Smith, D. W., Ward, C. H., Dyer, D. L. & Gafford, R. D. (1968). A solar-illuminated algal photosynthetic exchanger, pp. 1–19. Denver, Colorado, Martin Company, 1–19.

Nelson, E. B., Cenedella, A. & Tolbert, N. E. (1969). Carbonic anhydrase levels in *Chlamydomonas*. *Phytochemistry*, **8**, 2305–6.

Nichiporovich, A. A. (1967). Aims of research on the photosynthesis of plants as a factor in productivity. In *Photosynthesis of Productive Systems*, ed. A. A. Nichiporovich, pp. 3–36. Jerusalem, Isr. Progr. Scient. Transl.

Nichiporovich, A. A. (1969). The role of plants in the bioregenerative systems. *Ann. Rev. Plant Physiol.* **20**, 185–208.

Oesterlind, S. (1950a). Inorganic carbon sources of green algae. I. Growth experiments with *Scenedesmus quadricauda* and *Chlorella pyrenoidosa*. *Physiol. Plant.* **3**, 353–60.

Oesterlind, S. (1950b). Inorganic carbon sources of green algae. II. Carbonic anhydrase in *Scenedesmus quadricauda* and *Chlorella pyrenoidosa*. *Physiol. Plant.* **3**, 430–46.

Ohle, W. (1972). Gelöste organische Stoffe, Aufnahme und Abgabe durch Planktonorganismen. *Gewässerschutz, Wasser, Abwasser*, **8**, 1–56.

Platt, T. & Subba Rao, D. V. (1973). Some current problems in marine phytoplankton productivity. *Fish. Res. Bd Canada, Techn. Rep.* no. **370**, 1–90.

Reichardt, W., Overbeck, J. & Steubing, L. (1968). Free dissolved enzymes in lake waters. *Nature*, **216**, 1345–7.

Rodhe, W. (1965). Standard correlations between pelagic photosynthesis and light. *Mem. Ist. Ital. Idrobiol.* **18**, Suppl., 365–81.

Ruttner, F. (1947). Zur Frage der Karbonatassimilation der Wasserpflanzen. I. Die beiden Haupttypen der Kohlenstoffaufnahme. *Österr. Bot. Z.* **94**, 265–84.

Ruttner, F. (1948). Zur Frage der Karbonatassimilation der Wasserpflanzen. II. Das Verhalten von *Elodea canadensis* und *Fontinalis antipyretica* in Lösungen von Natriumbzw. Kaliumkarbonat. *Österr. Bot. Z.* **95**, 208–38.

Salageanu, N. (1967). Experiments with the mass culture of the alga *Chlamydomonas* in the laboratory and in the open. *Rev. Roum. Biol. Ser. Bot.* **12**, 211–17.

Schwarz, D. (1972). Entstehung des Thiamins und seine Bedeutung für Bakterien und Algen in aquatischen Biotopen. *Veröff. Inst. Wasserforsch. Dortmund*, **12**, 195 pp.

Sen, N. & Fogg, G. E. (1966). Effects of glycollate on the growth of a planktonic *Chlorella. J. Exp. Bot.* **17**, 417–25.

Šetlík, I., Šust, M. & Malek, M. (1970). Dual purpose open circulation units for large scale culture of algae in temperate zones. I. Basic design considerations and scheme of pilot plant. *Algol. Stud.* **1**, 111–64.

Slobodskoi, L. I., Sid'ko, F. Ya., Belyanin, V. I., Alypov, V. F. & Beresnev, G. F. (1968). Analytical expression of the effect of temperature on microalgae productivity. *Biofizika* **14**, 196–9.

Soeder, C. J., Hegewald, E., Pabst, W., Payer, H. D., Rolle, I. & Stengel, E. (1970). Zwanzig Jahre angewandte Mikroalgenforschung in Nordrhein-Westfalen. *Jahrb. Landesamt für Forschung, Nordrhein-Westfalen*, 419–45.

Soeder, C. J. & Stengel, E. (1974). Physico-chemical factors affecting metabolism and growth rate of algae. In *Algal Physiology and Biochemistry*, ed. W. D. P. Stewart, pp. 714–40. London, Blackwells.

Sorokin, C. & Krauss, R. W. (1962). Effects of temperature and illuminance on *Chlorella* growth uncoupled from cell division. *Plant Physiol.* **37**, 37–42.

Steemann Nielsen, E. (1966). The uptake of free CO_2 and HCO_3^- during photosynthesis of plankton algae with special reference to the coccolithophorid *Coccolithus huxleyi. Physiol. Plant.* **19**, 232–40.

Stengel, E. (1971). Die Massenkultur von Mikroalgen; Kulturverfahren und technische Anlagen. *Ber. Dtsch. Bot. Ges.* **83** (Heft 11), 589–606.

Strickland, J. D. H. (1965). Phytoplankton and marine primary production. *Ann. Rev. Microbiol.* **19**, 127–56.

Stumm, W. (1972). Die Rolle der Komplexbildung in natürlichen Gewässern und allfällige Beziehungen zur Eutrophierung. *Gewässerschutz, Wasser, Abwasser*, **8**, 57–88.

Talling, J. (1957). The phytoplankton population as a compound photosynthetic system. *New Phytol.* **56**, 133–49.

Talling, J. (1965a). Comparative problems of phytoplankton production and photosynthetic productivity in a tropical and a temperate lake. *Mem. Ist. Ital. Idrobiol.* **18**, Suppl., 399–424.

Talling, J. (1965b). The photosynthetic activity of phytoplankton in East African lakes. *Int. Rev. Hydrobiol.* **50**, 1–32.

Talling, J. (1970). Generalized and specialized features of phytoplankton as a form of photosynthetic cover. In *Prediction and Measurement of Photosynthetic Productivity*, pp. 431–45. Wageningen, PUDOC.

Talling, J. (1971). The underwater light climate as a controlling factor in the production ecology of freshwater phytoplankton. *Mitt. Internat. Verein. Limnol.* **19**, 214–43.

Tamiya, H., Hase, E., Shibata, K., Mituya, A., Iwamura, T., Nikei, T. & Sasa, T. (1953). Kinetics of growth of *Chlorella* with special reference to its dependence on quantity of available light and on temperature. In *Algal Culture from Laboratory to Pilot Plant*, ed. J. S. Burlew. *Carnegie Inst. Wash. Publ.* **600**, 204–34.

Tassigny, M. & Lefevre, M. (1971). Auto., hétéroantagonisme et autres conséquences des excrétions d'algues d'eau douce ou thermale. *Mitt. Internat. Verein. Limnol.* **19**, 26–38.

Tilzer, M. (1972). Dynamik und Produktivität von Phytoplankton und pelagischen Bakterien in einem Hochgebirgssee (Vorderer Finstertaler See, Österreich). *Arch. Hydrobiol. Suppl.* **40**, 201–73.

Vendlová, J. (1969). Outdoor cultivation in Bulgaria. *Ann. Rep. Algol. Lab. Třeboň for 1968*, pp. 143–52.

Vollenweider, R. A. (1965). Calculation models of photosynthesis-depth curves and some implications regarding day rate estimates in primary production measurements. *Mem. Ist. Ital. Idrobiol.* **18**, Suppl., 425–57.

Vollenweider, R. A. (1970). Models for calculating integral photosynthesis and some implications regarding structural properties of the community metabolism of aquatic systems. In *Prediction and Measurement of Photosynthetic Productivity*, pp. 455–72. Wageningen, PUDOC.

Wassink, E. C., Kok, B. & van Oorschot, J. L. P. (1953). The efficiency of light-energy conversion in *Chlorella* cultures as compared with higher plants. In *Algal Culture from Laboratory to Pilot Plant*, ed. J. S. Burlew, *Carnegie Inst. Wash. Publ.* no. 600, pp. 55–62.

Watt, W. D. (1966). Release of dissolved organic material from the cells of phytoplankton populations. *Proc. Roy. Soc. Lond.* B **164**, 521–51.

Westlake, D. F. (1963). Comparisons of plant productivity. *Biol. Rev.* **38**, 385–425.

Wetzel, R. G. (1965). Nutritional aspects of algal productivity in marl lakes with particular reference to enrichment bioassays and their interpretation. *Mem. Ist. Ital. Idrobiol.* **18** Suppl., 137–57.

Yentsch, C. S. (1962). Marine Plankton. In *Physiology and Biochemistry of Algae*, ed. R. A. Lewin, pp. 771–97. New York & London, Academic Press.

Yentsch, C. S. (1965). The relationship between chlorophyll and photosynthetic carbon production with reference to the measurement of the decomposition products of chloroplastic pigments. *Mem. Ist. Ital. Idrobiol.* **18** Suppl., 323–46.

Zarrouk, C. (1966). Contribution à l'étude d'une cyanophycée. Influence de divers facteurs physiques et chimiques sur la croissance et la photosynthèse de *Spirulina maxima* (Setch & Gardner) Geitler. *Thèse de Doctorat, Université de Paris*, no. A.O. **1064**, 85 pp.

Note added in proof

The yields of algal cultures in Thailand which were labelled as unpublished in Table 29.2 are contained in Payer, H. D. (1971). *First Report on the Production and the Utilization of Microalgae as a Protein Source in Thailand*, Kasetsart University, Bangkok. The maximal yield of *Scenedesmus* growing on sewage at Bangkok was calculated from McGarry, M. G. & Tongkasame, C. (1971)., *J. Water Poll. Contr. Fed.* **43**, 824–35.

30. Actual and potential photosynthetic production – conclusions

W. R. STERN

The preceding sections of this volume have considered levels of primary production in terrestrial and aquatic communities, the capture and utilization of incident radiation, photosynthetic processes and assimilatory activity and the influence of stress factors on these. Against this background, the present section considers the potential production of photosynthetic systems and the extent to which actual production falls short of this potential.

Actual and potential production

What constitutes potential photosynthesis or potential production is not easy to define. It is an elusive concept and definition will vary with the community under consideration. In the most general terms and for managed communities, it may be regarded as 'some possible rate of photosynthesis or yield, greater than that which is usually achieved using current knowledge and technology', In natural stands of vegetation, total dry matter production appears to be related to the type of community and tends to be higher for near-climax vegetation types (Billings, 1970). On a global scale, the annual influx of photosynthetically active radiation (PAR) at the earth's surface is of the order of 100×10^{22} joules. The total amount of biomass produced by autotrophic plants is estimated to be about 100×10^9 tonnes of carbon which is equivalent to about 170×10^{19} joules of energy. Thus the average coefficient of utilization of the incident photosynthetically active radiation by the entire flora of the earth is about 0.2%. Cooper (this volume, Table 27.3) tabulates efficiencies between 3% and 4% during the most active growing period of individual C_3- and C_4-crops. Efficiencies of more than 4% are shown for C_4-crops only. Mattei & Gibbon (p. 694) have reported values of about $5\frac{1}{2}$% for maize and sunflower.

Data concerning the highest rates of photosynthesis or 'best records of production' need to be accompanied by statements of the conditions under which such values were obtained. The evidence reviewed by

661

Cooper (Chapter 27) suggests that in the most favourable circumstances i.e. using well-adapted crop plants grown in environments of abundant radiation, water and a good nutrient supply, actual production is about half of what is considered theoretically attainable – i.e. about $4\frac{1}{2}\%$ conversion of PAR instead of the 9% theoretically possible. In order to derive estimates of what is theoretically attainable on the basis of energy capture, it is necessary to have a detailed understanding of the processes in the photosynthetic system. Because actual energy conversion is only about half of what is theoretically possible, it may be inferred that the complexities of the photosynthetic system are imperfectly understood and/or ineffectively managed. For the time being therefore, as plant biologists concerned with productivity we are dependent on actual field trials for our knowledge of the productive capacity of a species or an environment, though from time to time we may speculate on what the potential ought to be.

Actual productivity in plant communities is the resultant of interaction between genotype, environment and management, and productivity may be measured as dry matter production of either total biomass or economic product, or by net rates of photosynthesis of the biomass. In the present volume, both are considered. The inter-relationships between genotype, environment and management are so complex that generalisations concerning the *productive potential of an environment*, or the *productive capacity of a genotype* in an environment, cannot be made without reference to the management system of the community. On the other hand, enough is now known to be able to predict with reasonable confidence, the main seasonal trend of production in a community under an optimal management regime, and the effects on productivity of limiting factors, such as radiant energy, water and nutrient supply.

In his principles of limiting factors Blackman (1905) suggested that, where a process in influenced by a number of separate factors, 'the rate of the process is limited by the pace of the slowest factor'. From this principle the suggestion has come that as major limitations are overcome the productivity of a community might more nearly approach its potential. An interesting recent example of this principle comes from the work of Hardy & Havelka (1974) in which they attempted 'to break the nitrogen input barrier' in soybeans. They showed increased growth, nodulation and yield from the addition of CO_2 in the field.

Once major limiting factors are overcome however, this principle becomes an over-simplification. The net productivity of a plant stand

662

is the resultant of a vast array of factors affecting the photochemical, biochemical, and physical processes in a plant community.

The use of growth analysis methods

Classical growth analysis methods (Evans, 1972) have developed from intensive studies on the progressive accumulation of dry matter in crops. Growth curves have now been established for a wide range of species and environments and these have been analysed in a variety of ways (Williams, 1946; Radford, 1967; Hughes & Freeman, 1967). *Net assimilation rate, leaf area ratio* and the product of these two – *relative growth rate* – have been used extensively to interpret the influence of environmental factors on dry matter production. Net assimilation rate is defined as the net increase in total dry weight per unit leaf area per unit time, and leaf area ratio as the ratio of the total assimilatory surface to total plant weight (Watson, 1952). An extension of such growth analysis which offers distinct possibilities in the future, is the accurate partitioning of dry matter during growth and development, including the study of the carbon balance, to ascertain how and when assimilates are translocated and re-translocated (Robson, 1973; Ryle *et al.*, 1973; Monteith & Biscoe, 1971; Gallagher, personal communication). These studies have considerable bearing on such controversial questions as the contribution of current photosynthesis to grain filling, or regrowth after defoliation.

Blackman (1968) and Květ, Ondok & Jarvis (1971) have reviewed the applicability of growth analysis methods to the assessment of productivity. The value of growth analysis in interpreting the effects of short-term climatic influences on growth is limited (Watson, 1963). It is however useful in establishing seasonal trends (e.g. Blackman, Black & Kemp, 1955) and examining how a genotype might respond to a particular environment (e.g. Hearn, 1969) or to sudden changes in the environment (Thorne, Ford & Watson, 1967). Such a growth analysis approach may be useful in exploring new environments, in testing new species in an environment, comparing species in a different environment, or evaluating the adaptability and potential of a range of cultivars. Warren Wilson (personal communication), for instance, has studied the performance of sunflower in a wide range of environments over a long period of time and has proposed the relationship between NAR, solar radiation and temperature depicted in Fig. 30.1.

However, the amount of work entailed in undertaking growth analyses must not be underestimated and the purpose of the study must be clearly kept in mind when planning such work.

To relate productivity of crops and pastures to seasonal and climatic factors, the techniques of serial sowing to obtain overlapping growth curves may be effective. This has been used with ryegrass by Alberda & Sibma (1968), with ryegrass and white clover by Brougham (1959), with cocksfoot, perennial and short rotation ryegrass by Brougham & Glenday (1969), with cotton by Stern (1965) and more recently with

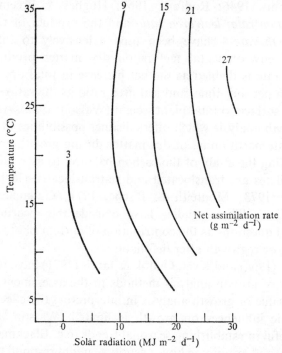

Fig. 30.1. Influence of solar radiation and temperature on net assimilation of *Helianthus annus* (from Warren Wilson, unpublished).

lupins by Perry & Poole (1975) and Perry (personal communication). The advantages of this technique is that it permits the derivation of growth rates without having to take account of excess non-assimilatory tissue. The relative importance of seasonal changes in light and temperature and their effect on the distribution of plant parts can be assessed without complications due to the changing age of the plant. Such a method also offers a means of evaluating a species' adaptation to the environment, determining the productive potential of species in that

664

environment, or establishing the relationship between productivity and environmental variables. This kind of information is necessary to provide a base line for simulation studies and might usefully be obtained before undertaking a modelling exercise of a particular crop.

Simulation

Recent developments in crop simulation, pioneered by de Wit (1965), enable us to put together the various components of the total photosynthetic system and may offer scope for analysing in what ways actual photosynthetic production falls short of potential production (Landsberg, 1972). It may also be useful in establishing the specifications of ideotypes, i.e. models of the most photosynthetically efficient forms of crop species (Donald, 1968).

Simulation is essentially a two-phase operation, involving modelling and experimentation. It involves setting up a model of a real system and performing experiments on the model. The model merely describes the behaviour of the system under a given set of assumptions and by experimenting with the model, approximate solutions can be obtained. Furthermore, when a model has been created it can be modified to analyse alternative pathways in a system, or to test the relative importance of various processes within the system. However successful the model may be, it must be remembered that at best it only represents an abstraction of reality. Because of the capacity of computers to handle large amounts of data, it is feasible to undertake iterative calculations, to undertake studies of a cyclic nature (e.g. diurnal or seasonal effects) and to attempt the simulation of total systems of great complexity. An important feature of the simulation approach is the ability to incorporate feedback mechanisms, which are so important in biological systems.

In setting up a simulation, the initial problem needs to be specified in some detail and the boundary conditions to be adequately defined (Lemon, 1969). The purpose of the simulation should be clearly borne in mind as well as the use to which the model is to be put. It must be remembered that the approach that is adopted may constrain subsequent thinking about the processes and may therefore need to be reviewed from time to time. For example, it is true of almost all the photosynthesis models in vogue today that they are dominated by physical functions concerned with the plant canopy and the shape of the light–photosynthesis curve. It is perhaps time that this approach be re-evaluated.

A suitable starting point in undertaking a systems analysis is a simple input–output statement that can be successively expanded to identify:

(a) the major components in the synthesis – the subsystems;
(b) the important specific relationships within each subsystem;
(c) the links between subsystems;
(d) the important external variables impinging on the simulation;
(e) the control points – or valves – in the simulation, which may operate in a similar way to the principle of limiting factors.

Once a suitable conceptual framework has been established, subsequent steps include coding and validation of the model by experiment to secure data that are independent of those that were used to create the model. In practice, few simulation studies appear to have progressed beyond the modelling phase.

At the Třeboň IBP/PP meeting (Šetlík, 1970) a good deal of time was devoted to crop photosynthesis models. As Monteith pointed out (Šetlík, 1970, pp. 145–6) fairly sophisticated models of light relationships in plant canopies were combined with rather elementary relationships of photosynthesis and respiration to produce estimates of canopy photosynthesis. Alberda and his colleagues (Chapter 28) have discussed some of the experimental programs which are now being undertaken to test some of the existing models. However, some of the large gaps referred to by several speakers at Třeboň, still remain, in particular with respect to the adequacy of physiological data. What is the variation in daily photosynthetic rates? What is the effect of leaf age? How many respiration components should we be dealing with? What is their magnitude? What does a plant do with its assimilates? How many reserve pools of assimilate can be identified in a photosynthetic system? Monteith's plea that 'new measurements and new ideas about physiological mechanisms are needed rather than new models' and Waggoner's observation (Šetlík, 1970, pp. 583–6) that physiologists have contributed too little to models of canopy performance are still valid four years later.

Variation in photosynthetic activity

The differentiation of plants into C_3- and C_4-species does not require elaboration here. The characteristics that distinguish these two groups have been summarized many times (e.g. Black, 1971) and thoroughly discussed in Hatch, Osmond & Slatyer (1971). Of relevance to this discussion, are the higher rates of net photosynthesis and comparative absence of CO_2 compensation point in C_4-species, leading to an apparently greater overall photosynthetic efficiency, as shown by Cooper (this volume, Table 27.2). Of interest also is the finding by Moss and his co-workers (Moss & Musgrave, 1971) that species do not in general deviate from either the C_3- or C_4-pathway so that there appears to be little prospect of enhancing photosynthetic efficiency by incorporating C_4 characteristics in C_3-species by breeding. In general, C_4-species are adapted to high radiation and therefore to warmer and higher transpiration environments and C_3-species to more temperate and cooler environments. It has been argued that C_3-species under regimes of lesser radiation but very intensive management may be as efficient in the conversion of PAR, as C_4-species in high radiation environments (Loomis & Gerakis, Chapter 6). Further studies are necessary to confirm this suggestion, and to determine which managements are necessary to achieve such efficient conversion by C_3-plants.

There appears to be scope, however, in selecting for higher photosynthetic rates within a species. In a study with over 100 barley varieties in current or recent use, Apel & Lehmann (1969) showed that the most adapted varieties were among those with higher photosynthetic rates. Using *Lolium perenne*, Wilson & Cooper (1969) established that there was variation in photosynthetic rates within species and that this was a heritable character. Using twenty-seven varieties of maize, Heichel & Musgrave (1969) recorded a threefold difference in photosynthetic rates between the highest and lowest values and it was shown subsequently that photosynthetic rate was a heritable character in this species also (Moss & Musgrave, 1971). However, it seems that a greater photosynthetic capacity of the individual leaf is not necessarily a guarantee of higher yields (Evans & Dunstone, 1970; Evans, Chapter 22) i.e. productivity, nor is it necessarily an indication of greater photosynthetic efficiency of the whole crop.

Adaptation and adaptability

There is no doubt that the adaptation of photosynthetic capacities to different environments – whether in the context of C_3 or C_4 photosynthetic pathways or of genotypic differences with a species – is capable of further exploitation. This is being attempted in practice; for example, the culture of maize is being extended into cooler climates (Bunting, 1968). In North America the boundary of this crop is creeping further northwards into Canada, and at the Plant Breeding Institute in the UK, there is an active programme of breeding maize for UK conditions. In seeking pasture species that are capable of producing more dry matter there is an intensive program at Palmerston North in New Zealand, to evaluate tropical pasture species (particularly C_4-plants) in a temperate environment in order to select lines that are better adapted and can grow satisfactorily in lower temperature and radiation regimes (DSIR, New Zealand, 1973).

The capacity of species to adapt to untested environments outside their normal limits of colonization or use, ought not to be overlooked. In addition to observing the usual criteria of developmental patterns in evaluating adaptability, it might be worth considering such other characters as photosynthetic rate (there are suitably rapid techniques now available), compensation points, stomatal and mesophyll resistance responses, maintenance respiration as a function of photosynthesis under different environmental regimes, the capacity to accumulate dry matter (seasonal growth rates), and the distribution and partition of dry matter (harvest index).

It is only when this level of detail in characterizing species and genotypes can be achieved that we can begin to unravel the complexities of the genotype–environment interaction and so assess the potential productivity of species or genotypes in different environments. This type of physiological data would greatly assist the plant breeder, and also enhance existing simulation models on photosynthetic production (Monteith & Elston, 1971). Only when we have such an array of data available for one species in several environments can we begin to speculate on its potential production. Perhaps this was the intention of IBP/PP, but while IBP has stimulated much discussion and thought, it does not appear to have produced for any one species, the global data that might be used to evaluate potential productivity. When the program was launched in 1964 the emphasis was on the study of environments, rather than on the study of *species in environments*; perhaps plant physiologists were not ready at that time to embark on such an exercise.

There are indications now that the study of species in different environments is developing on a firmer footing; obvious examples that come to mind are the extensive yield trials of wheat, maize, triticale and rice being undertaken by the International Maize and Wheat Improvement Centre (CIMMYT) and the International Rice Research Institute (IRRI) together with their supporting physiological studies.

Conclusions

In spite of the discrepancy between actual and potential production from photosynthetic systems, exceedingly high rates of photosynthetic production over short periods may be obtained with certain species, in certain environments, although these rates do not approach the calculated theoretical potential. As already mentioned, this gap implies either an imperfect understanding of the photosynthetic system or an inability to manage it effectively. Even so, yields of agricultural crops have been steadily rising (Eastin & Munson, 1971; Ishizuka, 1969,1971; Rohweder & Younts, 1967; Russell, 1973) and appear to continue to do so. This increase in yield involves increasing management skills in determining the most appropriate inputs, including their magnitude, i.e. what has sometimes been called 'engineering for higher yields'. To approach greater efficiency in production from photosynthetic systems, both the environment and the management need to match up closely with the requirements of the photosynthetic system for each developmental stage of the plant community.

In order to develop the understanding necessary to apply greater management skills, there is merit in combining studies in controlled environments and those in the field. Controlled environment studies in which a range of genotypes is exposed to a range of treatments, outside those normally experienced in the field, can indicate tolerance limits, define upper or lower limits of a wide range of plant characters or indicate trends in response to environmental change. From such data it should be possible to identify limiting characteristics which can then be tackled by the plant breeder, to assess the range of adaptability of a species, and to suggest the most effective strategy for further field testing – or maximum yield trials. An important example of this approach is the study currently being undertaken by the International Institute of Tropical Agriculture in Nigeria (IITA) and the University of Reading, UK, in connection with the development of cultivars of cowpeas and soybeans for the humid tropics (Summerfield & Huxley, 1973; Huxley & Summerfield, 1974). This study, among other findings, has revealed a sensitivity to night temperature over a narrow temperature range in a particular group of cultivars. In this way, the use of controlled environments could contribute substantially to our understanding of the factors that lead to the adaptability of different species and the speed with which they may respond to changing environments during their life cycle.

669

With this ability to test a much wider range of artificial and natural environments than ever before in history, the exploration of physiological processes and how they might contribute to photosynthetic production takes on new dimensions.

References

Alberda, T. & Sibma, L. (1968). Dry matter production and light interception of crop surfaces. III. Actual herbage production in different years as compared with potential values. *Journal of the British Grassland Society*, **23**, 206–15.

Apel, P. & Lehmann, C. (1969). Variabilität und Sortenspezifität der Photosyntheserate bei Sommergerste. *Photosynthetica*, **3**, 255–62.

Billings, W. D. (1970). *Plants, Man, and the Ecosystem*, 2nd edition, 160 pp. California, Wadsworth Publishing Co.

Black, C. C. (1971). Ecological implications of dividing plants into groups with distinct photosynthetic production capacities. *Advances in Ecological Research*, **7**, 87–114.

Blackman, F. F. (1905). Optima and limiting factors. *Annals of Botany*, **19**, 281–95.

Blackman, G. E. (1968). The application of the concepts of growth analysis to the assessment of productivity. In *Functioning of Terrestrial Ecosystems at the Primary Production Level*, ed. F. E. Eckardt, pp. 243–59. Paris, UNESCO.

Blackman, G. E., Black, J. N. & Kemp, A. W. (1955). Physiological and ecological studies in the analysis of plant environment. 10. An analysis of the effects of seasonal variation in daylight and temperature on the growth of *Helianthus annus* in the vegetative phase. *Annals of Botany*, **19**, 527–48.

Brougham, R. W. (1959). The effects of season and weather on the growth rate of a ryegrass and clover pasture. *New Zealand Journal of Agricultural Research*, **2**, 283–96.

Brougham, R. W. & Glenday, A. C. (1969). Weather fluctuations and the daily rate of growth of pure stands of three grass species. *New Zealand Journal of Agricultural Research*, **12**, 125–36.

Bunting, E. S. (1968). Maize in Europe. *Field Crop Abstracts*, **21**, 1–9.

Donald, C. M. (1968). The breeding of crop ideotypes. *Euphytica*, **17**, 385–403.

DSIR New Zealand (1973). Cold sensitivity of tropical cereals and grasses. *Report, Department of Scientific and Industrial Research, New Zealand for 1973*, pp. 25–6.

Eastin, J. D. & Munson, R. D. (eds.) (1971). *Moving off the Yield Plateau. ASA Special Publication No. 20*, 89 pp. Wisconsin, American Society of Agronomy.

Evans, G. C. (1972). *The Quantitative Analysis of Plant Growth*, 734 pp. Oxford, Blackwell.

Evans, L. T. & Dunstone, R. L. (1970). Some physiological aspects of evolution in wheat. *Australian Journal of Biological Sciences*, **23**, 725–41.

Hardy, R. W. F. & Havelka, U. D. (1974). The nitrogen barrier. *Crops and Soils Magazine*, **26**, 11–13.

Hatch, M. D., Osmond, C. B. & Slatyer, R. O. (1971). *Photosynthesis and Photorespiration*, 565 pp. New York, Wiley-Interscience.

Hearn, A. B. (1969). The growth and performance of cotton in a desert environment. II. Dry matter production. *Journal of Agricultural Science, Cambridge*, **73**, 75–86.

Heichel, G. H. & Musgrave, R. B. (1969). Varietal differences in net photosynthesis of *Zea mays* L. *Crop Science*, **9**, 483–6.

Hughes, A. P. & Freeman, P. R. (1967). Growth analysis using frequent small harvests. *Journal of Applied Ecology*, **4**, 553–60.

Huxley, P. A. & Summerfield, R. F. (1974). Effects of night temperature and photoperiod on the reproductive ontogeny of cultivars of cowpea and of soyabean selected for the wet tropics. *Plant Science Letters*, **3**, 11–17.

Ishizuka, Y. (1969). Engineering for higher yields. In *Physiological Aspects of Crop Yields*, eds. J. D. Eastin, F. A. Haskins, C. Y. Sullivan & C. H. M. van Bavel, pp. 15–25. Wisconsin, American Society of Agronomy.

Ishizuka, Y. (1971). Physiology of the rice plant. *Advances in Agronomy*, **23**, 241–315.

Květ, J. P., Ondok, J. & Jarvis, P. G. (1971). Methods of growth analysis. In *Plant Photosynthesis: Production Manual of Methods*, eds. Z. Šesták, J. Čatsky & P. G. Jarvis, pp. 343–91. The Hague: Junk.

Landsberg, J. J. (1972). Microclimate and the potential productivity of sites. *Scientific Horticulture*, **24**, 126–41.

Lemon, E. R. (1969). Gaseous exchange in crop stands. In *Physiological Aspects of Crop Yields*, eds. J. D. Eastin, F. A. Haskins, C. Y. Sullivan & C. H. M. van Bavel, pp. 117–42. Wisconsin, American Society of Agronomy.

Monteith, J. L. & Biscoe, P. V. (1971). Meteorological measurements of photosynthesis and transpiration. *Report University of Nottingham School of Agriculture for 1970–71*, pp. 66–75.

Monteith, J. L. & Elston, J. F. (1971). Microclimatology and crop production. In *Potential Crop Production – A Case Study*, eds. P. F. Wareing & J. P. Cooper, pp. 23–42. London, Heinemann.

Moss, D. N. & Musgrave, R. B. (1971). Photosynthesis and crop production. *Advances in Agronomy*, **23**, 317–336.

Perry, M. W. & Poole, M. L. (1975). Field environment studies on lupins. 1. Developmental patterns in *Lupinus angustifolius* L., the effects of cultivar, site and planting time. *Australian Journal of Agricultural Research*, **26**, 81–91.

Radford, P. J. (1967). Growth analysis formulae – their use and abuse. *Crop Science*, **7**, 171–5.

Robson, M. J. (1973). The growth and development of simulated swards of perennial ryegrass. II. Carbon assimilation and respiration in a seedling sward. *Annals of Botany*, **37**, 501–18.

Rohweder, D. A. & Younts, S. E. (eds.) (1967). *Maximum Crop Yields – The Challenge. ASA Special Publication No. 9.* Wisconsin, American Society of Agronomy.

Russell, J. S. (1973). Yield trends of different crops in different areas and reflections on the sources of crop yield improvement in the Australian environment. *Journal of the Australian Institute of Agricultural Science,* **39,** 156–66.

Ryle, G. J. A., Brockington, C. E., Powell, C. E. & Cross, B. (1973). The measurement and prediction of organ growth in a uniculm barley. *Annals of Botany,* **37,** 233–46.

Šetlík, I. (ed.) (1970). *Prediction and Measurement of Photosynthetic Productivity,* 632 pp. Wageningen: PUDOC.

Stern, W. R. (1965). The seasonal growth characteristics of irrigated cotton in a dry monsoonal environment. *Australian Journal of Agricultural Research,* **16,** 347–66.

Summerfield, R. J. & Huxley, P. A. (1973). Daylength and night temperature sensitivity screening of selected cowpea and soyabean cultivers. *Reading University – International Institute of Tropical Agriculture, Tropical Grain Legume Physiology Project.* Int. Comm. No. 5, 18 pp.

Thorne, G. N., Ford, M. A. & Watson, D. J. (1967). Effects of temperature variation at different times on growth and yield of sugar beet and barley. *Annals of Botany,* **31,** 71–101.

Watson, D. J. (1952). The physiological basis of variation in yield. *Advances in Agronomy,* **4,** 101–145.

Watson, D. J. (1963). Climate, weather, and plant yield. In *Environmental Control of Plant Growth,* ed. L. T. Evans, pp. 337–350. London: Academic Press.

Williams, R. F. (1946). The physiology of plant growth with special reference to the concept of net assimilation rate. *Annals of Botany,* **10,** 41–72.

Wilson, D. & Cooper, J. P. (1969). Diallel analysis of photosynthetic rate and related leaf characters among contrasting genotypes of *Lolium perenne. Heredity,* **24,** 633–49.

de Wit, C. T. (1965). Photosynthesis of leaf canopies. *Versl. Landbouwk. Onderz.* **663,** 1–57.

PART VIII

Conclusions

31. Photosynthesis and productivity in different environments – conclusions

E. C. WASSINK

Life on earth probably originated, and in any case is sustained, by virtue of the fact that solar energy, incident on the earth's surface, is temporarily accumulated, and stepwise degraded in passage through structures which collect part of this energy, thus delaying its dissipation into space. The result is a multitude of thermodynamically more or less improbable structures: organic molecules, organelles, living cells, multicellular organisms, and ecosystems with a rather definite composition of species and trophic levels.

As for the living units, single multipotential cells seem the most rigid structures, and allow the least variation, while retaining their vital functions; multicellular organisms seem to have more freedom for variation, and ecosystems still more.

Considering definitiveness of structure as information, this is highest in multipotential unicellular organisms, less for individuals, and still less for ecosystems. This 'level of generalization' should be considered in discussing experimental approaches and the precision of methods for research into systems of increasing complexity.

Energy conversion and growth

Life on earth depends largely on fixation of solar energy by photosynthesis of green plants, making it available for heterotrophically living organisms, as well as for their own growth, which results in 'primary production'. The efficiency of this production in various plant types and ecosystems is the main subject of this IBP volume, and is essential for estimating the total dry matter production on earth.

It is mostly accepted that photosynthesis may reach an efficiency of conversion of 20–30% of the absorbed light, i.e. 1 mol. of CO_2 assimilated for 8–10 quanta of light. On the other hand, in well-developed agriculture, dry matter is produced with an efficiency of no more than 1–2% of photosynthetically active radiation (PAR) over the entire growing season. Reasons for this low efficiency are: (1) loss of light between plants; (2) too high light intensities; (3) too low CO_2 concentration; (4) other limiting factors such as environmental stresses; (5) ageing effects, in part coupled with the use of energy for translocation processes (cf. Wassink, 1948).

It is uncertain whether 'growth' proceeds with an efficiency of solar energy conversion near to that of photosynthesis. Metabolism includes dark processes, leading to loss of accumulated energy, and measurable as 'respiration'. Energy yield of growth has been studied experimentally with algal cultures under light limitation, and attempts made to record complete energy balances (Kok, 1952); efficiencies of 12–21% were recorded, which are not much lower than those for photosynthesis proper. Sugar-beet crops reach an efficiency of 7–9% in the middle of the season when conditions are favourable, and 80–90% of the total dry matter is produced in 45% of the season (Gaastra, 1958). Similar values are reported by Caldwell (Chapter 3), by Loomis & Gerakis (Chapter 6) and by Cooper (Chapter 27). These efficiencies are close to those computed by van Keulen, Louwerse, Sibma & Alberda (Chapter 28), for 'potential production' under natural conditions. Maximum production of algal mass cultures with excess CO_2 supply also reaches efficiencies around 8% (Kok & van Oorschot, 1954; Stengel & Soeder, Chapter 29).

In using harvest data for terrestrial systems, it is dangerous to leave out subsoil parts, which may form a high fraction of total production; moreover, exchanges between subsoil and aerial parts may occur according to the stage of the growing season.

Terrestrial production

Primary (net) production in forests (Japanese and elsewhere) ranges from 20 t ha^{-1} yr^{-1} in the south to 5–10 t ha^{-1} yr^{-1} in cool-temperate regions; 20–25% may need to be added for subsoil production (Kira, Chapter 2). Net production in tropical forests may reach 30 t or higher; it differs much less with latitude than does gross production (net production + stand respiration); 40 t ha^{-1} yr^{-1} may be a ceiling. Efficiency of solar energy conversion is 2.0–3.5% for gross production during the growing season for all climatic zones, and <1% to 1.5% for net production.

Herbaceous plants (Caldwell, Chapter 3) show average efficiency values of 0.5 to 1%, although incidental figures over short periods may reach 10% of PAR (taken as 47% of total radiation). Net production ranges from 4–13 t ha^{-1} yr^{-1}. I consider many of the data difficult to

676

compare, owing to different durations of observation, presence of stress factors, etc. Most value should be attributed to data from careful experiments, or from observations with due evaluation of environmental factors. Whole season efficiencies mostly range from ~0.5 to 2–3% of PAR, in favourable parts of the season going up to 8–10%.

Tundra vegetation is characterized by temperature and water stress (Wielgolaski, Chapter 4); the same holds for desert and saline vegetations (Schulze & Kappen; Chapter 5). Tundra plants are capable of net assimilation at very low temperatures, and light saturation (e.g. in arctic grasses) is as high as 0.4 cal cm^{-2} min^{-1} (PAR). (In early spring diatoms we similarly observed that photosynthesis was not easily light-saturated, even at 6 °C). Above ground production in the tundra regions ranges from 50–200 g m^{-2} yr^{-1}, in the shrub zones from 225–450 g m^{-2} yr^{-1} (=2.25–4.5 t ha^{-1} yr^{-1}), and this may be doubled if subsoil production is included. Efficiency of PAR conversion is from 0.65% (lichen heaths) to 1.56% (subalpine birch forest), but neglecting subsoil production leads to heavy underestimation.

A natural salt-marsh vegetation, investigated by our group, also showed a low top–root ratio, and hardly any regular relation of production to light intensity in a (four-step) shading experiment; light intensity dependency could however, be brought about by increasing the mineral nutrient supply, indicating mineral stress (Fig. 31.1).

Production of non-polar deserts (Schultze & Kappen, Chapter 5) ranges from 10–20 g dry weight m^{-2} yr^{-1} (=0.1–0.2 t ha^{-1} yr^{-1}). Midday depression of photosynthesis occurs owing to closure of stomata; they may reopen upon a slight increase in air humidity later in the day. Zalensky (see Schultze & Kappen, Chapter 5) in the Karakorum desert, found no mid-day depression, and no light respiration; plants had a low, well-regulated water content.

For the fruticose desert lichen *Ramalina maciformis* a biomass of 73 g dry weight m^{-2}, and a yearly increment of 8.4% is estimated (Schultze & Kappen, Chapter 5) yielding a production of ~6 g dry weight m^{-2} yr^{-1} (0.06 t ha^{-1} yr^{-1}); crustose lichens may reach a biomass of ~300–400 g m^{-2}. The water content of these lichens is very low, even in the active state. Of special importance is their poikilohydric nature, enabling them to be rapidly activated when air humidity rises above a certain level, and to return to an anabiotic state for short or long periods, ensuring minimal loss of substance. Precipitation is less important than frequency and persistence of dew, fog, and high air humidity in the morning. Higher desert plants show structural and

Conclusions

strategic adaptation, the latter including leaf-, branch-, and shoot-shedders. 'When death is partial, it becomes a means of survival' (Schulze & Kappen, Chapter 5).

Maximum values of photosynthesis for tundra mosses are somewhat higher than for lichens (1.5 and 1.0 mg CO_2 g^{-1} h^{-1} respectively as an average, computed from data by Kallio & Kärenlampi, Chapter 17). Light saturation values in (arctic and antarctic) lichens are high

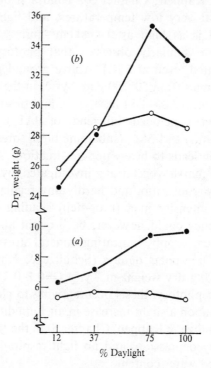

Fig. 31.1. Average dry weights over the entire growing season (11 May to 9 Sept. 1971) in relation to relative light intensity in a salt marsh ecosystem at the North Sea island Terschelling (Netherlands). (○) Non-manured; (●) with a balanced mineral nutrient supply. (a) Aerial dry weight; (b) subsoil dryweight (E. C. Wassink & M. E. van den Noort, unpublished data).

(10–20 klx, and up to 48 klx, even at 5 °C). Damage by high light intensity, at low temperature, may be more significant in laboratory experiments than in nature, where high light intensity mostly goes along with high temperature and desiccation. Lichens show temperature adaptation for optimal photosynthesis according to climate. Minima for net photosynthesis are very low, down to −10 °C, with rapid recovery after freezing; temperature maxima are relatively low (approx. 30 °C)

678

in the active state; in nature lichens can survive much higher temperatures when they are dry. Biomass of lichens in ungrazed areas is approximately 200–300 g m^{-2}, production $\sim 10\% = 20$–30 g m^{-2} yr^{-1} (0.2–0.3 t ha^{-1} yr^{-1}), in grazed stands much lower. Some lichens fix atmospheric nitrogen (e.g. *Stereocaulon*, *Peltigera*, which contain blue-green algae) but very low doses of mineral nitrogen prevent such fixation.

Among cultivated crops (Loomis & Gerakis, Chapter 6), C$_4$ plants are reported to give higher yields than C$_3$-plants. Solar energy conversion efficiency is considered to be much the same (e.g. 4.4% for C$_3$- and C$_4$-grasses). At low latitudes, however, tropical C$_4$-grasses are clearly superior in production to C$_3$-plants. In fodder crops, dry matter production increases with less frequent harvests, but the percentage digestibility decreases.

Aquatic production

Equal distribution of nutrients, high CO$_2$ solubility, and attenuation of light and temperature characterize aquatic environments (Talling, Chapter 10). The free-living unicellular alga is in fact, the most ideal primary production unit.

Freshwater macrophytes

These include emerged plants (with aerial parts), submerged ones, and submerged ones with floating leaves (Westlake, Chapter 8).

Emerged plants usually have over 50% fresh weight below the soil surface. In spring, material is transported from rhizomes to the shoots, in May the two are balanced, and in June transport towards the rhizome starts. Similar behaviour is well-known for terrestrial plants, and, in a modified form, also occurs in large seaweeds (Mann & Chapman, see below, and Chapter 9). Net production is 7–11 t organic matter ha^{-1} yr^{-1} for temperate zones and tropics, respectively.

Submerged plants have much lower yields: 0.8–2.0 t ha^{-1} yr^{-1}; net photosynthetic capacity, in terms of mg C g^{-1} dry weight h^{-1}, is given as 5 for submerged, 15 for emerged plants, and up to 150 for small algae. It seems questionable to me how far these data are strictly comparable. Westlake (Chapter 8) considers that the low productivity of submerged plants might be due to limited CO$_2$ supply and Jarvis has pointed out that CO$_2$ diffusibility in water is ~ 10000 times less than in air. Schindler & Fee (Chapter 14) have also drawn attention to

Conclusions

the fact that CO_2 in aqueous environments easily becomes a limiting factor.

Mosses are reported to require dissolved CO_2, Angiosperms may also use HCO_3^- directly; *Potamogeton lucens* is a carbonate user.

Most aquatic plants seem to be C_3-types; but the giant emergent *Cyperus papyrus* with haulms up to 6 m. (Thompson, p. 691) probably is a C_4-plant; in its natural habitat it produces 20–40 g dry weight m^{-2} day^{-1}, in hydroponic culture even 125 g m^{-2} day^{-1}. Květ has reported that in *Typha* removal of the haulm leads to more dry weight accumulation in the rhizome ($1-1.8$ kg m^{-2} yr^{-1}). Freshwater macrophytes in Malaysia are reported to have a standing crop (biomass) of 370–520 g m^{-2}, and a gross production of 25 g dry weight m^{-2} day^{-1}, sometimes still higher. Taking 25 % respiration loss, and 300 production days, this corresponds to ~ 60 t ha^{-1} yr^{-1}, and an efficiency of PAR conversion of 4–6 %.

Marine macrophytes

These may have very high production, e.g. 25–50 t CH_2Oh a^{-1} yr^{-1} in subtidal large brown algae of the genera *Laminaria* and *Macrocystis* (Mann & Chapman, Chapter 9), which probably means a conversion efficiency of PAR of 4–6 %. These algae show great increase in size in winter, with low dry weight content; it is suggested that they then use up material stored in summer, since Luning has demonstrated translocation of materials from older to younger parts. Intertidal brown algae, as *Fucus* and *Ascophyllum* commonly produce 500–1000 g C m^{-2} yr^{-1} ($= \sim 12-25$ t dry weight ha^{-1} yr^{-1}), sea and marsh grasses from 1500 down to 200 g C m^{-2} yr^{-1}.

Freshwater microphytes

These have an upper primary production level of 10 g C m^{-2} day^{-1} (Talling, Chapter 10). Dykyjová has quoted 10–20 g C m^{-2} d^{-1}, but taking 200 production days per annum this would mean $\sim 50-100$ t CH_2O ha^{-1} yr^{-1} which is extremely high, so that the figures are probably not long-term averages. An incidental figure by Schindler & Fee (Chapter 14) was 10–25 mg C m^{-2} h^{-1}, corresponding to $\sim 0.1-0.3$ g C m^{-2} d^{-1} or 0.5–1.5 t CH_2O ha^{-1} yr^{-1}, which is very much lower. With increasing biomass, production slows down (Javornický, p. 690) and limiting factors may differ for rate of production and standing crop size (Schindler & Fee, Chapter 14). In a heavy standing crop, dissolved

680

inorganic carbon is rapidly depleted shortly after sunrise, and production rate sharply declines. Very high primary net productions are reported from Indian temple ponds with permanent blooms of blue-green algae, namely, 13–24 g m^{-2} d^{-1} (40–70 t ha^{-1} yr^{-1}); the efficiency of solar energy conversion is 3.7–7% or even 10–14% (Ganapati & Kulkarni, p. 690). Reassimilation of excreted organic substances seems not excluded.

Mass cultivation of small freshwater algae

Czechoslovak workers report maximal daily yields with a *Scenedesmus* strain of 44 g dry weight m^{-2} d^{-1}, and averages for May to July of 22.8 g m^{-2} d^{-1}; providing an average efficiency of PAR conversion of 4.8% with maxima of 10–11%. Under suitable climatic conditions over 50 t dry weight ha^{-1} yr^{-1} may be obtained; values for eutrophic pelagic vegetation are only ~2 t ha^{-1} yr^{-1}, but may reach 9–15 t ha^{-1} yr^{-1} under favourable conditions in the temperate zone. Yields in tropics and subtropics may be twice this value, although in unpolluted standing waters they are mostly below 1 t ha^{-1} yr^{-1}. Potential productivity of aquatic ecosystems is linearly related to PAR input, and radiation also determines water temperature. Q_{10} is inversely related to the degree of light limitation.

Potential production in natural aquatic ecosystems or their artificial models (mass cultures) is determined by average daily PAR input and temperature; nutritional factors (phosphate, nitrogen, CO_2, organic micronutrients) decide in how far it is reached (Stengel & Soeder, Chapter 29).

Marine microphytes

Phytoplankton productivity for shelf conditions in the oceans varies between 0.4 and 0.9 g C m^{-2} d^{-1}; for offshore areas it is 0.15–0.3 g C m^{-2} d^{-1} (Platt & Subba Rao, Chapter 11). This corresponds to 3–7.5 t ha^{-1} yr^{-1} and 1–2.5 t ha^{-1} yr^{-1}, respectively (300 production days). The few reliable efficiency data existing range from 0.4–0.9% for, in part, polluted, coastal waters. Total primary production for the entire ocean is estimated at 31×10^9 t C yr^{-1}. In an earlier estimate I used 20×10^9 t. The new figure brings up the overall efficiency of oceanic primary production from 0.11% to 0.17%, and the total global efficiency from 0.16% to 0.20% (cf. Wassink, 1964). The lower efficiency of primary production in the oceans than on the land might be

681

z

presupposed since the ocean is much less 'green'. However, complicated relations between standing crop and production may obscure this picture.

Physiology of photosynthesis and production

Photorespiration and glycollate production

Lack of photorespiration has been considered responsible for the higher efficiency of light utilization in C_4-plants. When atmospheric pressure of O_2 is lowered from 21 to 1 %, light respiration in C_3-plants is completely suppressed and the efficiency of light utilization in C_3- and C_4-plants is similar. In production under field conditions, C_4-plants are not always better than C_3- or even CAM-plants (possessing crassulacean acid metabolism). Differences in adaptation to water stress seems to be important here (Caldwell, Chapter 3).

During photosynthesis, especially in C_3-plants, some carbon enters the glycollate pathway, leading to a release of CO_2. Glycollate biosynthesis is closely associated with the photosynthetic carbon dioxide cycle, requires high light intensity and is enhanced by high oxygen and low CO_2 concentration; high CO_2 may overcome the oxygen inhibition. In oxygen-free air the rate of photosynthesis may be enhanced by 25 % or more (Troughton, Chapter 16).

In unicellular algae, carbon fixed may leak out as glycollate from the Calvin cycle (Fogg, Chapter 19). This is very obvious with deficient mineral nutrition, probably especially with shortage of nitrogen. Glycollate appears to be dissipated when protein synthesis, cell division, and growth are curtailed. It is of interest to consider how far there are similarities between glycollate excretion and photorespiration in higher plants. Glycollate may well be reassimilated by algae under certain conditions as in the Indian temple ponds.

Transport and utilization of assimilates for growth

Conversion of primary photosynthates and their utilization for growth entails respiratory losses. Experimental evidence and calculations suggest that these conversions are very efficient, respiratory losses being not more than 25–30 % with addition of a few per cent for maintenance of essential structures (Penning de Vries, Chapter 20). Experiments with bacteria and fungi, and with germinating seedlings of higher plants, still growing on reserves, in many cases show efficiency figures (g g^{-1}, cal cal^{-1} or J J^{-1}) of around 0.6. Assimilates ultimately move from

682

source to sink. It is useful therefore to consider source strength and sink strength, i.e. size × activity (Wareing & Patrick, Chapter 21). Source activity can be expressed as leaf area × photosynthetic rate per unit leaf area, discounting respiration. Sink-strength may be differentiated into building the organ (i.e. its structure) and filling it with reserve materials. Growing shoot apices also act as active sinks. High C–N ratios seem to suggest sink-limitation, while low C–N ratios suggest source-limitation. Assimilates do not simply move in response to metabolic demand, but hormones also play a role. Troughton & Currie (p. 693) give examples of translocation rates, which in maize leaves are 3–6 cm min⁻¹, somewhat increased by shading, and in tomato ~1 cm min⁻¹, decreased somewhat by chilling or removal of the fruit, but with slight recovery when the fruit is replaced by hormones.

Rees (p. 692) reports direct transport of materials from the old to the new bulb in tulip, e.g. in forcing. Studies in bulb and corm plants in our laboratory showed that several aspects of production and morphogenesis of horticultural interest follow the sequence tulip, bulbous iris, gladiolus; for instance, the ratio of subsoil dry weight to total decreases in this order.

Photosynthesis in relation to environment

Shading, in *Teucrium scorodonia*, affects leaf area, chlorophyll content, number of chloroplasts, and chlorophyll content per chloroplast (Mousseau, p. 692). With the shading levels used, the light–shade ratios for the above items were 1, 1, 2 and 0.5, respectively, resulting in the same photosynthetic activity. In both *Calendula* and *Impatiens*, light saturation per cm² leaf area was higher in plants grown under higher light intensities. In *Calendula*, leaf size was little affected by the light intensity at which the plants were grown. *Impatiens*, at low light intensities, formed larger and thinner leaves, and measured at low light intensities, photosynthesis per entire leaf thus was much higher for leaves grown at low intensities; it was even slightly higher if measured at light saturation (Groen, 1973).

Temperature effects

Effects of 'normal' temperatures on photosynthesis and production have in part already been mentioned. Silsbury & Fukai (p. 690) report a negative temperature effect in *Trifolium subterraneum* in dense plantings; increase in dry weight slowed down sooner and reached lower values at

683

z*

Conclusions

30 °C than at 15 °C. Negative temperature relations ($Q_{10} < 1$) are of two main types, namely competition with another organ for assimilates (sink competition) and competition between a reaction and its reversal. In neither case do really negative temperature relationships in metabolic reactions occur. Other physiologically and ecologically important temperature relationships which should be recognized, and analyzed before being used in models are: the linear temperature curve of various physiological processes, brought about by gradual curtailing of a process by low Q_{10} reactions, and the effect of 'temperature sums' over prolonged periods of low temperatures (Wassink, 1972).

Light and CO_2 profiles in canopies, and plant density effects

In canopies, the *average* light intensity is lower than for single, widely spaced plants exposed to the same incident intensity, hence, light saturation of photosynthesis is reached at higher incident intensities in the first case than in the second. The same holds for dense algal suspensions compared with diluted ones. Saeki (Chapter 13) has pointed out that the decrease of light flux density in its passage through a canopy depends on density and structure of the canopy in a complex way; both the construction of models and field measurements may be helpful. Increase of diffuse skylight in the total sunlight contributes to uniform light distribution within the canopy. Important for the light climate within a crop are: leaf angle and orientation, LAI, gaps in the foliage and frequency and size of sunspots.

CO_2 distribution within a plant stand is quite different from that of light. In forests, a minimum often appears half-way down the canopy, owing to consumption of the downward flux from the atmosphere, and of the upward flux from the soil.

Further analysis of light effects may benefit from the classical plant physiological approach, namely, deliberate, serial variation of separate environmental factors. In our laboratory, we have compared serial variations of light intensity and plant density with respect to production and morphogenesis in bulbous irises. For a given dry weight production, a linear relationship was found between light intensity and log plant distance or log number of plants per unit field area (Fig. 31.2) This is reminiscent of Beer's law, with plant density acting as a concentration. Simple models of the decrease of light down a canopy start from this law (cf. Acock *et al.*, 1970). Anyhow, plant density variation acts largely as light intensity variation, as might be expected.

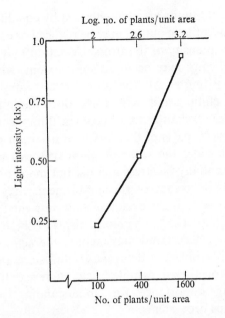

Fig. 31.2. Comparison of light intensity values and log plant density values producing equal dry weights in an average of the last 2 harvests of bulbous irises (cv. Wedgwood) in a field experiment with serial variation of both factors (E. C. Wassink & M. E. van den Noort unpublished data).

Stress effects on photosynthesis and production

A widespread stress is water deficiency, due to the resistanc structures to the water flux from the 'source' (the soil around the roots) to the 'sink' (the transpiring leaf/air surface) (Slavík, Chapter 23). The gaseous pathway of CO_2 is the same as that of water vapour efflux, in which stomatal resistance forms a major resistance; this depends on turgor of the guard cells, whose increase is now assumed to be chiefly due to ATP-dependent intake of cations, mainly K^+. Mesophyll resistance differs for water vapour and CO_2, where it may include carboxylation. ATP synthesis, NADP reduction, and PGA reduction are reported as resistant to even severe water stress, but water deficit causes rapid changes in cell microstructure, e.g. of membranes, and loss of RNA may be among the first effects of water stress. Cell division seems also very sensitive. Recovery depends on the degree of previous stress, and may be incomplete, except in poikilohydrous plants.

Temperature stress is manifest as effects of heat, chilling (above 0 °C and frost (Bauer, Larcher & Walker, Chapter 25), but after-effects also

685

occur. Heat and cold limits are characterized by equality of CO_2 output and intake. Photosynthetic output may be reduced or completely halted, dependent on the intensity of the stress. Cessation may be reversible or irreversible. Hardening may occur to some extent, with the effects of shifting sensitivity limits. All the above effects apply more or less similarly to heat, chilling and frost stress. Both the immediate and the after-effects on CO_2 exchange are of ecological importance.

Already in previous parts of this survey, it has been pointed out that mineral nutrients affect the rates of photosynthesis and production. They may not essentially be stress factors, but merely limiting factors; however, constant deficiency of specific elements may act as 'stress'. Evidence is available that deficiency of any nutrient depresses photosynthesis (Nátr, Chapter 24). The mechanisms of these actions are still largely unknown. They certainly may include interactions and effects on such features as chloroplast structure, CO_2 diffusion, and translocation of assimilates; altogether a complex field of research that may well acquire increasing importance for understanding production and efficiency in various ecosystems.

Final remarks

Primary production depends in the first place on the amount of light energy supplied; the efficiency of conversion for an entire season probably varies between 0.1 % (of PAR) and 2–3 %. Production and hence energy conversion are usually low in the first part of the season, e.g., because of insufficient leaf coverage, low temperature, etc., and also in the last phase of growth, e.g., because of ripening and ageing effects, water-stress, etc. In the 'middle' of the season, when both environment and plant capacity are at their optima, efficiencies may considerably exceed the average and reach up to approximately 10 %.

In several ecosystems, production seems usually limited by a stress factor; water, temperature, minerals or CO_2 may act individually or together, determining the type of ecosystem, its species composition and its development. In open ecosystems, especially in cold environments, plants are often characterized by very high levels of light intensity for saturation of photosynthesis.

It should not be overlooked that 'net primary production' per year in a stable ecosystem ideally approaches zero, since it is entirely consumed and/or mineralized, and the system starts at the same level as the year before.

Conclusions

The 'classical' plant physiological approach, considering the object as a complex 'black box', and studying the effect of deliberate serial variation of one important production factor at a time may certainly contribute to understanding production and morphogenesis both in field experiments and under controlled conditions. Factors that can be reliably varied in the field are relatively few, e.g. light intensity, light duration, and plant density; the latter, however, creates physiologically complex conditions. Extension of this series of factors by skilful thinking and experimentation appears worthwhile, because of the available high light intensity in the field. On the other hand, attempts to improve the intensity of illumination in controlled environments seem highly important. A whole programme of ecophysiological experimentation still seems open with single plants, monocultures, artificial competitions, spontaneous vegetations, and mass cultures of algae. Aside of this, extension of measurement of photosynthesis *in situ*, and characterizing the various factors in the field, seems highly desirable.

References

Acock, B., Thornley, J. H. M. & Warren Wilson, J. (1970). Spatial variation of light in the canopy. In *Prediction and Measurement of Photosynthetic Productivity*, ed. I. Šetlík, pp. 91–102. Wageningen, PUDOC.
Gaastra, P. (1958). Light energy conversion in field crops in comparison with the photosynthetic efficiency under laboratory conditions. *Mededelingen van de Landbouwhogeschool, Wageningen*, **58** (4), 1–12.
Groen, J. (1973). Photosynthesis of *Calendula officinalis* L. and *Impatiens parviflora* DC as influenced by light intensity during growth and age of leaves and plants. *Mededelingen Landbouwhogeschool, Wageningen, Nederland*, **73–8**, 1–128.
Kok, B. (1952). On the efficiency of *Chlorella* growth. *Acta Botanica Neerlandica*, **1**, 445–67.
Kok, B. & van Oorschot, J. L. P. (1954). Improved yields in algal mass cultures. *Acta Botanica Neerlandica*, **3**, 533–46.
Wassink, E. C. (1948). De lichtfactor in dephotosynthese en zijn relatie tot andere milieufactoren. (The light factor in photosynthesis and its relation to other environmental factors.) *Mededelingen. Directeur van de tuinbouw*, **11**, 503–13.
Wassink, E. C. (1964). Rendement van de omzetting der lichtenergie in laboratoriumproeven en bij de groei van gewassen. (Efficiency of light energy conversion in laboratory experiments and crop growth.) *Mededelingen Landbouwhogeschool, Wageningen, Nederland*, **64–16**, 1–33.
Wassink, E. C. (1972). Some notes on temperature relations in plant physiological processes. *Mededelingen Landbouwhogeschool, Wageningen, Nederland*, **72–25**, 1–15.

List of supplementary papers submitted at the IBP Aberystwyth Meeting, April 1973

I. Primary production in terrestrial ecosystems

1. Crop productivity in Rhodesia.
   Allison, J. C. S. (Department of Agriculture, University of Rhodesia, Mount Pleasant, Salisbury, Rhodesia) & Papenfus, H. D. (Tobacco Research Board of Rhodesia, P.O. Box 1909, Salisbury, Rhodesia)

2. Comparative photosynthetic production of Mojave desert shrubs.
   Bamberg, S. A. & Kleinkopf, G. (Laboratory of Nuclear Medicine and Radiation Biology, University of California, Los Angeles, California, USA)

3. Primary production in the Chaka project: a tropical deciduous forest ecosystem.
   Bandhu, D. (Department of Botany, Swami Shraddhanand College, University of Delhi, Alipur, Delhi, India)

4. Primary production in a Canadian grassland.
   Coupland, R. T., Redmann, R. E., Ripley, E. A. & Saugier, B. (Matador Project, University of Saskatchewan, Saskatoon, Saskatchewan, Canada)

5. Ecophysiological estimation of photosynthetic production of tree leaves in oak-hornbeam forest.
   Czarnowski, M. (Laboratory of Photosynthesis, Institute of Plant Physiology, Polish Academy of Sciences, Krakow, Poland)

6. Plant strategy, CO_2-exchange and primary production.
   Eckardt, F. E. (Section d'Ecophysiologie, CNRS, BP-5051, 34033 Montpellier, France)

7. Primary production and structure of halophyte communities in controlled environments.
   Horváth, I. & Bodrogközy, G. (Department of Botany, József Attila University, Szeged, Hungary)

8. Photosynthetic production in sown grassland.
   Leafe, E. L., Stiles, W. & Dickinson, S. E. (Grassland Research Institute, Hurley, nr Maidenhead, Berks, UK)

Supplementary papers

9. CO$_2$-exchange studies on Devon Island, NWT Canada.
Mayo, J. M. (Botany Department, University of Alberta, Edmonton, Alberta, Canada), Thompson, R. G. (Biology Department, Mount Alison University, Sackville, New Brunswick, Canada), Despain, D. G. (Box 227, Yellowstone National Park, Mammoth, Wyoming, USA) & Van Zinderen Bakker, E. M. (Botany Department, University of Alberta, Edmonton, Alberta, Canada)

10. Primary production of two annual pasture species in a Mediterranean environment.
Silsbury, J. H. & Fukai, S. (Waite Agricultural Research Institute, University of Adelaide, Adelaide, South Australia)

II. Primary production in aquatic ecosystems

1. Primary production of nannoplankton in Lake Jasne.
Bohr, R. (Institute of Biology, Nicholas Copernicus University, Torun, Poland)

2. Primary production in the Siddhanath Temple Tank at Baroda, India.
Ganapati, S. V. & Kulkarni, P. D. (Department of Biochemistry, M.S. University of Baroda, Baroda-2, India)

3. Primary production of freshwater macrophytes in Japan and Tropical Asia.
Ikushima, J. (Laboratory of Ecology, Faculty of Science, Chiba University, Chiba, Japan)

4. The changes of photosynthetic activity of fresh-water phytoplankton with the growing biomass.
Javornický, P. (Hydrobiological Laboratory, ČSAV, Vltavská 17, 15105 Prague, Czechoslovakia)

5. Primary production by phytoplankton in some lakes and coastal waters of Japan, specially in relation to nutrients, underwater light and standing crop.
Sakamoto, M. (Water Research Laboratory, Faculty of Science, Nagoya University, Nagoya, Japan)

6. Limnological studies of and primary production in temple pond ecosystems.
Sreenivasan, A. (Hydrobiological Research Station, 87, Poonamallee High Road, Madras 600010, India)

7. Productivity of a temperate and a tropical beach.
Steele, J. H., Munro, A. L. S. (Marine Laboratory, P.O. Box 101, Aberdeen, Scotland, UK) & Reddy, V. V. G. (National Institute of Oceanography, Karrikamuri Cross Road, Ernakulam, Cochin 11, India)

690

8. Primary production in the Gulf of St Lawrence.
   Steven, D. M. (Marine Sciences Centre and Department of Biology, McGill University, Montreal 101, Quebec, Canada)

9. Nutrients and phytoplankton in the Hauraki Gulf, Northern New Zealand
   Taylor, F. J. (Marine Research Laboratory, University of Auckland, Leigh, New Zealand).

10. Production of *Cyperus papyrus*
    Thompson, K. (Department of Botany, Makerere University, Kampala, Uganda)

11. Primary production at Ocean Weather Station India (59° 00′ N., 19° 00′ W.) in the North Atlantic.
    Williams, R. & Robinson, G. A. (Institute of Marine Environmental Research, Oceanographic Laboratory, 78, Craighall Road, Edinburgh)

III. Distribution of radiant energy and CO_2 in relation to community structure and stratification

1. Distribution of radiation within a Sitka spruce canopy.
   Norman, J. M., Jarvis, P. G. (Botany Department, University of Aberdeen, St Machar Drive, Aberdeen, Scotland, UK) & Landsberg, J. J. (Long Ashton Research Institute, Long Ashton, Bristol, UK).

2. Radiation and carbon dioxide fluxes in mixed grass prairie.
   Ripley, E. A. & Saugier, B. (Matador Project, University of Saskatchewan, Saskatoon, Saskatchewan, Canada)

3. Observed radiation and CO_2 profiles in loblolly pine.
   Sinclair, T. R. (School of Forestry, Duke University, Durham, North Carolina 27706, USA)

IV. Photosynthetic activity of individual plants and tissues

1. Effect of various daily rhythmic variations of the intensity of illumination on photosynthetic energy utilisation.
   Horváth, I. & Mihalik, E. (Department of Botany, József Attila University, Szeged, Hungary)

2. Response of Sitka spruce photosynthesis to environment.
   Jarvis, P. G., Neilson, R. E. (Botany Department, University of Aberdeen, St. Machars Drive, Aberdeen, Scotland, UK) & Ludlow, M. M. (Cunningham Laboratory, Division of Tropical Agronomy, CSIRO, St Lucia, Queensland, Australia)

691

Supplementary papers

3. The adaptation of photosynthesis of a shade-tolerant plant.
Mousseau, M. (Le Phytotron, CNRS, 91 Gif-sur-Yvette, France)

4. Summary of the gas exchange studies in arctic bryophytes at Barrow, Alaska.
Oechel, W. O. (Biology Department, McGill University, Montreal 101, Quebec, Canada) & Collins, N. J. (British Antarctic Survey, Botanical Section, The University, Birmingham, UK)

5. Assessment of photosynthetic adaptability to light regimes.
Prioul, J. L. & Bourdu, R. (Laboratoire Structure et Metabolisme des Plantes, Université Paris-Sud, Orsay, France)

6. Changes in the rate of photosynthesis as leaves of *Vicia faba* age.
Sunderland, R. A. & Elston, J. (Department of Agricultural Botany, The University, Reading, UK)

7. Contributions to the photosynthetic activity of lignifying shoot axes, by anatomical, ultrastructural and physiological studies.
Szujko-Lacza, Julia (Department of Botany, Museum of Natural History, Budapest 14, Hungary)

8. Photosynthetic capacity of conifers.
Żelawski, W. & Szaniawski, R. (Institute of Sylviculture, Warsaw Agricultural University, Warsaw, Poland)

V. Use of assimilates for maintenance, growth and development

1. The influence of the light factor on the distribution of assimilates.
Gopal, B. (Department of Botany, University of Rajasthan, Jaipur, India)

2. The effect of sink strength on the distribution of assimilates.
Moorby, J. (Glasshouse Crops Research Institute, Littlehampton, Sussex, UK), Troughton, J. H. & Currie, B. G. (Physics and Engineering Laboratory, DSIR, Lower Hutt, New Zealand)

3. Growth of bulbous plants.
Rees, A. R. (Glasshouse Crops Research Institute, Littlehampton, Sussex, UK)

4. Carbon fluxes in the graminaceous shoot.
Ryle, G. J. A. (Grassland Research Institute, Hurley, nr. Maidenhead, Berks, UK)

5. Gas exchange and productivity for *Opuntia* spp.
Ting, I. P., Johnson, H. & Szarek, S. R. (Department of Biology and

The Philip L. Boyd Deep Canyon Desert Research Center, University of California, Riverside, California 92502, USA)

6. Estimation of the speed of translocation in maize and some other species. Troughton, J. H. & Currie, B. G. (Physics and Engineering Laboratory, DSIR, Lower Hutt, New Zealand)

VI. Influence of stress factors and the use of assimilates

1. Some characteristics of photosynthesis in winter wheat, proceeding at temperatures around 0 °C.
Devay, M. (Agricultural Research Institute, Hungarian Academy of Sciences, Martonvasar, Hungary)

2. Influence of water stress on photosynthesis in *Glyceria maxima*, *Phalaris arundinacea* and *Alopecurus pratensis*.
Gloser, J. (Institute of Botany, ČSAV, Stará 18, Brno, Czechoslovakia)

3. Response of Sitka spruce photosynthesis to low temperatures.
Neilson, R. E., Jarvis, P. G. (Botany Department, University of Aberdeen, St Machar Drive, Aberdeen, Scotland, UK) & Ludlow, M. M. (Cunningham Laboratory, Division of Tropical Agronomy, CSIRO, St Lucia, Queensland, Australia)

4. (i) Seasonal patterns of CO_2 exchange in arctic bryophytes.
(ii) Comparative patterns of CO_2 exchange in two arctic bryophytes at Barrow, Alaska.
Oechel, W. C. (Biology Department, McGill University, Montreal 101, Quebec, Canada) & Collins, N. J. (British Antarctic Survey, Botanical Section, The University, Birmingham, UK)

5. Plant–water relationships in a Canadian grassland.
Redmann, R. E. (Department of Plant Ecology, University of Saskatchewan, Saskatoon, Saskatchewan, Canada)

6. Photosynthetic efficiency and productivity of rice in wet and dry seasons.
Sircar, S. M. (Bose Institute, 93/1 Acharya Prafulla Chandra Road, Calcutta 9, India)

7. Photosynthesis of sorghum and tobacco as affected by water stress.
Turner, N. C. (Department of Ecology, Connecticut Agricultural Experiment Station, New Haven, Connecticut 06504, USA)

VII. Actual and potential production in photosynthetic systems

1. Controlling factors of primary productivity in Lake Neusiedlersee.
Dokulil, M. (Limnologische Lehrkanzel, Universität Wien, Wien A-1090, Austria)

2. The influence of seasonal factors on the vegetative growth of *Helianthus annuus* and *Phaseolus vulgaris* in Freetown.
Eze, J. M. O. (Department of Botany, Fourah Bay College, University of Sierra Leone, Freetown, Sierra Leone)

3. Predicting crop climate and net carbon dioxide exchange – a resumé.
Lemon, E. (USDA, Bradfield Hall, Cornell University, Ithaca, New York, 14850, USA)

4. Agronomic potential and solar energy conversion in contrasting solar radiation climates.
Mattei, F. (c/o UCEA, Via del Caravita 7a, Rome, Italy) & Gibbon, D. (Division of Agricultural Research, Gaborone, Botswana)

5. Modelling the environmental effects on forest primary productivity.
Sinclair, T. R. (School of Forestry, Duke University, Durham, North Carolina, USA)

6. Studies on photosynthesis and related processes in the coniferous forest biome (US IBP).
Walker, R. B. & Waring, R. H. (Department of Botany, University of Washington, Seattle, Washington, USA)

Index

Index

aquatic plants: conclusions on production by, 281–2, 679–82; crop cover and photosynthetic activity in, 282–5; effect of methods on comparisons of, 290–1; factors determining production by, 285–9; internal factors affecting production by, 289–90; see also entries for freshwater and marine systems, and phytoplankton
Arachis, 163
Arbutus unedo, 573
arctic ecosystems, 75
Arctic Ocean, phytoplankton in, 257, 266, 270
arctic tundra subzone, 77; production in, 89, 91; semi-desert northern zone of, 77, 80, 82, 87; southern zone of, 80, 82, 87, 88, 89
Arctophila fulva, 96
arido-active and arido-passive plants, 121
Aristida karelini, 129, 130, 131, 132
Aristida pennata, A. plumosa, 59
Artemisia, 129n
Artemisia herba-alba: photosynthesis by, 108, 109, 110; production by, 60, 122–3, 124; root–shoot ratio in, 125; water stress effects on, 111, 113, 522
Artemisia–Poa sinaica steppe, 60
Artemisia porrecta, 60
Artemisia sieberi, 124, 125
Artemisia tridentata, 47, 59
Artemisietum communities I and II, 122, 123, 124, 125
Arundo donax, 197
Ascophyllum, 207, 680
Ascophyllum nodosum, 212, 213, 214, 215
ash content: of Chara, 199; of crustaceous lichens, 141
aspartate, first product of photosynthesis in C_4-plants (with malate), 362, 363
aspartate amino transferase, in CAM-plants, 364
aspect of habitat, and photosynthesis by lichens, 137–40, 142
Aspicilia, 133
assimilate: competition for, 492–3; efficiency of utilisation of, 682; loss of, in respiration, 502–3; total accumulation of, by whole plant, 484–6; translocation of, see translocation
assimilate, partition of: as determinant of production, 501, 607–10; mechanism of, 493–6; shoot–root balance in, 486–9, 626; source–sink relations in, 481–3, 485–6, 490, 503–6; stress and, 589; within shoot system, 490–2
assimilation number for phytoplankton, 250–1; effect of nitrogen content on, 251; figures for, in different oceans, 252–7;

for log phase and senescent populations, 259, 260
assimilation rate, net, 198, 663
Asterionella formosa, 238, 446
Astragalus paucijugus, 129, 130, 131
Atlantic Ocean, phytoplankton in, 252–3 262–4, 270
ATP, 361, 374, 376, 451, 476; active transport dependent on, 505; in C_4-plants, 363, 475; water deficit and synthesis of, 519–20
Atriplex: C_3- and C_4-spp. of, 65–6, 166; C_4-pathway evolved several times in? 381; hybrids between C_3- and C_4-spp. of, 362, 604
Atriplex confertifolia (C_4), 47, 48; compared with Eurotia (C_3), 66; production by, 123, 124, 125; root–shoot ratio of, 125
Atriplex dimorphostegia, 132
Atriplex halimus–Suaeda fruticosa community, 61
Atriplex hastata (C_3), 65, 521; photorespiration in, 375; photosynthesis in, 370, 372, 377, 559
Atriplex nummularia (C_4), 65
Atriplex patula, 377
Atriplex spongiosa (C_4), 65, 521; photosynthesis in, 363, 370, 372
Aulacomnium, 393
Avena, 605
Axonopus compressus (C_4), 166
Azolla, 199

bacteria: composition of, 461; and estimations of respiration by algae, 235; nitrogen-fixing, 220, 221; photosynthetic, in evolution, 378; remineralisation of waters by, 649; utilisation of glycollate by, 450, 453
Barbilophozia hatcheri, 410
bean: mineral nutrients and translocation in, 550, 551; nitrogen content and photosynthesis by, 539, 540, 545; water relations in, 525–7; see also Phaseolus, Vicia
benthos, phytomicro-, 225, 226
bermudagrass, see Cynodon
Beta vulgaris (sugar-beet): breeding for improvement of, 610; cation/anion balance in, 163; cross-grafts between spinach beet and, 286; energy conversion efficiency in, 156, 361, 596, 600, 601, 602, 603, 676; growth model for, 504; growth rate of, 156, 596; mineral nutrients and photosynthesis in, 539, 540–1; nitrogen assimilation by, 162; production by, 149, 151, 155; rate of sucrose storage in, 164; temperature effects on, 559; translocation

696

Index

calorific value of cells, decreases with age of culture of phytoplankton, 260

Campanula persicifolia, 566

Camptothecium philippeanum, 467

Canavalia ensiformis, 559

canopy, 178; ceiling of net production rate at closure of, 11; in crops, 157–60; CO_2 as limiting factor in upper part of, 314; distribution of CO_2 within, 23, 298, 309–12, 348, 684; distribution of light within, 19–25, 26, 297–8, 307, 350, 684; flux of CO_2 within, 298, 312–13; heat budget of, 306; micro-climate within, 183; models of function of, 26–31; specific leaf area within, 25; structure of, and penetration of light, 350; structure of, and production, 606–7; wind profiles under, 311

Caragana arborescens, 566

carbohydrates: amounts of, in different plant tissues, 461; storage of, in same sp. grown in Arctic and in England, 485; yield of (as cellulose), per g glucose, 460, 464

carbon: fractionation of isotopes of, by C_3- and C_4-plants, 362, 365–6, 378, 432; in large molecules in lake water, 335

carbon dioxide: aerodynamic studies on, 94, 298; in aquatic systems, 282, 328–30, 652–3, 679–80, 681; atmospheric, 346; atmospheric, supply to waters from, 329, 335, 339, 652; in canopy, *see under* canopy; labelled, for determination of photosynthesis, 426–7; light/dark ratio for production of, by desert plants, 129, 132; as limiting factor at high light intensity, 347; loss of, in photorespiration, 375; production of, in synthesis of plant constituents, 460, and tissues, 461; ratio of, to bicarbonate, 431; resistance to diffusion of, *see* resistance; supply of additional, to algal cultures, 676, to greenhouses, 347, and to outdoor crops, 347–8, 662; from soil, 310, 312, 313; from soil–plant system in darkness, 51; turnover times for, in lake at midsummer, 337, and for ocean/air and air/land, 346; used by RuDP carboxylase, 361, 369, 431

carbon dioxide assimilation: CO_2 concentration and, 370, 371; curves of, against light response, 474–8, (in mineral deficiencies) 539–43; differences in, with same incoming radiation, 349; different pathways of, *see* C_3, C_4, *and* crassulacean acid metabolism pathways; estimates of production from measurements of, 79, 93–4; by freshwater macrophytes, 191, 192–3; net rate of, 663, 664; prediction

of dissimilation rate from measurements of rate of, in steady-state system, 463–74; processes not detected by measurements of, 462; quantum efficiency of, 156, 347, 361, 675; resistances to, *see* resistance; stomatal aperture and, 112–13, 114, 115; by tundra plants, 93–4, 95–7

carbon dioxide concentration: and CO_2 assimilation, 370, 371; and CO_2 exchange rates, 372, 376, 427; and glycollate production, 438–9; and quantum yield, 361; and stomatal aperture, 349, 367

carbon dioxide exchange, 426–9; CO_2 concentration and, 372, 376, 427; estimates of production from measurements of, 236, 290; in lichens, 134–6, 138, 140, 399, 414, 415–17; in mosses, 401, 404, 408; model for, in lichens and mosses, 412–15; regulation of, 367–73, 376; temperature and, 557, (chilling) 567–71, (frost) 571–8, (heat) 558–9, 563–4

carbon/nitrogen ratio in plant, as indicator of source/sink relations, 485

carbonic anhydrase, in photosynthesis, 183, 369, 372, 373, 431; and utilisation of bicarbonate by algae, 652

carboxydismutase, *see* ribulose-1,5-diphosphate carboxylase

carboxylation enzymes: activity of, and CO_2 assimilation, 429–30; *see also* phosphoenolpyruvate *and* ribulose-1,5-diphosphate carboxylases

carboxylation resistance to CO_2 assimilation, 429–31, 519

Cardamine pratensis, 516

Carex, 129

Carex aquatilis, 90

Carex communities, 92

Carex ensifolia, *C. nigra*, 95, 96

Carex pachystilis, 121, 122, 124

Carex physodes, 130, 131

Carex stans, 90, 95, 96

carotenoids, protection of chlorophylls by, 359–60

Castanopsis cuspidata, 21, 23, 25–30; production by, 12, 16, 30–1

catalase, 440, 441

cation/anion balance, 163–4; constant for a species, 163

cellulose, 460, 464; energy cost of synthesis of, 475

Cenchrus ciliaris, 378, 605

Ceramium rubrum, 213

Ceratophyllum demersum, 193

cereals: energy conversion efficiency in, 599, 603; new cultivars of, 147, 609–10; spring-sown varieties of, 610–11; *see also* individual spp.

698

Index

crops: approach to improving efficiency of, 593, 612–13; energy conversion efficiency in, 15, 596–7, 675; genetic variation and improvement of, 604; ideotypes for, 665; maintain themselves only by intervention of man, 177; simulation of growth of, 625–6; *see also individual crops, and agricultural ecosystems*
cryptogams: in alpine belts, 81, 82, 83; in arctic tundra, 78, 80, 81; assimilation rates for, 96–7; biomass of, 82–3, 87
Cryptomeria japonica, 7, 9, 12, 16
Cucurbita, centre of origin of, 160, 161
Cylindrotheca closterium, 259
Cynodon dactylon (bermudagrass), 363, 601
Cynodon plectostachyus, 162
Cynodon spp., production by, 149, 151, 154
Cyperus papyrus, 193; growth rate and production of, 191, 198, 680
Cystoseira granulata, 211
cytoplasm of leaf: water stress and heat resistance of, in desert plants, 110

Dactylis glomerata, 377, 596
darkness: CO_2 distribution under plant canopy during, 310, 313; fixation of CO_2 during, by CAM-plants, 364–5
Datura metel, 108, 109
Daucus carota, 155, 156
decomposition rates: in deserts, 76; root-shoot ratio and, 84; in tundra, 76, 78, 85, 88, 93
Deschampsia caespitosa, 96
deserts: Central Asian, 129–32; Near Eastern, 121–7; Negev, 107–17; production in, 677, (by lichens) 133–42; thermostability of photosynthesis in plants of, 132; water relations in, 112–13, 114, 115
desiccation, of lichens, 134
Desmarestia aculeata, 211
desmids, killed by excretory products of *Microcystis*, 655
dew, used by lichens and mosses, 135–6, 137, 142, 394, 677
diatoms; autoinhibitors excreted by, 655; exponential population increase of, in spring, 238, 288; silicon and growth of, 237, 654
dicarboxylic acid pathway of carbon assimilation, *see* C_4
Dichanthium, 61
Dicranum, 393
Dicranum elongatum, 396, 398, 400, 404; temperature relations in, 407, 408, 409
dieback: correction for, in production estimate for tundra, 93; of desert plants, 127

diffusion resistance, *see* resistance to CO_2 exchange
Digitaria (C_4), 362
Digitaria sanguinalis, 363
Dioscorea, centre of origin of, 160
Diploschistes, 133
Diploschistes calcareus, 141
Distylium racemosum, 12
Ditylum brightwellii, 443
dormancy: summer, 129, 611; winter, 570–1, 575, 611
Drepanocladus uncinatus, 396
drought, resistance to, 512
dry weight of plants, 481–3; accumulation of, in whole plant, 484–6; CO_2 exchange in relation to production of (lichens), 415–17; growth of marine macrophytes in relation to amount of, per g tissue, 209; increase of, as growth, 460; model for calculating increase of, in grass sward, 626–31; production of, by desert plants, 125–7; production of, similar in different types of plant, 179; rate of production of, in algal cultures and reedswamp plants, 284; rate of production of, in grass sward, 631, 633, 634, 636; relation of CO_2 assimilation to, 79; relation of respiration to, 502, 641
Dryas, 86, 90, 93, 95
Dryas integrifolia, 90
Dryas octopetala, 95, 96
Dryas punctata, 90, 95
duckweeds, 199, 287, 288, 290, 291
Dunaliella tertiolecta, 259, 446

eddy diffusivity, in distribution of CO_2 in plant stands, 298, 310, 311, 313, 314, 348
Eichhornia, 199, 288
Elaeis guineensis: breeding to improve, 610; energy conversion efficiency in, 597, 598, 602; growth rate of, 597, 598; production by, 149, 152, 599; yield of, 602
ELCROS model for predicting production, 624
electron transport, photosynthetic, 360; ceases in darkness, 373
Elodea canadensis, 565, 652
energy conversion efficiency, 357, 598–604, 613; of absorbed PAR, 347, 675; in crops compared with single leaves, 623; highest values reported for, 52; methods of calculating, 63; and production, 11, 14–17; similar in all latitudes, 178; theoretically possible degree of, 662; in total flora of earth, 183–4, 661–2; *see also under individual ecosystems, plant groups, etc.*
energy inputs, in crop production, 146, 593–7

Index

Galathea expedition, estimates of production of oceans from data collected by, 260
generation time, and 'turnover time' of phytoplankton, 238, 291
genetic variation, and improvement of crops, 604, 613
genotype, interaction of environment and, 145, 147, 166, 176, 662, 663
geophytes, 176
Geum reptans, 572, 573
Gladiolus, 18, 23
glucose: amounts of, required for synthesis of different plant constituents, 460, 464; ATP formed per mol. of, 475; energy costs of reduction of CO_2 to, 475; oxygen consumed and CO_2 produced in conversion of, to different plant constituents, 460, 475, 502; uptake of, from natural waters, 450
glutamate-oxaloacetate transaminase, 364
glyceraldehyde-3-phosphate dehydrogenase, 363, 520
glycerate, from serine, 440, 445
glycerate dehydrogenase, glycerate kinase, in algae, 440–1
Glyceria maxima, 58, 192, 199
glycerol, excreted by *Dunaliella*, 446
glycine: glycollate transformed to, 440, 445; incorporation of labelled oxygen into, in leaves, 367; serine from, with loss of CO_2, 374, 440, 442
Glycine max: energy conversion efficiency in, 156, 596; growth rate of, 156, 157, 596; photorespiration in, 375; production by, 149, 152, 155; protein and oil storage in, seeds of, 163; rate of photosynthesis in, 545, 605; supply of extra CO_2 to, 662; temperature and respiration in, 559; water relations in, 513, 518, 521, 523–5
glycollate: algal production of, 437–41; excretion of, 443–6, 682, (in natural conditions) 446–9, 655; hypotheses on formation of, 366, 367, 451–3; in natural waters, 449; utilisation of, 450–1, 682, (in photorespiration) 442–3, (as substrate for growth) 441–2
glycollate dehydrogenase: glycollate excretion inversely related to activity of, 440, 444, 451; varying levels of, in algae, 440, 441, 442
glycollate oxidase, 374, 440
glycollate pathway, in photorespiration, 374, 438, 440–1
glyoxylate, oxidation of glycollate to, 374, 438, 451
Gomphrera globosa, 358
Gossypium, 160, 576, 664; growth and water stress in, 525, 527

Gossypium hirsutum: CO_2 supply and photosynthesis in, 348, 370, 372; chilling and respiration of, 568, 569; energy conversion efficiency and growth rate in, 597; maximum photosynthetic rate of, 605; photorespiration in, 375; shading and respiration of, 158; temperature relations in, 165, 371, 432, 566, 605; water stress and stomata of, 611
grapevines: higher rate of photosynthesis by, in fluctuating light, 302, 350
grass sward: determination of growth of, and photosynthesis by, 631–2; light intensity and photosynthesis by, 637; model for calculating increase in dry weight and transpiration of, 625, 626–31; photosynthesis by individual leaves of, 635, 639–40; production as observed and as predicted by model, 624–5, 638–40, 641–2; rate of growth of, 632–3; rate of photosynthesis by, 633, 635, 636; rates of growth and photosynthesis of, compared, 640–1
grasses, graminoids: C_3- and C_4-spp. of, 41, 45, 46, 47–8, 154; C_4-pathway evolved several times in? 380; cation/anion balance in C_3-spp. of, 163; legumes not successful against, except where nitrogen is limiting, 163; in deserts, 124; interception of light by sheaths and awns of, 308; of sea and marsh, 207; temperature effects in, 560; in tundra, 78, 80, 96; *see also* forage grasses
grasslands, grazing lands, 41; C_3- and C_4-plants in, 44–53; comparative studies of production and energy conversion efficiency in, 53–64, 67–8; production of, over growing season, 183; world production on, 42–4, 67
grazing animals: and evolution of plants, 176, 178, 180, 182; and freshwater macrophytes, 199, 200; in grasslands, 41; and lichens, 413, 417; and phytoplankton, 289; in tundra, 76
ground cover: by different lichens, on sites with different aspects, 139–40; estimate of production from extent of, in tundra, 79; leaf angle during establishment of, 606–7; *see also* crop cover in water
growing season, 595; in different grazing lands, 50, 51, 54–61; of kelps, 208–10, 218; methods of determining, 62, 63
growth: as dry weight increase, 460; efficiency of, 676; equations for, 488; investment of assimilate in, 501; model for, in grass sward, *see under* grass sward; often taken to include storage materials, 484; respiratory cost of, 158, 459–61,

Index

Parmelia olivacea, P. pachyderma, 397, 406
Parmelia physodes, 397, 410
Parmelia sulcata, 397
Parmelia tinctorum, 398
Paspalum dilatatum, 567, 568-9
Peganum harmala, 122, 124
Pelargonium, 516
Peltigera, 402
Peltigera aphthosa, 397, 405, 406
Peltigera polydactyla, 409
Peltigera praetextata, 397
Peltigera spp., nitrogen-fixers (contain blue-green algae), 410, 479
Pennisetum purpureum (C_4: Napiergrass), 162; energy conversion efficiency in, 597, 601; growth rate of, 597; production by, 149, 151, 154; yield of, 601
Pennisetum typhoides (C_4: bulrush millet): energy conversion efficiency in, 52, 54, 62, 156, 597; growth rate of, 156, 597, 598; roots of, 612; yield of, 601
pentose phosphate cycle, in evolution of biosphere, 175
penumbral effects, in light under canopy, 298, 301, 350
Peridinium westii, 234
permafrost, in tundra, 75
Perovskia–Agropyron steppe, 60
peroxisomes, 441, 442
pH: CO_2 content of water and, 239-40, 329-30; and glycollate excretion by algae, 439; and production in aquatic systems, 652-3
Phaeocystis poucheti, 446
Phalaris arundinacea, 58, 192, 193
Phalaris spp., 605
Phalaris–Trifolium pastures, 57
Phalaris tuberosa, 611, 612
Phaseolus, 163, 605; centre of origin of, 160, 161
Phaseolus vulgaris, 372, 566
Phleum commutatum, 86
Phleum pratense, in sward for testing of growth model, 632
phloem: energy cost of loading of, 462, 466, 502; pressure flow theory of translocation in, 488, 494-5; rate of flow in, in C_3- and C_4-plants, 506
Phoenix reclinata, 518
phosphate: in cation/anion balance, 164; fertilisation of lake with, 327, 334, 337; as limiting factor in aquatic systems, 654; molybdate method of estimating, 334; sea water, 209, 270; seasonal concentrations of, in lake, 331; uptake of, by roots of Zostera and Spartina, 220; see also phosphorus
phosphoenolpyruvate (PEP) carboxylase,

primary carboxylation enzyme in C_4-plants, outside chloroplast, 362, 363, 369; in bacteria and C_3-plants, 379; in CAM-plants, 364; inhibited by oxaloacetate, 373; not oxygen-sensitive, 379; temperature relations of, 558, 566, 567, 569; uses bicarbonate (not CO_2), 363, 369
phosphoesterases, excreted by some algae, 654
phosphoglycerate: C_4-acids converted to, in C_4-plants, 362, 363; first product of photosynthesis in C_3-plants, 361; from glycollate, 376, 441; from RuDP, 367, 437, 451; water deficit and reduction of, 420
phosphoglyceromutase, 363
phosphoglycollate: in photorespiration, 366-7; from RuDP, 374, 437, 451
phosphoglycollate phosphatase, 442
phosphorus: control of eutrophication by control of, 339; in large molecules in lake water, 335; and production and standing crop of freshwater phytoplankton, 327-8, 333; supply of, and grassland production, 53; supply of, and rate of photosynthesis, 540-1, 542, 547, 548; uptake of, by sea grasses, 220; see also phosphate
photocells measuring light in quanta, 327
photons, absorption of, 359-60
photoperiod, and onset of dormancy, 611
photophosphorylation, 363
photorespiration, 11, 369, 374-6, 502; absent from C_4-plants? 44, 604, 682; assimilation of CO_2 produced in, 430; in desert plants, 129, 132; favoured by high oxygen and low CO_2 concentrations, 375, 442, and suppressed at low oxygen concentrations, 375, 426, 427-8, 431, 682; in freshwater macrophytes, 190; glycollate in, 442-3, 451; in growth predictions, 463; methods used to estimate, 374-5; oxygen inhibition of photosynthesis linked with? 366-7; and ratio of $NADPH_2$ to ATP, 475; temperature and, 375, 559; wavelength of light and, 445
photosynthesis (general references only): activation energy for, 377-8; C_3-, C_4-, and CAM-pathways for, see C_3-, C_4-, and crassulacean acid metabolism pathways; constant rate of, during onto-genesis, 181-2; dark inhibition of, 323-4; determinations of, on single-leaf and whole-plant basis, 65; evolution of, 175, 378-80; in fluctuating light, 302, 350; in growth model, 624, 629; at low light intensity, favoured by low temperature, 90; method of measuring, in testing growth model, 632; model for, 26-8; net

Index

Index

silica: in ocean waters, 270; seasonal concentrations of, in lake, 331; water depleted of, by diatoms, 237, 654
sink, 481; accumulation of assimilate often limited by, 485; different types of, 505; relations of source and, 481–3, 485–6, 490, 503–6; storage organs as, 608
sink strength, 482, 483; components of, 683; hormones in regulation of, 495–6; relation between mobilising ability and, 493, 494–5; of whole plant, 484–5, 609
Skeletonema costatum, 259; excretion of glycollate by, 443, 447; utilisation of glycollate by, 441, 444, 451
sky: penetration of radiation from, into canopy, 300–1, 302, 308
slope vegetation, 123, 124
Smirnovia turkestana, 129, 130, 131
snow: on ice cover on lakes, 282; photosynthesis beneath, 86
soda lakes, microphytes in, 225, 230
sodium: requirement of blue-green algae for, in laboratory and field conditions, 324
soil: aeration of, increases available inorganic nitrogen, 161, 162; CO_2 from, 310, 312, 313; CO_2 from plants and, in darkness, 51; water potential of, 512, 513
Solanum lycopersicum, 361, 523, 683; centre of origin of, 160
Solanum melangena, 559
Solanum tuberosum, 164, 561; centre of origin of, 160; energy conversion efficiency in, 156, 596, 597, 600, 601, 603; growth rate of, 156, 596, 597; production by, 147, 149, 153; yield of, 600, 601, 603, 608, (record crop) 148
solar radiation: altitude and, 91; efficiency of conversion of, *see* energy conversion efficiency; as input of photosynthetic system in different areas, 593–5; *see also* light, photosynthetically active radiation
Solidago altissima, 17, 23, 307
Solidago virgaurea, 377
solifluction communities, in high altitude tundra, 78, 81
Solerina crocea, 397, 405, 406; as nitrogen-fixer, 410
Sorghastrum nutans, 46, 166
Sorghum (C_4): effects of chilling stress on, 567, 568–9; energy conversion efficiency in, 156, 597, 600, 601, 602; growth rate of, 156, 597, 598; leaf water potential and leaf resistance in, 515; mesophyll cells of, 358; production by, 149, 150; roots of, 612; yield of, 600, 601, 602, 603
Sorghum bicolor, S. sudanensis, 150, 154
Sorghum vulgare, 566

source, 481; relations of sink and, 481–3, 485–6, 490, 503–6
source strength, 482, 607; as leaf area × photosynthetic rate per unit leaf area, 683
soybean, *see Glycine*
Sparganium erectum, 195, 197
Spartina, 207, 208
Sphagnum, 88, 396
Spinacea oleracea, 574
Spirodela, 290
Spirulina, 646
Spirulina platensis: growth rate of, 646, 656; temperature and production curve of, 650, 651, 656; uses bicarbonate in preference to CO_2, 652, 656
spruce, CO_2 distribution in forest of, 311; *see also Picea*
starch: energy cost of synthesis of, 475; in photosynthesis, 374
stems: composition of woody and non-woody, 461; interception of light by, 309
Stephanodiscus hantzschii, glycollate excretion by, 439, 445, 449
Stephanodiscus tenuis, 447
steppes: arid and shrub, 59; dry, desert, mountain, and shrub, 42, 43; shrub, in US Great Basin, 47
Stereocaulon alpinum, 397, 405, 406
Stereocaulon paschale, 397, 406, 411
Stereocaulon spp., as nitrogen-fixers (contain blue-green algae), 410, 679
Stipa glaressa, 129n
Stipa spartea, 46
Stipa parviflora, S. retorta, 124
stipe of *Laminaria*, no laminarin in, 214
stomata: conductance of, 525, 526; frequency of, and transpiration rate, 606, 611
stomatal aperture, stomatal resistance, 348, 367–8; in C_3- and C_4-plants, 521, 612; CO_2 concentration and, 349, 368; in growth model, 629; light and, 349, 368, 369; mineral deficiencies and, 540, 541; stress effects on, 587–8; temperature relations of, 514–15, 559, 571, 577–8; water relations of, 514–16, 519, 529, 677, 685, (in desert plants) 110–11, 112–13, 117
storage materials: in calculating use of assimilate, 482, 484–5; in competition for assimilate, 493; in growth model, 626; may exert feedback effect on rate of photosynthesis, 501
storage organs of desert plants, above and below ground, 121, 123
Stratiotes aloides, 195
stress: climatic, responses to, 610–12; effects of, on photosynthesis, 587–9; resistance to, takes precedence over

712

Index